I0754432

REV. THOMAS ALLEN

1799

THE

HISTORY OF PITTSFIELD,

(BERKSHIRE COUNTY,)

MASSACHUSETTS,

FROM THE YEAR 1734 TO THE YEAR 1800.

COMPILED AND WRITTEN, UNDER THE GENERAL DIRECTION OF A COMMITTEE,

BY

J. E. A. SMITH.

BY AUTHORITY OF THE TOWN.

BOSTON:
PUBLISHED BY LEE AND SHEPARD,
149 WASHINGTON STREET.
1869.

Boston:
Stereotyped and Printed by Geo. C. Rand & Avery.

PREFACE.

At a town meeting held in the Town Hall, in Pittsfield, Aug. 25, 1866, Mr. Thomas Allen rose, and stated, that on the Centennial of the First Congregational Church and Parish, viz., April 18, 1864, he had been requested by a vote of the parish to prepare an historical memoir of that parish and church, embodying substantially, but extending, the remarks he made at that meeting. He stated, that, in looking over the records of the town and parish, he found them intimately connected, so that a history of the one would be also a history of the other; and he had found the history of the town highly interesting, and honorable to its inhabitants. True, there were no classic fields in Pittsfield, consecrated by patriotic blood spilled in battle in defence of the country, as in Lexington and Concord, simply because no foreign foe in arms had ever invaded its soil: but it was not the less true that Pittsfield had always promptly performed her part, and furnished her quota of men and means, in every war waged in defence of the country and the Union; and that in the intellectual contests through which the just principles of republican government, and civil and religious freedom, have been established in this country, the men of Pittsfield, on their own ground and elsewhere, have ever borne a part creditable alike to their wisdom, their sagacity, and their patriotism. Pittsfield, therefore, had a history which deserved to be written. The first settlers had all passed away; and their immediate descendants, witnesses of the earlier struggles, were whitening with the frosts of age, and were also rapidly disappearing. If the records of their history were to be gathered together, and preserved in a durable form, it was time that the duty be undertaken. He was satisfied that an honorable record would appear, and worthy of the place to which God had given so much that is beautiful in nature.

He therefore asked leave to introduce a resolution, of which the following is a principal part, which was warmly advocated, and, with great unanimity, at once adopted: —

"*Resolved,* That a Committee of five be appointed for the purpose of compiling, writing, and supervising the publication of, a history of the town, and that said Committee be authorized to select and employ a suitable person to aid them in the work."

The Committee, then immediately appointed, consisted of Thomas Allen, Stephen Reed, Phinehas Allen, James Francis, and James D. Colt. Dr. H. H. Childs was subsequently added, and an appropriation made to defray the expenses of the work. The Committee selected and employed Mr. J. E. A. Smith as a suitable person, qualified by experience as a writer, to aid them; and by him, the work, under their general direction and superintendence, and subject to their scrutiny, has been compiled and written. The work was commenced in September; documents and books in manuscript and print, and records from private and public sources, were gathered together; and Boston, Springfield, Hartford, Albany, and Lenox were visited to consult libraries, authorities, and public archives. Gathering information from so many and scattered sources, and reducing it to writing in chronological order, has been, of necessity, a work of time; but the result is that more of it has been obtained than was at first anticipated. On this account, the Committee have deemed it best to issue a first volume, bringing the history down only to the year 1800.

Dr. Childs having departed this life in March, 1868, and Dr. Reed not acting, John C. West and Thaddeus Clapp were at the April meeting, 1868, added to the Committee.

The Committee and Mr. Smith desire to put on record here an acknowledgment of their indebtedness to various persons for facts, and especially to mention the following as some of the chief sources from whence material for this History has been derived.

Rev. Mr. Allen left many papers of much historic interest, of which a considerable number have been preserved, and have been of the utmost service. Several of them we print in full.

Col. William Williams was one of the most prominent citizens of the town from its settlement until the close of the Revolution, and held offices which led him into voluminous correspondence regarding its affairs, and made him the custodian of valuable papers. A great mass of these was in existence within the last twenty years; but the larger portion have since been destroyed. Fortunately, however, while the work of destruction was going on, it came to the knowledge of Hon. Thomas Colt, who saved a considerable part, which forms the nucleus of his valuable historical collection, and has afforded us the greatest aid in our labors. Many other exceedingly valuable and serviceable documents, saved from the Williams papers, have been contributed by M. R. Lanckton and Henry Colt, Esqs.

The papers left by Col. John Brown to his family were inadvertently destroyed many years ago; but Henry C. Van Schaack, Esq., of Manlius, N. Y., a zealous and successful student of Revolutionary history, obtained a just conception of the character and services of that officer at a time when they were more obscure than they have since become, and has been for more than a quarter of a century earnestly engaged in collecting documents regarding them. His labors have been richly rewarded; and he has generously placed the results in our hands, together with his own interesting observations upon them. To Mr. Van Schaack we are also indebted for a large collection of interesting papers regarding his uncle, Major Henry Van Schaack, concerning the Shays Rebellion, the contest for religious equality, and other matters; many of them pertaining to the period the story of which is to be given in the second volume of this work.

We are also indebted, for valuable papers, to Messrs. John P. Brown, J. A. Foote, and Ambrose Cadwell, of Pittsfield; Mrs. J. V. C. Smith of New York; Mrs. Butler of Northampton;

H. W. Taft, Esq., of Lenox; and Charles J. Taylor, Esq., of Great Barrington.

We ought also to express our obligations to Mrs. Otis Peck for the loan of a file of "The Pittsfield Sun;" and to Mr. G. A. Murdock, civil engineer, who superintended the enlargement of the Pittsfield lakes as reservoirs, for aid in matters pertaining to his profession.

The records of Pittsfield are perfect from the incorporation of the plantation of Poontoosuck in 1753, with the exception of a few years during the last French and Indian War; and many papers of importance are preserved in the town archives. And these, of course, have furnished a general outline of its story. But perhaps the richest source of information has been found in the archives of the State at Boston, among which are preserved a large number of petitions, memorials, reports, and military rolls, pertaining to Pittsfield.

In addition to these, we have made use of the files of the Boston newspapers published during the Revolution, and preserved in the collection of the Massachusetts Historical Society; the files of "The Hartford Courant," in the collection of the Connecticut Historical Society; the files of "The Pittsfield Sun;" the county records at Springfield and Lenox; and the archives of the State of New York at Albany. A large number of printed volumes have also been consulted; most of which have been found to contain information valuable for our purposes.

In the course of these researches, we have received aid and courtesies from many persons, and cannot refrain from expressing our obligations especially to the gentlemen connected with the Massachusetts State Department, to Hon. Nathaniel B. Shurtleff and Wendell Phillips, Esq., of Boston, Hon. Richard Frothingham of Charlestown, J. Hammond Trumbull, Esq., of Hartford, Dr. E. B. O'Callaghan, and Joel Munsel, Esq., of Albany, and to Mrs. Thomas F. Plunkett of Pittsfield.

CONTENTS.

TOPOGRAPHY.

PART I. — BERKSHIRE.

PART II. — PITTSFIELD.

HISTORY.

CHAPTER I.

ABORIGINAL OCCUPATION.

CHAPTER II.

GRANTS. — SURVEYS. — SALES. — [1620–1741.]

CHAPTER III.

FIRST ATTEMPT TO SETTLE THE TOWNSHIP. — [1741–1749.]

CHAPTER IV.

CHAPTER V.

CHAPTER VI.

CHAPTER VII.

CHAPTER VIII.

CHAPTER IX.

CHAPTER X.

RESISTANCE TO PARLIAMENTARY AGGRESSION. — [MARCH-OCTOBER, 1774.]

CHAPTER XI.

A SEASON OF PREPARATION. — [SEPTEMBER, 1774-MAY, 1775.]

CHAPTER XII.

PITTSFIELD IN ETHAN ALLEN'S TICONDEROGA CAPTURE. — [DECEMBER-JUNE, 1775.]

CHAPTER XIII.

PITTSFIELD IN THE FIRST NORTHERN CAMPAIGN, AND AT THE SIEGE OF BOSTON. [MAY-NOVEMBER, 1775.]

CHAPTER XIV.

THE DECLARATION OF INDEPENDENCE. — THE TORIES. — BATTLES OF WHITE PLAINS AND THE DELAWARE. — [1776–1777.]

CHAPTER XV.

PITTSFIELD IN THE SECOND CANADA CAMPAIGN. — ARNOLD'S PERSECUTION OF BROWN AND EASTON. — [SEPTEMBER, 1775–1778.]

CHAPTER XVI.

THE INVASION OF BURGOYNE, AND BATTLE OF BENNINGTON. — [1777.]

CHAPTER XVII.

LAST YEARS OF THE REVOLUTION. — [1777–1783.]

CHAPTER XVIII.

THE BERKSHIRE CONSTITUTIONALISTS. — [1775–1780.]

CHAPTER XIX.

THE BERKSHIRE CONSTITUTIONALISTS (CONTINUED). — [1775–1780.]

CHAPTER XX.

THE BERKSHIRE CONSTITUTIONALISTS. — COMMITTEE GOVERNMENT OF THE INTERREGNUM. — [1774–1780.]

CHAPTER XXI.

THE SHAYS REBELLION. — [1781–1786.]

CHAPTER XXII.

PITTSFIELD IN THE SHAYS REBELLION. — PAROCHIAL DIFFICULTIES. — [1786–1789.]

CHAPTER XXIII.

COUNTY COURTS IN PITTSFIELD. — [1761–1787.]

CHAPTER XXIV.

THE MEETING-HOUSE OF 1790. — [1789–1793.]

CHAPTER XXV.

STRUGGLE FOR THE EQUALITY OF RELIGIOUS DENOMINATIONS. — [1772–1811.]

APPENDIX.

Explanation. — The initials T. C. C., refer to the Thomas Colt Historical Collection; H. C. C., Henry Colt Collection; Lanc. Col., Lancton Collection; Am. Ar., to the American Archives of Peter Force; H. V. S. C., to the Henry C. Van Schaack Collection.

TOPOGRAPHY.

"TOPOGRAPHICAL pursuits, my doctor used to say, tend to preserve and promote the civilization of which they are a consequence and a proof.

"They have always prospered in prosperous countries, and flourished most in flourishing times, when there have been persons enough of opulence to encourage such studies, and of leisure to engage in them. . . . Whatever strengthens our local attachments is favorable both to individual and national character. Our home, our birthplace, our native land, — think for a while what the virtues are which arise out of the feelings connected with these words; and, if thou hast any intellectual eyes, thou wilt then perceive the connection between topography and patriotism.

"Show me a man who cares no more for one place than another, and I will show you in that same person one who loves nothing but himself. Beware of those who are homeless by choice: you have no hold on a human being whose affections are without a tap-root." — SOUTHEY: *The Doctor.*

PART I.

BERKSHIRE.

Geography. — Physical Structure and Scenography. — Central Position of Pittsfield. — Manufactures. — Mineral Productions. — Aspect when first visited. — Geographical Nomenclature. — Derivation of the Name "Housatonic."

THE fourteen counties into which Massachusetts is divided are, most of them, distinguished by physical peculiarities, which shape the occupations of their inhabitants, and mould their habits of life and thought; and among these subdivisions of the Commonwealth, in forming which the statute has, often with nicety, followed the demarcations of Nature, not even the sandy Cape or metropolitan Suffolk — hardly even insular Nantucket — is marked by features so unlike those of its sister shires as are those which characterize the county of Berkshire.

The traveller who enters the mountain-walls of its upland valley soon recognizes the intense individuality of this region, and feels that he is among a peculiar people as well as amid novel scenes; and this notwithstanding the large infusion of foreign population into the manufacturing districts, and the constant tidal currents between city and country life, which have gone far to smooth away the strong although never very rugged lines that used to make the aspect of society no less picturesque than that of Nature. The stranger with a moderately observant eye will soon perceive that the old lineaments, however softened, are still there; and he may often find them starting into prominence, which leaves the lineal likeness unmistakable.

The people of Berkshire are the true children of their home among the hills. They are very much what its geographical and physical characteristics would naturally make the descendants of Massachusetts Puritans. Our first consideration, then, is of the influences of this kind which have tended to modify in them the common type of Massachusetts man.

Berkshire, the extreme western portion of the Pilgrim Commonwealth, is divided from the counties of Columbia and Rensselaer, in New York, by a right line[1] which runs for fifty-one miles along the summits of the Taconic Mountains.

On the north, a straight boundary of fourteen miles separates it from Vermont; but the town of Munroe, belonging to Franklin County, juts into its north-eastern corner. Immediately south of that point, the width of Berkshire is about eighteen miles. Thence a line, rendered very irregular by numerous attempts to rectify the boundaries of towns and counties, divides the Hoosac Mountains, between Berkshire on the west, and Franklin, Hampden, and Hampshire on the east. Upon the south, the line again becomes straight, and runs for twenty-four miles along the borders of Connecticut. Thus the four cardinal boundaries of Berkshire lie along four different States, including that of which it forms a part. The region thus defined, containing an area of a little over nine hundred and fifty square miles, forms a conspicuous feature in one of the most remarkable phases of New-England geography, as described, upon the authority of Prof. Guyot's observations, in Palfrey's history of that section: and no better basis for a clear comprehension of the physical conformation of Berkshire could be desired than a slightly condensed extract from that work: —

"Only moderate elevations," says Dr. Palfrey, "present themselves along the greater part of the New-England coast. Inland, the great topographical feature is a double belt of highlands, separated almost to their bases by the deep and broad valley of the Connecticut River, and running parallel to each other from the south-south-west to the north-north-east, till around the sources of that river they unite in a wide space of table-land, from which streams descend in different directions." . . .

"To regard these highlands, which form so important a feature in New-England geography, as simply two ranges of hills, would not be to conceive of them aright. They are vast swells of land, of an average elevation of a thousand feet above the level of the

[1] With the exception of a slight deviation at the south, caused by the cession of Boston Corner.

sea, each with a width of forty or fifty miles, from which, as from a base, mountains rise in chains or in isolated groups to an altitude of several thousand feet more.

"In structure, the two belts are unlike. The western system, which bears the general name of the Green Mountains, is composed of two principal chains,[1] more or less continuous, covered, like several shorter ones which run along them, with the forests and herbage to which they owe their name. Between these, a longitudinal valley can be traced, though with some interruptions, from Connecticut to Northern Vermont. In Massachusetts, it is marked by the Housatonic; in Vermont, by the rich basins which hold the villages of Bennington, Manchester, and Rutland; and, farther on, by valleys of less note. . . .

"The mountains have a regular increase from south to north. From a height of less than a thousand feet in Connecticut, they rise to an average of twenty-five hundred feet in Massachusetts, where the majestic Greylock, isolated between the two chains, lifts its head to the stature of thirty-five hundred feet. In Vermont, Equinox and Stratton Mountains, near Manchester, are thirty-seven hundred feet high; Killington Peak, near Rutland, rises forty-two hundred feet; Mansfield Mountain, at the northern extremity, overtops the rest of the Green-mountain range with an altitude of forty-four hundred feet.

"The rise of the valley is less regular. In Connecticut, its bottom is from five hundred to seven hundred feet above the level of the sea. In Southern Berkshire, it is eight hundred feet: it rises thence two hundred feet to Pittsfield, and one hundred more to the foot of Greylock; whence it declines to the bed of the Housatonic in one direction, and to an average height of little more than five hundred feet in Vermont in the other. Thus it is in Berkshire County that the western swell presents, if not the most elevated peaks, yet the most compact and consolidated structure."[2]

A region thus constituted could not fail to be filled with lovely vales; but unrivalled here, and with few rivals elsewhere, stands the fame of that occupied by the county of Berkshire. And nowhere else is the combination of its grand but unfrowning circumvallation of hills, with the varied beauty which it encircles,

[1] The Taconics on the west, and the Hoosacs on the east.

[2] Palf. Hist. N. E., i. pp. 3–5.

to be observed with such completeness of effect as from points near the centre of Pittsfield, where the perspective softens and shapes the outlines of the view into unity and proportion, and where you are free from that feeling of oppression which is apt to result from the too close proximity of mountains. The spectator standing on the observatory at Maplewood, on the commanding hill above Springside, or upon some similar elevation, finds no words in which to express his admiration of the scenes which surround him. On the west sweep the Taconics, in that majestic curve whose grace travellers familiar with the mountain scenery of both hemispheres pronounce unequalled. On the east, the Hoosacs stretch their unbroken battlements with white villages at their feet, and, if the sunlight favor, paths of mingled lawn and wood enticing to their summits; while from the north,

> "Greylock, cloud-girdled on his purple throne,"

looks grandly across the valley to the giant heights keeping watch and ward over the pass where the mountains throw wide their everlasting gates to let the winding Housatonic flow peacefully towards the sea.

On every side, the exquisite curves of this graceful stream, and the slender threads of its innumerable tributaries, embroider the rich green of the meadows and the more sombre verdure of the uplands; while not far away, although not all visible, sparkle the bright waters of six beautiful lakelets, companions to

> "The stream whose silver-braided rills
> Fling their unclasping bracelets from the hills,
> Till, in one gleam, beneath the forest's wings
> Melts the white glitter of a hundred springs."
>
> HOLMES.

Below, the not unfitting centre of this amphitheatre of beauty, lies the village of Pittsfield, with its mansions and humbler homes, its marts, schools, and churches, half hidden by noble trees;

among which, alas! no longer rises the gray old elm which used first to greet the traveller's eye.

A lovelier landscape one might not desire to see; and when, satiated with long, luxurious gazing, the spectator seeks to analyze the sources of his delight, all the elements of beauty justify his praise. To the eye, the valley here presents the proportions which architects love to give their favorite structures. The symmetry, too, with which point answers to opposing point, exceeds the power of art. Variety the most marvellous, but without confusion, forbids the sense to tire. Colors the richest, softest, and most delicate, charm the eye, and vary with the ever-changing conditions of the atmosphere. Fertile farms and frequent villages imbue the scene with the warmth of generous life; while over all hangs a subdued grandeur which may well have pervaded the souls of the great and good men who have made Berkshire their home since the days of Jonathan Edwards.

The emotion of sublimity is not often excited by Berkshire scenery, unless the feeling inspired by the excess and overwhelming profusion of beauty with which, under certain favoring circumstances, it overflows, may be properly so classed. Boldness, freshness, and variety are the traits by which it charms; and they are those which one would most desire to characterize his home, and under whose healthful influences he would wish his children to be educated. On the heights where Greylock lifts the topmost summit of the State, along the valleys of the Hoösac and the Housatonic, up the rude but flower-fringed wood-roads which penetrate the narrowing opes[1] of the Green Mountains, beauty is everywhere the prevailing element. The rapidly-shifting scenes — never tame, but rarely rugged; never altogether repulsive, but

[1] The reader will pardon to necessity the employment of a word of merely local authority and very infrequent use. A hope — or more descriptively, without the aspirate, an ope — is a valley, which, open at one end only, loses itself at the other, sloping upward to a point in the mass of the mountains. The word is quite indispensable in the description of scenery like that of Berkshire; and its disuse has resulted in the adoption of such vile substitutes as "hole," "hollow," or even worse. Thus we have Biggs's Hole and Bigsby's Hollow, or more probably "Holler." Surely neatly descriptive ope should not be displaced by such abominable interlopers as these.

WEBSTER has "HOPE, *n.* — A sloping plain between ridges of mountains. [*Not in use.*] *Ainsworth.*" — But English local topographical writers sometimes use the word in the sense given it in the text.

often filled with all that can please the eye — follow each other in infinitely multiplied combinations of mountain and valley, lake and stream, rock, tree, and shrub, mossy hillock and crystal spring.

"The delicious surprises of Berkshire" was one of the happiest phrases in the poetic rhetoric of Gov. Andrew, who knew well the scenes he praised; and the traveller along its winding roads recognizes at every turn how truthful and appropriate was the expression.

But we must not linger, where all love to linger, amid the exceeding loveliness of Berkshire scenery; but turn to those facts regarding the geographical structure of the county, which, although not devoid of scenographic interest, affect also its internal economy, and its relations to its county-seat and central market-town.

Pittsfield Park, which lies very near the centre of the town, and of the county as well, has an elevation above the level of the sea of one thousand and forty-one feet; and, omitting the small uninhabited mountain-districts, that is not far from the average altitude of the township.

Of the neighboring mountains, isolated Greylock, the highest point of Massachusetts (3,505 feet above the level of the sea), rises 2,464 above Pittsfield, from which it is about fourteen miles distant as the crow flies. Of the Hoosacs, some of the peaks near Vermont attain an altitude of two thousand feet above the valley at their bases; or perhaps fourteen hundred above Pittsfield. Among the Taconics, Berlin Mountain in Williamstown exceeds the latter level by 1,773 feet; Perry's Peak in Richmond, — famed for its superb over-view, — by 1,576; and, near the extreme southwest, Mount Everett, the dome of the Taconics, by 1,583.

Excluding from the computation these heights, which disproportionately excel their neighbors, the average elevation of the mountain-summits of Berkshire above Pittsfield Park may be about eight hundred feet; which is considerably less than their altitude above the level of the Berkshire Valley.[1] How slight is the depression of the transverse valleys between the several peaks, massive knobs, and table-lands of the Hoosacs, may be inferred from the fact, that, upon the eastern declivity of the range, the Western Railroad is

[1] Prof. Chester Dewey estimated the general average of the Hoosac Range above the bottom of the valley at sixteen hundred feet; that of the Taconics, at twelve or fourteen hundred.

compelled to almost double upon its track in order to find a gap through which it may enter the county by a valley-summit whose original elevation was 1,478 feet above tide-water at Albany, or 452 above Unkamet's Crossing.[1] The domelike summits of the Taconics are more sharply divided; but even between these the depressions are so slight, that, although the locomotive finds a passage at an elevation of only a hundred and twenty feet above the road-bed at Pittsfield, it is the only one that is practicable south of that through which the Hoosac River escapes.

Concisely to outline the geography of the Berkshire Hills, the grand uplifted table-land described by Dr. Palfrey must be considered as here cleft — above its solid substructure of a thousand feet — for a length of forty-eight miles, and to an average depth of fifteen hundred feet; while the longitudinal ridges thus formed are serrated by transverse valleys of less than one-third that average, supplemented by water-courses furrowed by the mountain-torrents.

Between the longitudinal ridges known as the Hoosac and Taconic Mountains lies the Berkshire Valley, having an average breadth of about six miles; although, except in Pittsfield and Sheffield, it is made to appear much more narrow by the spurs which protrude into it, and the isolated ranges with which it is thickly studded. In the basin formed by this valley and the declivities which incline toward it is concentrated the mass of population and wealth which lend character to the county.

The natural outlines which give unity to the region are sufficiently well defined; but practically it is divided into minor compartments, so arranged, however, as to form a homogeneous whole, with a common centre. In the northern section, the chief barrier which governs this division is the Greylock Range, which, beginning near the Vermont line, extends southward through Lanesborough. In the south, the less continuous Tom Ball Spur, thrown off by the Taconics at Alford, after being broken through by the Williams River at West Stockbridge, extends to Pittsfield, where it terminates abruptly in the Cliffwood terraces of South Mountain.

Between these intersections and the exterior walls of the county extend four valley-reaches, marked respectively by the east branches of the Hoosac and the Housatonic, by the west branches of

[1] Where the track crosses the east branch of the Housatonic in Pittsfield.

the same rivers, by the Housatonic after the junction, and by the track of the Western Railroad south-westward. Into these grand subdivisions of the Berkshire Valley open a multitude of others of minor importance.

Midway between the northern and southern boundaries of the county, the intersecting barriers disappear; and the confluent valleys merge in the six miles square occupied by the township of Pittsfield, the greater part of which is of moderately uneven surface, with large spaces approaching the character of plains. Only rarely do the highways have to climb greater heights than afford an agreeable relief to the traveller; and few sections of the town oppose more obstacles to level streets than are found in many cities and towns in those portions of New England not accounted mountainous. The Taconics impinge but slightly upon its western border; the Hoosacs still more slightly upon its eastern. The only formidable elevations are Oceola and South Mountain, which cover a small territory in the south.

It will readily be perceived that the peculiar divergence of the valleys which here find their common terminus make this favored locality the centre of the county in a sense and to a degree unknown in regions where the direction of roads is subject to hardly any other law than that which makes the shortest distance between two points a straight line. Among the hills, on the contrary, every boy who goes to mill knows that the farthest road round is often the shortest way home.

There are several flourishing centres of local traffic more convenient to their respective sections than Pittsfield is; but it needs only an inspection of the map to show how exclusively the disposition of the interior ridges of the county makes that the intersecting, radiating, decussating point of the great highways of Berkshire, — at once the only practical thoroughfare between her northern and southern divisions and the point where they meet each other. The traveller at one of the extreme corners of the county, wishing to reach that longitudinally opposite, will never attempt to do so by the most direct route, — if, indeed, any exist which at all approximate directness, — but, at whatever cost of *détour*, by one of those which intersect at the central town.

And, if this point is thus marked out by Nature as the centre of intercommunication by the highway, still more emphatically is it so for railway travel, which, by the necessities of the country, is compelled to wind among the mountain-defiles in a course so circuitous, that, of the thirty-one towns which compose the county, seventeen — containing 45,374 of its 56,966 people — are touched by the iron rails which unite at Pittsfield; while chartered roads soon to be built will add the most populous portion of the remainder to the connection.

In its intercourse with the world outside its mountains, Berkshire, before the introduction of railroads, was circumscribed almost as narrowly as in its internal thoroughfares. How formidable a barrier interposed between it and the rest of Massachusetts may be inferred from the fact that the least difficult access was by the Pontoosuck Turnpike. The Western Railroad now follows the general course of this route, sacrificing directness, sometimes, in order to lessen grades; and in a distance of twenty-five miles, between Tekoa Mountain and Washington Summit, — notwithstanding this sacrifice and the aid of the most skilful engineering, — it is compelled to ascend twelve hundred and eleven feet, of which eight hundred and thirty-seven are surmounted in the last half of the distance by a grade whose maximum is more than eighty-two feet to the mile. The Pontoosuck Turnpike in its best estate was considered, as it really was, a marvel of engineering skill, and encountered no such grades as rendered the great parallel highways which ran north and south of it almost impassable at certain seasons of the year. In the last years previous to the building of the railroad, the stage-route over this road was famed also for the luxury of its coaches and the excellence of its horses;[1] but Capt. Marryatt, in his "American Diary," having graphically described the horrors of stage-travel over the Hoosacs, even when mitigated as perfectly as they could be, exclaimed upon "the madness of certain crazy spirits who had conceived the idea of constructing a railroad through this savage region." Time soon removed the imputation of madness from the splendid scheme; but the traveller gazing from the car-windows as the locomotive with mighty throes toils up the Valley of the Westfield — now beneath overhanging cliffs, and now where the little river gleams far down the deep ravine — will sympathize with the admiration of his British predecessor for that daring spirit which conceived the possibility of such an achievement.

[1] The Albany and Boston stages, run by several noted contractors, among whom Jason Clapp, Esq., still a venerable citizen of Pittsfield, was prominent.

Upon those sides of the county which border upon other States, the passes were, as has been intimated, less difficult. The banks of the Housatonic opened a convenient avenue along which intercourse with the Connecticut towns was uninterrupted. So intimate was the connection of Berkshire with Hartford at the time of the Revolution that "The Courant"[1] was not only the medium through which the political contests of Pittsfield were carried on, but also contained the advertisements of the impounded cattle and runaway slaves of that town and of Great Barrington.

Hartford continued to draw to itself a large portion of Berkshire trade until the railroads opened new avenues in other directions; but even before that era, after the establishment of steamboats upon the Hudson, it was successfully rivalled by the towns upon that river: and the tide of traffic flowed through the West-Stockbridge gate of the Taconics to Hudson, Kinderhook, and Albany, and thence to New York. On the north-west, the pass of the Hoosacs, which, to the dismay of all Massachusetts, had long ago been found out by the French and Indian foe, in later times furnished a thoroughfare for more peaceful intercommunication; but, as no great markets then lay in that direction, it less affected the county.

These superior facilities for intercourse with other States than with Massachusetts colored not only the business-relations, but the general character of the people of Berkshire; and, although the traits inherited from "Old-Hampshire" ancestry still formed the groundwork of thought and custom, and were continually re-invigorated by fresh migrations from the old home, they were modified by much which had been spontaneously engendered in the isolation of the hills, or ingrafted from those with whom contact was more frequent than with kindred in the Connecticut Valley.

The Western Railroad has much reduced this disparity in the external communications of the county. The journey to Boston, which in the best times of staging consumed two weary days, now insensibly glides away in a comfortable ride of six hours. Berkshire, pleasantly conscious of the iron bands that bind her to the rest of

[1] The files of "The Hartford Courant," of which two sets, nearly or quite complete, are in existence, — one in possession of the present publishers of the paper, and the other in that of the Connecticut Historical Society, — are full of most precious matter for the historian.

the Commonweath, feels herself more truly than ever a part of the Old Bay State; but still three competing lines of railroad, re-enforced in summer by steamers on the Hudson and the Sound, cause the great mass of Berkshire trade and travel to seek New York as its metropolis; and, as a natural result, the county receives a powerful social and intellectual influence from the same centre.

Returning to the description of the interior geography of Berkshire : the bottom of the valley rises, with the bed of the Housatonic, about two hundred and sixty feet from Sheffield to the forks of that river at Pittsfield; thence the bed of the western branch rises over one hundred feet, to the foot of Greylock in New Ashford, where it finds the summit of that division of the main valley.

The many-headed eastern branch is formed by the confluence of innumerable rivulets, which spring up among the hills of Peru, Washington, Windsor, and Hinsdale. In Dalton, it is of sufficient capacity to drive the wheels of the large paper-manufactories of that town; and at Coltsville, where it enters Pittsfield, it furnishes one of the best water-powers of the Upper Housatonic.

At this point, it receives Unkamet Brook, a large tributary which rises in Partridge Meadow, in the north-eastern corner of Pittsfield. This meadow is a singular formation upon the summit of the eastern water-shed of the Berkshire Valley, and about fifty feet above the level of the Housatonic, at the junction of its branches. Filled with pools formed by boiling springs, — the common fountains of two rivers, — so level is its surface, that oftentimes it depends upon chance which of the drops that bubble up side by side shall flow into Unkamet Brook, and through the Housatonic to the Sound; and which into the Hoosac, and through the Hudson to the sea. So slight, indeed, is the rising of the valley-bottom in this vicinity, that a dam raised four feet above the level of the highway at Coltsville would turn all the waters that come in from Dalton, and from Unkamet Brook, northward, into the Hoosac.

Thus the summit of the Berkshire Valley, as it rises northward from Connecticut, and southward from the Vermont line, is formed by a ridge extending diagonally from New Ashford, across Lanesborough, to Coltsville; the descent from its highest point in New Ashford to Sheffield being nearly four hundred feet; and upon its opposite declivity five hundred feet, to its lowest point in Williamstown.

Berkshire, the mountain county of Massachusetts, is hardly less pre-eminently its lake shire; for no less than seventy natural sheets of water, — lakes, or ponds fed by springs, — varying in size from twenty acres to nine hundred, are laid down upon its map; some shimmering upon the very tops of the mountains, some reposing in the shadows of the valley. But, although they add a thousand graces to the landscape, we shall not stay to describe or even enumerate them.

They act, however, an important part in the economy of the county; being employed as reservoirs in which to store up the waters, which, in seasons of flood, the rivers pour with wasteful impetuosity to the sea. For this purpose, many of the lakes have been considerably enlarged by means of dams of stone masonry of sufficient strength to resist the immense pressure which is often imposed upon them. Their numbers have also been re-enforced by reservoirs, wholly artificial, formed by massive barriers of stone thrown, at great expense, across the outlets of mountain-rivulets. These *parvenus* of Nature often rival the ancient lakes in extent of surface, and sometimes, as in Wahconah Reservoir at Windsor, in depth.

The waters pent up with this costly economy, as well as those which in the free streams trip with rippling laughter to their tasks, are made to do giant's work before they escape out of the county. Mainly by their aid, manufactures have come to be the chief source of its material prosperity; so that seventeen millions, of the twenty-four million dollars returned as the value of its industrial products in 1865, were derived from that source.

The principal branches into which the manufactures of Berkshire are divided are, in the order of the comparative value of their products, woollen and cotton cloths, paper, crude iron, leather, flour, lime, and glass. There is one large paper-mill in Pittsfield; but Lee and Dalton are the great paper-making towns, each sending more of that product to market than any others on the continent. Cylinder glass is made at East Lanesborough and Cheshire, and plate glass at Lenox Furnace, from the purest and best granulated quartz known, of which inexhaustible beds are scattered in Berkshire. Iron to the annual value of seven hundred and twenty-six thousand dollars is made from a superior brown hematite, of which deposits are abundant. Lime is made from pure carbonates to the value of seventy-five thousand dollars annually; and the marble quarries of Berkshire are famous.

In agriculture, Berkshire ranks among the foremost counties of the State; although the climate of the more elevated sections forbids the culture of some products which flourish in the Valley of the Connecticut, and are not excluded from the farms of Sheffield and Great Barrington. Facilities for the intermixture of soils, and abundant deposits of marl and muck, favor the improvement of inferior lands; while the mountain-grazing tracts afford cheap pasturage for herds of cattle and sheep, to whose breeding much successful attention has been given. Still, in spite of the never glutted market furnished by the manufacturing towns and by the influx of summer visitors, the total value of the agricultural products of Berkshire in 1865 was only $5,374,163.

In addition to the sources of wealth of which the official statistician takes note, that of Berkshire is augmented by the attractions which its superb scenery and the purity of its atmosphere offer to permanent and migratory residents, summer travellers, and students in its numerous literary institutions. The expenditures incident to the working of the railroads which traverse the county are also a source of no little emolument to its citizens.

The great variety of resources, thus only partially enumerated, tend to prevent, in a great measure, those periods of distress which are apt to overtake whole communities, when, depending upon a single fountain of employment, they find that suddenly dried up. Diversity of occupation has also its beneficial effect upon the intellectual character of the people, in modes of operation which need not be specified.

Such, analytically, is the fair county, which, in the early pages of this chapter, we attempted to portray as a whole. Somewhat more cheerless must have been its aspect when the white man first began to penetrate its wilds; and especially when he found it shrouded in the snows of winter. There is extant an old Dutch map (it sends a shudder through one to remember it), upon which, across a ghastly expanse of white, denoting the whole territory which is now Berkshire and Vermont, stretch in frightful loneliness the frigid syllables, *Win-ter-berg-e,* — "Winter Mountains," — meaning the hills which we, with a pleasant fiction of perpetual summer, christen *Green:* a very dreary map, and surely not the work of any speculator in wild lands upon the Hoosac Mountains.

Yet even then Berkshire had a unity in its natural features, which to the observer overlooking it from some elevated spot, or threading its paths as a surveyor, must have marked it out for the home of a community with common interests and with a homogeneous character. Time has developed and strengthened these characteristics; but there is no reason to doubt, that, from the first, they were patent to such men as Wendell, Stoddard, Pomeroy, the Williamses, and others, who, with shrewdness as well as energy, pushed Massachusetts civilization towards the Hudson.

The name of the Winterberge suggests that the geographical nomenclature of Berkshire has undergone great changes since the days of the Dutch explorers. In the ancient records, deeds, leases, and the like, of this as of other localities, the aboriginal names are often spelled with lamentable carelessness or caprice; two or three forms of the same word often appearing in a single document. Every provincial scrivener held himself at liberty to satisfy his own notions of euphony by lopping off, eliminating, or selecting from the luxuriant syllables which were said to have been growing since the confusion of Babel. The result is, that the dismembered trunks of the unfortunate victims often defy recognition by any except the most patient and painstaking philology. The name Taconic, for instance, — however regretfully, we yield the guttural and natural *gh* to persistent innovation, — assumes more than two score of transformations in the archives of Massachusetts; now expanding to generous Taughkaughnick, and now shrinking to curt Tacon: while the original form, Taghkanak, is derived from *Taakhan*, or *Taghkan*, "a wood;" and *aki*, "place;" and, as applied to the mountains may be translated, "The Forest Hills."[1] Poontoosuck, the aboriginal name of the site of Pittsfield, appears to be derived from *Poon*, the Mohegan word for "winter;" *Attuck*, "a deer;" and *Suck*, the final syllable in which that language makes its plural, and signifies "the winter deer;"[2] or the terminal *ak*, which indicates the name of a place, being merged in the plural ending, — "the haunt of the winter deer."

But the problem which has longest and most profoundly perplexed the students of our aboriginal geography concerns the name of that beautiful river which is designated by syllables as intricate as the windings of its graceful curves, and, in the form which they have finally taken, are as musical as the murmur of

1 Trans. Am. Ant. Soc., v. 2, p. 337.

2 Dr. E. B. O'Callaghan.

its ripples. The whole difficulty has, however, we apprehend, arisen from the very natural mistake of seeking for the word "Housatonic" an aboriginal derivation, while its primitive form was, in fact, Dutch. In the writings of the early settlers and surveyors, and even of the missionaries, no word suffered more severely from the confused orthography of the period than this. Its transmutations were innumerable. Hubbard of Ipswich, the early New-England annalist, wrote, Ausotunnoog; which has a quasi Algonquin twang, and was, doubtless, communicated to him through the medium of Algonquin throats, whose owners could, nevertheless, have gathered from the grating sounds only a purely arbitrary meaning. If Mr. Hubbard had asked them *why* they so designated the river, they could have given him no better reason than that of the comic song, —

> "The reason why they called him John
> Was because it was his name."

In the papers preserved in the archives of the Commonwealth, the county, and towns, some of the more frequent forms which the word assumes are Housatunnuk, Houssatonnoc, Houstunnok, Hooestenok, Awoostenok, Asotonik, Ousatonac; and in all these forms, the consonants, except the final, are made double or single, and the terminal syllable is spelled indifferently, *ik*, *ak*, *ok*, or *uk*. Sergeant and Hopkins, the earliest preachers among the Indians, wrote Housatunnok; but comparison with other forms leads to the belief that what is now pronounced as the first syllable was originally two, —*Ho-us*. President Dwight preferred Hooestennuc, and, probably, with good reason; although the meaning which he ascribes to the word, "the river beyond the mountains," after the most patient and laborious research by the most competent students, finds nothing to give it color, either in the language spoken by the Mohegans or in that of their Iroquois conquerors. And yet, in a certain sense, this may have been the meaning attached to it by the Mohegans; for, if the name was bestowed while the tribe, dwelling in the Valley of the Hudson, were accustomed annually to cross the Taconics for hunting-seasons in the Valley of the Housatonic, the name of the latter river, whatever, may have been the original signification of its syllables, would have represented *to them*, in ordinary thought, the river beyond the mountains: precisely as when the Narragansett slaughter was called to mind, it represented the river of the massacre; or, in another mood of thought, the stream on whose banks the white man preached the Christian gospel. But in process of time the relation in which the river was most commonly contemplated would communicate its peculiar significance to its name. And thus, when President Dwight asked of some Mohegan, "What do you mean by Hooestenok?" it is altogether likely that the answer was, "The river beyond the mountains;" just as we should reply to a similar question, "The winding river of the Berkshire Valley."[1]

We can thus well understand how the learned president's habits of investigation, while they would lead him very near to accuracy in adjusting his orthography to the native pronunciation, would not necessarily protect him from falling into error in the translation.[2]

Those who read the traditions told by the Stockbridge Indians will suspect them of imaginations fertile in statements adapted to the tastes of their hearers; but, to do them justice, none of them (or, at least, none of any reputation) ever pretended to attribute a descriptive meaning to any of the forms which the name of the river of their homes put on. The chiefs Konkapot — or, not to dwarf their somewhat unmanageable patronymic, Poph-ne-hon-nuh-woh — were men of good natural parts, and received excellent educations. They were also profoundly versed in all the lore of their tribe. From them were obtained the names given by the natives to many features of Berkshire geography, and the translations of their meaning; but they could make nothing except an arbitrary appellation of the word "Housatonic;" nor could Hendrick Aupaumut, the professed chronicler of his people. Several missionaries familiarized themselves with the Mohegan tongue, and,

[1] Since the foregoing paragraphs were written, we have been informed by Mr. Charles J. Taylor, that, in the copy of the deeds of the Upper and Lower Housatonic townships, the name of the river is given once as the "Housatonic or Westanock," and again as the "Housatonic or Westonook." Mr. Taylor, who has given much thought and investigation to the subject, has no doubt, that, in the different deeds and patents of the Livingston Manor, the words, "Wawwichtonock," "Wawyachtanock," "Wawijchtanok," and "Wawijachtanook" are as correct representations of the Indian pronunciation of the word we call Housatonic as the writers of those papers could make with our alphabet.

[2] It must be remembered that Dr. Dwight's inquiries were made by him as a curious traveller, rather than as an exact philologist.

being men of cultivated and inquiring minds, would not have left so interesting a subject uninvestigated; but they extracted no interpretation of this word from their philological researches.[1] Mr. J. Hammond Trumbull, the most eminent student at the present day in the Algonquin dialects, and perhaps in all the aboriginal languages of North America, confesses himself unable to find a satisfactory interpretation for the refractory syllables. The most plausible suggestion, which considers the word as of Algonquin origin, is that of Dr. E. B. O'Callaghan, the able historian of the State of New York, who supposes it to be derived from *Husson*, "rock," and *Aki*, "place;" the *at* being introduced for the sake of euphony. This theory is favored by the fact that the Stockbridge chiefs, in their address to the Commissioners of the Provinces at Albany in 1754, characterized their home as "a rocky place." This interpretation is, however, met by the objection, that, had it been correct, it would have almost certainly been given by the native chroniclers, who translated with great precision the names of the Hudson and Connecticut Rivers, and affirmed the reasons for them with entire positiveness. And the still more serious difficulty lies in its way, that it is inapplicable to several of the more frequent forms which the word assumes.

Now, to abandon the field which has been so faithfully explored with such meagre results, let us turn to one which is at least fresh, if, at first thought, less promising.

Previous to the Revolution, then, a chorographic map of the Province of New York, including the disputed territory as far as the Connecticut River, was, by order of Gov. Tryon, compiled from actual surveys deposited in the patent office. This authoritative work was published at London in 1779, and reproduced in 1849, in the first volume of "The Documentary History of New York," where the reader may probably have access to it. And, upon inspecting the course of the Housatonic River, he will find, that near its source it is styled the Stratford, and above tide-water the Westenhok or Housatunnuk.

The difference, it will readily be perceived, between the Dutch

[1] Rev. Dr. Field, the accurate, learned, and painstaking historian of the county, is silent on this subject; and Rev. Dr. William Allen, the best authority upon matters pertaining to the early Berkshire divines, says in a note to his poem at the Berkshire Jubilee, "It is remarkable that none of the teachers of the Indians have in any of their writings given the meaning of the word 'Housatonic.'"

Westenhok and President Dwight's Hooestennuc, — or, as it is also written, Hooestenok, — is barely the transfer of the aspirate from the last syllable to the first.

The inference is almost irresistible, that the long-sought derivation of our musical Housatonic is found in the not unmusical Dutch of Westenhok; for it is hardly possible that so close a resemblance between the two names of the river was a mere accidental coincidence. The translation of the word is, "West corner," (or "nook"); and the appellation Housatonic is thus both truthfully and poetically descriptive of the winding river of our western nook among the mountains.

The origin and subsequent transformations of the name may easily be deduced from well-authenticated facts. The capital village of the Mohegans was at Schodac on the Hudson, but little farther than twenty-five miles from the Housatonic at Pittsfield. Here Hendrick Hudson, in 1609, visited them in "The Half-Moon," and, forming the chain of friendship, commenced an intercourse which was kept up from that time, with little intermission, by the Dutch of the New Netherlands. Trading and military posts were established at Castle Island[1] in 1614, and, three years later, at the mouth of the Tawasentha. In 1615, we find Jacob Elkins, an active and energetic commander and commercial agent, prosecuting a quiet traffic, already commenced, with the Mohawks and Mohegans; while his "scouting-parties were constantly engaged in exploring all the neighboring country, and in becoming better acquainted with the savage tribes around them, with all of whom it was the constant policy of the Dutch to cultivate the most friendly relations."[2]

These scouting-parties, traversing the forests in all directions, often visited the Valley of the Housatonic; where, indeed, the English pioneers a century afterwards found Dutchmen domiciled among the natives — who had made them gifts of lands — acting as interpreters, and possessing much influence. Now, the Mohegans, in their first intercourse with these winsome strangers, whenever they had occasion to speak of the winding-river-of-their-hunting-grounds-beyond-the-mountains, doubtless indicated it by some

[1] A locality now so completely merged in the city of Albany as to almost lose its insular character. The Tawasentha River, or Norman's Kill, enters the Hudson a few miles farther south.

[2] Brodhead's History of New York, pp. 55, 67, 81.

phrase in their dialect as cumbrous as that which we have just employed in English; for with them every name was a phrase, and was very likely to be a cumbrous one.

The clumsy appellation which we have supposed must have been extremely inconvenient for the busy fur-traders, who, instead of the more common practice of curtailing its undue proportions, succeeded in persuading the natives to adopt in its stead the simpler Westenhok; which was the name of a tract of land that lay between the Housatonic in Sheffield, and its large tributary, now known as Salmon Creek, which rises on the west of the Taconics, and joins the main stream at South Canaan in Connecticut. The river thus received its name in the upper part of its course from the district which it there washed, as, in the lower, it took that of the town which stood at its mouth, — Stratford. When it first began to be so called is uncertain. In the grant of the lands of Westenhook[1] in 1705, they are described as thus known; and both they and the river may have been so for a century before inquiry began to be made into the origin and meaning of the word "Housatonic." In the mean while, there was abundant time for it to suffer stranger changes than it actually underwent, in its transmission through four or five rasping generations of Algonquin throats. It may be added, in further explanation of the obscurity which hangs over this subject, that, if the truth concerning it ever became known to any Massachusetts investigator during the period when the New-York boundary was in dispute, he would have been almost sure to suppress it, as tending to support the Dutch claim to priority of occupation; and, for the same reason, he may have shrewdly favored that orthography which most effectually concealed the European features of Westenhook under an aboriginal mask.

The boundary disputes were not settled until the year previous to the breaking-out of the Revolution; and the jealousies which they engendered still linger in the more old-fashioned nooks of both New York and Berkshire: so that truths which are inconsistent with prejudice on either side are apt to be pushed out of sight.

[1] Westen*hook*, the more correct spelling of the word, is the least frequent upon the old maps of the river.

PART II.

PITTSFIELD.

General Description. — Adjoining Towns. — Lakes, Streams, Mountains. — Fish. — Manufactories. — Outlying Villages. — Central Village. — The Old Elm. — Maplewood. — Springside. — Churches. — Banks and Insurance Offices. — Railroads. — County Buildings. — Population and Valuation.

A CORRECT general idea of the position which the territory whose history we are about to narrate occupies in the geographical and physical system of Berkshire has, we trust, been conveyed by the preceding chapter. And to most readers the name of Pittsfield is familiar as that of one of the most charming country towns in New England, a favorite resort of the traveller in search of health or pleasure, a seat of thriving manufactories and flourishing institutions of learning, and as, from time to time, the home of men of note. A somewhat more minute description of some of its physical characteristics will, however, facilitate a comprehension of its story.

Pittsfield is fortunate in its neighboring towns, scarce one of which but possesses some attraction for the visitor peculiar to itself: while many are widely celebrated for rural loveliness and exquisite scenery; for literary, historical, and religious associations; for connection with gigantic physical enterprises; for mineral wealth, or for remarkable manufactures.

Of the towns which adjoin it, Lanesborough, its next northern neighbor, rivals in its natural scenery the most famous localities of Berkshire; is of fine agricultural capacity; has boarding-schools of much repute; possesses superior beds of brown hematite ore, and of granular quartz, with costly furnaces for their conversion respectively into crude iron and cylinder glass; and contains also many good quarries of marble and compact limestone.

Dalton — of paper-making fame, and containing more than one beautiful and wealthy village — lies upon the east. Mountainous and picturesque Washington encloses its south-eastern angle. Lenox, the favorite and famous summer resort, bounds it partially upon the south; on which side it is also joined by Richmond, a noble agricultural town, and rich also in iron mines and marble. On the west, the long and narrow town of Hancock — with its fertile and beautiful valley, its romantic hills, and its neat Shaker village, "the city of peace" — interposes a strip barely two miles wide between Pittsfield and New Lebanon, the seat of the popular mineral springs and the capital of the Shaker Church.

Pittsfield has already been described as of moderately uneven surface, and nearly surrounded by mountains, through which, by convenient passes, narrow but rich valleys stretch away to the extremities of the county.

The lakes and streams with which it abounds have as yet been, equally with its central position, the sources of its material prosperity; and we shall give them our next attention.

Six lakes or lakelets lie wholly or in part within the town: all of them beautiful, and some of them noted for their graceful outlines and the delightful combinations which they form with the surrounding mountains. All more or less directly feed streams which furnish motive-power to large manufactories; and four have had their capacities for this purpose artificially increased.

Fanciful legends attach to some of the prettiest; and all have a veritable history of their own.

Pontoosuc, the second in size, lies upon the northern border of Pittsfield, Lanesborough claiming more than half its surface. Previous to its enlargement, which took place in 1867, it was a mile and a quarter long, and at its broadest point three-quarters of a mile wide; covering an area of four hundred and twenty-five acres. It now covers five hundred and seventy-five; the increase being chiefly in Lanesborough.

Before this change, two little islets dotted its bosom; and the highway, after passing a noble grove of pines, — the relic of one of the finest forests which ever grew in Berkshire, — and some much admired isolated trees of deciduous growth, skirted close along the graceful windings of the whole eastern shore. The view from the southern approach was one to be remembered for its beauty, and was not deficient in grandeur as the eye, glancing across the quiet lake with its twin islets and grove-shaded banks, took in Constitution Hill, — its crown shaven like a monk's, — and then swept on through a vista of twelve miles formed by Prospect, St. Luke's, and Pratt's Hills, Round Rock, and other noble elevations, to that grand background of so many Berkshire views, —

> "where look majestic forth
> From their twin thrones the giants of the north,
> On the rude shapes, that, crouching at their knees,
> Stretch their broad shoulders, rough with shaggy trees." — HOLMES.

On the west, some two miles away, lay globe-crested Mount Honwee and other Taconic summits, often reflected by the glassy lake in mirror-like perfection, and if it chanced to be of a clear, still day, after the mountain sides had put on their October hues, presenting a spectacle of rare gorgeousness. Pontoosuc Lake, as it was, is a picture — nay, a cabinet of pictures — which lives among the choicest memories of thousands. It is, perhaps, not less lovely now; but all the nearer charms of the landscape are changed, and even the more distant assume a new aspect. Island and pillared grove are gone, submerged by the rising waters; and the traveller passing over the highway, now made to climb the neighboring hill, finds new beauties, but not the same. The landscape may in time become even more charming than it was of old; although neither the eye of man nor the dashing of the wavelet can at once accustom itself to the new demarcations.

But the Pittsfield lakes, great as have been the changes in their outlines, have been still more unstable in their nomenclature. Thus, the Mohegan name of Pontoosuc was Shoon-keek-moon-keek; and it was so designated in the deeds which conveyed its shores to their first white occupants. Some settlers from Middlesex County having planted New Framingham, Shoon-keek-moon-keek was, in accordance with the common fate of Indian names, soon lost in Framingham Pond. The plantation developing into the town of Lanesborough: then came Lanesborough Pond; although by the matter-of-fact people of Pittsfield, who always took their bearings from their meeting-house, it was often styled the North, as other sheets of water were called East, West, and South Ponds.

But, in 1824, the Pontoosuc Woollen Manufacturing Company

purchased the water-privilege and adjacent lands at its outlet, upon which they built the mill whose products have since made its name familiar, at least in commercial circles, the country over; and naturally Shoon-keek-moon-keek received probably its final transformation into Pontoosuc Lake.

One of its appellations has, however, been omitted from the catalogue; it having been for many years in familiar conversation called "Joe Keiler's Farm:" from the anecdote that a wag of that name once bargained it away, and actually made a deed of it, to a New-York citizen, who mistook it, when covered with snow and ice, for a level expanse, and had the good taste to be charmed with the singular and romantic situation of its broad surface among the hills.

Lake Onota, which lies in a pretty upland basin, a little more than a mile west of the Park, is the largest and most beautiful sheet of water in Berkshire; excepting, as regards size, one or two artificial reservoirs. Before its enlargement, which was made in 1864, it was a mile and three-quarters long, and three-quarters of a mile wide; having an area of four hundred and eighty-six acres, which is now increased to six hundred and eighty-three. The elevation of its surface caused great changes in the outlines of its northern and western shores; and destroyed its most marked feature, which was a division of its waters by a causeway into two independent lakes, of which the northern, and much the smaller,[1] was formed by a dam thrown across its outlet by those industrious builders of a race now long extinct, in Berkshire, — the beavers. Traces of their workmanship were distinctly visible until they were recently submerged by the labors of engineers as indefatigable and more Titanic than themselves.

On the western shore, the larger pebbles of the beach — some of which, indeed, might aspire to the title of boulders — were thrown up by the action of ice into a wall, which had all the semblance of a work of art. Indeed, it was the old-time faith of the neighborhood, that it was built by the Indians as a screen from behind which they might shoot the deer which were accustomed to resort to the lake, — not so much to drink, which they might have done as well at a hundred brooks, as to lie through the heat of the summer days in its cooling waves, with their nostrils, however, necessarily exposed. Certain it is, that this old wall was

[1] It had an area of about thirty-four acres.

used as a covert, not only by the aborigines, but by the deer-slayers among the early white inhabitants.

This curious illustration of the power of floating ice — like the causeway which used to divide the waters — is now hidden when the lake-surface is at its ordinary height; and possibly the same agency which built, may in time remove it to the new line of the shore.

But, great as have been the changes which Onota has undergone, they have affected its curious rather than its picturesque features; and its beauty is increased instead of being impaired. From the hill upon its south-western shore, which was fortified in the old French and Indian wars, a greater number of fine views are afforded than perhaps from any other spot of equal compass in Berkshire; and, of these, the most pleasing are those which embrace the lake and the mountains, which, beyond it, stretch away to ever-present Greylock.

Richmond Lake, which formerly lay about equally in the town of that name and in Pittsfield, was originally of a nearly circular form, and had an area of ninety-eight acres. In 1865, it was enlarged to two hundred and fifty, — the greater portion of the addition being in Pittsfield, — and lost that regular spherical figure by which it used to be pleasantly recognized from the mountain-tops. Upon the old maps, Richmond Lake is South Pond; and a small body near it, now long since drained, was designated Rathbun's Pond, in reference to Valentine Rathbun, who, about the year 1769, built clothiers' works near it.

Silver is the pretty but not over distinctive name of the pretty lakelet which the traveller over the Western Railroad observes, as, entering the village from the east, he passes its northern verge. It now covers about sixty acres, having been enlarged in 1843, as one of the reservoirs of the Pittsfield cotton-factory. It was known among the first settlers as Ensign's Pond, from Jacob Ensign, who built the first fulling-mill in Pittsfield, and owned the land along the eastern borders of the lake. In later days, a hat-factory was erected on its northern shore, and it took the name of Hatter's Pond. But the hatters went elsewhere; and the name, having lost its significance, gave place to the present less ugly although not strikingly novel appellation. The secluded lakelet, of some thirty acres extent, about a mile east of Silver Lake, and, like it, connected by a short outlet with the eastern branch of the

Housatonic, is laid down on Walling's generally very accurate map of Berkshire as "Sylvan Lake," although rarely so called. The meadow in which it lies was, on the earliest plans, named "Unkamet's;" and the lakelet was perhaps entitled to the same appellation. But it was early known as Goodrich Pond, from one of the most noted settlers, who owned large tracts of land in that vicinity; and there seems no good reason why the name of the stout old patriot and worthy magistrate should not continue to be preserved in the name of Goodrich Lake.

Last, and among the loveliest of the group, is Melville Lake, of perhaps thirty-five acres, lying east, a little to the north, of South Mountain, — a gem-like, crystal water, hidden among groves interlaced with frequent picturesque paths, that often debouch upon sunny lawns or gravelly beaches. It has for many years been a favorite haunt of some of the most celebrated men in politics and literature, while guests of the broad-halled mansion in whose grounds it is included, and which has been successively the hospitable home of Henry Van Schaack, Elkanah Watson, Thomas and Robert Melville, and J. R. Morewood. The lakelet has borne in turn the names of all these owners; but, on the county map, it appears as Lilly Bowl, an exceedingly descriptive although fanciful designation bestowed by the family of the present proprietor. The name of Melville is, however, surrounded by too many pleasant and honorable associations to be lightly abandoned; and the people cling to it with a pertinacity which promises to be lasting. Melville Lake it will doubtless continue to be in ordinary usage; while Lilly Bowl may be its pet or poetic title, — a result which is certainly not to be regretted æsthetically.

Melville Lake sends its surplus waters to the Housatonic through Wampenum Brook, a little stream, which, on its passage from above, touches its northern edge.

This brook, rising in the meadows on the north-west of South Mountain, passes through a little pond of the same name at the foot of the mountain, and crosses the highway a little south of the Housatonic Railroad. It furnishes a small water-power, but is here chiefly noted as a convenient landmark for future reference. It derives its name from Wampenum, who, with Mahtookamin and Cochecomeek, claimed the soil upon which Pittsfield is built, and leased it to Col. John Stoddard. By the terms of the lease, the land would have long since reverted to its red owners and their heirs; but the revival of a long-dormant interest in the name of these little waters is all they are likely to recover. Let us not begrudge them that.

The forks of the Housatonic River unite in Pittsfield, two miles north of the Lenox line, and a few rods south of the Pittsfield Cotton Factory. The eastern, formerly known as the main, branch has already been described, with its chief tributaries, Silver and Goodrich Lakes and Unkamet Brook. In addition to these it receives, from the eastern hills, Barton Brook at Coltsville, and Brattle near Goodrich Lake. The western branch rises in New Ashford, passes through Lanesborough, and enters Pittsfield in Pontoosuc Lake, which is properly an expansion of its waters. Issuing thence, it runs southerly, almost in a direct line, to Pomeroy's factories, where it turns abruptly to the south-east, and, after the passage of about a mile, joins the main stream. This branch was laid down on some of the old maps as the Pontoosuc River. Three-quarters of a mile north of the Park, it receives the waters of Lake Onota through Onota Brook, a beautiful streamlet which flows through the Pittsfield cemetery. A few rods south of Pomeroy's factories, it is joined by Shaker Brook; which rises in several fountains among the Taconics of Richmond and Hancock, and is swollen on its way by the drainage, through a canal, of Richmond Lake, and by the accession of several minor tributaries.

Down each of the Taconic gorges rushes a mountain brook, often of sufficient power to run a saw-mill; but, in order to give an intelligible delineation of these, it will be necessary to interrupt our tracing of the streams, that we may first fix the locations of the mountains, valleys, and opes, from which they flow.

Mount Honwee is the name given, on the authority of an Indian lease in which it is so called,[1] to the large rounded summit, — conspicuous in the Pittsfield view of the Taconics, — which, lying almost entirely in Hancock, juts into the little oblong notch in the north-west corner of the town boundaries. The word Honwee in the Iroquois tongue signified "men," and, as here used, is perhaps a fragment of the term *Ongwe Honwe*, — men surpassing all others, — a title which the Iroquois arrogated to themselves, and may have bestowed upon this eminence in token, that as the mountain of the Iroquois surpassed the neighboring hills in magnitude and symmetry, — in compactness as well, — so the nation excelled others

[1] Williams Papers.

in the same qualities. But, whether the name was assigned for this or some other reason, it would be in vain now to speculate. Writers of deeds in the busy times of Old-Hampshire land speculation were wont to mutilate names more destructively than by the clean elision of one half a cumbrous compound.

The mountain immediately south of Honwee was christened in this quaint wise: it was a part of the lands bequeathed by the founder of Williams College; and while, during the proceedings necessary to a legal transfer of the property, the title of the trustees was inchoate, they bargained with Capt. John Churchill to convey this hill to him, for a stipulated consideration, as soon as their interest in it was perfected. Capt. Churchill, in his turn, made similar agreements with his neighbors as to portions of the tract; and, the law's delays proving more tedious than had been anticipated, the mountain acquired, among the impatient expectants, the name of "The Promised Land;" which it still retains.

Lulu Ope lies between Mount Honwee and The Promised Land, and, with them, forms one of the most inviting regions in Pittsfield for the lovers of pic-nic. Having climbed to the western summit of The Promised Land, the excursionist finds himself by Berry Pond, in Hancock, a miniature lakelet, noted for the purity of its waters, as well as for its romantic location and the beauty of the surrounding landscape. It finds its outlet westward; but, down Lulu Ope, pleasantly shaded wood-roads, opening at intervals upon fine bird's-eye views, follow on either side the course of a streamlet, that through amber pools and over silvery shallows, with musical noises, tumbles down the steep descent, until, near the entrance of the ope, it plunges over a sharp and rocky shelf, in Lulu Cascade, — a foam-white column, which finds its base in a circular pool of black and glossy surface, overhung by a gray old bowlder and by masses of tangled foliage.

Issuing from the ope, the waters chary of their maiden beauty, too suddenly exposed to the ardent sunlight, plunge down a narrow chasm, and wholly disappear for the space of half a mile or more, while they rumble among the loose bowlders, through which they have wrought a passage by washing away the lighter earth.

Seven of the brooks which flow from the Taconic Opes assume a subterranean character at the base of the mountains; and their courses across the fields towards Lake Onota are marked by lines of coarse bluish gravel and small bowlders, resembling the beds of summer-dried rivulets.

Next south of The Promised Land is the Ope of Promise; which, after penetrating a little way into the mountain, bends north-westward to the summit, and affords the most direct, although an arduous path to Berry Pond. Then come Arbutus Hill and Ope, so-called from the profusion of that "darling of the forest," the sweet flower of May, with which they are covered in the spring, when their woods are musical with the hum of young voices and the laughter of children. Behind and overtopping them lies "Old Tower Hill," named from its observatory, which commands superb views.

Farther to the south, again, we come to Pine Mountain, famed for the forests of white-pine trees with which the early lumbermen found it covered, and of which they have left considerable relics to their successors. Pine Ope intervenes between this and May Mountain, across whose southern base the New-Lebanon highway runs, through Lilly Ope. These latter names have not quite so flowery derivations as one would naturally infer; the mountain having been christened in honor of one of its proprietors, and the ope for withered Mother Lilly, who used to live far up its recesses, and objurgate the mischievous anglers who disturbed her ancient solitude. But, if one inclines to romanticism, the Widow Lilly, like most widows and most lilies, "had once been fair."

South of the Lebanon Highway and Lilly Ope, swells the broad elevation known to fox-hunters as Doll Mountain, — derivation not traced. The Shakers, having appropriated a portion of it to their hill-top worship, call it Mount Zion; and "The World's People" often term it Shaker Mountain from the ownership of that peculiar sect. It is a favorite ground for fox-hunters and other sportsmen, and also for hunters of the precious metals; gold having been found mixed with other minerals in the quartz veins with which this, like most of the Berkshire hills, is seamed.

Beyond and indenting Doll Mountain are several opes, in which most of the branches of the Shaker Brook take their rise.

To resume our tracing of the Taconic brooks: the Daniels rises north of Mount Honwee, and, after receiving the Churchhill, flows into Lake Onota. The same reservoir gets the waters of Parker Brook — which rises in the Ope of Promise, and is joined by the Lulu — and also of the Arbutus. But the Wadham's, from Pine Ope, unites with the Lilly, and goes to swell Shaker Brook.

Of the tributaries to the Housatonic in Pittsfield, after the confluence of its branches, the most considerable is Sackett Brook, which comes in from Washington, having first received the Ashley from Lake Ashley, the fountain of the Pittsfield water-works. The Sackett, once a renowned trout-stream, is altogether exhausted by its too great reputation. The Seeley Brook is a branch of the Sackett, falling into it near its junction with the Housatonic; just below which the latter receives the Cameron, the last to be named of the Pittsfield streams; that next to it southward being the famous Roaring Brook of New Lenox.

The principal fish inhabiting the waters thus described, with perhaps tedious minuteness, are the pickerel, trout, sucker, perch, bullhead, dace, sunfish, and eel. The pickerel are not native to Berkshire, but were introduced from Connecticut. Linus Parker, who is still an inhabitant of the west part, placed the first ever brought to Pittsfield in Lake Onota about the year 1810. A few already swam in Lake Mahecanak;[1] and Pontoosuc received them two or three years later. Before 1829, they had become abundant; and they have since multiplied so prolifically that they not only afford a rich spoil for the angler, but contribute no mean addition to the resources of the table in an economic point of view.

Trout were formerly extremely abundant. The Housatonic was alive with them.[2] As late as the opening years of the present century, an hour's angling along this stream within half a mile of South Street was often rewarded by as many of this dainty fish as the sportsman could comfortably bear home. The stories told of Sackett Brook, although substantiated by the most reliable testimony, are almost incredible. Within thirty years, we are assured, the numbers of its trout were so incalculable that they were estimated by the "barrel-full;" and one veteran angler thinks he has seen that quantity in a single one of its pools. Another still retains the profile traced with his pencil

[1] Stockbridge Bowl.

[2] Statements made to the contrary are completely overthrown by the evidence of gentlemen like James Buell and John C. Parker, Esqs., the late Messrs. Samuel A. Allen, E. R. Colt, and others, whose means of knowledge were as ample as their testimony is unimpeachable.

around a trout caught in Onota Brook, which weighed when caught, some fifty years ago, five pounds and three-quarters; and, going over the Waltonian reminiscences of half a century, recalls others nearly as magnificent, which answered to his rod at other points.

The voracious and fastidious appetite of the pickerel, which will be content with nothing less delicate than a troutling, has now rendered the still waters untenable, except by those which find protection in their size. And in the rapids, where superior activity and power to resist the current give the trout the advantage of their more sluggish enemy, the refuse of the factories has driven them from their old haunts. But even these destructive agencies have been less efficient, than excessive, and not always legitimate, fishing; the laws for the protection of trout having been violated with impunity. Still there are few localities, so thickly settled, where this favorite of the sportsman and the epicure is so abundant as in the mountain brooks near Pittsfield; while, in the lakes and larger streams, specimens weighing from two to three pounds are not rare. The enlargement of the lakes proves very favorable to the increase of trout and pickerel, both in number and size.

The sucker, highly prized at certain seasons, is at others worthless for the table, and, being thus protected by nature's game-laws, thrives and multiplies. Others of the fish named as inhabitants of the Berkshire waters are plentiful, but have nothing about them locally peculiar.[1]

The edible tortoise, common in the lakes, often attains the weight of twenty pounds. One weighing thirty-three pounds after the loss of his head and much blood was, a few years since, caught in Lake Onota with a hook and line aided by a hatchet. It furnished twenty pounds of excellent meat.

We have lingered to trace the picturesque and curious features of the lakes and streams which we set out to describe as sources of the material prosperity of Pittsfield (and by these qualities they do contribute in no light measure to its wealth and population); but let us return to a more economic view.

Shaker Brook has a fall of one hundred and forty eight feet from Richmond Lake to the dam at Oceola, the lowest upon it; Onota

[1] In 1865, black bass and white fish were placed in Lakes Onota and Pontoosuc, but as yet without perceptible result.

Brook descends ninety-two feet from the lake to its junction with the Housatonic; the fall of the West Branch of the Housatonic from Pontoosuc Lake to Pomeroy's Factories is one hundred and twenty-eight feet: the comparison in each case being between the top of the upper dam and the foot of the lower.

The East Branch of the Housatonic — of which there are no complete measurements — descends about forty feet between its entrance of Pittsfield at Coltsville and its departure from it at New Lenox.

It was in reference to the streams we have attempted to describe, that Rev. Thos. Allen, in a sketch of Berkshire published in 1810, foretold that Pittsfield, then mainly devoted to agriculture, would become a successful manufacturing town: although there was not so much prophetic inspiration in this forecast as might appear at first sight; for the town had already shown no little enterprise in that direction, having maintained several forges for the manufacture of maleable iron from the ore during the Revolution, and having been early noted for its fulling-mills, to which the spinsters of the neighboring towns resorted with the produce of their looms. In fact also, at the time of Mr. Allen's prophecy, Arthur Schofield was about to set up in Pittsfield the first broad looms ever used in America; being already engaged, as Mr. Allen expresses it, "in forming machines to expedite the labor of spinning," — making the carding-machines, to wit, which preceded the looms by two or three years.

There was, however, in the minister's prophecy, — what was much more to the purpose than inspiration, — a clear foresight, resulting from native acumen, and thorough study of the natural advantages of the home which he loved with all the strength of his vigorous understanding as well as with all the warmth of his earnest heart.

His anticipations have been amply realized; and the streams of Pittsfield now furnish the motive power for eleven woollen manufactories, one large paper-mill, one cotton-factory manufacturing cloth and one making warps, and for three large flouring-mills. In addition to which, extensive manufactures of woollens, carriages, leather, looms, manufacturers' materials, iron machinery, musical instruments, and other articles, are carried on without the aid of water-power.

The aggregate extent of manufacturing operations in Pittsfield may be inferred from the following statement: —

STATISTICS OF THE WOOLLEN BUSINESS OF PITTSFIELD.

MILLS AND FIRMS.	Number of Sets.	Number of Looms.	Annual Production.	Kind of Goods.	Value of Production.	Number of Operatives.
J. Barker & Bros.	16	24 Broad 60 Narrow	650 000	Yards all wool and cotton warp cassimeres,	$500 000	230
L. Pomeroy's Sons	11	49 Broad 31 Narrow	225 000 200 000	Woollen cloth and satinets,	750 000	200
Pontoosuc W. M. Co.	10	75 Broad	130 000 35 000 5 000	Balmoral skirts, yds. Meltons and Skirtings, Carriage and car blankets,	475 000	200
Pittsfield W. Co.	8	40 Broad	175 000	Yds. 6-4 fancy cassimeres,	500 000	130
Taconic Mills	8	80 Narrow	450 000	" ¾ fancy cassimeres,	450 000	165
Stearnsville W. Co.	8	60 Narrow	450 000	" ¾ Union cassimeres,	225 000	130
S. N. & C. Russell	6	22 Broad 22 Narrow	250 000	" ¾ All wool cassimeres,	250 000	125
Tillotson & Collins	3	10 Broad	100 000	" ¾ Fancy cassimeres,	100 000	40
J. L. Peck	3	24 Narrow	350 000	" ¾ Flannels,	105 000	40
E. B. Whittlesey	2	11 Broad	100 000	" 6-4 Meltons,	100 000	25
Ashlar Mills	2	18 Broad	30 000	Balmoral skirts,	45 000	23

COTTON MANUFACTORY.

J. L. Peck, 3,392 spindles, warp. Annual production, $175,000. Hands employed, 75.
M. Van Sickler, 100 looms, manufacturing cotton cloth.

Around most of the manufactories named, little villages have grown up, some of them containing several hundred inhabitants. That known as Coltsville, in the north-eastern corner of the town, has a station of the North Adams Railroad, a hotel, and many residences of persons not connected with the paper-mill of Hon. Thomas Colt, from which it derives its name. Pontoosuc is a considerable village in size, and is of marked beauty. Below this, along the highway between Lanesborough and Pittsfield, lie Taconic and Wahconah; the boarding-houses of the Pittsfield Woollen Mill merging in the latter, which extends south to the junction of Onota Brook with the Housatonic.

Between the mouth of Onota Brook and Lake Onota lie, in the order in which they are named, Russell's, Peck's, and Peck and Kilbourn's villages. The dwellings connected with the Pittsfield Cotton Factory and Pomeroy's Woollen Mills form respectively the south-eastern and south-western verges of the central village of the town.

Upon Shaker Brook, about a mile and a quarter west of Pomeroy's, is Oceola. Upon the same stream, in the south-west corner of the town, is Barkersville; and, about half a mile farther north, Stearnsville, — both flourishing villages, containing not only the comfortable dwellings of the operatives, but the handsome residences of the proprietors of the mills. In Stearnsville is Emanuel Chapel, an outpost of St. Stephen's (P. E.) Church.

West of Stearnsville lies Shaker Village, or West Pittsfield, occupied mostly by a community of the religious sect whose name it bears.

Formerly, in some of the affairs of the town, Pittsfield was divided — as it often still is colloquially — into the East and West Parts, occasionally into the East and West Parts and the Centre. In ordinary conversation, the boundaries of these divisions are not very exactly defined; but as districts in the old time, for the collection of taxes and like purposes, if two only were made, the separating line was North and South Streets; if three, the Central was included between the Forks of the Housatonic. The North Woods embraced the region north-west of Lake Onota; and, although the woods have long since disappeared, the name is still retained.

The Central Village, to which we shall refer when speaking simply of "The Village," covers a space of something over a square mile, lying chiefly between the two branches of the Housatonic, and a little above their junction.[1]

Within these bounds are comprised nearly all the public and business edifices of the town, with the exceptions of the manufactories dependent upon water-power, and the buildings upon the Agricultural and Berkshire-Pleasure Parks. Here, too, are most of the private dwellings, other than those attached to factories or farms and a few costly country-seats. The Village is noted for the beauty of the views which it commands, for the broad and shaded avenues which branch from the pretty little park which adorns its centre, for its excellent educational institutions, and for some fine public and private edifices.

The Park, — hallowed of Pittsfield tradition, — which forms the central gem of the village cluster, is shaded by an elliptical grove of handsome elms, in the centre of which stood, until within a few years, a veteran of the same species, which was spared by the settlers from their sweeping destruction of the primeval forest. It early became the pride of the villager and the admiration of the stranger. Its fame went abroad. Every year added to the memories which had been clustering around it since the Old

[1] This thickly-peopled section is specially incorporated as "The Fire District;" having first been established for the support of a fire-department, but afterwards empowered to build and control water-works, sewers, sidewalks, and the like, and to maintain street-lights.

French and Indian Wars. But, in 1841, the lightning scored a ghastly wound down its tall, straight trunk, and began to dry up its life-blood. Limbs fell away from it from time to time; and the thunderbolt again scathed it. But still the little vitality which it retained was carefully cherished. In its palmiest days it had risen a smooth, bare shaft of ninety feet, bearing for capital a leafy coronal of branches which carried its height to one hundred and twenty-eight feet. In its days of blight, when a few green boughs and two or three withered and shattered limbs alone remained to crown it, the stranger still greeted it with admiration, and the citizen watched it with reverent love. And when, in July, 1864, it was found to be bending under its own weight, it was gently lowered from its place, literally amid the tears of the sternest men.

In the Park, the waters of Lake Ashley leap upward in a fountain whose spray might have washed the topmost leaves of the

MAPLEWOOD AVENUE.

Old Elm. Regard for the comfort of the neighborhood, however, dictates ordinarily a more modest display of its powers.[1]

1 Pittsfield is supplied with the purest water in great abundance from Lake Ashley, which lies upon the top of one of the Hoosac summits in Washington, at a distance of seven miles from the Park, and seven hundred feet above it. The lake is fed almost exclusively from springs in its own bed. The water descends about four miles in Ashley Brook to a reservoir in the south-western corner of Dalton, whence it is carried in pipes three miles one hundred and fifty-two rods, with a fall of one hundred and thirty-six feet, to the fountain in the Park. It is conveyed to all parts of the village, the length of main and distributing pipe being about fifteen miles.

The streets which branch from this centre are shaded in great part by fine elms and lindens; but an unfortunate partiality for rapid growth and luxuriant foliage has given a preponderance to the maples, long ago characterized by observant Spencer as "seeldom inward sound." Arbor-like streets, spacious court-yards overspread by patriarchal trees, and park-like grounds, almost embower a bird's-eye view of the village.

Of the latter, the most admired are those of Maplewood Young Ladies' Institute, whose graceful chapel, gymnasium, and half-

MAPLEWOOD CHAPEL.

vine-covered dwellings gleam white through avenues and groves of famed attractiveness.

An ample park, the seat of a school of a high grade for young men, occupies, with a profusion of arborage which almost rivals Maplewood, the southern declivity of a commanding eminence north of the village, which has received the name of Springside, from the abundant springs, whose waters have been turned to excellent purpose in adorning the grounds. The overview from Springside stretches across the lower Berkshire Valley to the Connecticut hills; glimpses of which, at a distance of twenty miles, are seen through the vista formed by the grander mountains which intervene.

Of the ten village churches, three are devoted to the Congregational form of worship; one of them being occupied by a colored parish. Two belong to St. Joseph's Roman Catholic parish; the sermons in one of them being alternately in the German and French languages. The Baptists, Methodists, and Episcopalians have one each; and one belongs to the German Lutherans, who form a considerable element in the population of Pittsfield, and have service in their own tongue.

In 1867–8, The Berkshire Life Insurance Company erected a large and costly building, one of the most perfect business structures in the country, upon the corner of North and West streets, long known as the site of the "Old Berkshire Hotel." In it is the central office of the proprietory corporation whose business ramifies into every portion of the northern section of the continent. It also affords spacious rooms for the post-office, luxurious banking-houses for the Pittsfield and Agricultural National Banks and the Berkshire County Savings Institution; halls for several Masonic bodies; the office of the Assessor of Internal Revenue for the Tenth Massachusetts District; many other offices, and several stores.

By law, the various railroads which intersect at Pittsfield are required to unite, previous to the year 1869, in a common passenger station: and a location has been selected for that purpose upon West street, about eighty rods west of the Park; and upon that site large and handsome buildings are about to be erected.

The Legislature of 1868 made Pittsfield the shire town of Berkshire County, requiring the town to furnish sites for the erection of the court-house and jail. For the former building, the beautiful elm-shaded grounds on East Street, between Park Square and Williams Avenue, have been purchased at the price of thirty-five thousand dollars; for the latter, ten acres of land are provided on North First Street, at a cost of five thousand dollars. The buildings will be commenced while this work is in press.

By the highway, the distance of Pittsfield from Boston is one hundred and thirty miles; from Albany, thirty-three. The windings of the railroad increase these distances to one hundred and fifty from the former city, and to fifty from the latter; requiring, respectively, six and two hours for the journey. New York is reached in about six hours.

BERKSHIRE LIFE INSURANCE COMPANY BUILDING.

Pittsfield has now a population of about eleven thousand, and is rated in the assessment of 1868 at a valuation of $3,473,061 in personal estate; $4,693,173, in real estate: a total valuation of $8,166,234. The number of polls returned was two thousand two hundred and ninety-three; the number of dwellings, fifteen hundred and four.

HISTORY.

HISTORY OF PITTSFIELD.

CHAPTER I.

ABORIGINAL OCCUPATION.

The Natives as found by the Pioneers. — Relics. — Villages and Burial Grounds in Pittsfield. — Scantiness of Native Population to be accounted for. — Mohegan Traditional History. — Wars of the Mohegans and Iroquois. — Changes in the Condition of the Mohegans of Berkshire.— Hunting-System of the Mohegans.— Berkshire a Hunting-Ground. — The Part of the Settlers of Pittsfield in various Indian Wars. — Remarkable Incidents.

WHEN, in the early part of the eighteenth century, the English of Massachusetts first became intimately acquainted with the mountainous district of its Far West, they found it teeming with the various species of game and fur-bearing animals then common in New England; which attracted occasional hunting-parties of the Mohegans and Schaghticokes, who, by tenures which will presently appear, held a sort of confused joint occupancy of the hunting-grounds.

The permanent native inhabitants were, however, sparse, even beyond the ordinary meagreness of Indian populations. The petty villages of a few insignificant squads, mostly of the Mohegan race, scattered at wide intervals, alone broke the solitude of the mountain wilderness. And of these little huddles of savage wigwams, too highly dignified by the title of village, one lay between Sheffield and Great Barrington; and the smoke of others curled up among the woods where Pittsfield, Stockbridge, New Marlborough, Dalton, and perhaps other towns, now stand.

The sites of those in Pittsfield are vaguely pointed out by tradition, with a somewhat less vague confirmation by the discovery of relics, as at Unkamet's Crossing, around the Canoe Meadows, and upon Indian Hill (the eminence immediately west of the Governor Briggs Homestead, and a little south-east of Lake Onota). It is altogether probable, however, that, in accordance with the universal practice of the aborigines, their lodges were removed from point to point, or, rather, that the costless things were abandoned for new, as often as convenience dictated, or a chance fire in the woods at once cleared and enriched new fields for their lazy husbandry.

Tradition speaks confidently of household implements of stone found abundantly in the olden time, especially near the Canoe Meadows, whose rich soil and neighboring river made them attractive; but such discoveries are rare now, although, in some fields, arrow-heads are not unfrequently found, —

> "The pointed flints that left his fatal bow,
> Chipped with rough art and slow barbarian toil,
> Last of his wrecks that strew the alien soil." — HOLMES.

It was for the chase or on the war-path, that the savage oftenest sought the wilds of the Winterberge. But the few memorials which he left of his presence on the soil of Pittsfield must be the more carefully recorded for their rarity.

On Indian Hill, in 1815, Capt. Joseph Merrick turned up with his plough a Jewish frontlet, which, being opened, displayed the usual sentences of Hebrew scripture, beautifully inscribed upon parchment, which had been kept in perfect preservation by leathern casings. The theory that the American Indians are the descendants of the lost tribes of Israel had then many ardent supporters, who, of course, hailed Capt. Merrick's waif as confirmation of their faith, in a double sense "strong as Holy Writ." Deposited with the Antiquarian Society at Worcester, it was learnedly discussed; and we still find it occasionally mentioned in books.[1]

[1] Memoir of Elkanah Watson, Hist. Stock., etc. Other like discoveries have since occurred. Dr. Lykin obtained the loan of a similar amulet which is still held in great repute by the Potawatamies of Kansas River; and the writer has seen one which was found about twenty-five years ago among the Penobscot (Taratine) tribe in Maine. One cannot account with perfect confidence for the dispersion of these sacred mementoes so widely among a people ignorant of their significance; but it is less difficult to assume a Hebrew shipwreck, than to inject the blood of Israel into Algonquin veins. The aboriginal superstition of ascribing

In 1850, a deep cutting was made in a peat-bed a few rods north-east of Indian Hill; and a number of poles, sharpened by the aid of fire, as if for the construction of wigwams, were found so far beneath the surface that they must have been deposited there long before Jacob Elkins's bold explorers could have penetrated the valley.

Indian Point is the name — handed down from the old time — of a projection into Lake Onota upon the west, where the red hunter delighted to lie *perdue* behind the singular rocky screen described in a previous chapter, and shoot the deer who took refuge in the delicious waters from the torments of the summer-heat and the swarming mosquitoes. And, doubtless, in the course of ages, erring marksmen left an armory of flint arrow-heads on the gravelly bed of the lake.

Along the Housatonic, east of the former residence of Dr. O. W. Holmes, stretch what the early settlers always called the Canoe Meadows; and from their level surface, upon the eastern bank of the river, rises a knoll which was once used as a burial-place by the Mohegans, who, after they were collected in one community at Stockbridge, were accustomed to make pious pilgrimages to this spot, leaving the birch-canoes, in which they had ascended the river, in the Meadows to which they thus gave name.[1]

Lake Shoonkeekmoonkeek, with its prolific waters, must have been a frequent resort for the guiders of the birch-canoe; and by its shores they buried their dead. Some of their skeletons were, a few years ago, exhumed from the eastern bank of its outlet, where they had been interred in the usual sitting posture.

The graves of the vanished race of which so many wild tales were told, of whom so many wild deeds were personally remembered, always had a strange fascination for the pioneers; and those of Pittsfield pointed out several in different parts of the town to their children. But these were wayside resting-places, to which their tenants seem to have been consigned without that reverential

the power of a "medicine," or charm, to whatever in civilized use was incomprehensible by savage simplicity, is well-known; and surely nothing would more probably acquire this mystic character than the curious frontlets which perchance some shipwrecked children of Abraham, miraculously preserved from the waves, may have been, by the wondering natives, observed to hold in religious veneration.

[1] Mr. William G. Backus, who, when a boy, assisted in clearing this burial-knoll for cultivation, states that the graves could then be distinctly *traced.*

care which the men of the woods were wont to bestow upon their dead.

Such are the scant memorials by which we are able to trace the aboriginal occupation of the soil of Pittsfield before its history as the home of civilized man commenced. But slender as these memorials are, and slight as may have been the red man's attachment to the spot as a permanent home, there can be no doubt that it was his choicest hunting-ground. That he has left recorded in the name he bestowed upon it; and, although another appellation has usurped the place of that which the Mohegan so significantly gave it, we still love to remember that this was the Indian's abundant Poontoosuck, his favorite chase for deer. The names the red men called them by still cling to mountain, lake, and stream, forbidding us to forget the race, which, a little more than a hundred years ago, imparted to this glorious landscape all of human interest that pertained to it. He must be dull of sentiment indeed, who does not feel that without the old Indian story, dim though it may be, the region of the Taconics and the Hoosacs, of Poontoosuck and the Housatonic, of Unkamet and Honwee, would lack a charm we should not willingly spare.

But aside from what may be considered mere sentimental interest, — although that, too, has its intrinsic worth, — a question of more material importance arises, and finds its answer in a consecutive, although not very minute, history of the Mohegan nation. The paucity of the native population found in Berkshire demands an explanation, and did, in fact, early attract the attention of the local historians, who, although in some respects favored, labored under great difficulties from the want of those archives to which later writers have access.

The native traditions declared, and with entire truth, that formerly a thousand warriors had answered to the Mohegan battle-cry, and distant tribes had sought and received the protection of their arms; but the first European explorers of their country, or certainly the first English surveyors, found but a few scant hundreds — men, women, and children included — remaining to tenant all the ancient empire of the tribe. And a patriotic shame forbade the native chroniclers to relate to the stranger the unvarnished story of their humiliation.

Those among the early settlers who interested themselves in such questions, — thus left to their own resources, if not actually misled, — in accounting for the decadence of the population which preceded them, adopted a theory utterly untenable. They fancied, that, when the remnants of the Pequots and Narragansetts, spared from fire and sword, were driven out of New England, the terror-stricken fugitives, passing through Western Massachusetts, so spread the fear of the white man's prowess and cruelty that the mass of the people joined in the flight to safer regions in the West.

By a strange negligence, the fact was overlooked, that the territory in question was inhabited by Mohegans, the inveterate enemies of both Pequots and Narragansetts, between whom and the New-Englanders they had been the chief instruments in stirring up strife. At the very moment when they are represented as joining the exiles in panic flight, they were pursuing them with a vindictiveness which their white allies were, for the sake of humanity, obliged to temper. It will be recollected that when, in 1676, the renowned Major Talcot overtook a fugitive band of two hundred wretched Narragansetts at Stockbridge, and visited them with great slaughter, he was guided in the pursuit by a Mohegan, and that the only man he lost in the affair was of the same race. It was with good reason that the Mohegans loved, and were faithful to, the white man; for by him they had been preserved from utter extermination, and, in the Valley of the Connecticut at least, restored to something of their old prestige as warriors. The sheep might as well have herded with the wolves flying from the shepherd, as the Mohegans have joined the Pequots and Narragansetts escaping from the New-Englanders.

So far from dwindling in these old wars, the population of Moheganland must have been swelled by the captives who, in accordance with their custom, were adopted into the victorious tribe; and, owing to the humane influence of the colonial officers, the number thus saved from death was greater than in most Indian wars. It does not, however, appear that the villages west of the Hoosacs received immediately much augmentation from this source. But the Iroquois, who had become the feudal lords of the old Mohegan empire, granted a refuge, in what is now the northern part of Rensselaer county, to a band of exiled Narragansetts, which grew to be the Schaghticoke tribe, and sent out little colonies to the Valley of the Housatonic.[1]

[1] The principal Indian village in Sheffield was styled Scatecook; and the presence of individuals of that race in the county was the cause of the only blood-

These accessions to the native population were, to be sure, not large; but they serve to strengthen our conception of the extreme desolation which must have prevailed anterior to them; and, even if they were altogether inconsiderable, the fact would still be plain, that such desolation was not the result of the New-England wars.

The error in solving the problem arose from the mistake of seeking the key — if, indeed, it was sought in any documentary evidence — among the records of Massachusetts; while the Mohegans were, especially at the period of their decadence, essentially a New-York tribe.

Turning to the historical collections of the latter State, we find that destruction came to the aborigines of Berkshire from the west, and not from the east, — from the red man, and not from the white: in what manner, we shall endeavor to show.

The Mohegan — one of the most prominent in the history of the Algonquin races — was, like the others, divided into tribes or nations, bearing distinctive names; which, again, were subdivided into bands, —a political organization into whose constitution we do not purpose to inquire. The great tribe to which the appellation of Mohegan is commonly applied, and who may hence be held to represent the parent stock, occupied in 1609, when they were first visited by the Dutch under Hendrick Hudson, the whole territory now the counties of Berkshire, Columbia, and Rensselaer; having their chief village, or "castle," at Schodac (more musically pronounced by themselves Eskwatak, — the place of fires; i.e., council-fires), on the Hudson. And they had also, at what is now Greenbush, a strongly fortified post — according to their notions of engineering — against their hereditary enemies, the Mohawks, whose territory came down to the opposite bank of the Hudson.

The name by which they called themselves, as nearly as English type can represent its multitudinous syllables, was Mo-he-ka-neew, — in the plural, Mo-he-ka-neok; signifiying "the people of the great waters which are continually in motion," — that is, which ebb and flow. This unwieldy patronymic was mellowed by the Dutch to Mahican, as it is written in the early Pittsfield deeds;

shed between the colonists and the children of the soil which ever occurred among its hills.

by the English to Mohican; and, finally, has passed into poetry and history as the sonorous Mohegan. The national tradition is, that the progenitors of the race on this continent, having crossed the great waters at a point in the North-west where the opposite coasts approach very near to each other, were compelled by famine to disperse through the wilderness, and thus lost whatever of civilized arts and manners they had previously possessed, — "apostatized," as their Christianized chronicler expresses it.[1]

Pursuing their way to the south-east,— still driven by hunger, or impelled by that centrifugal restlessness which urged the nations away from their cradle, — they crossed many great waters, but none which ebbed and flowed like Mohekunnuk, "the river of their nativity," until they reached the Hudson. Pleased with the resemblance of that noble stream, in this respect, to that which ebbed and flowed in their Asian home, they called it Mahicanittuck; anticipating a bad American practice by reduplicating, in the land of their adoption, the name which had been dear in the land of their birth.

Finding, in addition to the charm of association, that the shores of the great river abounded in game, and its waters with fish, while the soil and climate favored their easy-going agriculture, the way-worn and hungry people determined here to fix their permanent habitation.

Flourishing in this new home, the Mohegans ran the usual career of successful Indian nationalities. Carrying carnage and desolation among neighbors as savage as themselves, they destroyed some weaker tribes, protected and affiliated others. The terror of their name spread far to the east and west; and probably it was at this era that one of their tribes penetrated into south-eastern Connecticut, and, there establishing themselves, achieved among the natives of that region the proud title of Pequots, — the destroyers.

On their western border, the Mohegans reduced the six nations — not yet confederate — to the utmost straits. They even threatened that afterwards-powerful empire — or, rather, most of its then independent parts — with total extinction. But at that unknown epoch when the wonderful league was formed which constituted the Iroquois in war one people, — one ambitious, revengeful, and irresistible nation, — the fortunes of the Mohegans

[1] Hendrick Aupaumut in Hist. Stockbridge.

began to wane; and they were soon glad to accept the alliance, for mutual defence, of the Wappingers, and other river-tribes, with whom, up to that time, they had been at continual war. But the combined forces of the eastern shore proved too weak to withstand the enemy, to whom a wise union had suddenly given the almost undisputed empire of the forest. The allies were defeated by the Iroquois, in a decisive battle fought near Rhinebeck on the Hudson, at a date so recent that the first Dutch farmers found their fields still strewn with the bones of the slain.

The defeated party was reduced to vassalage, which, although not of so degrading a character as that imposed on the unfortunate Leni Lenape, — who descended from the rank of warriors to the political condition of squaws, — must have been sufficiently galling; especially in cases like that of the treaty of Tawesentha, when the belt of friendship, held at one end by the Dutch and at the other by the Iroquois, rested upon the shoulders of the Mohegans and of "the nation of women," in token of their common subjugation.

Fretting under the yoke, the conquered but still high-spirited race soon rebelled; and in 1625 we find them again in arms against their ancient enemy. The attempt to regain their independence on their own soil miserably failed. The uprising was suppressed; and, after a merciless war of three years' duration, the greater portion of the Mohegans were either killed or captured, and the remainder were driven into the Valley of the Connecticut. Here they were hospitably received by their kinsmen of the previous migration, — the Pequots. But difficulty soon arose from the ambition of Uncas. A separation ensued, and then those intrigues at Boston and Hartford which brought destruction upon the Pequot branch.

If, as has been said, there was any feudal subjection of the Mohegans in the Connecticut Valley to the Iroquois, it must have been an uneasy and often interrupted relation; for Arnold Montague, who wrote of the last days of the Dutch dominion on the Hudson, and published his account in 1671, reports the Mohawks as constantly at war with the Mohegans, which latter also maintained "a constant animosity against the Dutch."

At last, in 1664, as the English fleet was approaching to convert the New Netherlands into New York, the Mohegans were emboldened, perhaps instigated, to harry the Province upon its opposite frontier; and thus the old fire again broke forth. The Mohegans attacked the Mohawks, destroyed cattle at Greenbush, fired a barn at Claverack, and ravaged that eastern bank of the Hudson which had been the home of their fathers. But, on the 8th of the following September, — this devastation having occurred in July, — the Dutch governor surrendered Fort Amsterdam, and the New Netherlands ceased to be. Thenceforward the governments of New York and Massachusetts, subject to the same crown, strove to stanch the feuds which prevailed between the tribes within their borders; so that the Mohawk and the Mohegan did not again meet in battle until the war of the Revolution, when the former adhered to the king, and the latter espoused the cause of the people.

After the forced exodus of the great body of the Mohegans, in 1628, their ancient hunting-grounds upon the hills seem to have been occupied by the few who were released from captivity, or who crept back from exile and hiding; and, after such fierce conflicts and such general expatriation, the wonder is, not that so few, but that any remained. The components and form of Indian communities are, however, proverbially fluctuating as the sand-hills of the desert; and, in the disturbance produced by colonial agencies, sources were found from which, in some small degree, to replenish dispeopled Moheganland. Along the river-shore at Claverack, Kinderhook, and Greenbush, the Dutch began to spread their settlements, and press the natives to the hills. On the north, the Schaghticokes prospered, and threw out their branches along the Housatonic. Straggling Horikans, perhaps, wandered down from the Upper Winterberge. Meanwhile, the relations between the Iroquois and their Mohegan feudatories became more intimate and genial, — doubtless through the kind offices of the Oneidas, who, before their incorporation into the Six Nations, had incurred a debt of gratitude to the then-powerful Mohegans, which they seem now faithfully to have discharged. "The Mohawks, Onondagas, Cayugas, and Senecas are our uncles," said the Stockbridge chroniclers; "but the Oneidas and Tuscaroras are our brothers."

Still the statement of the exceeding meagreness with which the Indians peopled Western Massachusetts needs no qualification; and what inhabitants there were, were mostly Mohegan. Even when an attempt was made, about 1750, to introduce Mohawks into the mission settlement at Stockbridge, the effort met with no success, notwithstanding the strenuous exertions of the commissioners, sustained by lavish appropriations of money by the General Court.

We have few data upon which to found an estimate of the number of natives who, before its settlement, occupied the territory now known as Berkshire. When the mission was established at Stockbridge, an effort was made to gather all of the nation into one community in that town; and, in 1736, ninety had thus been collected. One hundred and twenty were reported in 1740; and, by 1747, these had increased to two hundred. In 1785, when they were about to remove to the Oneida country, the community had grown to the number of four hundred and twenty souls. But of these, a majority had come from beyond the Hoosacs upon one side, and the Taconics on the other.

There is, indeed, no reason to believe, that, even in the palmiest days of Mohegan empire, any considerable number of the tribe ever dwelt permanently in the mountainous regions of their country. Indeed, we have positive evidence to the contrary in an account written by Capt. Hendrick Aupaumut, one of their later chroniclers, and preserved by President Dwight. As the customs of the nation are described in this paper, the business of the chase was pursued with system. The sanop, to be sure, might replenish his larder from the neighboring woods, whenever appetite or opportunity suggested. But the red deer did not, as an ordinary morning occurrence, bound by the Indian village, and receive an invitation in the guise of a flint arrow-head to the wigwam dinner. The year was, therefore, divided into two great hunting-seasons, — one in the fall, when they hunted the deer, bear, beaver, otter, raccoon, fisher, and martin, for winter clothing, and drying-meat; the other in the spring, when they chased the moose upon the Green Mountains, — the Taconics and Hoosacs. The latter season commenced about the first of March, and was succeeded by a supplementary trapping of otter, beaver, and other amphibious animals, as soon as the ice broke up in the streams and lakes. Good care was, however, taken that the stay among the mountains should not exceed two months.

The conclusion which we reach, then, is, that the few Mohegans who kept their lodges permanently at Poontoosuck lived amid an abundance of game, which, throughout the year, they shared with such hunting-parties of their countrymen as chose to join them, which many probably did at the time of the fall hunt. But, in the early spring, the whole valley, with its surrounding hillsides, was alive with the hunters of the moose,—the broad-horned "winter-deer;" and, as the ice melted from the waters, their banks were lined with the forms of the trappers, as, now bending, now creeping, they cautiously examined their thick-set snares.

Of what wild adventure, of what wily craft, the scenes now familiar to us were witnesses in those grand hunts, or during the desperate struggles for tribal independence which have been portrayed, imagination only can tell; unless, indeed, antiquarian research shall yet discover some fragments of the story, imbedded perhaps, as much which goes to make up this chapter was found, in documents otherwise dry as dust.

We need not here pursue the topic further. The fairest era in the Mohegan's story — that of his introduction to Christian civilization — belongs to the annals of Stockbridge. But, while Pittsfield may well envy her beautiful sister-town, the memories of that noble missionary enterprise, and of the great men who were connected with it, happily she has also little of that tragic interest, so far as events occurring upon her own soil are concerned, which connects the red man so sadly with the early history of many New-England towns. The first inhabitants and their fathers had already, in other places, borne their full part in the dangers, sufferings, and losses inflicted by savage warfare, as, in all respects, they had contributed their full share in laying the foundations of the commonwealth. The names they bore were not strange to Massachusetts history, but had been hallowed in that baptism of blood which, for a century of cruel years, was poured out over the Valley of the Connecticut.

Military rolls — almost lost among similar memorials of honor which war after war has accumulated in the archives of Massachusetts — still preserve the names of some, afterwards among the founders of Pittsfield, who, when younger men, of Springfield, Northampton, Westfield, and other towns, fought in "the old Indian wars." But the record of individual suffering and achievement is scant; while of the daring women, who, with husband and son, braved the dangers of that lurid frontier, only here and there an incident is told: of which one, in which an ancestress of the Janes-Brown families of Pittsfield was the heroine, must suffice for an illustration. This lady, the wife of Benjamin Janes, was, says Rev. Frederic Janes (the historian of the family), conspicuous in the tragic perils and sufferings at Pasconiac, near Northampton Village, in 1704, — saw her four children murdered by the savages, and was herself tomahawked, scalped, and left for dead; but recovered, after two years of suffering, and bore four other children. One of her grandsons, Elijah, settled in Pittsfield about 1763, and other of her descendants at various times.[1]

[1] In the foregoing chapter, the accounts of the customs and pre-historic migrations of the Mohegans are gathered from the traditions preserved by President Dwight. For the story of their wars with the Iroquois, I have depended chiefly upon the documentary history of New York, and the histories of that State by Dr. E. B. O'Callaghan and John Romeyn Brodhead.

CHAPTER II.

GRANTS. — SURVEYS. — SALES.

[1620–1741.]

Advance of Population Westward in Massachusetts. — History of the Western Boundary of Massachusetts. — First Settlement on the Housatonic. — Disposition by the General Court of Wild Lands in Hampshire County. — Jacob Wendell. — John Stoddard. — Grant to Stoddard. — Grant to Boston. — Boston sells to Wendell. — Adjustment of the Rights of Wendell, Stoddard, and Philip Livingston. — Cost, Form, and Dimensions of the Township.

THE tide of population, setting westward from Plymouth Rock, in the brief space of twenty-six years advanced to the shores of the Connecticut, where Springfield was founded in 1636. Thirty additional years carried it forward but barely ten miles to Westfield, where, stayed at the base of Tekoa Mountain, it paused for more than half a century, until suddenly, in 1725, it overleaped the Hoosacs, and the village of Sheffield was planted upon the broadest and most fertile meadows of the Housatonic. Twenty-seven years more elapsed before a permanent settlement was effected at belated Poontoosuck. Thus one hundred and sixteen years intervened between the settlement of Springfield and that of Pittsfield. The Connecticut Valley, with its people decimated by repeated massacre and harried by hordes of savages, whose apparent numbers were enhanced by their mode of warfare, — this valley, with fields more abundant than husbandmen, — had small temptation to offshoot its scanty population into a region whose frowning mountains even now turn eastward their most rugged front, and which then lay in most provoking contiguity to the war-path of the Canadian foe. This, however, was by no means the sole or even the chief cause which postponed the western settlements. It was little effect, except when war actually existed, that such obstacles were wont to have in staying the progress of Massachusetts population when the interests of the Province demanded that it should advance.

The impediment which proved effectual was the uncertainty of the New-York boundary, which a series of conflicting royal grants and charters had involved in a curious complication that was only finally disentangled by what New York called "intrusion," but Massachusetts a bold assumption of just territorial rights.[1]

The antagonistic positions maintained by the two Provincial Governments may, perhaps, be best exhibited in dialogue, thus: —

MASSACHUSETTS. — Under royal charter granted A.D. 1691 by King William and Queen Mary, of blessed memory, my territory extends as far west as that of Connecticut, in virtue of the words following; to wit, "westward as far as our colonies of Rhode Island, Connecticut, and the Narragansett countrie."

NEW YORK. — Nay; but these words refer to the eastern and not to the western bounds of Connecticut: rightfully construed, they do not bring you even to the Connecticut River. However, up to that line, it is no concern of mine; but observe, in 1674, — seventeen years antecedent to your charter from William and Mary, — Charles the Second granted, among other territories, to his brother, the Duke of York, "all the lands from the west side of the Connecticut to the east side of Delaware Bay." And to the Duke's title my government succeeds.[2]

MASSACHUSETTS. — True, as to Charles's grant; and that was not the only portion of my proper territory the royal rascal tried to steal for his brother, the sometime papist tyrant, before his corrupt judges robbed me legally, or at least with some of the forms of law, of the whole.

NEW YORK. — But you will not deny, that, your charter having been vacated in chancery, it was competent for the King to dispose as he pleased of the lands reverting to him.

MASSACHUSETTS. — We need not discuss that. The decree in chancery issued in 1684. It could have no effect upon transactions in 1674, when, if at all, the Duke's rights must have accrued from the last confirmation of his grant of which there is any pretence. By the King's patent, only such title could have passed as was then in him, not that which he may afterwards have acquired. Now,

1 Resulting, however, in an amicable adjustment of claims.

2 New York also contended that the boundary established between that Province and Connecticut was not that contemplated by the original patents, but was conceded by a special agreement between the parties, for reasons not applicable to the case of Massachusetts; among which, one was the actual occupation of the territory by Connecticut colonists.

in 1674, I was living under the grand old charter which made the Atlantic and Pacific seas my eastern and western bounds.

New York. — Hold! Not so fast! Remember that your 'grand old charter" — that of the first Charles, in 1628, I suppose you speak of — limits itself by this restriction: "Provided also that the said islands, or any the premises by the said letters-patent intended or meant to be granted, were not then actually possessed or inhabited by any other Christian prince or state." Now, about the year 1608, "as appears from the book entituled 'The British Empire in America,'" Henry Hudson discovered the lands of this province; and, by virtue of that discovery, the Dutch — whose title is merged in mine, and under whom, as well as the Duke, I claim — possessed and occupied the same as far north-easterly as the Connecticut River, near which, I doubt not, it may be made to appear many Dutch people were settled.[1]

And thereupon Massachusetts made an issue of fact, denying any such sufficient occupation by the Dutch as was alleged, except as regarded a narrow strip of territory along the Hudson.

The controversy continued many years, and was finally terminated, without an adjudication upon its original merits, by an agreement entered into by the parties, after an amicable conference by their representatives at Hartford, in 1773. The boundary then consented to was substantially that claimed by Massachusetts; but, instead of being a continuation due north of the Connecticut line, it was made to deflect considerably towards the east by a corresponding divergence in the course of the Hudson River, between which and Massachusetts it was provided that a space of twenty miles should at all points intervene.

Until this arrangement was effected, the uncertain dividing-line was a constant source of trouble, vexation, and anxiety; sometimes resulting in violence, and once at least in bloodshed, between parties who acted under conflicting patents from the rival Governments. In general, however, the influence of the royal governors prevented a resort to extreme measures. Massachusetts maintained her jurisdiction up to the boundary which she claimed. New York ruled beyond it. Conflicts arose only in the few cases in which the two Governments had granted the same tracts to

[1] Papers relating to the Livingston Manor and the New-Hampshire Grants, N. Y., Doc. Hist., and Col. Docs.

different parties, and principally as to those now mostly included in the towns of Sheffield, Mount Washington, and Egremont, but which were known to New-York colonial geography as the tracts of Taghkanik and Westenhook in the manor of Livingston.

Previous to the conference of 1773, New York, nevertheless, did not in terms relinquish her pretensions to any of the territory claimed by Massachusetts west of the Connecticut River. On the contrary, she rather insisted upon their validity; and, while hinting that equity might require the Crown to confirm to individuals the lands actually possessed and improved by them, she clogged this concession by insisting upon the quit-rents which lands in her patents paid to the royal revenue. These rents had sometimes furnished corrupt officials with a pretext for extortion, and had always been fruitful of discontent, even among those who had accepted grants specifically charged with them.

In Massachusetts, no such tribute was known. Her settlers boasted themselves freeholders, — a title which conferred not only substantial rights, but much-prized burgher dignity. They therefore especially dreaded transfer to a government whose lands were universally held under what they deemed a feudal tenure. The New-York officials, on the other hand, were contemplating with impatient longing the sums which the quit-rents due upon the lands unjustly withheld by Massachusetts ought to bring into their treasury; Gov. Hardy estimating them, in 1756, at £2,000 *per annum*, and Lieut.-Gov. Colden, in 1764, being content with the more moderate demand of £1,200. We can thus well comprehend the relief which must have been afforded to the people of Pittsfield, as well as of her sister towns, by the result of the Hartford conference, which was doubtless one of the causes that, in the ensuing ten years, vexed as they were with war and financial disorder, nearly doubled her population.

The line agreed upon in 1773 was not, however, finally run until 1787, when Congress, at the request of the States interested, appointed a commission for the purpose, consisting of Rev. Dr. John Ewing, a distinguished *savan* of Philadelphia; David Rittenhouse, the celebrated astronomer; and Thomas Hutchins, the national geographer-general. All the science of even this distinguished triad was, however, insufficient to correct the variations of the magnetic needle among the iron-laden hills of Taconic; and the line was not precisely that contemplated by the parties: but the error was of trifling moment as compared with the amity of contiguous States. The line, therefore, remains as it was then fixed, with the slight exception caused by the cession of Boston Corner to New-York in 1855, which, although made for the convenience of those living upon that little tract, incidentally rectified, in part, the error of 1787.[1]

We must now return to the period when the pioneer civilization of Massachusetts, after its long pause upon the banks of the Connecticut, was about to advance at one bound to those of the Housatonic.

Between the years 1717 and 1722, it became apparent, from the course of New York, that the boundary between that Province and Connecticut, agreed upon in 1683–4, must soon be run.

Roughly, that agreement was upon a line about twenty miles east of the Hudson; and it was manifest, as well from observation as from the express declaration of the representatives of New York, that Connecticut, in obtaining a boundary so far westward of that originally conceded to her, had been mainly aided by boldly pushing forward her population to the farthest limits which she claimed.

Every consideration, then, urged Massachusetts to a similar course; while the precedent of Connecticut imparted confidence to settlers in the titles founded upon a basis which had proved sufficient in the southern Province. Nine years of peace since Queen Anne's War had also reinvigorated the frontier, and filled it with young men impatient for a new advance into the wilderness.

In 1722, therefore, one hundred and seventy-seven citizens of Hampshire County petitioned the General Court for a grant of lands in the Valley of the "Housatunnuk or Westbrook." Some of the best minds[2] in the councils of the Province then represented the old county, and strongly favored, if they had not indeed suggested, the petition: and accordingly the townships

[1] The extension of Massachusetts a little farther westward than Connecticut, notwithstanding her claim to only coequal bounds, is accounted for by the cession, by the latter State, of a strip from her western border as an equivalent for a tract added to Fairfield County from New York.

[2] Among these, one of the most active and influential was Ebenezer Pomeroy, an ancestor of the Pomeroy family of Pittsfield.

afterwards designated as the "Upper and Lower Housatunnuk" were granted; their ample limits embracing the present towns of Sheffield, Great Barrington, Mount Washington, and Alford, with a great portion of Stockbridge, West Stockbridge, and Lee. The settlement of this tract commenced at what is now Sheffield, in 1725, simultaneously with the survey of the New-York and Connecticut boundary-line; but the enterprise lagged until the completion of that survey in 1731. About that time, an informal understanding appears to have been at least tacitly established between New York and Massachusetts; for a New-York historian of that period exultingly records that "it was left for the year 1731 to be distinguished for the complete settlement of the boundary disputes, — an event, considering the late colonizing spirit and extensive claims of the New-England people, of no small importance."

Something very like a Western fever, and speculation in "the unappropriated lands of the Province, in the county of Hampshire," now sprang up. The General Court, eager to occupy the disputed territory, made liberal grants to actual settlers upon payment of sums barely sufficient to extinguish the Indian title, and defray the expenses of formally establishing the plantations. To other purchasers, lands were sold at a moderate price per acre. Public men were rewarded for services to the State by gifts of forest tracts; institutions of learning were endowed with townships; and towns at the east, upon which an unfair proportion of the general burdens fell, were relieved by drafts upon the same treasury of public wealth.[1]

But, whatever might otherwise be the nature of the grant, provision — generally in the form which we shall find in the case of Pittsfield — was almost invariably made for a speedy, thrifty, and defensible settlement by *Massachusetts subjects*, and for the support of schools and public worship.

[1] There was no division of the territory into townships by general survey; but grants were made of a certain number of acres, sometimes of a prescribed compactness, to be selected from the unappropriated lands of the Province in the county of Hampshire, "to be surveyed, and a plat thereof returned to the General Court" within a specified time, "for confirmation." Afterwards, the nooks between these selections were granted. This practice, the variation of the western boundary of the State from the line at first expected, and the mountainous ridges which intersect the county, are the chief, although not the only causes of the very irregular shapes and sizes of the Berkshire towns.

There was no lack of men ready to accept lands, even upon an exposed frontier, and with Indian claims to be extinguished, when the terms were otherwise so easy as those described above. Nor were there wanting many, with strong muscles and intelligent minds, although of feeble purse, who were willing to encounter danger, exposure, and the most arduous labors, that they might build up homes in the newly-opened country.

The system of large farms and scant culture — natural to new countries, and not without its benefits in diffusing population — left many young men, even in the fertile valley of the Connecticut, with no alternative but to till an inferior soil, or bravely win a richer from the forest. We know what class chose the latter: the advancing wave of civilization bore the noblest spirits on its crest. Persons of a riper age and more ample means, whose professional or political success had not equalled their ambition, or perhaps their conscious merit, were tempted, if of elastic temperament and persistent resolution, to new fields of effort in the rising plantations, where their experience, serviceable to the community, would be welcomed and rewarded. Men of public spirit and unemployed capital at once gratified their tastes, and found a profitable investment for their money, in furthering the settlement of townships, whose acres were certain to increase many fold in value by the labors and outlays of those who purchased a small portion, often for almost as much as the first cost of the whole tract.

The Provincial archives of the period are full of papers concerning wild lands, new settlements, and dealings regarding them; and, among the names which most frequently recur in these documents, are those most conspicuous also in the transactions preliminary to the settlement of Pittsfield, — Cols. Jacob Wendell of Boston, and John Stoddard of Northampton.

These gentlemen were both men of property, members of the Provincial Council, and colonels of the militia in their respective counties. Col. Wendell, born at Albany in 1691, of Dutch lineage, connected with some of the most prominent families in that ancient burgh, early transferred his prosperous fortunes to Boston, where he became one of the wealthiest merchants of the port, a director of the first banking institution established in America, and a successful politician. He married a daughter of Dr. James Oliver of Cambridge, and by her became the father of a son more distinguished than himself, — Oliver Wendell, the bold and ardent Revolutionary leader; — and the ancestor of two men of brilliant intellectual fame in our own day, Wendell Phillips and Oliver Wendell Holmes.

Col. Stoddard was one of the most remarkable men in the Provincial history of New England, if we may credit so eminent a eulogist as President Edwards, who ascribes to him "the highest native gifts of mind, a peculiar genius for public affairs, a thorough political knowlege, great purity of life, incorruptible principles, and sincere piety." He adds, that, "upon the whole, there perhaps never was a man in New England to whom the appellation of 'a great man' did more properly belong." This is, to be sure, the language of eulogy, uttered by one mourning the newly dead, to whom he had been bound by the ties of kindred, and the closest sympathies of religious opinion; but the assenting judgment of unbiassed contemporaries of Col. Stoddard, and the record of his public life, permit us to deduct little from President Edwards's high estimate of his character.

There were but few public undertakings of much consequence, in his time, in which he had not some part; and, among other commissions upon which he served, were those to open the settlement at Sheffield, and to establish the celebrated Indian mission at Stockbridge; in both of which he was joined with Ebenezer Pomeroy. During Queen Anne's War, his command of the militia, in the most exposed portion of the Province, was creditable; and, at its close, he was sent to Canada to effect the restoration of the New-England captives who were scattered among the savages of that region.

In 1734, the General Court granted to this faithful servant of the Province one thousand acres of its "unappropriated lands in the county of Hampshire," to be by himself selected in some convenient place. The grant was asked in consideration of Col. Stoddard's "great services and sufferings for the public in divers journeys to Canada, Albany, and the eastern parts, upon public affairs; his serving in war with good success; his transactions with the Canadian and other western Indians; and his entertaining of them at his own house without any expense to the Province."

It was required that the thousand acres should be laid out by surveyor and chain-men, under oath, and a plat returned to the General Court for confirmation within twelve months of the passage of the act which bore date Dec. 17, 1734. The Legislature were, however, not rigid as to lapses of time when conflicting claims did not accrue in the interval; and the grant was duly confirmed, although the survey was not submitted until June 22, 1736. The bounds of the patent are thus defined:—

"Lying on the main branch of the Housatonic River, about sixteen miles north of Capt. Konkapot's house: beginning east ten degrees, south eighty perch from two hemlock-trees, marked (which trees stand upon a ridge of upland running northerly), and coming to a point a few rods from said trees, which are about ten rods from a sand-bank on the east side of said Housatonic River, just above Unkamet's or Antankamet's Road, where it crosseth said branch: and, from the end of the aforesaid eighty perch from said trees, it runneth north ten degrees, east two hundred and forty perch: thence west ten degrees, north four hundred perch; thence south ten degrees, west four hundred perch; thence east ten degrees, south four hundred perch; and thence north ten degrees, east one hundred and sixty perch, to the eastern end of the first eighty perch."

Konkapot's house stood upon the north bank of Konkapot's Brook, in Stockbridge. Unkamet's Road extended from Northampton to Albany. It was probably an ancient Indian trail, improved by passing parties of soldiers and surveyors, so as to admit the use of pack-horses, upon which supplies for the army and the settlers were transported. It crossed the eastern branch of the Housatonic, near where the highway, Unkamet Street, next south of the Western Railroad, now bridges it.[1] As the meadows at that point were called "Unkamet's," and a neighboring brook bore the same name,[2] it is fair to surmise that some Mohegan guide, whose wigwam stood in the vicinity, acquired among the travellers who passed that way, in Col. Stoddard's time or earlier, the sobriquet of Unkamet, or Old-Path-Over-Yonder, from the phrase which was perpetually recurring in their intercourse; the translation of the word "Unkamet" being simply "the path over there."

Col. Stoddard, in his frequent visits to Albany, Sheffield, and Stockbridge, as well as in his military oversight of the district, must have become thoroughly acquainted with the region; and he manifested his knowledge of it shrewdly in selecting his thousand acres, which hardly had their equal within the bounds of his choice. Lying in the form of a square at the western terminus of the most

1 Plan of the town in 1752, and deed in Henry Colt's collection.

2 Vulgarly corrupted in later times to Huckamuck.

convenient pass through the Hoosac Mountains, it included some of the most luxuriant meadows and fertile uplands in the Province. One of the best water-privileges on the Upper Housatonic added to its wealth; and its location rendered it likely to become the intersecting point of the county roads. Stoddard's thousand acres must be borne in mind: they will have their distinctive part in our story.

But even this fine tract, encumbered as it was by Indian claims, and with its value largely in anticipation, would, in modern judgment, be considered an inadequate recompense for the array of public services which we have quoted of Col. Stoddard. And there are indications that, even with his more primitive notions, he entertained a similar opinion of his reward. He certainly contemplated an extension of his patent, either by grant or purchase, to a full township; and, with this view, obtained deeds and leases from different Indian claimants, by which their title to a tract six miles square, nearly identical with that now covered by Pittsfield, was transferred to him. One of these leases is preserved in the collection of Hon. Thos. Colt, and the material portions are given below: —

To all People to whom these shall come. GREETING:

KNOW YE, That we, Jacobus Coh-qua-he-ga-meek, Matakeamin, and Wampenum, formerly of Menanoke,[1] or the island in the Hudson below Albany, now planters in the Indian town on Housatonic River, have demised, granted, and to farm-letten (*sic*), and by these presents do farm-let unto John Stoddard of Northampton, in the county of Hampshire and Province of Massachusetts Bay, in New England, Esq., all that tract and parcel of land, of six miles square, lying and being in the county of Hampshire and Province of Massachusetts Bay aforesaid, on the main or principal branch of Houseatunnick River, so called, about sixteen miles northward of the place where Cuncupot now dwells, and at the place where Unkamet's Road, so called, that leads from Albany to Northampton, crosseth said branch, beginning at said crossing, extending thence two miles eastward and four miles westward, three miles northward and three miles southward, extending every way from said point until it embraces six miles square of land, . . . to have and to hold for the term of nine hundred and ninety-nine years. [The yearly rent was fixed at "six pounds, in public bills of the Province, or its equivalent in silver, according to the present worth or estimation," payment to be made upon the 20th of October annually; and the lessors to have the right to re-enter and take possession, if payment was delayed,

[1] A Mohegan word, meaning "island place."

twenty-one days from that date. The lease was executed "in the eleventh year of our sovereign Lord, King George the II., and *Anno Domini* 1737.]

his
JACOBUS × COOCHEECOMEEK.
mark.

his
MAHTOOKAMIN. O
mark.

his
WAMPENUM. Q
mark.

Signed, sealed, and delivered in presence of
TIMOTHY WOODBRIDGE.
JONATHAN WHITE.
ABIGAIL WOODBRIDGE.

In other parts of the instrument, the names of the lessors are spelled Coquahegameek, Metakamin, and Wampenon. The description given of the premises would carry their bounds one mile east of the corresponding limits of Pittsfield; taking in Cranesville on the east from Dalton, and excluding Shaker Village on the west.

But, before Col. Stoddard was able to procure a legislative confirmation of his Indian purchase, a grant of the same tract to other parties compelled him to change his plans.

In June, 1735, a memorial from the town of Boston to the General Court — representing the heavy expenditures of that municipality in supporting its poor and maintaining its free schools, and also that its citizens paid one fifth part of the entire annual tax of the Province — asked, in consideration of these burdens, for "three or four townships" of Hampshire wild lands, "to be brought forward and settled as the circumstances of the petitioners might seem to require, or upon such conditions as the Court might deem meet."

In response to this request, three townships, each six miles square,[1] were bestowed, but not without the usual provisions for a speedy and rightly-conducted settlement. These conditions, which proved of unexpected moment to the settlers of Pittsfield, were thus expressed in the grant, immediately after the clause requiring a survey, and the return of the several plats within twelve months for confirmation: —

[1] Afterwards Coleraine, Charlemont, and Pittsfield.

"Provided the town of Boston do, within five years from the confirmation of said plats, settle upon each of the said towns sixty families of His Majesty's good subjects, inhabitants of this Province, in as regular and defensible manner as the lands will admit of, each of said families to build and finish a dwelling-house upon *his* home-lot, of the following dimensions, viz., eighteen feet square and seven feet stud at the least; that each of the said settlers, within the said term, bring to and fit for improvement five acres of said home-lot, either for ploughing or for mowing, by stocking the same well with English grass, and fence the same well in, and actually live upon the spot; and, also, that they build and finish a suitable and convenient house for the public worship of God; and settle a learned orthodox minister in each of the said towns, and provide for their honorable and comfortable support; and also lay out three house-lots in each of the said towns, each of which to draw a sixty-third part of said town in all future divisions, — one to be for the first settled minister, one for the ministry, and one for the schools."

In order that these provisions "might be more effectually complied with," a committee was appointed (consisting of John Jeffries, Jacob Wendell, and Samuel Welles, of the Council; and Elisha Cooke, Oxenbridge Thatcher, Thomas Cushing, jun., and Timothy Prout, of the House), who were authorized to admit settlers, taking from each a bond of £25 for the performance of his proportion of the duties enjoined, — the lot also to revert to the Province in case of non-compliance with the prescribed conditions.

The requirement that the settlers should be inhabitants of Massachusetts was intended to guard against the introduction of Dutchmen from New York, against whom the boundary quarrels had created a prejudice, and who might defeat one prominent object of the General Court, — to fill up the western territory with a population willing to defend the Massachusetts claim.

The grant was made June 27, 1735; but, notwithstanding the language of the act, the time allowed for survey and return of plat, either by some construction or subsequent provision of law, did not expire until Dec. 29, 1736. And, in June of that year, Col. Jacob Wendell, one of the commission appointed to supervise the settlements, purchased at public auction the inchoate rights of Boston in one of the townships; "relying upon the goodness of the Great and General Court to give him further time to lay out the same, and return a plat for confirmation." This reliance did not fail him; and he obtained an extension until the 6th of January, 1738. That he should obtain this favor was, perhaps, one of the conditions of the bid at vendue; for it was not until the 13th of

PLAT OF TOWNSHIP, 1738.

Hemlock Tree.
So. Wt. Corner.

So. 20d. Wt. 462 Chains and 31 links.

Beach Tree.
N. Wt. Corner.

Et. 20d. So. 520 Chains.

A Platt of a Townſhip Granted by the General Court to the Town of Boston, and by the Said Town of Boston Sold to the Honble. Jacob Wendal, Esqr., of the contents of Six Miles Square, Including in Said Plat a Grant of 1000 acres made to the Honble. John Stoddard, Esqr., which contains in the whole 24040 acres. The whole whereof is thus bounded; viz., Beginning at a Stake with Stones about it, the So. Et. corner, nigh a Small Run of water, about a mile and Halfe Eaſt of Houſea Tunnic River, from Sd. Stake the line Extends No. 20d. Et. 462 Chain 31 Links to a Hemlock tree marked on a Hill the No. Et. Corner. From thence the line Runs Wt. 20d. No. 520 Chain to a Beach tree marked upon a steep Hill, with Ston's about it, the No. Wt. Corner. From thence So. 20d. Wt. 462 Chain 31 links to a Hemlock Standing by a little brook, mark'd with Stones about it, being the So. Wt. corner. From thence Et. 20d. So. 520 Chain, to the Stake and Stones firſt mention'd, which sd. Townſhip is Lying About Five Miles No. No. Et. From the Indian Town on Houſatunnick River, in the County of Hampſhire. Platted by a Scale of 48 Chain in an Inch. Septemr. 27, 1738.

Per JOHN HUSTON, Surveyor.

Wt. 20d. No. 520 Chains.

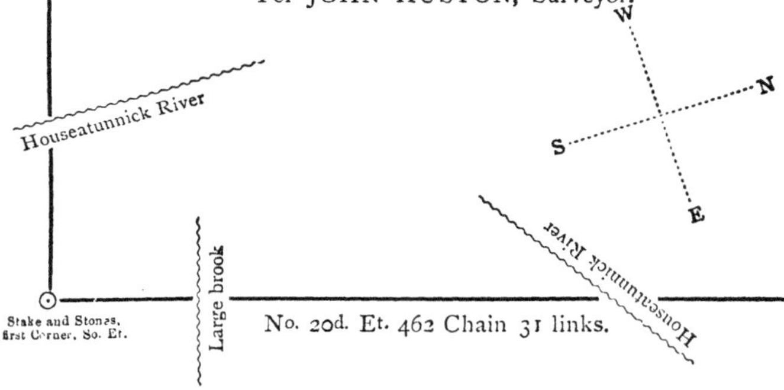

Stake and Stones,
first Corner, So. Et.

No. 20d. Et. 462 Chain 31 links.

Hemlock Tree,
N. E. Corner.

Hampſh., Ss. SPRINGFIELD, Octobr. 4th, 1738.

John Huston appearing, made oath that in Platting and Surveying the land Deſcribed in the platt aforesaid, he acted therein Indifferently and Impartially, according to his best skill and Judgment.

Examd. Per Ebene. Burrill.

Before me,

WM. PYNCHON, JUNR., Just. Pea.

Plat accepted and allowed, Decr. 8th, 1738.

March, 1737, that the deed in which these facts are recited, and which conveyed the township, still not laid out, to Col. Wendell, was executed by John Jeffries, Jonathan Armitage, David Colson, Alexander Forsythe, Caleb Lyman, Jonas Clark, and Thomas Hutchinson, jun., selectmen of Boston." [1]

The survey was made in September, 1738, by John Huston, a Northampton civil engineer of repute; and the plat, here inserted, was returned to and accepted by the General Court in the following act: —

"In the House of Representatives, Dec. 5, 1738, read and ordered, 'That the plat be accepted and allowed, and the lands therein delineated and described be and are hereby confirmed to the town of Boston and their assigns forever (exclusive of the one-thousand-acres grant made to the Hon. John Stoddard, Esq., within mentioned), and is in full satisfaction of one of the three townships granted by this Court to the said town of Boston at their session begun and held at Boston, May 28, 1735; provided the said town of Boston, or their assigns, effectually comply with and fulfil the conditions of the grant, and that the plat exceeds not the quantity of twenty-four thousand and forty acres of land, and interferes not with any other or former grant.'"

The plat thus allowed and described as containing twenty-four thousand and forty acres of land included the six miles square granted to the town of Boston, the thousand acres given to Col. Stoddard, and also a strip sixty-eight rods wide upon the west; the last item being added as compensation "for the waste ponds comprised in the township." The good people hardly foresaw, that, within little more than a hundred years, these contemned waters would be held of higher value than the same amount of surface in what they classed as "first-rate arable land," and that rich meadows would be submerged to increase their area.

The little oblong notch observable in the north-west corner of the map of the town does not appear in the plat, but it is found in the plan of 1752. Mount Honwee here juts into the angle of the territory, as laid out by Huston; and probably it was considered that its steep declivities would be an undesirable possession.

More than two years elapsed, after the confirmation of Col. Wendell's title, before his claims and those of Col. Stoddard were

[1] Copy of the deed in possession of Mr. J. A. Foote, certified by "William Cooper, Town Clerk," "as of record on the Boston Registry of Deeds."

adjusted; and then, a third person appearing in interest, — Philip Livingston of Albany,[1] — deeds were interchanged, by virtue of which the three gentlemen became joint and equal proprietors of the township. The deed from Wendell to Livingston, after quoting the grantor's patent from the Province, thus recites the mutual agreement, in brief: —

"Whereas the said John Stoddard hath not only a just and complete title to the thousand acres aforesaid, but hath also, at great expense, purchased several grants and leases from the natives, of the lands above described; and afterwards, this very day (March 29, 1741), the said Jacob Wendell and the said John Stoddard, for an amicable settlement of their mutual claims and interests in the township aforesaid, agreed that the said Jacob Wendell should have two thirds of the thousand acres aforesaid, and the said John Stoddard should have one third of the rest of said township; . . . and whereas, also, the said Jacob Wendell, in all these transactions, purchased as well for Philip Livingston of Albany, in the Province of New York, Esq. (by agreement not mentioned therein), as for himself, in equal halves, and, in his first purchase and after-gratuities to the natives for their satisfaction and other charges upon the premises, disbursed the sum of fourteen hundred and sixteen pounds three shillings and threepence, and for that now hath two third-parts of that whole tract of land surveyed and platted as aforesaid: now, therefore, know ye, that the said Jacob Wendell, in faithfulness to his trust aforesaid, and in consideration of the sum of seven hundred and fifty-eight pounds one shilling and sevenpence half-penny in hand, received of said Philip Livingston in full of his part of said purchase-money and other disbursements aforesaid, doth hereby convey . . . to the said Philip Livingston one half of his above-mentioned interest." [2]

Thus the cost of the township up to this time — if we allow Stoddard's public service to count in the ratio of Wendell's purchase-money[3] — was precisely two thousand one hundred and seventy-four pounds four shillings tenpence and two farthings.

[1] The lord of Livingston Manor, a kinsman of Col. Wendell, and father of him who signed the same name to the Declaration of Independence. The elder Philip, and after him his eldest son, Robert, claimed Westenhook and Taghkanik as parts of their manor, and were prominent in the troubles which arose concerning those tracts.

[2] Copy of deed in possession of Mr. J. A. Foote, certified by "Ewd. Pynchon, Regr.," from the Hampshire Registry of Deeds.

[3] Col. Wendell paid to the town Boston £1,320 for its rights in the township.

CHAPTER III.

FIRST ATTEMPT TO SETTLE THE TOWNSHIP.

[1741-1749.]

Settling-lots laid out. — Description of Lots and Roads. — Philip Livingston to procure Settlers. — Efforts to introduce Dutchmen fail. — Huston induces a Company from Westfield to purchase Forty Lots. — Pioneers commence a Clearing. — Poontoosuck as it appeared in 1743. — Work suspended by News of War. — Col. William Williams. — The War of 1744-8. — Building of Fort Massachusetts. — Hardships of Settlers in the War.

WHEN the township was platted by Capt. Huston in 1738, sixty-four home (or house) lots were laid out, each intended to contain one hundred acres, and, except where irregularities arose from the indentations of Onota and Silver Lakes, to be uniformly of eighty rods front and two hundred deep. Careless surveying, however, caused some variations from this standard; the lots in the middle tier, for instance, proving to be, in fact, two hundred and two rods deep.

Two roads, each seven rods wide, intersected each other near the centre of the township. One of these, now East and West Streets, ran from boundary to boundary;[1] the other, in that part of its course which is now North Street, extended two hundred rods above the Crossing, and, on the old direct line of South Street, four hundred and six rods below it.

A third road, four rods in width, was laid out parallel to the first, and two hundred and two rods south of it. East of its intersection with South, this is now Honasada Street. West of that point, only portions of it have been opened.

Along the first and third of these thoroughfares, or what were intended to be such, the home-lots designed for settlers and for

[1] Owing to obstacles in the nature of the ground, East Street has been actually opened only to the distance of half a mile from the Park.

public purposes were ranged in three tiers, running east and west. Of these the middle, containing twenty-seven lots, lay between East and West Streets and Honasada Street, and extended completely across the township. The northern fronted south upon East and West Streets, contained nineteen lots, and, beginning at the Hancock line, reached to Goodrich Lake. The southern tier, facing north upon Honasada Street, numbered seventeen lots, and extended from the Dalton line to where Oceola Village now stands.

The territory thus set apart for the proposed plantation formed about one quarter of the whole township, and embraced its fair proportion of good arable lands. It is now far more valuable than all the rest of the township. The northern boundary of the Settling-lots would be indicated by an extension of Burbank Street; the southern, by a line drawn through South Mountain Street at its intersection with South, passing a little north of Melville Lake.

The numbering of the lots, which was peculiarly arbitrary and puzzling, recognized in them but two classes,—Lots North and Lots South. "No. 1, North," was the most westerly in the upper tier. From this, the regular numerical order was followed up to 13, which denoted the Ministry Lot, embracing nearly all the territory which lies between the west branch of the Housatonic and North Street.

No. 14 was found by a diagonal transit to the lot in the middle range, south of what is now the Park, whence the numerical order is preserved to 25 at the Dalton Border. No. 26 designated the Minister's Lot, north of the Park, and the next in territorial proximity to 13. Nos. 26 to 31, counting east, completed the surveyor's tier of "Lots North."

Lot No. 1, of the technical southern tier, was the most westerly in the middle range. Thence arithmetical regularity prevailed up to No. 15, on the corner of West and South Streets. No. 16 dropped diagonally again to the southern range, where it indicated the lot on the south-eastern corner of South and Honasada Streets, which extends across the Housatonic River. Thence the enumeration again proceeded in due order to 27, on the eastern line of the town. No. 28 was found next west of 16. Thence the figures increase westward to Lot 33, the highest in the list, which was laid out in addition to the prescribed sixty-three. In conveyances, leases, and similar instruments, the premises were generally designated as

"Lots North, or South," as the case might be. Sometimes, however, the form, "Lot No. —, North (South or Middle) tier," was used: but here the number referred to the relation of the lot to its *class*, north or south; the mention of the tier in which it was actually located was mere collateral description.

As soon as the terms of the joint proprietorship were fixed, in 1741, the whole matter of complying with the requisitions attached to the grant was intrusted to Livingston; and, either through ignorance or wilfulness, setting at naught one of the provisions of the act, he at once visited the township with seventy *Dutchmen*, whom he hoped to induce to purchase sixty of the lots "at a moderate lay" in money, with the further consideration that they should perform all the duties imposed by the General Court upon the entire tract of twenty-four thousand acres.[1]

The requirement that each settler must take the good, bad, or indifferent lands which might fall to him by lot in the confined tiers which had been set apart for that purpose, was unsatisfactory to the Dutchmen; and perhaps the soil of Poontoosuck did not compare so favorably with the broad fertility of the Valley of the Hudson as it did with that of the regions from which the eastern emigrants came. Perhaps, also, the strangers at whom it was aimed, observing the clause in the Boston patent excluding them from its benefits, may have conceived a doubt as to the validity of the title which they were to receive. They certainly, upon hearing the terms proposed, peremptorily refused "even so much as to accept the lands if they were offered as a gift, not to speak of the conditions attached to them," unless they might select each his hundred acres where it pleased him; which would have left but a barren remainder to the original proprietors.

The Dutchmen — wisely for themselves, as the event proved — returned as they came, leaving Mr. Livingston and his partners sadly broken up in their plans, and, owing to previous delays, sorely pressed for time.

Upon this Capt. Huston, who had surveyed the township and was familiar with its good points, learning how affairs stood with

[1] Petitions to the Provincial Government from the settlers, in 1762–6, alleged that Wendell and Stoddard left it to Livingston to obtain settlers, with the express expectation that he would procure them from the Dutch, as the place lay near their country, whence they could bring provisions, etc., until they could raise it; "and thus they would have a Dutch town at once."

his old employers, induced a number of his acquaintances in Westfield and thereabout to visit the place. Their inspection proving satisfactory, a company was formed, which sent Capt. Huston, Joseph Root, and John Lee to Albany, "empowered to agree with Mr. Livingston for forty of the aforesaid Dutch-despised lots." Livingston was so well pleased with Huston's proceedings, that he gave him three good lots as a gratuity; and he so successfully plied the committee, that, instead of merely making an agreement for the forty lots, — getting a bond for a deed, as was probably the expectation of the company, — they bought them outright, giving their note for the purchase-money, which was fixed at £1200, current money of the Province; "as much, within £120," the settlers were fond of boasting, as Col. Wendell paid to Boston for the whole township.[1] These statements, although *ex parte*, are probably substantially correct, as the answers of the respondents to the memorials do not attempt to controvert them.

The committee also bound themselves, or the settlers under them, to perform two-thirds of all the duties enjoined by the conditions of the grant upon the whole township. Certainly, taking into view all the circumstances, these Connecticut-River Yankees did not drive a shrewd bargain with the lord of the Livingston Manor. The Dutchmen were the sharper of the two parties.

The lots obtained by this purchase were Nos. 1 to 8 inclusive, in both classes; Nos. 9 to 32 south, inclusive, except 14, 16, 17, and 27; and Nos. 16, 17, 18, and 19, north.

Most of these lands were deficient in pine timber, of which there were rich forests in the "Commons," as the lands outside the Settling-lots, held in common by the original proprietors, were called. Marble and limestone, also abundant in many localities, were not universally distributed. It was therefore provided in the deed of the forty lots that the settlers "should have free right to cut wood, dig stone, and carry away the same from any part of the township, sufficient for building, fencing, and fuel." Afterwards, it was one of the grievances complained of by The Plantation, that Wendell's and Stoddard's heirs repudiated this portion of

[1] See Appendix A, regarding the values of Massachusetts bills of credit. The facts concerning the dealings of Livingston are collected chiefly from two memorials sent by the Pittsfield settlers to the Governor and General Court, — one in 1762, now preserved in the Massachusetts archives; the other in 1766, found among the William Williams Papers.

their solemn indenture, on the pretence that Livingston had not been empowered to enter into any such agreement. The increasing value of pine-lands perhaps helped them to the conclusion.

The indenture was made in November, 1742: and it was agreed that each of the grantees should begin a settlement upon his home-lot during the next spring or summer, and continue it, unless in the mean time war should ensue between France and England; in which case the settlement was to be commenced within one year after the declaration of peace. Accordingly, in the spring of 1743, their lands having been distributed to them by lot, the pioneers of Pittsfield promptly took possession of the spot where they hoped soon to welcome their young wives to homes, which, if not free from danger and discomfort, were such as those in which their mothers, through much love and high resolve, had braved the terrors of the old frontier. Most of the forty were young men; and, with many, the marriage-day waited only the promised home in the wilderness. We may imagine with what forms the fancy of the stout-hearted pioneers peopled the changing scene, as, with strong arm and ringing axe, they attacked the fastnesses of the forest in that half-hopeful summer of 1743. Half hopeful: for anxious forebodings must have continually oppressed the workers; knowing, as they did, the disturbed state of Europe, and that the intrigues of the Stuarts (name of ill omen to Massachusetts, even though those who bore it no longer ruled), favored by circumstances, were likely at any moment to embroil France and England. In the fall, came closer foreshadowing of evil. Word was sent by Col. Stoddard that hostilities were immediately imminent; and, taught by the sad experience of former wars that the first intimation of their actual existence might come from the war-whoop of Canadian savages surrounding their clearing at midnight, the pioneers abandoned their labors, not to resume them for five tedious years. It was the old story, — the ambitions of corrupt courts and powerful capitals working woe in the most insignificant and remote corners of their vast empires.

There is no absolute certainty as to the names of those who took part in this first attempt to plant a settlement at Poontoosuck; although it seems clear that a majority of those who engaged in the second essay also took part in the first. But, between 1744 and 1748, many of the pioneers doubtless enlisted in the military expeditions to which Massachusetts contributed so liberally; and, in those peculiarly exhausting campaigns, some must have fallen by disease or in battle. Others relinquished their purpose of settling at Poontoosuck in the five years which elapsed before another effort could be made to carry it out.

Only a few of the deeds from Huston, Lee, and Root can now be found either in the original copies, or in the registry at Springfield. One of these conveys to Samuel Root, jun., of Westfield, Lot No. 5, South, to which his son Oliver — the major of Revolutionary fame — succeeded, Mr. Root dying before he could carry out his intention of removing to Poontoosuck. David Mosely, "gentleman," got Lot No. 7; Aaron Dewey, 8; Hezekiah Jones, 19; John Tremain, 29, — all in class South — the consideration in each case being £30. The grantees also severally bound themselves each to perform his proportionate part of the obligations which had been assumed by the grantors, and, specifically, to begin settlements upon their respective lots in the spring or summer of 1743, — with the war proviso, as in the Livingston indenture; to continue the same in such manner, that, at the end of two years, there should be a dwelling-house, and family living in it, upon each lot, and to keep possession by similar occupancy for at least the two years next succeeding.

The half-forgotten story of the first brief intrusion of civilized life into the red man's Poontoosuck is peculiarly alluring to the pen of the chronicler. Nor will it be uninstructive, if, in the best light which we can get, we seek to portray the township as it appeared to those who, before "the old French wars," were striving with busy axe, and musket near at hand, to prepare in its wilds a home for those scarcely less hardy — certainly not less brave — than themselves.

If, from some neighboring mountain-top, the pioneer, as he approached, gained a view of the amphitheatre which lay below, the scene was one to enchant even the most prosaic heart. All the minor irregularities, all the sharper angles, were softened and rounded by an enamel of forest, in which were embossed the rolling outlines of hill and valley. The landscape, stretching through a range of fifty miles, presented, until all other hues were lost in the blue of distance, the unbroken green of waving tree-tops, — save where, through a few chance openings, the Housatonic flashed back the sunlight, or some shimmering glimpse of lakelet revealed its lonely surface, upon which, perhaps, still lingered the graceful bark of a wandering Mohegan. At intervals, in the sea of green, a spot of darker verdure, where the boughs stirred more stiffly to the breeze, betrayed the lurking-places of the gloomy and frequent hemlock-swamps. Around the southern borders of Lake Shoonkeekmoonkeek, and on some of the Taconic hills, glowed those noble groves of pine whose fame, attested by a few not unworthy relics, remains to this day. Elsewhere the practised eye of the woodsman recognized the maple, the elm, the beech, the birch, the linden, the hickory, the chestnut, the red (and infrequently the white) oak, the cherry, the ash, the larch, the fir, the spruce, and every tribe of New-England forestry except the cedar, whose spicy aroma never mingles with the odors of our groves.

Thus the scene must have burst upon the pioneer, as, with hope's elastic step, he approached it in leafy June. How much more glowingly it lay outstretched, as, sick at heart with hope's deferment, he turned away from it in many-colored October!

As he descended the mountain-side by Unkamet's Road, or such other rude path as might offer, it would have been strange had his ear not been greeted by the growl of the bear, the howl of the wolf, or the cries of the lynx [1] and the loup-cervier; [2] for all these had their dens among the tumbled rocks of the neighboring ravines.

As he proceeded, he might have caught a vanishing glimpse of a fox's brush, or the bristling quills of a porcupine. He was pretty sure to startle a brace of rabbits, and send a woodchuck burrowing to his hole; while squirrels — red, black, gray, and striped — gambolled by scores up and down the shaggy sides of the great trees. The skunk made his presence known; and perhaps a raccoon, on some fallen mossy trunk, challenged a shot from the ever-ready firelock. But that, no doubt, the marksman would have reserved for the moose which might presently peer at him from the recesses of the forest, the deer that was almost sure to dash across his path, or the wild turkey stalking among the ferns. Above him, the eagle and the hawk swept in dizzy circles. From the dank borders of the lake, the shrill scream of the loon and the harsh note of the heron saluted him. The black duck swung upon the still waters; and possibly a sea-gull, which had wandered inland with the mist of the

[1] The Bay-lynx, or American wildcat. [2] The Canadian lynx.

Sound, dipped its white wing along their surface. All the feathered host which, with bright hues or melodious song, make glad New-England woods, fluttered among the overhanging branches.[1]

On every side resounded the drumming and the whirr of the grouse,[2] to be succeeded at nightfall by the complainings of the whip-poor-will, the solemn to-whoo of the great white owl, and the dismal screech of his ill-omened cousin, prophetic of St. François war-whoops.

But while some harmless striped or green snake may have glided across his path, or the black (now long since exterminated) have lain coiled near by, or perhaps the milk-adder lurked in the under-brush, the wayfarer listened in vain for the warning rattle of the dread of New-England fields, against which the soil of Northern Berkshire is charmed, by the prevailing virtues of the ash-tree, as the popular faith avers.

All the denizens of the Green-Mountain forests, save the rattle-snake, might thus have come to salute or dismay the stranger, who, in a little while, was to usurp their ancient domain. His reception, however, was likely to be less tumultuous. The more conspicuous members of the forest-guild may, indeed, have absented themselves entirely from the assemblage; for sometimes, although the wood was populous with game, even the skilled Indian hunter, familiar with all its haunts, sought it in vain, and went supperless to his bed of turf, which perhaps might nevertheless, at the very moment, be indented with the foot-prints of a hundred deer. The scout found his only trusted commissariat in a bag of pounded corn; and the commanders of outposts in deer-forests, acknowledging gratefully the receipt of a dried codfish, complained that it was impossible to obtain meat in their vicinity. When one reads of " a country swarming with game," it is necessary to remember that nevertheless it may oftentimes be hard to come at, and that hunting is always a precarious mode of subsistence, even for a savage.

Still, all that we have suggested might have occurred to the pioneer, as, descending from the Hoosac Mountains, he trudged to

[1] Mr. James H. Butler, in 1867, made a collection embracing more than one hundred varieties of the smaller birds which inhabit the woods and fields of Pittsfield, — some of them of brilliant plumage, and others of exquisite grace of form.

[2] The ruffed grouse, invariably but erroneously called by New-Englanders the partridge, the name of a species of pheasant not native to this region.

his claim, perhaps beyond Lake Onota; and doubtless, in his camp of logs, he often welcomed to a savory meal of game the Dutch fur-trader, the Eastern surveyor, or the messenger who bore, between Boston and Albany, intelligence of French and Spanish movements, and propositions for mutual defence in the foreshadowed troubles. News of wars and rumors of wars were eagerly discussed over plentiful viands supplied by the neighboring hunting-grounds.

If Unkamet's Road passed — where the favorable nature of the ground invited it — along the northern verges of Goodrich, Silver, and Onota Lakes, and directly from base to base of the opposing mountains, it afforded a path, which, although narrow, was free from any serious obstacles. But if the pioneer bent his course south of the lakes, by the road — now East and West Streets — laid out by the surveyor, traversing the whole range of the settling-lots, he would have been obliged to struggle through no less than five swamps, which, uninviting as they appeared from the mountain-top, were still more repulsive upon nearer acquaintance. But, frequent and inconveniently located as these sloughs were, they did not cover a very large portion of the surface; and some of them afterwards became valuable meadow-land. The pioneer, if he were fortunate in his guidance, was able to avoid them by winding paths of no very violent *détour;* and, in doing so, he came upon rich, loamy uplands inviting the plough; lawnlike openings, suggestive of cottage homes; and meadows weary of waiting for the English grass prescribed by The Great and General Court. The richer soils were found covered with massive maples, huge oaks, and spreading beeches; the thinner, with gigantic pines, enormous trunks, fit to intimidate even the sturdiest logger. Except in the case of the pine, or where individual trees of other species were specially adapted to, or convenient for, the purposes of building or fencing, the settlers were, indeed, not accustomed to attempt these monsters of the forest by fellage with the axe, but by the slower process of girdling and burning.[1] The pioneers at Poontoosuck in 1743 spent the summer

[1] Removing a circlet of bark around the tree, so as to interrupt the ascent of the sap. The tree thus became dry and ready for the fire, which was generally applied to it at the end of twelve months. This process was only less laborious than fellage with the axe; it being necessary to collect the fragments of the fallen trunks in piles, heap brushwood and other lighter fuel about them, and repeat the burning until all was consumed, — leaving, however, a ghastly array of stumps, to be disposed of by time.

in the preliminary labor of girdling; but, for six dreary years following, the dead trees spread their leafless limbs above the young, green boles, and no man came to apply the torch.

The interval was, however, not without events of interest to the embryo plantation. In 1746, the enemy pressed, more cruelly than in any other year of the war, upon the frontiers of the Province; but, in that year, Capt. Huston sold the three lots given him by Livingston — viz., No. 12, North, called the "mill-lot," between what is now Onota Street and the river — to Zebediah Stiles, for £40; No. 16, South, to Eldad Taylor, gentleman, for £57; No. 2, South, to Thomas Noble, saddler, for £49, — the purchasers all being described as of Westfield, and the conveyancer in each case contriving to spell the name of the plantation, Puntusick. The apparent advance in prices must be attributed, not to an increase in the market value of the lands, but to the depreciation of the currency.

But the event, among these early movements towards a settlement, of the most moment to the after-fortunes of the plantation, was the connection with them of William Williams, who, from that time until the Revolution, was the most prominent personage in the place, holding the most important offices in town and county; sometimes being at once chief justice of the common pleas, judge of probate, colonel of militia, representative, selectman, assessor, moderator of town-meeting, clerk, and hog-reeve, besides serving upon several committees. He was the son of William Williams, a successful pastor at Weston, and grandson of the eminent divine of the same name who was ordained at Hatfield in 1685. Robert Williams, the founder of the family upon this continent, was admitted a freeman at Roxbury in 1638, where he maintained a respectable position, and became the ancestor of the long array of politicians, soldiers, and divines bearing the name of Williams, who flourished especially in the Colonial and Revolutionary periods of our history. His son Isaac, the father of the Hatfield minister, was of some local prominence, and represented Newton in the General Court. William of Hatfield first married a daughter of the distinguished theologian, Dr. Cotton, from whom the Pittsfield settler thus traced his descent. For his second spouse, the gallant old divine succeeded in winning the younger sister of his son's (the Weston minister) wife, who was the daughter of another noted theological controversalist, Rev. Solomon Stoddard, and sister of the colonel of multitudinous public service. William, of Pittsfield, who thus piqued himself upon a very reverend and honorable ancestry, was born at Weston in 1711, and graduated at Harvard College in 1729, as his father before him had done in 1705, and his grandfather in 1683. In college, from a liberal spirit and a meagre allowance of means, he formed a habit of anticipating his income, which clung to and cruelly embarrassed him through life. After graduation, he applied himself to the study of medicine; but, having commenced practice, he abandoned it "as by no means consonant with his genius."[1]

While in the practice of his profession, he married Miriam Tyler, a daughter of an old Boston family, and a lady "of good sense," whose memory he appears never to have ceased to cherish. By the aid of his wife's friends, he established himself in mercantile business at Boston. This enterprise failing, Williams, in 1740, obtained an ensign's commission under Gen. Oglethorpe, in the unjust and unsuccessful expedition against St. Augustine. The next year, he took part, with the same rank, in Admiral Vernon's still more ill-fated armament against Carthagena. Like others, he was led into this disastrous affair by the promised plunder of the rich Spanish-American cities; but he was fortunate in escaping with life from the yellow fever, which ravaged the fleet with fearful malignancy: and he gained nothing from his southern adventures, except an ensign's half-pay on the retired list of the British army, and the military education acquired in two campaigns under accomplished officers.

He now returned to Massachusetts, where his abilities commended him to his uncle, Col. Stoddard, and to Col. Wendell, who, in consideration of the benefits which his connection with it would confer upon the plantation at Poontoosuck, entered, in 1743, into a written agreement to give him one of the settling-lots, not disposed of previously by Mr. Livingston, and also one hundred acres

[1] "While the doctor was in the practice of physic, a person who had been blind from infancy applied to him for a cure. Dr. Williams, fertile in inventing, pulverized a small quantity of a stone jar, and placed it on the eye of the patient, which soon ate off the film, so that the blind man received his sight. This anecdote we have mentioned to show that he was not deficient in his profession, and that he did not despair of healing the wounds and infirmities of mankind, which, to common minds, seem incurable." — BERKSHIRE CHRONICLE, *published at Pittsfield in* 1789.

adjoining, provided that he would settle upon the lot and perform the duties attached to it.[1]

Ensign Williams appears to have visited Poontoosuck in 1743; but, upon the breaking-out of the war in the following spring, he received a commission in Col. Stoddard's regiment of Hampshire militia, and was detailed to construct "the line of forts between the Connecticut and Hudson Rivers" determined upon by the General Court, and located by their commissioners; viz., Fort Shirley at Heath, Fort Pelham at Rowe, and Fort Massachusetts at Hoosac, — now Adams, — near the present Williamstown line. This service he performed to the satisfaction of the Government, being promoted major while the work was in progress.[2]

In the spring of 1745, he raised a company from among the men of his command for the expedition against Louisburg; but he was not permitted to accompany it, as his services were considered more valuable in the position he then occupied. In June, however, re-enforcements for the besieging army being urgently demanded, "an express was sent one hundred and fifty miles through the wilderness to Major Williams, at Fort Massachusetts," directing him to repair with the utmost despatch to Boston, bringing with him as many men as he could induce to enlist. In six days he reported to the Governor with seventy-four men, and was immediately commissioned lieutenant-colonel of the Eighth Massachusetts Regiment, Col. John Choate; which sailed for Cape Breton on the 23d of June. Louisburg capitulated before their arrival; but the regiment, under the command of its lieutenant-colonel, — Col. Choate having returned home, — garrisoned the place till the following spring.

The easy success of Louisburg revived in the Colonies the long-deferred hope of relieving themselves, by the conquest of Canada,

[1] Papers in the T. Colt and Lancton Collections.

[2] This service has been ascribed to Col. Ephraim Williams, the founder of Williams College; but I have before me, in the collection of Hon. Thomas Colt, the memorials of Col. William Williams to the commander-in-chief and the General Court, who must have known the facts, in which he reminded them that he built the works in question. A letter to Mr. C. Kilby, a relative of his wife, and a well-informed Boston merchant, makes the same statement, which is further corroborated by other papers in the same collection. In his order for building Fort Shirley, he was directed to call upon the company of Capt. Ephraim Williams for aid.

from a constant source of danger; and a grand expedition with that object was at once set on foot. But, instead of the promised English naval contingent, the most powerful French fleet which had ever floated in American waters appeared off the coast of Nova Scotia, under the command of the Duke D'Anville; and the Colonial plans for invasion were transformed with haste and trepidation to measures of defence. It was apprehended that Massachusetts would be assailed simultaneously on her coast and her north-western frontier; and, while a large force was collected for the protection of Boston and other seaports, smaller corps watched, and attempted to guard, the other extremity of the Province.

But, in this as in every hour of New England's peril, He who rides upon the storm and guides the whirlwind proved her surest helper. The September gales crippled the French fleet; D'Anville died; his successor in command committed suicide; and, of the proud armament which, boastful of irresistible might, in May set sail from Brest, only a shattered remnant crept back in November, having succeeded only in postponing the fate of Canada.

In the mean time, however, continual incursions of French and Indian marauders harassed the northern settlements. Fort Massachusetts was, in August, captured and destroyed; Deerfield again suffered massacre; and prowling bands of St. François savages infested all Upper Hampshire.[1]

The officer highest in rank in Western Massachusetts was Brig.-Gen. Joseph Dwight of Brookfield,[2] who had served with great credit at Louisburg, and, returning home at the close of the siege, had raised a regiment, principally from the Connecticut Valley, for the expedition against Canada. To this corps — of which Gen. Dwight, in accordance with a custom of the army, was the titular, and when not on actual brigade-duty the acting colonel — Lieut.-Col. Williams was assigned. It had been recruited for special service in the proposed campaign; but, much to the disgust of both officers and men, it was ordered to other duties, not only in the exigency of the D'Anville alarm, but subsequently. Early in

[1] Until 1761, the present Hampshire, Berkshire, Hampden, and Franklin were all included in the old county of Hampshire.

[2] Gen. Dwight removed, about 1756, to Great Barrington; but he had a temporary residence at Stockbridge in 1752, where he was addressed in the petition from Poontoosuck, requesting him to call the first meeting of the plantation.

October, when the coming of the hostile fleet was announced, "five companies were sent to Boston, and five to the most exposed western frontier;" but, intelligence of the disasters to the enemy arriving soon after, the regiment was re-united in Northwestern Hampshire, where it was employed during the winter in detached parties, scouting, garrisoning the block-houses, creating new defences, watching the movements of the enemy, rallying to the support of threatened outposts, and in every way guarding the endangered section.

Late in the fall of 1746, Massachusetts and New York resumed their preparations against Canada, and, undeterred by the near approach of winter, began to concentrate men and munitions of war at Albany; but the more cautious counsels of Connecticut prevailed, and the expedition was given over, as the event proved, for that war.

The Massachusetts troops were, however, still kept under pay; and, on the 21st of April, Gen. Dwight assigned to Col. Williams three companies and part of a third for the purpose of rebuilding Fort Massachusetts, adding, "I suppose Capt. Ephraim Williams will send all or part of his, if you desire it, who, I think, ought to do their part of this duty." The rebuilding of the fort was by order of the General Court, and under the direction of a commission appointed for that purpose, consisting of Cols. Stoddard and Porter, and Oliver Partridge, Esq. The Indians made some attempts to impede the work, amounting, in one instance, to a not very spirited skirmish; but, by the 2d of June, it was completed, and the command transferred by the following order:[1] —

FORT MASSACHUSETTS, June 2, 1747.

Major EPHRAIM WILLIAMS.

Sir, — Intending, by the leave of Providence, to depart this fort to-morrow, which, through the goodness of God towards us is now finished, I must desire you to take the charge of it; and shall, for the present, leave with you eighty men, which I would have you detain here till the barracks are erected, which I would have you build in the following manner, viz., seventy feet in length, thirty in breadth, seven-feet post, with a low roof. Let it be placed within five feet of the north side of the fort, and at equal distances from the east and west ends.

Let it be divided in the middle with a tier of timber; place a chimney in the centre of the east part, with two fire-places to accommodate those rooms. In the west part, place the chimney so as to accommodate the two rooms on

[1] Lancton Col.

that part, as if the house was but twenty feet wide from the south; making a partition of plank, ten feet distance from the north side of the barrack, for a storeroom for the provisions, &c.

The timber, stone, clay, lath, and all materials, being under the command of your guns, I can't but look upon you safe in your business, and desire you to see every thing finished workmanlike; and, when you have so done, you'll be pleased to dismiss Capt. Ephraim Williams, with his men, and what of my company I leave. You'll not forget to keep a scout east and west, which the men of your company are so well adapted for, and can be of very little service to you in the works.

Sir, I shall not give you any particular directions about maintaining the strong fortress or governing your men, but, in general, advise you always to be on your guard, nor suffer any idle fellows to stroll about. Sir, I heartily wish you health, the protection and smiles of Heaven on all accounts, and am, with esteem and regard, sir,

Your most humble servant,[1]

Wm. Williams.

Gen. Dwight's regiment was broken up Oct. 31, 1747; and it appears that Col. Williams had previously secured an appointment as sub-commissary,[1] which, as more lucrative, he preferred to the command of Fort Massachusetts, for which he was also named. But his inveterate ill-fortune in pecuniary matters continued to pursue him, and even as a quartermaster he failed to make money. The military profession, indeed, proved to him as barren of substantial profit as the medical and the mercantile had been. He complained, that, for his services "as commander and inspector in building the line of forts from Northfield to Hoosac, he received only eight pounds per month, Old Tenor;" that, as lieutenant-colonel commanding a regiment in the Louisburg garrison, his pay had been less than what a captain was afterwards allowed, — "the miserable Province pittance, not enough to buy a cabbage a day in that dear place;" and that his salary as commissary was so long in arrears that he was obliged to borrow £1400, for twelve months, of Col. Stoddard and Moses Graves. He did not, however, rest quiet under this ill-requital of his public labors, but was often at

[1] The major to whom the command was thus transferred was the founder of Williams College. Capt. Ephraim Williams, to whom allusion is made by both Gen. Dwight and Col. Williams, was probably a Connecticut officer in command of one of the companies sent by his colony in aid of the common defence.

[2] He seems to have received his appointment as early as February, 1747, but not to have entered upon its duties until his regiment was disbanded.

Boston in the intervals afforded by his military duties, engaged, with other officers of the Louisburg expedition, in pressing their claims upon the consideration of the British Government through correspondents and agents in London. The matter lingered long, and was never determined to the satisfaction of the officers, who finally, in individual instances at least, appealed with no better success to the General Court.

Such was the story of that one of the early settlers of Pittsfield who had the best opportunity to make a subsistence as a soldier during the interruption of the plantation by the war which closed with the treaty of Aix-la-Chapelle in the summer of 1748. How it fared with those who enlisted in the ranks may be inferred from the following extract from a representation made to Gen. Dwight by the captains of his regiment in behalf of the private soldiers, at the close of their term of service. After reciting other "particulars in which they conceived themselves injured," the memorial proceeds: —

> "In regard to their pay: as these levies were raised for a particular expedition, they expected, as according to proclamation, to receive the King's pay; so, as they were marching forces, 6*d*. per day, clear of any stoppages. But, by his Excellency's letter, they perceive they are to be paid as garrison-soldiers at the very lowest establishment in the nation, which is very distressing to them; many of them having been obliged to expend much more for clothing since they have been enlisted in said service than the amount of their pay, and must return to their families without any thing for their relief and support, and, indeed, without a penny in their pockets to carry them home, after having marched hundreds of miles at their own or their officers' expense, in obedience to your orders." [1]

[1] The story narrated in the preceding pages, so far as it is of a local character, is collected from original letters, orders, and memorials in the T. C. and L. Collections.

CHAPTER IV.

PERMANENT SETTLEMENT.

[1749–1754.]

Return of the Pioneers. — The First White Woman in Poontoosuck, and her Trials. — David Bush. — Nathaniel Fairfield. — Alone in the Woods. — A Bridal Tour in 1752. — Zebediah Stiles. — Charles Goodrich. — Partition of the Commons made and annulled. — Col. Williams settles on Unkamet Street. — His Property there. — The Plantation organized. — Powers of Plantations. — Votes with regard to Meeting-house, Preaching, Bridges, and Highways. — The First Bridge built. — Propositions for a Saw and Grist Mill.

THE peace introduced by the treaty of Aix-la-Chapelle, although brief and troubled, enabled the settlers of Poontoosuck to gain a foothold upon its soil, which was never afterwards wholly relinquished. Only the purchasers of the forty lots sold by Livingston participated in the abortive labors of 1745;[1] and these, with such changes as time had wrought among them, and joined by the three buyers of Huston's gift, returned in the summer of 1749, to "find that their clearing and girdling were of little or no advantage to them, as the young growth had covered the ground in a surprising manner."[2]

In the same year, Col. Stoddard having died in 1748, his widow, Madame Prudence, was, upon the petition of Col. Wendell, authorized by the General Court to act for her minor children in disposing of the seventeen "rights" which remained unsold, and in all matters which pertained to "bringing forward the settlement." In June, the joint proprietors of the township, who now by inheritance and purchase had increased to thirteen, appointed Col. Oliver Partridge of Hatfield their agent, who sold several lots;

1 Mem. of Col. Wendell, Mass. Ar., V. cxv. p. 504.

2 Mem. of settlers in 1762, Mass. Ar.

among which were two to David Bush, which extended from South Street, along Honasada, one hundred and sixty rods. Jacob Ensign, in 1752, purchased Lot 29, North, through which Beaver Street now runs. Col. Williams received by gift No. 31, in the same range.

Among those whom tradition points out as engaged in the settlement of 1749, are David Bush, Solomon Deming, Nathaniel Fairfield, Gideon Gunn, Timothy Cadwell, David Ashley, and Samuel Taylor. So, also, there is reason to believe, were Daniel Hubbard, Stephen Crofoot, Simeon Crofoot, Jesse Sackett, Josiah Wright, Hezekiah Jones, Abner and Isaac Dewey, and Elias Willard.

By these pioneers, and others whose names cannot now be ascertained, the busy scenes of the previous occupation were renewed, with chastened hopes, and forebodings yet more sombre than had haunted them six years before: for all the tidings which reached them betokened how hollow and treacherous was the peace which had been patched up at Aix-la-Chapelle; while they well knew that the emissaries of France were tempting the savages of their own neighborhood, who as yet gave no sufficient assurance of resisting their wiles. Many indeed, even of the Mohegans, found delight and profit in enhancing the value of their alliance with the English by exaggerating their inclination to transfer it to their enemies.

But by the summer of 1752, which is usually accounted the birth-year of Pittsfield, some of the settlers had log-cabins ready to receive their families. And first came Solomon Deming, from Wethersfield, with his wife Sarah behind him on the pillion. She was a maiden of seventeen when Solomon first essayed to provide them a dwelling-place in the wilderness of the Green Mountains. Now a brave young good-wife of twenty-six, she entered Poontoosuck, the first white woman who ever called it home.[1]

[1] The town of Pittsfield has erected a neat obelisk of marble to the memory of Mrs. Deming, in the little burial-ground on Honasada Street, near the spot where she fixed her home in 1752. The following inscriptions embody the traditions handed down regarding her: —

SOUTH SIDE. — This monument is erected by the town of Pittsfield to commemorate the heroism and virtues of its first female settler, and the mother of the first white child born within its limits.

NORTH. — Surrounded by tribes of hostile Indians, she defended, in more than

Mr. Deming's farm was on the north side of Honasada Street, in the eastern outskirts of the township, a region much frequented by the Indians, who were accustomed to make themselves a terror and an annoyance to the wives of the settlers, calling at their cabins in the absence of the men, and, with insolent threats, demanding food and drink. It was considered impolitic, in the precarious state of public affairs, to offend the red nuisances by well-deserved punishment; and the only recourse — one to which only the bolder dames dared resort — was to shut and bolt the door in their impudent faces: and this was probably the extent of the defence against the savages commemorated by Mrs. Deming's monument; for nothing more serious occurred between the natives and the settlers, except in a single instance.

David Bush, a native of Westfield, where his ancestors had long resided, purchased, as has been related, the two lots, 16 and 17 South. He was one of the more "well-to-do" settlers, and was the first to commence a clearing in 1749, on which he "had cut several tons of hay before the first white woman came to town." The honor of first penetrating the soil of Pittsfield with a plough is claimed both for Capt. Bush and Nathaniel Fairfield; but, as is the case with most claims of priority based upon tradition, there is nothing to determine which is rightly entitled to it, if either be. Nathaniel Fairfield's early connection with the settlement is, however, sufficiently noteworthy. He was born at Boston in 1730; and his father, who had a large family, having suffered severe pecuniary losses, he was adopted by a Mr. Dickinson of Westfield; but in 1748, at the age of eighteen, becoming impatient to seek his own fortune, although war still lingered on the border, he went with Dan Cadwell[1] to examine the settling-lots at Poontoosuck, and probably other land in that vicinity.

one instance, unaided, the lives and property of her family, and was distinguished for the courage and fortitude with which she bore the dangers and privations of a pioneer life.

Sarah Deming, born at Wethersfield, Conn., February, 1726. Died in Pittsfield, March, 1818, aged 92.

East. — A mother of the Revolution and a mother in Israel.

West. — Sarah Deming, born in Wethersfield, Conn., Feb., 1726. Died in Pittsfield, Mass., March, 1818, aged 92 years.

[1] In 1745, Amos Root had sold one of the forty lots purchased of Livingston to Dan Cadwell, whose descendants still reside upon it, and retain the original deed conveying it to him.

Before they were satisfied with their exploration, their provisions gave out, and Mr. Cadwell returned to Westfield for a fresh supply; leaving young Fairfield for three nights alone in the forest, as regarded white companions, but with a disagreeable co-tenantry of savages, whose unmusical voices he heard plainly on every side as he lay in the hollow log which served him for nightly lodging, and hiding-place by day.[1]

As a result of this exploration, he purchased lot No. 18 south, on the south-west corner of Wendell Square.[2] Having built here his log-cabin and opened his clearing, Mr. Fairfield revisited Westfield, and, having married Miss Judith ——, returned in 1752, with his bride, to their new home. On this bridal tour, the story of which may serve for that of many that were made by the fathers and mothers of Pittsfield, the young couple were accompanied by a yoke of oxen, and a dray bearing their household goods; and, pursuing their way by the aid of marked trees, they reached the house of Solomon Deming on the third evening, and there passed the night. The traveller by the Western Railroad now makes the same journey in less than two hours; but it is not necessary to suppose that the trip of the Fairfields proved tedious. The region through which they came was designated, even in the formal descriptions of the conveyancer, by the pleasant name of "the green woods between Westfield and Poontoosuck;" and perhaps — since summer days are very genial — the bridal party dallied a little leisurely in the fragrant shade.

In the same summer, Zebediah Stiles found companionship in a like humble home, on the corner of West and Onota Streets.

Then, also, came Charles Goodrich, "driving the first cart and team which ever entered the town, and cutting his way through the woods for a number of miles." It is of tradition that he reached the last of the Hoosac summits which he had to pass, just at nightfall; and, fearful of missing the path if he attempted to proceed in the dusk, tied his horses to a tree, and kept guard over them all night against the wild beasts, walking around to prevent himself from falling asleep, and "munching" an apple, his sole remaining ration, for supper. Goodrich, who became one of

[1] Family tradition.

[2] The two branches of the Housatonic River form their junction in this lot, which lies on the south side of Honasada street, and just below the Pittsfield Cotton Mills.

PLAN OF 1752.

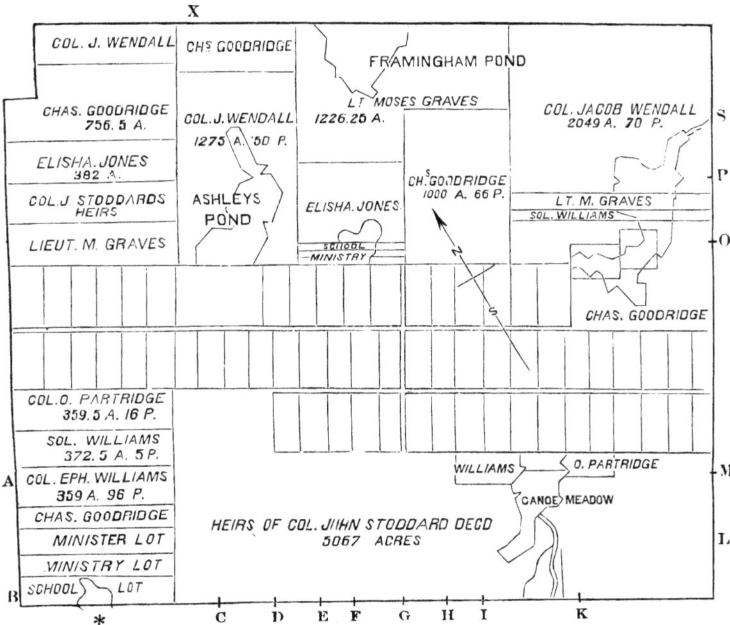

This is a Plan of the Township of Poontoosuck as it was taken by the Committee some time in December, 1752.

Test. BENJA. DAY, *Surveyor.*

A, A large Mountain the line ran upon, near half way from the settling-lots to the south-west corner.
B, A large Brook.
C, Ye foot of the Mountain.
D, The top of the Mountain.
E, A small Brook.
F, Foot of a large Mountain.
G, Ye Road.
H, Stockbridge Road.
I, The River.
K, The foot of the Mountain.
L, The corner of the 9,000 acres.
M, A large Brook.
O, Northampton Road.
P, A small Brook.
S, The River.
X, Mountain Land from here to the river.
* A large Pond.

The original of this plan is in the archives of the State at Boston, and a copy in the Town Clerk's office at Pittsfield. Some of the minutiæ of the original have been omitted by the engraver, chiefly relating to the area of the allotments to the several proprietors.

Framingham Pond is stated on the plan to contain 186 acres. Ashley's Pond, now Lake Onota, is represented as containing 284 acres.

the most conspicuous figures in the history of the town, was born at Wethersfield in 1720, and "obtained a hope" says his epitaph, "under Whitefield in 1741." He was the first man of considerable property who joined the settlement, and long continued the wealthiest citizen of the town, as well as one of those most distinguished for enterprise and intellectual ability. Both before and after his removal to Poontoosuck, he dabbled a good deal in land speculations, and had large interests in what are now Hancock and Lanesborough. In June, 1752, he bought of Col. Wendell "one third-of his one-third part" of the "Commons, or undivided lands," of Poontoosuck, for £473 7s. 4d. And being, unlike the other proprietors of those lands, desirous of immediately enjoying his portion, he applied to the next September term of the Superior Court, sitting at Springfield, for the appointment of commissioners to make partition; and the following gentlemen were accordingly named for that duty: Timothy Dwight, Eldad Taylor, David Moseley, Benjamin Day, and Obadiah Dickinson. The lands were alloted by them to the several proprietors in accordance with the plan here given, which was accepted and confirmed by the Court at its next session. It did not, however, prove acceptable to Colonel Wendell, and he petitioned the General Court that it might be annulled: alleging that no proper notice of the proceedings in the Court at Springfield having been served upon him, his only knowledge of them was transient and accidental; that only four out of the five gentlemen named by the Court had acted on the commission; that only the meadow-lands had been surveyed by them, — a general view merely being taken of the uplands, — and that, in part, when they were covered with snow; and that, returning home, the four commissioners, in their winter leisure, set out the allotments to the several proprietors, which in the spring were surveyed by only two of their number, as the four had protracted them upon the plan. He considered, that, if any justice had been done by such a process, it must have been the effect, not of judgment or understanding, but of accident; which accident had not happened, as the division was very unjust and unequal, and greatly injurious to himself, — all which he conceived would appear to the Court from an inspection of the plan.

Notice of Col. Wendell's memorial was ordered in "The Weekly Post-boy." The commissioners responded, that — the law requiring all the proprietors to be notified of the proceedings, that they might, if they wished, be present at the making of the division — they sent word to Col. Wendell and Elisha Jones, by Col. Partridge, who was going to the General Court, in October; that, Mr. Dickinson being unable to join them, it was necessary to proceed without him; that they "had obtained an exact accompt of the upland, and the situation and laying of the meadow, as it is interspersed and intermingled among the upland; and examined, as far as they thought needful, the quality of the soil, the form of the surface of the ground, and the timber growing upon it;" that the subsequent proceedings were properly had, and the commissioners unanimous in all their acts.

The General Court sustained the objections of Wendell, and in June, 1754, resolved that the partition was, "of course, null and void."[1]

But Goodrich had already — as soon, at least, as the partition was confirmed by the Superior Court — built upon a portion of the land set off to him, which now forms a part of Hon. Thomas Allen's farm.

Col. Williams, at the close of the war, wavered in his intention of settling at Poontoosuck; and in October, 1749, obtained from his friend, Gov. Benning Wentworth of New Hampshire, an authorization[2] which subsequently resulted in the grant to him and sixty-three other persons — of whom nine bore the name of Williams — of the township which afterwards became Bennington in Vermont, with whose fame that of Pittsfield is so gloriously associated in Revolutionary story.

But in November, 1752, — "Col. Williams having already been at Poontoosuck in order to bring forward a settlement, and intending to return early the next spring to reside permanently at the place" — Madame Stoddard addressed a note[3] to "The Hon. Timothy Dwight and the other gentlemen commissioners," desiring them, in apportioning her share of the township, to "have respect to the design of her deceased husband; that his kinsman, William Williams, settling at Poontoosuck, should have one hundred acres of his lands there."

Through the agreement thus acknowledged, — Col. Wendell afterwards joining in the gift, as he had joined in the original

1 Mass. Ar. v. 116, p. 491. 2 T. C. C. p. 86.
3 Madame Stoddard's letter in Lancton Col.

promise, — Col. Williams finally obtained a rectangular tract, one hundred and twenty by one hundred and thirty-four rods in area, lying upon Unkamet Street, west of the meadow.[1]

He also received in the same way the "original home-lot," No. 31 north, which lay about one hundred and twenty-five rods farther west, and contained some valuable meadow and upland. But he built his log-cabin, and commenced his clearing, in 1753, on the north side of Unkamet Street, and not far from the river.

On the 23d of June, 1753, a petition was presented in the General Court "from the inhabitants of the township on the Housatonick River, commonly called Poontoosuck,"[2] setting forth the difficulties they were under in bringing forward their settlement, and praying for directions and assistance. In response, the Court incorporated them as a plantation under the name of "The Proprietors of the Settling-lots in the Township of Poontoosuck," with the power to assess and collect taxes, but only upon the

[1] Although it is clear that Col. Williams finally obtained this Unkamet-street property in virtue of the Wendell and Stoddard promise of 1743, yet some obscurity rests upon the intermediate transactions. The tract was allotted by the commissioners to Wendell and the heirs of Stoddard; but was understood "to be and belong to William Williams," who thus recited his title in a mortgage-deed of 1754. This title, of course, failed when the partition upon which it was founded was annulled. But conveyances are extant, — in the H. C. C. and the Springfield Registry, — which indicate that agreements regarding tracts in the vicinity of Unkamet Street, made among the joint proprietors previously, were carried into effect in the final partition of the Commons in 1759–60. Thus Wendell and Mrs. Stoddard, although their exclusive title to the lands in question does not appear by the record to have become perfect until 1760, gave a deed of them, with warranty, to Col. Williams in 1758; and, in like manner, Charles Goodrich sold him two contiguous acres in May, 1759.

In the final division of the township, as in the first, the hundred acres were assigned to Wendell and the heirs of Stoddard, although they actually became the property of Williams; but the latter, in regard to some undivided right which he had acquired in the Commons, obtained — besides large tracts near Poontoosuck Lake — a narrow strip containing twenty-five acres, and lying in the form of the letter L, on the north and west sides of the Unkamet-street property, and also a straight strip of sixteen acres on the south of it.

The apparently detached location and inconvenient shape of Col. Williams's lands, as exhibited by the plan of 1759, are thus explained by the fact, that he really owned the intervening lands as well. The allotment of the one hundred acres jointly to Wendell and Stoddard — the only instance upon the plan in which they are joined — is also thus made clear.

[2] It was also often styled Wendell, or Wendell's Town, and sometimes Wendell and Stoddard's Town.

sixty settling-lots; excluding the lands reserved for the first minister, for the perpetual support of the ministry, and for schools, as well as the "Commons."

Plantations, under the old statutes, although embryo towns, yet, in their powers and duties, resembled private more nearly than municipal corporations.[1] The officers which they chose were only a moderator, a clerk, a treasurer, a collector, and assessors. And they were simply empowered, through these agents, to assess and collect province, county, and plantation taxes; appropriating the last to fulfil the conditions upon which they held their lands, and to make such improvements in building bridges, making highways, and the like, as, by "bringing forward the settlement," would enhance the common value of the home-lots.

Any community of Massachusetts men, associated as the people of Poontoosuck were, would certainly have united, if it became expedient, in measures for the protection of the public morals, and the promotion of the general safety or comfort; and they would have been likely to resolve upon them in Proprietors' meeting. But the statute gave such resolutions no legal effect; and, in fact, the only allusion in the Poontoosuck records to matters of local police is a vote that "hogs shall not run at large."

Among graver matters, appropriations for the support of public worship — sincerely as the people individually prized "the ministrations of the Gospel" — in Proprietors' meeting, were, of necessity, purely business transactions, done in fulfilment of contracts; and even provision for the burial of the dead was to be considered as adding to the value of the home-lots, whose occupants were thus assured of the chamber whose narrow bed all must one day need.

On the 30th of July, Simeon Crofoot, Charles Goodrich, Jacob Ensign, Solomon Deming, Stephen Crofoot, Samuel Taylor, and Elias Willard requested Joseph Dwight, Esq., to call the first meeting of "the Proprietors of the Settling-lots in the Township of Poontoosuck," to act upon certain articles specified in the request. That magistrate accordingly issued his warrant to Stephen Crofoot, "one of the principal proprietors, etc," directing him to warn the meeting, to be held at the house of Elias Willard at two o'clock in the afternoon of Sept. 12, by posting up the

[1] Especially in cases like that of Poontoosuck, where their jurisdiction was confined to a single section of the township.

request and warrant, twenty days at least before the day of the meeting, in some public place in the township.

The Proprietors met at the appointed time, and, Gen. Dwight presiding, chose Hezekiah Jones as moderator; after which the plantation was organized by the choice of the following officers: *Clerk*, David Bush; *Assessors*, Deacon (Stephen) Crofoot, Hezekiah Jones, Jacob Ensign; *Treasurer*, Charles Goodrich; *Collector*, Samuel Taylor, 2d.

It was voted to assess a tax of three shillings upon each lot "for the support of preaching among us," and to raise, in lawful money, £40 for building a meeting-house, and £15 for making highways, building bridges, and "for other necessary expenses that shall come upon us."

Deacon Crofoot, Charles Goodrich, and Jacob Ensign were appointed "to agree with some suitable person or persons to preach among us"; Jacob Ensign, Josiah Wright, and Abner Dewey "to dispose of" the appropriation for bridges and highways; Hezekiah Jones, Israel Dewey, Elias Willard, Deacon Crofoot, and Charles Goodrich, "to manage the whole affair of the meeting-house," which last did not prove an affair to be easily "managed."

It was of much importance to the plantation, that saw and grist mills should be erected, as the nearest point at which the farmers could have their grain ground was Great Barrington, twenty-one miles distant; and it does not appear how sawed lumber could be obtained at all within any practicable distance. Deacon Crofoot, who seems to have been an active and enterprising man, wished to supply the deficiency, and, for this purpose, asked the plantation to exchange that portion of the school-lot which included the water-privilege now occupied by the Pittsfield Cotton Mills, for a section of his home-lot, which adjoined it upon the east. Articles to consider this proposition, and also "to see what the Proprietors will give Deacon Crofoot for setting up the mills," were inserted in the warrant. But, the record curtly informs us, the meeting refused either to make the proposed exchange, or to "give Deacon Crofoot any thing for setting up his mills." It is nowhere explained why the plantation did not encourage an enterprise which seems to have been so much for the common interest. But Deacon Crofoot, although he afterwards built his mills, was never popular as a miller.

Finally, it was ordered that succeeding meetings should be called "by posting up notifications at the house of David Bush, in the township, at least fourteen days before they were to be held." Mr. Bush's house stood on the south side of Honasada Street, about one hundred rods west of Wendell Square; and, as the Proprietors' meetings were also held in it, its location must have been considered fairly central, although its selection for the purposes named was in part due to its owner's office of Proprietors' clerk.[1]

Proprietors' meetings were held in March, May, and August, 1754; and the records show progress in the plantation. It was voted to double the tax upon each lot for the support of preaching. The dimensions of the meeting-house were fixed "to be thirty feet long and thirty-five wide," and it was determined to go on with the work the next fall. The troubles concerning the erection of this building, which afterwards became chronic, seem already to have commenced; for the May meeting resolved that Stephen Crofoot and Hezekiah Jones, who had tendered their resignations, should nevertheless continue to "stand committee about the meeting-house."

The enterprising Deacon Crofoot had built a bridge, the first public work ever completed in Pittsfield, across the river, in his lot, a little east of the present Elm-street iron bridge; and it was agreed to give him £9. 1*s*. 4*d*. for it, including a road, which, care was taken to provide, should extend as well from East Street to the bridge as from the bridge to East Street.

The warrant calling upon the Proprietors to decide whether they "would hire Mr. Smith to preach any certain time with them, or call him as a probationer," the second alternative was adopted.[2]

The "Mr. Smith" to whom this call was extended was Rev. Cotton Mather Smith, father of Hon. John Cotton Smith, afterwards Governor of Connecticut. He was a graduate of Yale, and studied theology with Rev. William Williams of Hatfield. In 1752–3, he was an instructor in the Indian school at Stockbridge,

[1] As the crossing of Wendell and Honasada Streets is a point of which frequent mention occurs, we shall, for the sake of conciseness, speak of it as Wendell Square.

[2] It is a noticeable fact, although not peculiar to Poontoosuck, that, while the records accord the title of *Deacon*, wherever it is due, with great precision, the prefix *Rev.* is never connected with the names of any of the clergymen with whom negotiations were had, — not even in the case of Mr. Allen until after his ordination.

and had probably, before this call, preached occasionally at Poontoosuck, and perhaps the first sermon ever delivered in the township.

Eight pounds were voted at one meeting, and twenty at another, for highways and bridges; and Jacob Ensign, Josiah Wright, and Abner Dewey were chosen to dispose of this money, and also empowered "to make exchanges of lands, so that the Proprietors may be better suited, if occasion requires." But no record of their acts remains. Unkamet's Road appears to have been overgrown; for in 1753, according to the very reliable authority of Judd's "History of Hadley," "a horse-road was marked out from fifteen miles east of Albany," — where the carriage-road probably commenced, — "through Poontoosuck, to Northampton; but it was not much used." "The way from Hampshire and Hartford to Albany," says the same work, "was through the villages of Westfield and Kinderhook, and the territory now in Blandford, Sheffield, etc. A later road crossed Great Barrington." But many of the settlers of Poontoosuck appear to have come by the most direct route practicable, through the woods, guided by marked trees. And this was more easily done than we are apt to suppose, on account of a practice which prevailed, both among the aborigines and the pioneers, of burning the underbrush, in order to facilitate hunting, as well as to destroy the lurking-places of prowling enemies, and, by the natives, in order to prepare some portion of the ground for their rude culture.

It is a mistake to picture the aboriginal forest of New England as a scene altogether or chiefly of sombre shades and tangled thickets. "The dark-haired maiden loved its *grassy dells*," where, when the swift servant, Fire, had roughly done his work, kindly Nature had followed, "touching in her picturesque graces." The hunters of a labor-hating race, courting neither difficulty nor danger in the chase, did not choose that their grounds should be cumbered with thickets which at once impeded their pursuit of game, and afforded concealment to hostile braves; and so, since it cost but the kindling of the spark, the annual fires swept them clear. Even the patient squaws were not enamored of hard work, and the same ready agent helped them to prepare the meadow for the hoe. Thus immense tracts were swept of their undergrowth, while the more massy trees were unharmed; so that it is related that a deer could often be seen, in a heavily-timbered country, at a distance of forty rods. And many of the upland forests were passable — with a little occasional aid from the axe — for carts and drays, like those with which Goodrich and Fairfield entered Poontoosuck.[1] These burnings were, perhaps, not so universal in the times of the Indians, upon the western mountains, as in other parts of Hampshire; and these may have been, as the name Taghkanik intimates, more deeply wooded. But the same reasons which had originated the burnings by the natives operated still more powerfully upon the settlers, and fire swept the way before advancing civilization; while, even in tracts where it did not reach, —

Old winding roads were frequent in the woods,
By the surveyor opened long ago,
When through their depths he led his trampling band,
Startling the crouched deer from the underbrush. — STREET.

And so it happened that the pioneers found less difficulty in traversing the woods, and in many instances better preparation for their clearings, than, without considering these facts, we should suspect.

[1] Hist. Hadley.

CHAPTER V.

SECOND FRENCH AND INDIAN WAR.

[1754–1759.]

State of the Plantation. — Position of Housatonic Indians. — Homicide of Waumpaumcorse. — Indian Massacre at Stockbridge and Hoosac. — Flight from Poontoosuck. — Poontoosuck Military Post. — Building of Fort Anson. — Garrison-Life at the Fort. — The Settlers during the War. — Fort Goodrich. — Fort Fairfield. — Fort at Onota. — Oliver Root. — William Williams.

THE Plantation of Poontoosuck had, in August, 1754, made respectable progress; and the proprietors were ready, as the votes we have quoted show, to prosecute their corporate work with increasing vigor. Most of the sixty home-lots had been taken up; and, although in some instances two or more were purchased by a single settler, the population of the place must have been nearly two hundred. The dwellings were as yet all of logs; but Charles Goodrich was preparing to build on Wendell Square, if he had not already partially erected, the first frame-house in the township. The pioneers of 1743 still felt the depressing effects of the failure of their enterprise, but were gradually overcoming the difficulties which it placed in their way. The settlement was attracting men of substance, and some of that class had already joined it. Had no new misfortune intervened, it would have been close upon that prosperity which it only actually attained after long struggles with poverty and pecuniary embarrassments, — struggles whose marked influence upon the character of the people of Pittsfield was especially manifest in the internal political troubles which accompanied the Revolutionary War.

Between the years 1725 and 1754, the territory now embraced in Berkshire gained a population of perhaps something more than fifteen hundred,—almost all of it south of Poontoosuck. The towns of Sheffield and Stockbridge were incorporated; and settlements were planted in New Marlborough, Sandisfield, Tyringham, Alford, Egremont, and Mount Washington. Northward, a few families had made their homes in Williamstown and Lanesborough; and a little land was cultivated, at times, under the guns of Fort Massachusetts. Here and there, among the green woods, solitary hunters and trappers — hardier even than the pioneer farmer — planted patches of vegetables in the scant clearings where they built their lonely cabins, — seminaries which produced the boldest and most successful scouts in the coming war.

The Indians formed a more considerable element in the population of the Valley than at any previous date since its settlement by the English, showing a census of probably about three hundred.

The mission commenced in 1734, and established at Stockbridge in 1735, had in twenty years produced an admirable change in the condition of the Mohegans; but it had not wrought a miracle upon them. Ever well disposed towards the white man, and, upon the whole, well treated by him, they received at his hands the gifts of education and religion with a readiness which was not to be expected in tribes whose experience had been of a different character; and they adopted the usages of civilized life with astonishing facility. They did not, however, leap at once from the depths of barbarism to the plane which the Saxon race had reached only after ages and generations of painful climbing. Much less did they elevate themselves above the human passions and frailties from which their teachers were not themselves free.

There was, moreover, as in all such cases there inevitably must be, a vagabond class, who had lost the virtues of savage life without submitting to the restraints of civilized society,—loose fellows, who hung around the settlements, selling the fruits of their hunting and trapping for rum, and then roaming from farm-house to farm-house, committing the annoyances of which mention has been made. They were frowned upon by the more respectable and numerous class of the tribe; but they created a bitter prejudice in the minds of the unthinking against all of their color. The inhabitants of the Mission Village were collected from many sections of country, some of them as distant as the banks of the Susquehannah;[1] and,

[1] Rec. Gen. Court, Jan. 27, 1752.

although this long pilgrimage in search of Christian instruction afforded a presumption in their favor, a few disappointed the hopes formed of them, and all, in those days of suspicion, were objects of jealousy as strangers. Nor were the annoyances to which the settlers were subject wholly unprovoked on their part. The Provincial Government, its agents, and the better part of the people, did, indeed, treat the Mohegans, not only with scrupulous justice, but with tender and earnest regard for both their temporal and spiritual welfare, and with generous forbearance towards the frailties and perversities of their wild neophytes. But there were too many exceptions to this rule, even among men in some small authority, who had come from sections of the Province where the Indian, without distinction of person or tribe, was known to the masses only to be detested. And, if the Mohegan suffered injustice from the hands of those who should have been in some degree restrained by the well-known wishes of the government, the treatment was simply intolerable which he received at the hands of a rude soldiery, hereditary haters of every red-skin, and ignorant or regardless of the long-tried fidelity of the tribe of Uncas to the English cause.[1]

In addition to these just causes of complaint, the Mohegans had become discontented with the disposition which they had made of their lands, and alleged, although apparently without truth, that, in bargaining them away, they had been misled by false representations,[2] and that, in some cases, they had been seized without purchase.

1 "They say, and we are, and too often have been, witnesses of the many insults and abuses which they (the Mohegans) have suffered from the English soldiery, — their lives and scalps threatened to be taken, and they called every thing but good, charged with the late murders, and actually put into such terror as to not know which way to turn themselves." — *Col. Dwight to Col. Israel Williams, October*, 1754.

2 "We would say something respecting our lands. When the white people purchased from time to time of us, they said they only wanted the low lands: they told us the hilly land was good for nothing, and that it was full of woods and stones. But now we see people living all about the hills and woods, although they have not purchased the lands. When we inquire of the people who live on these lands what right they have to them, they reply to us, that we are not to be regarded, and that these lands belong to the King. But we were the first possessors of them; and, when the King has paid us for them, then they may say they are his." — *Speech of the Stockbridge Chiefs to the Commissioners of the Six Provinces, at Albany, July* 8, 1754, N. Y. Doc. Hist., Vol. ii. p. 599.

The means thus offered for fomenting distrust and ill-will in the jealous minds of the savages were not neglected by the agents of France, who contrived to inspire in many of them the belief "that the English were on a design of exterminating the Indians within their reach."[1]

In the spring of 1753, an unhappy event occurred, which was used with surprising effect to increase the ferment, and strengthen in the minds of the natives the belief that the English designed their destruction. It appears that one Wampaumcorse, a Schaghticoke Indian, domiciled at Stockbridge, being in Sugar Camp at Hop Brook in Tyringham, saw two men, Cook by name, passing by with horses which he suspected to be stolen. Pursuing them, and an altercation arising, he was shot dead. The Cooks were thereupon arrested, and tried at Springfield. One was convicted of manslaughter, and the other acquitted; which seems to have been what the law and the evidence required. But in the minds of the Schaghticokes, as in those of the exiled Pequots, murderous resentment against the English was always ready to be aroused; and this affair was used with the utmost success to exasperate the Indians. Its effect was soon apparent "in the surly behavior of several in whom it had not before been observed;" in the stealing of guns; in more frequent intercourse with distant tribes, and the consorting together of the worst-tempered and worst-behaved fellows, who had a drunken pow-wow, which was kept up, in the woods some six miles west of Stockbridge, with fresh supplies of rum from Kinderhook; and finally some negro slaves reported a plot, in which they had been invited to join, for the massacre of as many of the whites as possible, and flight to Canada.

Upon this, the wildest excitement prevailed at Stockbridge, and not less, of course, in the more exposed outpost of Poontoosuck. The people of the former place wisely determined to call the Indians together, let them know their apprehensions, and endeavor to ascertain what foundation there was for them.

It appeared, as had been anticipated, that "the great body of the tribe were entirely unacquainted with the secret plot, but that the thing was real with regard to so many that the authorities looked upon themselves as in a worse state than in an open war."[2]

[1] Jona. Edwards to Prov. Sec. Willard, May, 1754, Mass. Ar., vol. xxxii.

[2] Gen. Dwight and Capt. Woodbridge to Gov. Shirley, March 26, 1754, Mass., Ar., vol. xxxii, p. 483.

Gen. Dwight and Timo. Woodbridge, Esq., therefore represented this condition of the frontier to Gov. Shirley, adding that there seemed to be no pique against any person in particular, but against the English in general for the killing of Wampaumcorse; and, in order that the people "might not be exposed to the murderous strokes of savage resentment," they earnestly begged his Excellency to recommend to the General Court an increase of the sum of £6 which had been granted "to wipe away blood,"[1] and that it might be sent by a special embassy; which would add to its efficiency as a peace-offering.

This request was so far granted, on the 22d of April, as to vote £20, to be placed in the hands of Gen. Dwight, to be distributed among the relatives of Wampaumcorse.

But, on the 22d of May, Jonathan Edwards, apparently in the greatest anxiety, found it necessary to write to Secretary Willard, requesting his influence that "the money which had been granted to Wanaubaugus, the uncle of the man that was killed, might be speedily delivered." "It was manifest," he said, "that it was a matter of the greatest importance, not only to the people in Stockbridge, but to all New England, that the Indians should be speedily quieted in that matter. It was evident that the ill-influence of that affair had a wide extent, reaching to tribes at a great distance, — that it would be a handle of which the French at that juncture would make the utmost improvement." It "seemed to affect the Mohawks, no less than the other Indians."

The money was accordingly paid, and the excitement among the natives in some degree subsided. The delegates of the Stockbridge Mohegans, as vassals of the Iroquois, attended the conference of that confederacy with the commissioners of the Provinces at Albany, in July, and joined in the league formed, very much through the influence of Sir William Johnson. The Stockbridge chiefs seized the opportunity to make the complaints given in the note on page 99; but alliance with the English was traditional with them, and doubtless their disposition was more favorable to it since the intimate relations created by the mission settlement. The influence of the French emissaries appears to have had effect

[1] In accordance with the Indian custom of compounding for homicide by a fine to the relatives of the slain.

only upon the baser sort, and perhaps chiefly upon those (not of Mohegan blood) who had been attracted to the mission. At this time, the relation of the Mohegans to the Iroquois, although still of a feudal character, approached nearer to equality than at earlier periods, and, in token of its amicable nature, had assumed the typical form of kinship. And the two nations, both of which, in spite of exceptional cases, had experienced kindness and protection from their respective Provinces, mutually influenced each other in favor of English alliance.

Although the storm of war, which had been lowering all through the clouded peace of Aix-la-Chapelle, seemed now about to burst upon the Colonies, apprehensions of immediate danger to Western Massachusetts, from the Indians of its own vicinity, were thus in some measure allayed.

But on the evening of Thursday, the 29th of August, some Stockbridge Indians, who had been northward on a hunting-excursion, returned in haste with the startling report, that, on the previous day, they had, in concealment, witnessed the total destruction of Dutch Hoosack by a band of six hundred strange savages.[1]

The excitement immediately became intense, and messengers were sent to spread the alarm in every direction. On Saturday, an express, bearing information of the troubles, reached Col. Worthington at Springfield, where Gen. Dwight, with Capts. Ashley and Ingersol, as well as other leading citizens of the Housatonic Valley, were attending court. The latter gentlemen at once hastened to take charge of the defence of their homes; and Col. Worthington only waited to raise a company of seventy men, with whom he set out on Monday evening to the aid of the threatened settlements.

In the mean time, by Saturday night, several hundred men were under arms at Stockbridge, some of them from Connecticut. The

[1] A settlement of Dutch farmers in the Province of New York, north-west of the present site of Williamstown. Seven houses, fourteen barns, and a large quantity of wheat, were burned; many cattle and hogs slaughtered, and the latter thrown into heaps to rot. The damage was estimated at "£50,000, York currency." One man, Samuel Bowen, was killed, and another "captivated." The number of the enemy was greatly exaggerated by the fears of the settlers, as well as by the Stockbridge witnesses of the affair.

same neighborly colony also sent a large number of horses to bring off the women and children from Poontoosuck.[1]

Even yet, however, there appears to have been no apprehension, at Stockbridge, of danger from any of the Indians then in the town; and timely notice was expected, from the scouts who were scouring the woods, of the approach of any others. The people attended church as usual; and, in the absence of their neighbors for that purpose, the family of one Chamberlain, who lived in the retired locality of "The Hill," appear to have considered themselves in perfect safety, until they were suddenly attacked at about three o'clock in the afternoon. Col. Worthington, on the authority of a despatch from Capts. Ashley and Ingersol, describes the murderous scenes which ensued, as follows:[2] —

"There was in the house Chamberlain, his wife, three children, and another man, named Owen. Two Indians only attacked the house, — fired immediately upon entering, one at Chamberlain's wife, and missed her; the other at Owen, and shot him in the arm. One immediately attacked Owen; and the other, Chamberlain's wife. As Owen was more than equal to the Indian who engaged him, the Indian called his fellow to his help, and both beset Owen; so that Chamberlain's wife escaped, as did her husband coming out of an inner room, and left the two Indians (as we have the account) combating with Owen, who fought them like a man for a considerable time, but was so cut and wounded by them that he was obliged to yield, and he died soon after. He was scalped

[1] The following bill was presented to the next General Court: —

PROV. OF MASS. BAY,

To ABNER DEWEY, of Poontoonsuck, Dr.

To keeping 130 horses in his field of corn and grass, one night, which came from Connecticut to fetch off the women and children belonging to said place, at 4*s*.	£26 00
To entertaining 15 men three days, each at 3*s*.	6 15
Old tenor,	£32 15 0
Lawful money,	4 7 4

Charles Goodrich presented a similar bill for keeping sixty horses one night at five shillings each; for one hundred and fifty meals of victuals "to Connecticut men when they came to our relief to carry us off;" together with "sundry of the Province men at fourpence a meal, and for keeping ten men left by Capt. Ashley for our protection, for four days, at five shillings fourpence per week."

The Court allowed Dewey £2 10*s*. 6*d*. lawful money (silver); and Goodrich, £3 8*s*. 6*d*. (Mass. Ar., vol. lxxiv. pp. 337–343.)

[2] Report to Prov. Sec. Willard, dated Springfield, Sept. 8, 1754: Mass. Ar. vol. liv. p. 323.

by them, as was also one of the children whom they killed. A second child they carried out a quarter of a mile; and there, being discovered by a party of English coming from Poontoosuck, they knocked it on the head, and, mortally wounding it, left it in the woods, where it was picked up by these people."

The party from Poontoosuck was a portion of the whole population of that place, who, mounted on the Connecticut horses, were flying to the stronger settlements of the south. On their way, tradition says (and there is no reason to doubt) that they were repeatedly fired upon from the woods: and some of the fugitives, — particularly the heroic first female settler, who had perhaps specially provoked the vengeance of some of the rascals whose attacks upon her larder she had repelled, — narrowly escaped the bullets of the hidden foe. But the only person who was killed was one Stevens, or Stearns, — the accounts give the name in both forms, — said to have been a laboring man from Canaan, Conn., who had been at work in Poontoosuck during the summer. On the pillion behind him was a daughter of Sylvanus Piercey, whom he had perhaps married, as some of the reports speak of her as his wife. Stevens was shot while passing through Lenox; but his companion was rescued by the first settler of that town, Jonathan Hinsdale. The settlements above Stockbridge were completely abandoned.

It is a prevalent opinion that only the two Indians who made the attack upon Chamberlain's house were engaged in firing upon the fugitives from Poontoosuck; but the weight of evidence is opposed to this theory. The woods were full of prowlers. A scout sent out from Fort Massachusetts towards Albany ascertained, that, "on the 25th or 26th of August, forty-two canoes of Indians, of five, six, or seven in a canoe, crossed the lake" (either Lake George or Lake Champlain), "with a design to make a descent on our frontier." On the 6th of September, a man who had ventured to return to Poontoosuck was "shot at by three Indians, and the bullets penetrated his clothes in several places." He returned the fire and "shot one down, but did not get him." [1]

The reliable local tradition is, that the white combatant, having procured a re-enforcement, traced his opponent by his blood to the shore of Lake Onota, and found a pebble wrapped in cloth, which had evidently been used to stanch the wound. But the injured

[1] Col. Worthington to Willard.

man had disappeared; whether carried off by his friends, or plunged into the lake to save his scalp from his pursuers, is uncertain. The latter was the belief of the time.

On the same day, two men were fired upon, west of Sheffield, and another north of that town. All these events, occurring in the week ending on the 7th of September, were amply sufficient to rouse suspicion of the complicity of the resident Indians, especially in the minds of the soldiers who came from a distance to the relief of the settlers; although the latter were not entirely free from the injustice.[1]

Gen. Dwight, after careful investigation, warmly defended the Mission Indians; showed them to be innocent of all blame in the matter, and, if properly treated, ready to join with their white neighbors in the war. The guilty parties proved to be Schaghticokes, of whom a few were domiciled at Stockbridge. And doubtless some of the rascal red population which hung round the place also participated in the mischief done.

The Schaghticokes had, like the Mohegans, pledged themselves to the league formed at Albany in July; but they had hardly returned home before they proved faithless to their obligations. In October, Col. Timothy Woodbridge held "a talk" with the Canadian sachems, whose bands had perpetrated the outrages at Hoosac, Stockbridge, and Poontoosuck, and drew from them that they had acted under the joint instigation of the French and the Schaghticokes. He asked them, "Why they had made war upon the settlements, while the princes under which they respectively lived were at peace?" They replied, that "The Schaghticokes had sent to the Orondocks and the Onuhgungoes, to come and revenge themselves for the death of several of their men who had been killed by the English, and to help them — the Schaghticokes — to Canada."

Others reported that the Onuhgungoes waited upon the Governor of Canada, and said, "Father, the English have abused us in driving us from our lands and taking them from us."[2]

[1] The worst of the outrages mentioned by Gen. Dwight, in his letter of Oct. 4, — quoted in the note on page 99, — were the results of this suspicion; although treatment of the natives of a similar character, however less gross in degree, had prevailed, as stated in the text, long before the date in connection with which the letter is first quoted.

[2] Col. Woodbridge explains in parenthesis, that "the Onuhgungoes were inhabitants of the Connecticut Valley driven away in former wars, the same as the

The Governor replied, "Children, the land is not mine, but yours: you must assert your right."

Upon this hint they acted, and sent out an expedition, which, as they confessed, numbered one hundred and twenty men.[1]

To the people who, driven out from the homes, which, after one cruel interruption, they had just begun to build up, were collected, in doubt and confusion in the lower towns, it was a momentous question, whether the murderous outbreak which had visited them was only a sudden freak of savage fury, which would soon pass away, or one more of the accumulating proofs that France had secured the alliance of the Indians in another bitter, and probably prolonged contest, for the extension of her dominion in America. The conference of the St. François chiefs with Col. Woodbridge was considered conclusive against the French, who were then still keeping up treacherous professions of peaceful purposes. But the Government could have previously had no doubt upon the subject: the conference is only mentioned here, as showing the conjunction of causes which produced so serious an interruption to the settlement of Berkshire.

The alarm on the border was pitiable. Every hour brought rumors of outrage, which, although oftenest false, served to keep alive the public excitement. "I never knew," wrote Israel Williams on the 6th of September, "in all ye last war, the people under so great surprise and fear." But Col. William Williams, probably after consultation with Gen. Dwight and Col. Worthington, returned with some of his neighbors and a detachment of Connecticut troops to his house on Unkamet Street, which at once was stockaded. On the 9th, Col. Israel Williams, who commanded the Hampshire militia, wrote from Hatfield to the Provincial Secretary, that he "hoped they would maintain their guard at Poontoosuck, and be some protection to the towns and places within."

As soon as communication could be had with head-quarters, Col. William Williams received orders from Gov. Shirley of Massachusetts, and a request from Gov. Fitch of Connecticut, to make a stand at Poontoosuck: the former sending him a sergeant and eight men; the latter, twenty-eight men, under command of Capt. Hinman.[2]

Schaghticokes." The ghosts of murdered nations were rising it seems, to plague their destroyers.

[1] Lieut.-Col. Woodbridge, Oct. 9, 1754

[2] T. C. C. p. 217.

FORT ANSON.

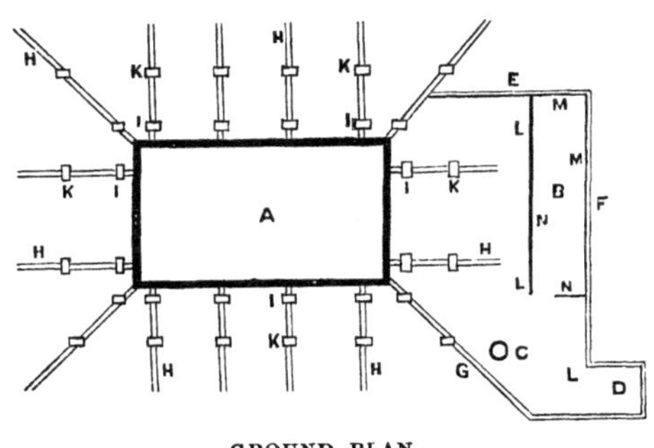

GROUND PLAN.

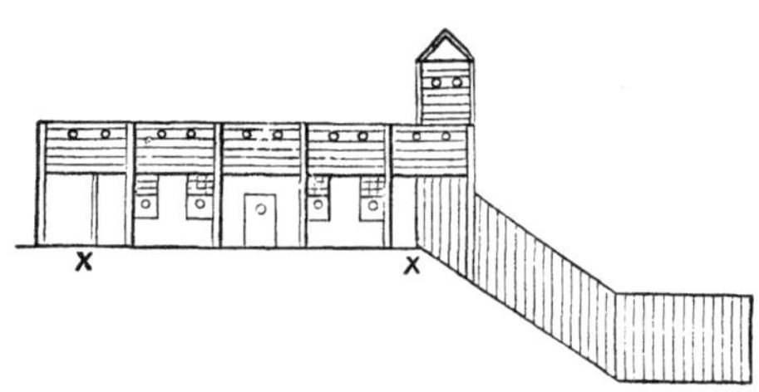

SOUTH PROSPECT.

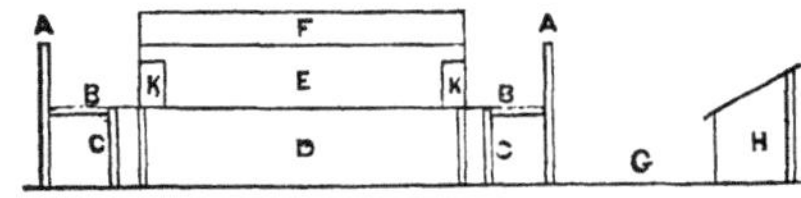

PROFILE FROM THE CENTRE.

FORT ANSON,

Built by William Williams, at Poontoosuck, September, 1754.

EXPLANATION OF GROUND PLAN.

A, The House, 40 by 24 feet, nine-feet posts, with a gambrel roof, the walls filled with four-inch white-ash plank.

B, The Storehouse, 35 by 10 feet; the outside, M, M, 14 feet high; the inside, at N, 7 feet; double-covered with boards up and down, salt-box fashion, drooping inwards.

C, The Well.

D, A Flanker, to defend the dead-wall F.

E, *G*, Dead-Walls, scoured from the upper works.

H, *H*, Large Sills, let into the ground, to support the pillars I, K.

I, *I*, Large Pillars, let into the sills, just eight inches from the house, in every part, that reach as high as the eaves, and support plates that go all around the house, and are locked at the corners.

K, *K*, Large Pillars, 16 inches square, 7 feet higher than the top of the plate, supported by the pillars. Each girted to his fellow, and cross-girted to the plate.

L, *L*, The Yard, floored all over.

A SOUTH PROSPECT OF FORT AT POONTOOSUCK.

X, *X*, the ends of the House.

A PROFILE FROM THE CENTRE OF THE HOUSE, EAST AND WEST.

EXPLANATION.

A, *A*, Pillars filled with square timber, let in with a groove from the girt, I, to the top; being 7 feet all round ye house.

B, *B*, A Platform, 8 feet wide, round the house.

C, *C*, Pillars that support the plates that support one side of the platform; the other side being supported by the girts that pass from ye pillars A, A, sideways.

D, The lower part of the house.

E, The Chamber, or soldiers' lodging-room.

F, The space of the Gambo.

G, The Yard.

H, The Storeroom.

K, *K*, Doors, out of which the soldiers may run and cover any or every part of the house.

The home-lots being too widely scattered for defence, the settlers who returned with Col. Williams repaired to his house,[1] and entered into a compact to work together on the lands protected by its defences, holding the produce in common, and "cheerfully agreeing, that, if any thing remained beyond what was necessary for their own support, to give it for the soldiers which might be allowed them." The petition to the General Court, in which they stated this plan, asked only that the same protection might be granted them which was accorded their brethren of the Province, "considering their situation," and that allowance might be made them for the expense incurred in fortifying, in case their scheme should be approved.[2]

Correspondence ensued, of which the following letter formed a part: —

COL. ISRAEL WILLIAMS TO COL. WM. WILLIAMS.

HATFIELD, Sept. 28, 1754.

Sir, — Major Williams is returned from Boston, by whom I have my orders renewed for ye strengthening ye frontiers and raising a greater number of forces for that purpose and scouting, if I judge needful, but no orders for building forts anywhere. The Governor will report that matter to ye General Court: but yet he is desirous of having ye people maintain their ground, and has given me sufficient orders to defend the garrisons they build; and, as I wrote to you heretofore, so I would again press your people to fortify somewhere in ye westerly part of Poontoosuck. By what I have been informed, Ashley's house is well situate: but, if they incline to fortify further west, I like it well; and, if they go cheerfully and do it, there is reason to think they will meet with ye favor of the Government; and, if they do, the

[1] No man appearing to provide for the forces aforesaid but Col. Williams, we repaired to his house, who, at his own expense, had fortified the same. — *Poontoosuck Petition, T. C. C. p.* 98.

[2] The following memoranda, made by Col. Williams two years afterwards, gave these transactions more in detail, and with a little different coloring: —

"MEMORANDUM. — That, upon the mischief, protection was sent us both from this Province and Connecticut. Upon their arrival, I offered to join them with all my strength, in fortifying wherever they should choose; but none of them would undertake, either to billet or build. Upon which, rather than no stand should be made, I proposed, if they would fortify with me, I would billet them, the inhabitants and soldiers, pay the broad-axe men three shillings and narrow-axe two shillings per diem: which they accepted, and I performed, and built a handsome, strong, and very tenable fort [Anson]; and, if I had not thus done, the soldiers would have all returned, and no one soul would now be at P. And now, since they find the war is like to last longer than they expected, and that the Bryars and Bushes will get up too high, they want the Province to pay them and support them, while they cut them down [alluding to the custom of alternate mustering in as soldiers]. It can be nothing else. Behold their situation. The ingenuity, gratitude, and requital." — *Lancton Coll.*

men that are now there must, some of 'em, guard whilst they are about ye work; and, if the inhabitants can supply themselves with provisions, Col. Partridge will supply ye soldiers with necessaries.

We have no news of ye enemy.

I suppose Col. Partridge will send to you to come in, when I shall confer with you about some other matters. The Governor has given ye command of the men at Fort Massachusetts and Poontoosuck to Major Williams[1] for ye present.

With proper salutations,

Your affectionate friend and servant,

ISRAEL WILLIAMS.

But Col. Williams, at Poontoosuck, had already begun to strengthen the defences on his own Unkamet-street grounds, by the erection of a formidable fort, in accordance with the plans here reproduced from the original copies, which are still preserved in the State archives. And instead of abandoning this site, which had no natural advantages, for the fine and commanding eminence on the south-west shore of Lake Onota, which was the location of "Ashley's House," he persisted in his first intention, and built the work which he christened Fort Anson, probably in honor of the admiral with whom he sailed on his first military campaign under Oglethorpe, but which is known in the Provincial records, sometimes as the fort at Poontoosuck, and sometimes as Williams's Garrison."

The refusal to adopt the district-commander's suggestion in regard to the location of the fort did not prevent its acceptance by the General Court as one of the Province garrisons; but its builder was allowed only £63 for it, although it cost him, as he alleged, £91. During its erection, apprehensions of a lurking enemy rendered it necessary to keep up a vigilant scout of the neighborhood; and there were other difficulties to encounter. The uncertain state of affairs will appear by the following letter from Col. Oliver Patridge to Col. Williams,[1] which also is of interest as illustrating the scarcity of certain articles of merchandise, as well as the writer's distrust of Col. Williams's business capacity: —

HATFIELD, Sept. 21, 1754.

Dear Brother, — I received yours by Chandler; have procured you ten pounds of ginger, a door-lock, and two padlocks, small, but the biggest in

[1] Major Eph. Williams, the founder of Williams College.

[2] Col. Partridge married Col. Williams's sister, and appears to have entertained a warm friendship for his brother-in-law.

town. Shall send ye hinges, staples, &c., you sent for; also, twenty-one and half gallons of rum and six gallons of molasses. Upon advising with Col. [Israel] Williams, he let me know that rum would not be allowed soldiers, except those destined for scouting. I thought molasses would be profitable in the article of Bar. One half-pound pepper and a quire paper I also send. There is no Commissary appointed for your place, and who it will be I know not; but I will be so free with you (and I trust I may so advise you), to be very wary and careful how you proceed in the article of billeting: else difficulties may arise. Poontoosuck inhabitants, who, I understand, are with you, will not be allowed billeting until they are mustered as soldiers, which probably they will alternately. What store of pork you have at Poontoosuck among your people, and at what rate it may be bought, I don't know. I would advise you not to give any extravagant price: there is enough to be had here reasonably. As to their wheat which is upon the straw, you certainly (if you want) may get at a moderate price. We have heard this morning (Sept. 22) a man was shot upon at Southampton, and we have no news from any other quarter. I hope you will use prudence as to yourself and men with you, for we know not where ye enemy lurks.

I am your brother and servant,

OL. PARTRIDGE.

N. B.—I have sent eight and three-quarter pounds of sugar, though I had *none* to part with.

Besides superintending, and providing the means for, the erection of Fort Anson, Col. Williams attended to the commissariat of both the soldiers and the returned settlers,—a department for which he seems to have had a predilection, if not an aptitude. We have his "Gentlemen's, Soldiers', and Laborers' Account Book, 1754, whilst building Fort Anson at Poontoosuck,"[1] and also his Sutler's Book for the month of November. And they furnish some curious recollections of life at Unkamet's Crossing. The former shows a deal of hard work, sustained by regular although not excessively frequent potations;[2] the latter, commencing after the families of some of the settlers had repaired to the fort, is of more curious interest. Nine-tenths of its charges are for spirituous liquors, in drams of rum, bowls or half bowls of punch, and mugs of flip. But it must be considered that every potation was here recorded, and that an allowance of two or three daily, and the average did not reach the smaller number, although it was then considered moderate drinking, made a formidable show if stretched

[1] Lanc. Coll. [2] T. C. C., p. 286.

out through a month's accounts. Persons lower in rank took their drams; their superiors revelled in punch; while the more staid, and the gentler sex, — for the ladies did not totally abstain, — were generally content with the mild beverage of flip: if "sower," then the more luxurious.

Capt. Hinman appears to have been a jolly fellow, with a relish for liquid delicacies, and in his element when Nathaniel Tyler got credit for sixty shillings by one hundred limes delivered the commissariat. Sometimes, too, a pleasant party relieved the sombreness of the times over the social glass. On the 20th of November, the gallant Capt. Hinman is charged with a "mug of flip for Mrs. Piercey." On the same day we have the following startling entry: "The wife of Deacon Crofoot for a mug of flip, — a kiss." There must have been a merry party of fair women and brave men that chill November evening in the old fort. But it may be as well to mention that the good deacon's good wife was then sixty-six years old. It is not recorded that the score so deliberately set down against her was ever liquidated. The red men, too, came in for their share of the fire-water. Wanonpe is made debtor to a gill of rum. John Wawampequeenont to a mug, a gill, and a glass. John got a pound of shot as well.

The soldiers in 1754 could not have been such multitudinous letter-writers as those of 1861–6. The only charges for paper, on Col. William's book, were one sheet to Stephen Parsons, and a half sheet to Moses Alexander, — the latter coupled with a dram. But opportunities of communication with home were then rare.

The larder of the fort was occasionally replenished with venison at five pence a pound, and wild turkey at a shilling. An ox weighing six hundred and forty pounds was bought of Sylvanus Piercey for twelve pence a pound, making £32; and a yoke was sold for £60 by Hezekiah Jones. The rations of thirty men for a month were estimated at twenty bushels of flour, four hundred and twenty pounds of pork, five hundred and twenty-five pounds of beef, four and a half bushels of pease, and twenty-four gallons of rum. No mention is made in the book of tobacco in any form.

There seems to have been much flitting to and from the fort, and the quartermaster entertained all comers. On the 14th November, "Capt. Hinman and Somers" came before dinner, and five more before supper. Sarah Williams, "Sylvanus Piercey, his wife and four children, and his three men," are registered on the same day. Nov. 16, "an Indian scout and two of Capt. Hinman's men before supper." "Clerk Stone and Tyler *ante prandem*" on the 19th, &c.

We are grateful for the light thrown by these little book; upon life in Poontoosuck while it was held as a military outposts for documentary accounts become scant after January, 1755, when Col. Williams, who had before been acting as a half-pay officer under special orders, accepted a captaincy in the regiment which his old commander, Sir William Pepperell, was raising for the Canada expedition of Gen. Shirley.

From the archives of the Commonwealth, however, we gather, that, between the opening of the war and the year 1759, the settlers of Poontoosuck, were maintained by the Province in a sort of semi-military capacity. The supposition of Col. Partridge, that they would be "mustered in alternately," proved substantially correct, and was doubtless in accordance with custom. In order that they might live, and hold their post as "a protection to the towns within;" pay, for garrisons of a limited number of men, was allowed to the forts which were built from time to time; and this was shared by as many of those who most needed it as could agree upon a division of service and remuneration. Thus a fort which was allowed a garrison of eight men, really had more than twice that number, who eked out their subsistence by agricultural and other work in common, or otherwise.

Nor were individual interests altogether forgotten. In 1756, Charles Goodrich represented to the General Court that the Fort [Anson] was located so far from his clearing as to afford no protection to it — a fact which shows how close to its walls the enemy were supposed to lurk, and how great was the terror which they inspired. Goodrich received the promise of support for a garrison of eight men, provided he would build "a fortified place at his own expense." He accordingly erected — on an eminence southeast of Wendell Square, and about two miles south of Fort Anson — a stout block-house, which went by the name of Goodrich Fort, of which he was appointed commander, with the rank of sergeant. Goodrich, owning much land in the vicinity of his fort, made it profitable to lease or sell small sections of it to less favored settlers, who were glad to be "mustered in alternately" as soldiers of the garrison, and to cultivate little patches of earth so near the fort that they could take refuge in it in case of danger.

In November, 1757, a petition similar to that of Goodrich was sent to the General Court by Stephen Crofoot, Solomon Deming, Ebenezer Holman, Nathaniel Fairfield, Jesse Sackett, Abner Dewey, Ephraim Stiles, Simeon Crofoot, Hezekiah Jones, Eli Root, Israel Dewey, Benedict Dewey, and David Bush.

The petitioners stated, that, before the war, they had made considerable improvements on their lands; but, having no place of defence to secure their families, were obliged to remove them "on the first mischief by the Indians;" that the men sent by the Connecticut Committee of War were employed by Col. Williams to garrison his own house, which stood about two miles from their improvements;[1] that some of the petitioners had been at said fort [Anson] in the pay and subsistence of the Province, in the hope of a re-settlement of the town: but, as it was situated, it was of no advantage to the settlers; and they could not improve their lands unless they were protected by works properly located for that purpose. These they stated their willingness to build, and only asked that a suitable number of themselves and others, — of which there were about eighteen, — who wished to re-settle the township, might be put under the pay and subsistence of the Province, and some disinterested person appointed to the command.

In January, the same parties, together with Moses Miller, Ezekiel Phelps, Benjamin Goodrich, Abner and Israel Dewey, and Jacob Ensign, informed the Court that they had built "a good defensible garrison, eighty feet in length and sixty in breadth, with mounts at the opposite corners, with comfortable and convenient housing within, and suitably situated for the settlement." This work stood between Honasada Street and the river, near the bridge, and upon the land of Nathaniel Fairfield, whose name it took. This was not far from the four corners, now Wendell Square; and the expressions of the memorialists sustain the tradition that that was then considered "The Centre."

The General Court granted the pay and subsistence of ten men to the garrison of Fort Fairfield, from the 1st of March to the 1st of November next ensuing; and provision was afterwards made for it, from time to time, in the establishment for the western frontier. Hezekiah Jones was appointed commandant, with the

[1] The centre of the lands owned by the petitioners was about where Honasada Street crosses the Housatonic River.

rank of sergeant. A fourth place of defence was afterwards built upon the eminence on the south-west shore of Lake Onota,[1] which had been recommended for that purpose by Col. Israel Williams in 1754. At what date it was actually occupied does not appear. In 1755, Gen. Dwight reported to Gov. Shirley the arrival of sixty-five Connecticut soldiers at Stockbridge, of whom twenty-five were destined for Poontoosuck, to take the place of those who had refused to work at fortifying. And he suggested that some of the new comers were "specially enjoined" for work of that kind; and as Massachusetts — contrary to the expectation both of himself and Gov. Shirley — was required to furnish them subsistence, he recommended that they should be employed in erecting a good fortress in the western part of Poontoosuck.[2]

Col. Israel Williams had, in 1754, urgently pressed the building of works on Ashley's Hill, which he pronounced "situated best for a garrison for ye protection of Stockbridge and for scouting from;" and — Gen. Dwight giving his earnest opinion, in February, 1756, that "a fort there, if kept well-manned, would be of the greatest service" — it was probably built in the following summer. When finished, it was the especial Province fort of this portion of the valley; looking more to the general defence, while the others, although affording great protection to the towns and places within, were located, as we have seen, with primary reference to the defence of the settlers in their agricultural labors.

All these forts were mere block-houses; and there is no intimation that any of them mounted so much as a swivel in the way of cannon: but they were of much more skilful and elaborate construction than is commonly supposed, as will appear from the minute description we are able to give of Fort Anson and the more scanty outlines of Forts Fairfield and Massachusetts.

The "establishment on the western frontier," as the garrisons of the forts in that quarter were officially styled, fluctuated in numbers, as fear and the spirit of economy alternately prevailed among the legislators; but often a new alarm reversed an order to reduce the establishment before it could be carried into

[1] Then called Ashley Pond, from the residence of one Ashley, afterwards a noted Tory, upon the site of the fort.

[2] Mass. Ar. v. 54, pp. 380–1.

effect. The forces were divided between headquarters at Fort Massachusetts, and some half-dozen smaller works. Probably five hundred men could have been rallied to defend a given point; and so perfect a scout was kept up through the woods, that it was impossible for any considerable body of the enemy to approach without timely discovery. In this service, the men found constant and active employment when not otherwise engaged in garrison duty or in erecting new fortifications.

The largest garrison was usually stationed at Fort Massachusetts; and another, of from thirty to fifty men, at West Hoosack, now Williamstown. At Lanesborough, the inhabitants held their own, by the erection of a fort, or block-house, in the southern part of the township, in which their plantation was organized in 1759. Poontoosuck was usually allowed a garrison of about thirty men; to which Connecticut sometimes added a detachment of the troops which she maintained in Massachusetts for the defence of her own frontier. The settlers, mustered in alternately as soldiers, were occasionally employed upon detached service at Fort Massachusetts, Stockbridge, and probably at other points: once, at least, at Blandford, for a few weeks in 1755. With the exceptions mentioned, the country northward from Poontoosuck to Canada was an unbroken wilderness; and although the few posts above diminished in some degree the perils of those who guarded the lower passes, yet, in scouting their own wild neighborhood, the soldiery at Poontoosuck must have been subject to no small danger, as well as to privation and fatigue. It was at the risk of his scalp that the hunter from Fort Anson singly chased the deer to the foot of the Hoosacks; and, if he sought his venison along the bases of the Taconics, it became an interesting question whether he might not himself furnish material for the roast. Luckily, the trout leaped by thousands in the rivers and lakes; for the mountain brooks dashed through tabooed ground, and Lulu Cascade might have proved as fatal as a fountain in the desert to the adventurous sportsman who was tempted by its pool.

Tradition is garrulous of encounters in the township, both before and after the breaking out of the war, between the white man and the red, with fatal results to the latter; but these stories are happily discredited by the fact, that no mention of them is made in contemporary reports, in which every indication of the presence of the enemy on the border was scrupulously noted, and whose writers were well informed of every incident which happened at Poontoosuck. Two Indians were, however, killed near the Fort at Lanesborough; [1] and the universal belief that the woods, up to the very walls of the forts, were full of hostile savages, must have had some foundation in fact.

During the war, several of the regiments destined for the various expeditions against Crown Point, Ticonderoga, and Canada, passed through Poontoosuck; among them, in 1755, that of Sir William Pepperell, in which William Williams served as captain, and, in 1758, that which the latter officer commanded as colonel. Most of these bodies halted for rest at Poontoosuck; and Williams showed his interest in the plantation by persuading Gen. Pepperell to leave twenty-six men for its protection, — a detail which was disapproved by the General Court, who requested Gov. Shirley to order its discontinuance. Relics of the presence of the troops of the Province in Poontoosuck during this war are still occasionally found. Very recently buttons bearing the inscription, "Massachusetts 8th Reg.," were dug up near Lake Onota. It is said, that, some forty years ago, a veteran passing this way, declared that he had belonged to one of the regiments which halted here in the the second French and Indian war, and related that the colonel, finding that his men suffered from the lack of exercise, marched them to a spot where stood three gigantic white oak-trees, one of which they cut down. On being put to the test, he pointed out the spot; and the stumps of the trees, which are of a kind rare in this vicinity, were found as he had described them.

It was on these marches that some who were subsequently citizens of Pittsfield first became acquainted, perhaps more intimately than was agreeable, with its soil. Names afterwards familiar to its history are found on the muster-rolls of the towns of Westfield, Springfield, and Northampton. Among those from Westfield were David Noble, who organized and led the company of minute-men which marched from Pittsfied on the news of Lexington fight; and Oliver Root, a noted officer of the Revolution. The latter was the son of Samuel Root, one of the forty pioneers, who had died before completing his plans of removal to Poontoosuck. Oliver was born at Westfield, Nov. 24, 1741, and, when of a proper age, was apprenticed to a worthy shoemaker of that town. When the war of 1754 broke out, he was, of course, a mere child; but he

[1] Holland's Hist. West. Mass.

soon grew a stout youth, and, taking advantage of the law which permitted apprentices to enlist, he joined a company raised in his native place, and marched to Albany by the road cut in 1753, along the Westfield River and through Poontoosuck.

This road was but a narrow path for pack-horses; and Col. Root described that portion of it which lay in Poontoosuck as in horrible condition. No less than five hemlock swamps, some of them most formidable bogs, lay between the Hoosacs and the Taconics. In these the horses were constantly mired; and the men were compelled to carry the poor beasts through, with their burthens upon them, by main strength. This was effected by a file of soldiers on each side, who passed the bands by which their muskets were commonly slung, under the bellies of the animals, and so went marching along. Perhaps it was in consequence of this same shocking state of the road, that Capt. Edward Ward, in his account with the Province, still preserved in the State archives, has an extra charge of "£1. 10*s.* to cash paid for transporting my baggage through Poontoosuck."

Reaching the seat of war, Oliver Root had the good fortune, as the brave and adventurous young soldier esteemed it, to be assigned to the famous Corps of Rangers organized by Major Robert Rogers. Into this corps, the strictest care was taken to admit none but men of the hardiest constitution, accustomed to hunt and travel in the woods, and in whose courage and fidelity the utmost confidence could be placed. Among its officers were John Stark and Israel Putnam, with others of the same character, and a rank and file of similar material; who, together, made up the most splendid Corps of Rangers known in history.

Besides their arms, their only accoutrements were a tin cup and a single blanket for each man; their simple rations a little parched corn pounded to a coarse meal.

Singly, or in parties, they lay down to rest wherever inclination and opportunity found them, with no shelter but their blankets. Their strength was sustained, and their unpampered appetites satisfied, with a little corn stirred in their cups with water dipped from the wayside brook or spring; although they did not forbear to forage for choicer viands when circumstances favored, nor disdain the game with which the forest abounded, when prudence did not forbid the noise necessary for its capture, or the smoke which would arise in cooking it.

Throughout the war, the Rangers performed the most perilous services; and their exploits were as important to the expeditionary forces as they were dashing in their gallantry and thrilling in their hairbreadth adventures. The fate of Braddock had taught the British commanders a lesson not easily forgotten; and the Rangers, in every battle of the armies to which they were attached, were placed in the van. In all marches, they piloted the way, and, scouting along the edges of the columns, rendered surprise or ambuscade impossible. Always on the alert, they patrolled the forests in all directions; making prisoners of unwary enemies, skirmishing with exposed outposts, rescuing captured friends, and giving warning to those in danger, until they surpassed the red man in his own craft, and became the terror of Frenchman and hostile Indian. For the dangers and privations inseparable from such a life, the Rangers found compensation, not in the slight superiority of their pay to that of the soldiers of the line, but amply in the wild and adventurous life which they led, and in the privileges and exemption from military routine which their corps enjoyed, although held to the severest discipline in their own line of duty.

In such warfare as this, the future Col. Root, like many other officers of the Revolution, found his military school, and became familiar with hardship and danger, as well in the recesses of the forest as on the ensanguined ground before Ticonderoga.

With the advent of peace in 1760, he returned to Westfield. The law freed enlisted apprentices from all claim by their masters upon their earnings: but our young Oliver did not find it consistent with his notions of integrity to avail himself of its provisions; and, upon his return home, he brought his bounty-money, and as much of his pay as by careful economy he had been able to save, and delivered them to his master, saying, in substance, "This money I might legally retain, but justly and rightfully it is yours: take it."[1]

It is pleasant to know, that, when his apprenticeship was completed, Oliver was taken by his master to Pittsfield, and there established by him upon the farm inherited from his father.

[1] The same simple-minded integrity characterized Col. Root throughout life: and, in his old age, he refused to apply for the pension to which he was entitled as an officer of the Continental army; maintaining that the act of Congress could only have been intended for the benefit of those veterans who had no other means of support, while he, although not wealthy, was comfortably well off.

An inspection of the rolls, in connection with corroborating circumstances, leads to the belief that nearly all the settlers of Pittsfield who were of a suitable age served in the last French and Indian war, either in the marching regiments or in the resident garrisons.

The services of Col. Williams were conspicuous. In January, 1755, he received a letter from his old friend and commander, Sir William Pepperell (Lanc. Col.), which, after some moderately-bitter complaint of the ill requital of their services at Louisburg, expressed his intention to overlook past ingratitude, and raise a regiment for the first expedition against Canada in the new war, in which he offered Lieut.-Col. Williams a captaincy, regretting that he could at the time do no better by him, but promising him his influence for future promotion. Col. Williams accepted the proposition, and served for three campaigns without advance of rank. This deferment of promotion arose from a difficulty into which Capt. Williams fell with Sir William Johnson; whose pets, the Iroquois, he had grossly insulted and enraged, by charging them with treachery to the English cause, disarming them, and threatening extreme measures if they were in his power. For this he was imprisoned by Johnson at Albany, but seems to have defended or excused himself to the satisfaction of the Massachusetts authorities; for, in the spring of 1758, he received a colonel's commission from Gov. Pownal, and raised a regiment which, in camp at Poontoosuck, June 5, 1758, numbered 906 men.[1] With this corps he took part in Abercrombie's unsuccessful expedition against Ticonderoga, and was in the memorable and sanguinary attack upon that post, July 5, 1758; of which he wrote a most thrilling and interesting account. With this campaign ended his active career as a military man.

[1] In August, William Williams, son of the colonel, who had been surgeon's mate in Col. Ephraim Williams's regiment at the time that gallant officer was slain, and had behaved very creditably in that affair, was appointed surgeon in his father's regiment. He died a few years later of small-pox.

CHAPTER VI.

THE PLANTATION ORGANIZATION RESUMED.

[1759–1761.]

Proprietors'-Meetings, 1759–60. — Vote to sell the Lands of Delinquent Tax-payers. — Committees to hire a Minister. — Col. Williams's First Election as Clerk. — Highways and Bridges. — Highway-Surveyors' Districts formed. — Condition of the Settlers at the Close of the War. — Partition of the Commons.

THE last item of the plantation records prior to their suspension on account of the Indian troubles was the oath subscribed, Aug. 12, 1754, by Hezekiah Jones and David Bush, faithfully to perform their duties as assessors; to which office they, with William Wright, had been elected. The next entry was the warrant of those gentlemen, issued Sept. 16, 1758, for a meeting of the Proprietors, to be held on the 2d of October, at the house of Nathaniel Fairfield, — the same which the General Court accepted the next winter, as "one of its garrisons."

The meeting chose Stephen Crofoot moderator, and Eli Root collector of taxes; continued the old assessors in office; appointed Deacon Crofoot, Sergeant Jones, and Ephraim Stiles a committee to hire a minister; laid a tax of six shillings upon each lot to pay him; and instructed the assessors to sell the lands of such as refused to discharge their rates. The apparent object of the meeting was to procure a chaplain for the fort, as no inhabitants of other parts of the plantation seem to have taken part in it; but a suspicion of sharp practice attaches to the vote to sell the lands of those who refused to pay their rates, at a time when many of the proprietors were dispersed at a distance, — some of them with the army at the front, — and others were straitened in their resources by the unsettled state of the country.

In the fall of 1758, the colonists had cause to be inspirited; but the more thoughtful rejoiced with trembling. The advantages gained by the English arms in the campaign just closed inspired confidence in their ultimate success, which the event justified; but, as late as the spring of that year, murders had been committed by the Indians at Coleraine, and many months passed before the inhabitants of towns much farther within the border experienced a sense of safety. It is not merely in the gloom of the sufferings which they actually underwent, that we are to consider the plantations; but in the shadow of those which they had abundant reason to dread as well. And not until the fall of Quebec, — not, indeed, fully until the cession of 1763, — could their fears be entirely dispelled. Stockbridge, in 1759, applied with earnestness to the General Court for aid; stating that it "had fifty men in the service, which weakened its garrison for home defence, and left it *almost as much exposed as Poontoosuck*."

Plainly the time had not come for any proceedings, in plantation-meeting, which would seriously affect the owners of lands not immediately under the protection of the forts; and the voters at the meeting in question confessed as much, by refusing to make appropriations for highways and bridges.

Affairs, however, began gradually to resume the aspect which they had worn before the war. A second meeting of the Proprietors, held Jan. 29, although it did little more than repeat the action of that in October, was less limited in its attendance. It was resolved that the old assessors, clerk, and collector should continue to "stand" in their several offices; but Jesse Sackett was made treasurer, in place of Charles Goodrich. David Bush, Jacob Ensign, and Josiah Wright were substituted for the former "committee to hire a minister." An increasing sense of security from savage prowlings was manifested by holding the meeting at the house of the clerk, David Bush, some rods west of the fort, and by restoring that as the place designated for posting up legal notices.

At the next meeting, — May 21, adjourned to May 30, 1759, — matters began to take more definite form. Col. Williams, having returned from the wars, began his long course of civil service in the office of Proprietors' clerk, taking the qualifying oath, "*Coram* John Ashley, Jus. Peace." The preaching of the gospel was put upon a little more permanent footing by the appointment of Charles Goodrich, Stephen Crofoot, and William Williams "to hire some man, from time to time, to preach among us." The committee was to have some fixedness, however it might prove with the minister. The attention of the meeting was specially given to highways and bridges. Some good beginning had been made in this direction before the war; and during its continuance, although the more remote roads must have retrograded in condition, those favorably situated for protection, and those required for military purposes, were improved. Prior to 1753, some county roads had been laid out and worked; including that now Wendell Street; and that which, commencing near the present junction of Wendell and Elm Streets, formed the east road to Lanesborough. Changes had also begun to be made in the rectangular town-roads, which it would be a laborious task now to trace. Doubts already existed as to the true line of West Street, and encroachments upon all the highways were complained of. Three bridges were standing, — that described in the previous chapter as built by Deacon Crofoot, and those respectively near the present crossings of the Housatonic by West and South Streets. The record of the action of this meeting concerning highways and bridges exhibits clearly the manner of doing that kind of town business; and, as it is in other respects characteristic, we quote in full: —

"Voted: That eighteen pounds be raised for repairing the public and private ways within this township this year; and that twelve pounds be raised to build a bridge over the river in the country road, where it runs through Nathaniel Fairfield's lot; and that Jacob Ensign, Eli Root, and Abner Dewey be a committee to procure the materials, inspect the work, and see it forthwith accomplished, and empowered to let said work out by the great, or employ the proprietors at day-labor; that nine pounds fifteen shillings be raised and allowed to Charles Goodrich, as it shall become due from him for his rates upon his settling lots, he building a good and sufficient bridge over the river, in the country road, near his house. He giving bond (according to his own proposal) to the Proprietors' clerk to finish it in two months from this day, and keep it in repair twenty years next ensuing; and that the builders of the South Bridge should be paid for it, at the rate of highway work, on condition that David Bush, to the Proprietors' clerk, gives bond to keep an open road, during their pleasure, two rods wide, from the highway or town-road down the river, where the path is now trod, two rods wide, to said bridge; and from the said bridge southerly, two rods wide, to the aforesd. road; and that the builders of the west bridge be paid at the same rate, upon condition Josiah Wright gives bond as aforesd. for free passage to and from it with horses, carriages, &c., during pleasure, in case it proves to stand on his lot.

"Voted: That £9. 1. 4. be now raised to pay Deacon Crowfoot for building the bridge over the river in his lot; and that the assessors forthwith make a rate, including all the aforesd. grants of money; and that the builders of the south and west bridges, as soon as may be, bring in their accounts to the assessors, or be excluded in this present assessment."

At this meeting, the first division of "all the public and private roads" into Highway-surveyors' districts was made, with the following bounds; and the surveyors, whose names are given, were assigned to them for the following year:—

No. 1.—From the west line of the township to the West River. Daniel Hubbard, surveyor.

No. 2.—Between the East and West Rivers, including the two bridges, east and west. Sylvanus Piercey, surveyor.

No. 3.—All the roads east of the East River, and the county road. William Williams, surveyor.

The building of bridges, the re-arrangement of the roads, and the adjustment of taxes so that they might be conveniently paid in labor or material, occupied a very prominent place in the early plantation-meetings, even when compared with the large space which kindred subjects claim in the town-business of the present day.

While affairs at Poontoosuck were resuming the routine which the Indian mischief had so rudely interrupted, the conquest of Canada was finally accomplished; and when, soon afterwards, the storm of war ceased, the threatening cloud, which, through every former peace, had lowered along the northern horizon, was dissipated forever. In 1759–60, the omens were so auspicious that the most timorous and exposed settlers began to take heart for the future, and enter upon measures to repair their losses.

A very large proportion of the proprietors had kept their residence more or less closely with the plantation through all its dangers; and some, if not the majority, had, in this perilous sojourning, the companionship of their wives. Others removed their families to the old Connecticut-Valley homes, and held themselves in readiness, either to serve in garrison at Poontoosuck, scout the neighboring forests, or join in the more distant and formal expeditions. Thus, it is narrated of Nathaniel Fairfield, that, on the first mischief by the Indians, he escorted his wife to Westfield, somewhat less leisurely than on their bridal tour they had come through the Green Woods, and, leaving her there, served for six months in the army. At the expiration of that term he re-visited his clearing, and "found his cow and oxen safe, but grown so fat as to be unfit for use:" but let us hope particularly nice eating for the gallant garrison.

The planters found the advantage of their persistent clinging to the place, in the comparatively slight deterioration of their farms; although some, and especially those in the western part of the plantation, suffered from the neglect compelled by their exposed location.

Those settlers who could cultivate their lands at all during the war may have found some compensation for the difficulties under which they labored, in the near and profitable market afforded by the army commissariat; but whether this relief was experienced to any appreciable extent, we are unable to say. It is certain, that, if any losses were thus lightened, they were those which without this mitigation would have been least ruinous to the sufferers. The lands under the protection of the forts belonged to the wealthier planters. The diversion of their industry from the purposes upon which they intended to bestow it, and the idleness in which they were compelled to leave their capital, impoverished the settlers generally in proportion as their interests were confined to, and their capital invested in, Poontoosuck. But, upon the whole, the plantation was in a better condition than was to have been anticipated to resume its progress, and rapidly increase to proportions which would justify its incorporation as a town. Preliminary to that measure, however, and as a means of still further adding to the population, a new partition of the Commons, in place of that which had been annulled, became necessary,— a proceeding which was also demanded by the greatly increased number of the joint proprietors, several of whom were desirous of immediately enjoying their rights in severalty.

As early as June, 1743, Philip Livingston, in consideration of £3000, current money, sold his third of the Commons lands to Ephraim Williams, Esq., of Stockbridge, John Brewer of Township No. 1 (Tyringham), near Stockbridge, Elisha Jones of Weston, Israel Williams and Moses Graves of Hatfield. Jones immediately sold a quarter part of his purchase to Col. Oliver Partridge of Hatfield, and Rev. William Williams of Weston; and the latter, in 1756, "in consideration of love and affection," transferred his rights to his son Solomon, who, dying soon after, left them to his brother, Col. William. Ephraim Williams, one of the founders of Stockbridge, died in 1754, leaving his Poontoosuck lands to his more distinguished son, the colonel of the same name, who was killed the next year in battle. The lands in 1759 were in the hands of Cols. John Worthington and Israel Williams, as trustees for the legatees of Col. Williams; of which the chief was the free school, that, afterwards established at Williamstown, became Williams College.[1]

Col. Wendell had, as has been related, sold one-third of his interest — that is, one-ninth of the Commons — to Charles Goodrich.

Col. Stoddard dying in 1748, left issue, — Mary, Prudence, Solomon, Esther, and Israel, who, with their mother and guardian, Madame Prudence, inherited his property. The daughters had their portion of the estate assigned elsewhere: all the children, except Israel, had become of age in 1759. Only the widow and her sons received lands in the partition of the Poontoosuck Commons.

Capt. Brewer's right had been transferred to some of the other proprietors.[2]

Wendell, Jones, William Williams for his brother's heirs, and Graves, probably with the consent of their co-tenants, applied to the Superior Court, Hampshire September Term, 1759, for a commission of freeholders to make partition of the lands held in common at Poontoosuck; and the following gentlemen, having been accordingly appointed, took the qualifying oath previous to the 1st of January: Major John Ashley, Capt. Ebenezer Hitchcock, Capt. Nathaniel Dwight, John Chadbourne, and Daniel Brown. The warrant for division was dated — *pro forma* at Boston — Oct. 20, 1759. The Commissioners' Report, according to the plan

[1] The Promised Land, described among the hills of Pittsfield, formed part of the allotment to the heirs of Col. Ephraim Williams in the partition of the Commons, as did also the beautiful place now known as "Onota," — the noble grounds attached to the residence of Wm. C.Allen, Esq., on the south-eastern shore of the lake of that name.

[2] The costs of partition, £70, were assessed one-third each to Wendell and the heirs of Stoddard; one-ninth to Moses Graves; one-twelfth to Charles Goodrich; one-eighteenth to Elisha Jones; one-thirty-sixth to Col. Partridge; and the same proportion to the heirs of Col. Ephraim and Dr. Solomon Williams, respectively. Probably Col. Wendell, in his sale to Goodrich, had agreed to pay the cost of partition; and the amount assessed to the latter may have been upon an interest purchased by him of Brewer.

here given, was received at the Registry of Deeds in Springfield, Feb. 6, 1761; and recorded by Edward Pynchon, in Book 2, p. 510.

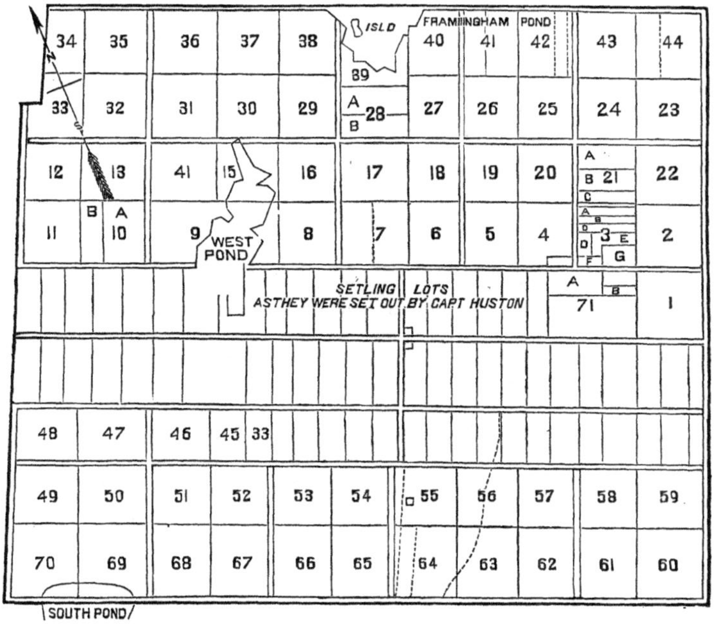

PLAN OF 1759.

A Plan of the Township called Poontoosuck, in the County of Hampshire and Province of Massachusetts Bay; viz., of all the settling-lots, as they were surveyed by Capt. John Huston: and also a lands in said township were surveyed and bounded out by Nathaniel Dwight, in of the year 1759, and as it was set out to each proprietor in January, in the year 1760, with each proprietor's name set on his lot, with the number of the lot, and the number of acres therein contained, by John Ashley, Esq.; Capt. Eben Hitchcock; Nathaniel Dwight, Esq.; John Chadwick; and Daniel Brown,—a Committee appointed for that purpose by the Court of Assize, held at Springfield in September last. Planned on a scale of one hundred and twenty perch in an inch.

Per Nathaniel Dwight, Surveyor.

Signed, NATHANIEL DWIGHT, by order of the Committee.

Jan. 4, 1760.

[On the original plan, each square is marked with the name of the proprietor to whom it was assigned, the number of acres it contained, and the quality of the land. These particulars are transferred to the table below. Some other inscriptions, added by a later hand, are included in parentheses.]

Square No. 1. — Mr. Charles Goodrich, 230 acres, 1 rod, 24 perch. 2d rate.
" No. 2. — Col. Elisha Jones, 230 acres, 1 rod, 24 perch. 2d rate.
" No. 3. — [This square, and part of adjoining land, were subdivided, for reasons which are explained in the text. The subdivisions are indicated by letters.]
A. — Col. Jones, 35 acres.
B. — Col. Partridge, 19 acres.
C. — Col. Eph. Williams's heirs, 21 acres.
D. — Goodrich, 31 acres.
E. — Col. Wm. Williams, 25 acres, 2 rods.
F. — Goodrich, 17 acres.
G. — Wendell and Sol. Stoddard, 100 acres.
" No. 4. — Charles Goodrich, 230 acres, 1 rod, 24 perch. 1st rate.
" No. 5. — Col. Jacob Wendell, 230 acres, 1 rod, 24 perch. 1st rate. (Sold Dickinson.)
" No. 6. — Sol. Stoddard, 230 acres, 1 rod, 24 perch.
" No. 7. — Ministry, 115 acres, no rods, 32 perch.
Minister, 115 acres, no rods, 32 perch. 1st rate.
" No. 8. — Col. Partridge, 230 acres, 1 rod, 24 perch. 1st rate.
" No. 9. — Col. Jacob Wendell, 222 acres, 1 rod, 20 perch. 1st rate (I. W., — E. R.)
Col. Eph. Williams's heirs, 86 acres. 1st rate.
" No. 10. — A. — Mr. Israel Stoddard, 170 acres. 1st rate.
B. — Mr. Sol. Stoddard, 60 acres, 1 rod, 24 perch. 1st rate.
" No. 11. — Mr. Sol. Stoddard, 230 acres, 1 rod, 24 perch. 2d rate.
" No. 12. — Col. Jacob Wendell, 230 acres, 1 rod, 24 perch. 2d rate. (I. M. W. — O. W. ×.)
" No. 13. — Mrs. Prudence Stoddard, 230 acres, 1 rod, 24 perch. 1st rate.
" No. 14. — Sol. Stoddard, 230 acres, 1 rod, 24 perch. 1st rate.
" No. 15. — Col. Jacob Wendell, 199 acres, excluding pond. 3d rate. (J. W.)
" No. 16. — Col. Jacob Wendell, 230 acres, 1 rod, 24 perch. 1st rate. (Hn. W. — O. W. ×.)
" No. 17. — Col. Elisha Jones, 230 acres, 1 rod, 24 perch. 1st rate.
" No. 18. — Col. Jacob Wendell, 230 acres, 1 rod, 24 perch. 1st rate. (Sold Easton ×.)
" No. 19. — Israel Stoddard, 230 acres, 1 rod, 24 perch. 1st rate.
" No. 20. — Lieut. Moses Graves, 230 acres, 1 rod, 24 perch. 1st rate.
" No. 21. — A. — Mrs. Prudence Stoddard, 85 acres, no rods, 35 perch.
B. — Sol. Stoddard, 85 acres, no rods, 35 perch.
C. — Lieut. Moses Graves, 66 acres.
" No. 22. — Sol. Stoddard, 230 acres, 1 rod, 24 perch. 2d rate.
" No. 23. — Col. Stoddard, 242 acres, 1 rod, 24 perch. 1st rate.
" No. 24. — Mrs. Prudence Stoddard, 242 acres, 1 rod, 24 perch. 3d rate.
" No. 25. — Prudence Stoddard, 242 acres, 1 rod, 24 perch.
" No. 26. — Col. Jacob Wendell, 242 acres, 1 rod, 24 perch. 1st rate. (O. W. cleared 60 acres.)
" No. 27. — Prudence Stoddard, 242 acres, 1 rod, 24 perch.

Square No. 28. — 1st rate. A. — Lieut. Moses Graves, 310 acres, 2 rods, 21 perch.
B. — Col. Elisha Jones, 103 acres, 2 rods, 21 perch.
" No. 29. — Col. Jacob Wendell, 242 acres, 1 rod, 24 perch. 2d rate.
(H. N. W. — O. W. ×.)
" No. 30. — Lieut. Moses Graves, 282 acres, 3 rods, no perch. 2d rate.
" No. 31. — Col. Jacob Wendell, 242 acres, 1 rod, 24 perch. 1st rate.
(J. W. M. P.)
" No. 32. — Col. Jacob Wendell, 242 acres, 1 rod, 24 perch. 2d rate.
(J. W. J. W., Jr's, heirs.)
" No. 33 — Col. Wendell, 223 acres, 2 rods 25 perch. 3d rate.
(J. W. A. & S. W. — m 6 — 100.)
" No. 34. — 3d rate. A. — Col. Partridge, 23 acres.
B. — Lieut. Graves, $6\frac{3}{4}$ acres.
C. — Col. Eph. Williams's heirs, 119 acres, 2 rods, no perch.
" No. 35. — Lieut. Moses Graves, 254 acres. 3d rate.
" No. 36. — Mrs. Prudence Stoddard, 254 acres. 2d rate.
(Janes & Brown.)
" No. 37. — Col. Jacob Wendell, 296 acres, 3 rods, no perch. 2d rate.
(J. W. — A. & S. W.)
" No. 38. — Mrs. P. Stoddard, 251 acres. 2d rate.
" No. 39. — Col. Wm. Williams, 103 acres, 2 rods, 21 perch. 1st rate.
" No. 40. — Wm. Williams, 248 acres. 1st rate.
" No. 41. — 2d rate. A. — Sol. Stoddard, 90 acres.
B. — Col. Wendell, 163 acres.
(E. M. W. O. W. ×.)
" No. 42. — 2d rate. A. — Partridge, 207 acres.
B. — Col. Jones, 26 acres.
" No. 43. — School-land, 262 acres, 3 rods, no perch. 3d rate.
" No. 44. — 3d rate. A. — Ministry, 112 acres, no rods, 8 perch.
B. — Minister's Lot, 151 acres, 2 rods, 8 perch.
" No. 45. — Mr. Charles Goodrich, 150 acres. 1st rate.
" No. 46. — Mr. Israel Stoddard, 240 acres. 1st rate.
" No. 47. — Mr. Sol. Stoddard, 240 acres. 1st rate.
" No. 48. — Lieut. Moses Graves, 240 acres. 1st rate.
" No. 49. — Mr. Charles Goodrich, 230 acres, 1 rod, 24 perch. 2d rate.
" No. 50. — Col. Jacob Wendell, 230 acres, 1 rod, 24 perch. 1st rate.
(Sold ×.)
" No. 51. — Lieut. Moses Graves, 230 acres, 1 rod, 24 perch. 1st rate.
" No. 52. — The heirs of Col. Eph. Williams, 239 acres, 2 rods, no perch. 1st rate.
" No. 53. — Col. Jacob Wendell, 230 acres, 1 rod, 24 perch. 2d rate.
(Sold.)
" No. 54. — Col. Jacob Wendell, 230 acres, 1 rod, 24 perch. 3d rate.
(I. M. W. — O. W. ×.)
" No. 55. — Col. Elisha Jones, 230 acres, 1 rod, 24 perch. 2d rate.
" No. 56. — Col. Jacob Wendell, 230 acres, 1 rod, 24 perch. 1st rate.
(I. M. W. — O. W. ×.)

Square No. 57. — Col. Jacob Wendell, 230 acres, 1 rod, 24 perch. 1st rate.
[N. B. — Across lots 56 and 57 is the following : " Col. Wendell's meadow included in these two lots, chiefly valuable."]
" No. 58. — Mr. Sol. Stoddard, 230 acres, 1 rod, 24 perch. 2d rate.
" No. 59. — Gol. Jacob Wendell, 230 acres, 1 rod, 24 perch. 2d rate.
(I. M. W. — O. W. ×.)
" No. 60. — Col. Jacob Wendell, 298 acres, 3 rods, 8 perch. 2d rate.
(J. W. — S. H.)
" No. 61. — Mr. Sol. Stoddard, 298 acres, 3 rods, 8 perch. 3d rate.
" No. 62. — Col. Jacob Wendell, 298 acres, 3 rods, 8 perch Some meadow in this lot. 1st rate. (J. W.)
" No. 63. — Mr. Israel Stoddard, 298 acres, 3 rods, 8 perch. It is meadow included. 1st rate.
" No. 64. — 1st rate. A. — Mr. Charles Goodrich, 248 acres, 2 rods, 32 perch.
B. — Lieut. Graves, 49 acres, 1 rod, 11 perch.
" No. 65. — Mr. Israel Stoddard, 298 acres, 3 rods, 8 perch. 2d rate.
" No. 66. — Mrs. Prudence Stoddard, 298 acres, 3 rods, 8 perch. 3d rate.
" No. 67. — Lieut. Moses Graves, 311 acres, 2 rods, no perch. 2d rate.
" No. 68. — Col. Jacob Wendell, 298 acres, 3 rods, 8 perch. 1st rate.
" No. 69. — Col. Jacob Wendell, 272 acres, 1 rod, 24 perch. 2d rate.
(I. M. W. O. ×. — Sold part.)
" No. 70. — Mr. Sol. Stoddard, 287 acres, 3 rods, 24 perch. 1st rate.

The mode of division adopted, which was much more likely to secure an equitable result than that followed in 1752, was this: Nathaniel Dwight, the professional surveyor to the commission, first divided the land into "squares," generally of from two hundred and thirty to three hundred and twenty-six acres in extent, although some, either from the encroachments of the lakes, or as make-weights, were much smaller. The squares were then classified in regard to their arable qualities, as first, second, and third rate. The three sixty-third parts reserved in the patent of the township for the first settled minister, and for the perpetual support of the schools and of the ministry, were then set off; and the commissioners proceeded to apportion the remaining lands to the several proprietors, square by square, in proportion to their interests. Either by previous agreement, or by courtesy, the spots upon which some of the proprietors had made improvements were included in their allotments; and no dissatisfaction appears to have arisen with the report of the commissioners.

Among the more noticeable allotments, Col. Wendell received the squares which contained the valuable Canoe Meadows, and the fine knoll upon which his grandson, Oliver Wendell Holmes, built his villa. Col. Williams got one hundred thirty-two acres on the south, and two hundred and forty-eight upon the west shores of Poontoosuck Lake; of which he boasted a few years later, as the finest pieces of pine-land in all this region, and "certain always to supply New Framingham (Lanesborough), as that place was entirely destitute of this tree." The beautiful rural cemetery of Pittsfield occupies the larger portion of two semi-squares, of about one hundred and fifteen acres each, which fell to the minister and the "ministry;" the former getting the oblong upon Wahconah Street, the latter that upon Onota.

The Commons lands, now no longer Commons, were thus opened for settlement; and population soon began to extend to them.

CHAPTER VII.

PITTSFIELD INCORPORATED.

[1761-1774.]

Towns receive Names from the Governor. — Berkshire County erected. — First Pittsfield Town-Meeting. — Town-Officers. — Highways and Schools. — Pauperism. — Slavery. — Crimes and Misdemeanors. — Cattle restrained. — Wolves. — Anecdote of Mrs. Janes. — Grist-Mills, Saw-Mills, Fulling-Mills, and Malt-House. — Growth of the Settlement. — Col. Williams's House and Garden. — Other Dwellings. — Early Settlers' Names. — Condition and Prospects of the Town. — Taxation of Non-resident Proprietors.

MANY evils arose from the peculiar system adopted in the settlement of Poontoosuck; and among others, less easy of remedy, was the limitation of corporate powers and duties, under the plantation, to the proprietors of the sixty settling-lots. In reference to the difficulties springing from this cause, it was represented to the General Court, in 1761, that incorporation as a town would greatly contribute to the growth of the place, and remedy many inconveniences to which the inhabitants and proprietors might otherwise be subjected.

The movement was made by Col. Williams, who was then at Boston urging the erection of the county of Berkshire; and an act of incorporation was introduced in the Council, read three times, passed to be engrossed, sent to the House and there read once, all upon the 10th of April. It passed the House on the 13th, was enacted on the 16th, and approved by the governor (Sir Francis Bernard) on the 26th. James Otis, as speaker, attested the passage of the bill by the House.

The act of incorporation conferred the usual powers, but with the provision, that "no inhabitant or proprietor, excepting the original sixty settling-proprietors, or those holding under them, should be obliged to pay any part of the charges towards building a meeting-house, settling the first minister, or the other charges which the said original settling-proprietors were obliged to perform, either according to the tenor of their grant, or by any agreement made by or among themselves."

A further provision was made by amendment, adopted after the passage of the bill by the Council, excluding the new town from representation until the year 1763.

The privilege of conferring names upon towns at their incorporation belonged, under the Provincial *régime*, to the royal governor, who generally, in selecting them, consulted the wishes of the parties interested. In cases, however, where these differed among themselves, the contestants most in favor at Province House prevailed; and, where no satisfactory name was proposed by any party, his Excellency availed himself of the opportunity to indulge his own taste, — and that of Sir Francis Bernard was not to be questioned, — or to compliment some personal friend or patron: a fact which may aid some towns in finding a godfather responsible for their unaccountable names.[1]

Three plantations were made towns on the same day with Poontoosuck; and in each instance a space, which has never been filled, was left blank in the records of the Court, for the name of the place. In the copy, among the rolls of the commonwealth, of the act regarding Poontoosuck, the word "Pittsfield" is inserted in a different handwriting, and with different ink, from those

[1] The following letter — Hon. Thomas Colt's Collection, pp. 335 — affords a curious illustration of this statement, in connection with the incorporation of the Plantation of Queensborough, in 1771. Queensborough was made the town of West Stockbridge in 1774.

SIR,— We have now a petition in the General Court to have the west part of Stockbridge set off, and made into a district; which I suppose will meet with no opposition. We now call the place Queensborough: should be glad to have it retain that name if it is agreeable to his Excellency. I forgot to desire 'Squire Woodbridge to mention it to the governor; and, had I have thought of it, I suppose he would have been too negligent to have done any thing about it. I would therefore now beg the favor of you, sir, to request of his Excellency to call the place Queensborough if it is agreeable to him.

I am, with respect, sir, your very humble servant,

ELIJAH WILLIAMS.

QUEENSBOROUGH, June 4, 1771.

The letter was addressed to Col. William Williams, then Representative from Pittsfield, and high in Gov. Hutchinson's favor.

used in the body of the document. By whom, or upon whose suggestion, the name was selected does not appear. In the act, another blank left for the name of the magistrate authorized to call the first town-meeting was filled by that of Col. Williams; and in June, writing to a friend in London, that gentleman remarked, "The name of Pitt is most agreeable to me; and, as the plantation in which I dwell grew numerous, the government, last spring, saw cause to incorporate it into a town, which Gov. Bernard was pleased to call Pittsfield." Doubtless the writer had some voice in securing for his home the name which was so agreeable to him.

But William Pitt, by his vigorous conduct of the war against France, had made himself the idol of all parties in New England; and, however modern sentiment may regret aboriginal "Poontoosuck," it was not without reason that the men of 1761 thought it seemly to commemorate the British minister who had in troublous time manifested the most earnest solicitude for the defence of the western frontier of Massachusetts, in the name of the first town incorporated in that section after the triumphant close of the war: and it was incidentally fortunate that this town also occupied the site of one of the most exposed military outposts, and was one of those whose safety most closely depended upon the conquest of Canada. And thus, while happily the name of Pitt grew more and more endeared to the whole American people, until the last great statesman who bore it ceased to live, it had, when applied to Pittsfield, an earlier and a local fitness which should not be forgotten.

On the 1st of October, 1760, the proprietors of New Framingham (Lanesborough), fifty-one being present, voted, "That, as the westerly towns of the county of Hampshire are about petitioning the Great and General Court that said county may be divided . . . by the west line of the town of Blandford, . . . we do heartily join with them in their request, and now appoint Wm. Williams, Esq., our agent to solicit the same . . . at their next session, or at any time hereafter, when the other towns, by their agents, shall move in the matter."[1]

There is no record of the action which Poontoosuck undoubtedly took, similar to that of her sister plantations; but, on the same 13th of April on which the act to incorporate the town of Pittsfield

[1] T. C. C., p. 196.

passed in concurrence to be engrossed, Col. Williams — having, as the agent of several towns, petitioned for the division of Hampshire county — had leave to bring in a bill for that purpose; and, on the same day that the act to incorporate the town passed to enactment, that to erect the county of Berkshire passed to be engrossed.[1]

The name "Berkshire" was given to the new county by Gov. Bernard, and was probably suggested by his personal connections with the shire of that name in England.

The towns of Sheffield, Stockbridge, Egremont, and New Marlborough, the plantations of Poontoosuck, New Framingham, and West Hoosuck, and the Districts Nos. 1, 3, and 4, were enumerated in the act; while the rest of the territory of the county was lumped as "all lands within" certain described limits. There were, however, settlements, and some of them considerably advanced, in all the present towns of Southern Berkshire, except West Stockbridge.

Sheffield was declared to be, "for the present, the shire or county town;" and it was enacted that courts of the General Sessions of the Peace and inferior courts of Common Pleas, should be held in the North Parish of that town, on the last Tuesday of April and the first Tuesday of September; and at Poontoosuck on the first Tuesday of December and the first Tuesday of March.

A court-house and jail were built at Sheffield, North Parish, which was, in June, 1761, incorporated as the town of Great Barrington. The courts at Pittsfield were held in a large room set apart for that purpose in Fort Anson, which was dismantled, and, a little after that time, became the property and residence of Lieut. Moses Graves, one of the more wealthy settlers. The terms of the Superior Court of Judicature (corresponding to the present Supreme Judicial Court) were directed to be held at Northampton, in connection with those for Hampshire; and they were so held until 1783.

In 1770, the General Court having submitted certain proposed changes in the times of holding the Berkshire courts to the consideration of the towns of the county, Pittsfield voted that the term held at Great Barrington on the first Tuesday in September had been found inconvenient, as that was the season of the year when every experienced farmer chose to sow his wheat, and because it

[1] Rec. Gen. Court, Lib. copy, vol. xxiii.

gave the clerk so little time that he was perplexed to make out his copies for the Superior Court; and recommended a change to the third Tuesday in August, "as that was a time when all had done reaping, and none began to sow." It was further recommended that the courts held at Pittsfield should, on account of the travelling, sit on the third instead of the last Tuesday of February. And, generally, the town advised that courts should be held at Great Barrington on the last Tuesdays of May and August, and at Pittsfield on the third Tuesdays of November and February. The proposition as to the Great-Barrington September term was adopted by the Legislature; the others rejected. But it will be observed, by the wording of the Pittsfield vote, that changes had already taken place between the erection of the county in 1761 and the meeting of 1770. The agricultural reader will note the prominence given to the farming-interest; and particularly to the culture of wheat, which has since become an insignificant item in the produce of town and county.

Pittsfield having been made a town, and established as one of the two seats of the county courts, entered upon a new era of her history; of which the first few years were marked by organization and formation, when the affairs of the place — social, personal, municipal, and religious — assumed the characteristics which they bore at the opening of the Revolution, and some of which outlasted that convulsion.

The first town-meeting was held in the forenoon of the 11th of May, 1761, at the house of Deacon Stephen Crofoot, which stood near the western end of Elm Street. The business centre was already, it seems, creeping westward. The only business transacted was the election of the following officers: Moderator, David Bush; Clerk, Wm. Williams; Treasurer, David Bush; Selectmen and Assessors, David Bush, William Williams, and Josiah Wright; Constable, Jacob Ensign; Highway-Surveyors, Gideon Goodrich, David Bush, and Eli Root; Fence-viewers, Nath'l Fairfield, Wm. Francis; Sealer of Leather and of Weights and Measures, Simeon Crofoot; Wardens, Solomon Deming and David Noble; Deer-reeves, John Remington and Reuben Gunn.

The Deer-reeves were elected annually to enforce the law which forbade the killing of deer in certain seasons.[1]

[1] By the law of 1698, between Jan. 1 and Aug. 1. Afterwards the dates were slightly changed. In 1763, prohibition began on the 21st December. — *Hist. Hadley*, p. 356.

The meeting was held under a precept from the magistrate named in the act, directed to "Charles Goodrich, one of the principal inhabitants, &c," requiring him to "notify and warn the freeholders and other inhabitants qualified to vote in town-meeting." Various modes were adopted in warning subsequent meetings, as the town, from time to time, gave directions. The custom of the Province — by posting up copies of the warrant at certain prescribed places — was generally followed; but sometimes, when the necessity of calling meetings in sudden and important emergencies was anticipated, the constables were required to serve personal notice upon every voter. To facilitate the performance of this duty, and also the collection of taxes, the inhabitants were classed as belonging to either the East or West Part; and separate constables and collectors were assigned to the two sections.

The right of voting in town-meeting belonged only to such as "had a ratable estate in the town, besides the poll, amounting to the value of twenty pounds, by the following method of estimation, viz.: real estate to be set at so much only as the rents or income thereof for the space of six years would amount to, were it let at a reasonable rate; and personal estate and faculty to be estimated according to the rule of valuation prescribed in the acts from time to time made for assessing and apportioning public taxes."[1]

A practice prevailed, for which no good reason appears, of bestowing a plurality of offices upon a single individual when there was no lack of others, equally qualified, from whom to choose.

As in plantation, so in town meetings, highways and bridges occupied a large share of attention: but it would be impossible, without the aid of a practical engineer, to follow in detail the changes which were made; and, even with such aid, the labor would be difficult and the result voluminous. The roads reserved in the division of the township were laid out at uniform distances and at right angles; so that the changes which were required by the frequent streams, lakes, swamps, and hills, which the right lines encountered, were innumerable, — the discussion of them interminable.

The first appropriation for schools was of £22. 8*s*., in March, 1762, to be equally divided between the East and West Parts. Sixteen

[1] Act of 1743.

pounds only were voted in 1764; and a proposition to build two school-houses, once passed, was reconsidered and defeated. But, the next year, the town was divided into the east, west, and centre districts, and a school-house voted for each. William Brattle engaged to build the eastern; James Easton, the middle; Caleb Wadhams and David Noble, the western.

These engagements were not kept; and, in 1766, a committee was appointed to select sites for three school-houses, to be built by James Easton for £36; one to be twenty-two feet square, the others seventeen, and all "to be well shingled, doors made and hung, with floors and good chimneys, and glazed with four windows, and twelve squares in each window." The largest stood north of the eastern end of the park, in what is now the travelled street of Park Place. Deacon Easton was finally allowed £25. 8*s*. 7d. for building it.

In 1764, the appropriation for schooling rose to £30, to be divided among the districts, as nearly as might be, in proportion to population. In 1771, two new districts having been created, £60 were divided, — £15 each to the east, centre, and middle districts; £7. 10*s*. apiece to the others. In 1773, a new interest in schools was inspired by the exertions of Rev. Mr. Allen, who offered to give six pounds yearly, for five years, towards their support. The town accepted the offer with thanks, increased its appropriation for schooling to £100, and ordered new houses to be built in the north-east and south-west districts; so that, before the Revolution, Pittsfield had five school-houses.

The selectmen — acting as the superintending school-committee — had in hand £100 from the appropriation, £6 from Mr. Allen, and £6 from the rent of the school-lot, — £112: of which each of the larger schools received £28; each of the smaller, £14.

The districts managed their affairs independently: and, on the settlement of their annual accounts, some were usually found to have overdrawn their allowance, while some left a "balance" in the town treasury; both, of course, to be adjusted in the coming year.

As to the character of the instruction afforded, we have no means of judging, except from the facts here stated. There was, however, a good omen in the liberal interest taken in the schools by the clergyman of the place, engrossed as he was in the troubled politics of the times.

We have the names of only three of the teachers, — Mr. John Strong; Mrs. Phineas Parker, who taught in the west district; and a son of Col. Partridge, probably the same who afterwards settled on the lands, in the north-eastern part of the town, which his descendants still cultivate.[1]

Young as the town was, helpless poverty and vagabond pauperism soon made their way to it. There were frequent votes of money for the relief of the former class; and aid was also otherwise extended to needy persons, as for instance, by permission granted to a widow for building a house in the highway. Ten pounds were appropriated, in 1764, for a workhouse. Itinerant pauperism was prevalent to a degree which betrayed the imperfection of the laws designed for its prevention. But the town instructed its selectmen to enforce them by "warning out in general all persons who shall hereafter come into town;" or, as the warrant expressed it, "all, without discrimination, not possessed of a freehold." Of course this instruction is to be understood with more limitation than can be found in the language, literally interpreted; but, at the best, it had a severity of meaning, upon which we shall have occasion to remark hereafter.

Chattel slavery existed under the Province laws; and not only was property in human beings recognized by that code, but manumission was trammelled by the requirement of a bond from the master that the freedman should never become a public charge "by reason of sickness, lameness, or any other incapacity."[2]

Many of the early citizens of Pittsfield held slaves. Col. Williams owned several. It appears from bills of sale still extant,[3] that, in 1761, he purchased, for fifty pounds, "a negro girl named Pendar," whom he sold a few years later for seventy-five, — a very pretty speculation in human muscles. Pendar afterwards married Simon Bow, and joined the First Congregational Church in 1795, under the "half-way covenant." As late as the Revolution, adver-

1 HATFIELD, March 21, 1768.

Dear Brother, — I hear my son lives with you, taking care of a little school. I desire your fatherly care of him, and advice to him. He is now in the forming age for future usefulness. I know not that he is addicted to any vice; but you are sensible how our hearts are concerned for the good of our offspring. — *Col. Partridge to Col. Williams, March,* 1768, *T. C. C.*, p. 226.

2 Province Laws, ed. 1815, p. 745.

3 T. C. C. Lanc. col., and one in possession of Hon. H. Chickering.

tisements of runaway slaves were inserted in "The Hartford Courant," by Pittsfield masters. Slavery in Berkshire differed in no essential particular from the same institution, when of a household character, in other sections. The incident which led to the judicial recognition of its abolition by the Bill of Rights was an act of gross — although, perhaps, suddenly-provoked — cruelty, perpetrated in the kitchen of a prominent citizen of Berkshire upon the slave-widow of a Revolutionary soldier killed in the service.

Rev. Thomas Allen wrote in 1810, "Perhaps the whole of sixty roll, original settlers, did not contain a single vicious person."[1] These, however, did not comprise the whole of even the permanent population of the place: while from thirty to forty transient agricultural laborers were annually hired;[2] and among this class, and the tramps who were largely recruited from it, an amount of vice existed, which, at the present day, would seem alarming in a country town of no greater population than Pittsfield then had.[3] Crimes of incontinence crowded the records of the Quarter Sessions of the Peace; and, when committed by those of the lower class, were treated as venial offences, incident, perhaps, to their condition in life. The first indictment tried in the county was for fornication, which the offender confessed, and expiated by a fine of thirteen shillings. In 1762, Sarah Pratt, a married woman, convicted of adultery, was fined fifteen shillings and costs of court. A hundred years before, the penalty was death. Misdemeanors, with which the magistrate now rarely meddles, then often occupied the attention of the criminal courts. John Williams, charged in 1764 with "prophaning the name of God," was returned *non est inventus.* The probable penalty of his blasphemy was severe enough to scare John into ignominious flight. Another John — by surname Pell — travelled upon the Lord's day, and was mulcted

[1] Hist. Sketch, p. 12.

[2] "Every spring we hire in this town between thirty and forty laborers, generally for the term of six months; and, as the late law obliges us to take our lists on the 1st of September, it enables us to recover the small pittance their polls are set at, when, in a month or two later, they carry away from us between £300 and £400. — *Town-Committee's letter, May,* 1767, *Lanc. Coll.*

[3] What is said of the state of morals must not be understood as peculiar to Pittsfield, whose record in the Quarter Sessions was no worse, at least, than that of other towns.

therefor in the sum of ten shillings. A party of young men, belonging to respectable families, engaged one night at a tavern in "the unlawful game of cards," escaped out of the window on the approach of the officers, but were indicted and fined for their offence "and evil example." And so in numerous instances of a similar character.

As a matter of economy to the county and of convenience to all parties, — including the offender, — a large proportion of the complaints for misdemeanor were summarily disposed of by a single magistrate,[1] who either imposed a fine, or sentenced the prisoner to the stocks or the whipping-post. The punishment of minor offences by stripes or exposure in the stocks, which universally prevailed, was attended by many evils; but, under the circumstances which then existed, — and especially the brutalizing system of prison discipline, — it was not without some plausibility of reason that magistrates inflicted it in preference to incarceration in the miserable jails. It is questionable, however, whether many of those worthies thought further in the matter than to follow the precedents which similar tribunals had kept unbroken from the time when the memory of man runneth not to the contrary.

In 1764, James Easton and Josiah Wright were allowed by the town nine shillings and sixpence for building the stocks and whipping-post in Pittsfield; but whether these indispensable auxiliaries in the teaching of morals and the administration of justice were set up on the meeting-house common, — as was the prevailing custom — or near some of the places where the courts were commonly held, is not of record or tradition. Rev. Mr. Allen was no great friend to the penal system then in vogue for the repression of vicious naughtiness; and perhaps its ugly servants found a more congenial location out of sight of his windows.

Owing, probably, to the imperfection of enclosures, the least

[1] The justices of the peace in the county, who together constituted the Court of General Sessions, had jurisdiction singly in complaints for misdemeanor, and in civil cases where the value in dispute did not exceed forty shillings. Four justices were commissioned for Berkshire in 1761, — Joseph Dwight of Stockbridge, William Williams of Pittsfield, John Ashley of Sheffield, and Timo. Woodbridge of Stockbridge. Perez Marsh of Dalton was added in 176–; John Chadwick of Tyringham, and Daniel Brown of Sandisfield, in 1764; Elijah Dwight of Great Barrington, and Israel Stoddard of Pittsfield, in 1765; Mark Hopkins of Great Barrington, in 1766; and David Ingersol of Great Barrington, in 1767.

possible liberty was allowed to wandering cattle and hogs. That the latter "should not run at large," was one of the town regulations most frequently and earnestly re-enacted. To restrain the former, forty shillings were voted in 1761 for a pound forty feet square, "to be built and kept by Zebediah Stiles, near his house," on West Street. Other votes, from time to time, directed the building of pounds in other places. But the cattle and sheep of different owners were so herded together, or so liable to become intermixed, that special means for their identification were provided; the inhabitants being required annually "to bring into the clerk's office the artificial marks which they put upon their creatures, that they may be recorded." A volume of these curious "earmarks" remains in the clerk's office, of which representations are given.

Wolves abounded to such a degree that unprotected pasturage was resorted to at great risk; and, indeed, few folds were safe from their ravages.[1] The town offered bounties in some years for wolf-scalps.

It was the custom among newly-settled places to encourage the introduction of mechanical arts by the grant of special privileges; and three instances of the kind are recorded of Pittsfield. In 1763, William Brattle was privileged to "set up lengthwise in the road against his house, a malt-house eighteen feet wide, and keep it there as long as he made good malt." The inhabitants were accustomed to brew a mild ale, of sufficient strength to preserve the brewage healthful and palatable for the week's time which it was intended to last; and Willam Brattle was expected to furnish good malt for it.

Notwithstanding Deacon Crofoot's ill success in obtaining encouragement from the Proprietors, we infer from a letter of Col. Partridge that, before the Indian disturbances, he built some sort

[1] It is related of Mrs. Seth Janes, whom some of the oldest citizens of Pittsfield remember as a kind-hearted and genial old lady, whose fine, erect form, clad in a satin pelisse, made an impression upon their youthful imaginations, as her amiable and gentle manners did upon their hearts, — it is related of this ladylike old person that once, when a young wife, alone in her home at the West Part, she heard the sheep rushing wildly against her cabin-door, and, looking out in alarm, saw a huge, gaunt, and hungry wolf in eager pursuit; whereupon she quietly took down her husband's loaded gun, and shot the intruder dead. — *Hist. Janes Family.*

The Pittsfield ladies at that time were, many of them, familiar with the use of firearms. Mrs. Judith Fairfield was reputed an excellent shot.

SHEEP MARKS.

Eli Root.
Benj. Keilar.
J. Keilar.
J. Goodrich.
James Easton.
John Dickinson.
Sol. Allen.
N. Robbins.
Ezek. Root.
Wm. Francis.
Charles Goodrich.
Jno. Kingsley.
J. Ensign.
Oliver Root.
Daniel Hubbard.
Josiah Wright.
Eph. Little.
E. Tracy.
D. Ashley.
Aaron Blinn.
Joshua Robbins.
James Hubbard.
James Noble.
Oswald Williams.

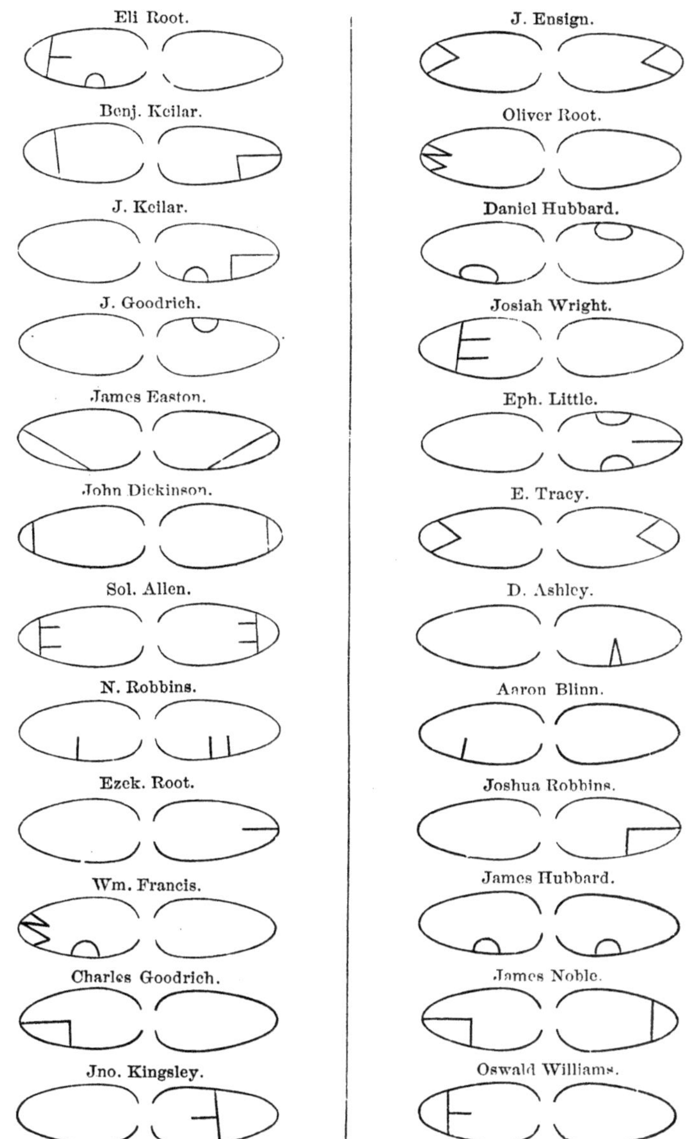

of a grist-mill, upon a dam which he erected near the site of the present Elm-street bridge. But it was of insufficient capacity; and the first plantation and town meetings after the war were agitated with propositions "to see whether Deacon Crofoot will come into such measures that the Proprietors may be well accomodated with good grinding and bolting; and if not, then to let the dam to those that will." Finally, after a world of tribulation, the Deacon, under the award of arbitrators, obtained a lease of the dam for fifteen years. But his mills were never popular; and after his death, which occurred before the expiration of his lease, his heirs were relieved from their obligation to keep the mills in repair. In 1778, the mill-privilege and neighboring land passed into the hands of Ebenezer White, under a lease for 999 years. In 1767, Jacob Ensign, having previously agreed with Deacon Crofoot, obtained from the town a grant of the west end of the mill-dam for fifteen years; conditioned that "he should, within one year, begin and exercise the feat of a clothier, and attend to said service, and do the business of a clothier at such place, during said term;" the town reserving the right to remove the dam farther down the stream, if it saw fit, at the expiration of Crofoot's lease: in which case Ensign's rights to be transferred to the new location.

In 1768, Valentine Rathbun, from Stonington, Conn., built similar works on the outlet of the pond which then lay between Richmond Lake and Barkersville. Fulling-mills had for many years a place in the business of Pittsfield not unlike that which the woollen manufactures, of which they were the germ, now occupy; although in the last quarter of the eighteenth century they were over-shadowed by the production of iron, and still earlier by the manufacture of lumber. In answer to the pressing demands of the settlement, saw-mills — often associated with grist-mills — began, soon after the peace, to spring up in all quarters. In 1762, Joseph Keeler purchased two hundred and forty acres of Col. Williams's great pine tract, on the south shore of Poontoosuck Lake, and extending forty rods down the outlet, upon which he built a saw and grist mill. About the same time a saw-mill was built at Coltsville. About 1767, saw and grist mills were erected near the present site of the Pomeroy Lower Factories, by Ezra Strong and others. A saw-mill was early built where the Pontoosuc Factory stands; and, previous to 1776, another at Wahconah, in connection with a fulling-mill owned by Deacon Matthew Barber.

While the new town was taking form, as we have seen it, under its municipal organization, and introducing the necessities and conveniences of village-life, its inhabitants were exchanging the log-huts of former days for comfortable and comely dwellings.

When the first partition of the township was annulled, Charles Goodrich and Col. Williams abandoned their intention of creating a business-centre near Unkamet Street, and transferred their interests to Wendell Square, with regard to which they entered upon a similar design in connection with Elisha Jones, Nathaniel Fairfield, and Eli Root. It was arranged that Fairfield, Root, Goodrich, and Jones should erect handsome frame-houses on the four corners of their respective settling-lots, which met at the Square; while Williams was to build a little farther to the east, on Honasada Street.

But an unlooked-for obstacle presented itself in the nature of the land, whose soil was so completely underlaid with ledges of solid rock, that no wells could be sunk which would afford any but surface-water. In this dilemma, Charles Goodrich displayed his wonted energy and determination by building the first water-works of Pittsfield, — an aqueduct some two miles long, extending from his farm to the hills at the east. It was constructed of huge logs divided into quarters, bored, bevelled at the ends, and bound together at the connecting joints with heavy iron bands. The enterprise failed, according to one account, in consequence of a fault in construction, which caused the logs to crack. Another tradition has it that an unpleasant person, through whose lands the pipes passed, soothed his temper and proclaimed his territorial lordship by tearing them up.

The lack of water thus proving irremediable, the owners of the Four Corners were compelled, in building their new houses, to withdraw from the companionable neighborhood for which they had anticipated so much distinction; but it was long before the ambitious project was altogether abandoned, although the building of the meeting-house, the parsonage, and mills soon began to attract the business centre, so far as the business of the town was then capable of centralization, towards its present position.

Col. Williams built on Honasada Street, about a mile east of Wendell, the curious mansion known for many years throughout Western Massachusetts as "The Long House," — a rather showy structure for those days, being eighty feet in length, and two stories high, with a gambrel roof. A broad hall ran through the centre from front to rear; on one side of which was "The Long Room," in which the owner held his Justice's, and sometimes his Probate Courts, and where, if tradition is correct, the county courts also, at one time, sat. On the other side of the hall, were "two smaller rooms, besides a buttery and bedroom."

The whole house was adorned with a profusion of carving, panelling, and other ornamental work; and the grounds were not neglected. The decorations were especially elaborate in the hall and The Long Room, which were entered from without by twin doors of twenty-six panels each, through which a negro slave ushered the visitor into one apartment or the other, as his visit was one of courtesy or business. The whole establishment betokened the owner's proverbial magnificence of spirit, and accorded with his portly person, and that dignity of demeanor which distinguished him at home; however certain peculiarities may have tempted his friends on the Connecticut to style him irreverently, in familiar letters, "Colonel Billy."

Col. Williams's schedule of the cost of his house is preserved in the Collection of Hon. Thomas Colt, p. 271, and is here given: —

COST OF MY HOUSE.

Glass, £15; Nails, 19; Brads, 2; Paint, 9,12; Oyl, 6; Locks, Hinges, etc., 11. — £62,12.

Boards, £40,10; Clapboards, 10,16; Shingles, 10,4; Laths, 3; Slitwork, 18; Carpenters' bill, 26,16,6; Carpenters' board, 9; Joyners' bill, 64,4; Joyners' board, 21,12. — £204,2,6.

Cellar digging, £6,6; Masons' bill, 23; Masons' board, 4,10; Masons' attendance, 31,16; Masons' attendants' board, 9; Stone carryers' bill, 34; Stone carryers' board, 2,2. — £110,14.

Paper, £6; Lime, 18,15; Clay, 1,4; Loom, 1,10; Sand, 0,10; Lead, 2,10; Hair, 1,2. — £31,9.

House, £408,17,6; West lot, 430; East lot, 305; Laid out in labor, 140. Total, £1373,17,6.

The reader may form some idea of the vegetables to be found in a Pittsfield gentleman's garden of that period, by the following list of seeds minuted by Col. Williams for purchase in Boston: —

"Cabbages and Cauliflowers, Yorkshire, Early Dutch, Savoy, and Common; Lettuce, Goss and Cabbage; Carrots, Orange, Yellow and Purple; Turnips, English and French; Onions; Dedham Squash; Cucumber;

Squashpepper; Peas, Dwarf, Hotspur, Marrowfat, and round gopher; Radish; Double parsley; Stow and pole beans; Sage; Balm; Fennil; Dill; July flower (Gilliflower); Pink; Stertion (Nasturtium); Crounations (Carnations); Hyssop; Thyme; Sweet Marjoram; Summer-Savory; Parsnip and Asparagus."

A goodly catalogue.

We are not so precisely informed as to the building-up of other parts of the town; but houses of some pretension were soon scattered over the various sections. Israel Dickinson built upon the grounds now attached to the summer residence of Hon. B. R. Curtis; Israel Stoddard, the youngest son of Col. John, selected the eminence about a mile north of that estate. James D. Colt bought a thousand acres in the south-west corner of the township, and made his residence there. Rev. Mr. Allen's house was built in 1764, on the site on East Street now occupied by the residence of his grandson and namesake. Woodbridge Little, the first lawyer to settle in the town, built the cottage, which still stands, north of the crossing of the Western Railroad by Beaver Street.

It is impossible to give with accuracy the years in which individuals became residents of the town, except in a few instances; but the appearance of names upon the record makes us sure of dates previous to which those who bore them became citizens, and, to some extent, indicates their prominence in town affairs. Most of the leading settlers have already been mentioned in connection with events in which they took part; but we cite a few other entries from the town and provincial archives.

The persons who affixed the following signatures to a petition to the General Court, in 1766, assumed to represent the forty purchasers from Livingston; but the interest of some of them had been acquired by transfers of various kinds: William Wright, John Remington, Charles Goodrich, Josiah Wright, Charles Miller, John Waddams, Elizur Deming, David Ashley, William Francis, Oliver Ashley, Joshua Robbins, James Lord, Erastus Sackett, David Bush, Daniel Hubbard, Amos Root, Eli Root, Dan Cadwell, Hezekiah Jones, Gideon Gunn, William Brattle, Abner Dewey, Nathaniel Fairfield, Zebediah Stiles.

The following names, not previously mentioned in any other connection, appear on the first list of jurymen, reported Aug. 18, 1761: Lemuel Phelps, Wm. Phelps, David Noble, Jesse Sackett, Thomas Morgan. John Morse was a fence-viewer in 1762.

Israel Stoddard, Israel Dickinson, Phinehas Belding, Joseph Wright, and Joseph Wright, jun., signed a petition in 1762. Caleb Wadhams was deer-reeve in 1763; James Easton, school-committeeman in 1764.[1]

The influx of new citizens brought with it a good deal of wealth, as well as of business capacity and enterprise, which soon, in a measure, relieved the depression bequeathed from less happy days. A growing sense of the natural advantages of the place contributed, also, not a little to that local pride, and confidence in the future of their home, which has always characterized the most thoughtful and intelligent people of Pittsfield. A notable and amusingly exaggerated expression of this sentiment and faith appears in a letter from Col. Williams to his brothers-in-law,[2] in which he endeavors to persuade them to remove from Deerfield to Pittsfield. We quote a portion: —

PITTSFIELD, March 28, 1767.

DEAR BRETHREN, —

These wait on you by Mrs. Williams, with my hearty sympathy on the poor state of health I understand you at present enjoy. Languor, sickness, and excruciating pain were my portion, while I chose, or rather was obliged, to tabernacle in the narrows between the west and east mountains of Deerfield.

Since my removal to this place, I challenge any man in the government, that has not had half the fatigue, to compare with me for health, or freedom from pain. All my doctor's bill has been a gallipot or two of unguent for the itch. And never have I but two half-days been absent from public worship for fourteen years; and then 'twas not because I wasn't well. But what may in a more general way convince you of the temperature and goodness of our air may be demonstrated by the records of the probate-office, the avails of which, in near about six years, has not amounted to ten pounds to the judge. And another indisputable proof of the goodness of the country is the prolific behavior of the female sex among us. Barren women beget (if not bring forth) sons. Women that have left off for 5, 6, 7, and 9 years, begin anew, and now and then bring one, but as many two, at a birth, after residing a suitable time among us. And, to mention but one thing (though I might many more), no man or woman of but common understanding, that ever came and got settled among us, wished themselves back.

[1] Rev. Dr. Field made inquiry into the dates of the settlements of the early families at a time when the means of information were more abundant than they now are. See Appendix.

[2] H. C. C.

The air suited them, they felt frisk and alert, or a something endeared their situation to them: this with regard to the women. The men perceived soon the difference of the soil; and, put what you would upon it, it would yield beyond what they were acquainted with. This prompted them to labor; and when they came in, either by day or night, their wives would give them a kind, hearty welcome, so that they chose to stay where they were, — and they chose well. If your patience would suffer me, I would fill this paper with instances of growth in estates in a few years. And, as you go along, take this with you; viz., that the oldest town in the county is but a few years above thirty.

And now to come to instances, and only of such persons as you have known: Capt. Brewer came to Tyrringham with £2,200 Old Ten. He lived but seventeen years there, and had, when he died, upwards of £19,000 upon interest; and his lands, appraised at little more than one-half their value, swelled his estate to £50,000. His son-in-law came into the same town years after, and was not worth £5; is now judged to be worth as much as his father was: I mean Capt. Chadwick. Col. Ashley came to Sheffield with less money than your minister carried to Deerfield: he is now worth more than any man in your county. And, since I have mentioned a minister, I will mention another; viz., Mr. Hubbard of Sheffield.[1] He came as poor as church mouse, to a people poorer than himself: he died the other day; has left sufficient to support his widow, and settle his five sons well. Come to Stockbridge, and see the advance that Col. Williams, Mr. Jo Woodbridge, and Deacon Brown have made in their estates. Come to this town and see Goodrich, Brattle, Bush, Hubbard, Wright, Crowfoot, and Ensign, who, strictly speaking, were in debt when they came. . . . But I suppose I have tired you. I have confined myself to such as I supposed you knew. Come and see, and then I will say and convince into the bargain.

But delays are dangerous: we have had five wholesome families come in this winter; and last week Coult of Hadley bought, and is coming directly. Uncle Benjamin Dickinson told me, not a month ago, that it was his fixed determination to be here with his brood before the year was out if he liked the land. And I can assure you our land grows in repute faster than any around us.

Col. Williams, in committee with James Easton and Woodbridge Little, pleading for a remission of the Province tax, managed to tone down a good deal the prosperity so glowingly depicted. The inhabitants of Pittsfield were compelled, owing to their great distance from Massachusetts markets, to carry to

[1] Rev. Jonathan Hubbard of Sheffield, the first minister of Berkshire County, and grandfather of Hon. Henry Hubbard, for many years a prominent citizen of Pittsfield.

smaller,[1] which were already glutted, what little surplus produce they raised: "and moreover," say the committee, "although our lands in the valuation are esteemed to be of considerable value, yet the labor we are compelled to bestow upon them in cutting off the old [girdled] trees blown down, picking up the fallen limbs, burning, etc., amounts to a large tax on our best farms;" and as to uncleared lands, "the expense is prodigious which we must be at before they can be rendered in any degree profitable, by reason that there is such a growth of such sort of timber upon them, that, unless we *cut* it all off, — which costs £4 per acre, — we can't improve them, at the shortest, under three years."[2] Rather a graphic delineation this of the difficulties in early Pittsfield farming.

In the lights and shades of these two representations, colored to suit opposite purposes, the reader will form for himself a conception of the town in the first decade after its incorporation, as a community struggling under many embarrassments and against many impediments, but with a large preponderance of favoring circumstances, and towards an assured prosperity.

A more intimate acquaintance with its people and their affairs would reveal to him a greater inequality of pecuniary condition than was usual in newly-settled places, and that the wealthiest men were exempt from the heaviest burdens of taxation.

The duties assumed by the proprietors of the sixty settling-lots, as part of the consideration in their purchase, would have been cheerfully performed, had the state of the country immediately permitted it. But as year after year rolled on, and the proprietors were compelled to hold their lands, so far as they could hold them at all, by military occupation, foregoing any profitable enjoyment of them, and as the expenditure of £170 which they had made previous to 1762 upon the highways had much increased the value of the commons, they conceived that "the great service they had been to the gentlemen proprietors — not to mention any benefit they may have been to the Province" — entitled them, in equity, to some mitigation in the severity of their contract; although its rigid enforcement had been carefully provided for in the act incorporating the town. And this the more, since Livingston's grant,

[1] Hartford, Kinderhook, and Albany.

[2] Committee's Letter, May, 1767.

in his deed to the agents of The Forty Pioneers, of "the right to dig stone and cut timber on any land in the township not within fence," had been repudiated.

For these reasons, the sixty settling-proprietors, through a committee,[1] sought relief from some of the consequences of their ill-considered bargain, at the hands of the General Court; applying for an act to subject the lands not alienated by Cols. Wendell and Stoddard, and not included in the hundred-acre lots, to a tax — to be limited in duration and amount by the Court — for the support of preaching, and making highways.

To this application, Oliver Partridge and Moses Graves objected that it was an attempt to re-impose upon the original proprietors duties which the petitioners had, for a valuable consideration, covenanted to perform; and, moreover, that the tax asked for was "surprisingly partial," as the lands upon which it was proposed to assess it did not include several thousand acres, some of them cultivated, which had been "alienated" by the original proprietors to Charles Goodrich and others, — the petition being so framed as not to cover the commons lands of those who were also proprietors of settling-lots.

These objections proved fatal to the petition; but the controversy between the tax-paying and the exempt proprietors long continued, and was imbittered in 1765 by the heirs of Col. Stoddard, who brought an action of ejectment against one of the settlers, on the ground of non-compliance with the tenure by which he held his home-lot. This was intended as a test-case by which to try the titles of the whole sixty: and they again appealed to the General Court, and again recited their story and its hardships; declaring, in conclusion, that the man against whom the action was brought had "done more than ten times the duty which was required by the General Court of any one lot;" and begging that the petitioners, at their own expense, might have a committee of the Court "to view their settlements and improvements," and, "if these were found not to answer the expectations of the Honorable Court, then that they would be good enough to let them know it, — otherwise, to confirm them in the quiet and peaceable enjoyment of their possessions."

[1] Consisting of Stephen Crofoot, David Hubbard, Jesse Sackett, David Bush, and Josiah Wright.

The title which the settlers had so dearly earned was finally confirmed in them; whether by the General Court in compliance with their reasonable request, by a judicial decision, or by agreement of the parties, it is impossible to say. By whatever methods this and other specific controversies between the settling-proprietors and the representatives of Stoddard and Livingston were terminated, the feuds which they engendered did not end with them, but had their influence afterwards in the division of parties at the Revolution, when the great majority of the settlers proved ardent Whigs, — their adversaries still more unanimously arraying themselves with the Tories. And it is to be noted that the heirs of Col. Wendell, who are not recorded ever to have pressed their legal and perhaps just rights against the settlers, afterwards sympathized with them in the ardor of their patriotism, and maintained a place in the good-will of the town, which is retained by their descendants.

CHAPTER VIII.

FIRST MEETING-HOUSE AND MINISTER.

[1760–1768.]

Massachusetts Laws for the Support of Public Worship. — Their inharmonious Operation in Pittsfield. — Differences between Resident and Non-resident Proprietors. — The Meeting-house raised. — Difficulties in finishing it. — First Sale of Pews. — Dignifying the Seats. — Description of the Meeting-house. — Burial-Ground. — First Attempts to settle a Minister. — Ebenezer Garnsey. — Enoch Huntington. — Amos Tomson, Daniel Collins, Thomas Allen, called and settled. — Church formed. — Sketch of Rev. Mr. Allen.

THE obligations imposed by Massachusetts upon those who settled her townships, to provide out of the lands which they received a decent and honorable establishment of public worship, were prompted, not so much by a desire to compel the reluctant and therefore perfunctory performance of sacred duties, as to repel from her Israel those to whom such duties were unwelcome. It was a policy which, well-suited to the times of its founders, has left a rich legacy of happy results to our own. The political principles and religious dogmas transplanted from the church, which was the nursery of two commonwealths, grew together, inseparable until after the red harvest of the Revolution; and, till then at least, whatever harmed the one was hurtful to the other.

Whatever evils attended the compulsory support of religious worship, perpetuated under circumstances to which it was not applicable, it worked little but good to those upon whom its requirements rested while it was essential to the future of Massachusetts, that her Puritanism should be preserved incontaminate. Not to dwell upon its direct and palpable influence in preventing that deterioration of morals and manners incident to all frontier life, the attention to religious institutions, which Massachusetts plantations were forbidden to postpone, was of unbounded benefit in securing rapidity and unity of municipal organization, in elevating the tone of local sentiment, and by investing the new abode, however rude its cabins, with the sanctity of home.

Nor was the inharmonious action in building the Pittsfield meeting-house the fruit of these laws. The mischief there arose, not from the obligations imposed upon the township by the General Court, but because, after the assumption of those obligations by the settling-proprietors solely, so long an interval elapsed before they could be fulfilled, that events transpired, which, in the opinion of the covenanting party, destroyed the equity of the contract. And to this view the non-resident proprietors, at least partially, assented, as will appear by the following paper:[1] —

Whereas the proprietors of the sixty settling-lots in the township of Poontoosook propose speedily to build a meeting-house and settle a minister; and whereas their present circumstances will not enable them to build a large meeting-house, neither will they have occasion for such an one: but, inasmuch as there is a prospect of a considerable number of others that will soon settle in said township, they have been advised to think of building a house of fifty-five feet one way, and forty-five feet the other, and at present only to cover the same, and to finish the same hereafter, which may probably accommodate all that may hereafter settle in said township; which they are ready to comply with, and pay their full proportion of, so far as may be judged reasonable, provided the non-resident proprietors will be so good on their parts as to encourage the same upon this proposal. We, who are ye non-resident proprietors, upon condition a house of ye aforesaid dimensions be built, will give towards the same, provided the proprietors will give to each of us a pew in said house, what we have respectively affixed to our names, as witness our hands, this 3d of January, 1760.

MOSES GRAVES,
Half ye glass.
SOLOMON STODDARD,
Half ye glass.

These offers did not satisfy the settlers, who voted, Jan. 17, to build the house forty-five feet long, thirty-five wide, twenty post; and "to raise forty-five shillings on each lot to accomplish the work, half to be paid this year, half next."

[1] This agreement, which was found among the Col. Williams Papers, is in the possession of Mr. J. A. Foote. A similar instrument, signed by Oliver Partridge and other non-resident proprietors, agreeing to furnish other material, was in existence a few years since, but is unhappily lost.

Partridge and Graves, in their petition of 1762, considered that a house of the dimensions given would "scarcely hold the people when sixty families should be in town;" and alleged that "one of the inhabitants, not a proprietor of the settling-lots, begged of the settlers to allow him to add twenty feet to the length, at his own charge, which they utterly refused, greatly to the damage of the original proprietors and their assigns, upon whose lands, in various parts of the town, many were [1762] settling; so that it was probable that the meeting-house would soon be useless."

The settlers, however, voted, Dec. 8, "That the committee be allowed to build the meeting-house fifty-five feet long, and forty-five broad, with proportionate post, provided the non-resident proprietors will give £80, lawful money, towards enabling them to build, cover, and close the same; they, in consideration, to have four pews."

This arrangement being declined, a proposition was introduced, May 29, 1761, for a house probably intended to serve a temporary purpose, — to be forty feet long, thirty broad, and fifteen-feet post, and to be covered with feather-edged boards only. This plan, also, was voted down; and, June 15, it was resolved, "That four shillings be raised on each lot, to pay for raising the meeting-house; and every man who comes early to have three shillings credit, *per diem*, till the house be raised, and the committee to take account of each man's labor, — the other shilling to be paid for rum and sugar."

And so, with labor duly cheered according to the custom of the day, the first Pittsfield meeting-house was raised in the summer of 1761; and covered and floored before the first of the next March, when a town-meeting was held in it. At a meeting of the proprietors, May 3, Mr. Jesse Sackett having greatly neglected to comply with his agreement to "clear, close, and clean an acre and a half for a meeting-house spot," the building was stated to be in great peril from wind and fire; but Mr. Sackett, promising to fulfil his engagement as soon as possible, was allowed until the 1st of November to do so.[1]

[1] A reason appears in this statement for the completeness with which the pioneers were wont to denude their farms, which does not imply that lack of taste of which they are often impeached. Even in burnings of less extent than those fearful conflagrations which sometimes swept over the new country, the flames might readily be communicated, by means of a few trees, to the buildings of the

And probably, by the time specified, the meeting-house lot was denuded of all its trees; and the building was only shaded by the grand old elm, which, standing in the street before it, had, with a single smaller companion, been spared for its majestic beauty.

Nothing further appears to have been done towards finishing the meeting-house until May, 1764, when Col. Williams obtained the privilege of building a pew upon lot No. 16 in the ground-plan, for the use of himself and family, but to be relinquished to the town, if, upon the completion of the house, it did not fall to him of right. Capt. Charles Goodrich had lot No. 1 upon the same terms.

Other gentlemen craved similar privileges; and, in December, it was determined to finish the house below and the front seats of the gallery, defraying the expense by the sale of pews. The first

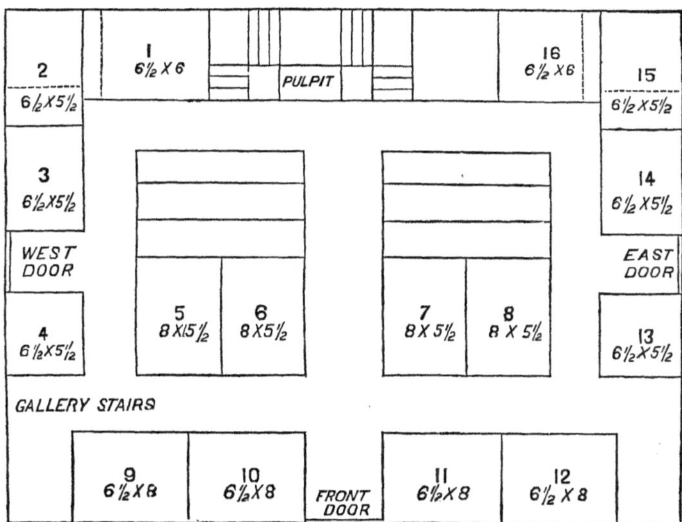

PLAN OF THE FIRST PITTSFIELD MEETING-HOUSE.

farmer who permitted himself to be seduced by their beauty to spare them. And a still further wisdom in thorough clearing appears from the necessity of laying bare to the cleansing sunlight as much as possible of a soil matted with a sponge-like covering of decaying leaves, dank with putrid moisture, and charged with noxious vapors, which even the pure sunlight could not cast out, without first, for a time, redoubling their malignancy.

sale of pews in a Pittsfield meeting-house accordingly took place on Monday, Feb. 4, 1765, by auction, to the highest bidder.[1]

The result was as follows: —

No. 1.	Sold to David Bush & Co.	£10 5 0
" 2.	Caleb Waddams & Co.	4 15 0
" 3.	Joseph Keelar & Co.	4 10 0
" 4.	Zebediah and Ephraim Stiles	2 10 0
" 5.	Amos Root & Co.	4 0 0
" 6.	James Easton & Co.	4 0 0
" 7.	Daniel Hubbard & Co.	8 5 0
" 8.	Gideon Goodrich & Co.	4 0 0
" 10.	Wm. Williams & Co.	6 10 0
" 11.	Capt. Charles Goodrich & Co.	6 15 0
" 13.	Wm. Williams	2 10 0
" 14.	Eli Root & Co.	5 0 0
" 15.	Daniel Hubbard, jun., & Co.	4 10 0
" 16.	David Noble & Co.	9 0 0

Nos. 9 and 12 were not sold; and an unnumbered square next to the pulpit was reserved for the minister's family. It was voted that William Williams should have the proceeds of the sale (£83 15), and the two spaces for pews left unsold; he finishing the house in the usual manner within twelve months, and allowing the market-price for lime and boards to those who had bought pews, should they incline to furnish the same.

One would think that the long-desired end might now have been anticipated with tolerable certainty; but one of those lapses which seem to have been inevitable in the history of the early public works of Pittsfield intervened, and it was many twelvemonths before the house was completed in even an imperfect manner. In 1768, Col. Williams was called upon by the town to "finish the meeting-house according to contract," Deacon Easton, as sub-contractor, having failed to do so. But, Nov. 16, 1770, as if in despair of ever seeing any other end of the matter, it agreed to "accept the house as it stood, although not completed according to contract." Besides the work performed in accordance with Col. Williams's contract, Caleb Stanley and other young men had leave, in 1765, on paying thirty shillings into the treasury, to build a pew over the

[1] A plan of the pews and seats, as they were to be made, was presented to the town, and transcribed on the record-book, from which the representation here given is copied.

gallery stairs; and, in 1770, the young men generally, after several refusals, obtained a vote permitting them to build four pews in the front gallery, with the proviso "that they should be under the direction of the selectmen."

The practice of seating the young men in one of the galleries, prevailed for many years; and it is related of Rev. Mr. Allen, that on one New-Year's Sunday, after reading the usual parochial statistics of the preceding twelve months, and remarking upon the meagre record of marriages, he glanced his eye along the delinquent ranks, and shaking his head, as much as to say, "This will never do," he remarked quietly, "Young men, young men, you are expected to do your duty."

A custom known as "dignifying" or "seating" the meeting-house existed at this time, and long after, in almost every New-England town; which is thus described in Caulkins's excellent history of Norwich, Conn.: "When the meeting-house was finished, a committee was appointed to dignify the seats, and establish the rules for seating the people. Usually the square pew nearest the pulpit was the first in dignity; and next to this came the second pew, and the first long seat in front of the pulpit. After this, the dignity gradually diminished as the pews receded from the pulpit. If the house was furnished, as in some instances, with square pews on each side of the outer door, fronting the pulpit, these were equal to the second or third rank in dignity. The front seat in the gallery, and the two highest pews in the side-galleries, were also seats of considerable dignity.

"The rules for seating were formed on an estimate of age, rank, office, estate-list, and aid furnished in building the house. These lists were occasionally revised, and the people reseated at intervals of three or four years. Frequent disputes, and even long-continued feuds, were caused by this perplexing business of seating a congregation according to rank and dignity."

One can well conceive that such a result would follow. Indeed, the church-going customs and laws of early times would intolerably gall the spirit of a man of our day, especially if his religious faith did not accord with that of the majority. To be taxed for the building of a temple not of his own mode of worship, and the support of a minister whom he believed the preacher of heresies; to be compelled, on penalty of the stocks, to "go to meeting"— "attend on the stated ordinances of the gospel," the law phrased it — within certain intervals, and when there to take the seat assigned him, as an indication of his social status, by a committee for whom his respect may have been of the slightest, — such, in Provincial times, was the fate of the dissenter, and, in some of its particulars, of the Orthodox Congregationalist as well.

In Pittsfield, the "system of dignifying the house" was disturbed without being ameliorated by the sale of the pews, which left only the long seats to be periodically classified. The honors of the pew-holders bloomed perennially. This distinction was only an additional source of discontent and irritation; but, notwithstanding many attempts to do away with their invidious privileges, the proprietors held on to their pews until within a few years of the demolition of the meeting-house in 1792.

Seventeen years having passed away since the first vote of "The Proprietors of settling-lots in Poontoosuck" regarding it, the meeting-house was at last, in 1770, after some rough fashion, finished; and we have the data from which to reconstruct it, with little aid of the imagination.

FIRST MEETING-HOUSE, SCHOOL-HOUSE, AND PARSONAGE.

East street then ran straight through to West; and close upon its north side, immediately in front of the present location of the First Congregational Church, stood, broadside to the street, the little meeting-house, which had come of the great travail of so many years, — a plain, angular building, "forty-five feet long, thirty-five wide, and twenty feet post;" two stories high, with roof peaked after the ordinary modern style; covered with rough, unpainted clapboards, with square windows, and, in the middle of the south, east, and west sides, doors of the same Quakerish pattern; without belfry, portico, pilaster, or bracket; with no ornamentation whatever, but soon with a plentiful display of broken window-panes, — the ugly little barn-like structure, about to be consecrated by words and acts for freedom as bold, as pure, and as ardent as any that were ever spoken or done in American history.

The visitor entering on the Sabbath, by the south door, confronted, at the north end of the broad aisle, the plain but elevated pulpit, with its earnest preacher. Below, upon a slightly-raised platform, stood a deal-table, used alike for the communion service and as the clerk's desk at town-meetings. Behind it, two chairs, high backed, and, as related to the present era, antique, but modern enough then, and by no means Gothic or massive. The pews, arranged as in the plan, and the six "long seats" before the pulpit, occupied the floor of the house. Galleries extended on the east and west ends, and along the front. The pew-holders and their families sat together as now; but, in the galleries and long seats, the men and women were separated, Shaker fashion.[1]

The majority of the congregation were hardy, well-to-do farmers of respectable carriage, betokening good New-England sense and education, and weather-beaten in other fields as well as those of peaceful labor. There were some of greater wealth and refinement; and a few of aristocratic pretension (for aristocratic pretension budded bravely under Provincial rule); a few, also, whose intellectual culture and ability are still held in remembrance. Nor did the lower seats lack for those less favored by fortune in respect to social position and the possession of this world's gear: while behind the singers, who occupied the front seats in the front gallery, were bestowed the Philises, the Dinahs, the Pendars, the Blossoms, the Hartfords, the Simons, and the Hazels; for, where equality was denied to the white race among themselves, no civil rights bill could be expected to accord it to the blacks.

Retiring with the congregation, at the close of a service some-

[1] In 1773, John Strong was, by vote of the town, allowed to purchase for eight pounds "the hind seat on the woman's side," in order to build a pew where it stood; and, three years afterwards, he received permission to exchange this for "half the two hind seats," on the same side, he preferring the dignity of a square pew.

what less protracted than was customary in other pulpits of that day, the visitor found himself under the shadow of the elm which reared its grandly graceful form in the street, directly before the southern door. On the other three sides of the house, spread a widely-cleared space, still cumbered with stones and stumps, and extending to the woods upon the north, all distinction having been lost between the "meeting-house common" and the burial-ground. Here, if it were summer, at the tables offered by the broad stumps, or in the shadow of the near woods, the people, in the brief nooning between the two services, discussed their luncheons and the gossip of the week; the men, however, not failing to step across the way to sip their Sunday flip at the Deacon's tavern, — a custom always held in honor until the iconoclastic days of the Temperance Reformation.

The people had come together in the morning, some on foot, many on horseback with women on their pillions, a few in wagons, and possibly one or two with more stately equipage; and all dispersed promptly upon the afternoon benediction: for the late Sunday-dinners were waiting sharpened appetites; and, after that, the farmer's chores must be finished by sunset. The young men and maidens had other engagements for the evening.

In such a temple as we have described, and to a congregation like this, Thomas Allen preached those sermons, and taught those lessons, which, to this day, powerfully influence the character of Pittsfield; and the earlier of which were among the chief instrumentalities in giving the town that proud position which it holds in Revolutionary story. Here, too, was the theatre of that bold and spirited action by which Pittsfield, under the inspiring eloquence of its pastor, and the leadership of such men as Brown, Easton, Childs, Noble, Root, Goodrich, Strong, and Rathbun, responded to Faneuil Hall. As we shall recount the story, let it be remembered that its scene was in the little, plain, brown, Quakerish-looking meeting-house under The Elm. Nor let it be forgotten that near or in it rallied the minute-men on Lexington alarm; the soldiers who followed David Noble to the armies of Washington, and died in the pestilence at Lake Champlain; those who followed James Easton to Canada, and those who in Patterson's regiment fought in the battles of the Delaware; the volunteers who conquered at Bennington, and the militia who were decimated when John Brown fell at Stone Arabia. The soldiers of Pittsfield in the Revolution made their rendezvous on the same spot — now her beautiful, elm-shaded Park — whence, in later times, those whom she sent to a mightier but not more glorious conflict took their departure.

The dead, in the early years of the settlement, were buried in some convenient spot near their residences when living; and some of these primitive cemeteries still remain. At the first meeting of the Plantation in 1753, the committee intrusted with "the affair of the meeting-house was also instructed to report, for the consideration of the Proprietors, 'a place or places to bury the dead;'" and the fact that no record of it appears affords no evidence that their report was not actually made and adopted. There is no means of determining when, how, or by whom, the site of either the meeting-house or the burial-ground was finally fixed. In 1767, a proposition either to change the location of the latter, or to fence and clear it, was referred to Deacon Josiah Wright, Capt. Israel Stoddard, and David Bush; with whom it lingered in Committee until November, 1769, when it was voted, "forthwith to clear the ground for a burial-place, and that David Bush be a committee to see it perfect, and also fenced, and the timber thereon to be employed therefor; and that he give every man a chance to work out their proportion if they attend according to his warning." In the previous year, Eli Root was directed to provide "a spade, a howe (hoe), and a peck for digging graves, and to take charge of the same." Aaron Stiles, a person dependent, on account of some infirmity, upon public support, was employed for many years as "saxton," both as grave-digger and in the charge of the meeting-house; and, in the latter work, seems to have had a world of trouble in keeping things in decent order.

The meeting-house commons and the graveyard, which were soon merged in each other, covered all the space embraced within North street, the old line of East Street (including the present Park Place), a line drawn past the north side of the Baptist church, and another drawn near the west side of St. Stephen's to meet it at right angles.[1] The land thus described was the south-west corner of the home-lot held in trust by the town for the minister who

[1] The eastern part of the "Old Burial-ground" was not added until about 1812, when it was obtained from the heirs of Mr. Allen to offset the encroachment of stores upon the west.

should first be settled in it. It was probably taken for the purposes named, under the authority granted to towns of appropriating private property to certain public uses; paying therefor a reasonable compensation. There may have been some doubt as to the legality of the proceeding under the circumstances; but when the title vested in Mr. Allen, upon his ordination in 1764, he made a deed of gift, conveying it to the town.[1]

Pittsfield found hardly less difficulty in settling its first minister than in building its first meeting-house; but it arose from theological instead of pecuniary obstacles. What the differences of opinion which agitated the town were, or precisely how parties were arrayed in respect to them, we are not informed; but doctrinal controversies of much bitterness had long disturbed the congregational fold in New England; and among those who entered most vehemently into the strife were distinguished laymen, no less than eminent divines, of the Stoddard and Williams names. And it is hardly to be questioned that the representatives in Pittsfield, of those intimately-allied families, partook of their theological acerbities, and that out of this grew the opposition to several of the unsuccessful candidates for the first pastorate of the town.

The roll grew tedious before the right man presented himself. The committee of 1759 employed a Mr. Clark, who preached some time as a candidate, — or, as the phrase of the day was, "a probationer," — but was not honored with a call. In 1760, Rev. Ebenezer Garnsey preached four months, "to almost universal acceptance," said the proprietors; "but, that they might not be taxed with rashness in attempting to settle him, they desired that he would offer himself to the examination of the Upper Association of Ministers in Hampshire County," and "upon their recommendation," the Proprietors promised "to give him £90, in three annual instalments, to enable him to settle himself, and £60 salary annually, to be

[1] The statement that the land was thus given was made by Rev. William Allen, D.D., in a pamphlet published during the lifetime of his father and of many others who were conversant with the facts, some of whom were in a temper promptly to deny the assertion if any doubt of its correctness could have been conjured up. But we are not aware that either Dr. Allen's account, or the tradition which accords with it, was ever questioned. The deed, however, has disappeared; and, by an omission not singular in the old time, no record of any transactions concerning the lands in question was ever made in the registry of deeds; so that the precise terms of the gift are unknown, or whether any limitations were attached to it.

increased forty shillings yearly until it should reach £80." Mr. Garnsey left for the purpose of obtaining the required sanction; but, learning on his way that "Col. Williams was mistaken in supposing such a proceeding necessary," he wrote that he "had almost no objection to the settlement and salary, but that no offers must tempt him to do what appears better omitted; that they must be aware that the steps taken are quite out of the common method; and that he is unwilling to take too much pains, or to appear too forward, to settle among them." He had "several other objections, among which ill health was not the least;" but, as he positively declined to comply with the condition of examination which the Proprietors had proposed, he did not think it necessary to specify them.

Upon this the Proprietors acknowledged their mistake, declared that "their affections were still toward him," and requested him "to preach some time longer with them, in order that they might obtain a further acquaintance with him, and knowledge of his principles." Mr. Garnsey complied, and "a more personal acquaintance" with the man and knowledge of his principles having only "still further endeared him to the people," they unconditionally renewed their call in December. A month later, he replied that "the turn of thinking he had discovered among some particular persons, he considered in such a light as rendered a happy union very difficult, and almost utterly impossible." He thought himself "happy that the discovery was made so timely that he was able to extricate himself from the difficulty in which he was like to have been involved."

Mr. Garnsey returned to his native town, Durham, Conn., and ultimately retired from the ministry. What the objectionable turn of mind he had discovered in some at Pittsfield was does not appear: but the machinations of a small though powerful minority, operating shrewdly upon a sensitive mind, are apparent in the affair and the effect must have been unhappy upon the little community which had so earnestly, and with such seeming unanimity, declared its respect and affection for the preacher of their choice.

In August, 1761, the town, having been incorporated, invited Rev. Enoch Huntington of Middletown, Conn., to become its pastor. In December, Mr. Huntington replied, that "although the temporal encouragements held out at Pittsfield"—the same which had been tendered Mr. Garnsey—"were larger and better than could be offered or expected at Middletown, yet Providence seemed to point at his tarrying there." The circumstances which were urged by "the judicious," and which weighed upon his own mind, in favor of this determination, were "the great numbers and unity of the people of his charge, and the danger, that, if he left them, they might become divided; and the more so, as there was a separate church and meeting which might draw away numbers from that to which he ministered if it were left for a time destitute. "God, in his providence, had called him to Middletown when there seemed to be no manner of reason for refusing to go; and the longer he stayed, the more difficult it proved for him to leave, although he confessed a great liking and affection for the people of Pittsfield." Evidently a noble-hearted and conscientious Christian minister, this Mr. Huntington; true to his calling, and a man whom any people might have been glad to receive or to retain.

The next effort to supply the place with a settled minister, of which we have knowledge, was in May, 1762, when Rev. Amos Tompson was called as a probationer. We know nothing of this gentleman, except that he met a more decided opposition, as a candidate, than any of his predecessors had encountered. In September, twelve legal voters represented to the selectmen that "uneasiness subsisting between Mr. Amos Tompson and some of the town, who liked neither his principles nor his performance," they had mutually agreed to submit their differences to the determination of Rev. Messrs. Raynolds, Bellamy, Brinsmade, Woodbridge, and Ashley; "the dissatisfied promising, on their part, if the council advised the settlement of the candidate, to make no further stir in the matter;" Mr. Tompson, on the other hand, consenting "to quit the town" in the event of a decision adverse to him. No proper case, however, could be made up for the council without the action of the town, to obtain which a town-meeting was demanded.

The meeting was held; but it promptly refused to accede to the proposed arrangement, and proceeded unconditionally to invite Mr. Tompson "to settle in the work of the gospel-ministry among them." But, either that he considered himself bound by his agreement with the dissatisfied, or that he thought the place undesirable with so powerful a minority arrayed against him, — we hear no more of him.[1]

[1] The signers of the petition for a town-meeting, who may be presumed among the leaders of the dissatisfied, were Joseph Wright, Joseph Wright, jun., Thos.

Mr. Daniel Hopkins was then invited to preach on probation; and, nothing coming of this, Mr. Daniel Collins preached in like manner until the first of September, 1763, when the town voted, thirty-two to three, to invite him to settle; but an adjourned meeting, four days afterwards, was so thinly attended, — and eight appearing against Mr. Collins, — that it was considered useless to make him any offers; and so the minority again triumphed.[1]

On the 9th of December, 1763, the town decided to invite Mr. Thomas Allen of Northampton to preach as a probationer; and his ministry in that capacity was signalized by the formation of the church, — a duty which it seems had, up to this time, been singularly neglected. On the 7th of February, 1764, "a number of members belonging to different churches" met at the house of Deacon Crofoot; Rev. Samuel Hopkins of Great Barrington, Rev. Stephen West of Stockbridge, and Rev. Ebenezer Martin of Becket (then No. 4), being also present. A Confession of Faith and a Covenant were drawn up, and signed by eight male members, "who then and there united so as to form a church of Christ in this place.[2]

The eight names signed to the covenant and articles of faith are, Stephen Crofoot, Ephraim Stiles, Daniel Hubbard, Aaron Baker, Jacob Ensign, William Phelps, Lemuel Phelps, Elnathan Phelps. Col. Williams, Capt. Goodrich, and other prominent inhabitants, were connected with churches in other places, but did not transfer their membership until some months later.

After the proceedings at Deacon Crofoot's house, those who had

Morgan, John Waddams, Phinehas Belding, Lemuel, William, and Elnathan Phelps, Israel Dickinson, Israel Stoddard, Israel and Elisha Jones, of whom the last four, at least, were of the Williams-Stoddard connection, while William Williams was one of the Selectmen to whom the petition was addressed.

[1] Mr. Collins was afterwards, for many years, the minister of Lanesborough, dying in office, at the age of eighty-four, in 1822. He was a worthy man, but was suspected of Toryism in Revolutionary times. His election as minister of Pittsfield might have somewhat changed the complexion of the town's story.

[2] The designation, "The Church of Christ in Pittsfield," was assumed in accordance with the custom of similar bodies where but one existed in a town. It was the only form used until 1817, when after the re-union of the parish, which had been divided in 1809, the present name of "The First Congregational Church" was adopted, partly because the old style, other churches having been formed in town, savored too much of asserting an exclusive claim to the Christian name, and partly because circumstances rendered it expedient for the organization to re-assert its adherence to the Congregational form of church-government.

taken part in them repaired to the meeting-house, where Rev. Mr. Hopkins "preached a lecture," from 2 Cor. viii. 5: "And this they did, not as we hoped; but first gave themselves to the Lord, and now to us by the will of God." The new organization was then formerly "declared to be a church of Christ."

By the incorporation of the town, the concurrence of two distinct bodies became requisite in settling a minister; and now, by the organization of the church, a third was added.

It was the province of the church to select the minister; of the town, if it approved, to ratify the choice, and fix the salary; and of the Proprietors of the sixty lots, to provide the "settlement," or outfit, of the pastor elect.

The church not disappointing the hope hinted in Mr. Hopkins's text, and doubtless more fully expressed in his lecture, proved a harmonizing and not a disturbing element in the electoral triad. Meeting at the house of Deacon Crofoot, on the 5th of March, 1764, it unanimously elected Mr. Thomas Allen to the pastorate, and immediately announced its choice to the town; which on the same day, as promptly and unanimously concurring, resolved to tender Mr. Allen a salary of £60 *per annum*, to be increased £5 yearly, until it should reach £80, which was then to become his stated stipend.

The Proprietors also, upon the same day, voted him £90, in three annual instalments, "to enable him to settle himself among them; and appointed Col. Williams, Capt. Goodrich, James Easton, and Josiah Wright, a committee to wait upon him with the several votes; and, if he accepted the pastorate on the proffered terms, to agree with him upon a time and council for the ordination, and make the necessary preparations.

The committee having executed their trust, Mr. Allen responded in the following letter: —

To the People of Pittsfield.

Dear Brethren, — Your invitation of me to settle among you in the gospel ministry, I have received by your committee chosen for that purpose; and I apprehend I have duly considered the same. In answer to this, your invitation, I would say, that having sought divine direction, taken the advice of the judicious, and duly consulted my own judgment, I cannot but think it my duty to accept; and, accordingly, do now declare my cordial acceptance of the same.

I take this opportunity to testify my grateful sense of your respect, shown in that unexpected good agreement and harmony that subsisted among you in the choice of one less than the least of all saints to preach among you the unsearchable riches of Christ.

Nothing doubting but that, at your next meeting, you will freely grant forty or fifty cords of wood annually, or as much as you shall think sufficient, and some small addition to my settlement, either by grant in work, or whatever, out of generosity, by subscription or whatever way you please, I now stand ready to be introduced to the work whereunto I am called, as soon as a convenient opportunity shall present itself.

These from your affectionate friend,

Thomas Allen.

PITTSFIELD, March 20, 1764.

The addition of forty cords of wood to the proposed salary was granted; and the mode in which it should be procured was long one of the annual items of town-business, the duty being sometimes assigned to a committee, and sometimes alternating, year by year, between the East and West Parts. Finally it was commuted with Mr. Allen for an allowance of money. The Proprietors had in previous years bestowed some labor upon girdling the trees on "the minister's home-lot;" and the requested addition to the settlement was made by further aid in continuing the clearing.

The ordination of Mr. Allen took place on the 18th of April, the following named clergymen being present, "besides several neighboring ministers:" Jonathan Ashley of Deerfield, Timothy Woodbridge of Hatfield, John Hooker of Northampton, Samuel Hopkins of Great Barrington, Thomas Strong of New Marlborough, and Adonijah Bidwell of No. 1 (now Tyringham). The first prayer was made by Mr. Hopkins, the second by Mr. Woodbridge; Mr. Ashley gave the charge, and Mr. Bidwell the right hand of felfowship. Mr. Strong offered the concluding prayer. The sermon was preached by Mr. Hooker, who had been Mr. Allen's preceptor in his divinity studies; and it was one of the only two productions of that clergyman which were ever printed. "The whole," says Mr. Allen's record, "was carried on with decency and order." "Thirty-one members were added to the church in the first year of Mr. Allen's ministry," says Dr. Field.

The young clergyman who was so auspiciously introduced to the stage upon which he was to be conspicuous for nearly half a century was descended from an honorable ancestry of industrious, virtuous, pious men. His earliest ancestor in this country was Samuel Allen, a native of England, probably of Essex, who died at Windsor, Conn., in 1648; whose son, Samuel, was one of the first settlers of Northampton in 1657. The third of the name was a deacon in the Northampton church when Jonathan Edwards was its pastor, and died in 1739. Next came Joseph Allen, the father of the Pittsfield minister, — a neighbor of Mr. Edwards, and his steadfast friend in the difficulties which drove that great man from Northampton. The wife of Joseph, and the mother of Thomas Allen, was Elizabeth Parsons, a descendant of Joseph Parsons, an eminently pious early settler. She died in 1800, more than eighty years old.

Thomas Allen was born at Northampton, Jan. 17, 1743, — the same year in which the abortive attempt to settle Poontoosuck was made. Through the bequest of a grand-uncle, whose name he bore, ample provision was made for his education at Harvard University, where he was graduated in 1762, with a very high reputation for scholarship, especially in the classics. He studied theology under the direction of his pastor, Rev. Mr. Hooker.

His son, Rev. William Allen, D.D., in a sketch of his life printed in Sprague's American Annals, portrays the character of the first minister of Pittsfield so vividly, and so entirely in accord with all the evidence within our reach, as well as with the report of those who knew Mr. Allen in his last years, that we transcribe it with the full conviction that it owes little to the partiality of a filial pen.[1]

"My father was of middle height, and slender, vigorous, and active; of venerable gray hairs in his age; of a mild, pleasant, affectionate countenance; hospitable to all visitors, and always the glad welcomer of his friends. As he was very honest and frank, and had a keen sense of right and wrong, and as he lived when high questions were debated, it is not strange that those whom he felt called upon to oppose should have sometimes charged him with indiscreet zeal; but he cherished no malice, and his heart was always kind and tender. Simple and courteous in his manners, sincere in his communications, and just in his dealings, he set his parishioners an

[1] We are also indebted to the same source for the ancestral record of Mr. Allen.

example of Christian morals. The atonement of the Divine Redeemer, the evangelical doctrines of grace, and their application to the practical duties of life in the various relations of society, were the favorite subjects of his public sermons and private conversations. He explained them without the formality of logic, but with a happy perspicuity of style, and recommended and enforced them with apostolic zeal. As he wrote out most of his sermons in Weston's shorthand, he usually, in his preaching, read them from his notes; but he threw into them, with but little action, great fervor of spirit. Sometimes, in his extemporary addresses at the Communion-table, his trembling voice and kindling eye and animated countenance were quite irresistible.

Nothing need be added to this as a portrait. But popular tradition — which always preserves that in a man's character which in the popular comprehension seems odd, to the neglect of what is intrinsic and sterling — gives prominence in its memories of Mr. Allen, not to his deep religious sentiment, nor even to the purity of his patriotism and his advanced ideas of political rights, but to the mode in which his earnest and straightforward nature led him to manifest those great qualities. It remembers him as a politician devoted to his party, — as a Whig of the Revolution, whose zeal led him to take up arms in an emergency; but it forgets the reasoning, which, in Mr. Allen's conscience, justified a departure from ordinary clerical etiquette at the crisis in which he was placed.

History is not likely to fall into this error, as regards the secular principles upon which he acted; but as he did not obtrude the inner springs by which he was governed when occasion did not require their display, and as that which it falls within our province to record of him is chiefly of a secular character, justice to his reputation as a minister of religion demands that we should bear testimony in advance to what cannot well be connected with the thread of the story, — that his political was an outgrowth of his religious life. The memoranda — mostly intended only for his own eye — show, that in the commonest, as well as in the most conspicuous of his secular acts, he was moved by a religious spirit.

In the private exercises of devotion he was constant; and, however he may have at times thrown off the etiquette of his sacred profession, there is abundant evidence that its essential spirit was preserved and its essential duties were performed in the most trying moments of military and political excitement, as the reader will have opportunity to note in one or two remarkable instances.

Nor does even tradition hint a single word or deed of Mr. Allen inconsistent with the purest Christian morals. His peculiarity — which was the joint result of his temperament and of the epoch in which he lived — was, that he held in small respect any religious faith which did not manifest itself in outward acts, and especially in those done for the common good, and that he esteemed resistance to every form of oppression, and devotion to the political principles best adapted to the preservation of equal rights, to be among the most sacred duties. In the Revolution, moreover, while his ardent temperament, without any other inspiration, would have made him as fervid a patriot as his kinsmen of Ticonderoga fame, he had the additional incitement, that, with the majority of New-England clergymen, he believed that the cause of pure and unfettered religious worship was bound up, as it really was, in that of the colonies, and that that cause was therefore holy.

This view of Mr. Allen's character, which accords strictly with the evidence, is also necessary in order to its consistency, and to explain facts which could not be made clear by any theory of eccentricity, — a solution of biographical problems which is oftener due to the laziness of the investigator than to any idiosyncrasy of his subject.

VIEW OF THE PARSONAGE.

In 1768, the three annual instalments of Mr. Allen's outfit having come due, and been paid, and his house having probably been built, he married Elizabeth, daughter of Jonathan Lee of Salisbury, Conn., a descendant of William Bradford, the Pilgrim Governor of Plymouth Colony, and one of the most illustrious of the leaders who came over in the May Flower. Mr. Allen brought his bride home to Pittsfield, through the narrow wood-roads, mounted on a pillion behind him.

CHAPTER IX.

ANTE-REVOLUTIONARY POLITICS.

[1761–JUNE, 1774.]

Public Sentiment. — Its Leaders in Pittsfield. — Israel Stoddard. — Woodbridge Little. — William Williams. — Rev. Thomas Allen. — Elder Valentine Rathbun. — James Easton. — William Francis. — Josiah Wright. — Oliver Root. — David Noble. — John Strong. — Charles Goodrich. — Israel Dickinson. — Dr. Timothy Childs. — John Brown. — Eli Root. — Daniel Hubbard. — Census of 1772. — Censorship of the Town Records. — Revolutionary Measures. — Instructions to Representatives. — Action regarding the Boston Tea-party.

WHILE home-affairs were taking shape under the town-organization of Pittsfield, the storm of revolution was gathering over the Province. Writs of Assistance, the Stamp Act, the Townsend Revenue Acts, the British garrison in Boston with its consequences, followed each other in evil procession, and were met by resistance in the courts of law, by legislative protest in the General Court, by the spirited action of Boston and other towns, and by the more or less tumultuous outbreaks of the metropolis. In the contests and divisions which arose among the people concerning the wisdom and the rightfulness of these several modes of resistance to the royal and parliamentary will, Berkshire, although isolated upon the extreme verge of the Province, intensely sympathized. Few, perhaps none, of her citizens wished the parliamentary schemes to be persisted in; but many hoped for redress from a returning sense of justice in Great Britian, and believed that a portion, at least, of the measures adopted at Boston hindered that result. It was hardly to be expected that they could comprehend how deeply considered was the ministerial policy, and how perfectly it coincided with the popular feeling of the kingdom. Even the most advanced Whigs owed their position to long contemplation of the radical evils which the substitution of the Provincial for the Colonial charter had introduced into the Constitution of Massachusetts; from which they regarded the new encroachments of the home-government to be a natural and inevitable outgrowth. While they found it expedient to direct popular opposition, for the time, exclusively against immediate and palpable wrongs, they—if they did not from the first look forward to absolute independence—anticipated no permanent security for their political rights from any measure short of a substantial restoration of the charter of 1628. And the tenacity with which the Revolutionary leaders in Berkshire—more firmly than those in other sections of the Province—clung to this idea afterwards led to consequences of great importance to the county.

On the other hand, the opinions of many were warped by the possession or the hope of the offices which the Provincial charter placed mostly at the disposal of the royal governor. The sympathy of others was conciliated to the party of the Government by sentiments a little more generous: by the ties of long and friendly association, gratitude for past favors, family tradition, lessons of loyalty and reverence for the king's representative learned in childhood. The sweet influences which Province House so well knew how to throw out had a peculiar charm for the secluded magnates of Western Massachusetts, upon whom they had long been sedulously brought to bear, and not unfrequently with success.

But here, as elsewhere, while principle, temperament, or interest arrayed some classes at once and decidedly upon one side or the other of the rising strife, the great body of the people were slow in uniting upon the measures rightful and proper to be adopted, in regard to parliamentary acts, by which, as few ventured to deny, their liberties were invaded. In the minds of individuals, the issues of the day hung balanced; and the inclination of the scale was often determined by a very slight preponderance. Every fact, every principle, all precedents of history at all pertinent to the discussion, were brought into it by the pamphleteers, the newspaper writers, the orators, and the preachers, upon one side or the other, and gravely and anxiously scanned, as well by those who finally adhered to the king, as by those who decided for the colonies. And, after all, the sentiments of men ranged through all shades of feeling, from the loyalty of the most obstinate Tory, to the fervor of the Revolutionist, who, from the beginning, foresaw and rejoiced in the end.

The letters which passed between confidential friends showed how undetermined some of the most upright men long remained, how well they discerned the difficulties of the situation, and how thoroughly they appreciated the responsibilities which pressed upon themselves. This responsibility lay heavily upon the leaders of public sentiment in towns, — a class of men even more powerful then than now: and few took their stand without long and severe thought, a profound consideration of consequences, and protracted consultation with those, in the phrase of that day, so significantly styled "the judicious;" not many without trustful and earnest prayer.

In reading their letters, we, of course, discover the writers to have been influenced by their several natural temperaments, habits of thought, associations in life, and, whether consciously or not, biassed by private interests; but, in a vast majority of instances, nobler considerations dominated.

These municipal magnates were, almost without exception, men of some property, which must needs be endangered in such a conflict as resistance to the king's authority was sure to provoke. Many were rising and ambitious men, and well aware, that, as they chose their sides now, their aspirations would be brought to bloom or blight. Some, as officers under the royal commission in the old wars, had been trained to habits of military subordination and submission to royal authority which it was hard to throw off, and none the less so when it happened that there was half-pay on the British peace-establishment to be forfeited in so doing. Some, in subscribing the oaths prescribed to be taken by those appointed to civil and military office, had assumed obligations whose repudiation they found it difficult to reconcile with their consciences.[1]

[1] The oath included the following clause: "And I do swear that I will bear faith and true allegiance to his Majesty King George, and him will defend to the utmost of my power against all traitorous conspiracies and attempts whatsoever which shall be made against his Person, Crown, or Dignity. And I will do my utmost endeavor to disclose and make known to his Majesty and his successors all treasons and traitorous conspiracies which I shall know to be against him or any of them. . . . And all these things I do plainly and sincerely acknowledge and swear according to the express words by me spoken, and according to the plain common sense and understanding of the same words, without any equivocation, mental evasion, or secret reservation whatever." The latter clause was framed with special reference to the Jesuitical interpretation of the oath by the Jacobites; but it bore hard upon the position of the Massachusetts office-holders, as many of them thought.

There is matter for wonder in the bold, far-seeing wisdom and unselfish patriotism which finally prevailed with so large a majority of those who were required to stake large personal interests upon the doubtful issue: there is none that many, even of those afterwards among the truest and most uncompromising, were not at once ready to unite with their more ardent and impulsive compatriots, or with those whom close observation had enabled early to detect the fatal canker in the Provincial Constitution.

The event proved that wisdom accorded with the impetuosity of youth and the ardor of radicalism; but even then Massachusetts councils needed a retarding power, lest, by too rapid strides, she might dangerously disconnect herself from colonies whose patriotism, although not less sincere, had not been spurred by the same sharp contact with tyranny, and whose loyal traditions were not so obliterated from the popular heart.

But, besides the conservative men who were at heart and essentially Whigs, — who soon ripened into brave and decided Whigs, — there was a considerable party whom no provocation on the part of the British government could repel from their allegiance; and nowhere did the patriotic spirit encounter, in this class, a more bitter, powerful, and subtle enemy than in Pittsfield. The influence of age, wealth, and official position was nearly united here against all the measures, except perhaps very humble remonstrance, with which the usurpations of the mother country were met.

The Williams and Stoddard families, with their numerous connections by blood and marriage, were, with few exceptions, attached to the Tory interest. Israel Stoddard, who had inherited from his father, the early proprietor, a large property in the town, was a young man, having been born in 1741; but he was major in the Berkshire regiment of militia, was appointed in 1765 one of the justices of the Quarter Sessions, and was prominent in town-affairs. He was a graduate of Yale in the class of 1758, and appears to have possessed a cultivated mind.[1]

[1] The consideration in which Major Stoddard was held is curiously illustrated by the following article in the warrant for a town-meeting in December, 1768: "To choose a committee to wait upon Israel Stoddard, Esq., to know of him the foundation of his resentment, and by what means he can be accommodated to his satisfaction." The town, however, resolved that it had no right to act upon the

Moses Graves and Elisha Jones were both large landholders in the township, and both allied to the Williams and Stoddard blood But the ablest and shrewdest of the Tories was Woodbridge Little, the first lawyer who settled in the town. This gentleman was a native of Colchester, Conn., where he was born in 1741. He was graduated at Yale in 1760; studied theology with Rev. Dr. Bellamy; was licensed to preach, and officiated for two years as "a probationer" at Lanesborough.[1] He then abandoned divinity for the study of the law; and, having been admitted to the bar, established himself, in 1770, in practice at Pittsfield, where he had become a resident at least as early as 1766, in which year he was elected hog-reeve, in accordance with the waggish welcome which towns used to give young gentlemen of dignified pursuits as well as young bridegrooms. Many a worse prank was played upon the worthy lawyer in the license of war-times.

Mr. Little was a man of varied learning, and profoundly versed "in the art of putting things." Most of the political papers of his party were drawn by him; and nothing could have been fairer than their case as he stated it. His character also was such as to give weight to his argument. Indeed, although he was far from ingenuous and although his position, until 1777, was reprehensible, there is no reason to doubt that his opinions were honestly held, and that what he did was justified by his own conscience. His associations gave rise to grave suspicions, which received confirmation in the public mind, from acts which may have been prompted merely by natural timidity, instead of a consciousness of guilt; and it is not probable that he ever gave direct aid and comfort to the enemy after the actual breaking out of hostilities. He was regarded by the patriots of Pittsfield as their most dangerous opponent, not because he was the most malignant, but as the ablest and most subtle of the Tory leaders.

article. Among the customs copied from the English aristocracy, by their callow Provincial imitators, was the practice of arranging names in college catalogues, not, as now, alphabetically, but according to the social rank of the students. Thus John Adams, upon entering Harvard, found himself the twelfth man of his class in degree; which his son thought due to the standing of his mother's family, the dignity of the house on the paternal side not entitling him to that position. In Yale, this practice continued until 1768; and, by its scale, Israel Stoddard ranked *first*, Israel Dickinson twenty-fifth, in a class of forty-three. Woodbridge Little stood tenth in a class of thirty-three.

[1] Dr. Durfee's Hist. Will. Coll.

The position of Col. Williams was peculiar. He was elected representative to the General Court in the years 1762, '64, '69, and '70,[1] and preserved the friendly relations with the royal governors which he had enjoyed previous to the incorporation of the town. In 1771, Gov. Hutchinson counted him — with Israel Williams, John Worthington, and Timothy Woodbridge — among the eight gentlemen whom the recent elections had left in the House, who, in common times, would have had great weight on the side of the Government, but who were paralyzed by the hopelessness of the minority in which they found themselves. Williams also held, by appointment of the governor, the offices of chief-justice of the Common Pleas and judge of probate for Berkshire, — places which, given to the father of James Otis for the poorer county of Barnstable, Hutchinson thought ought to have secured both father and son for the Government party. Williams, like the elder Otis, had, moreover, been permitted "to name many of his friends for other offices;" and enjoyed, in addition, — what to him was a great enjoyment, — the dignity of colonel in the Berkshire regiment of militia; and, still to accumulate the ties which bound him to the royalist party, he was a half-pay officer on the retired list of the British army.

By the charter of William — as it was then in force — all civil and military officers of the province were appointed by the governor, and confirmed by the council: but the former had no power of removal in civil cases; and opportunities to make new appointments could only occur by the death or resignation of incumbents, or upon the demise of the king, which vacated all commissions. Col. Williams, therefore, if he had wished to support the popular cause, had little to fear from the resentment of the appointing power, or from any other quarter, so long as he refrained from treasons which would have forfeited his half-pay. The obligations of gratitude and old association were, however, strong, and the family influences which surrounded him were mostly Tory: although his cousin, Major Hawley of Northampton, was one of the ablest of the Whig leaders; and his favorite brother-in-law, Col. Partridge, finally arrayed himself upon the same side. But Hawley was always a timid councillor, and Partridge was alarmed

[1] By some means, the exclusion of Pittsfield from representation until 1763 appears to have been done away.

and disgusted by what he deemed the unjustifiable excesses at Boston.

All through the ante-Revolutionary troubles we are called upon to remark the extreme sensitiveness of "the River-Gods of the Connecticut," and their no less magnificent kindred among the Berkshire Hills, to the slightest infractions of law, order, and public decorum, on the part of the Sons of Liberty, — a fastidiousness which, creditable enough within certain limits, when carried to extremes made some very worthy men Tories, and rendered others very lukewarm Whigs. They seem to have belonged to the class of moralists who consider political rascality the exclusive privilege of eminent respectability. Col. Partridge gave expression to this feeling with no exceptional force in the following extract from a letter, dated "Hatfield, March 21, 1768," referring to the refusal of the House of Representatives to notice a severe attack by Dr. Joseph Warren upon Gov. Bernard, which was published in "The Boston Gazette" on the 29th of the preceding month.

"The Green-villain spirit against America rather increases;[1] and the late wretched doings at Boston, about the beginning of this month, will increase that spirit in England. I mean the scurrilous libel against ye Governor, not much, if any, short of a blasphemy, and the disregard with which the House treated it. I am settled in my opinion, that the late conduct of ye House will bring on a demolition of our charter, unless we are treated by King and Parliament as a people insane, and so not to be punished until we come to our wits."[2]

Few men in the Province had stronger or more numerous bonds of attachment to the Government party than Col. Williams; and surely such inspiration from his Whig friends as that to be derived from the above quotation was not likely to weaken them.

But, however pleasant his relations had been with the royal authorities of Massachusetts, his experience of the English commanders in the army had been galling in the extreme; and the remembrance must have been bitter. His desire, also, to stand well with the people was strong; and it is evident that he had a secret understanding with the local Whig leaders. The tradition is, that when partisan jealousy ran high, as the outbreak of hostil-

Col. Partridge had just received some "prints" from Boston, with news from England of the change in the ministry and the state of public feeling there.

[2] T. C. C., p. 226.

ities approached, or perhaps immediately after they had actually occurred, he was summoned before the Committee of Inspection, in order to explain his position, and that he succeeded in convincing that rather exacting conclave of his loyalty to the popular cause; and moreover, that, being too old for military service, it was for the public interest that he should avoid any overt act that would forfeit the half-pay which he received in gold, and spent among his neighbors. It soon, however, became impossible to serve two masters, and we find him filling positions inconsistent with allegiance to the King.

That he was early reluctant to come in conflict with the popular feeling was shown in the convenient illness which prevented him from holding a Probate Court while the Stamp Act was in force.[1]

Still, in that momentous period, when the patriots who early comprehended the conspiracy of the royal closet against the liberties of the colonies were painfully moulding a public sentiment which should have boldness, determination, strength, and unity sufficient to meet and thwart that conspiracy, — in the doubtful years of that great moral struggle which preceded the appeal to arms, — William Williams, holding the chief offices of the county, and possessed of far more personal consideration than any other man, in Pittsfield at least, gave the weight of his influence to the party of submission. While the patriot leaders were establishing the people in the principles of constitutional liberty, animating them with the warmth of a righteous indignation, and instilling into them its confidence in their military strength, — calling, in fine, from chaotic elements that mighty power which we name "The Spirit of '76," — Williams was uniting his voice with those who palliated, if they did not justify, the encroachments of Great Britain; who forbade every hope of redress except from the grace of king and parliament; whose perpetual theme was the inability

[1] In a letter to the Registrar, Hon. Elijah Dwight, of Great Barrington, now in the possession of Henry W. Taft, Esq., Col. Williams says, "My state of ill-health has prevented my attention to almost any sort of business; but, *the Stamp Act being repealed*, and being some better, desire you, as soon as may be, to disperse the following advertisement among the several towns." The advertisement announced Probate Courts in Stockbridge, at the house of Mr. Benjamin Willard, Innholder, on the last Tuesdays of April, June, August and October; in Pittsfield at the house of Deacon James Easton, Innholder, on the last Tuesdays of December and February. The letter is dated Pittsfield, June 14, 1766.

of the colonies to cope in arms with the mother country; and who carped at every display of spirit by the people, the towns, or the Provincial legislature.

Thus on the side of the submissionists in Pittsfield were the strong conservative sentiment of the Williams-Stoddard connection, the wealth of Israel Stoddard, Moses Graves, the Jones brothers, the Ashley's, and others, the subtlety and legal learning of Woodbridge Little, and the personal and official influence of Col. Williams. In meeting this array, the Whig cause had gained, previous to 1774, several able champions, who gave in their adherence to it, from time to time, as party-lines were more and more sharply drawn by the progress of events.

With the first to declare themselves was Rev. Mr. Allen, who, from zealous non-conformist ancestors, had inherited the purest principles of the English commonwealth, and believed in a church without a bishop hardly more implicitly than he did in a state without a king: so that, while he meditated no treasons for the sake of abstract theories of government, the princely name had for him no sanctity to deter from resistance to royal iniquity. An innate hatred of oppression and injustice, a zealous devotion to any cause to which his sense of right attached him, a personal character which carried weight with the people, and a happy faculty for enforcing his opinions both with the tongue and the pen, completed the qualities which eminently fitted him to be a leader in times of revolution. Placable towards his own enemies, he was an excellent hater of the foes of his country, chief among which he classed the Tories and George the Third. He charged — and modern investigation proves him to have been correct in so doing — upon the monarch, personally and primarily, rather than upon his ministry, the wrongs which his government inflicted upon America. An entry in his diary, so long after the conclusion of the war as 1799, shows how lasting and intense was his resentment for these wrongs. Being in that year at London, and having seen King George pass in state from the palace to Parliament House, he recorded the incident with the following comment: —

"This is he who desolated my country; who ravaged the American coasts; annihilated our trade; burned our towns; plundered our cities; sent forth his Indian allies to scalp our wives and children; starved our youth in his prison-ships; and caused the expenditure of millions of money, and a hundred thousand precious lives. Instead of being the father of his people, he has been their destroyer. May God forgive him so great guilt!"

The evil deeds thus denounced, of course occurred after the era which we are now considering; but their place as an incitement to feeling was then supplied by political wrongs and the immediate presence of the conflict: and we have introduced the incident, out of the order of time, as showing something of the manner and spirit of the minister who made the Pittsfield pulpit one of the foremost of those which, throughout New England, rang with denunciations of the oppressor and the invader, and preached the gospel of liberty to apt listeners.

Elder Valentine Rathbun, the pastor of the Baptist church, organized in 1772, was no less ardent in his patriotism than his Congregational brother. A clothier by trade, he had — without abandoning that pursuit, and without the advantages of a classical or theological education — formed the church to which he ministered from proselytes made by his own preaching in his own house. The results of his public speaking indicate that its style was effective: the temperament of the man suggests that it was fiery, vehement, and nervous. His fellow-citizens manifested their esteem for his character and his talents by electing him to important county "Congresses," — over which he often presided, — and, at interesting crises, to the General Court: although his extremely radical principles, and passion for ultra, not to say violent, measures, may have had something to do with his popularity when the blood of the people was heated even beyond Revolutionary fervor, as it often was when Valentine Rathbun was a successful candidate.

James Easton was a builder, and also kept a store and a tavern, a little south of the present corner of Bank Row and South Street, the latter of which became historical in connection with the Ethan Allen capture of Ticonderoga. He was a native of Hartford, but removed from Litchfield, Conn., to Pittsfield, in the year 1763. He joined the church by letter in May, 1764, and was chosen deacon the next September. He was, from the first, a prominent citizen; and his letters show sound sense well expressed, great promptness and energy of character, and a remarkable combination of zeal and judgment. We know him best as an officer in the early years of the war; but he was among the first to range himself with Mr. Allen upon the Whig side.

Among the other prominent men who early committed themselves to the party of liberty were Oliver Root, William Francis, Deacon Josiah Wright, David Noble, and John Strong. Our information concerning these patriots — except Col. Root, whose early life has already been sketched — is slight. William Francis was a native of Wethersfield, and was among the first settlers of Poontoosuck. Not only before the Revolution, but for many years afterwards, he was held by his townsmen in extraordinary esteem for his discretion and integrity. "Governor Francis," the *soubriquet* by which he was known in his later years, is still remembered with reverential respect by persons now living. Of somewhat similar character was Deacon Wright, afterwards one of the earliest Methodists in Pittsfield. He had served as a sergeant in the French and Indian Wars.

David Noble — than whom no Pittsfield patriot has left a brighter record — was a native of Westfield, from which town he was a volunteer in 1755. He was a farmer, trader, and tavern-keeper, living in the eastern part of the town, and had accumulated considerable property, most of which he sacrificed for his country. John Strong was also a tavern-keeper, living where the Pomeroy Homestead now stands. He is remembered as a genial and popular landlord, but, at the time of which we write, was often chosen to places of civil, as well as military trust, which required more than a common share of intellectual ability; and he seems to have been quite competent to fill them.

Charles Goodrich, — who continued a prosperous citizen, and had attained the rank of captain in the militia, — although he owned large tracts of what had been the commons lands, had allied himself closely in town-affairs with the party of the settling proprietors, and was, in 1764, 1769, and 1770, chosen to represent the town at Boston. Naturally averse, as a man of large property, to dangerous agitation, his sympathies were, nevertheless, sincerely with the people, and not altogether, or chiefly, because his political hopes, which were active, rested upon them. Prompt, even to a proneness to litigation, in maintaining his personal rights, the same quality roused him equally when the chartered privileges and immunities which he shared with his countrymen were attacked. A man of independent thought, and of discriminating as well as decided opinions, while adhering firmly to the principles which commended themselves to his judgment, he was disposed occasionally to differ in detail from those with whom he agreed in essentials; and he may have maintained a peculiar position, as regarded the Pittsfield patriots — in the formative period of Revolutionary sentiment, as he did afterwards upon the question of civil government in the new commonwealth. But we find him in full favor with the Whigs as soon as they came into power; and it is to be presumed that his influence had previously been exercised in harmony with them. Such men as he are more apt to break with their party in the hour of victory than while the struggle is on.

The only person in Pittsfield, at all connected with the Williams and Stoddard families, who is known to have sided with the patriots before hostilities actually commenced, was Israel Dickinson. This gentleman was born at Hatfield in 1735, and graduated at Yale College in 1758; afterwards receiving his master's degree as well from the College of New Jersey, of which his kinsman, Dr. Jonathan Dickinson, had been the first president, as from his own *Alma Mater*. In college, he was the class-mate and chum of Israel Stoddard; and both were the friends of Woodbridge Little, who was two classes below them. This early college intimacy led to the settlement of the chums, and, soon after, of Little, upon three adjoining estates in a pleasant section of Pittsfield. And there the ante-revolutionary troubles found them, in the enjoyment of cultivated and harmonious intercourse, interchanging reminiscences of college-life, and, as the books preserved by their descendants prove, indulging and cherishing their taste for intellectual pleasures. Nothing remains to show when this delightful union was interrupted by the political differences which estranged the friends, if they were estranged; but immediately after the Lexington fight, when Stoddard and Little were taking refuge in New York from the rage of the people, we find Israel Dickinson prominent in the military operations of the patriots.

In 1771, the Whigs received a valuable accession in the person of Dr. Timothy Childs. This noted patriot was born at Deerfield in 1748; entered Harvard College in 1764, but did not graduate; studied medicine in his native town with Dr. Thomas Williams, and established himself in practice at Pittsfield in 1771. The young physician soon won popularity and influence; proved himself an effective speaker,[1] and by these qualities, as well as by the contagion of his youthful zeal, gave a new impulse to the cause which he espoused.

About three years after Dr. Childs had planted himself at Pittsfield, a similar acquisition was made by the removal to the place of John Brown, a young lawyer of commanding talents, of noble personal appearance, well connected, and, withal, a true man, — one destined to win fame, but not such as equalled the promise of his youth, or was commensurate with the deserts which appeared even in his brief career. His father, Daniel Brown, a native of Haverhill, settled at Sandisfield in 1752; and his prosperity there was remarked by Col. Williams in a letter already quoted. His respectable position among the gentlemen of the county was attested by the commission of the peace which he received in 1765. His son, in 1777, spoke of himself as having "had a birth and education of some consequence." John, the youngest of five brothers, was born at Haverhill, Oct. 19, 1744; was graduated at Yale in 1771; studied law at Providence with his sister's husband, Hon. Oliver Arnold, and commenced practice at Caghnawaga, now Johnstown, N.Y., where he held the place of king's attorney. After a brief stay there, early in 1773 he transferred his residence to Pittsfield, where Woodbridge Little had previously been the only man of law. His radicalism at this time does not appear to have been quite up to the Boston standard; but his principles were fixed, and, proving bold as well as prudent, he soon received from the people the most distinguished marks of their confidence, and never gave them reason for one moment to repent their trust.

Among those, who, from the positions in which we soon find them, are presumed to have been early adherents to the Whig cause, are Deacon Daniel Hubbard, a wealthy citizen of The West Part, and Eli Root, one of the richer residents near Wendell Square, and after the Revolution a worthy magistrate: both men

[1] It is related that Dr. Childs's manner, on town-meeting days, was to halt on his professional rounds, enter the meeting-house, stand patiently waiting until the subject which specially interested him came up for action, when he presented his views quietly but with precision and force, after which, without waiting for reply or result, he left the house, and resumed his calls. But, doubtless, when subjects momentous as those which in Revolutionary times claimed the attention of towns were under discussion, this nonchalant manner was greatly modified, if it did not entirely disappear.

of sterling character, whose determination, energy, and place in the community, made them of eminent service to their party.

By the nearly perfect census of the population, which is preserved,[1] the number of families living in Pittsfield in 1772 was 138; of inhabitants, about 828. The leadership which swayed the two parties in this little community, shut up, with a few others of like composition, among the hills, shows a remarkable proportion of liberally-educated men as well as others of decided intellectual character and ability. That they should, in some greater measure than towns at the east, work out their own political problems by their own processes was natural. That while reaching the same result with their compatriots at Boston, while sympathizing with their struggles in defence of invaded rights, and according to them the respect and influence which was due their vanship in the conflict, they should not always adopt the prevailing color of metropolitan sentiment, nor always applaud the measures which that sentiment dictated, was inevitable. Aside from the diverse habits of thought which ordinarily prevailed in the two sections, and setting aside for the moment the absence in Berkshire of immediate incitements to feeling, the lack of those means of intimate, and in some degree secret, communication with the masses, which the Boston leaders possessed at home, would alone have secured this result. Thus the reasoning which made clear to the Boston clubs the essential difference between the sacking of Hutchinson's house and the swamping of the Honorable East India Company's tea was not so apparent to the comprehension of secluded farm-houses in Pittsfield. It was otherwise with fundamental maxims of government, concerning which public discussion, in the press and upon the rostrum, was able to effect unity both of assent and application. And it was otherwise, also, with regard to parliamentary and executive acts, obnoxious functionaries, and Tory statesmen, — objects against which it was quite possible for the central revolutionists to concentrate the unbroken opposition of their party, and finally to bring that party to comprise so large a majority, that it, not without good right, assumed to be The People.

While the revolutionists in Pittsfield, as elsewhere, were growing up to this estate, an unfortunate custom existed of keeping

[1] See Appendix D.

the minutes of town-meetings upon sheets of paper loosely stitched together, which, with other town-archives, were, at intervals of a few years, inspected by committees appointed for that purpose, who directed what should be permanently recorded, what kept on file, and what destroyed. It will readily be comprehended how fatal such a process would be to all evidence of tergiversation on the part of the inspectors.

In the record of town-meetings there are, in fact, previous to June, 1774, but two entries bearing upon the unsatisfactory state of affairs with the mother country. One of these was in March, 1768, when William Williams, Josiah Wright, Stephen Crofoot, James Easton, and Rev. Mr. Allen were appointed "to examine the Boston letter to the selectmen." This was the circular sent out in accordance with the vote of a large meeting held at Faneuil Hall, on the 28th of the previous October, to consider the recently-passed Townsend Revenue Acts. It proposed an agreement to discontinue the importation, and, except in cases of absolute necessity, the consumption, of British goods, and to encourage American industry, economy, and manufactures. The Pittsfield committee was politically divided, and there was an excellent prospect for two reports and excited action; but it is simply recorded, that the article in the warrant, "to receive the report of the committee," was dismissed.

The other vote was in the following December; and merely, in obedience to an act of the General Court, appropriated £12 for a town-stock of ammunition, to be placed in charge of Deacon Crofoot.

A few significant papers of 1774 — "kept on file, but not recorded" — remain in the town-archives, and indicate, that, until the summer of that year, the Tories, by professing to "be as averse as any of the patriots in America to taxation without their own voluntary consent," maintained their ascendency. The balance of power was held by those who, afterwards driven by the continued encroachment of Great Britain into the Whig ranks, — where they belonged, — as yet shrank from co-operation with their radical brethren, and, in preference to so dangerous alliance, acted with the party of professions. Timid, but dreading political rather than personal danger, hoping against hope, reasoning against reason, they clung to their trust in the old English love of justice and liberty; and, patiently waiting until that mythical existence should manifest itself, shuddered more convulsively over the slightest exhibition of manly spirit in Massachusetts than at the most atrocious usurpations of king and parliament. And yet they were patriots at heart, and, when driven to the wall, often brave and good ones. It was in assuming their position, not in defending it, that they lacked courage.

The nature of the association of the conservative Whigs with the Tories is shown in the instructions which the town gave its representative in the matter of the Boston Tea-Party;[1] although the illustration is not altogether perfect, as many firm Whigs in the interior towns — and, outside the clubs, in Boston as well — did not fully comprehend the necessity for a measure which it was so easy for the ill-disposed to stigmatize as a riot.

The paper is, however, interesting, and notwithstanding its legal phraseology, which is due to the authorship of Woodbridge Little, is readable.

The town, having adopted the report, seems to have conceived a suspicion that it might at some time, if spread upon the records, become the subject of unfriendly criticism; and so resolved that it should "be placed on file and not recorded," — a proceeding which marks the sensitiveness of the public mind at this juncture, as, without any vote to that end, it had never been the practice to record similar documents. It is singular that no sharp-eyed inspector of the archives ever marked it "to be burned," — a mode in which many a less obnoxious witness of changed opinions was, doubtless, put out of the way.

INSTRUCTIONS OF THE TOWN OF PITTSFIELD TO ITS REPRESENTATIVE REGARDING THE DESTRUCTION OF TEA IN BOSTON HARBOR, Dec. 16, 1773.

The inhabitants of the town of Pittsfield being alarmed at the extraordinary conduct of a number of disguised persons who, on the evening follow-

[1] It was an old custom of towns, upon the choice of a representative, or whenever new and important legislative questions arose, to give him instructions, drafted by a committee (to whose selection much care was given), and adopted by the voters. These instructions had no binding effect, but, of course, carried great weight with the representative, who was generally, but far from invariably, governed by them. The practice was a relic of times when the legislative function was exercised by the whole body of the freemen, and suggests the reluctance of the people wholly to delegate it.

ing the sixteenth day of December last, entered on board the ships commanded by Captains Hall, Bruce, and Coffin, lying in the harbor of Boston, then and there breaking up and destroying three hundred and forty-two chests of tea belonging to the Honorable East India Company, a number of the said inhabitants petitioned the selectmen of said town that a meeting of the freeholders and other inhabitants of said town might be called, which was accordingly done; and, at a meeting holden on the tenth day of January last, the said town appointed a committee of five persons to prepare instructions for their representative relative to said conduct, and adjourned said meeting to the twentieth day of said month; at which time the said committee reported as follows, viz.: —

That the said conduct was unnecessary and highly unwarrantable, every way tending to the subversion of all good order and of the Constitution, as we determine that the king himself hath two superiors; to wit, his heavenly King, and his own laws: nor was there ever a more flagrant instance that even the perpetrators of the fact viewed themselves as enterprising an act in itself unlawful and unjustifiable; otherwise they would not have disguised themselves, or have attempted it in the night.

At the same time, we are as averse as any of the patriots in America to being subjected to a tax without our own free and voluntary consent, and shall, we trust, always abide by that principle. And, was there not an alternative between the destruction of said tea and the people's being saddled with the payment of the duty thereon, we should not have the like reason to complain; but, as far as we live in the country, judge otherwise.

And as great damage hath been sustained by the owners of said tea in the destruction thereof, and as they will doubtless seek some compensation therefor, and as the inhabitants of this Province have heretofore been obliged to pay large sums of money by reason of the like unjustifiable conduct and proceedings of individuals not duly authorized thereto, —

We do therefore enjoin it upon you, that, by all prudent ways and means, you manifest the abhorrence and detestation which your constituents have of the said extraordinary and illegal transaction, as also of all the other public transactions which have been leading to, or in any degree countenancing, the same; and especially that you do not directly or indirectly consent to any proposals which may be made, or any measures which may be taken, to render your constituents chargeable to any payment or satisfaction which may be required to be made to the owners of said tea, as we have determined, at all events, never to pay or advance one farthing thereto; and, if your assistance is called for, that you exert yourself to the utmost of your power to bring the persons connected in the destruction of said tea, and other such-like offenders, to condign punishment; and it is the expectation of this town, that you strictly adhere to these, their instructions, as you value their regard or resentment.

WILLIAM WILLIAMS.
WOODBRIDGE LITTLE.
DAVID BUSH.
ELI ROOT.
JNO. BROWN.

Committee.

To Capt. CHARLES GOODRICH.

Jan. 19, 1774.

CHAPTER X.

RESISTANCE TO PARLIAMENTARY AGGRESSION.

[MARCH – OCTOBER, 1774.]

Boston Port-Bill and Regulating Acts. — First Revolutionary Town Action of Pittsfield. — Committee of Correspondence appointed. — The League and Covenant adopted. — Pittsfield contributes in Aid of the Sufferers by the Port-Bill. — Obstruction of the King's Court. — Seth Pomeroy. — Oliver Wendell.

THE spring of 1774 brought events which everywhere consolidated the Whigs, and made broad the dividing lines between those who would defend, and those ready to surrender, the liberties of the Province.

The act of Parliament which soon became infamous as "The Boston Port-bill" — excluding commerce from the harbor of that town, and removing the seat of government to Salem — received the royal assent on the 31st of March, and was printed in the Boston newspapers of May 10.

The acts "for the better regulating the government of the Province of Massachusetts Bay," and "for the impartial administration of justice" in the same, followed closely, and wrought an entire abrogation of the charter in all those particulars by which it afforded protection to civil or personal liberty.

Under the new laws, councillors created by royal mandamus, and the superior judges appointed by his Majesty's governor, held office during the king's pleasure. All other officers, judicial, executive, and military, were appointed by the governor, independently of the Council, and — except the sheriffs, who could only be displaced with consent of the Council — were removable by the same sole authority. The governor's appointing power, — a grievous fountain of corruption, even with the checks provided by William's charter, — now concentrated with the new right of removal in the unchecked control of the king and his automatic representative, was fearfully augmented.

Town-meetings, permitted to be held for the election of municipal officers and representatives, were strictly confined in their functions to the bare casting of the necessary ballots; and special meetings were allowed only with license first had of the governor, designating what matters alone they might consider. The selection of jurors — previously made, as now, by the selectmen, with the ratification of the towns — was given to the king's sheriffs. Acts, passed almost simultaneously with the others, provided for quartering troops in America, and for the transportation to England for trial of persons charged, like the soldiers implicated in the Boston massacre, with murders committed in the support of the royal authority. The enactment of despotism was complete. In the new system of government, hardly a vestige remained of those safeguards, which, in the Colonies even more absolutely than in Great Britain, were essential to the preservation of liberty. Practically, nothing whatever in the perverted Constitution interposed between the people and the sovereign's will: for the House of Representatives, mighty as it proved by its advice, was, in its legislative capacity, reduced to utter impotence by the governor's inexhaustible prerogative of prorogation and dissolution; by the unqualified veto which he, as well as the puppet Council, might exercise upon all its acts; and by the independence of its appropriations, enjoyed by the governor and judges, who, by another still recent innovation, received their salaries directly from the Crown.

Thus two departments of the Provincial Government — the judicial and the executive, including the council and the military — were the mere registrars and instruments of the king's will; while the third, if it consented to assume the *rôle* to which it had been assigned, was more insignificant for good than either.

Heretofore the people of the Colonies had been alarmed by measures of Parliament, which, not otherwise oppressive, were taken in violation of their privileges, either under the charter or as English subjects. They had detected, in the occasional exercise of powers which infringed upon colonial rights, the insidious design of overthrowing them altogether. Now the very citadel of all right was attacked, not by veiled advances, nor by sapping hidden foundations, but by bold and crushing assaults upon its most jealously-guarded defences.

Thanks to the prescient leadership which had kept Massachusetts alive to the impending danger, she was ready to meet it when it came. The excitement, with the news of the obnoxious acts of Parliament, spread inward from the capital, and everywhere roused the same spirit of indignation and determined resistance. In every direction, nothing was heard of but meetings and patriotic resolutions. May 12, — two days after the publication of the Port-bill, — the delegates of eight neighboring towns, summoned by the Boston committee, met at the selectmen's room in Faneuil Hall, and adopted spirited measures to unite the colonies in defence of the common liberties; [1] and it was, perhaps, to a missive sent out by this little assemblage, that the petition for the first Pittsfield town-meeting held in this emergency alludes. The petition, however, was dated on the 24th of June; and, early in that month, rough drafts of the regulating acts, and news of their probable passage, were received by the Boston committee, and dispersed over the country with so good effect, that, on the 20th, "The Boston Gazette" was able to pronounce "the aspect of affairs highly favorable to American liberties" . . . "the whole continent seeming inspired by one soul, and that a rigorous and determined one." [2] It was due partly to its remoteness from the capital, and partly, doubtless, to the still potent Tory influence, that Pittsfield manifested a dilatory spirit that never again appeared in her patriotic councils. But, on the 24th, a petition was presented to the selectmen, requesting them to convene a town-meeting, "to act and do what the town think proper respecting the circular letter sent out by the town of Boston and other towns in this Province; and such other matters as the town shall think proper in regard to the invaded liberties and privileges of this country."

This petition was signed by James Easton, John Strong, Ezekiel Root, Oliver Root, Timothy Childs, John Brown, Matthew Wright, David Noble, Daniel Weller, and James Noble; and the selectmen to whom it was addressed were David Bush, William Francis, Dan Cadwell, Eli Root, and Israel Dickinson. The warrant for a town-meeting on Thursday, the 30th of June, was signed by all the selectmen except Cadwell; [3] and it was accordingly held, Josiah Wright presiding as moderator.

[1] Frothingham's Life of Warren, p. 301.

[2] Frothingham's Warren, p. 333.

[3] David Bush had scruples as to taking up arms against the king, to whom he had, as a militia captain, sworn allegiance; but he acted, generally, with the

The first action taken was to appoint "a standing committee to correspond with the correspondent committees of this and other Provinces;" and it was thus constituted: Rev. Thomas Allen, Deacon James Easton, Mr. John Brown, Deacon Josiah Wright, Mr. John Strong, Capt. David Bush, Lieut. David Noble.

The meeting then adopted the "Worcester Covenant," — the most stringent form of the solemn league and covenant, by which individuals bound themselves, and towns their citizens, not to purchase or use any goods, the production of Great Britain or her West-Indian Colonies, or which had been imported through her companies trading to the East; and, generally, agreed to act together in resisting the aggressions of the mother country. Dea. James Easton, John Brown, and John Strong were chosen delegates to a county congress,[1] to be held at Stockbridge, on the sixth of July; and the meeting adjourned to the 11th, to await their action, but not without first resolving to keep the 14th as a day of solemn fasting and prayer.

Col. John Ashley of Sheffield presided in the congress at Stockbridge; and Theodore Sedgwick, then a young lawyer of the same town, was clerk.

Thomas Williams of Stockbridge, Peter Curtis of Lanesborough, John Brown of Pittsfield, Mark Hopkins of Great Barrington, and Theodore Sedgwick, were appointed to consider the obnoxious acts of Parliament, and "report their sense of them." Whatever their report was, — and it was certainly patriotic, — it was unanimously adopted.

Whigs, and once or twice took the field, in cases of alarm. Dan Cadwell was a loyalist of the better sort, and seems not to have lost the esteem of the people, who elected him to town-offices, and once to the Committee of Safety, during the war. The case of Ezekiel Root is a singular one. He was a very pronounced Tory in his conversation, and even went so far as to name his children for the British commanders; but all his recorded *acts* are on the Whig side, as in signing the above petition, in serving on the Committee of Safety, and in volunteering for Bennington and other fields. He was often elected to important town-offices, and once at least by the extreme radicals to represent them in county congress. Indeed, although both Mr. Cadwell and Capt. Root were sometimes disciplined for a too loud expression of their Toryism, — to the offence of sensitively patriotic ears, — it seems to have been regarded by the community as the eccentricity of worthy men, which would never stand seriously in the way of their duty. They certainly never lost the good will of a people who were not famed for charity towards political opponents.

[1] Assemblies of town delegates were then styled indifferently congresses, conventions, or committees.

The following delegates were appointed to draft "an agreement to be recommended to the towns of the county for the non-consumption of British manufactures:" Timothy Edwards, Esq., of Stockbridge, Dr. William Whiting of Great Barrington, Dr. Lemuel Barnard of Sheffield, Dr. Erastus Sergeant of Stockbridge, and Deacon James Easton. And they reported the subjoined league and covenant, which was unanimously adopted, "paragraph by paragraph."

LEAGUE AND COVENANT.

WHEREAS the Parliament of Great Britain have, of late, undertaken to give and grant away our money without our knowledge or consent; and, in order to compel us to a servile submission to the above measures, have proceeded to block up the harbor of Boston; also have, or are about to vacate the charter, and repeal certain laws of this Province heretofore enacted by the General Court and confirmed to us by the King and his predecessors: therefore, as a means to obtain a speedy redress of the above grievances, *we do solemnly and in good faith covenant and engage with each other:* —

1st, That we will not import, purchase, or consume, or suffer any person for, by, or under us, to import, purchase, or consume, in any manner whatever, any goods, wares, or manufactures which shall arrive in America from Great Britain from and after the first day of October next, or such other time as shall be agreed upon by the American Congress; nor any goods which shall be ordered from thence from and after this day until our charter and constitutional rights shall be restored, or until it shall be determined by the major part of our brethren in this and the neighboring Colonies, that a non-importation or non-consumption agreement will not have a tendency to effect the desired end, and until it shall be apparent that a non-importation or non-consumption agreement will not be entered into by the majority of this and the neighboring Colonies — except such articles as the said General Congress of North America shall advise to import and consume.

2d, We do further covenant and agree, that we will observe the most strict obedience to all constitutional laws and authority, and will at all times exert ourselves to the utmost for the discouragement of all licentiousness, and suppressing all disorderly mobs and riots.

3d, We will exert ourselves, as far as in us lies, in promoting peace, love, and unanimity among each other; and, for that end, we engage to avoid all unnecessary lawsuits whatever.

4th, As a strict and proper adherence to the non-importation and non-consumption agreement will, if not seasonably provided against, involve us in many difficulties and inconveniences, *we do promise and agree*, that we will take the most prudent care for the raising of sheep, and for the manufacturing all such cloths as shall be most useful and necessary; and also for the raising of flax, and the manufacturing of linen; further, that we will by every prudent method endeavor to guard against all those inconveniences which might otherwise arise from the foregoing agreement.

5th, That if any person shall refuse to sign this, or a similar covenant, or, after having signed it, shall not adhere to the real intent and meaning thereof, he or they shall be treated by us with all the neglect they shall justly deserve, particularly by omitting all commercial dealings with them.

6th, That if this, or a similar covenant, shall, after the first day of August next, be offered to any trader or shop-keeper in this county, and he or they shall refuse to sign the same for the space of forty-eight hours, that we will from thenceforth purchase no article of British manufacture or East-India goods from him or them until such time as he or they shall sign this or a similar covenant.

It was further resolved that the delegates should severally recommend the distressed circumstances of the poor of Charlestown and Boston to the charity of their constituents, and that their contributions should be "remitted in the fall in fat cattle."

Pittsfield, at its adjourned meeting, voted that "the county covenant should be esteemed similar to the Worcester."

The record of its donations "in fat cattle" is not preserved; but in the town-archives is the following receipt: —

BOSTON, Nov. 30, 1774.

Received from the town of Pittsfield, by the hand of James Easton (in cash) a donation of six pounds, twelve shillings, lawful money, for the relief and support of the poor sufferers in the town of Boston, by means of the Boston Port-bill.

By order and in behalf of the Committee of Donations.

£6, 12, 0. ALEX. HOGSDEN, *Clerk*.[1]

The meeting of the 11th had a peculiar termination; being "dissolved, except in reference to the general Congress," but, as to that, adjourned to the third Monday in October. The first Continental Congress was to meet on the first of September; and the people, looking eagerly to its wisdom for guidance, feared that in the interval the new laws would take effect to prevent the calling of a new meeting to consider its advice. The omnipotence of

[1] This donation was also acknowledged in "The Boston Gazette," Dec. 5, and with it a private contribution of twelve shillings from Deacon Easton.

Parliament was fairly matched by the vitality of an adjourned town-meeting. That any thing, calling itself law, could intervene to prevent their re-assembling with unimpaired powers under a fair and regular adjournment, was beyond the comprehension of New-England townsmen.

But events crowded responsibilities upon Massachusetts patriots that would not wait the advice of Continental wisdom. The Regulating Act, and that "for the more impartial administration of justice," — bitterly nick-named "The Murder Act," — were, early in August, known to have received the royal signature, and their promulgation was daily expected.[1]

Popular resistance to the organization of the courts under the new acts was threatened in many counties. Worcester was ablaze; and "a flame sprang up at the extremity of the Province" which Gov. Gage attributed to the machinations of the Boston committee, and especially to a letter, a copy of which fell into his hands. "The popular rage," wrote his Excellency immediately after the events we are about to relate, "is very high in Berkshire, and makes its way rapidly to the rest."[2]

"And all," thought the bewildered governor, "from that pestilent Boston clique"! As though the spark were more essential to the flame than the fuel, or kindled that which was not prepared for it.

It was true, however, that the patriotic rage of Berkshire was fed by the advice and appeals sent abroad by the same men who, at Boston, were troublesome to Gage and his master. It is true, too, that the people "at the extremity of the Province," intending to act in co-operation with their brethren at the east, placed themselves, as far as it was necessary for that purpose, under the same great and wise leadership. At this particular juncture, we have their own authority for saying that they "acted in conformity with the advice of the wisest men in the Colony."[3] And it adds to, rather than diminishes, the glory of the Berkshire fathers, that, when unity was essential to success, the step taken by them, in advance of the other counties, was part of the great plan by which zeal tempered with discretion made up the issues of the Revolution.

The first County Court to be held in the Province, after the

[1] They were officially received by Gov. Gage on the 6th, but, for prudential reasons, not immediately proclaimed.

[2] Letter to the Earl of Dartmouth, Am. Ar., Ser. 4, vol. i. p. 742.

[3] County memorial drafted by Rev. Mr. Allen.

reception of the acts of Parliament for perverting the charter, was that appointed for the third Tuesday in August, at Great Barrington; and a county convention, held at Pittsfield on the fourth of that month, probably took measures for its obstruction.

Whatever the recommendations of the convention were, the town of Pittsfield, being called together for that purpose on the 15th, promptly accepted them; and then proceeded to choose Capt. Charles Goodrich, William Francis, and the moderator, Deacon Josiah Wright, — three of the most stout-hearted, as well as the most substantial citizens, — "to prefer a petition to the Honorable Court not to transact any business the present term."

Dr. Tim. Childs and Mr. John Strong were appointed to draw up the petition; and soon reported the following, which was adopted.

To the Honorable His Majesty's Justices of the Inferior Court of Common Pleas for the County of Berkshire: The Petition of the Inhabitants of the Town of Pittsfield, assembled in Town-meeting on Monday the fifteenth day of August, 1774: —

Humbly Sheweth,

That whereas two late acts of the British Parliament for superseding the charter of this Province, and vacating some of the principles and invaluable privileges and franchises therein contained, have passed the royal assent, and have been published in the Boston paper, that our obedience be yielded to them.

We view it of the greatest importance to the well-being of this Province, that the people of it utterly refuse the least submission to the said acts, and on no consideration to yield obedience to them; or directly or indirectly to countenance the taking place of those acts amongst us, but resist them to the last extremity.

In order in the safest manner to avoid this threatening calamity, it is, in our opinion, highly necessary that no business be transacted in the law, but that the courts of justice immediately cease, and the people of this Province fall into a state of nature until our grievances are fully redressed by a final repeal of these injurious, oppressive, and unconstitutional acts. We have the pleasure to find that this is the sentiment of the greater part of the people of this Province; and we are persuaded that no man that only understands the state of our public affairs, who has business at the approaching term, but will advise and consent to the same, and willingly undergo personal inconvenience for the public good. We do therefore remonstrate against the holding any courts in this county until those acts shall be repealed; and we hope that your honors will not be of a different opinion from the good people in this county, Our reasons for holding no courts in the present situation of affairs, are as follows: —

Some reasons why our Inferior Court cannot be held in its ancient form, and agreeable to charter, now the new acts are published: —

1st. If they are now held in the ancient form, this will be in direct violation of those laws, and in defiance of them.

2d. Whatever business shall be transacted in the ancient form, now those laws are in force, will be illegal, and liable afterwards to be wholly set aside.

3d. The honorable judges will expose themselves, by not submitting to the new acts, by transacting business in the old form, or agreeable to our charter, to an immediate loss of their commissions.

4th. It will be much greater contempt of those laws to transact business in the ancient form, or agreeable to our charter, than to do none at all.

5th. This course of procedure will tend to bring matters to a more unhappy crisis, which we would choose by all means to avoid, than to neglect to do any business.

6th. The new acts will insensibly steal in upon us under pretence of doing business after the ancient Constitution: therefore, as soon as the new acts are in whole or in part in force, as they now are, no court ought to be held in the ancient form.

Our reasons why our Inferior Courts ought not to be held at the approaching term are as follows: —

1st. We have undoubted intelligence from York and Boston that the said acts have passed the royal assent.

2d. We also are informed of their arrival in Boston.

3d. It is highly probable they are published in form by the governor by this present time in order that our obedience be rendered to them.

4th. We ought to bear the most early testimony against those acts, and set a good example for the other part of the Province to copy after.

5th. Some parts of those acts have taken place already, — that part of which dissolves the council by whose advice the former commissions were granted out; and that part of which empowers the governor to grant new commissions without advice of the council; and also that which respects town-meetings. For these and other reasons, it plainly appears to be of dangerous consequences to do any business in the law till the repeal of those acts, as would most certainly imply some degree of submission to them, the least appearance of which ought not to be admitted.

The honor of the Court has good grounds to neglect to do business in the law, and the people just occasion to petition for it, and insist upon it without admitting a refusal."

A somewhat larger deputation than the action of the town contemplated waited upon the Court. At the time appointed for it to sit, about fifteen hundred men assembled, unarmed, at Great Barrington, and "filled the Court House, and the avenues to the seats of justice, so full that no passage could be found for the judges." "The sheriff commanded the people to make way for the Court; but they gave him to understand, that they knew no Court, or any other establishment than the ancient laws and customs of the country; and to none other would they give way on any terms."[1]

They were assured that the new acts had not arrived, and that, consequently, business would proceed in the usual manner: but everybody knew that the judges' commissions were already revocable at the governor's pleasure; and that the aggressive laws — likely to reach Great Barrington at any moment — might be proclaimed as soon as the Court was well benched. The assemblage therefore insisting that the judges should forthwith quit the town, they complied, lest worse might befall them;[2] and no Court ever again attempted to sit, under royal commission, in Berkshire. The last which actually transacted business in the king's name was the May term at Great Barrington in 1774.

About three hundred of the assembled people were from Litchfield County, Conn.; and these, upon their return, took with them David Ingersol, Esq., a particularly obnoxious Great-Barrington Tory, and a magistrate of the General Sessions. For this they were arraigned by a Connecticut sheriff before "the Honorable Eliphalet Dyer, Esq., who, with great solemnity and severity, reprimanded the delinquents," and bound them over to the court above; by which their case was continued until the offenders and their prosecutors changed places. David Ingersol, Esq., went, the next fall, to England as a refugee. Col. Williams of Pittsfield was the chief-justice of the obstructed Court of Common Pleas; and, although he was fond enough of his place, was not likely to very strenuously resist the will of the people, energetically expressed. Major Stoddard, a man of a different stamp, was a magistrate of the General Sessions: but any opposition to so determined a multitude as surrounded the Court House, further than a manly remonstrance, would have been folly; and even that involved greater risk than it was worth, unless the whole

[1] Massachusetts Gazette and Newsletter, Sept. 1, 1774.

[2] Great-Barrington Letter, Sept. 18, 1774.

magistracy had joined it, as there was no likelihood of their doing.

The proceedings against the perverted courts worked grandly for the patriotic cause. Everywhere throughout Berkshire the Revolutionary feeling was roused and united in action as it could have been in no other way so effectually. The great object of committing the western frontier of the Province, devotedly and enthusiastically, to the cause of liberty was at once and perfectly accomplished, in spite of obstacles which would have interposed a dangerous delay to any less vehement advance. The beneficial effects of the achievement were manifest from the very opening of the war to its close.

Elsewhere the patriotic spirit was braced with new vigor, as the news spread that the usurpations of Parliament had, on the first suspicion of an attempt to enforce them, met a bold, and, for the time at least, successful resistance. The example proved contagious, and was held up for imitation even in Boston.[1] At Springfield, at the assembling of the courts on the 30th of August, the Justices, with Israel Williams, the chief of the Tories, at their head, in the presence of three thousand persons, "very willingly" signed a solemn agreement not to accept or exercise any office or commission "under or by virtue of, or in any degree derived from, any authority pretended or attempted to be given by the late acts of Parliament." Everywhere, where the courts were not surrounded by British troops, the story was the same. The counties which had stood ready to set the example, if the privilege had fallen to them, were no less prompt to follow it when set by the youngest of their sisterhood. In Suffolk, where the courts sat under the protection of the soldiery, the jurors found means hardly less effectual, and even more annoying, to thwart the "taking place" of the dangerous innovations. The movement initiated in Berkshire spread, in some form, throughout the Province; and although it can by no means be claimed that this initiation and that adoption of the movement were strictly cause and effect, the relation of the one to the other was sufficiently close to justify the traditional county pride in "the first obstruction of King George's Courts."

The Pittsfield records of town-meetings, as transcribed after

[1] Frothingham's Siege of Boston, p. 10.

the erasures of the inspecting committees, afford no intimation of any opposition to the Revolutionary measures which prevailed; but a few minutes, chance-preserved in the archives, show that the struggle was, nevertheless, violent, and the debates which arose personal and acrimonious. The most suggestive of these papers is one containing the following resolutions, which were "passed in full," probably at the meeting of the 15th of August: —

"Whereas [the name of Col. Wm. Williams was here inserted but erased] Major Israel Stoddard, and Woodbridge Little, Esq., have exhibited several charges against the Rev. Thomas Allen, thereby endeavoring to injure his reputation, in respect to what he said and did in a late town-meeting, in defence of the rights and liberties of the people; wherein they charge the said Thomas with rebellion, treason, and sedition, and cast many other infamous aspersions, tending to endanger not only the reputation, but the life of the said Thomas, —

Voted, That all the foregoing charges are groundless, false, and scandalous; and that the said Thomas is justifiable in all things wherein he hath been charged with the crimes aforesaid; and that he hath merited the thanks of this town in every thing wherein he hath undertaken to defend the rights and privileges of the people in this Province, and particularly in his observations and animadversions on the Worcester Covenant."

This paper is indorsed "To Col. Williams and others, — to lie on file:" from which it may be inferred that the erasure of Col. Williams's name from the resolutions was made subsequently to their passage.

Some months later, in November, the town, through its clerk, Israel Dickinson, addressed a letter to Rev. Mr. Collins, the loyalist minister of Lanesborough, stating that, it having been suggested in public town-meeting that he had at divers times, when in Pittsfield, "censured and disapproved their reverend pastor, Mr. Allen, in regard to his conduct in some public matters of late," which, whatever Mr. Collins's intention may have been, seemed to them to have a tendency to promote, rather than settle, the differences arising therefrom, they requested him to desist from that sort of comment in the future.

Mr. Collins replied with spirit, denying that he had done more than give it as his opinion, and his reasons for it, "that it would be well for gospel ministers, in their public discourses, to avoid entering very far into a consideration of state policy;" and he hoped the town of Pittsfield would not be offended if he held himself at liberty to defend that proposition whenever occasion arose. The belief in the intimate relations between civil and religious liberty, which, in Mr. Allen's opinion, identified the safety of the one with the jealous defence of the other, has already been stated; and the papers above quoted are introduced merely to show the influence attributed to the first pastor of the town in moulding its patriotic sentiment and action, as well as the esteem in which he was held by his associates of the popular party.

What was the exact nature and amount of the counsel and inspiration which the Pittsfield Whigs received from the East is uncertain; but, after the occurrences of August, influences from abroad were more needed to restrain than to incite.

In addition to Mr. Allen's large official correspondence with the committees of other towns in Massachusetts as well as the neighboring colonies, his interchange of letters was frequent with his personal friends, and particularly with Major Hawley and Col. Seth Pomeroy of Northampton.[1] John Brown also, after the meeting of the Provincial Congress, was in confidential communication with Warren, Sam. Adams, and others of like position.

Oliver Wendell, son of Col. Jacob, the early proprietor of Poontoosuck, although a very young man, attaining his majority about this time, was one of the most glowing and impetuous of the Sons of Liberty, and a prominent member of the Committee of Safety in Boston. His family, who still retained considerable estate in Pittsfield, were liked by the people for their genial, free-hearted, ungrasping disposition; and it would have been singular if the young and active committeeman had not turned his popularity to account in winning support to the cause which he had at heart. The evidence that he did so, although strong, is, however, only traditional.[2]

[1] Col. Seth Pomeroy, grandfather of the late Lemuel Pomeroy of Pittsfield, was a gallant officer in the last French and Indian War, and, early in the troubles with Great Britain, took rank with the foremost of the patriots. He was one of the four brigadiers appointed by the first Provincial Congress, of which he was an influential member; but declined that rank, and fought at Bunker Hill — like Warren, who had been voted a similar commission — as a volunteer. He afterwards served as colonel until 1777, when he died in command of the post at Peekskill. "A good friend of his country," is the epitaph that Mr. Allen inscribed in his pocket diary upon receiving the news of his friend's death.

[2] Among the traditions in this connection is one, that Oliver Wendell, then owning the farm on Wendell Street where his grandson, Oliver Wendell Holmes,

afterwards built his villa, leased it to a tenant for a moderate rent, on condition that if Gen. Gage should, as he threatened, make Boston too hot for men of the Wendell stamp, the premises should at once be surrendered, with the furniture, standing crops, etc. The tradition is probably not accurate in all its particulars; and a more consistent version of it would be, that Mr. Wendell placed a tenant in his farmhouse, who would receive him in the anticipated emergency: for it is averred with great positiveness, that, from the arrangement then made, arose the custom in the Wendell family of an annual summer pilgrimage to Pittsfield.

Some of the older inhabitants of the place still remember the visits of Judge Wendell, who, whatever he may have done before, for many years after the Revolution exercised a potent social and political influence in Berkshire, as will appear in the consideration of that era. His epicurean tastes excited the admiration of his rural neighbors; but his keen relish for the country luxuries, and the simple although skilful cuisine of good Mrs. Backus, who marshalled the affairs of the Judge's farmhouse, showed an unperverted palate. His nice sense, however, revolted at the barbarism of country taverns, where fowls were served up before the life had been an hour out of their bodies. And so, when he set out upon his leisurely journeys of four or five days between Boston and Pittsfield, a freshly-killed chicken was placed under the seat of his carriage; which, at the end of twenty-four hours, was delivered to the cook of the wayside inn, and another substituted to undergo a like seasoning. A wholesome good liver was Judge Oliver Wendell.

CHAPTER XI.

A SEASON OF PREPARATION.

[SEPTEMBER, 1774–MAY, 1775.]

John Brown elected to the Provincial Congress.—Pittsfield adopts Congressional Advice.—Adopts the Articles of Association.—Revolutionary Committees.—Pittsfield Militia.—Generous Patriotism of Capt. Noble.—The Minute-Men.—Spinning-Matches and Clothing-Bees.—News of Lexington Fight.—March of the Minute-Men.—Changes in Capt. Noble's Company.—Proceedings against the Tories.—Patriotic Labors of Rev. Mr. Allen.

MASSACHUSETTS, in the fall and winter of 1774–5, was busy with preparation for the impending conflict. Gov. Gage issued his precept for a General Court, to be held at Salem on the 5th of October. The committee of Worcester suggested an assembly of the towns, by their delegates, in Provincial Congress; and the Suffolk Convention fixed upon Concord as the place, and the 11th of October as the time, for the meeting.

Pittsfield, like many other places, refused to send a representative to Salem; but chose John Brown delegate to the congress, and appointed, as committee of instruction, Capt. Charles Goodrich, Deacon Josiah Wright, Dr. Timothy Childs, Deacon James Easton, and Lieut. Eli Root.

Gage, angered and alarmed at the spirited attitude of the towns, revoked his precept of assembly, and announced that he would not meet the representatives. Ninety of them were, however, present in Salem at the appointed time; and having, with studious regard to etiquette, waited all that day for his Excellency to appear, resolved themselves into a Provincial Congress, "to be joined by such other persons as had been, or should be, appointed for that purpose, to take into consideration the dangerous and alarming situation of public affairs in the Province, and to consult upon measures to promote the true interest of his Majesty, and the peace, welfare, and prosperity of the Province."

After a consultation of two days, the congress issued an address, advising its constituents of the "unconstitutional, unjust, disrespectful, and hostile conduct," by which the governor had deprived the Province of its accustomed legislature; and adjourned to merge itself in the assembly, which was, by the will of the people, convened at Concord on the following Tuesday.

In the latter body, John Brown took his seat as representative from Pittsfield. It did not assume to enact laws: but its advice, given to towns, committees, and the people at large, was respected as statutes rarely are; and no town responded to these counsels with more zeal and promptitude than Pittsfield.

Thus the congress having advised that the Province tax should be paid over, not to Harrison Gray, the governor's treasurer, but to Henry Gardener, whom it elected receiver-general, Pittsfield, at its next meeting, so instructed its collectors; and in the spring, some of the loyalists disputing Mr. Gardener's warrant, the town directed its officers, if any man refused to pay his rates, to apply for aid to the Committee of Inspection, who had a happy knack of enforcing congressional advice.

The Continental Congress was treated with no less deference than the Provincial; and, Dec. 5, the town voted "to adopt the Continental resolutions in full, and particularly the 11th article." These were the famous Resolutions of Association, signed by the delegates in Congress, Oct. 20, 1774: by which, in a series of fourteen articles, they bound themselves and their constituents not to import any of the productions of Great Britain or her dependencies after the 1st of the following December, not to export to those quarters after the 10th of September; to entirely discontinue and discountenance the slave-trade; "to encourage frugality, economy, and industry, and promote American agriculture, arts, and manufactures, especially that of wool;" to discourage every species of extravagance and dissipation, especially horse-racing, gaming, cock-fighting, and play-going; to wear no mourning on the death of a friend, "more than a black ribbon on the arm or hat for a gentleman, and a black ribbon and necklace for a lady," and to give no more gloves and scarfs at funerals. Finally the "Associators" bound themselves not to take advantage of the scarcity produced by non-importation to raise prices. Some of the articles of agreement were devoted to the means of enforcing the others; and the 11th, which Pittsfield specially adopted, provided that a committee should be appointed in every town, county, and colony, whose duty it should be "to observe the conduct of all persons within its precinct concerning the Association;" and if any delinquency was proved to the satisfaction of a majority of its members, "to publish the name of the offender in 'The Gazette,'—to the end that all such foes to the rights of British America might be publicly known, and universally contemned as the enemies of American liberty; and that all patriots might thenceforth break off all intercourse with him or her."

The persons chosen to compose this formidable committee in Pittsfield were, Eli Root, Timothy Childs, Charles Goodrich, Dan Cadwell, Josiah Wright, James D. Colt, and Stephen Crofoot. This was the Committee of Inspection, and as yet distinct from that of Correspondence; to which latter Messrs. Goodrich, Childs, Root, and William Francis were added at the next meeting. In addition to these two bodies, there was a committee appointed upon the suppression of the courts, "to sit as arbitrators, to regulate disturbances and quarrels, and to take the Province law for their guide." This consisted of Deacon Wright, William Francis, Lieut. Root. Capt. Bush, Capt. Israel Dickinson, Ensign John Brown, and Capt. Goodrich.

The Pittsfield militia—probably under the advice of the Central Committee of Safety—had early exchanged its organization under commanders appointed by the governor, for one under officers of its own choice. How this was effected, or at what time, does not appear. But on the 1st of September, Gov. Gage having sent out a detachment to remove to Boston the Provincial military stores deposited at Charlestown, a report arose during the excitement which ensued, that the British were firing upon the former town. The alarm—which is supposed to have been a feint of the patriot leaders to try the spirit of the people—spread with marvellous rapidity; and it was estimated that forty thousand armed men were the next morning on their march to defend or avenge their brethren. The alarm, having served its purpose, was checked, and the militia returned to their homes.

In this affair a company of minute-men, commanded by Capt. David Noble and Lieut. James Easton, went from Pittsfield to

Westfield; and the town voted to each private and non-commissioned officer two pounds "for himself and horse." The captain and lieutenant received six pounds apiece for their services, but were refused extra compensation for continuing their trip to Boston.

What the organization of the militia was at this time is not known; but the town-records are significant of the readiness which the leaders of Whig sentiment manifested to defend with the sword the principles which they had advocated on the old meeting-house rostrum. Thus, in addition to the two gallant officers named, we find, before the close of September, Deacon Wright, Israel Dickinson, and James D. Colt, captains; Eli Root, a lieutenant; and John Brown, — commencing at the lower round of the ladder of promotion, with Dr. Timothy Childs, — an ensign.

In the latter part of October, the Provincial Congress took measures to impart vigor to the militia; and, among other recommendations, advised companies which had not completed their organization to do so at once, and that the captains and subalterns then forthwith choose field-officers.

Under this advice, James Easton — the deacon of our previous story — became colonel of the Berkshire militia; Col. Williams's royal commission being set aside for one with a seal much less exquisitely cut. At the same time, two regiments of minute-men were put in effective readiness to take the field on the most sudden alarm, — one in the northern and middle section of the county, under Col. John Patterson of Lenox; the other in the south, under Col. John Fellows of Sheffield: both the commanders being members of the Provincial Congress, and afterwards reputable brigadiers.

Capt. Noble's company of Pittsfield and Richmond men, in Col. Patterson's regiment, continued to increase in numbers and discipline; and, before it was called into service, numbered fifty-one men from the former town, twenty-one from the latter, all well drilled, armed, and equipped. Pittsfield voted in January to pay each man from that town who enlisted in this "Piquet" company one shilling and sixpence a day; "he equipping and furnishing himself with proper and sufficient arms and accoutrements fit for war, and standing ready at a minute's warning to march and oppose the enemies of the country if called thereto." Every minute-man was required to appear and exercise for three hours, four times a month, on penalty of a fine of three shillings for every neglect to do so, for which an excuse "satisfactory to the officers of said Piquet" was not furnished. The annual meeting in March continued this establishment of the company "till further orders."

The company was, however, indebted for its arms and equipments to the generous enthusiasm of its commander, — one of the most splendid displays of patriotism in the Revolutionary story of Pittsfield. Capt. Noble, in the alarm of September, went to Boston, and there became more thoroughly impressed with the imminence of the conflict, and the necessity of the earliest preparation for it. Upon his return, he sold two farms in Stephentown, N.Y., and one or two in Pittsfield, receiving pay, for the former at least, in gold, — a circumstance which his son was enabled to recollect in his old age, from the fact that the purchaser brought the coin to Pittsfield quilted into every part of his under-garments, from which the narrator's aunt had a serious task in ripping the glittering pieces.

With the money obtained by this sacrifice of his property, Capt. Noble supplied his company with one hundred and thirty stand of arms, and uniformed them in neat and substantial "regimentals;" their breeches being of buckskin, and their coats "of blue, turned up with white." To obtain the material for these, he went to Philadelphia, where he also hired a breeches-maker, who returned with him to Pittsfield; and the uniforms were made up during the winter at his own house.[1]

The company, thus generously equipped, drilled with corresponding zeal, and acquired an efficiency which was soon called into exercise.

Nor was the patriotic activity of the town confined to Capt. Noble and his minute-men. In almost every family, excepting the fifteen or twenty Tory households, all were busy in fitting out

[1] No repayment was ever made of the sums expended by Capt. Noble for the support of his company at this or other times; but, in 1841, his heirs presented to Congress a claim for the seven-years' half-pay granted to the widows and children of officers who died in the service. This claim, although favorably reported upon, was postponed by technical impediments until 1858, when it was allowed upon a report, full of patriotic sympathies, made by Hon. H. L. Dawes of Pittsfield, from the Committee upon Revolutionary Claims; to which we are indebted for many of the facts given in this volume concerning Capt. Noble.

the young soldiery for the field; so that, for one campaign at least, something of the comfort of home might be communicated to the camp. That winter saw busier scenes than were ever before witnessed even in New-England kitchens; while the click of the loom and the hum of the spinning-wheel made music harmonious with that of the drum and fife. Then (for in 1774 no thousand-spindled factories clothed armies by contract) there were "spinning-matches" and "clothing-bees;" parties of "the fair daughters of Pittsfield"—the married against the single, the West against the East Part, dames, or however the match might be made up—contending for the palm in those now lost domestic arts; the product going to clothe the army. And the laughter, although louder and more frequent than when such gatherings had been held in token of good will to the minister, had an undertone which showed that none were cheated of their forebodings. Then the village pastor—the very embodiment of patriotic ardor, but full of the tenderest sympathies for the suffering which must needs be that the right might prevail—went from gathering to gathering, and from house to house, and everywhere left a new sense of the holiness which invested the impending strife for liberty.

In measures of preparation like these, the Pittsfield patriots passed that anxious winter; and, when the call to arms came, it found them ready. The news of the battle of Lexington—or, more probably, the alarm set on foot by Paul Revere on the night preceding the "excursion of the king's troops"—reached Pittsfield on the 21st of April, at noon;[1] and at sunrise the next morning, Capt. Noble's minute-men, the flower of the youth of Pittsfield and Richmond, were, with the regiment to which they were attached, on their march to Cambridge. Dr. Timothy Childs was one of its lieutenants,[2] but was soon detailed as surgeon; and the commissioned officers became, Capt. David Noble, First Lieut. Joseph Welch of Richmond, Second Lieut. Josiah Wright of Pittsfield. In this form the company served for twenty-six weeks. Col. Pat-

[1] Tradition, with its usual inaccuracy, makes this date the 20th, which is physically impossible. Revere's alarm, starting from Boston in the evening preceding "the excursion of the king's troops," as the Provincials called the affair in quaint derision, could have barely reached Pittsfield on the noon of the 21st; and the rolls of the minute-men date their service from the 22d.

[2] His father, of the same name, commanded the minute-men who at the same time set out from Deerfield.

terson's regiment was then re-organized, a majority of the men enlisting for a term of eight months; Capt. Noble's company retaining its officers. Dr. Childs was made regimental surgeon; and Dr. Jonathan Lee, also of Pittsfield, and a brother-in-law of Rev. Mr. Allen, was associated with him as assistant, and afterwards succeeded him as full surgeon.

The Pittsfield Tories, although, after the passage of the regulating acts had unmasked the designs of the British Government, ceasing to be a power in town-meetings, continued to be a source of annoyance and alarm. Rev. Mr. Allen, in a letter of May 4, 1775, to Col. Seth Pomeroy, characterized them as among "the worst in the Province:" an opinion which was, however, probably colored by the excitement of the hour. Other towns would, doubtless, in the vexation of their troubles, have put in a similar claim for their black sheep. Still, the position of the town upon the doubtful frontier of Columbia County (then King's District), which was supposed to harbor several "nests of Tories," rendered it unsafe to tolerate any of their complexion in politics, and compelled the utmost rigor against them on the part of the committees.

As early as December, 1774, Woodbridge Little and Israel Stoddard were charged with disaffection "to all the measures into which the people in general were coming." It was proved that they had opposed, and refused to sign, "The League and Covenant," which alone was sufficient, under the resolutions of the Continental Congress, to stamp them "the enemies of American liberty;" and they, further, confessed that they had advised a meeting of loyalists, who applied to them for counsel, to send their names to Gen. Gage, — to become "addressers," — in order to secure their property from confiscation in the anticipated hour of British and Tory vengeance. "As for themselves," they had declared, when giving this counsel, "no such precaution was necessary, as they were already well known to Gage as sufferers for Toryism." The not unnatural inference was, that they were in secret communication with the governor, and constantly conveying information to him of the revolutionary movements in which their neighbors were engaged. The town, therefore, on the second of January, "passed in full the writing of complaint against Woodbridge Little, Esq., and Major Stoddard." The latter thereupon took refuge in the city of New York; and "on the same night the news came of the Lexington battle, the said Little took his flight to Kinderhook, the place of Tories, and thence to New York," where he joined his friend. The "hue and cry" was raised upon them; and Little, venturing to Albany, was recognized through the advertisement, and, after being imprisoned a while in the City Hall, was sent home. Here he was put under keepers until Stoddard returned, preferring to trust himself to the mercy of his townsmen, rather than endure further exile, and risk the confiscation of his estate. Having then been again brought before the committee, and convicted of being unfriendly to the common cause, "they humbly confessed their faults, asked forgiveness, and promised reformation." After this experience, "they seemed awed from open acts of inimical conduct, but did not at all times satisfy the people that they were the true friends of the American cause; but associated among themselves, and others of the town and elsewhere of the same kidney, and not with people in general." [1]

Moses Graves and Elisha Jones, whose sympathies with the enemies of their country were more pronounced and practical than

[1] Report of the committees to the General Court in 1776 (Mass. Ar. vol. lvi. p. 193). Some of the evidence adduced against Major Stoddard in this report, we have not alluded to in the text, as it does not clearly appear to have been a part of the same upon which the verdict of 1775 was framed, or to have been necessary to its conclusions. Indeed, if the expressions reported by the witnesses to have been used by him had been believed by his townsmen to represent his genuine sentiments, they would have found no room for forgiveness. They probably regarded the language which he was proved to have used as — what it doubtless was — the ebullition of a bitter partisan in a towering passion; and, although it proved him a virulent Tory, by no means convicted him of cool approval of the atrocities threatened. The evidence is, however, a part of the picture of the times, and is essential to its truthfulness. As such we quote it: —

"The evidence of William Cady, of lawful age, and sober life and conversation: testifyeth, that, just before the Lexington battle, he saw Israel Stoddard Esq.; heard him say that those minute-men would not fight; if they were called, they would not go, for they would not engage in so bad a cause; if they did go, that they would all be killed; that they had no courage; that there was a plan laid to have them all cut off; said that the enemy could cut off our people by spreading the small-pox; said there was nothing too bad for the Whigs; said Stoddard held up his hands, and thanked God he was not a Whig. Joseph Chamberlain testified that sometime since these troubles came upon us, he heard Israel Stoddard say, he knew where the regulars would strike upon ye countrie, for he heard from them every day. . . . Capt. Zebulon Norton had heard Stoddard say, that the people would all be sorry they signed the covenant; that they would all lose their estates; that the regulars would come on our front, and the Indians in our rear, and it would be easy to subdue us."

were those of Little and Stoddard, were, in the latter part of April, committed to Northampton jail, where they remained until July, when Graves was released upon hollow professions of repentance, only to get himself into trouble again in December; being drummed out of the town of Westfield for loud-mouthed Toryism, and sent home to be disciplined in his own precinct. Jones was also released, joined the King's army, and suffered confiscation of his estate.

The annual town-meeting in March manifested the peculiarities of the times. It was voted, first, to take the Province law as the guide of the meeting, ignoring the regulating act. No money was appropriated for schools. The votes before noted, regarding taxes and the continued pay of the minute-men, were passed. Col. Williams, Deacon Wright, Matthew Barber, Aaron Baker, Jacob Ensign, and James D. Colt were chosen Wardens, and appointed "a committee to take care of disorderly persons."

Israel Dickinson, Josiah Wright, Wm. Francis, Col. Easton, and Capt. Goodrich were elected selectmen; and Capt. Dickinson was also made town-clerk and treasurer.

John Brown being employed on other service, Capt. Charles Goodrich was chosen delegate to the Provincial Congress to be held at Concord, March 22.

In the mean time, Rev. Mr. Allen was active in advocating Whig doctrines in King's District; speaking at Canaan, Kinderhook, Claverack, and elsewhere, to the delight of the radical patriots and the vehement displeasure of their opponents, against whom he advised the strongest measures, including a confiscation of debts due them to the Continental treasury.

With regard to his own movements, and the general state of affairs in his vicinity, he wrote to Gen. Pomeroy on the 9th as follows: —

"Our militia this way, sir, are vigorously preparing for actual readiness. Adjacent towns and this town are buying arms and ammunition. As yet, there are plenty of arms to be sold at Albany; but we hear, that, by order of the Major, etc., no powder is to be sold there for the present. The spirit of liberty runs high at Albany, as you have doubtless heard by their own post to our headquarters. I have exerted myself to spread the same spirit in King's District; which has, of late, taken a surprising effect. The poor

Tories at Kinderhook are mortified and grieved, are wheeling about, and begin to take the quick-step. New-York Government begins to be alive in the glorious cause, and to act with great vigor."

Thus determined, self-sacrificing, and indefatigable, were the patriots of Pittsfield in that era of preparation for the Revolutionary struggle.

CHAPTER XII.

PITTSFIELD IN ETHAN ALLEN'S TICONDEROGA CAPTURE.

[DECEMBER — JUNE, 1775.]

John Brown in the Provincial Congress. — On the Canada Committee. — Selected to go to Canada. — Perilous Journey. — Report of his Mission. — Recommends the early Capture of Ticonderoga. — Arranges it with Ethan Allen. — Connecticut plans the Capture. — Connection of the two Schemes. — The Commissioners visit Pittsfield. — John Brown and Col. Easton join the Party. — Its Plans modified on their Suggestion. — Col. Easton raises Men for the Expedition. — Councils of War in Vermont. — Rank of the Officers fixed. — Ethan Allen. — Benedict Arnold claims the Command, and is resisted. — Important Letter from Arnold. — Allen captures the Fort. — Easton and Brown announce the Victory to the Continental and Provincial Congresses. — Reports of Col. Allen and Capt. Mott. — The great Services of the Pittsfield Officers officially acknowledged.— Malignant Course of Arnold. — He receives Troops, captures a King's Sloop, and sets up a rival Command. — Is placed under Col. Hinman of Connecticut by the Provincial Congress, and resigns. — Col. Easton appointed to fill the Vacancy. — John Brown commissioned Major. — Arnold embezzles the Pay of Capt. James Noble's Pittsfield Company.

ON the 6th of December, 1774, the Provincial Congress appointed, as a committee to open a correspondence with Canada, and obtain frequent intelligence of movements there, Major Hawley, Col. Seth Pomeroy, John Brown, Sam. Adams, Dr. Warren, and Dr. Church.[1] The selection of so many eminent men showed the magnitude which Congress attributed to the business assigned them; and the committee also recognized it by intrusting to one of its own members the difficult and dangerous task of personally sounding the disposition of the Canadians, instituting a revolutionary party among them, and organizing a

[1] Jour. Prov. Cong., p. 59.

system of secret communication with its leaders. John Brown's selection for this mission was due not less to his admirable diplomatic qualities, and the cool daring which in no emergency left them at fault, than to that adventurous ardor which continually led him to seek the most dashing and dangerous — not necessarily the most conspicuous — fields of patriotic service.

Immediately upon receiving his appointment, he returned to Pittsfield, resigned his seat in the Provincial Congress, made preparation for his journey, and, as soon as the pamphlets and papers intended for use in Canada reached him, set out for Albany. There he learned that Lakes George and Champlain were impassable; but after waiting a fortnight, although their condition was not improved, he set out, accompanied by two experienced guides, and, after fourteen days of "inconceivable hardships," reached St. John's-on-the-Sorel.

The perils as well as the hardships of this journey were extreme. Lake Champlain, swollen by an extraordinary freshet, flooded a great portion of the country for a space of twenty miles on each side, and especially towards Canada. The rivers and streams were lost in the overflow, and the guides missed their accustomed landmarks; and, still worse, the broadened surface, partly open, was in part covered with dangerous ice, a field of which, miles in extent, breaking loose, caught the frail craft of our daring voyagers, and drove them against an island, where they remained, frozen in, two days, and "were then glad to foot it on shore."[1]

At Montreal, Mr. Brown was cordially welcomed by the Committee of Correspondence, already organized, and obtained from them and from other sources a thorough comprehension of Canadian character and politics, and also of the movements of the military; all which he communicated to the Committee at Boston, together with an outline of Gov. Carleton and his policy, drawn with striking truthfulness in a few rapid sentences.

At Montreal, he met a delegation of the Quebec Committee, and consequently did not visit that city; but he travelled through a considerable portion of the interior, in order to disseminate patriotic sentiments, and personally observe the disposition of the people.

The guides who had crossed the lakes with Mr. Brown were

[1] Letter to Adams and Warren, Mass. Ar., vol. cxciii. p. 40.

from "the New-Hampshire Grants,"[1] — one of them an old hunter familiar with the St. François Indians and their language; the other had once been a captive among the Caughnawagas. These men he sent to those tribes respectively, and obtained positive evidence (hostilities having then not commenced) that the royal commanders were intriguing to bring the savages upon the colonists. They also obtained from the chiefs assurances of neutrality, which, although they were afterwards violated, were probably as sincere as an Indian's pledges ever are.

Mr. Brown reported that there was no prospect that Canada would send a delegate to the Continental Congress, and gave no hope of any uprising there, independent of the presence of a colonial army. The rivalry of races, and the character of the Canadian French, whom the British Government were assiduously courting, forbade both.

But he closed his letter of March 29[2] with these words: —

"*One thing I must mention as a profound secret. The Fort at Ticonderoga must be seized as soon as possible, should hostilities be committed by the king's troops. The people on New-Hampshire Grants have engaged to do this business, and, in my opinion, are the most proper persons for the job. This will effectually curb this Province, and all the troops which may be sent here.*"

This was the whole gist of the plans which resulted in the capture of Ticonderoga; and it was undoubtedly written after consultation with Ethan Allen, who had lands on Grand Isle, and upon Shelburne Point, now Colchester and Burlington, which juts into Lake Champlain directly across the route pursued by the Canadian envoy. Allen, a cousin of the Pittsfield minister, was probably known to Brown, and, as the commander of the Green-Mountain Boys, was clearly the only person competent, in their behalf, to undertake the very serious "job" of surprising the great fortress of the lakes.

As Mr. Brown was writing the postscript to this letter,[3] the messenger was impatiently waiting to be gone with it; and it reached Boston, at the latest, by the middle of April.

[1] Vermont.

[2] This letter, of which I have made free use in the foregoing pages, was addressed to "Samuel Adams and Dr. Joseph Warren, of the Committee of Correspondence, Boston." It is preserved in the Mass. Ar., vol. cxciii. pp. 40–44.

[3] This postscript announced Gov. Carleton's prohibition of the export of wheat from the St. Lawrence.

Plans for the capture of Ticonderoga were at once rife in the secret councils, not only of Massachusetts, but of Connecticut. And to the latter belongs the honor of initiating and organizing the expedition which successfully executed the plans concocted by Brown and Allen, of furnishing for it the requisite funds, and of entrusting it to a commission which wisely represented its sovereignty, sagaciously avoiding the perils which beset an undertaking authorized by one colony, to be carried out in another, by troops collected from a third and fourth.[1]

The Connecticut expedition was "projected and undertaken" by Col. Samuel H. Parsons and five other gentlemen, who, on the 27th, sent forward Messrs. Phelps and Romans, procuring for them £300 from the colonial treasury, upon their personal responsibility for its judicious use. Capt. Mott arrived the next day at Hartford, and, having recently been at Cambridge, was questioned as to the best method of obtaining a supply of artillery for the siege of the British army in Boston. He at once proposed the surprise of Ticonderoga, which he pronounced perfectly feasible: upon which he was informed of what was on foot, and consented to assume the lead of the party which had gone on, adding to it five or six trusty volunteers.

The project had been suggested to Col. Parsons by a conversation with Benedict Arnold, who had, or pretended to have, an exact account of the cannon at Ticonderoga, and the condition of defences there. It is possible that both his proposition and that of Mott might have been traced to rumors of recommendations contained in Mr. Brown's letter to Adams and Warren. Capt. Mott's recent return from the camp where those leaders were the moving spirits favors the supposition, but I am aware of no evidence which proves it correct. The immediate object of the Connecticut expedition — to supply the pressing demand for siege-artillery —

[1] This commission consisted of Edward Mott, Noah Phelps, and Bernard Romans, the latter of whom appears not to have contributed his full share to the good sense of the management. Capt. Mott, although not appointed until the others had set off, acted as the head of the commission, and has left two accounts of the expedition, — one in his diary recently published in the Transactions of the Connecticut Hist. Soc.; the other in a letter to the Provincial Congress of Massachusetts, in whose journals it is printed with other papers relating to the surprise of Ticonderoga. Upon these two collections, two letters from Rev. Mr. Allen to Gen. Pomeroy, and a few isolated papers, named when referred to, we have founded our account of the capture of Ticonderoga and events connected with it.

was certainly original with its projectors; and the entire independence of their scheme, in its inception, of that proposed by Mr. Brown, may be conceded without at all diminishing the honor due to his connection with the exploit. That his was the first proposition for the seizure of the post is unquestioned; and it is proof of his political and military sagacity, that he so early perceived that for one campaign, if no more, Great Britain would operate against her ancient colonies from the new possessions which they had helped her to win from France; that the old antagonistic military bases of North America were to be restored; that the old war-path must be trod anew; and that the utmost advantage would accrue to the party which should first secure the great fortress, that, for half a century, had been familiar to New England as the key of Canada. It was by recommending action founded upon these observations; by discerning at a glance the method in which, and the soldiery by whom, that action could be successfully taken; by enlisting the fittest commander for the enterprise; and by the aid which he rendered personally in executing the scheme which he had planned, — that he connected his fame with the patriotic measures of Connecticut and the memorable exploit of Ethan Allen.

It is by no means necessary to impeach the claim of Messrs. Parsons and Mott to originality, in suggesting the Ticonderoga expedition, in order to trace its triumphant success, link by link, directly back to the chance-meeting of John Brown and Ethan Allen on the flooded shores of Champlain.

Capt. Mott set out on the afternoon of Saturday, April 29, to overtake his associates; [1] and on the morning of that day, or the evening previous, John Hancock and Samuel Adams, members of the Massachusetts committee to correspond with neighboring colonies, reached Hartford on their way to attend the Continental Congress.[2] The great undertaking on foot was naturally communicated to them, and received their approval, as well as that of the Governor and Council of Connecticut, who were, perhaps now for the first time, officially apprised of it.[3]

[1] Con. Hist. Col., vol. i. p. 167.

[2] Am. Ar., ser. 4th, vol. ii. p. 401.

[3] Rev. Mr. Allen, Chairman of the Pittsfield Committee of Correspondence and Inspection, in a letter of May 4, speaks of the "plan" of the expedition as having been "concerted" at this interview. He obtained his information from the verbal,

It may be that Capt. Mott now first learned the recommendations of John Brown; for, even if loose talk of the capture of Ticonderoga as desirable had arisen in the Cambridge camp from the Montreal letter, its details were, as the writer requested, kept a profound secret. But it would have been strange indeed, and most unlike the man, had Mr. Adams allowed the Connecticut leader to depart on such a mission as he was sent upon, without the aid of all the information pertinent to it which his position upon the Canadian committee enabled him to impart. It is incredible that he left him in ignorance of facts so essential to the business which he had in hand, as the measures already taken and proposed by John Brown in the same direction. It is clear, from Capt. Mott's subsequent proceedings, that Mr. Adams was guilty of no such culpable and thoughtless oversight.

Having been joined by their leader, who left Hartford on the 29th, the Connecticut party, increased in number to sixteen, reached Daniel Dewey's tavern in Sheffield, and thence sent a delegation of two to Albany to "discover the temper of the people at that place," — so uncertain, at that time, were the people of different colonies of each other's patriotism. The same night they reached Pittsfield, and took quarters at the tavern then kept by Col. Easton, about eighty feet south of the present corner of Park Square and South Street.

"They had intended to keep their business secret, and ride through the country unarmed, until they came to the new settlements on The Grants;" but at Col. Easton's they found John Brown,[1] and determined to take him into their councils, as well as their landlord, the colonel of the Berkshire militia.

Mr. Brown's opinion that the Green-Mountain Boys were the proper persons to undertake the "job" at Ticonderoga, will be

and not very precise or minutely detailed statements of the Connecticut commissioners during their brief stay in Pittsfield. Plans for the expedition were, as the reader knows, concerted previously; but they were, without doubt, in some degree modified by the advice and information received from Hancock and Adams, and especially the latter. Mr. Allen's letters to Gen. Pomeroy, referred to in this chapter, are printed in the Am. Ar., ser. 4th, vol. ii. pp. 507, 546.

[1] Mr. Brown, after establishing "a channel of communication, which could be depended upon," from Canada, "through the New-Hampshire Grants" had just returned home; and his presence in Pittsfield was probably neither known to Mr. Adams, nor expected by Capt. Mott, — a supposition which explains passages in the latter's diary, otherwise obscure.

remembered. It had probably been communicated by Mr. Adams to the Hartford Committee. Capt. Mott certainly left Hartford with instructions not to increase his party of sixteen until he reached The Grants.

Circumstances, aided no doubt by sympathy with Col. Easton's desire that his Berkshire regiment should have a part in the achievement, had modified Mr. Brown's views; and he now concurred with the colonel in representing, that "as there was great scarcity of provisions in The Grants, and the people were generally very poor, it would be difficult to raise a sufficient body of men there."

The commissioners yielding to this advice, Mr. Brown, Capt. Dickinson, and four or five others from Pittsfield, were admitted to the party; and Col. Easton's offer to assist with some men from his regiment was accepted. To preserve secrecy, however, it was thought advisable to raise no more men in Pittsfield; but, while their associates proceeded to Bennington, Col. Easton and Capt. Mott crossed the mountain into Jericho, now Hancock. There they, with the aid of Capt. Asa Douglas, an active and noted patriot of that place, enlisted twenty-four men, to whom fifteen were added in Williamstown. Col. Easton's regiment contributed in all forty-seven men to the expedition.

Leaving Capt. Douglas to follow with his company, Messrs. Easton and Mott hastened forward to Bennington, where they found that a part of their advanced delegation were staggered by the report of some nameless fellow, who pretended that he had just come from Ticonderoga, and that the garrison, re-enforced and alert, were diligently repairing their works. A messenger had even been sent to advise Capt. Mott to dismiss his recruits, and abandon his project; but, by his eloquence and personal influence, he soon revived the drooping spirits of his comrades; telling them that it would never do to go back to Hartford with a story like that; and that, as for himself, he would not fear, with the two hundred men which they proposed to raise, to go round the fort in broad daylight. Even were its garrison five hundred, they would not dare follow them to the woods. Others of his companions responding in the same tone, the disheartened few were reassured; and all determined to go forward except Bernard Romans. Of him they were well rid: he "had been but a trouble."

At Bennington, Ethan Allen came to them, evidently to meet

his old engagement with John Brown. There is no hint of any new negotiation; and it seems to have been expected, as a matter fully provided for, that, when the great partisan received the signal that the hour for action had come, he would be found prompt at the rendezvous, and ready to assume the chief burden of the undertaking.

A council of war, Col. Easton presiding, directed Col. Allen, who was rapidly calling his Green-Mountain Boys around him, to send forward patrols on the northern road, and prevent news of their approach preceding them.

They then advanced to Castleton, — twenty-five miles, by the route pursued, from Ticonderoga, — and there, on the 8th of May, held a general council, at which they considered their methods of further procedure, and of retreat in case of repulse. It was agreed that Capt. Herrick should proceed to Skenesborough, and capture Major Skene and his party; take what boats they found there, and, the next night, drop down to Shoreham,[1] there to ferry the attacking party across the lake. This party consisted of about one hundred and forty men: and in fulfilment of a promise made to them when enlisting, that they should be commanded by their own officers, Ethan Allen was placed first, James Easton second, and Seth Warner third in command; the rank of these officers being fixed in proportion to the number of men they respectively procured. In addition to these arrangements, Capt. Douglas was sent to Crown Point to hire the king's boats at that post, if he could do so by some stratagem, aided by his brother-in-law, who lived there.

The whole plan having been harmoniously "settled by a vote of the committee," and the time fixed when "he must be ready, and must take possession of the garrison at Ticonderoga," Col. Allen left to make some arrangements at Shoreham.[2]

That evening, mischief appeared at Castleton, in the ill-omened shape of Benedict Arnold. This man was already odious in Connecticut; but he had led a volunteer company from New Haven to Cambridge, and had there obtained from the Committee of Safety

[1] Major Skene, a half-pay British officer, of the French and Indian wars, and supposed to be the confidential agent of the government, had built up the flourishing village of Skenesborough — now Whitehall — at the head of Lake Champlain. Shoreham is twenty-five miles below Whitehall, and nearly opposite Ticonderoga.

[2] Mott's Diary.

Gentlemen Rupert 8th May 1775

By the best Information I can get there Is One hundred Men, or more, at Ticonderoga who are Alarmed & keep a good look Out. I am also Informed, the Sloop is gone to St. Johns for Provisions, that She has Six Guns Mounted, & Twenty Men. We have Only One hundred & Fifty Men gon On, which are not Sufficient to Secure the Vessell & keep the Lake, this Ought by all Means to be done, that we may Cut of their Communication, & Stop all Supplys Going to the Fort untill we can have a Sufficient Number Men from the Lower Towns. – I beg the favour of you Gentlemen, as far Down as this shall Reach to exert your Selves & send forward as many Men to Join the Army here as you can Posably Spare there is Plenty of Provisions Engaged, & on the Road for five hundred men Six or Eight Weeks, Let Every man bring as much Powder & Ball as he can Also a Blanket their Wages are 40/ pr. Month. I humbly engaged to See paid also the Blanket,

I am Gentlemen your Humb

To the Gentlemen In the Southern Towns

Benedict Arnold, Commander of the Forces.

Am. Photo-Lithographic Co. N.Y. (Osborne's Process)

a commission as "colonel and commander of a body of forces, not to exceed four hundred, to be raised for the reduction of Ticonderoga."

He proposed to obtain his forces in Berkshire, and is said to have authorized enlistments in Stockbridge. But, on reaching Pittsfield, he learned of the expedition which was anticipating him, and hastened to overtake it, determined, with his accustomed effrontry, to assume command; although the troops — enlisted by Connecticut, receiving her pay, and operating beyond the bounds of Massachusetts — owed no more allegiance to the committee at Cambridge, than Capt. De la Place's garrison in Ticonderoga did.

He needed to move quickly who would overtake Ethan Allen in the execution of his plans; but Arnold, when spurred by the promptings of selfish ambition, was equal to any achievement. In his haste, he, however, found time to send back the following letter[1] to the committees of the Berkshire towns:—

REUPORT, 8th May, 1775.

GENTLEMEN, — By the best information I can get, there is one hundred men, or more, at Ticonderoga, who are alarmed, and keep a good lookout. I am also informed, the sloop is gone to St. John's for provisions; that she had six guns mounted, and twenty men. We have only one hundred and fifty men gone on, which are not sufficient to secure the vessels, and keep the lakes; this ought by all means to be done, that we may cut off their communication, and stop all supplies going to the fort, until we can have a sufficient number of men from the lower towns.

I beg the favor of you, gentlemen, as far down as this reaches, to exert yourselves, and send forward as many men to join the army here as you can possibly spare. There is plenty of provisions engaged, and on the road, for five hundred men six or eight weeks. Let every man bring as much powder and ball as he can, also a blanket. Their wages are 40*s*. per month. I humbly engaged to see paid; also the blankets.

I am, gentlemen,
Your humble servant,
BENEDICT ARNOLD,
Commander of the forces.

TO THE GENTLEMEN IN THE SOUTHERN TOWNS.

[1] This letter, whose authenticity is beyond dispute, was found in 1844 by the late Hon. E. R. Colt of Pittsfield, among the papers of David Dunnels, a Revolutionary pensioner of Cheshire. It is now in the Hon. Thomas Colt's collection of historical documents.

Nothing surely could be more unlike to Arnold's plan of operations than that which had been agreed upon at Castleton, in which he expressed his utter want of confidence. Capt. Mott and his friends were "shockingly surprised" — as they well might have been — "when Col. Arnold presumed to contend for the command of the forces they had raised," in the manner, and upon the conditions which have been stated: but that master of impudent assumption, having been generously told all their plans, continued strenuously to insist upon his right to command; which was as strenuously resisted. Defeated here, Arnold, the next morning, proceeded to overtake Allen, with the rather desperate hope of inducing that hero to surrender his rights. It seems that even the members of the expedition did not yet quite understand the nature of the man who led them; for the moment Arnold started, the whole party, leaving Capts. Mott and Phelps, with a single companion, to care for the baggage as they best could, followed, pell-mell, "for fear he should prevail with Col. Allen." [1]

If Arnold's conduct shocked the leaders, it bred a mutiny amongst the soldiers, and almost "frustrated the design they were upon." [2] "Our men," wrote Capt. Mott to the Massachusetts Council of War, "were for clubbing their firelocks and marching home: but were prevented by Col. Allen and Col. Easton, who told them that Arnold should not have the command of them; or, if he had, that their pay should be the same as if they were under their own command. But they would damn the pay, and say they would be commanded by no other than those they had engaged with." And so Arnold at last, perceiving the folly of issuing commands which none would obey, consented, although still meditating mischief, to join the party as a volunteer. An honorable position was assigned him by the magnanimity of those towards whom he had shown none; and the little army moved on to the execution of its appointed task.

They reached Shoreham on the evening of the 8th of May, but found none of the boats which they had hoped to receive either from Skenesborough or Crown Point. Capt. Phelps also, who had visited the fort in disguise, was detained with the baggage, and had not yet come up. It was determined, however, to lose no time. Nathan Beman, a boy of the neighborhood, who was familiar with every nook and crany of the fort, was engaged as guide;

[1] Mott's Diary. [2] Jour. Prov. Cong., p. 697.

and, availing themselves of such scant ferriage as was at hand, the party began to cross the lake. Barely eighty-three men had reached the Ticonderoga shore when day began to dawn, and there remained no safety but in an immediate advance. The boats were hastily despatched for the rear division. Allen, drawing his corps up in three columns, made them a brief, earnest harangue, such as he well knew how to address to his followers, and then, with Nathan Beman by his side, led them, rapidly and in silence, up the steep ascent. Before sunrise, he entered the gate; the sentinel snapping his fusee, which missed fire, in his face as he passed. The surprise was complete. The flying guard guided the Americans directly to the parade-ground within the barracks, where a second sentinel made a bayonet thrust at Col. Easton, inflicting a slight wound; for which attention to his friend, Allen repaid the unlucky soldier with a sword-cut on the head, which induced him to beg quarter.

The victors were then drawn up on the parade, and gave three rousing cheers; which not sufficing to bring out Capt. de la Place, the post-commander, Col. Allen mounted to the door of his apartment, which was reached by a flight of stairs on the outside of the barracks, and there, in full view of the party below, ensued the famous scene which resulted in the surrender of Ticonderoga to the demand made in the name of Almighty God and the Continental Congress.

The Connecticut Committee, through their chairman, Capt. Mott, thus recognized the services of Col. Easton and John Brown, in their report to the Massachusetts Congress: —

"Col. James Easton was of great service, both in council and action; raising men for the expedition, and appearing to be well qualified, not only for colonel of militia at home, but for service in the field.

"John Brown, Esq., of Pittsfield, we recommend as an able counsellor, and full of spirit and resolution. We wish they may be both employed in the service of their country in a situation equal to their merits." [1]

Col. Allen, in his report to the Congress, wrote, —

"The soldiery were composed of about one hundred Green-Mountain Boys, and near fifty veteran soldiers of the Massachusetts Bay. The latter were commanded by Col. James Easton, who behaved with great zeal and fortitude, not only in council, but in the assault. The soldiery behaved

[1] Jour. Prov. Con., p. 697.

with such resistless fury, that they so terrified the king's troops that they durst not fire on their assailants; and our soldiery were agreeably disappointed. The soldiery behaved with uncommon rancor when they leaped into the fort; and it must be confessed that the colonel has greatly contributed to the taking of that fortress, as well as John Brown, Esq., who was personally in the attack." [1]

Col. Easton, in his report, wrote, —

"As to other regimental officers, Capt. Israel Dickinson and John Brown, Esq., distinguished themselves very highly, both in council and in action, and, in my humble opinion, are well qualified to command in the field." [2]

The news of so brilliant and unexpected an exploit as the capture (without the loss of life, and at so trifling a cost of treasure) of the famous fortress of Lake Champlain, with its vast military stores, sent a thrill of joy and courage through the land. And, as the imminence of a grand campaign on the northern frontier loomed on the popular apprehension, a cooler estimate of the gains which had accrued to the Colonies enhanced their value.

In reference to the primary object of Connecticut, to secure heavy artillery for the siege of Boston, Rev. Mr. Allen, on the 9th of May, wrote to Gen. Pomeroy at Cambridge, —

"Should the expedition succeed, and should the Council of War send up their orders for the people this way to transport by land twenty or thirty of the best cannon to head-quarters, I doubt not but the people in this county would do it with expedition. We could easily raise a thousand yoke of oxen for the business."

In view, however, of the hostilities from the north which John Brown had predicted, and which were now seen to be almost inevitable, it was considered unadvisable to weaken the defences of that frontier; and although some of the cannon were removed to Fort George, at the upper end of the lake of that name, Ticonderoga was not dismantled, but greatly strengthened in its works.

John Brown was sent to announce the capture to the Continental, and Col. Easton to the Provincial Congress. Both were cordially received, and introduced to the floors of the bodies to which they were respectively accredited, that they might give the details of the glorious enterprise in which they had taken prominent parts. After listening to Col. Easton, the Congress at

[1] Am. Ar., 4th ser., vol. ii. p. 556. [2] Jour. Prov. Con., p. 713.

Cambridge passed suitable resolutions, with which he was despatched to Hartford, where he was again received with enthusiasm, and handsomely entertained by the Connecticut authorities.

His mission to the two governments was managed with discretion and ability; and the favorable impression which he made at Cambridge was soon manifested by substantial tokens. All parties acted towards each other with consideration and magnanimity, except Arnold. It was the complaints which he was pouring into headquarters that gave Col. Easton's visit there the character of something more than mere congratulation.

The surrender of Ticonderoga had no sooner taken place than Arnold renewed his pretensions to command, and insisted that Allen was acting under no proper authority; upon which Capt. Mott, in the name of Connecticut, drew up and signed a commission, placing Allen in command of the party, and directing him to keep the possession of Ticonderoga and its dependencies until further orders from the Colony or from the Continental Congress.

In the mean time, under the requisition sent from Rupert, a considerable body of levies from the Berkshire militia had reached Arnold; among them a detachment, composed of fifteen men from each company in Pittsfield and vicinity, led by Capt. James Noble of that town, a brother of him who marched the minute-men to Cambridge. With a portion of the troops which he had thus received, Arnold made the capture of the king's sloop, upon which he had laid so much stress in his Rupert Circular,[1] and thus was enabled to establish a rival command upon the lake.

While engaged in these legitimate, although not always magnanimous operations, the embryo traitor was flooding the Massachusetts Congress, the public press, and influential individuals, with letters vilifying, in the most malignant terms, the heroes who had just met the approval of so glorious success; and it was in counteracting the effect of these vile missives, that Col. Easton's mission at Cambridge and Hartford required all his tact, temper, and ability; and it was by successfully exercising these qualities, that the colonel laid the foundation of that enmity with which Arnold followed him until he drove him from the army.

The Provincial Congress, greatly perplexed by the conflicting

[1] Capt. Noble did not personally take part in this exploit, having been sent to Albany by Arnold for supplies for his army.

reports from Ticonderoga, could, with certainty, infer from them one truth; and that was, that the state of affairs upon the lakes was such as could not safely continue. It therefore, on the 13th of June, sent a joint committee to the post, charged, among other duties, to inform themselves of the manner in which Arnold had executed his commission. They found him, at St. John's, with the sloop which he had taken, and claiming, also, "the command of all the posts and fortresses at the south end of Lakes Champlain and George; although Col. Hinman of Connecticut was at Ticonderoga, with near a thousand men under his command at the several posts."

The committee informed Arnold of the commission intrusted to them, and handed him their instructions; which authorized them to continue him in the service of Massachusetts, with such orders as they saw fit, "provided . . . he and his men were willing to remain at one, or both, of the lake-posts, under such chief officer as Connecticut might appoint."

Then the spirit of Arnold broke forth. "He seemed greatly disconcerted, declared that he would not be second in command to any person whomsoever;" and, after considering the matter a while, disbanded the men he had raised, and handed the committee his resignation. They immediately appointed Col. Easton to fill the vacancy, and soon after gave him John Brown for his major. The unwarrantable and petty conduct of Arnold, in spitefully disbanding the men which he had raised at the expense of the colony, caused some little annoyance for a time. But Capt. Noble, who was at Crown Point with some of the disbanded soldiers, expressed in their behalf a willingness to return to the service; and, being intrusted with one hundred pounds to be used as advance pay, he succeeded in re-enlisting a company of fifty-one. Col. Easton's command soon assumed respectable proportions.

With one more incident, we close this first chapter of Benedict Arnold's dealings with the Pittsfield soldiery. His "humble engagement to see paid the wages" of the recruits who responded to his call from Rupert will be remembered. How that promise was kept will be best told by an extract from the records of the General Court, dated four months after he had disbanded and abandoned, at Ticonderoga, the men who had trusted him.[1]

[1] Mass. Ar., vol. ccvii. p. 200.

In the House of Representatives,
Nov. 9, 1775.

The Committee on Col. Arnold's account have examined Capt. Noble's pay-roll, and find that the said Arnold has charged this colony with said Noble's pay-roll, and has received the whole amount thereof. It further appears that the balance due the said Noble, which the said Arnold has received, amounts to £36. *5s. 5d.;* and as it appears that the said Noble and his men are in great want of their money, and the said Arnold is now in the Continental service, and cannot at present be come at, to pay the sum he received for the use of the said Noble and his company — therefore resolved, that there be allowed and paid by the Treasurer of this colony to the said Capt. James Noble the sum of £36 *5s. 5d.*, being the full balance of his muster-roll; he giving security to pay the men made up in said roll the sums severally due to them.

And it is further resolved that this court prefer to Gen. Washington a charge of the sum aforesaid against the said Arnold; that a stoppage of so much as is before ordered to be paid to said Noble may be made for the benefit of the Continent.

CHAPTER XIII.

PITTSFIELD IN THE FIRST NORTHERN CAMPAIGN, AND AT THE SIEGE AT BOSTON.

[MAY — NOVEMBER, 1775.]

Rivalries at Ticonderoga. — Col. Easton proposes an Invasion of Canada. — He raises a Regiment. — Pittsfield Companies in it. — Gen. Schuyler appointed Department Commander. — First Visit to Ticonderoga. — Opinion of the Troops there. — Major John Brown's Second Scout in Canada. — Returning, he urges an immediate Advance. — Appointed to command the Lake Fleet. — Hastens the March of the Army. — Siege of St. John's commences. — Major Brown again sent to Canada. — Reports to Schuyler. — Major Brown the first to lead a Detachment into Canada. — Captures Stores near Chamblee. — Unsuccessful Plan to capture Montreal. — Takes Fort Chamblee. — St. John's surrenders. — Col. Easton's Regiment advances to the St. Lawrence. — Entrenches at Sorel. — Its Sufferings. — Blockades the British Fleet. — Brilliant Services of the Pittsfield Officers acknowledged. — Close of the Campaign. — Col. Patterson's Regiment at Cambridge. — Extraordinary Transmission of Sounds.

THE rivalry which attended the capture of Ticonderoga and its dependencies was not merely for the command of a few hundred men in retired posts upon the lakes. The American army had no more restless spirits than those who met in that old historic fortress; and, to the imagination of each, it was the gateway to a grand campaign, soon to open, in which they foresaw unwonted opportunities of distinguishing themselves.

John Brown had observed, on his first visit to Canada, that the countenance of a continental army was essential to the party there in league with the patriots; and he considered the earliest possible moment the best for a march to Montreal. Allen and Easton partook of the same ideas; and no less so did Arnold, to whose quick perception they would have been suggested by the possession of Lake Champlain, if they had not been before conceived.

It was plain that Gen. Carleton could not permit the Americans quietly to retain possession of the advantages they had gained; and the first plan to anticipate his movements was a removal of the armament from the newly-acquired works to safer places of deposit. But this weak policy was quickly abandoned; and, from the determination to hold and strengthen the forts, the advance was rapid to the purpose of operating from them against Canada. This was, indeed, the dream of Allen and Arnold, Brown and Easton, from the beginning.

The first distinct recommendation of the invasion of Canada, of which we have record, was that of Ethan Allen to the New-York Congress on the 2d of June. But Col. Easton was at least as early in advising the measure; for, in a letter of June 6 to the Massachusetts Congress, — referring to a previous communication, made probably during his visit to Watertown in the middle of May, — he wrote, "I still retain my sentiments, that policy demands that the Colonies should advance an army of two or three thousand men into Canada, and environ Montreal."[1]

In June, Philip Schuyler, a distinguished New-York officer of former wars, was, upon the recommendation of his colony, appointed a major-general of the Continental Army, and assigned to the command of the Northern Department. After some delay at New York and Albany in making arrangements for supplies, he reached Ticonderoga on the night of the 18th of July, and found the garrison to consist of a thousand Connecticut men under Col. Hinman, and Col. Easton's small Berkshire corps. Of the six incomplete companies which composed the latter, one contained twenty-seven Pittsfield men, — including its officers, Capt. James Noble and Lieuts. Joel Dickinson and John Hitchcock. The quartermaster, William C. Stanley, was also from Pittsfield. Col.

[1] In a letter of May 30, Col. Easton had "hinted to their honors" his willingness "to serve his country in the capacity he stood in at home; i. e., with the rank of colonel. "Should you," he added, "gratify me with the command of a regiment for the fortifying and garrisoning said fortress," [Ticonderoga], "you may depend upon my most faithful exertions to defend it against the whole weight of Canada, and on the most punctual observance of your orders. And I shall be ready to make such further acquisitions as shall be in my power, consistent with wisdom and prudence, for the safety of what are already made, that you, in your wisdom, shall direct."[2]

[2] Jour. Prov. Con., p. 713.

Easton and Major Brown were absent, probably attempting to increase their force.

To Gen. Schuyler, the garrison appeared " good-looking people, and decent in their deportment; not lacking in courage," but with a shocking laxity of discipline. The sentinel on duty when he arrived at the landing, on being informed that the general was in the boat, did not hesitate to leave his post, to make a vain attempt to rouse his companions sleeping soundly by the watch-fire. The new commander met a similar experience at other posts of the guard; but he, nevertheless, thought he could make excellent soldiers out of the Connecticut and Berkshire levies "as soon as he could get the better of that nonchalance of theirs." [1]

But Schuyler had small opportunity to make good soldiers of raw militia-men. It was well understood that Gen. Carleton was meditating an attempt to regain the command of the lakes, with a view to the invasion of the country below; and it was feared that the incursion was only delayed in order to obtain the alliance of the savages. As well, therefore, to anticipate this movement, as to take advantage of the favorable disposition reported to exist among certain classes in Canada, the immediate advance into that Province of such a corps as had been suggested by Cols. Allen and Easton was urged on every hand.

Men and material for such an enterprise were, however, tardily supplied; and the department commander was, moreover, greatly perplexed by the difficulty of obtaining reliable information from the proposed field of operations, in which all reasonable hope of success depended upon conditions of which he was profoundly ignorant. On the 21st of July, he wrote to the Continental Congress, that the only man upon whom he could rely to proceed to Canada had suddenly fallen ill; [2] but, about that time, Major Brown returned to head-quarters, and, on the 24th, set out on his second visit to Canada, commissioned to obtain the fullest intelligence of the military preparations making by the king's troops, the Canadians, and the Indians; to learn the situation of St. John's, Chamblee, Montreal, and Quebec; and the number of troops with which each was garrisoned, whether any re-enforcements had come to the Province; whether the Canadians designed

[1] Schuyler to Washington, Am. Ar., 4th ser. vol. ii. p. 1085.

[2] Am. Ar., 4th ser. vol. ii. p. 1302.

taking up arms against the Colonies; and whatever else it was of consequence that an invading general should know."[1]

Major Brown took with him four men, one of them a French Canadian, and reached the border in six days, after a tedious march, on the west of Lake Champlain, through a vast swamp, in whose dank recesses the party were compelled to camp three nights. Issuing from this comfortless tract, and assuming the guise of a horse-dealer, he penetrated the country, remained four days, and obtained a great amount of information, which proved correct, and of untold value to the army. The kindness of the French Canadians, while he was thus engaged, Major Brown spoke of as "indescribable;" and he confessed, that, but for their protection, he must have fallen into the hands of the enemy. The shrewd country-people did not, nevertheless, fail to observe that "he was an odd sort of jockey, who never got a nag to his liking;" and some fellow, not so discreet as his neighbors, or less well disposed, communicated his suspicions to the military police. The result was, a large squad of red-coats surrounded the house where the major lodged. He, however, contrived to escape through a back window, and make good his flight, although hotly pursued for two days. Two scouts, of fifty men each, were sent after him; but, being kept accurately informed of their movements by the friendly Canadians, he evaded both, and got out of the country on the 3d of August. A further flight of three days brought him to the Bay of Missisquoi, where he found a small canoe, with which he proceeded up the lake, and arrived at Crown Point on the 10th,—just one day later than he had fixed with Gen. Schuyler for his return.

What Major Brown had learned in Canada rendered him still more impatient of delay. Writing, four days after his arrival at Crown Point, to Gov. Trumbull, of the Canadians and their affairs, he said,—

"They wish and long for nothing more than to see us penetrate their country with an army. They engage to supply us with every thing in their power. . . . Now is the time to carry Canada. It may be done with great ease and little cost; and I have no doubt the Canadians would join us. Should a large [British] re-enforcement arrive in Canada, it would turn the scale immediately. The inhabitants must then take up arms, or be ruined. It seems that some evil planet has reigned in this quarter this year;

[1] Maj. Brown to Gov. Trumbull, Am. Ar., 4th ser. vol. iv. p. 135.

for notwithstanding the season is far advanced, and a fine opportunity presents for making ourselves masters of a country with the greatest ease, which I fear may cost us much blood and treasure if delayed, in New York [they] have played a queer part, and are determined to defeat us if in their power. They have failed us both in men and supplies."

The evil planet continued to reign. New York delayed, and finally in great part withheld, her promised contingent, in order to hold her own Tories in check. Massachusetts, absorbed in the siege of Boston, furnished to the all-important northern expedition only the small corps which Col. Easton could raise in Berkshire, after the county had already sent two regiments to Cambridge. It numbered barely two hundred men, of whom fifty-three were from Pittsfield, which early in August had sent a second company of twenty-four men, including its officers, — Capt. Eli Root, Lieuts. Stephen Crofoot and James Easton, jun.

Connecticut, threatened with an invasion of her coast, furnished over a thousand men, — less than she wished, but all that she could safely spare. The troops from all the colonies were imperfectly armed, and miserably provided with the most necessary equipments and stores. Illness prevailed, both from this cause and from lack of the restraints of discipline. The regiments of Cols. Hinman and Easton returned a startling proportion of sick, — the latter more than one third of its entire number.

Nevertheless, the last of August found Schuyler, weak and ill appointed as his army was, eager for advance and hopeful of success. There might, however, have been still further delay, had it not been for information received from Major Brown, who, after his return from his Canadian mission, had immediately been placed in command of the flotilla upon the lake, against which a formidable antagonist was known to be preparing on the Sorel, at St. Johns.[1]

Among the things which he had accomplished in Canada, one of the most valuable was to open correspondence with James Livingston, an intelligent, active, and patriotic gentleman, then resident at Chamblee, who thenceforward furnished the most correct, timely, and important information to the American commanders.

Major Brown now ventured personally on a scout, as far as the

[1] The Sorel is often laid down, especially in modern maps, as the River Richelieu, and sometimes as the St. Johns.

Isle Aux-Noix,[1] whence he sent messengers to his friend Livingston, who returned with intelligence upon the strength of which he addressed a letter to Gen. Montgomery, who had arrived at Crown Point, and was acting as Schuyler's lieutenant, for the "dictatorial style of which"[2] he made the extreme exigency of the occasion his apology. It represented that the vessels building on the Sorel were in such a state of forwardness, and were so formidable in their armament, that unless the army moved within ten days, at the latest, it would be necessary to fortify either at Isle Aux-Noix, or, better in his opinion, at Windmill Point,[3] otherwise there would be the most imminent danger that the British fleet would sweep the lake, and compel the abandonment of the expedition against Canada for that year at least.

This letter hastened affairs at Crown Point; and on the 31st of August, seven days from its date, Gen. Montgomery embarked with twelve hundred men; and, Schuyler having overtaken him, the army appeared before St. Johns on the 6th of September, nearly two thousand strong.

The siege proved long and tedious. We shall, of course, only be expected to recite the services of the Pittsfield soldiery in connection with it, and that portion of the general story which is necessary to their comprehension.

Arrived before St. Johns, Gen. Schuyler began to manifest that irresolution and timidity in meeting difficulties of the military situation, which, in spite of his undoubted personal bravery, so often fatally marred his northern campaigns, and led the people of Berkshire to distrust, not only his capacity, but his fidelity. The Americans landed on the 6th of September, were fired upon without effect by the garrison, and had a slight skirmish with a small party of Indians. In the evening, "a man who appeared to be friendly and intelligent," visited the general: stating that the whole British force in Canada, except fifty, were in garrison at

[1] The Isle Aux-Noix is a small, low island in the Sorel, a few miles below St. Johns. It is an important locality in our story. It is now strongly fortified by the British Government.

[2] Am. Ar., 4th ser. vol. iii. p. 468. There is nothing disrespectful or assuming in the letter.

[3] The Windmill Point here alluded to is at the entrance of Lake Champlain into the Sorel, and must not be confounded with the point of the same name on the west side of the lake.

St. Johns, which, as well as Chamblee, he represented to be strongly fortified, and well prepared for a siege; that a hundred Indians were in the fort, and a large body under Sir John Johnson hovering near; that a sixteen-gun vessel was at St. John's, ready to weigh anchor; and that not a single Canadian would join the "insurgent standard."[1] The greater part of this stuff was afterwards proved to be pure invention: but Schuyler gave it full credence; and a Council of War, to whom it was submitted, determined to fall back to Isle Aux-Noix, to await re-enforcements, and prevent the passage into the lake of the sixteen-gun ship, which would have effectually cut them off.

While these events were transpiring, Major Brown was absent; having been sent by Schuyler, with Ethan Allen and some interpreters, to go through the woods into Canada, and there disseminate among the people his address assuring them that the designs of the Americans in entering their country were solely against the English garrisons, and not at all against the property, religion, or liberties of the inhabitants.

This arduous and dangerous service having been faithfully and successfully performed, Col. Allen and Major Brown found Livingston, who collected a small body of Canadian recruits, with which they attempted, on the 8th, to return to the army, but were deterred by learning that a body of Indians lay in wait for them. Major Brown, however, made his way through, with a communication from Livingston, demanding a party of men from Schuyler's army to cut off communication between St. Johns and the country; explaining his position at St. Terese, and expressing his belief, that, on the arrival of the men he asked for, they would be joined by a considerable number of Canadians.[2]

In compliance with this request, Col. Ritzema was ordered to proceed, on the 10th, to a point on the road from La Prairie to St. Johns, as near to the latter place as he deemed prudent; but a succession of disgraceful panics thwarted the execution of the plan.

On the 16th, Gen. Schuyler, compelled by prolonged ill health, returned to Ticonderoga. But it had previously been arranged, that, on the 15th, a second advance upon St. Johns should be com-

[1] Lossing's Field-book of the Revolution, vol. i. p. 169.

[2] Am. Ar., 4th ser. vol. iii. p. 740.

menced by the army led by Montgomery. In anticipation of this movement, that general, on the day before that assigned for its execution, despatched Major Brown, with one hundred Americans and thirty-four Canadians, towards Chamblee, in order to keep up the spirits of their friends in that quarter.

This little detachment was the first of the American army which could be said to have entered Canada; and, with it, Major Brown penetrated to the gates of Chamblee. There he left one-half his force; while, with the remainder, he cut off communication between St. Johns and the interior, took several prisoners, and intercepted eight carts, going to the fort, laden with rum and gun-carriages for the armed vessels which threatened the lake. Gen. Montgomery's departure from Isle Aux-Noix was delayed by a storm until the 17th, on the evening of which day he encamped before St. Johns. The next morning, he crossed with five hundred men to the north side of the Sorel, where he had instructed Major Brown to rejoin him. But Brown, trusting to his earlier arrival, had imprudently thrown his little company before a superior force of king's troops, and been repulsed. Montgomery's corps, which had been retarded by the inexperience of its raw recruits in marching, came up in a few hours: the king's troops were, in their turn, defeated; and the captures, which Major Brown had bethought himself to hide in the woods before engaging in his unsuccessful conflict, were secured.[1]

The siege of St. Johns having been formally established, Ethan Allen and Major Brown were ordered to La Prairie and Longueil to recruit corps of Canadians for the American army, — a service in which James Livingston had already been so successful as to be commended by Montgomery to Congress.

Allen and Brown also had the most gratifying and encouraging success in this service; and Major Brown was, moreover, lucky enough to take a quantity of stores designed for the Indians, who had been induced by Gov. Carleton to go to La Prairie to operate against the Americans.[2] On the 20th of September, Allen had two hundred and fifty Canadians under arms, and boasted to Montgomery, that, in a week or two, he could obtain one or two thousand. Major Brown had also enlisted between two and three hundred. Every thing was going prosperously, and with the most

[1] Montgomery to Schuyler, Am. Ar., 4th ser. vol. iii. p. 797.

[2] Am. Ar., 4th ser. vol. iii. p. 840.

encouraging promise, when the all-important work was interrupted by the unhappy issue of one of those audacious but tempting enterprises, opportunities for which Allen and Brown seem to have been incapable of resisting.

Allen wrote to Montgomery, on the 20th of September, that he would join him in three days with five hundred men, after which, if it were necessary, he would return and recruit. "By the Lord!" said he, "I can raise three times the number of our army in Canada, provided you continue the siege: it all depends upon that." He was, in fact, crazed with the desire to take part personally in the operations against St. John's;[1] and, on the 24th, he set out for that place with a guard of eighty men. He had gone, however, but about two miles from Longueil, when he was met on the banks of the St. Lawrence, nearly opposite to Montreal, by Major Brown, who proposed a plan for the surprise of that city, which he thought could be easily effected by the combined action of their forces. No project could have been more fascinating to the captor of Ticonderoga; and although, upon its failure, it was denounced as rash and impracticable, it would probably have succeeded, had neither of the parties failed to meet his engagement.[2]

The proposition was readily assented to, and a plan of operations agreed upon. Allen, returning to Longueil, was to procure canoes, and cross the river at night, a little below the city. At a point a little above it, Brown was to cross, with his corps of two hundred men; and, upon the signal of three huzzas from the latter party, a simultaneous attack was to be made. The night was so rough, and the canoes to be obtained were so small and frail, that Brown supposed Allen would defer the attempt. At the appointed time, however, the latter having, by the addition of thirty Anglo-Americans, increased his force to one hundred and ten men, was over the river, and impatiently waiting the signal for action. He continued to expect the arrival of the promised co-operating corps until the sun was two hours high, when he "began to suspect that

[1] Am. Ar., 4th ser. vol. iii. p. 754.

[2] Montgomery, to whom the design was communicated too late for his interference in it, although distrusting its success, did not absolutely condemn it. In a letter to Schuyler, he wrote, "Allen, Warner, and Brown . . . have a project for making an attempt upon Montreal. I fear the troops are not fit for it. Mr. Carleton has certainly left that town, and it is in a very defenceless condition."

he was in a *premunire*."[1] It was then too late to retreat. A prisoner had escaped from his guards, and given the alarm in the city; the boats which had brought them over were insufficient to carry one-third of Allen's men back; and, although all but thirty-eight finally deserted him, he could not reconcile it with his sense of honor to abandon any. He therefore sent off messengers to Major Brown and a Mr. Walker, asking aid; and stood his ground manfully, for an hour and three-quarters, when attacked by about forty regulars, and a rabble hundred or two of armed citizens. A smart skirmish occurred, with some loss of life on each side; but, no re-enforcements appearing, the hero of Ticonderoga was obliged to capitulate, and, in violation of the terms of his surrender, to enter upon that long and cruel imprisonment which has awakened the sympathy of every reader of Revolutionary story.

Allen attributed his disaster to Major Brown's failure to keep his engagement; but the commander-in-chief, and all the officers who mentioned the subject in their correspondence, fixed the blame upon his own rashness and obstinacy. This, to be sure, was not an absolutely fair test, as Allen's associates did not manifest the same indulgence towards his infirmities of temper, which posterity, with a grateful memory of his heroic virtues, has accorded. But, with whatever undue harshness of judgment Allen's contemporaries may have visited his leadership in this affair, the uniform conduct of John Brown compels us to believe, that, if all the circumstances of the case were known, they would fully justify his course. If he had failings as a commander, they certainly did not lie in the direction of excessive prudence, sluggishness in action, or remissness in duty. Of treachery, he was incapable.

September passed, and the siege of St. Johns advanced but slowly. Discontent began to show itself in the army, which constantly embarrassed Montgomery by its disposition to interfere with his proper functions. About the 12th of October, he was informed by Major Brown that the general dissatisfaction was so great, that, unless something was soon done to allay it, there was danger that it would break out in open mutiny.

He therefore called a council of war, in which he found his own opinion opposed to that of every field-officer present. His views

[1] Allen's narrative.

were unchanged by this result; but, while deeply regretting the decision of the council, he declared that he would not oppose the general sense of the army, but enforce it by every effort in his power.[1] And Montgomery was always as good as his word.

But the siege continued to be retarded, as it had all along been, by the want of ammunition, and particularly of powder. It was even feared that this cause would compel the abandonment of the expedition altogether. In this dilemma, Schuyler, on the 29th of September, made an earnest application to the New-York Congress for at least five tons, to be sent forthwith to St. Johns. The Congress exerted itself zealously; but all that it could procure from its own resources was fourteen hundred pounds, and this only by resorting to the dangerous expedient of exhausting the county arsenals of the reserve stores, which they were, by law, required to keep. Gov. Trumbull, who was asked for a loan, had none to spare. The Continental Congress, "learning that Gen. Schuyler was in great distress for powder, ordered a single ton to be sent him from New-York City." But all which he received from any source furnished Montgomery but a temporary supply; and a few days from the 18th of October would have entirely exhausted it.[2]

Happily, a mode of relieving the army from this serious strait was suggested to Major Brown; affording him an opportunity for another of those daring and dashing exploits in which he delighted, and which so often proved of signal service to the country. At Chamblee, on the Sorel, stood a strongly-constructed fort, containing a considerable amount of stores, and a large quantity of powder, but feebly armed and garrisoned. Carleton believed that the Americans could not approach its walls with artillery, unless they first captured St. Johns, which commanded the river twelve miles above.[3] But some of Livingston's Canadian recruits — experienced oarsmen — volunteered to place cannon upon bateaux, and take them at night past the fortifications of the latter place. Their offer was accepted; and, on a dark night, the plan was successfully put in execution. Major Brown had been intrusted by Montgomery with the charge of the undertaking, and personally

1 Am. Ar., 4th ser. vol. iii. pp. 1097–8.

2 Schuyler to Washington, Am. Ar., 4th ser. vol. iii. p. 1095.

3 The River Sorel descends from Lake Champlain to the St. Lawrence.

directed and took part in the perilous feat of the boatmen. At the head of the Chamblee Rapids, the guns were mounted upon carriages, and soon placed in position for attack. Major Livingston re-enforced the besiegers with three hundred Canadians,—there were but fifty Americans engaged in the affair; and Major Stopford, the commander of the fort, was surprised to find it closely invested. He had no reason to expect relief—but among the articles of capitulation which he proposed to Major Brown was one containing the extraordinary condition that the garrison should not be made prisoners, but be permitted to march out unmolested, drums beating, colors flying, with their arms, accoutrements, and twenty-four rounds of ammunition each, and carts and provisions sufficient to pass by the shortest route to Montreal, or any other place in that Province at the option of Major Stopford.

VIEW OF FORT CHAMBLEE.

This proposition was of course entirely inadmissible; and Major Brown, at once declining it, demanded a surrender of the place upon the usual terms granted in honorable warfare. There was no alternative but to accede to this, or sustain an assault without hope of making a successful defence; and the fort was given up, with its garrison, on the morning after the demand, Oct. 19.

One major, three captains, three lieutenants, a commissary, and a surgeon, with eighty-three non-commissioned officers and privates of the Royal Fusileers, were made prisoners. The stores found in the fort were eighty barrels of flour, eleven barrels of rice, seven barrels of peas, six firkins of butter, one hundred and thirty-four barrels of pork, one hundred and twenty-four barrels of gunpowder, three hundred swivel-shot, one box of musket-shot, six thousand five hundred and sixty-four musket cartridges, one hundred and fifty-four stand of French arms, three royal mortars, sixty-one shells, five hundred hand-grenades, rigging for at least three vessels, and the arms and accoutrements of the eighty-three Fusileers. Gen. Montgomery was overjoyed at this glorious acquisition, which he foresaw would give an early and successful termination to the lingering siege of St. Johns. He announced it to Gen. Schuyler in the following terms: —

"Dear General, — I have the pleasure to acquaint you with the surrender of Chamblee to Majors Brown and Livingston. . . . I send you the colors of the Seventh Regiment and a list of stores taken. Major Brown assures me we have gotten six tons of powder, which, with the blessing of God, will do our business here. Major Brown offered his service on this occasion. Upon this and all occasions, I have found him active and intelligent."

A report of the achievement was transmitted to the Continental Congress, which instructed a delegation it was about sending to the Northern army, to assure Majors Brown and Livingston "that the Congress had a just sense of their important services, and would take the first proper opportunity to reward them." [1] Livingston was made colonel of a regiment of Canadians. Brown waited for his reward.

St. Johns surrendered on the 2d. Both during the siege, and previously while in camp at Ticonderoga, Col. Easton's regiment suffered severely from sickness, induced by insufficient shelter, improper food, and lack of medical stores. One hundred and sixteen of its men were sent home, invalided, between the 20th of July and the 25th of September; and the returns of the 12th of October carried up the number to one hundred and forty-three. This loss had been in some measure repaired by new recruits, of whom one hundred and forty were sent forward at one time; and, at the close of the siege of St. Johns, the regiment numbered about three hundred men. We have no certain knowledge of what its services were up to that time; but Major Brown had been almost constantly employed on detached and adventurous duty, to aid in which, he would naturally have selected tried men from his own neighborhood, except when Canadians were better adapted to the work in hand.

The moment, however, that the surrender of St. Johns was sure,

[1] Jour. Cont. Cong., Nov. 7, 1775.

Col. Easton — Major Brown having rejoined him — pushed his small corps, augmented by Livingston's larger regiment of Canadians, down the Sorel, driving before him Allen McLean, who, without a commission, commanded an irregular body of king's men. McLean attempted to intrench at the point in the St. Lawrence formed by the debouching of the Sorel; but was driven from his works by Easton, who proceeded at once to complete and strengthen them. In a few days they were mounted with three twelve-pounders, one nine, and two sixes, and effectually commanded the passage of the St. Lawrence.

All the night of the 6th, Major Brown patrolled the north side of the river near Montreal, and captured several prisoners, from one of whom he learned that Gen. Carleton had announced to the citizens his determination to quit the place within a couple of days; and that they had thereupon resolved to apply to the American commander for protection. This intelligence changed the major's intention of remaining on the north side, to raise a party and cover Montgomery's landing; and, returning to Sorel, he wrote to the general, informing him what he had learned, and begging to be permitted, if his regiment was to remain at Sorel, "to have the honor of entering the city of Montreal with the army."

Montgomery marched into the city on the 13th. Carleton had, the night before, embarked with his garrison, certain prominent loyalists, and such stores as he could take, on board a fleet of eleven small vessels, with the expectation of dropping down the river to Quebec, but was unable to pass the batteries at Sorel. On the 17th, he was still engaged in vainly attempting to effect a passage; and Montgomery wrote that Col. Easton not only "prevented it, but had twice compelled him to weigh anchor, and move up the river."[1] He added that he was making all despatch to attack the fleet from his own side. It capitulated on the 19th; and, with it, there fell into the hands of the Americans Gen. Prescott, — infamous for his ill-treatment of Ethan Allen, — thirteen other officers, one hundred and twenty privates, and several prominent loyalist gentlemen. Gen. Carleton, in a boat with muffled oars, succeeded in passing the batteries under cover of an unusually dark night. Of ordnance, the vessels were found to contain two nine and two six-pounders, and two or three

[1] Am. Ar., 4th ser. vol. iii. p. 1633.

smaller guns; of ammunition, three barrels of gunpowder, a large quantity of artillery cartridges and ball; twenty-three hundred musket cartridges; of small arms, eight chests, besides those borne by the prisoners; of other stores, seven hundred and sixty barrels of flour, six hundred and seventy-five barrels of beef, three hundred and seventy-six firkins of butter, two hundred pairs of shoes, a quantity of entrenching tools, &c.

"Col. Easton's detachment," wrote Montgomery to Schuyler, "while employed in this important service of stopping the fleet, were half naked, and the weather was very severe. I was afraid, not only that they might grow impatient, and relinquish the business in hand, but I saw the reluctance the troops in Montreal showed to quit it. . . . By way of stimulant, I offered, as a reward, all public stores taken in the vessels, to the troops who went forward, except ammunitions and provisions." But this stimulant induced only Bedel's New-Hampshire regiment to forsake their comfortable quarters in the city, to share the labors and the honors of the half-naked and almost shelterless Berkshire men at Sorel.

With the surrender of the fleet on the upper St. Lawrence, the first northern campaign ended; for, although the war in Canada was prosecuted with little interruption, Arnold's arrival gave to the succeeding operations a character distinct from that of the advance to Montreal.

The brilliant services rendered to the expedition by the chief Pittsfield officers were handsomely acknowledged. Montgomery wrote to Schuyler, Nov. 22, "Col. Easton has shown so much zeal and activity in the important service he has been employed upon, that I think myself obliged to speak of him in the warmest terms of acknowledgment; and, as his character suffered in the public opinion by some unfortunate transaction last summer,[1] I hope you will be kind enough to do him the justice which his conduct with me merits."

Other letters in which Col. Easton was eulogized by his commander will be referred to in another connection. For Major Brown, Montgomery formed the warmest friendship and esteem; and even Schuyler wrote to Congress that he "had certainly, in in the course of the last year, done extraordinary services."[2]

[1] Probably this refers to a dispute regarding the accounts of the Ticonderoga expedition.

[2] Jour. Cont. Cong., Aug. 26, 1776.

In October, 1776, Cols. James Livingston and Timothy Bedel, Major Robert Cochran, and Capts. Gersham Mott and William Satterlee of the Northern Army, certified, that, during the campaign of the previous year in Canada, Major John Brown "was the most active man in the army; being employed in the beginning of the campaign in long tedious scouts, and, in the latter part, before the army with a detachment. Major Brown was scarcely off duty day or night during the campaign."

Of the services and sufferings of the other officers and men in Easton's regiment, Montgomery's praises were earnest.

While their brethren were thus winning honor in Canada, Col. Patterson's regiment remained with the army employed in the siege of Boston, and built Fort No. 3 on Prospect Hill in Charlestown,[1] which it also garrisoned. On the day of the Battle of Bunker Hill, Patterson's regiment, with three others, was held in reserve for the protection of Cambridge; and late in the afternoon, being ordered to re-enforce the exhausted defenders of the Hill, failed to reach the lines before they were carried by the enemy.

Some time in November, four hundred British troops landed at Lechmere Point, now East Cambridge, for marauding purposes, and were bravely repulsed, although under cover of a frigate, by an American force to which Washington paid the following compliment: "The alacrity of the riflemen and others did them honor, to which Col. Patterson's regiment and some others are equally entitled." He praised them again in the general orders of the next day.[2]

A tradition has been handed down in Berkshire, regarding the Battle of Bunker Hill, which, strange as it seems at first thought, is supported by such abundant and indisputable evidence, that we cannot refuse it credence. It is to the effect that the cannonading from the British fleet was distinctly heard by many persons in Pittsfield, and elsewhere among the hills. At Lee, persons digging a well heard the reports with peculiar clearness. In Pittsfield, among many others who distinctly heard the booming of the cannon, were Capts. Israel Dickinson, Jared Ingersol, and Hosea Merrill, — men of unquestioned veracity. By placing the ear near

[1] Now Somerville.

[2] Frothingham's Siege of Boston, p. 268.

the earth, the loudness of the sounds was much increased. In considering the probable truth of this tradition, it must not be forgotten that the intervening space between Charlestown and Pittsfield was, in 1775, free from the disturbing noises of railroads, manufactories, and cities, which now abound.[1]

[1] Another remarkable instance of the transmission of sounds among the hills occurred on the 26th of November, 1822. On that day, Samuel Charles, an Oneida Indian, was hung at Lenox for the murder of a negro in Richmond; and the Berkshire Greys, a Pittsfield military company, attended as sheriff's guard. At the hour fixed for the execution, Dr. Oliver S. Root was in a field, near where the Medical College in Pittsfield now stands, when he heard the sound of a drum and fife apparently close at hand. Surprised at the early return of the Greys, he went to the brow of the declivity made by the road at that point, expecting to see them on its southern slope, but was still more surprised when he found no signs of the company there. It afterwards appeared, that it was at that moment just leaving Gallows Hill, seven miles distant. On the same occasion, fishing-parties at the north end of Pontoosuc Lake, ten miles from the place of execution, heard, as distinctly as though in the next street, the mournful strains as the procession wended its melancholy way to the gallows, and the lively notes struck up on the return.

Since the above was written, I have seen an account in "The Springfield Republican," that persons in that city heard distinctly the sound of three explosions, which, following each other in rapid succession, recently destroyed a powder-mill at Poughkeepsie, N.Y. These instances go far to remove any improbability which might otherwise attach to the old tradition.

CHAPTER XIV.

THE DECLARATION OF INDEPENDENCE.—THE TORIES.—BATTLES OF WHITE PLAINS AND THE DELAWARE.

[1776–1777.]

King George's Name expunged from Military Commissions. — The Town instructs its Representative in Favor of Independence and a Free Republic. — Committees of Correspondence, etc. — Their Rules of Practice. — The Tories. — The Hue and Cry. — Hiding-place of the Tories. — The Ban of Community. — Its Effect illustrated by an Incident. — John Graves aids the Escape of a Royal Officer, and is punished therefor. — An *ex-post facto* Fright. — Infliction of Confiscation and Banishment. — Case of Elisha Jones and Others. — Enlistment of a Slave. — Woodbridge Little and Israel Stoddard. — Six Tories induced by Energetic Measures to take the Oath of Allegiance. — Anecdote of a Soldier returned from a British Prison. — Mr. Allen's Diary at White Plains. — Patterson's Regiment rejoins Washington. — Its reduced Condition.

"VOTED, That the field-officers proceed to regulate the North District or Regiment with the erasement of George's name." Such was the quiet resolution by which, on the 25th of March, 1776, — more than three months previous to the Declaration of Independence, and two months before the famous resolution of the Continental Congress, "that the exercise of every kind of authority under the king ought to be suppressed," — the people of Pittsfield signified that they were done with his Majesty King George the Third, and regarded him much as their Puritan ancestors did "the man Charles." Independence was, with them, a foregone conclusion; and, for their part, they were sick of the sham of fighting the king under his own commission. For the person of the man George, it was absurd any longer to profess affection; and they had early learned a theory of government which paid hardly more regard to the royal office. They had also acquired among the hills a habit of carrying political principles to their full legitimate conclusions, with a hopeful belief that a higher Power would take care of the consequences, — a habit and a pious faith which we shall find them exercising in other relations of state, as well as in this.

Having passed the vote which practically renounced all allegiance to the king, — but which is recorded with no more note or comment than that by which the same meeting enacted that "hogs should not run at large," — the town went on with its ordinary business. Two months later, in May, it gave to Valentine Rathbun, its representative in the General Court, the following emphatic instruction: —

> "You shall, on no pretence whatever, favor a union with Great Britain, as to becoming, in any sense, dependent upon her hereafter; and we instruct you to use your influence with the Honorable House, to notify the Honorable the Continental Congress that this whole Province is waiting for the important moment which they, in their great wisdom, shall appoint for *the Declaration of Independence and a free Republic.*"

A town thus impatient for the birth of the nation must have hailed its actual occurrence with enthusiastic joy. But no account has been handed down, even by tradition, of the mode in which it was celebrated. Even the great Declaration, which the General Court ordered to be "spread upon the records of the several towns for a memorial forever," does not appear on those of Pittsfield; probably on account of the practice, to which allusion has been made, of keeping the minutes of town-meetings for a long while upon loose sheets of paper. The permanent records at that time appear to have been written up at long intervals.

The General Court having recently sanctioned the committees of correspondence, inspection, and safety, consolidated them in one, and ordered the towns to choose them annually, the Pittsfield March meeting elected to the office, Dea. Josiah Wright, Valentine Rathbun, William Francis, Stephen Crofoot, Joseph Keilar, William Barber, and Aaron Baker: Capts. Eli Root, James Noble, and John Strong were added at the May meeting.[1]

[1] The committees of subsequent years were as follows: —

1777. — Lieut. William Barber, Valentine Rathbun, Col. John Brown, Capt. Eli Root, Joshua Robbins, Dea. Josiah Wright, Capt. William Francis, Lebbeus Backus, Lieut. Stephen Crofoot.

1778. — Valentine Rathbun, Caleb Stanley, Lieut. Stephen Crofoot, Dea. Josiah Wright, Capt. William Francis, Lieut. Rufus Allen, Lebbeus Backus. Re-elected in 1779.

The unhappy Tories who were "handled," as it was quaintly phrased, by the Revolutionary committees, were never satisfied, whoever might compose them; but they took advantage of the change of persons to demur to the jurisdiction of the new body in cases commenced before the old; whereupon the committee made application to the town, at its March meeting, for "directions how to recover pay for handling persons that appeared inimical to their country." The subject was referred to Valentine Rathbun, David Bush, William Francis, William Williams, Charles Goodrich, James Noble, and John Strong, on whose report the town determined, —

"*First*, That said committees, consisting, or having consisted, of whom they may, are one and the same, from their first appointment to this day; and that all their transactions and determinations ought to be considered the acts and proceedings of an adjourned court; consequently, all matters and things that have not been finally determined, still have day with them; and, if there be any matters and things before them that are not yet determined upon, they, the committee as it now stands, have as full power and authority to act upon them as ever they had; and if any person upon trial appeared inimical to his country, or hereafter upon trial shall appear so, they are hereby empowered, so far as our united influence can support them, to tax such persons for their time therein expended on trial, and all other necessary charges, and, on refusal, to be committed to the common jail, or be otherwise confined, till the same be paid; and, in all other respects, to deal with them, as to punishment, according to the direction of the Continental Congress, Provincial Congress, or General Assembly.

Second. Voted, That if said committee shall apprehend and convene before them any person or persons whom they suspect to be inimical to their country, or to be guilty of any other misdemeanor, and upon trial are found innocent, in that case the said committee have no pay for their time or cost.

Third. Voted, That if any complaint shall be brought before said committee by any person or persons, and supported, then the offender shall pay all costs, and, refusing, shall be confined in the common jail, or elsewhere, until he comply and pay the cost, together with the confinement, with the costs thereof; and, in case any complainant shall not support his complaint, said complainant shall be holden to pay all costs, and, on his refusal, shall be holden and committed as aforesaid."

These rules, perhaps, made as fair a provision for impartial justice as could be then attained; but it still left an inducement for

1780. — Lieut. Stephen Crofoot, Col. John Brown, Col. James Easton, Capt. Eli Root, Capt. William Francis.

The State Constitution being adopted in 1780, no more committees of this character were chosen.

the committee, sitting as judges, to sustain their own suspicions as prosecutors, and thus obtain their costs. The confusion of functions rendered this difficulty inevitable.

The period from the spring of 1776 until the victories at Saratoga in Oct. 1, 1777, was one of those in which the spirit of Toryism was most rampant in Berkshire and the neighboring districts. The miserable failure of the Canada expedition, from which so much had reasonably been expected, spread dissension and mutual distrust in the Whig ranks, disheartening the patriots, and giving courage to those "inimical to their country." The Declaration of Independence, while it gave firmness and consistency to the Whig party, and inspirited its clear-sighted and determined members, disaffected not a few half-hearted men, who could not even yet admit the impossibility of reconciliation with the mother country upon honorable terms, or who, weary of the conflict, were willing to seize upon any pretext for abandoning it. The disasters to the army of Washington near New York, which looked more like utter ruin and disintegration than simple defeat, spread a gloom over the country, so discouraging that many were seduced by the liberal offers of pardon and favor which the royal commanders extended; and the danger that the defection would become infectious was so great that the sternest measures for its repression were justified. Of those measures, the favorite was to place the offender under the ban of the community, by proclaiming him in the public prints to be an enemy of his country, and raising the hue and cry upon him.[1] The effect of this proceeding was to deprive the culprit of the protection which law and public sentiment ordinarily accord against petty depredations and annoyances, and, holding him up to the contempt and hatred of his

[1] The hue and cry was not literally a pursuit with shout and halloo, although that sometimes came of it; but an advertisement, like the following from "The Hartford Courant:" —

"Whereas, Major Israel Stoddard and Woodbridge Little, Esq., both of Pittsfield, in the county of Berkshire, have fled from their respective homes, and are justly esteemed the common pests of society, and incurable enemies of their country, and are supposed to be somewhere in New-York government, moving sedition and rebellion against their country, it is hereby recommended to all friends of American liberty, and to all who do not delight in the innocent blood of their countrymen, to exert themselves, that they may be taken into custody, and committed to some of his Majesty's jails, till the civil war, which has broken out in this Province shall be ended.

"By order of the Committees of Inspection in the towns of Pittsfield, Richmond, and Lenox. JOHN BROWN.

"PITTSFIELD, April 27, 1775."

neighbors, to invoke upon him those petty and irritating persecutions which the baser sort of villagers are at all times sufficiently prone to visit upon the objects of their dislike. It further excluded Tories from intercourse with each other, and from business communication with all; and placed them under the strict surveillance of the committee's police, and the jealous watchfulness of a suspicious public. Fines and costs of court were the inevitable concomitants of this state of ban; and the sufferer might think himself lucky if he escaped imprisonment. On the frequent occasions when public feeling was roused by the approach of invasion, when rumors of treasonable plots were rife, or when news of such Tory atrocities as the massacre of Wyoming were received,—then it behooved the loyalist, however circumspect his conduct had been, and however little implicated in political intrigues, to beware.

Many of those in Pittsfield, in anticipation of unwelcome visits at times like these, prepared themselves hiding-places. That of Woodbridge Little was in the open space left, according to custom, around the chimney of old-fashioned houses. The cottage occupied by Mr. Little is still standing in good preservation, being the pretty residence of Mr. F. C. Peck, where the Tory's hiding-place may still be seen. One of the brothers Ashley — the only Tories in The West Part — had his refuge in a crevice among the rocks, at the base of the Taconics, known as the Diamond Cave. Another was accustomed to fly to a cavern in the rocky banks of Roaring Brook, in New Lenox.

An instance of the minor troubles to which "inimical persons" were liable is related of Ashley. West Street, on which he resided, is legally seven rods wide; but less than one-half that width suffices for the purposes of travel, and, from time immemorial, it has been the privilege of the farmers on each side to mow and sometimes to cultivate the superfluous space. In early times, it was permitted them to enclose their crops until harvest. This Ashley, in 1776, had done with the portion which lay along his farm; and it was covered with a fine growth of corn, when, for some reason he went into hiding. But unluckily for him, while thus absent, a party of young ploughmen took their nooning near by; and one of them, of mischievous wit, suggested that it would never do to permit such encroachments upon the highway, especially by a Tory, and that it was no more than their duty to maintain the rights of the town. No second suggestion was needed. "In the twinkling of a goad-stick," says the rustic tradition, "the fence was on the original limits;" and the cattle of the neighborhood feasted that afternoon at the expense of George's friend. But the end was not yet. That night the volunteer conservators of the integrity of the highway carelessly left their plough standing in the field; and, on the next morning, the tongue was found to have been chopped completely off. It had been hacked and mangled in a manner which showed it to have been the work of weak hands; and, as it was known that only Ashley's wife and daughters were at the house, there was no difficulty in fixing upon the authors of the mutilation. A "council of war" was at once called; and the party proceeded to the house, where, undeterred by the screams of the girls, they searched until the mother was dragged from the closet in which she had ensconced herself, when they escorted the frightened dame to one of the horse-blocks, which, for the convenience of mounting pillions, then stood before every door. On this they compelled her to stand while the plough was brought, and its wounds bound up in bandages, as if it were a mangled human limb.

When overt acts of treason against the liberties of America were proved, the punishment was more severe. In May, 1776, John Graves, son of Moses,[1] aided in the escape of Capt. McKay, an officer of the royal artillery, and his servant, one McFarlane, from the Hartford jail; which must have been effected in some mysterious way, the doors and windows being afterwards found secured as usual. Graves piloted the fugitives through the country, lodging at the house of fellow Tories, until he reached Pittsfield. Here they recruited at the house of Graves and his brother, who furnished them with horses, with which they set out in the hope of reaching Canada. But at Lanesborough they were suspected, knocked down, and, according to their own story, "beaten and abused in the grossest manner after being tied."[2] That was not the manner of "the country fellows" of that section; and the probability is, that Capt. McKay, who was a brave and spirited man, resisted his captors strenuously, and got soundly mauled for his pains.

Be that as it may, the recapture created a sensation in the neigh-

[1] Brother of the Moses Graves known to the last Pittsfield generation.

[2] Major French's Journal, Coll. Conn. Hist. Soc., vol. i. p. 207.

borhood, and Graves was sent back with his friends. An examination showed that he was not only concerned in McKay's escape, but had made two similar trips between Pittsfield and Hartford. The Connecticut committee, however, thought that, although he had committed an offence in that colony, it was better that he should be tried at home, and wrote to the Massachusetts Board of War a letter in which they described him as "appearing to be a low-spirited, insidious fellow, and to entertain strong prejudices against the liberties of America."[1] The board ordered the sheriff of Berkshire to receive and commit him for trial.[2] He was finally banished. An anecdote connected with this affair illustrates the feeling of the people towards the Tories. McKay was entertained at Stockbridge by Gideon Smith, a notorious loyalist; and, the fact coming to the knowledge of the committee, it was deemed necessary to "handle" him. The hue and cry was raised; and a party, of which Sharpshooter Linus Parker was one, repaired to the delinquent's house. His family reported him not at home; but the seekers, confident that he was secreted in the barn, summoned him, with a promise of quarter, to surrender. Upon this he appeared at a half-open door, peered curiously around, and, after some parley, came out and gave himself up. Smith and Parker were, nevertheless, on very friendly terms; and after the war, the former being, with his wife, on a visit to the latter's house, Smith reverted to the incident described, and said that when he opened the door of the barn, being an extraordinary runner, he felt certain of effecting his escape; but, seeing Parker with his famous rifle in hand, he was afraid to make the attempt. "And now, Parker," said he, "I want to know if you would really have shot me." — "As quick as I ever shot a deer!" was the reply. "Then it would have been all over with me," said his friend, trembling with emotion at the memory of the danger he had escaped.

Confiscation and banishment were inflicted in several instances; but generally those who received these punishments had already joined the king's forces. In 1778, the General Court passed "an act to prevent the return to the State of certain persons who had left it, or either of the United States, and joined the enemies thereof." The list of those thus proscribed contained, in all, three

[1] Mass. Ar., vol. clxv. [2] Mass. Ar., vol. ccx. p. 270.

hundred and eight names, of which the following were from Pittsfield: Jonathan Prindle, Benjamin Noble, Francis Noble, Elisha Jones, John Graves, and Daniel Brewer. Francis Noble settled at St. John, New Brunswick, and was one of the refugees to whom the lands upon which that city is built were granted, in compensation for their sufferings for the Crown. His twin-brother, Benjamin, was banished at the same time, and repaired to New York, where he was killed before the return of peace.[1]

The commencement of Jones's troubles has been related.[2] In May, 1776, the Pittsfield committee, "in observance of an order from the Great and General Court, dated April 23, directing them to take possession of all the estates of absconding Tories," made return, as regarded Jones, that "they had the greatest reason to think he had fled to the ministerial army, and joined the same against the Colonies," and that they had accordingly "taken possession of his real and personal estate." The former embraced three hundred acres of land and four lots, upon one of which was the homestead, a very superior farm-house, on Wendell Square; and, on another, saw and grist mills. These they had leased, according to the legislative order, for one year from April, "with some small reserve for the proper support of Mrs. Mehitable Jones, wife of said Elisha, and their six children." An inventory of the personal property "found in the hands and possession of the said Mehitable" was also returned; and in the list are enumerated "one negro man named Prince, about twenty-four years old, who left his master Jones about a year ago, and enlisted in Col. Sargent's regiment,[3] and Titus, negro boy, aged eleven."

Woodbridge Little and Israel Stoddard, after their experience in the spring of 1775, had maintained a circumspect course, and, as they claimed, complied outwardly with all the requirements of the national and State legislatures. But they had been watched with suspicious jealousy by the local committees: and a post-bag, which passed secretly back and forth between the Tories of Berkshire and their friends in New-York City, was captured by High Sheriff Israel Dickinson;[4] and the contents showed that all the loyalists

[1] Sabine's American Loyalists.

[2] See chap. xiii.

[3] Enlisted as Prince Hall. In 1772, Jones advertised two runaway mulatto slaves in the "Courant."

[4] This post-bag is still in possession of the sheriff's grandson, Israel Dickinson, Esq., of Lafayette, Ind.

of the county, for some purposes at least, were closely banded in a secret organization, — the high with the low; those who outwardly maintained a show of respect for the Revolutionary authorities, as well as those who malignantly opposed them. Probably on account of the evidence thus obtained, Messrs. Little and Stoddard were "handled" with a severity from which they appealed to the powers at Boston. But, in the spring of 1777, the increasing depression of American affairs, and the dangers which threatened the patriotic cause, still more emboldened the Tories, who had, through the disasters of the previous year, been gaining confidence, and showing themselves in their true colors; so that it became necessary to deal with them in earnest. And, in June, William Williams, John Brown, and Stephen Crofoot, selectmen of Pittsfield, — being, as they declared, "obliged thereto by an act of the General Court," — called a town meeting for the express "purpose of discovering who are the internal enemies of this and the other United States of America," and also "to hear what Jonathan Hobby and Jonathan Weston have to offer."

This action brought matters to a crisis; and, at the meeting, "Woodbridge Little, Israel Stoddard, Moses Graves, J. Hobby, J. Weston, and Joseph Clark made their appearance before the town, and upon their confession, declaration, and taking the oath of allegiance to the United Independent States of America, were received as the friends of these States." The allegiance thus sworn appears to have been faithfully maintained; and Mr. Little, at least, received the favor and confidence of his fellow-citizens, being elected selectman, and delegate to the county conventions in 1781 and subsequent years, and representative in 1788, 1789, and 1790.

But this happy reconciliation was preceded by an incident of not so pleasant or creditable a character. Under the orders of the legislature, fifteen Tories were arrested, and placed under guard at the tavern of Col. Easton; and it is related that a soldier, whose temper had been soured by ill-treatment when a prisoner in the hands of the enemy,[1] begged the privilege of standing sentinel over them. His request being granted, he imposed perfect silence upon those under his charge, and prohibited intercourse among them on penalty of instant death. On the slightest pretence of infraction of his orders, he presented his loaded musket at the head

[1] In the diary of Mr. Allen, the return of several soldiers, broken down by the cruelties practised in the British prison-ships, is noted.

of one or another of the frightened party. It was evident that the man was seeking a pretext for killing one of them; and the greatest terror prevailed, especially, it is said, on the part of Mr. Little. It is to be hoped that so ill qualified a guardsman was relieved as soon as the facts came to the knowledge of his officers.

During the military operations in Westchester County, after the retreat from Long Island in the fall of 1776, Col. Simonds of Williamstown led a corps of levies from the three Berkshire regiments to re-enforce the army of Washington. Of this regiment, which served from the 30th of September until the 17th of August, Rev. Thomas Allen was chaplain; and Pittsfield also contributed Lieut. William Barber and fifteen men to its ranks. We know nothing of its service there except what is contained in the following extract from Mr. Allen's diary, regarding the battle of White Plains, and the few days immediately preceding it: —

"WEDNESDAY, Oct. 23. — This day I went with Rev. Mr. May and Dr. Guitteau, to Frog's Neck, and brought off a colt. On our return, I saw our men bringing in a Hessian on a sort of bier, who was wounded in the leg. There had been an action just before between a party of our men and the enemy, of whom we killed ten or twenty, and took two prisoners. The wounded Hessian's leg was broken; and, as our men brought him in, the surrounding multitude behaved in the most rude, inhuman, and unmanly manner; some calling out, "Dash out his brains," others damning him, and still others upbraiding and insulting him in an indecent manner. But the poor Hessian behaved like a man, and pulled off his hat to the multitude. He was a rifleman, dressed in green, faced with white, and wore a green cockade upon his hat. He was of dark complexion, caused, I suppose, by the long passage which he had of twenty weeks, he having arrived but three weeks before.

"THURSDAY, Oct. 24. — At night, struck our tents, and moved up four miles towards White Plains. This night, encamped without a tent upon the ground.

"FRIDAY, Oct. 25. — All day under arms, in expectation of an attack from the enemy, who now appeared, paraded in sight, marching and countermarching. A great battle appeared to be at the door. This night, also, lay on the ground, under a brush shelter.

"SATURDAY, Oct. 26. — The sun rose clear. The enemy near; a great battle drawing on. Our soldiers this morning brought in a regular, James Marrow, of the Thirty-fifth Regiment. Gen. Leslie commands the brigade; Col. Kerr commands the Thirty-fifth Regiment, one of the four which make up the brigade. This soldier affirms that the regulars' muskets were all charged; and it was his opinion they would attack us before to-morrow morning. He further deposed that there were ten brigades of regulars in this neighborhood. Yesterday forgot to dine; to-day made an excellent dinner on bread and butter only, being in continual expectation of a cannonade from the enemy, who lay in plain sight, at the distance of a little more than half a mile. Kindled up the fires at dark; and, soon after, began our retreat, with Gen. Bell's brigade, in most excellent order, keeping out on flank guard.

"LORD'S DAY, Oct. 27. — Arrived at break of day at White Plains, having performed a march of above twelve miles in the night. Lay down after daylight for sleep on the ground. This day, thirteen Hessian prisoners were taken, and two were killed. Yesterday, Dr. Danielson, surgeon's mate to Dr. Mather, was killed within our encampment on Valentine's Hill. He refusing to stop, they fired upon him, and he fell dead. Dr. Wright of New Marlboro' was buried this day at White Plains. Such a confused Sabbath I never before saw. This day encamped on White Plains, in our tent again, having been marvellously preserved in our retreat.

"MONDAY, Oct. 28. — About nine o'clock, A.M., the enemy and our out-parties were engaged. About ten, they appeared in plain sight, filing off in columns to the left and towards our right wing, but no additional force of ours was as yet directed that way. At length, the enemy came up with our right wing, and a most furious engagement ensued, by cannonade and small arms, which lasted towards two hours. Our wing was situated on a hill, and consisted of, perhaps, something more than one brigade of Maryland forces. The cannonade and small arms played most furiously, without cessation; I judged more than twenty cannon a minute. At length, a re-enforcement of Gen. Bell's brigade was ordered from an adjacent hill, where I was. I had an inclination to go with them to the hill where the conflict was raging, that I might more distinctly see the battle, and perhaps contribute my mite to our success. Just as we begun to ascend the hill, we found our men had given away, and were coming off the hill in some confusion, at which moment elevated shot from the enemy's camp came into the valley, where we were, very thickly, one of which took off the fore part of a man's foot, about three rods from me, of which I had a distinct view, as would be supposed. I saw the ball strike and the man fall; and, as none appeared for his help, I desired five or six of those who had been in battle to carry him off. Others I saw carrying off wounded in different parts; and, with the rest, I retreated again to the main body on the hill, which was fortified, from which I had just before descended. Our men fought with great bravery: they generally, one with another, shot seven cartridges before they were ordered to retreat. They were sore galled by the enemy's field-pieces. Our loss in killed, wounded, and missing, from the best information I can obtain, is about two hundred. The enemy's loss" . . .

The fragment of Mr. Allen's diary closes here.

In November, at about the time when Col. Simonds's regiment

returned to Berkshire, that of Col. Patterson, leaving its fatal encampment at Mount Independence, repaired to Albany, where it took shipping for Esopus, on the Hudson. Marching thence across the country, it joined Washington at Newtown, Pa., just in season to take part in the battles of Trenton and Princeton.

But such had been the sufferings of the corps, that leaving Washington at New York, on the 21st of April, a well-appointed regiment more than six hundred strong, it returned to him in November with barely two hundred and twenty men, many of whom were greatly enfeebled; and yet it had seen less than two months' service in the field. Of the brave men who were missed from its ranks, some were invalided at home; but the greater portion, victims of disease, battle, or the tomahawk of the lurking savage, were in their graves, — if graves were accorded them.

CHAPTER XV.

PITTSFIELD IN THE SECOND CANADA CAMPAIGN. — ARNOLD'S PERSECUTION OF BROWN AND EASTON.

[SEPTEMBER, 1775–1778.]

Arnold arrives at Quebec. — Montgomery arrives. — Projected Assault on the City. — Brown charged with creating Dissensions. — The Charge considered. — Assault on Quebec. — Death of Montgomery. — Arnold continues the Siege. — Brown's the most advanced Post. — Expects to be a Uriah there. — Small-Pox in the Army. — Attempt to set up Inoculation in Pittsfield. — Patterson's Regiment marches to Canada. — In the Affair of the Cedars. — Evacuation of Canada. — Miserable Condition of the Army at Crown Point. — Schuyler and the Berkshire Committees. — Arnold's Charges against Brown and Easton. — They demand a Court of Inquiry. — Singular Difficulty in obtaining it. — Brown impeaches Arnold of Treason and other Crimes. — Appeals to the Public. — Publishes a Hand-Bill against Arnold. — Remarkable Interview between Brown and Arnold. — An *ex-parte* Trial. — Gross Injustice to Brown. — His spirited Remonstrance and Resignation.

EARLY in August, 1775, Washington found that he could very well spare from the army at Cambridge a detachment of a thousand or twelve hundred men,[1] for a movement against Quebec by the way of the Kennebec River. This expedition had been suggested by Col. Brewer of Massachusetts; but the commander-in-chief placed at its head Arnold, who was at Cambridge, filling the camp with his loud-mouthed complaints of the treatment which he had received at Ticonderoga.

The little army which was intrusted to him consisted of two regiments of infantry and three companies of rifles, — about eleven hundred men in all.[2] Leaving Cambridge on the 15th of Septem-

[1] Am. Ar., 4th ser. vol. iii. p. 214.

[2] Jabez Chandler (?), John Gardner, and Jonathan Bill enlisted out of Capt. Noble's minute-men into Arnold's expedition.

ber, it arrived at Point Levi, opposite Quebec, on the 9th of November, with less than nine hundred effective men, who, in their march through the wilderness, had endured the severest suffering, and encountered innumerable dangers.

Eager to obtain distinction for himself, Arnold made some bold demonstrations against the city; but, learning that Carleton was approaching from Montreal, he retreated to Point Aux-Trembles, on the St. Lawrence, twenty miles above Quebec, where, on the 1st of December, Montgomery, with a beggarly remnant of the army of St. Johns, arrived, and took command of the combined forces, numbering not so many effective men in all as Arnold had brought with him to Point Levi: so rapidly were their battalions reduced by the expiration of enlistments and by disease.

Montgomery soon discovered that an attempt to enter Quebec by storm was a necessity; and a plan was arranged of which the essential points were simultaneous night-assaults upon the upper and lower towns, by divisions led respectively by Montgomery and Arnold in person, with feints in two other quarters. But the general was greatly chagrined, when the corps selected for the attack were ordered to report for that duty, to find three companies of Arnold's detachment refusing to serve under him, although eager for service in either of the other parties. Montgomery had been greatly struck with the superior discipline and subordination which Arnold's troops exhibited in contrast to his own, and was loath to encourage a proceeding which might lead to deterioration in qualities the lack of which he had deeply felt in his own command; and he was, moreover, convinced that the dissatisfied companies had no just cause of complaint against their commander. He therefore refused to make the change which they demanded; but their dissatisfaction was so great, that the proposed plan of assault was abandoned.

Montgomery attributed the disaffection of the three companies to a certain "Capt. ———, who had incurred Arnold's displeasure," and to a field-officer, who, as he thought, desired separate command of the recusant corps; and he added, "I am much afraid my friend ——— is deeply concerned in this business. I will have an *éclaircissement* with him on the subject." The names given in blank are carefully erased in the original letter;[1] but it has

[1] Am. Ar., 4th ser. vol. iv. p. 754.

been assumed that the friend alluded to was Col. Brown, and that he was actually the originator of the trouble. There are many circumstances to favor the supposition that his name should actually fill the blank, although there is no evidence of it. But it will be observed, that the general expresses only a suspicion, which the *éclaircissement* which he intended might have entirely removed. If it had been well grounded, it could not have escaped the knowledge of the vigilant Arnold, who, if he had been able to prove so serious a military offence, would not have failed to make it prominent among the charges which he brought against his enemy in the acrimonious controversy which they carried on for the ensuing two years. So reckless was he in his accusations, that one cannot believe he would have waited even for a semblance of proof, had the rumor come to his ears, that Major Brown had been guilty of a crime so odious to every commander, and especially to Washington and Schuyler, as incitement to mutiny.

Brown had had opportunity, in private life, before the war, to obtain an insight into the vileness of Arnold's character,[1] and had learned him thoroughly. After-intercourse had revealed to him in the officer the same selfish wickedness which had characterized the jockey and tradesman. He was informed of his petty embezzlement of the wages he had "humbly engaged to see paid" to Capt. Noble's poor Pittsfield soldiers; he was familiar with the arrogance, slanderous malignity, and even worse, which he had manifested at Ticonderoga; and he fully believed that the incipient traitor, after learning that the Massachusetts committee would refuse him the place he claimed there, would, had he not been prevented by Col. Easton with a strong hand, have betrayed the little flotilla to the British commandant at St. Johns.

With this opinion of Arnold, Major Brown dreaded the consequences of the favor which so dangerous a man was winning with his superior officers. His deep feeling upon this point had been freely communicated to his friend and general, and hence probably, if Brown was the person alluded to in Montgomery's last letter, arose his fear that one whom he loved and esteemed had been so imprudent as to tamper with Arnold's soldiers. Col. Brown's subsequent heroic and patriotic subordination of his just

[1] His brother-in-law and legal preceptor, Oliver Arnold, was first cousin to the traitor.

sense of his own personal rights to the interest of his country renders it impossible to believe that he was guilty of the conduct of which he was hastily suspected.

As the time approached when the term for which Col. Easton's men had enlisted would expire, Gen. Montgomery urged Major Brown to remain in the service, and attempt to raise a regiment from those about to be disbanded from his own and other corps. Brown consented; and, considering the difficulties which lay in his way, mustered a respectable number of men, among whom Capt. Eli Root, Lieut. Joel Dickinson, and Lieut. Joseph Allen, with six privates, enrolled themselves, on the 1st of January, as from Pittsfield, which sent four additional men on the 23d of the same month.

Col. Easton's regiment was discharged on the 31st of December. On the day previous, the disastrous assault on Quebec, which cost the American armies the noble Montgomery, was made. The troops were ordered to parade at two o'clock in the morning. The first division, commanded by Montgomery in person, comprised the New-York regiments and part of Col. Easton's; the second, under Arnold, embraced the detachment he had brought from Cambridge, and Lamb's artillery. Besides these were Livingston's small corps, and a detachment of ninety-four men from Major Brown's newly-organized battalion, under command of Capt. Jacob Brown.[1]

The four divisions paraded separately; and the two latter amused the enemy, while Montgomery and Arnold led the real assaults at divers points. We need not enter into the sad details. Montgomery fell mortally wounded, while gallantly fighting at the head of his men. Arnold, while no less gallantly leading his, was wounded in the leg, and carried off the field. The attack was abandoned. By the death of Montgomery, Gen. Wooster succeeded to the chief command in Canada; but kept his quarters quietly during the winter at Montreal, while Arnold doggedly maintained the siege of Quebec, chiefly by keeping up a blockade which excluded supplies. Carleton, confident of his ability to hold out until the breaking-up of the ice in the spring should permit re-enforcements from England to reach him, as doggedly defended his position within the walls.

[1] Capt. Jacob Brown was brother of the major, and father-in-law of David Bush of Pittsfield.

During this winter's siege, Col. Brown was posted with his regiment at the advance post, within cannon-shot of the city fortifications. "A plenty of thirty-six-pound balls," said he, in a letter of Feb. 7 to his father, "come to our door without hands: two of them we use for hand-irons." In a letter of March 15 to his wife, he expressed great pleasure in a rumor that Gen. Lee was near at hand. "Gen. Arnold and I," said he, "do not agree very well. I expect another storm soon, and that I must be a Uriah. We had [manuscript illegible] yesterday. The enemy made a sally on our working-party, it was said with five hundred men. Gen. Arnold immediately ordered me, being on the advance post, to attack them with my detachment, which consists of about two hundred men, more than half of whom were sick in hospital. I accordingly marched against the enemy, who retired into their fort too soon for me to attack them. I expect to be punished for disobedience of orders next. . . . I suppose all letters are broken open before they reach the Colonies; but as this goes by a friend, Capt. Pixley, it will come safe."

New England having responded to an earnest appeal for reenforcements, Gen. Wooster's force was, by the 1st of April, increased to three thousand men, of whom, however, about eight hundred lay sick with small-pox. No preventive was then known for this malady, — then the most dreaded of pestilences, — except inoculation of the patient with its own virus, after his system had undergone a severe regimen and a peculiar medical treatment. Those who submitted to this process generally survived the ordeal; but a considerable percentage died, and all were subjected to more or less suffering. There was, besides, great danger, that, from the inoculating pest-houses, the disease might extend to the surrounding community.

There was, therefore, the most intense prejudice against the practice in the minds of the people; and the special vote of the town, which was required before it was permitted, was always obtained with the utmost difficulty, and accompanied by the most stringent restrictions, which the physicians were required to give bond to respect, while a committee of the most prudent citizens was appointed to supervise their conduct. Even this, indeed, was a revolutionary assumption of authority on the part of the towns, for there was a law of the Province prohibiting inoculation, except in the town of Boston; and the Council in July, 1776, expressed their unwillingness to credit the report that Gen. Ward had granted liberty to some of the Continental troops to receive it at Winter Hill, to the great dread of the good people of Medford.[1]

In the spring of 1774, Dr. Childs, foreseeing the war, and anticipating the infection to which the army would be exposed, asked permission "to set up inoculation" in Pittsfield; but it was refused. He renewed his application with increased earnestness before the town-meeting of April, 1775, which again denied him. It was not until after sad experience, that in September, 1776, the requisite license was accorded, and then only with hesitancy, and accompanied by the most embarrassing conditions. Only those who had the thoughtfulness, as well as the means, to visit other places for the purpose, went to the war protected against the fearful contagion. Rev. Mr. Allen, on entering the service, visited Sheffield, and there submitted to inoculation.

Patterson's regiment, in the latter part of April, proceeded to Canada *via* New York and the Hudson; and a detachment of sixty-seven, taken from several of its companies, were included in the cowardly capitulation at the Cedars, where, on the 19th of May, three hundred and ninety-six Americans were surrendered by Major Butterfield to Capt. Foster, who led a force of forty British regulars, one hundred Canadians, and five hundred Indians, the latter commanded by Brant in person. Major Sherburn, arriving near the scene soon after the surrender, having been sent to the relief of Butterfield, fell into an ambuscade, and, after making a splendid fight, was also obliged to capitulate. But Foster, in violation of the terms he had granted, permitted his savages to plunder both detachments of the American prisoners, and to murder many of Sherburn's corps, which lost in the battle and the massacre fifty-eight men. In Butterfield's detachment were two of Capt. Noble's company, — Elisha Kingsley and Tristram Story.

Burgoyne arriving early in May, with succor for Quebec, the Americans were compelled to retreat, and soon entirely to evacuate Canada. All that dash and enthusiasm, inspired by a reasonable hope of great results, — in spite of imperfect discipline, meagre numbers, and the scantiest appointments, — had enabled the army of 1775 to win, was lost in a few brief weeks of 1776.

The remnant of the retreating forces reached Crown Point in

[1] Am. Ar., 5th ser. vol. i. p. 146.

June, in a state of demoralization which is thus vividly and truthfully depicted in a letter of John Adams, dated July 7:—

"Our army at Crown Point is an object of wretchedness, enough to fill a humane mind with horror: disgraced, defeated, discontented, dispirited, diseased, naked, undisciplined, eaten up with vermin, no clothes, beds, blankets, no medicine, no victuals but salt pork and flour. . . . I hope that measures will be taken to cleanse the army at Crown Point from the small-pox; and that other measures will be taken in New England, by tolerating and encouraging inoculation, to render the disease less terrible.

Capt. Noble, of the minute-men of 1775, died at Crown Point from the secondary effects of small-pox, having previously written home the following letter, which finds its illustration in the above extract from Mr. Adams's:—

CROWN POINT, July 1, 1776.

DEAR WIFE,—I would inform you, that, through Divine Providence, I am alive, but not over-well; for by reason of hard fatigue before I had the small-pox, by marching and unsuitable diet, the distemper has left me in a poor state of health, though I had it very light. Ten days ago I was sent, with the sick, from Isle Aux-Noix to this place, and have grown worse rather than better since I came here. Our army is very distressed by reason of the small-pox. We have had four thousand sick at once. I have not lost one of my company, though some of us had it very severe. Sergeant Colefix is now very bad, and it is doubtfnl if he ever recovers. I had two men taken by the Indians in Major Sherburn's party, which are redeemed; and one Samuel Merry, of my company, is either killed or taken by the regulars, going down on a raft from Montreal to Sorel. The distress of our sick is so unaccountable that I cannot paint it out by pen and ink. (All of my company have had it.) If it was not for the danger of the small-pox, I should like to have brother James or David come up and see me, and bring my horse; for I intend to try to come home if I remain so poorly. I believe one of them may come safe by taking good care when he gets here. I suppose there are about four thousand of the well of our army at Isle Aux-Noix; and whether they will remain there or come here I do not know. Tell Crowner's wife that he has had the small-pox, and has got well over the distemper, but has had the misfortune to have it fall into one of his eyes; so that I am afraid he will lose the sight of one eye. He remembers his kind love to her and child. He intends to try to come home when I come: he cannot write for want of paper. It is very hard living here. Wine one dollar per quart, spirits one dollar per quart, loaf-sugar three shillings per pound, butter one shilling and sixpence, none to be had for that: no milk. All of the above articles hardly to be had. Vinegar three shillings per quart. I shall write no more at present, but remain your loving husband,

DAVID NOBLE, *Captain.*

The calamitous termination of the invasion of Canada brought to its culmination the opposition to Schuyler, which in the county of Berkshire, in King's District, and on the New-Hampshire Grants, had been growing ever since his appointment to the northern command.

An unblemished patriot, a gallant soldier, and no mean statesman, Schuyler was yet distinguished by qualities, both positive and negative, which rendered him, if qualified for any departmental command, remarkably ill-adapted to that which was assigned him, between a majority of whose people and himself there existed an incompatibility which resulted in antagonism fatal to the public interests. An aristocrat of the aristocrats, he hated the nonchalant and robustuous democracy of Massachusetts, and the still ruder independence of the settlers upon The Grants. A New-Yorker of the New-Yorkers, jealous of the rights of his Province, he participated to the full in the feeling excited by the alleged encroachment of the New-Englanders upon her eastern border, and was prepared to resist, at any cost, the new invasion of her territory under pretence of patents from New Hampshire. Intimate, socially and personally, with many of the higher class of loyalists in King's District, he could not be made to believe them guilty of the secret plots against their country, and the violation of their solemn pledges, of which they were popularly accused. Annoyed and embarrassed by the machinations of the malignant Tories, he was willing to proceed strenuously against them; but he was indignant at the harshness with which his friends, the Van Schaacks, and others of like stamp, had been "handled" by the committees. The ill blood which arose in the district on this account between him and a "certain class of Whigs" was perhaps more bitter than his differences with the same class in Berkshire, or even upon the Grants.

Coming to his command with a nervous horror of partisan warfare, he attributed that character to the proud-spirited and ambitious militia of the hills, who, prone to hardy and independent enterprise, were not easily controlled, but kept him in perpetual terror of some rash adventure; while they failed him in executing his best-laid schemes of falling back for an indefinitely postponed advance. And he refused to renounce his prejudices against them, even when he found that they alone won victories in his department, and, having won them, showed a regard for the amenities of honorable warfare, and observed its laws with a scrupulous nicety, which put to shame the regulars whom they encountered.[1] He failed to perceive a courtesy which was not expressed in courtly phrase, or to recognize chivalry except in those of gentle blood, — as gentility went in Provincial America. As a soldier, his courage was proved; as a general, few in the American armies could better set a squadron in the field, or were more familiar with the rules of their art. As a commander of department, none labored more arduously, or gave themselves with more untiring zeal and industry to the unthankful task of providing material of war; none did so more unselfishly, as was grandly shown in his ceaseless exertions to supply the northern army when forbidden to hope for any large share in the glory of its anticipated achievements. But he was destitute of that great element in generalship, which, given a certain soldiery with whom to accomplish a specific end, takes them as it finds them, with all their faults and with all their excellences, wins their confidence, and makes the most of what is in them. Schuyler, on the contrary, fretfully magnified the imperfections of the men committed to him, and was perversely blind to their good qualities as soldiers. Assigned to a position surrounded by innumerable difficulties, he possessed nothing of the spirit which delights to encounter obstacles, the energy which turns them to its own account, and, least of all, that calm strength which endures without complaint what cannot be avoided or changed.

Much of that which was to be regretted in him was the result of the depressing influence of ill health; and, reviewing his career, we cannot fail to recognize the true patriot and statesman, and the general whose abilities would have given him perhaps brilliant success in almost any other field than that in which he was placed.

The radical Whigs, who controlled the politics of his department, were hardly to be expected so clearly to perceive his merits. Between the Revolutionary committees of that region and such a man as we have described, conflict was inevitable. Of political and social sentiments the very reverse of those which characterized Schuyler, the committees were also extremely unlike him in temperament and habits of thought. Impetuous, sometimes even to rashness, in their zeal, they and their followers were ever ready

[1] See, in illustration, the story of Ethan Allen and Gen. Prescott.

to rally in sudden emergency, or for the execution of dashing enterprises; but, if the opportunity to meet the enemy was not speedily accorded them, they grew impatient of the necessary restraint of military discipline. In their theory of the art of war, retreat was omitted from the list of contingencies. As a general, Fabius was by no means a model in their esteem. Judging the readiness of all men to make sacrifices for their country by their own, they underrated the impediments which Schuyler found in raising armies and accumulating stores. Intolerant of the lukewarmness of moderate Whigs as well as of the misdeeds of the loyalists, they denounced the former in no measured terms, while they advocated and practised the most rigid discipline of the latter. Many of them of narrow experience in affairs, and wanting that liberality towards opponents which contact with the great world brings, they could not explain the perhaps over-generous sentiments of Schuyler towards some of those whom they classed indiscriminately as the enemies of American liberty, except upon the hypothesis of his sympathy with their Toryism.

When, therefore, information came to Berkshire and King's District of the sad aspect which affairs wore in Canada, and finally that all which had been gained there, at such great cost, was wrested from the Americans, — smarting under the disappointment of hopes which with them had been more sanguine than elsewhere, — the people of those districts were ready to charge the commander who, although not long personally in the field, had from the first been nominally at the head of operations, with the responsibility for their miserable failure. Among its prime causes, they ranked the brief delay before St. Johns, to which he had been persuaded by the report of a treacherous informer to the neglect of the truthful representations of John Brown and James Livingston. Other missteps of the expedition were attributed to him, oftenest unjustly, through the malignancy of his enemies, who played upon the popular feeling through unscrupulous emissaries, who found powerful auxiliaries in Schuyler's unfortunate peculiarities. In the frame of mind thus produced, the community was ready to credit the most absurd statements which jumped with its humor of the hour. Even before the defeated and pest-stricken army reached Crown Point, the excited feeling among the people at home had risen to a height which invited, what men thus frenzied will always find, witnesses of the Titus Oakes stamp, ready, for the sake of a sorry notoriety and a petty reward, to play upon their fears and fancies. The chief among these was an informer, whose name, like that of the other witnesses, was withheld, on the pretence, that, if it was known, his life would be in danger, and who related what one George Hindsdale had told him that he had heard from one McDonald, an agent who had been sent to view the lead-mines at Canaan. Most or all of the evidence was of this hearsay character, having often passed through three or four mouths before it was deposed before the committees; eleven of which listened to the informer just mentioned at Richmond, Valentine Rathbun presiding.

The informers were credulously favored by the most violent and radical of the committee-men, whose prominence and popularity were augmented by whatever deepened the general hatred of the Tories, and brought odium upon the moderate Whigs. Out of the evidence elicited, this class formed the outlines of a "hellish plot," of whose reality they succeeded in convincing both themselves and a majority of the community. This plot, they imagined, had been concocted between Gen. Schuyler, the British Government, and the New-York Tories, among whom, it was alleged, were included the whole Provincial Congress, with two exceptions only. The gist of the plan was, that Schuyler's New-York forces, or as many of them as would not excite suspicion, were to be stationed in a line of forts along the Hudson River, from Canada to New-York City; who, on an appointed day, were to raise the British flag, and permit the king's troops to ascend the river, and cut off communication between the Southern and Eastern Colonies.

So earnest was the faith of the people in this fiction, that there was the most unbounded terror throughout Berkshire, the northern part of which was patrolled by the militia night and day. Letters were also sent to Gen. Washington, some of them charging Schuyler with downright treason; some, like one of Matthew Algate, chairman of the King's-District committee, only "discovering" to the commander-in-chief "a glimmering of such a plot as had seldom appeared in the world since the fall of Adam by the grand deceiver and supplanter of truth." [1] Others left it an open question, whether Schuyler was traitorous, or simply

[1] Am. Ar., 4th ser. vol. vi.

incompetent. But all alike were handed over by Washington to Schuyler, with the warmest expressions of his continued confidence, both in his integrity and ability. Nothing, probably, could have been better adapted, than the course of the committees, to strengthen his affection for the accused, who, whatever other faults he may have possessed, he knew could not be untrue to the country which trusted him.

The New-York Congress, to whom Capt. Douglas went personally to prefer charges against the commander of the department, dismissed them as scornfully as did Washington. Schuyler demanded a court of inquiry; but it was refused as unnecessary.

Such, briefly, was the famous affair of Schuyler and the Berkshire committees.

We resume the account of the events which caused the loss of Col. Easton and John Brown to the Continental Army; one of the most remarkable records of wrong, and the refusal of justice, in the history of that time, or perhaps of any other.

Soon after the death of Montgomery, Major Brown, claiming the rank of colonel, which had been given him by that commander, was refused it by Arnold. He demanded the reason of the denial, and then first learned that their great enemy charged Col. Easton and himself with certain military crimes, of which the chief was plundering the baggage of British officers at Sorel. Conscious of his entire innocence, being joined by Col. Easton, he immediately demanded a court of inquiry, and challenged Arnold to prove aught against him inconsistent with the character of an officer or a gentleman. Arnold refused to order the court, but said that the commander-in-chief at Montreal would doubtless give him the satisfaction of a trial. Brown then applied for permission to send an officer for that purpose to Gen. Wooster. Arnold assented, but delayed the departure of the messenger until he had forestalled Brown's application by a request that it might be denied;[1] and he had sufficient influence at headquarters to prevent this simple act of justice. At the same time, Arnold had written to the President of Congress, making the same charges against Brown and Easton; alleging that Gen. Montgomery had himself refused the promised rank of the former on the ground that he was pub-

[1] A copy of the letter in which this request was made, afterwards fell into Brown's hands.

licly impeached of the plundering at Sorel, and urging Congress to refuse the application which he anticipated that the two officers would make for promotion.[1] Gen. Wooster had put off Col. Brown's application with the promise to attend to the matter on his arrival at Quebec; and there, on the 1st of April, Brown renewed his petition, strongly urging immediate action, as an act of justice, and deprecating further delay, on the ground of the uncertain future of war.[2] But Wooster still neglected the investigation. Brown then applied to the commissioners sent by Congress to Canada; and they, too, refused their intervention.

On the 1st of May, Gen. Thomas took command of the army, and readily promised to grant the court of inquiry as desired by Brown. But the sad death of that commander by small-pox, on the 2d of June, defeated this, like many other good results which had been hoped from his presence.

Col. Brown now appealed for the justice which he could not obtain from the sources below, to the commander-in-chief of the department; but Schuyler, an admirer of Arnold, and bitterly prejudiced against every Berkshire man, "deemed it inexpedient to call a court."

July came; and, the term for which Col. Brown's little corps had re-enlisted having expired, he visited Philadelphia, and, in a firm and respectful petition, demanded the inquiry which he had not been able otherwise to procure; and, on the 30th, Congress "resolved that so much of the petition of Col. Easton and Major Brown, as prays that the charges against them, of having been concerned in plundering the officers' baggage taken at Sorel, be submitted to a court of inquiry, is *reasonable;* and that Gen. Schuyler is desired to order courts of inquiry on them as soon as possible."[3]

On the 1st of August, on the recommendation of the Board of War, to whom Brown's petition had been referred, Congress determined that he should be allowed the rank and pay of lieutenant-colonel from the 20th of the previous November; and that "James Easton was entitled to the rank of a colonel from the first day of July, 1775, and to the pay of a colonel from that date until he should be discharged, which ought to be done as soon as a court of inquiry should report in his favor, or a court-martial should

[1] Am. Ar., 4th ser. vol. iv. p. 907. [2] H. C. Van Schaack.

[3] Jour. Cont. Cong., 1776.

determine upon his conduct, and their sentence be carried into execution—there being no vacancy to which he could be appointed; but, should he be honorably acquitted, his past services would recommend him to the confidence of Congress for future employment."[1]

In the previous February, after his regiment was disbanded, Col. Easton wrote to Gen. Washington, requesting to be again appointed to the command of a regiment in the northern army; alleging that the application was made "in faithfulness to the dear deceased Gen. Montgomery and his commands, and obliged by a love of liberty and his country." "You will see, sir," said he, "by the letters and orders enclosed, the minds of the generals who wrote them." Washington replied, through his aid, that, not knowing how matters stood with regard to Easton's command, he thought it necessary to refer the case to Congress, if Col. Easton wished to raise a new regiment, and advised him to repair to Philadelphia, and produce there the honorable testimonials of his merit which he had sent for his own examination. "The services you have done your country in the last campaign," said the writer, "mentioned in the letters to you from the late gallant Gen. Montgomery, merit the acknowledgment of the public."

Col. Easton accordingly repaired to Philadelphia in April, and there laid before Congress, not only the request which he had made to Washington, but also petitions regarding other matters, which will appear from the action of that body upon them.

Col. Easton's claims for his services in the surprise of Ticonderoga were referred to the committee of Albany, the claims of all other persons engaged in that affair having been disposed of in the same manner. It was resolved, that "as, from the testimonials produced by the petitioner, it appeared that he and his battalion behaved with great diligence, activity, and spirit, in the successful enterprise against Gen. Prescott, and the vessels and troops under his command," after the surrender of Montreal, and that, "to encourage the parties employed in that important service, Gen. Montgomery promised them all the public stores, except ammunition and provisions, which should be taken in the vessels; and as the petitioner alleged that no part of those stores was delivered, nor any composition made to the troops concerned in the acquisi-

[1] Am. Ar., 5th ser. vol. i. p. 1597.

tion,"— therefore it was recommended to the general commanding in Canada to appoint commissioners to estimate the stores, and pay the value thereof to the officers and men employed in that service, in such proportions as the commissioners should determine. As the petitioner's account of regimental receipts and disbursements on which he claimed a balance due could only be adjusted in Canada, the settlement was referred to the Congressional commissioners in that Province. But, as Col. Easton was in want of money, two hundred dollars were ordered to be advanced him.

With regard to Col. Easton's request respecting a court of inquiry concerning his own conduct and that of Major Brown in the Sorel affair, "as Gen. Arnold had, on the first of February, alleged to Congress that both officers were accused of acts which would bring great scandal upon the American arms, and produce great disgust in the army in general, if either of them were promoted until these matters were cleared up; and as Easton asserted his innocence, declaring that he neither plundered, nor directed, nor was privy to the plundering of any prisoner, or other person whatsoever; considering, therefore, on one hand, the aggravated nature of this charge, which was an impediment to the petitioner's promotion, and, on the other, the great confidence reposed in him by Gen. Montgomery, and the essential service which he had rendered his country,"— Congress instructed its commissioners in Canada to institute an inquiry, by court-martial or otherwise, into the charges against him, giving him an opportunity of making his defence, and to transmit their proceedings thereon to Congress, in order that justice might be done the petitioner if he had been accused without sufficient reason.[1] But a new difficulty here beset the unfortunate colonel, whether by the instigation of Arnold does not appear. He was arrested, and thrown into prison, for a debt of fifteen hundred pounds, "York currency," and had no remedy but to apply to Congress, which he did in the following terms, after acknowledging his indebtedness for the sum for which he was sued, and nine hundred pounds in addition :—

"I have due two thousand pounds lawful money. My creditors have a landed security of what I value at three thousand pounds lawful money. In several letters they have received from me since I came to this place, I have offered my land and my outstanding debts at an honest appraisal;

[1] Am. Ar., 4th ser., vol. v. p. 1690.

in short, I have done every thing in my power to get a settlement, but have heard nothing from them. There is no such thing as obliging people to pay their debts in the Massachusetts by the resolves of the honorable Congress. I ought to be on my way to Canada. This settlement with the commissioners appointed by Congress requires it; a settlement of my regimental accounts of five captains still in the service at Canada, the getting the stores and vessels taken by the regiment appraised, the court of inquiry to be holden there in regard to Major Brown and myself, and many other important matters, all urge it; in short, I am in pain to see the event of Quebec."[1]

Congress granted the enlargement requested by Col. Easton, and he returned to Canada; but, before he reached that Province, it had been evacuated by the American forces, and he appears to have profited nothing by the Congressional orders in his favor. From that time he seems to have abandoned in despair the attempt to obtain justice, at least against Arnold, and remained inactive, save when volunteering in the militia, which he did as often as opportunity presented.

Col. Brown was more persistent; and having armed himself with the order of Congress passed in July, for a court of inquiry in his case, and its confirmation of his rank as lieutenant-colonel in August, and being assigned to Col. Elmore's Connecticut regiment, — he returned to the army in the latter month, and forwarded his papers to Gen. Gates, who had, for a time, supplanted Schuyler in the northern command. From him, he asked a compliance with the directions of Congress: but Arnold, who had acquired even greater influence over the new and less manly commander than he had possessed with Schuyler, was able to ward off the investigation, which, with good reason, he dreaded; and, on his instigation, Gates had the assurance to refer the matter to the Board of War.

Wearied with vain efforts to obtain a vindication of his character by a court of inquiry upon his own conduct, and hopeless of effecting it in that manner, Col. Brown now adopted a new line of procedure, and preferred to Gen. Gates the following serious charges against Arnold, whom he insisted should be arrested, and tried upon the several specifications: —

[1] Am. Ar., 4th ser., vol. v. p. 1234.

To the Honorable HORATIO GATES, ESQ., *Major-General in the Army of the United States of America, commanding at Albany.*

Humbly sheweth, that, in the month of February last, Brig.-Gen. Arnold transmitted to the honorable Continental Congress, an unjustifiable, false, wicked, and malicious accusation against me, and my character as an officer in their service, at the time when I was under his immediate command; that, had there been the least ground for such an accusation, the author thereof had it in his power — indeed, it was his duty — to have me brought to a fair trial by a general court-martial in the country where the pretended crime is said to have originated; that I was left to the necessity of applying to Congress, not only for the charge against me, but for an order for a court of inquiry on my own conduct in respect thereto; that, in consequence of my application, I obtained a positive order of Congress to the then general commanding the Northern Department for a court of inquiry, before whom I might justify my injured character; that the said order was transmitted to your Honor at Ticonderoga, in the month of August last; and, notwithstanding the most ardent solicitations on my part, the order of Congress has not yet been complied with; that, upon my renewing my application to your Honor for a court of inquiry, you were pleased to refer me to the Board of War.

Thus I have been led an expensive dance, from generals to Congress, and from Congress to generals; and I am now referred to a Board of War, who, I venture to say, have never yet taken cognizance of any such matter; nor do I think it, with great submission to your Honor, any part of their duty. I must therefore conclude, that this information, from the mode of its origin, as well as from the repeated evasions of a fair hearing, is now rested upon the author's own shoulders.

I therefore beg that your Honor will please to order Brig.-Gen. Arnold in arrest for the following crimes, which I am ready to verify, viz.: —

1st. For endeavoring to asperse your petitioner's personal character in the most infamous manner.

2d. For unwarrantably degrading and reducing the rank conferred on your petitioner by his (Gen. Arnold's) superior officer, and subjecting your petitioner to serve in an inferior rank to that to which he had been appointed.

3d. For ungentlemanlike conduct in his letter to Gen. Wooster, of the 25th of January last, charging your petitioner with a falsehood, and in a private manner, which is justly chargeable on himself.

4th. For suffering the small-pox to spread in the camp before Quebec, and promoting inoculation there in the Continental army.

5th. For depriving a part of the army under his command of their usual allowance of provisions ordered by Congress.

6th. For interfering with and countermanding the order of his superior officer.

7th. For plundering the inhabitants of Montreal, in direct violation of a solemn capitulation, or agreement, entered into with them by our late brave and worthy Gen. Montgomery, to the eternal disgrace of the Continental arms.

8th. For giving unjustifiable, unwarrantable, cruel, and bloody orders, directing whole villages to be destroyed, and the inhabitants thereof put to death by fire and sword, without any distinction to friend or foe, age or sex.

9th. For entering into an unwarrantable, unjustifiable, and partial agreement with Capt. Foster for the exchange of prisoners taken at the Cedars, without the knowledge, advice, or consent of any officer then there present with him on the spot.

10th. For ordering inoculation of the Continental Army at Sorel, without the knowledge of, and contrary to the intentions of, the general commanding that Northern Department; by which fatal consequences ensued.

11th. For great misconduct in his command of the Continental fleet on Lake Champlain, which occasioned the loss thereof.

12th. For great misconduct during his command from the camp at Cambridge, in the year 1775, until he was superseded by Gen. Montgomery, at Point Aux-Tremble, near Quebec.

13th. For disobedience of the orders of his superior officers, while acting by a commission from the Provincial Congress of the Province of Massachusetts Bay; and for a disobedience of the orders of a committee of the same Congress, sent from that State to inspect his conduct, and also for insulting, abusing, and imprisoning the said committee; as also for *a treasonable attempt* to make his escape with the navigation men, at or near Ticonderoga, to the enemy at St. Johns, which obliged the then commanding officer at Ticonderoga and its dependencies to issue a positive order to the officers commanding our batteries at Crown Point, to stop or sink the vessels attempting to pass that post, and by force of arms to make a prisoner of the said Gen. Arnold (then a colonel), which was accordingly done.

JOHN BROWN, *Lieutenant-Colonel.*

ALBANY, 1st. Dec., 1776.[1]

Col. Brown transmitted this impeachment to Congress as well as to Gates; but such was the reputation and favor which Arnold's dash and gallantry, shrewdly turned to account by his meanly intriguing spirit, had won for him, that nothing came of either presentment.

Congress allowed its admiration for one bold and active officer to lead it into gross injustice towards another. Nothing, therefore, was left to Brown but to appeal to still another tribunal, — the people of the country. This he did in a paper which was

[1] H. C. V. S. Col.

published at Pittsfield, April 12, 1777.[1] The substance of its contents is contained in the foregoing pages, and we quote but one paragraph: —

"I appeal to every person of common understanding, whether in a military character or not, that, if Gen. Arnold did not know himself guilty of the charges laid against him, he would not have endeavored to bring himself to a trial, to clear up his character, which, had he been able to do, he certainly might have called his impeachers to account for false and malicious charges, and put the saddle upon the other horse; but, very far from this, he has used every possible art to prevent a trial, as if his character was not worth a sixpence."

In the winter of 1777 occurred an incident which is thus related in Col. Stone's Life of Brant: —

"During the winter of 1776–7, while Arnold and many of the officers were quartered at Albany, . . . Arnold was at the head of a mess of sixteen or eighteen officers, among whom was Col. Morgan Lewis. Col. Brown having weak eyes, and being obliged to live abstemiously, occupied quarters affording greater retirement. . . . Col. Brown published a handbill, attacking Arnold with great severity, rehearsing the suspicious circumstances that had occurred at Sorel; and upbraiding him for sacking the city of Montreal while he was in the occupancy of that place. The handbill concluded with these remarkable words: '*Money is this man's God; and, to get enough of it, he would sacrifice his country.*'

"Such a publication could not but produce a great sensation among the officers. It was received at Arnold's quarters while the mess were at dinner, and read aloud at the table; the accused himself sitting at the head. Arnold, of course, was greatly excited, and applied a variety of epithets, coarse and harsh, to Col. Brown, pronouncing him a scoundrel, and declaring that he would kick him whenever and wherever he should meet him. One of the officers present remarked that Col. Brown was his friend, and that, as the remarks just applied to him had been so publicly made, he presumed there could be no objection to his repeating them to that officer. Arnold replied, 'Certainly not;' adding, that he should feel himself obliged to any officer who would inform Col. Brown of what he had said. The officer replied, that he should do so before he slept. Under these circumstances, no time was lost in making the communication to Col. Brown. Col. Lewis himself called upon Brown in the course of the evening, and the matter was the principal topic of conversation.

"The colonel was a mild and amiable man, and he made no remark of particular harshness or bitterness in respect to Arnold; but, towards the close of

[1] H. C. V. S. Col.

the interview, he observed, 'Well, Lewis, I wish you would invite me to dine with your mess to-morrow.'

"'With all my heart,' was the reply. 'Will you come?'

"Brown said he would, and they parted.

"The next day, near the time of serving dinner, Col. Brown arrived, and was ushered in.

"The table was spread in a long room, at one end of which the door opened directly opposite to the fireplace at the other. Arnold was standing at the moment with his back to the fire; so that, as Brown opened the door, they at once encountered each other face to face. It was a moment of breathless interest for the result. Brown walked calmly in, and, turning to avoid the table, passed around with a deliberate step, and, advancing up close to Arnold, stopped, and looked directly in his eye. After the pause of a moment, he observed, '*I understand, sir, that you have said you would kick me. I now present myself to give you an opportunity to put your threat into execution.*" Another brief pause ensued. Arnold opened not his lips. Brown then said to him, 'Sir, you are a dirty scoundrel.' Arnold was still silent as the Sphinx: whereupon Brown turned upon his heel with dignity, apologized to the gentlemen present for his intrusion, and left the room.

"This was certainly an extraordinary scene; and more extraordinary still is the fact that the particulars have never been communicated in any way to the public. Arnold certainly did not lack personal bravery; and the unbroken silence preserved by him on this occasion can only be accounted for upon the supposition that he feared to provoke inquiry upon the subject, while at the same time he could throw himself upon his well-attested courage and rank as excuses for not stooping to a controversy with a subordinate officer. But it still must be regarded as one of the most remarkable personal interviews to be found among the memorabilia of military men. [1]"

Arnold in May, 1777, forwarded to Congress a copy of Brown's Pittsfield appeal, which was referred to the Board of War, "together with such complaints as had been lodged against Gen. Arnold." But the Board, acting entirely *ex parte*, giving no notice to Brown, or any other complainant, that they might appear and substantiate, if they were able, the truth of their charges, acquitted Arnold on the strength of his own assertions, corroborated by the statements of Carroll of Carrolton, who had been one of the committee to visit Canada, but had had no opportunity personally to know the facts. And the Board not only acquitted Arnold in this strange way, but convicted Brown without a hearing — notwithstanding his long seeking for open trial and even-handed justice —

[1] The particulars of this story were derived by Col. Stone from the lips of Col. Lewis himself.

of having "cruelly and unjustly aspersed the character" of the man who had as sedulously avoided scrutiny as his accusers had courted it.

Col. Brown knew nothing of these proceedings until the following November. On the 22d of the previous February, he had resigned his commission in the Continental army, being "determined that no power on earth should force him to serve with an officer who was impeached of treason and every thing else, unless he was brought to justice." He now forwarded to Congress the following spirited remonstrance[1] in which he exposed pointedly and forcibly the absurdity and illegality of their conduct in the case, and the gross injustice which had been perpetrated against himself.

To the Honorable the Congress.

The Memorial and Remonstrance of John Brown of the State of the Massachusetts Bay humbly sheweth, That in the month of March, 1777, your petitioner was passing through Yorktown to the southward, when he waited on the Honorable Charles Thompson, Esq., Secretary to Congress, who favored your petitioner with a copy of the very extraordinary trial of Gen. Arnold, from which the following is an extract: —

"In Congress, May 20, 1777. — A letter of this date from Gen. Arnold, with a printed paper enclosed, 'signed John Brown,' was read. *Ordered*, That the same be referred to the Board of War, together with such complaints as have been lodged against Gen. Arnold."

By this your petitioner would suppose, that the Board of War were directed, not only to take into consideration his complaint, but all others that had been lodged against Gen. Arnold, particularly those lodged by a general court-martial, composed of thirteen of the principal officers at Ticonderoga, in the year 1776, as well as those lodged by Col. Hazen and others, although it does not appear that any other matter of complaint was determined upon but that contained in the handbill, signed John Brown, on which the Board of War reported, —

"That the general laid before them a variety of original letters, orders, and other papers, which, together with the general's account of his conduct, confirmed by Mr. Carroll, one of the late commissioners in Canada, and now a member of this Board, have given entire satisfaction to this Board concerning the general's character, so cruelly and groundlessly aspersed in the publication."

Your petitioner begs leave to affirm, that Mr. Carroll, whatever he might wish, knew nothing, more or less, as a witness concerning the charge laid against Gen. Arnold, owing to an unlucky *alibi* which happened with respect to him, in regard to all the charges laid in the complaint. Still, how far his

[1] Collection of H. C. Van Schaack, Esq.

evidence might go in assisting General Arnold in proving his negatives, I do not pretend to say, as this is to me an entirely new mode of trial. First, because one of the parties was not notified, or present at the same, consequently *ex parte*, unconstitutional, and illegal on every principle. Secondly, because there was not one witness present at the trial who ever had it in his power to know any thing of his own knowledge respecting one of the charges laid in the complaint. Thirdly, with great submission to the honorable Congress, they had not the least right to take cognizance of the crimes mentioned in my complaint. For the truth of this assertion, I beg leave to refer them to the military laws by them composed and instituted for the regulation of the army, which are the only security and protection of the officers and soldiers belonging to the same; consequently no other court or tribunal can have any right to take cognizance of the crimes mentioned in my complaint, but that of a court-martial, and therefore the trial of the general, above recited, was a nullity, to all intents and purposes.

However, should your Congress be of a different opinion respecting this matter, and that the trial of Gen. Arnold was legal and constitutional, he then expects that Congress will give him the same indulgences and latitude, and that he may be heard by Congress on the subject of his impeachment of the general, in which case the general's presence and witnesses will not be necessary.

Your petitioner therefore esteems it a great grievance, that Congress, by the trial aforesaid, have resolved and published, and authorized Gen. Arnold to publish to the world, that he, your petitioner, has been guilty of publishing false and groundless assertions and complaints against a general officer, when, at the same time, every article in the impeachment was sacredly true, and could have been proved so could a proper trial have been obtained, of which Gen. Arnold was well apprised, or he would have been as fond of his trial in the army as his impeachers were. It is possible that Gen. Arnold might have suggested to Congress that your petitioner was not an officer at the time he solicited his trial. As to this matter, your petitioner has not as yet been informed whether his resignation has been accepted or not. Indeed, he cannot suppose it compatible with the wisdom and dignity of Congress to discharge any of their officers for the reasons set forth in your petitioner's letter accompanying his resignation, as he then stood impeached by the same Gen. Arnold of high crimes, which, if true, affected the reputation of the United States; and Gen. Arnold's sacred character stood impeached by your petitioner of thirteen capital charges, which, in the opinion of those most knowing, might have effected the loss of that honest man in consequence of a proper trial before a generous court-martial. Your petitioner presumes his resignation was not accepted by Congress. Let this matter be as it may, Congress is sensible that he was not out of service from the commencement of the war until the reduction of the British army under Gen. Burgoyne, in which he arrogates to himself some share of credit (since no one else is willing to give it to him.) Your petitioner is sensible, that

Congress, at the time of Arnold's application for a trial, were embarrassed on all questions, and no doubt labored under high prejudice with respect to your petitioner's character, owing, perhaps, to representation made there by Gen. Gates, who, it is possible, has been mistaken in his friend Arnold; which prejudices your petitioner hopes time and events have eradicated. He can assure Congress that he hopes and wishes for nothing but common justice, although the history of the war, and his present infirmities incurred therein, might entitle him to something more. But to stand convicted, by a decree of Congress, of publishing cruel and groundless libels, without a hearing, while actually fighting for liberty, is intolerable in a free country, and has a direct tendency to check the ambition, and even disaffect those men by whose wisdom, valor, and perseverance America is to be made free, not to mention the dangerous precedent such trials may afford. Your petitioner, therefore, implores your House to reconsider their determination on his impeachment of Gen. Arnold, as there cannot, at this date, exist a possibility of doubt that the same was presented, and furnished Gen. Arnold with a foundation to establish a character on the ruins of a man, who, to speak moderately, has rendered his country as essential service as that dangerous general, whose reasons for evading a trial at a proper tribunal are very obvious, and fully suggested in my impeachment on which the general had his trial, by which it appears that Gen. Arnold was rescued out of the hands of justice by mere dint of authority exercised by Gen. Gates. Your petitioner, relying on the wisdom and justice of Congress, begs leave to subscribe himself most respectfully

Their very obedient, humble servant,

JOHN BROWN.

Having now rid himself of connection with a service in which its most corrupt, treacherous, and dangerous officer was able to wield so potent and mysterious an influence, Col. Brown returned to Pittsfield, was appointed colonel of the middle regiment of Berkshire militia, and in that capacity sought, and, as we shall see, not in vain, to serve his country faithfully, and win honor for himself.

Three years afterwards, John Brown lay dead on the battle-field, where he fell fighting for the country which had refused him the simplest justice. Benedict Arnold was a fugitive in the army of her enemies; and all men believed what had been vainly charged upon him in 1777.

CHAPTER XVI.

THE INVASION OF BURGOYNE, AND BATTLE OF BENNINGTON.

[1777.]

Pittsfield Soldiers for the Continental Army. — Apprehensions of Invasion from Canada. — A Petition of 1775. — Pittsfield responds to Calls for Men. — Sends Companies to Ticonderoga in December and April. — Burgoyne approaches. — Extracts from Mr. Allen's Diary at Ticonderoga. — He addresses the Soldiers of the Garrison. — Evacuation of Ticonderoga. — Feeling at Pittsfield regarding it. — Correspondence of Gen. Schuyler. — Schuyler and the Berkshire Militia. — Baum's Expedition marches on Bennington. — Met by Stark. — Rally of the Berkshire Militia. — Pittsfield Volunteers. — Anecdote of an Indian Scout. — Anecdotes of Rev. Mr. Allen. — He fires the First Gun at the Bennington Fight. — Anecdote of Linus Parker. — Route of the British Forces. — Effect of the Victory on the Country. — Col. Brown's Lake George Expedition. — His Brilliant Success. — Surrender of Burgoyne. — His March through Pittsfield. — Quaint Patriotic Verses.

THE year 1777 was distinguished in the Revolutionary annals of Pittsfield for the extraordinary sacrifices and exertions required of her people, as well as for the brilliancy of the exploits in which they conspicuously shared. At midsummer, after months of incessant anxiety, hostile troops approached nearer to her borders than at any other time since the close of the French and Indian Wars; bringing her within the purposed scope of an invasion characterized in an unusual degree by elements designed and well fitted to spread terror among the non-combatant population. From April to November was a period of continued excitement and alarm; of frequent calls upon her militia, promptly met, although at the most inopportune moment for the farmer; of disasters which only inspired new vigor and patriotic devotion; of successes which flashed hope and light over the nation at the moment of its deepest despondency and gloom.

The feeble remnant of the splendid company, which, under David Noble, had joined Patterson's regiment in 1775, after participating, during the last days of its service, in the glories and dangers of Princeton and Trenton, had been dismissed on the last day of 1776. Only six Pittsfield soldiers remained in the Continental service during the succeeding winter; but these formed part of that noble though crippled army with which Washington baffled the superb legions of Howe in New Jersey, and finally drove them from that State.

In the spring, Pittsfield responded to the call made upon her in common with the other towns of Massachusetts, by furnishing to the depleted armies of Washington twenty-four men, — more than one-seventh of the entire number enrolled in her militia. It was also voted by the town to purchase for each a shirt, a pair of shoes and stockings, and "that the assessors take the town's money in the hands of Col. Williams, and purchase the same immediately." Capts. Goodrich and Rufus Allen were also directed to forward the money and clothing collected for the soldiers by Rev. Mr. Allen, who appears to have managed what answered for a Christian and Sanitary Commission.

At the moment when the town was thus so liberally performing its duties as regarded the national armies, it was justly apprehending the approach of an invader which it would tax all the resources of the section to which it belonged to resist, and whose success would be fraught with misery, even beyond that which ordinarily awaits a conquered people.

In the earliest stages of the Revolutionary contest, among the threats with which the Tories had exasperated, while vainly attempting to intimidate, the patriots, the most odious was, that the savages would be brought upon their rear, while the regulars assailed them in front; and the committees obtained evidence that it was really the purpose of the king's commanders to effect an alliance with the Indians, which they suspected to be for the purpose of an incursion as well as for the defence of Canada, to which the honorable scruples of Carleton confined it.

John Brown, while a representative from Pittsfield and Partridgefield, in February, 1775, presented to the Provincial Congress a petition — of which he was one of the signers, and probably the author — from the committees of the several towns in Hampshire and Berkshire, asking for a better supply of arms to their militia, and stating their reasons in the following paragraph: —

"The enemies of these Colonies frequently throw out that administration have concluded a bloody plan for mustering great numbers of French Canadians and remote tribes of savages, and to bring them against this Province, in order to effect their system of tyranny and despotism of these Colonies; and the inhabitants of these counties apprehend that the first attacks of said Canadians and Indians will be made upon them."

The war carried into Canada postponed the realization of these fears; but the operations with which the British commander followed the expulsion of the American forces from that Province left no room to doubt that the following spring would be signalized by the long-dreaded irruption. The unfortunate relations between the department commander and the militia within his precinct contributed, however, with other causes, to obstruct the measures which ought to have been taken in anticipation of it.

John Adams wrote on the 29th of April from Philadelphia, doubtless relying upon Schuyler's reports, "Every man in the Massachusetts quota ought to have been ready last December; and *not one* man has yet arrived in the field, and not three hundred at Saratoga. I have been abominably deceived about the troops. If Ticonderoga is not lost, it will be because it is not attacked; and, if it should be, New England will bear all the shame and all the blame of it." Of the neglect thus charged, Pittsfield was not guilty; nor probably was Berkshire generally, notwithstanding the distrust in which Schuyler was held in the county. Lieut. James Hubbard, with nineteen men from Pittsfield, was kept at Ticonderoga from December to the latter part of March; and, on the 25th of April, the town sent Lieut. Stephen Crofoot with fourteen men, Richmond and Lenox probably making up the full company.

An average of about one-sixth of the enrolled militia of the town were in the military service of the country from the 1st of December to the 1st of May after which the proportion began to increase, until, in July, it actually exceeded the whole number on the rolls, which was only one hundred and forty, while at one time one hundred and forty-five were returned as in service, including the clergyman, and others exempt by law.

None of the Pittsfield militia appear to have remained at Ticonderoga after the 22d of May; but Rev. Mr. Allen was there, as chaplain to a Continental regiment, from the 13th of June until the evacuation; and has left a diary of what transpired in connection with that event, which throws light upon the feeling manifested in Berkshire regarding it.[1]

The invasion which that summer threatened the portions of New York and Massachusetts which were protected by Ticonderoga was such as might well have kept alive the most anxious solicitude for the safety of that fortress, and the most lively apprehension whenever it was endangered. The king and his cabinet, determined no longer to be balked in their purposes by the old-fashioned chivalry of such soldiers as Carleton and Howe, had sent over, in the person of Burgoyne, an officer, who, if he had any natural repugnance to bringing the horrors of savage warfare upon the homes of the rebellious colonists, was willing to yield all weak scruples to the instructions of the royal closet.

Arriving in Canada, and entering upon his schemes of invasion, his deliberate purpose was to inspire the people through whose country he intended to march with the terror of his red allies as well as of his military police.

On the evening of July 1, Burgoyne's army debarked before Ticonderoga, mustering, rank and file, 3,724 British soldiers, 3,016 Germans, and 250 Provincials, besides which there were 473 picked cannoneers, with the finest park of artillery which had then ever accompanied any army. In addition to these were the savages, on which the king so strongly relied.

The character of the warfare carried on by these auxiliaries may be learned from the following paragraphs in Rev. Mr. Allen's diary of June 26:—

"This day, as John Whiting and John Batty were returning from Lake-George Landing, they were fired upon by a number of Indians; the former of whom was shot through the head, and then stabbed in his throat, breast, and belly, and, in addition to all, he was scalped. He was a likely lad of about eighteen years of age, and belonged to Lanesborough.

"The other, John Batty, had two balls pass through his thigh, one through the small of his back, and one obliquely through his breast, and his scalp taken off during all which he was quite sensible, and was obliged to feign himself dead during the stripping him of his armor, and taking off his scalp, which caused great pain. After the Indians retired, he got up, and ran and called for help, and was soon carried in. He was living the day before the retreat, and, it was said, was left behind."

[1] Published in The Hartford Courant, Sept. 1, 1777.

The whole civilized portion of Burgoyne's army was perfect in soldiership and appointments, and was commanded by able and ambitious officers.

The garrison of Ticonderoga, under Gen. St. Clair, consisted of barely 3,300 men, one-third of them not efficient, and only one man in every ten of the rest furnished with a bayonet. Notwithstanding this great disparity, the American soldiers were able to remember, that, twenty years before, an army of twice the number of that of Gen. Burgoyne, and with a reputation nearly as splendid, had been repulsed from before those very walls by a garrison not comparatively larger than their own.

Gens. Schuyler and St. Clair expressed the utmost confidence of defending the post; and the former continued to accumulate stores until the last, while the latter, by the orders of his superior, retained his men there until the favorable moment for retreat was passed. Yet Schuyler, at least, was well aware of a not improbable contingency, which, if it should occur, would render it utterly impossible to hold the works for a single day.

The original selection of Ticonderoga as a military post was made with reference to the exigencies of the old forest-warfare, and its retention had been a matter of tradition, without any skilful re-examination of its position. On the retreat of the Canada expedition in 1776, it had, however, been observed that Mount Independence commanded the old lines; and that elevation had been fortified, in great part by the Berkshire soldiers.

But across the outlet of Lake George from Mount Independence, and across a narrow portion of Lake Champlain from Ticonderoga, the chain of hills which separates the two lakes terminates in an abrupt eminence, six hundred feet high, which in 1776 bore the name of Sugar Mountain.

Its distance from Mount Independence was but fifteen hundred yards; from Ticonderoga, fourteen hundred: but it had been neglected by French, English, and American engineers, as too distant to be dangerous, or too precipitous to be occupied. But Col. John Trumbull, when at Ticonderoga, on Gen. Gates's staff, in 1776, had demonstrated that it was quite practicable for an enemy to occupy it with a battery, and that, if he should do so, Ticonderoga would become utterly untenable. He had further shown, that a small but strong fort, mounting twenty-five heavy guns, would effectually command the lake passage, then the only one by which an invading army could enter New York or Massachusetts from the north. Col. Trumbull furnished Schuyler and Gates with drawings and specifications explanatory of these facts; and surveys were made for the erection of works in accordance with them upon Sugar Mountain, but nothing came of it. The hope indulged seems to have been, that, as the weak point in the defence had so long escaped observation, it would continue to do so.

It quickly, however, attracted the notice of a lieutenant of Burgoyne's engineers; and, on the night of the fourth day of the siege, a party of infantry ascended Sugar Mountain, and were so delighted with its commanding position that they at once hailed it *Mount Defiance*,— a name which it still retains.

When the day broke, the Americans were startled to see a crowd of red-coats busily engaged in levelling the summit for a battery whose guns were already half-way up the steep acclivity. In a few hours, they would command every nook and corner of the works spread out below.

Gen. St. Clair hastily summoned a council of war; which, of course, had no alternative but to resolve upon an immediate evacuation, and it was ordered for the same night.

What preparations could be made during the day, without attracting the attention of the enemy, were effected, and the retreat was begun under cover of the night. The true object of these preparations does not seem to have been at first communicated to the body of the army. Mr. Allen having, in obedience to orders, removed his baggage to Mount Independence, was returning with the intention of taking part in the defence of Ticonderoga, when, meeting his regiment in full retreat, he was astonished and indignant to learn the true condition of affairs. Ignorant of the examination made the previous year by Col. Trumbull, he, like the great majority of the army, held to the traditional belief that Ticonderoga was, for all practical purposes, out of artillery range from Sugar Mountain. "All the king's artillery," said he in his diary, "on the high mountain behind us could never have obliged us to evacuate the place; for what they could make reach us would have been falling shot, and never risen after they struck the ground. The distance was judged to be about three miles from Independence, and two from Ticonderoga. Did not our people lie nearer the army at Boston than that, without receiving damage either from bombs or cannon-shot? Even had they have lifted up their eighteen-pounders to the summit of that craggy mountain, we might have sat under our own vines and fig-trees, and not been afraid."

Had Mr. Allen been informed of Col. Trumbull's thorough investigation of the matter, his opinion would have been changed; but the council of war explained their action to their subordinates, only by the pleas of a scarcity of ammunition, and the danger of re-enforcement to the enemy. The true reason which justified their decision appears only to have been thrown out casually and without authority.

Of the general feeling in the army, Mr. Allen says, "This event was surprising to the whole garrison, and unexpected by us all. Neither officers nor soldiers indulged the most distant apprehension of such a measure. The garrison in general seemed to be filled with astonishment, grief, and indignation. Some vented their grief in tears and lamentation; others, by execrations and bitter reproaches of this sad catastrophe."

Mr. Allen has left an abstract of an address made to the regiment to which he was chaplain, a few hours before the determination to abandon the fortress was made public; and from it we may learn how astonished he must have been by such a proceeding. The enemy's fleet in full sight, he said in substance as follows: —

"VALIANT SOLDIERS, — Yonder are the enemies of your country, who have come to lay waste and destroy, and spread havoc and devastation through this pleasant land. They are mercenaries, hired to do the work of death, and have no motives to animate them in their undertaking. *You* have every consideration to induce you to play the men, and act the part of valiant soldiers. Your country looks up to you for its defence; you are contending for your wives, whether you or they shall enjoy them; you are contending for your children, whether they shall be yours or theirs; for your houses and lands, for your flocks and herds, for your freedom, for future generations, for every thing that is great and noble, and, on account of which only, life is of any worth. You must, you will, abide the day of trial. You cannot give back whilst animated by these considerations.

"Suffer me, therefore, on this occasion, to recommend to you, without delay to break off your sins by righteousness, and your iniquities by turning to the Lord. Turn ye, turn ye, ungodly sinners; for why will ye die? Repent, lest the Lord come and smite with a curse. Our camp is filled with blasphemy, and resounds with the language of the infernal regions. Oh that officers and soldiers might fear to take the holy and tremendous name of God in vain! Oh that you would now return to the Lord, lest destruction come upon you, lest vengeance overtake you! Oh that you were wise, that you understood this, that you would consider your latter end!

"I must recommend to you the strictest attention to your duty, and the most punctual obedience to your officers. Discipline, order, and regularity are the strength of an army.

"Valiant soldiers, should our enemies attack us, I exhort and conjure you to play the men. Let no dangers appear too great, let no suffering appear too severe, for you to encounter for your bleeding country. Of God's grace assisting me, I am determined to fight and die by your side, rather than flee before our enemies, or resign myself up to them. Prefer death to captivity; ever remember your unhappy brethren made prisoners at Fort Washington, whose blood now cries to Heaven for vengeance, and shakes the pillars of the world, saying, 'How long, O Lord, holy and true, dost thou not avenge our blood on them that dwell upon the earth?' Rather than quit this ground with infamy and disgrace, I should prefer leaving this body of mine a corpse on this spot.

"I must finally recommend to you, and urge it upon you again and again, in time of action to keep silence; let all be hush and calm, serene and tranquil, that the word of command may be distinctly heard and resolutely obeyed. And may the God of Heaven take us all under his protection, and cover our heads in the day of battle, and grant unto us his salvation!"[1]

The retreat was planned to be made in two divisions. A flotilla, commanded by Col. Long, was to pass up the narrow lake to Skenesborough, conveying the wounded, the sick, and the non-combatants, together with such artillery and stores as could be saved. The main body of the army, under Gen. St. Clair, was to cross to Mount Independence, and thence proceed south by land. A premature discovery of the evacuation transformed the retreat into something very like a flight. Both divisions were compelled to set off in haste. Col. Long was overtaken at Skenesborough, lost his artillery and stores, and pushed on southward; but, turning upon his pursuers, he made a gallant and almost successful stand near Fort Ann. Finally compelled to retreat, he reached Fort Edward, where Schuyler had fixed his headquarters.

St. Clair's army, after severe fighting and heavy losses by its

[1] In a note to Mr. Allen's abstract of this address, written shortly after his return home, he says, "In about five hours afterwards, the garrison was evacuated, and our vast army fleeing before their enemies with the utmost precipitation and irregularity, leaving behind, for the use of the enemy, an immense quantity of baggage, artillery, ammunition, provisions, and every warlike necessary. How are the mighty fallen, and the weapons of war perished!"

rearguard at Hubbardston, plunged into the woods, and, by a circuitous route, reached a point about fifty miles east of Fort Edward on the 10th. From the 7th, when they had disappeared in the woods, no tidings had been received of them. Reaching Fort Edward, although as way-worn, haggard, and reduced a corps as is often seen, they were received with joy by Gen. Schuyler, who had fully shared the apprehension, which everywhere prevailed, that they had all been made prisoners.

This suspense had added to the consternation that had fallen upon the whole region which the loss of Ticonderoga laid open to the inroads of the enemy, — a consternation which Burgoyne sedulously sought to enhance through his proclamations and the Tory emissaries, open or concealed, who ingeniously magnified the numbers of his army, and enlarged upon the ferocity of the savages, who committed their atrocities under the shelter of his commission.

In the minds of the neighboring people, the mysterious evacution of the traditional stronghold to which they and their fathers had looked for protection could not but create, in addition to the other terrors of invasion, doubts of the ability or integrity of the officers upon whom its defence devolved. St. Clair and his brigadiers were bitterly charged with cowardice; and the graver allegations against Gen. Schuyler, which his enemies had hardly suffered to slumber, were revived in all their unjust malignancy.

If, however, the people of Pittsfield gave any thought to the suspicions against the department commander, they did not suffer them to impede, in the least, their co-operation in repairing the breach made in their defences. A letter proffering aid was, on the 9th, sent to Gen. Schuyler, who, the next day, gratefully acknowledged it, and specified the modes in which the town could best render him assistance. This communication was forwarded to the General Court, with an explanatory note from the selectmen. Both letters are characteristic; and the latter is illustrative of the spirit and feeling of the town at that exciting crisis. We therefore reproduce them here.

[*From the Selectmen and Committee of Pittsfield to the General Court.*]

TO THE HONORABLE THE COUNCIL AND HOUSE OF REPRESENTATIVES IN GENERAL COURT ASSEMBLED.

As the unparalleled, infamous, ignominious, and cowardly evacuating of Ticonderoga and Mount Independence, and hasty retreat therefrom, must give astonishment to all humanity, so must it also give the utmost perplexity and remorse to the United Independent States of America, and greatly reproach their general officers. To think that out of four there was not one of so much firmness and resolution as to confine the others there, when all the field-officers and others, with the men, would have stood by him for the support and maintenance of the key of North America; supplied with ammunitions and provisions sufficient for thirty or forty days' siege, and within reach of twenty thousand men, who might, in all probability, have been with them in twenty days! But so it is, truly a lamentation, and will be for a lamentation; and they that have the watch must look out; and we shall still hope and trust that the All-wise Governor of the world will give that wisdom to the Congress and to the several assemblies of the States to lead us into such measures as that we may surmount all the difficulties that attend us, and, in some measure, rectify the mistakes which have been made. It gives us no small pleasure to see *no countenance changed*, unless it be with a spirit of resentment and indignation. And as we have just received a letter from Gen. Schuyler, in which he mentions the want of a very necessary article, we thought it our duty to enclose it, fearing that, in his hurry and broken situation, he may have omitted sending to you.

You will pardon us, if we unburden ourselves by letting you know what is heavy on our minds, as the keeping of officers of whom even the common soldiery have a jealousy, especially such as have showed the greatest cowardice. They never will follow with that cordiality, fearing that they will leave them to themselves, or, to regain their credit, charge them on with impetuosity to needless ruin and destruction. And we are apprehensive, that if those officers who made the late inglorious flight are not brought to trial, and then, not justifying themselves, are not brought to condign punishment, officers will run at a very low ebb; and it will not be worth while to attempt any great things for the future.

And, if it is true that we have lost three hundred cannon at Ticonderoga, it cannot be supposed that there are many near or at headquarters. Suffer us to suggest that some of the brigades marching to Fort Edward take along with them some of the field-pieces paraded at Springfield.

We shall be glad if our ebullition of resentment against the late northern conduct has not run us into indecency or impertinence. But we trust that you will forgive us, as it comes from hearty well-wishers to the common cause of America.

We are your most obedient and very humble servants,

Wm. Williams, *in behalf of the Selectmen.*

Josiah Wright, *in behalf of the Committee.*

Pittsfield, July, 13, 1777.

[*Gen. Schuyler to Col. Williams and Josiah Wright, Esq.*]

Headquarters, Fort Edward, July 10, 1777.

Gentlemen,—Your favor of yesterday's date I have this moment received. The evacuation of Ticonderoga and Mount Independence is, unhappily, too true. I am informed that it was done in consequence of a resolution of the general officers in council. I have not yet been so happy as to see any of them, and cannot therefore inform you on what principle the resolution was founded. I am sorry to learn from Col. Williams of White Creek, and other gentlemen, that it is imputed to me as having given an order for that purpose. If such order was ever given, I should not dare to deny it, as the means of detection must be very easy, even if principle were no restraint to asserting a falsehood. Gen. Learned has seen the originals of all my letters to Gen. St. Clair; for they were returned unsealed by Col. Long, having never reached Ticonderoga. They hold up ideas widely, nay directly, repugnant to the orders I am so unjustly charged with giving. You will please, therefore, give my own words in contradiction to such report, should it have taken place with you. The enemy have appeared at Fort Ann, but at present none of them are there, except a few lurking Indians, or white men disguised like Indians, of which we are assured the enemy have many, in order to intimidate. I am in hopes, that when Gen. St. Clair and Gen. Nixon, with the troops respectively with them, arrive, that I shall be able to stop their progress in the vicinity of this place, provided we are properly supported by the militia. I am accordingly thankful for your offers of assistance, and will accept of any you can give. Carriages are greatly needed; and any number you can expedite to me, however small, will be of service. I need not inform you that the more men there are sent to me, the better. If, perchance, there should be any lead attainable by you, I wish to have it sent to me with all despatch, as we are greatly straitened in that necessary article.

I am, gentlemen, with much respect,
Your obedient, humble servant,

PH. SCHUYLER.

Col. WM. WILLIAMS, JOSIAH WRIGHT, Esq.[1]

The assistance proffered by Pittsfield to Gen. Schuyler, in its most essential particular, went before its offer. When news first came that Burgoyne was advancing up the lake from Canada, Capt. John Strong and Lieut. Caleb Goodrich led fifty-four men, on the 30th of June, to Fort Ann; and, if tradition is correct, they took part in Col. Long's sanguinary and almost successful fight. And it must have been immediately upon learning the disaster at Ticonderoga, that, on the 8th July, Capt. William Francis and Lieut. Stephen Crowfoot marched with forty men to re-enforce the army at Fort Edward. Ten days after, Lieut. James Hubbard led a detachment of ten men to Manchester. On the 18th of June, these corps were all in the field, making, with the thirty-two men

[1] Mass. Ar.

and several officers in the Continental service, more than one hundred and forty soldiers in the armies of the country.

Gen. Schuyler, on the 26th of July, dismissed one-half of the militia of New England, and of Albany County in New York; and the greater portion of the rest a month later. The company of Capt. Strong returned home under the first order; the two others, on the 26th of August, under the second. Schuyler's pretence for this course, while there was the severest need of men, was, that the militia of Berkshire and Albany were so impatient to return to their fields, that he released a part lest he might lose the whole; and then, having dismissed the one-half, he sent home the other. The explanation he gave in private was, that he considered every one of the Southern soldiers, whom he was importuning Washington to send him from his own too meagre force, to be worth two of the men of New England.[1] Possibly the fundamental reason lay in the distrust in which he knew himself to be held by the militia of Berkshire and Albany Counties, and in hardly a less degree by those of all the Eastern States. The contemned soldiery shortly had a noble revenge, in proving upon the fields of Bennington and Saratoga, and on the shores of Lake Champlain, that, under officers in whose ability they could trust, they had few superiors in arms. Had Schuyler possessed, like Stark and Brown, the magnanimity to overlook their faults, that sympathy with their rude virtues which taught those leaders how to win the confidence of their men, and the genius which enabled them to render even their failings useful to their country, he might, with the soldiery whom he so grossly underrated, have forestalled the successes which soon shed lustre on the northern army, and have escaped the bitterness of removal from a command in which he believed victory almost within his grasp.

With the triumphs attending his pursuit of the flying garrison of Ticonderoga, the fortunes of the British commander culminated; and even these were achieved at an expense in men which he could ill afford, and which could by no means be made good from the loyalists who flocked to him at Skenesborough. Here his blunders became more palpable, and his perplexities began to accumulate. Following the most impracticable routes, it was not until the 30th of July that he found himself at Fort Edward with

[1] Brancroft, Hist. U. S., vol. ix. p. 373.

a wearied army, and surrounded by ever-increasing difficulties. Before leaving Canada, he had directed a co-operating column to proceed by the way of Oswego and the Mohawk. This body, he now learned, was already before Fort Stanwix. The defeat which it there met was not within his purview of possibilities; and it behooved him to make all haste down the Hudson, in order to form the proposed junction before the occupation of Albany, which was confidently assigned for the 22d or 23d of August. But his transportation was utterly inadequate to such a movement. Carleton, still governing in Canada, confined his assistance strictly to the letter of his instructions, and acted, even within that limit, with the reverse of zeal. The wagons contracted for in that Province, unfaithfully made, were so rickety as to be of little service; the horses, insufficient in number, arrived in wretched condition. The subsistence which could be ordinarily obtained from all sources barely sufficed for the daily consumption: it was rare good fortune when a magazine of four days' supply was accumulated.

In this strait, Burgoyne was prepared to welcome any suggestion which promised relief. Our old friend Skene of Skenesborough was in his camp; and Burgoyne, trusting to the intimate acquaintance with the country which he was supposed to possess, had latterly relied much upon his counsels, raised him to the rank of colonel, and made him titular governor of the regions thereabout.

This man represented, to say the least with great exaggeration, that the Americans had established large depots of supplies, and especially of horses at Bennington in Vermont, which he asserted might easily be captured by surprise.

The veteran generals, Phillips and Reidesel, protested warmly against the scheme, as attended with too great risks. The affairs in which they had recently engaged the retreating Americans had probably persuaded them, that, whatever might be the condition of the opposing army as a whole, there were in it corps sufficiently intact, and commanded by officers of sufficient dash and ability, to render them extremely dangerous to a detached column.

Burgoyne's necessities were, however, imperious; and he not only eagerly embraced the proposed plan, but enlarged its scope. The final written instructions to Lieut.-Col. Baum, the German officer who was assigned to the command, defined the purposes of the expedition to be, — to scour the country, with Peters's corps (Tories) and the Indians, from Rockingham to Otter Creek; to get cattle and horses, and mount Reidesel's Dragoons; to go down the river as far as Brattleborough, and return by the great road, which passed through the extreme north-west corner of Berkshire to Albany, there to rejoin the army of Burgoyne; to endeavor to make the country believe that it was the advance guard of the general's army, who were to cross the Connecticut, and proceed *via* Springfield to Boston; to make prisoners of all civil, as well as military officers, holding under Congress; to tax the towns where they halted for whatever they needed, taking hostages for their performances; to bring all horses fit either to mount the dragoons or for battalion service, with all the saddles and bridles which could be found. The number of horses, besides those for the dragoons, ought, it was the British general's modest opinion, to be thirteen hundred; but, if more were to be obtained, so much the better.

Verbal orders were given to send back the spoils of Bennington at once to Burgoyne's camp, which, in order to be nearer to Baum in case of necessity, had been advanced down the river to a point opposite Saratoga, and near the mouth of the Batten Kill. It is clear that Burgoyne's march down the Hudson could only be facilitated by such transportation as could be obtained at Bennington; for the fruits of the marauding beyond that point would only reach him at Albany. It will be perceived how large a share of the labors and dangers of the expedition were submitted to for another purpose. The raid beyond the first point named was an outgrowth of that system of terror which Burgoyne, in council with his royal master and the most infamous of his ministers, had devised as the fittest expedient to restore the rebellious people of the Colonies to their allegiance.

Nothing, surely, could be a more efficient adjunct to such a system, than a raid of mercenaries, ignorant of the language of the people, instructed to live upon the country, and with unlimited power to make prisoners, supplemented by a "scouring" of Indians and exasperated Tories. And nothing could be more conducive to the permanence of submission — supposing terror competent to induce it — than a military police, well mounted upon horses stripped from the conquered territory. But, whatever may have been the object prominent in the mind of the British commander when sending out this ill-starred expedition, the belief that it could safely march through the route indicated, much less carry out the programme laid down for it, betrays that pitiable misconception of the people with whom he had to deal which characterized his leadership from first to last.

But, in fact, he looked upon that whole region as virtually subdued, and only needing to be made sensible of the fact by a vigorous application of the rod. In the absence of all active opposition from the American forces, the natural obstacles he was obliged to encounter did not suffice to disabuse him of the fatal fallacy. As the British camp advanced from post to post, until it was established on the banks of the Hudson, less than forty miles above Albany, Schuyler, although pure in purpose and eager to meet every personal danger, yet dispirited, irresolute, fretted by unjust imputations, and doubtless conscious of grave errors with which he was not yet charged, fell back from Fort Edward to Fort Miller, thence to Saratoga, and finally to Stillwater and the Mohawk River.

Washington, alarmed at the hopeless tone of his letters and his perpetual complaints of the New-England militia, robbed his own already depleted army to furnish him re-enforcement, which an officer like Stark would have rapidly drawn and organized from the surrounding country; and sent to his aid Arnold, whom he regarded as the ablest of the major-generals, and who certainly did not lack in dash, as well as Lincoln, who had the confidence of the militia, upon whom the sagacious commander-in-chief well knew all must finally, in a great measure, depend.[1]

But it was left to an independent commander to carry out, although ignorant that it had been made, the suggestion which Washington in vain wrote to Schuyler, that, "if the enemy continued to act in detachments, one vigorous fall upon one of those detachments might prove fatal to the whole expedition." After a brilliant record from the very inception of the present war, as well as in that of 1754, Col. John Stark of New Hampshire had retired from the Continental service in the March of 1777, disgusted with the omission of his name from the list of newly-appointed brigadiers, in which those of far inferior men figured. This circumstance, untoward as it then appeared, in good time proved to be of inestimable advantage to the country, which profited by the blundering injustice of its representatives.

[1] Bancroft.

Upon the irruption of Burgoyne, New Hampshire being one of the frontiers threatened, the patriotic legislature of that State, roused by the imminence of the danger, determined to raise two brigades of militia for its defence. Stark was tendered the command of one of these, and of the whole, when in combined service, by virtue of seniority; and with this force was directed to "proceed to the new State,"[1] and "check the advance of Burgoyne."

The task was one from which commanders of more abundant resources were shrinking; but Stark was willing to undertake it, although only upon the indispensable condition that his command should be an entirely independent one, responsible to the legislature of New Hampshire solely, and in no way subject to the Continental generals. Such was the estimation in which his ability, as well as his patriotism and sound sense, was held by the legislature, that, unprecedented and dangerous in principle as was his demand, it was complied with without hesitation. That demand and that compliance fought and won the battle of Bennington.

Stark had hardly reached Manchester, when Gen. Lincoln arrived at the same place, charged by Gen. Schuyler with orders to bring the militia in that quarter to the west bank of the Hudson, where he was concentrating his army to oppose the progress of Burgoyne; or fall back before him. Stark, in whose judgment, as in that of Washington, the better policy seemed to be to hang heavily on the enemy's flank and rear, flatly refused to comply, and, on the 9th of August, established his headquarters at Bennington.

Baum set out from Batten Kill early on the morning of the 13th, the general showing his interest in the expedition by riding with him across the stream. The force consisted of four hundred Brunswick dismounted dragoons, a detachment of Hanau artillerists with two field-pieces, Capt. Frazer's English marksmen, all the French Canadians, a considerable body of the Queen's Royal Rangers (Peters's corps), and bands of savages to the number of perhaps one hundred and fifty. Those who have examined the huge long sword, the ponderous musket, and brazen helmet, now in the Massachusetts Senate Chamber, which were worn by the German troops in Baum's expedition, will comprehend how utterly unfit such a body were for a rapid movement. Surprise is an effect

[1] Vermont, which had then just assumed its independent rank and its beautiful name.

which they seem to have only been capable of producing in the minds of those who witnessed their selection for such a movement as the present. Their tactics, also, were as cumbrous as their armor; and the British officers affirmed, that, in forest-roads which incessant rains had rendered beds of unfathomable mire, the German officers halted their men ten times an hour to dress their ranks.

The distance from the mouth of the Batten Kill to Bennington, by the route pursued, was probably little more than thirty miles. The presence of the Indians at Cambridge, twelve miles from Bennington, where they were committing their usual outrages, was reported to Stark late in the afternoon of the 13th; and Lieut.-Col. Gregg, with two hundred men, was sent out to check and chastise them. During the following night, word was received that the savages were merely the advanced scouts of a large body of troops pushing directly for Bennington. Stark immediately put the whole force at headquarters under arms, sent express to Gen. Lincoln in command of the forces collected at Manchester, and dispersed messengers in all directions to summon the local militia to the rescue.

The tradition has long been current, that the alarm reached Pittsfield on the Sabbath; that the messenger coming to the door of the meeting-house, where the people were still engaged in divine worship, announced the approach of the British; that thereupon the pastor descended from the pulpit, and, standing on the little platform beneath it, called upon his people to go forth with him to do battle with the enemies of his country.

The tradition is not one of those current among Mr. Allen's descendants; and it is disproved by the fact that the battle was fought on Saturday. The origin of the story probably was, that, when the alarm reached town, the citizens, as was their custom, assembled in the meeting-house to take measures for an effectual response; and that there the minister, with his heart full of the emotions excited by his late experience at Ticonderoga, made an address whose eloquence and power were remembered long after the attendant circumstances became obscured.

This explanation is rendered the more plausible by that portion of the legend which affirms that Mr. Allen spoke musket-in-hand; while, since the days of Indian surprises, the most belligerent clergymen had given over the practice of making an armory of their pulpits.

A large portion of the able-bodied men of the town were already in the field; others had just returned, and were scattered upon their farms, deeply engrossed in their too long-delayed agricultural labors. But the exigency was felt to be of the most pressing and alarming nature; and the best citizens of the town pressed forward to meet it, irrespective of legal exemption from military service, or any other personal consideration.

Twenty-two men enrolled themselves in all, under the command of Lieut. William Ford, an officer who saw much service in those days. With him served the veteran Col. Easton, Rev. Mr. Allen, Capts. Charles Goodrich, James Noble, and William Francis, Lieuts. Joseph Allen (second in command), Josiah Wright, and Rufus Allen.

On the 16th, and of course before news of the battle was received, a second detachment of seventeen men, under Lieut. James Hubbard, set out for Bennington; and this, too, was peculiarly constituted, for in its ranks were Capts. Isaac Dickinson and John Strong and Lieut. Oliver Root. Major Israel Stoddard and Woodbridge Little, Esq., also signalized their newly-sworn allegiance to the "Independent United States of America" by volunteering in Lieut. Hubbard's detachment; and we find in its rolls, as well, the name of Ezekiel Root.

The first detachment hurried to the threatened point in hot haste. Possibly every man got there as best he could. Certainly there was no superfluous weight of armor, and no dressing the ranks on the march. Mr. Allen set out in the old sulky, the wonted companion of his pastoral visits; going to war in his chariot, like the heroes of classic and scriptural story.

Of the Berkshire militia districts, Col. Symonds, of that nearest the scene of action, marched his full regiment. Col. Brown, the commander of the middle district, in which Pittsfield lay, was absent; and the detachment of his corps was led, and commanded with great spirit and military skill, by Lieut.-Col. David Rossiter of Richmond. From southern Berkshire, several towns sent volunteers. Meanwhile, as the people of the surrounding district were rallying to his support, Stark, on the 14th, had checked Baum's forces at a point in Hoosac, N.Y., five miles from Bennington Church, and near the Wallamsac, a little winding branch of the Hoosac River. On a small elevation near this stream, Baum occupied a strong position, which, during the heavy rain of the 15th, he was able to fortify with two lines of breast-works, although suffering severely from Stark's skirmishers. On the 14th, these sharp-shooters succeeded in killing or wounding thirty of the enemy, with no loss to themselves; and, on the 15th, the woods where the Indians had camped were so thoroughly scouted, that the savages, declaring the forest full of Yankees, began to desert in large numbers.

Among the volunteers of Southern Berkshire was a company of Stockbridge Indians, who, although civilized, retained, for the convenience of the service, their national costume, and were among the most valued of Stark's scouts. An incident of the battle was related by Linus Parker, which illustrates the double danger to which these faithful allies of the colonists were subjected. On the night previous to the fight, which was dark and dreary, Parker was on picket, and was induced to take double duty, and remain unrelieved at his post until morning. When the light broke, he found himself near a heavy belt of pines and hemlocks, which at once struck him as an admirable covert for lurking savages. He accordingly betook himself to watch behind a large tree; and, sure enough, a huge Indian with war-paint, musket, tomahawk, and scalper, soon showed himself, and, after taking a wary observation, walked straight towards Parker's hiding-place. The latter drew his musket to his shoulder; but, bethinking himself that a party of Mohegans were out on scout, determined to challenge, and shouted, "Who comes there?" — "A friend," was the reply. "A friend to whom?" After a painful hesitation, "To the Congress!"— "Advance, and give the countersign!" — "I can't," exclaimed the stranger, advancing and trembling with emotion: "O Parker! thank God, it is you! If it had been anybody else, they'd never stopped to talk to poor Indian. I'd been a dead man, sure."

The stranger proved to be Capt. Solomon, a Stockbridge chief, who had been out three days with a scouting-party, who had exhausted their provisions. "Now, Solomon," said Parker, "give me your gun, tomahawk, and scalper, and sit down yonder. Play my prisoner, and we'll get a drink." The guard soon came along; and, to the inquiry of the sergeant, "Who have you there?" Parker's reply was, "You can see, can't you? ask him." But Solomon, having been duly instructed, could talk nothing but Indian; and was taken, with his "captor," to the colonel, who at once recognized the scout. The drams were produced; and

Solomon was soon on his way back with supplies for his famishing tribesmen.

Stark continually gained strength by the arrival of the militia, by inuring his raw troops to danger, and by organizing the fragmentary squads in which some of the most ardent of his recruits had come.

The Berkshire militia arrived during the night, thoroughly drenched, of course, with the rain, and clogged with the mire through which they had trudged thirty miles, but having kept their powder dry, and full of heart for immediate action. The frequent tedious marches, which, in the midst of harvest-time, they had recently made, only to be sent home again without the opportunity to face the enemy, had left the militiamen in no very good humor; and the alarm of Bennington had been regarded by many as the old cry of "Wolf." Only the splendid reputation of Stark as a fighting commander obtained the effectual rally which was made to his standard. And even his name could not altogether dispel the distrust which had become chronic in the militia. This was the origin of the following scene, which is related by Edward Everett in his Life of Stark, and is probably as truthfully told as such traditions ever are: —

"Among the re-enforcements from Berkshire county came a clergyman [Rev. Mr. Allen] with a portion of his flock, resolved to make bare the arm of flesh against the enemies of his country. Before daylight on the morning of the 16th, he addressed the commander as follows: 'We, the people of Berkshire, have been frequently called upon to fight, but have never been led against the enemy. We have now resolved, if you will not let us fight, never to turn out again.' Gen. Stark asked him 'if he wished to march then, when it was dark and rainy.' — 'No," was the answer, 'not just this minute." — "Then," continued Stark, "if the Lord should once more give us sunshine, and I do not give you fighting enough, I will never ask you to come again.'"

The morning of the 16th of August dawned bright and clear; and Stark prepared to make good his promise of action. A close reconnoisance, together with the report of scouts, showed that the enemy were carefully, if not at all points skilfully, posted. The artillery, protected by Baum's dragoons and Frazer's sharpshooters, occupied the hill which rose from the Wallamsac, just within the borders of New York. The Loyal Rangers and French Canadians were stationed behind the first line of breastworks, in front of the hill, and on the same side of the river with the Americans. The little stream was, however, fordable at all points, and exercised but small influence upon the fortunes of the day which made it famous. The hill was quite abrupt upon its south-eastern face, but fell off more gently to the north and west; a fact of which Stark promptly availed himself, sending Col. Nichols with two hundred men, and Col. Herrick with three hundred, to simultaneously assail the right and left rear of the dragoons and sharp-shooters. The manœuvre was successfully executed, notwithstanding the outlying of the Indian scouts, who, finding themselves between the two detachments, and terrified by the experience of the two past days, broke through the lines and fled, although not without leaving a considerable number of dead and wounded on the field. Bancroft affirms that Baum mistook the militia, stealing behind him in their shirt-sleeves and with fowling-pieces, for loyalists of the country seeking the protection of his lines.

In the mean time, as Nichols and Herrick were marching to the real point of attack, small detachments made diversions in other quarters.

The Berkshire militia were with the reserve of some three hundred, who, under Stark in person, were slowly approaching the Tory breastworks by marches and countermarches, and getting familiar with the noisy terrors of the Hanau artillery; while the commander impatiently awaited the rattle of Nichols's musketry, which was to be the signal for his advance.

In the morning, the Berkshire men would not leave their encampment until Mr. Allen had prayed to the God of armies that he would "teach their hands to war, and their fingers to fight." The prayer was offered with that fervent earnestness for which its author was remarkable; and it inspirited the men like the harangue of a trusted commander. There were many who attributed the glorious success of the following day to the efficiency of the Berkshire parson's morning prayer. And who that, even in these days of less faith, trusts in the effectual fervent prayer of the righteous man, shall rebuke them for superstition in so believing?

As the regiment to which he was attached approached the Tory outworks in its countermarching, Mr. Allen, who knew that some of his old neighbors must be there, was moved by a sense of duty which he could not resist, although conscious of the extreme danger, to go still nearer, and, standing in full view upon a fallen tree, to conjure them to come out from the enemies of their country, and save the effusion of blood, while he warned them of the consequences of persisting in their hostility.

The answer was what might have been expected. "There's Parson Allen: let's pop him!" exclaimed some one who perhaps still smarted from the lash of the minister's plain preaching; and, although a few were of a more merciful mood, a shower of bullets whistled around him, riddling the tree on which he stood, but sparing his person — a piece of good luck which he owed more to the nervous markmanship of the musketeers than to their merciful compunctions. The undaunted parson, having satisfied his conscience, and no doubt feeling that the blood of the traitors would now be upon their own heads, turned coolly to his brother, Lieut. Joseph Allen, who had followed him under cover of the tree, and said, "Now give me a musket: you load, and I'll fire!" And fire he did, — the first gun in that glorious fray, — it must be confessed a little in advance of orders.

In a few moments, however, Stark heard the welcome sound of Nichols's attacking musketry, the word was given, and his men rushed eagerly to the attack, pouring in, as they advanced, a continuous fire, which soon rendered the first line of entrenchments too hot for its defenders. Panic-stricken, the unhappy Tories, expecting little mercy at the hands of their incensed countrymen, attempted to gain the protection of the works above by scaling the steep face of the hill, which had been rendered extremely slippery in digging for the earthworks during the heavy rains of the preceding days. Hardly able to maintain a precarious foothold at the best, constantly exposed to the relentless and unerring aim of the forest-trained militia, the wretched fugitives were indeed in pitiable plight. Linus Parker, afterwards the famous Pittsfield hunter, then a volunteer from Lenox, describes the scene as horribly ludicrous when a glimpse was caught, through the veil of smoke, of the black figures scrambling desperately up the smooth acclivity, and, one after another, killed or wounded, tumbling helplessly back to its base. "I could not," he said, "have kept from shaking with laughter if I had known that I was to be shot dead the next minute." The horror of the scene did not strike him at the moment as it did when he reviewed it in memory. The conflict soon became general, and "lasted," says Stark in his official report, "two hours, and was the hottest that he" — he who could remember, not only Bunker Hill and Trenton, but the fierce fights before Ticonderoga in the old French and Indian Wars — "had ever seen : it was like one continued clap of thunder."

The German dragoons and the English sharp-shooters defended their position gallantly, but the impetuous daring of their assailants was irresistible. The American musketeers rushed madly up the steep ascent to within a few paces of the cannon's mouth, the more surely to pick off the cannoneers. Attacked in front and rear, and his ammunition nearly expended, Baum ordered his dragoons and infantry to cut their way through the militia, who were almost destitute of bayonets. The charge was bravely made, but was as bravely met. The British commander fell, mortally wounded; and those of his men who survived were mostly made prisoners.

The soldiers of Stark now dispersed in various directions. Some were detailed to guard the numerous prisoners; others were employed in tending the wounded, and in seeking and caring for the dead; many, exhausted with the fatigues of the day, went in search of refreshment; and not a few betrayed the instincts of irregular troops, and devoted themselves to the plunder of the British camp. Even those who cared nothing for the spoils as booty desired to have some trophy of the great militia battle-field. It was while the victors were thus variously occupied that Col. Breyman approached with a body of troops which had been despatched by Burgoyne in response to Baum's demand for re-enforcements, but had been delayed by the inability of heavy German troops to act efficiently as light infantry in a pitched fight with American forest-mire.

It was impossible readily to recall a large portion of the scattered militia, and there was great danger that the fortunes of the day would be reversed.

Col. Rossiter distinguished himself by coolness, zeal, and courage in his exertions to collect the men and restore order; but all would have been in vain, had not Col. Seth Warner's regiment, which had not previously been engaged, arrived at the critical moment.

They had been stationed with the militia which Gen. Lincoln was collecting at Manchester; but, on Stark's application, had promptly been despatched to his aid, and had arrived, on the 15th, near Bennington, where they had been delayed by the condition of their arms and the scantiness of their ammunition. They now came fresh from repose; and, although they had been reduced to less than one hundred and fifty men by the Battle of Hubbardston, proved adequate, with the aid of what militia Stark could bring into action, and the captured cannon, to rout the force of Breyman, although that, too, was accompanied by two field-pieces.[1]

The rout was complete and precipitate. The enemy abandoned his artillery and many of his wounded; and, during the pursuit, the Americans took a considerable number of prisoners and a large quantity of small arms. Darkness preserved the broken remnant, who were received, with what feelings may be imagined, by Burgoyne, who was advancing to their relief with the Forty-seventh British Regiment.

The victory was perfect. In all the engagements, the Americans had lost only about thirty killed and forty wounded; while the loss of the enemy, in killed, wounded, and prisoners, was more than a thousand. The prisoners alone were at least six hundred and ninety-two, of whom four hundred were Germans, and one hundred and seventy-five were Tories. They exceeded in number the whole force which Burgoyne acknowledged to have been sent out in Baum's party.

The material fruits of the victory were four brass cannon, nine hundred dragoon swords, one thousand stand of excellent arms, and four ammunition-wagons, besides what the militia secured individually.

After the battle, Rev. Mr. Allen found a German surgeon's horse, loaded with panniers full of bottled wine. The wine was at once administered to the wounded and exhausted soldiers; but Mr. Allen retained two of the large square bottles as trophies of his three days' "tour;" and they were long kept as heirlooms in his family, some branch of which probably still have them in their possession.

The prisoners were sent, under charge of Gen. Fellows, to Boston; but a portion were left on the way, in Berkshire and Hampshire Counties; and these, except one servant to every officer who

[1] For an account of the Battle of Bennington, by Rev. Mr. Allen, see Appendix.

chose to have one at his own expense, were ordered by the General Court to be consigned to the care of the committees of some of the towns in those counties, and to be permitted to hire out to labor on such terms as the committee might think equitable. Quite a number did so, to the relief of the great scarcity of laborers; and some became permanent settlers of the country.

No battle in the Revolution took a more powerful and permanent hold upon the hearts of the people than that of Bennington. To this end a variety of circumstances combined. The dark background which it relieved contributed much to the effect. At the moment when the news of its glorious success flashed over the country, the aspect of affairs, to the popular eye, was one of almost unbroken gloom. The serene mind of Washington, indeed, contemplated the star behind the cloud; but he was, with a far inferior force, vainly combating the passage to Philadelphia of the superb army of Sir William Howe, by a system of tactics which, although it commands the admiration of posterity, had no splendor for the multitude in that day, and was even denounced as too "Fabian" by eminent statesmen.

Burgoyne, almost utterly unopposed, was advancing upon Albany with an army whose power and terrors were studiously magnified by every art in the reach of its general. Marauding parties upon the Hudson indicated that the fleet and forces below only waited the arrival of Burgoyne at Albany, to advance to the same point, and complete the armed barrier which was to divide the East from the South and West.

On this night of gloom, the eye of Washington, eagerly watching for the morning star which his trusting spirit prophesied, did indeed recognize it in the noble exploit of Herkimer's New-York militia, and that most mirth-provoking termination to the siege of Fort Stanwix. But the connection of St. Leger's column with Burgoyne's scheme was too remote to be comprehended by the masses; and, in fact, his success was not essential to that of his principal. Herkimer's gallant exploit, therefore, both for this reason and because of its incompleteness, although to Washington's eye "it first relieved the gloomy scene of the northern campaign," had not the effect on the country which he desired and confidently expected from the cutting-off of some detached body of Burgoyne's army, — the restoration of lost spirit and courage. That remained to be effected by the Battle of Bennington.

This had in it all the elements which seize upon the popular mind. Standing out from the dark background we have rudely sketched, it glowed with the perfect halo of victory. It impressed itself upon the imagination also in other ways. It occurred in a region which, romantic in itself, had just become associated with the thrilling tragedy of Miss McCrea. The wounded and the slain of the enemy were the abettors of her savage murderers; perhaps among them were the miscreants themselves. The victors were her avengers. The defeated, also, were a portion of the most boastful and arrogant army which the king had sent over. The victors were militia,— the most popular branch of the military service,[1] and of a portion of the militia, which to those at a distance especially, was invested with a sort of quaint fame. A large portion were the Green-Mountain boys who had once been led by Ethan Allen. All were men of the mountains, and were led by Stark, the story of whose exploits in the old wars now passed — nothing lost in the telling — from mouth to mouth. Hardly a less prominent figure in the well-wrought scene, as it was pictured by a thousand firesides, was that of the bold parson who went with his flock to share the dangers of the battle-field; satisfied that the war which was holy enough for him to advocate from the pulpit was righteous enough for him to take part in with his musket.

Such were some of the elements which enabled the Battle of Bennington to obtain and keep so large a place in the national heart.

But the first great thrill of joy and hope, that went all over the land, was inspired by the fact that a large detachment of that proudest of armies had been utterly routed by a hastily collected body of husbandmen, half armed, and imperfectly organized; that no small quantity of munitions of war had been acquired; and that the march of Burgoyne had been seriously interrupted.

In effects like these the Battle of Bennington may justly be classed, and not in any particular as inferior, with those of Lexington and Bunker Hill, Princeton and Trenton; and no prouder rank could be accorded it among the battle-fields of the Revolution.

In addition to the moral effect, the material loss inflicted upon

[1] Although in form and organization militia, the Pittsfield volunteers were, it ought to be stated, individually almost all veterans; some of them having served in two wars. But few, if any, of them had never been under fire.

Burgoyne was serious. Out of his small force, more than a thousand men — a majority of them among his best troops — were gone, besides those he had lost in the skirmishes of July. His scanty transportation was still more diminished ; and, although the captured arms and ammunition would not be much missed from his plentiful supply, it was a serious consideration that they went to replenish the depleted armories of the Americans, who, consequent upon the evacuation of Ticonderoga, had lost no less than 128 pieces of cannon, and an immense quantity of warlike stores.

Three days after the Battle of Bennington, Schuyler was succeeded, or rather supplanted, in the command of the northern army, by Gates, — a man with few of his noble qualities, but with many of his weaknesses. The new commander was, however, governed by a selfish ambition, which sometimes, at a pinch, stood him in the stead of personal courage and the spirit of a resolute commander.

Emboldened now by the recent disasters to the enemy, and by the augmenting strength of his own forces, Gates, upon the 9th of September, turned the faces of his men again towards the invaders, and moved his camp northward to a strong position which commanded the passage of the Hudson at Stillwater.

In the mean time, Burgoyne, by the most arduous exertions, had succeeded at length in bringing from Lakes George and Champlain one hundred and eighty boats, which, laden with one month's supplies, to that extent made every thing ready for the long-delayed advance upon Albany.

But now the occupation of Stillwater by the Americans had made that movement impracticable, unless they were first dislodged from that commanding position. To accomplish this, Burgoyne could at the best muster less than six thousand men, rank, and file ; and, in order to swell his numbers to the utmost of his capacity, he resolved to draw in the garrisons stationed at Skenesborough, Fort Edward, and Fort Miller, and abandon his communication with the lakes.

The necessity of such a measure on the part of the British general had been foreseen ; and a plan to take advantage of it had been arranged between Gates and Gen. Lincoln, who still commanded the depot for militia at Manchester.

The execution of this scheme, so congenial to his tastes, was committed to Col. Brown, who, with a detachment from his militia regiment, had left Pittsfield on the 6th of September, and was stationed at Pawlet, to which place Lincoln also removed his headquarters. It is probable, that, when setting out for this rendezvous, he contemplated something of an adventurous nature; for the Pittsfield company which attended him, under the command of Capt. John Strong and Lieut. James Easton, is recorded to have gone "every man with a horse and a bag of meal."

From Pawlet, Gen. Lincoln sent out three detachments of five hundred picked light troops each. To one of these Col. Brown was assigned, with directions to proceed to Fort George, to destroy the British stores collected there, and release the American prisoners for whom that post had been made a depot. While this attempt was making, Col. Johnson was ordered to create a diversion at the northern end of the lake, and, if opportunity offered, to attack Mount Independence.

With so much discretion and spirit was Col. Brown's expedition conducted, that, leaving Pawlet on the 13th of October, by the morning of the 18th, he had not only accomplished the objects designated in the general's orders, but, passing up Lake George, he had surprised all the outworks between its northern landing-place and the main fort of Ticonderoga, including Mount Hope, Mount Defiance, an isolated block-house, and the old French lines. Besides these, an armed brig, several gunboats, and two hundred bateaux, had fallen into his hands. He had made two hundred and ninety-three prisoners; embracing four companies of regular infantry, and nearly as many Canadians, besides the officers and crews of the flotilla. Five cannon, and small arms in proportion to the number of captured soldiers, were among the spoils; and, to complete the gratifying character of the achievement, one hundred American soldiers were released from captivity, and the Continental standard, which had been left behind in the unseemly haste of the late evacuation, was recovered.

Having accomplished this, Col. Brown summoned the commandant of Ticonderoga to surrender; but he had neither siege-artillery nor men to enforce a compliance; and, after making demonstrations against the works for a few days, he withdrew his forces, and, destroying the captured vessels, returned safely with his trophies to headquarters, having lost in killed and wounded only nine men.

Meantime the conflict went on between the armies of Gates

and Burgoyne at Saratoga and Stillwater; and, in compliance with the order of the General Court requiring one-half of the Berkshire militia to take the field, Capt. William Francis with thirty men marched on the 30th of September to Stillwater, where they remained until the 10th of October. What part they took in the battles which ccurred in that interval is not stated. Dr. Timothy Childs, who accompanied the detachment as surgeon, remained with the army until the capitulation of Burgoyne; which was signed on the 17th, when five thousand seven hundred and ninety-one men, including officers, laid down their arms. Eighteen hundred and fifty-six, previously made prisoners of war, were not included in the articles of capitulation.

The army of Burgoyne marched through Berkshire to Boston, — twenty-five hundred of them by way of Pittsfield.[1] The march of these long-dreaded and now but half-humbled enemies through the country impressed itself strongly on the memories of the people, and still mingles largely in their vague traditions. It is indicative of the almost total absence of specie in those days, that the possession of gold and silver, in what seemed profusion, by the passing prisoners, and their readiness to spend it for such luxuries as the impoverished country afforded, was what took the most powerful hold of the imagination of the Berkshire folk; and this to such a degree as to tinge some of the legends, which they handed down, with superstitions akin to those which attach to the piratical hoards of Capt. Kidd. Men, at a not very remote date, have been known to engage in the search for hidden treasure along the route of Burgoyne's men.

Upon the surrender of the British army, the garrison of Ticonderoga withdrew into Canada: the excitements and alarms which had so long pervaded the territory of which Berkshire formed a part ceased, and comparative quiet reigned. The exultation of the people over the successes of 1777 are quaintly expressed by some ingenious writer of that day in the following verses, which were found among the papers of Gen. Stark after his death: —

[1] Rev. Mr. Allen's diary.

GEN. BURGOYNE'S OVERTHROW AT SARATOGA,
OCTOBER, 1777.

Here followeth the direful fate
Of Burgoyne and his army great,
Who so proudly did display
The terrors of despotic sway.
His power and pride, and many threats,
Have been brought low by fort'nate Gates,
To bend to the United States.

British prisoners by convention . .	2,442
Foreigners by contravention . . .	2,198
Tories sent across the lake . . .	1,100
Burgoyne and suit, in state . . .	12
Sick and wounded, bruised and pounded Ne'er so much before confounded	528
Prisoners of war before convention .	400
Deserters come with kind intention .	300
They lost at Bennington's great battle, Where glorious Stark his arms did rattle	1,220
Killed in September and October . .	600
Taken by brave Brown, some drunk, some sober,	413
Slain by high-famed Herkiman . . . On both flank, on rear and van . .	300
Indians, sutlers, and drovers, Enough to crowd large plains over, And those whom grim death did prevent, From fighting against our continent; And also those who stole away, Lest down their arms they should lay, Abhorring that obnoxious day.	4,413
The whole make fourteen thousand men, Who may not with us fight again	14,000

This is a pretty just account
Of Burgoyne's legions' whole amount,
Who came across the northern lakes
To desolate our happy States.
Their brass cannons we have got all, —
Fifty-six, — both great and small;
And ten thousand stand of arms,

To prevent all future harms;
Stores and implements complete,
Of workmanship exceeding neat;
Covered wagons in great plenty,
And proper harness no way scanty,
Amongst our prisoners there are
Six generals of fame most rare;
Six members of their Parliament,—
Reluctantly they seem content;
The British lords, and Lord Balcarras,
Who came our country free to harass.
Two baronets of high extraction
Were sorely wounded in the action.

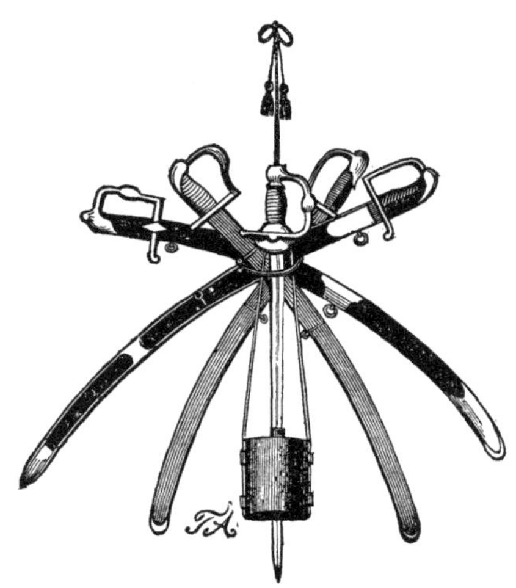

CHAPTER XVII.

LAST YEARS OF THE REVOLUTION.

[1777-1783.]

Battle of Stone Arabia. — Death of Col. Brown. — Major Oliver Root defends Fort Paris. — Pittsfield Militia. — Pittsfield Soldiers in the Continental Army. — Action of the Town in filling Quotas. — Hosea Merrill. — Interesting Incidents. — Material Contributions of Pittsfield to the War of the Revolution. — Collection of Taxes. — Curious Papers relating thereto.

FROM the year 1777 to the close of the war, the military record of Pittsfield is meagre, as compared with that of the earlier years of the Revolution. While the patriotism of its people continued as ardent, and they were as prompt as before to respond to the calls of their country, the war was in a great measure turned from the neighboring frontier; the demand for extraordinary service ceased; the contributions of men were mostly to the regular Continental army, and we can rarely follow them in their scattered and distant service. Even could we trace them from field to field, we should find, in the story of their conflicts, that the exploits of the few were merged in the achievements of the many; and that not only was the individual lost in his company, and the company in its regiment, but that, in most instances, the corps hid the regiment.

A few incidents of special local interest are, however, saved from this generally unmarked period; and it was distinguished by the sad but not inglorious fight in which many of the sons of Pittsfield participated, and the most illustrious soldier which she furnished to the armies of the Revolution fell.

But, even concerning an event so conspicuous as the Battle of Stone Arabia, one is compelled to rely very much upon tradition, both for the events of the day and their immediate causes. Fortunately, however, the story comes to us through so many trustworthy sources which corroborate each other, and was so minutely related many times by the chief actor who survived the slaughter, to gentlemen from whom we have received it directly.[1]

In the autumn of 1779, Gen. Sullivan, by the orders of Gen. Washington, had inflicted a terrible chastisement upon the Mohawks, and other hostile tribes of the Six Nations; burning their villages, destroying their orchards, and laying waste their fields, — a devastation whose record shows that these tribes had sufficiently advanced in civilization to feel keenly the severity of their punishment.

During the ensuing winter, this visitation was bitterly retaliated upon the friendly Oneidas, whose homes were desolated, and their families driven in upon the Americans for protection and support. Not content with this, the Indians and the Tories, impelled by a common resentment, banded together under Sir John Johnson and the chiefs Brant and Corn-Planter, prepared to pursue their schemes of vengeance in the valley of the Mohawk, a luxuriant farming-country, in whose population there was a convenient infusion of Tories, although the great majority of its inhabitants were ardently patriotic.

The hostile league was formidable; and the alarm was general, although, until fall, apprehension of its nature and designs was vague. The horrors of Indian warfare, under British instigation, had exceeded the atrocities incited by the French foe. The massacre at Wyoming in 1778 was still fresh in the memory of the people; and, in the summer of 1780, the danger became apparent, that similar scenes, and even more dreadful, might be witnessed in the valley of the Mohawk, — the fair home from which Sir John Johnson and many Tories had been driven, and where, moreover, a harvest of unusual abundance was ripening, upon which Washington's commissariat was known to place much dependence. Policy and exasperated feeling alike devoted this lovely region.

Prominent among the troops which rallied to its defence was a Berkshire regiment, commanded by Col. John Brown; in which there was a company of seventy-nine Pittsfield and Richmond men under Capt. William Ford, the same who, as lieutenant, had led the Pittsfield detachment at Bennington.

[1] Dr. O. S. Root and Franklin Root, Esq., grandsons of Major Oliver Root. We have also consulted the accounts of Lossing and Stone, and valuable papers in Mr. Henry C. Van Schaack's collection; but tradition is the foundation of all these reports.

The regiment was composed of levies from the three, into which the militia of Berkshire was divided. John Ashley, who commanded in the southern part of the county, was the senior officer. John Brown had commanded the middle regiment until 1778, when he resigned, and was succeeded by Lieut.-Col. Rossiter. In 1780, the new State Constitution went into operation; and, in accordance with it, the choice of regimental officers was intrusted to the captains and subalterns, who, in their turn, were elected by the privates of their respective companies. At the first election under this law, Col. Brown was restored to his old position.

About the same time, the levy for the Mohawk was made, and Ashley was assigned to the command, and proceeded to Albany. There he was seized with an illness which afterwards proved fatal; and Col. Brown, being in the city upon private business, consented to relieve him, being assured by his senior and friend, that the Berkshire troops, especially since his recent success at Lake George, would follow him more readily than any other man.[1]

Col. Brown accepted the position probably with the more readiness, because his old home, Caughnawaga, where he commenced the practice of the law, was in the district he was called to defend. The other regimental officers were Major Oliver Root, Adjutant James Easton, son of the colonel of the same name, Quartermaster Elias Willard, and Surgeon Oliver Brewster. All were from Pittsfield, except Dr. Brewster, who was from Partridgefield, now Peru, but was the ancestor of two prominent Pittsfield physicians.[2]

Col. Brown assumed the command on the 14th of July. We learn nothing more of the regiment, until, on the 18th of October, we find it posted at Fort Paris, a small blockhouse about three miles north of the Mohawk River, and in that part of the district of Stone Arabia which now forms the town of Palatine. Four days previous, Sir John Johnson's hordes had set out upon a grand mission of destruction through the fine valleys of the Schoharie and

[1] It is related in connection with this change of commanders, that Col. Brown, being without his pistols, borrowed, and gave his receipt for, those of Ashley; which, when he fell, became the booty of some plundering savage. Ashley dying soon after, the receipt was found among his papers, and his administrators collected payment from the estate of the man who was killed in his place.

[2] Surgeon Brewster was born in Lebanon, Conn., in 1760. He was reputed an excellent physician, and a man of marked piety. He was grandfather of the late Dr. Oliver E. Brewster, of Pittsfield, surgeon of the Fortieth Massachusetts Regiment, in the civil war of 1861-5.

Mohawk; and, wherever they had passed, the devastation was complete. The destroyers left unburned not one house, barn, or stack of grain, which was known to belong to a Whig; and hundreds of the patriotic inhabitants — men, women, and children — were pitilessly murdered while flying, or begging for mercy.

DR. OLIVER BREWSTER.

On the 18th, Gen. Robert Van Rensselaer, an exceedingly sluggish and incompetent commander, coming tardily, with a considerable body of militia, to the relief of the distressed region, reached Caughnawaga, which flourishing village he found still in flames. Learning here that Fort Paris, which is about twelve miles distant, was to be attacked the next day, he sent orders to Col. Brown to march out in the morning, and form a junction with his own force at an appointed rendezvous, in order to anticipate the enemy's plans by a joint attack.[1]

Many of the garrison seem to have considered the movement a dangerous one; and some of the officers even counselled disobedience of the order. The same feelings of distrust extended to the

[1] The reason assigned for Van Rensselaer's order is not so clear as one could wish; and it is not bettered by adopting the other version, that it directed Brown to attack the rear while Van Rensselaer assailed the front of the enemy,— which is inconsistent with the story of the ambuscade. The whole account leaves the impression that neither officer supposed that any body of the Indians lay between them.

men. One of them, — Giles Parker of South Adams, — whose courage had often been tried by the severest tests, came to the colonel in the morning, and warned him to forego his march; relating, at the same time, an ominous dream of the previous night, which depressed his spirits. "What!" exclaimed his commander, "are *you* afraid to march with me? Then stay behind." The soldier indignantly protested "that he had fought by his side many a time; that it was not for himself he feared, but his colonel." Finding him fully impressed with the belief that evil would attend the march, Col. Brown seriously advised him to remain in the fort; but the noble fellow claimed his right to share the danger of his comrades, and was among the first to fall under the murderous fire of the savages.

The one thing that Col. Brown feared was, that a battle in which he had a right to take part would be fought without him.

Early on the morning of the 19th of October, — his thirty-fifth birthday, — he therefore left Fort Paris, with about three hundred men, to form a junction, in obedience to his orders, with Gen. Van Rensselaer. The detachment had marched perhaps two miles, when a house was discovered, at a distance of perhaps a quarter of a mile upon the right, before which was a family group, surrounding a man just mounting his horse. This person rode directly to Major Root, who was in advance, and inquired if he commanded the party; Col. Brown, who was in the rear, was pointed out; and, riding up to him, the stranger stated that he was directed by Gen. Van Rensselaer, to inform him, that by proceeding down a road which turned to the left, instead of that he was then pursuing, he would reach the general's army.

The proposed route seemed to be a convenient detour around the region where the presence of the enemy began to be indicated by the smoke of burning buildings; and, the well-arranged family scene doubtless helping to ward off suspicion, unfortunate credence was given to the stranger, without demanding further guaranties, and without detaining him as a surety for his good faith.

The route was changed in accordance with his directions, and soon led into a long and narrow clearing, extending to the river, — near a ruined work called Fort Keyzer, — and surrounded by heavy woods. The detachment had well advanced into this treacherous *cul-de-sac*, — the colonel and major both being at the head of the column, — when a sergeant near them exclaimed, "See that damned Indian!" and immediately discharged his musket. At once the woods resounded with savage yells; and a thousand muskets, gleaming from behind sheltering trees, poured in a rapid and murderous cross-fire upon the entrapped and bewildered troops. Col. Brown, who was conspicuous by his fine person and his official sash, was shot through the heart at the first fire, and fell upon his face without a word or a struggle.[1]

Any attempt to restore order among the panic-stricken troops would have been worse than futile; and officers, as well as men, fled precipitately towards the fort. There was no lack of vigor in the pursuit; but the irresistible impulse to tomahawk and scalp the wounded delayed the savages, and enabled a large portion of the fugitives to escape. Major Root saw one man crawl into the woods and conceal himself, while his over-eager pursuers passed on without heeding him; but he thought almost every man of the seriously injured was killed and scalped. Forty were reported slain.

The fort was filled with women and children, who, upon the approach of the savages, had fled to it from the neighboring country; and their shrieks and moanings added to the confusion, as the flying soldiers crowded in disorder into the gates. Fortunately, Major Root had been trained in a school which rendered him familiar with such scenes, as well as with the character of the enemy with whom he had to deal. The fort, he knew, was not at all competent to sustain an assault from the forces which now thronged into the edges of the clearing around it, and were evidently eager for an attack. But he was well aware of the terror with which "big guns" inspired the savages, and was convinced, by the temerity with which they exposed themselves, that they believed him unsupplied with artillery. The wretched little fortress, however, was, by chance, supplied with one poor dwarf of a four-pounder; although its ammunition was limited to a solitary ball and three charges of powder.

With this the major determined to make a demonstration; and,

[1] Lossing relates the following anecdote: "On his way to the Mohawk country, Col. Brown called upon Ann Lee, the founder of the sect of Shaking Quakers. He assured her, by way of pleasantry, that, on his return, he should join her society. A fortnight after his death, two members of the society waited upon his widow, told her that her husband, in spirit, had joined 'Mother Ann,' and that he had given express orders for her to become a member. She was not to be duped, and bade them begone."

wheeling his gun to the gateway, he sent the lonely missile bowling among, or at least towards, the astonished groups. A charge of horse-chains next went singing through the air. But in the mean while, by order of the major, a huge old cast-iron dinner-pot had been broken up; and, when its fragments came shrieking and screaming among the besiegers, it completed their dismay, and they withdrew rapidly within the shelter of the woods. Even the Tory officer who commanded them does not seem to have noticed the scarcity of ammunition which the strangeness of the missiles would have indicated to one of more shrewdness or experience; for he gave over his purposed attack, remarking, that "he had a mind to take that fort by storm; but it would cost too many lives."

The militia rallied to the support of Gen. Van Rensselaer in such numbers, that, there being no longer need of the services of the Berkshire regiment, it returned home at the expiration of its term of three months, on the 21st of October.

The affair of Stone Arabia was the only occasion, subsequent to 1777, when the Pittsfield militia met the enemy in actual conflict. It responded promptly, however, when called upon in various alarms.

While Johnson was invading the Mohawk Valley, Lieut. Joel Stevens led a small detachment to Fort Edward, where signs of danger appeared; and, at the same time, Capt. Rufus Allen, with twenty-six men, "marched forty miles," probably to the same point.

When Connecticut was invaded by Gov. Tryon in the summer of 1779, Lieut. Stevens went with fourteen men to New Haven. In October, 1781, the same officer, having been promoted to a captaincy, repaired, with Lieuts. Lebbeus Backus and Nathan Warner, to Saratoga upon an alarm in that quarter.

There may have been other occasions when the militia of the town were called out in the closing years of the war; but, if so, they were unrecorded, and probably bloodless, campaigns, and with no remembered adventure.

The reader who has followed us thus far will not attribute it solely to local pride, that we claim for the Pittsfield militia a record of peculiar brilliancy and usefulness. From the spring morning when Capt. Noble's minute-men, with rattling drum and scream of fife, took up their march for Cambridge, until Capt. Stevens's volleying musketry welcomed the return of peace, its able-bodied men — with those of all Berkshire as well — had been, and the General Court practically recognized them to be, virtually a frontier garrison posted behind the ramparts of their hills, but ever ready to sally out to any point where danger gathered. Their fame is indissolubly connected with the names of Ticonderoga, Bennington, Lake George, and the fields of Canada, which they helped to make historic; and more sadly, but hardly less gloriously, are they associated with the ambuscade of Fort Keyser.

The Continental soldiers furnished by the town, so far as we can learn, served with credit; but little has been preserved of their individual record. The story of the demand and supply of men for that service is, however, of curious interest; and we have a general statement of the several calls, of the bounties paid, and of the other means used to raise the men.

In the spring of 1778, Pittsfield had in the Continental service thirty-two men, all enrolled within the two years immediately preceding, for terms either of three years or during the war. A call for six additional having been made, the town, on the 20th of May, authorized the commissioned officers "to promise to the Continental soldiers now to be raised, the sum of £180; it having been granted to the town by the General Court, provided it procure six able-bodied men to serve in the Continental army for the term of nine months."

The next call was for seven men for nine months' service; and on the 30th of June, 1779, a committee of seven was appointed to hire them, with power "to plight the credit of the town" for whatever sums they might promise as bounty.

On the 2d of July, the committee reported that they had made the following enlistments upon the terms specified: —

John Wright and Ozem Strong, £200 Continental money each, and £9 each in neat cattle at the rate at which they were selling in the year 1775.

David Johnson and Samuel Smith, £300 Continental money each, on their passing muster.

Jeffrey Hazzard (colored), £200 Continental money, and nine pounds' worth of merchantable wheat at 4*s.* 6*d.* per bushel, to be paid to Nathan Robbins by Dec. 1, 1779, provided Hazzard passes muster.

Isaac Morse, £200 Continental money, and £10 worth of wheat, or corn at the rate of wheat, by Feb. 1, 1779, at 4*s.* per bushel, provided he passes muster. Morse entitles the town to his State bounty.

Daniel Bates, £115 Continental, and £13. 10*s.* worth of wheat at 4*s.* 6*d.* per bushel, by Dec. 1, 1779, provided he passes muster.

The town proceeded to tax itself £2,700 to meet these bounties, and directed the tax to be assessed and collected as soon as possible. It was also provided, " that, if any person is disposed to pay either of the soldiers so raised what said person's rate shall be, on his producing said soldier's receipt to the collector he shall cross the same."

The matter was, however, not yet disposed of; for, in the warrant for town-meeting on the 2d of the following August, an article was inserted, "To see what measures the town will come into, to recover three of the nine-months' men that have been enlisted, mustered in, and received their bounty, but have since absconded: if not recoverable, to see by what means their places shall be supplied." The town authorized the selectmen to send some person after the runaways, and passed over the article looking to the possibility of their absolute loss; but voted, that if Capt. John Strong should deliver Joshua Chapell to the superintendent of this county, and procure a certificate that the said Chapell is received as a nine-months' man, the treasurer of this town shall pay to Lieut. Rufus Allen eight hard dollars." Which of the seven were the deserters is not stated. All finally served in that contingent, except Ozem Strong and Jeffrey Hazzard, whose places were filled by Joshua Chapell and Jonathan Morey. Hazzard's name appears afterwards on the Continental rolls as having been mustered on the 14th of November, 1779, into service "during the war."

In December, 1780, came a more formidable requisition. No less than sixteen men were wanted to serve for three years or during the war; and, at a meeting on the 14th, a committee of nine men, chosen from different parts of the town, was appointed to devise the most eligible mode of procuring them. It consisted of Joshua Robbins, Eli Root, Esq., Joseph Fairfield, Lieut. Wm. Barber, Woodbridge Little, Esq., Capt. Rufus Allen, Capt. David Bush, and Daniel Hubbard, who, on the 20th, reported the following elaborate plan: —

That the town choose two good and faithful men to hire the said sixteen men, and to obligate themselves, on the credit of the town, to pay each man whom they shall so hire and procure the sum of thirty pounds in hard money, over and above all State and Continental pay and rewards, within three weeks, or otherwise to such person's acceptance and satisfaction.

2d. The officers of the three militia companies into which the town was divided, were requested to assemble their companies at the meeting-house at nine o'clock, the next Monday morning, and to use their utmost exertions to obtain a full attendance of their men.

3d. That the aforesaid committee of two attend the above meeting, and use their utmost endeavors to procure the required number of men for the aforementioned sum; at the same time giving information of the State and Continental pay and rewards.

4th. That a committee of five be chosen from the several parts of the town, for the purpose of dividing the ratable polls and estate into as many classes as there shall be men wanting after the committee of two have made their trial aforesaid.

5th. That the committee of two, immediately after their trial aforesaid, make report to the committee of five, who, thereupon, shall immediately proceed to class the town.[1]

6th. That, in forming said classes, the committee shall be governed by the last valuation or list, which was taken by the assessors, having no regard to the dormant lands.[2]

7th. That the committee shall consult the convenience of the inhabitants by classing together persons who live in the same neighborhood, so far as is practicable; and shall transmit to some principal member of each class a list of the persons contained in their respective classes, together with the amount of each person's estate.

8th. That it shall be the duty of each class, so made and formed, to procure an able-bodied, effective man, to the acceptance of the muster master, to serve in the Continental Army for three years or during war.

9th. That each class, unless they otherwise agree among themselves, shall tax its members to such an amount as shall be found necessary in order to procure such men, one third thereof to be assessed on polls, and the other two-thirds upon estates.

10th. That reference be had to the resolve of the General Court of the 2d of December, 1780, for the compelling the respective classes, or individuals of classes, to comply with their respective duties on the premises.

The report was made by David Bush, and was adopted, with the exception of the clause excluding the dormant lands from a share in the taxation.

It was also resolved that the classes should "exhibit to the town what each soldier cost its respective class, which sums shall be made a town debt."

[1] The towns were authorized by the General Court to divide their inhabitants and estates into as many classes as there were men in their quota, and to compel each class to produce its man.

[2] Lands of non-resident proprietors, unimproved, and by the old law not subject to town taxation.

The town selected Capt. James Noble and Mr. Joseph Fairfield for its "committee of two good and faithful men," and the following five to class the town: Woodbridge Little, Eli Root, Rufus Allen, James D. Colt, and Oliver Root.

The "utmost endeavors" of the first committee did not suffice to persuade any of the militia that thirty pounds, even in hard money, was an adequate bounty; and the town was divided into sixteen classes, fifteen of which procured their men previous to the first of January. The bounty paid in six cases was £50; in five cases, £55; in one, £55. 7*s.*; in three, £60, — all of course in specie or its equivalent.

The class nominally delinquent, according to a certificate of the selectmen April 20, 1781, paid to its head their respective assessments, sufficient to procure a man, to his full satisfaction; and he undertook to hire a soldier and idemnify the class, but, for some reason unexplained, failed to do so.

The last call upon the town during the Revolution was in July, 1781, when thirteen men were required for the service of the Commonwealth, not the Continent, for three months. The town was classed by a committee consisting of Woodbridge Little, Eli Root, Lebbeus Backus, and Capts. William Barber, Joel Stevens, and James D. Colt; and the men were promptly raised.

HOSEA MERRILL.

The name of Hosea Merrill is borne on the Revolutionary rolls as having served for Pittsfield in 1780. Mr. Merrill was born at Hebron, Conn., in 1761, and removed to Pittsfield at the age of twelve. The family tradition is, that, at the age of nineteen, he and several other boys, providing themselves with old guns, powder-horns, and bullets made by melting down pewter spoons, proceeded to Washington's headquarters on the Hudson, and offered their services; and, when asked by the commander-in-chief what they came for, young Merrill replied for them, "To fight the British;" and to the question, what position they desired, his answer was, "The post of danger." Boys of nineteen were worth too many pounds of "hard money," in filling quotas, to permit us to accept this story literally; but it indicates the opinion which prevailed of Mr. Merrill's gallantry. It is better authenticated, that he was on patrol on the night when Major André was brought in a prisoner; that he was selected as one of his guards, and was afterwards posted in the room with him during his last night on earth, and witnessed the sad spectacle of his execution.[1]

The contributions of material, as well as those of men, made by Pittsfield to the war of the Revolution, were large. Rev. Mr. Allen speaks of the demands made upon the county of Berkshire as being extraordinary, in proportion to those upon the rest of the State; which is explained by her proximity to the theatre of war. In several exigencies, portions of the county were stripped of almost all means of transportation. In others, as in the alarm of 1777, every article of lead or pewter which could be laid hands upon was seized: cattle and grain were demanded in large but not in so exhaustive quantities. There were resolutions of advice from the Provincial Congress, and orders from the General Court, — of equal authority in Berkshire, — that the town should furnish certain articles of clothing, and equipments for its soldiers, and they were always forthcoming; there were special voluntary contributions for the comfort of the sons of the town in the army, and they were liberally made.

The taxes, as in most towns, were sometimes in arrears. The political disorders of the times created the utmost financial confusion;[2] and, when the imposts came to be enormously increased, some

[1] Mr. Merrill was in after-life a fine specimen of the Revolutionary soldier returned to private life, — a calm, even-tempered, collected, and thoughtful man; kind and affectionate; speaking ill of none; quiet, industrious, and economical; spending a long life without reproach, and fearing no man.

[2] Some idea of the depreciation of the currency, even in the earlier years of the

irregularity in their collection was to be expected, especially among a people largely dependent upon their daily labor, while a majority of its able-bodied middle-aged and young men were in the military service. Still the efforts of the town to collect the dues of the State were unremitting and fairly successful. There were, however, some difficulties in the matter which called for the aid of legislation. The exemption from local taxation of the unimproved or "dormant" lands of non-resident proprietors in the town had long been a source of complaint, and, the State tax upon them being now refused payment, produced troubles which are explained in the following preamble and resolutions, introduced, and probably passed, in the General Court of 1781: —

"Whereas it appears that Joel Dickinson and Joseph Wright, constables and collectors in the town of Pittsfield, labor under difficulty, and are likely to suffer damage in their estates, on account of the dormant lands of the non-resident proprietors, as the law now stands, as no purchasers appear to bid off said lands when they are offered for sale; therefore —

"*Resolved*, That the sheriff of the county of Berkshire is authorized and directed to levy the execution or executions which he may have against said collectors upon said proprietors' lands in the several rate-bills, in the hands of said collectors and constables, and cause so much of the lands so taken to be apprized, by three indifferent men, under oath, as will pay the sum or sums set upon their lands, and the costs, and the lands so apprized to become the property of this Commonwealth; which shall discharge such part of the aforesaid executions as shall be levied upon such dormant lands."

Another difficulty, which it must have puzzled the legislative wisdom to resolve, will appear from the following draft of a petition to which we can find no other allusion nor any response:[1] —

STATE OF MASSACHUSETTS BAY.

TO THE HONORABLE THE COUNCIL AND THE HONORABLE HOUSE OF REPRESENTATIVES IN GENERAL COURT ASSEMBLED.

The petition of the assessors of the town of Pittsfield humbly sheweth, That your petitioners have received an act from your Honors requiring them to inquire into the ratable property of the State, and that they have possessed themselves of the same as to the town of Pittsfield; but that they are so unhappy as not to agree what is the real value thereof, — varying equal to their numbers.

war, may be found by consulting the comparative table of prices left by Rev. Mr. Allen, and given in the Appendix to this volume.

[1] T. C. C., p. 250.

Such being our situation, we most humbly entreat your Honors would be pleased to give us the value of our currency; or else we must be subjected to the fine you have enjoined, or lie at your mercy to be doomed.

We are, with all deference,

Your Honors' most obedient servants.

PITTSFIELD, Sept. 1, 1778.

Peace and acknowledged independence came to the Colonies in 1783, and the event was celebrated in Pittsfield with great rejoicings. The militia paraded, and fired volleys of musketry. There is a dim tradition of a salute said to have been fired from a cannon cast at Lenox furnace; but that is doubtful.

Rev. Mr. Allen preached a Thanksgiving discourse, glowing with fervent gratitude to the God of nations, and not failing to inculcate the great principles by which he believed the republic ought to be governed. The glorious future which he predicted for his country long dwelt in the minds of those who heard him. A rare opportunity was afforded for the unchecked display of his hopeful and enthusiastic nature.

The quaint old gambrel-roofed house, afterwards known as the Chandler-Williams place, and now standing a little east of its original location, had been commenced, a few years previous to that date, by Col. Easton, who intended it for the residence of his son. It was not quite finished: but in it a great feast, known to tradition as the Peace Party, was held; among the viands for which, half a roasted ox figured conspicuously between platoons of geese and turkeys. Punch stood in huge tubs; wine and cider flowed in sparkling abundance.

Young and old flocked from every direction to the gathering. The joyous merriment of the occasion, the gayety of the dance, and the rustic splendors of the preparations, impressed themselves upon the memory of children who witnessed the scene with a vividness which did not fade until their dying day.[1]

Among the incidents told in connection with the occasion was one which very strikingly illustrates the customs of that period. The ladies came from far and near, mounted on their pillions, and dressed in fabrics suitable for the ride. But they brought with them the more costly robes in which they were to be arrayed

[1] The late venerable Madam James D. Colt, who related the story to the writer in 1863 with an enviable vigor of description, was a child of ten years when she looked on with admiring eyes at the great Peace Party of 1783.

for the party; trusting to the house of some hospitable villager, or the neighboring tavern of Capt. Strong, to furnish room for making their toilet. Now, few in those days totally abstained from intoxicating beverages; and one good lady was so profuse in her patriotic libations, that, before the close of the festivities, her sense of the proper use of things was so confused, that she unconsciously wrapped a huge piece of roast beef, reeking with gravy, in her rich brocade,—with what consequence to its lustre need not be told.

CHAPTER XVIII.

THE BERKSHIRE CONSTITUTIONALISTS.

[1775–1780.]

Political Status of the County. — Its Origin in the Organization of the Provisional Provincial Government. — The Provincial Congress. — Plan devised by the Continental Congress for the Government of Massachusetts. The Western Counties oppose it, but yield. — Reasons for reviving their Opposition. — Feeling against the Provincial Charter accounted for. — Rev. Mr. Allen's Position. — The Judicial System of the Province oppressive. — The Civil Administration excluded from Berkshire. — The Memorial of Pittsfield. — Delay of other Counties in re-organizing their Courts.

WE must now retrace our steps, in order to review the political history of the town, and in some sort that of the county, during the vexed years which transformed the people of Massachusetts from colonial subjects of a distant prince to citizens of an independent, constitutional State, — a review which, owing to the peculiar relations borne for the greater part of this period by the county to the Commonwealth, requires a very exact statement of facts and the nicest discrimination of motives.

From the summer of 1775 until the adoption of the State Constitution in 1780, a party composed of the vast majority of the people of Berkshire, under the acknowledged leadership of the first minister of Pittsfield, ruled the county in open resistance, so far as civil government was concerned, to the authority set up at Boston.

The political status of Berkshire during all that time was entirely anomalous. The nearest parallel which history affords is found in the position of those feudal barons who acknowledged an obligation to support their sovereign in his foreign wars, while maintaining against him their own assumed rights of internal government. In like manner, the people of Berkshire, while for more than five years refusing to admit the civil administration of the State within their limits, granted it military aid by a more prompt and liberal contribution of men than any other county, paid their taxes as readily as the circumstances of a community upon an impoverished and disturbed frontier permitted, and sent their representatives to the General Court, in which, however, they recognized powers much more limited and temporary than that body claimed. Unsurpassed in their devotion to the cause of national independence, they responded with ardor to every call made upon them in that behalf; but, not less earnest in their desire for constitutional liberty at home, they believed it insecure if any State government capable of perpetuating itself should be erected, except upon the basis of a constitution and bill of rights established by the express consent of a majority of the people.

So thorough were their convictions on this point; so essential did they deem these guaranties of civil and personal liberty, — that, in order to obtain them, they resorted to measures justifiable only in the last resort, and "utterly refused the admission of the course of law among them" until their demands were complied with.

This course subjected them to the disapprobation of the greater portion of their brethren at the east, and to the displeasure of the General Court. It will be for the reader to judge whether the course of the county was too hasty or too violent; but candid criticism will concede to the men who adopted it the meed of pure motives, a sincere love of popular liberty, and a riper trust in the people than had then been generally attained.

That we may better comprehend their motives, as well as their measures, let us endeavor to place ourselves where they stood, and attempt to realize as they did the evils which experience had revealed in that form of government whose re-establishment they resisted.

The part taken by the town and the county in the suppression of the king's courts in 1774 has already been related. That example, followed throughout the Colony, was approved by its results. Coupled with the enforced resignation of the councillors created by royal mandamus, it had effectually thwarted the parliamentary scheme for establishing in Massachusetts a government in contravention of her charter.

On the other hand, the refusal of Gov. Gage to exercise his

functions in conformity to the charter, or to perform those duties incumbent upon him in order to give the General Court a legal organization, as effectually prevented the operation of government under the ancient forms.

In this lapse of all authority recognized by either party, Gov. Gage, on his part, resorted to absolute military rule. The natural recourse of the people was to those powers assumed by the representatives elect, under the name of "The Provincial Congress;" and, in the first fervor of the Revolution, the ready assent yielded to Congressional recommendations gave them practically, while that assent continued, the validity of law. It was not, however, even then forgotten by considerate men, that authority of this kind was liable to be interrupted at any moment — it might be the most critical — by one of those sudden and often unaccountable impulses to which masses of men are subject.

In addition to the defects of the improvised government, incident to its unstable foundation, even for the purposes of war, in which alone it exercised its functions, much difficulty was encountered, especially in the commercial and maritime districts, on account of the suspension of the courts of law; for, while less trouble than was to have been expected was found in restraining crime and maintaining public order, — a task which had been taken in hand by the town authorities and Revolutionary committees, — the sacredness of property and the obligations of contracts were seriously impaired in the absence of the courts designed for their protection. The attention of the statesmen in the Provincial Congress was, however, first drawn to the insufficiency of the existing government, by the danger arising from the presence of a large army in the Province, with no civil power to provide for and control it.

With reference to this solely, the Provincial Congress,[1] on the 16th of May, 1775, applied to the Continental Congress for directions. The terms in which the application was made are to be noted for our present purpose: —

"We are happy in having an opportunity of laying our distressed state before the representative body of the Continent, and humbly hope you will

[1] In the remainder of this chapter, to avoid confusion with the Continental Congress, we shall denominate this body the Massachusetts Convention, as it was frequently called in 1775.

favor us with your most explicit advice respecting the taking up and exercising the powers of civil government, which we think absolutely necessary for the salvation of our country: and we shall readily submit *to such a general plan as you may direct for all the Colonies; or make it our great study to establish such a form of government here* as shall not only promote our advantage, but the union and interest of all America."

John Adams was in Congress when this petition was presented; and the subject which it brought to the attention of that body had, before he left home, lain with great weight upon his mind as the most difficult and dangerous business which there was to do.

When it was introduced on the floor of Congress, however, he approached it in no coward spirit, but seized the occasion for one of those bold but logical harangues by which he was paving the way to independence. He entreated the serious attention of all the members, and of all the Continent, to the measures which the times demanded. He declared that there was great wisdom in the adage, "When the sword is drawn, throw away the scabbard;" "but," he added, with startling emphasis, "whether thrown away or not, it is useless now, and will be useless forever."

He earnestly advocated, therefore, the prompt formation of State governments in every Colony; since the case of Massachusetts, although now the most urgent, must soon become that of all. This, he considered, could only be accomplished through conventions of delegates chosen by the people for this express purpose; and he urged Congress at once to recommend to the several Provincial assemblies the immediate calling of such conventions, so that each Colony might set up government under its own authority.

But these were new, strange, and terrible words to most of the members; and rejecting this sound and statesmanlike counsel, whose adoption would have saved infinite trouble in the future, Congress, inharmonious in its views of the relations in which the revolt of the Colonies had placed them to the mother country, postponed the subject to the 3d of June, when it was referred to a committee, whose report was adopted on the 9th. The committee had frequent interviews with the Massachusetts members of Congress, and doubtless received promptings from other citizens of the Province: but, from whatever source it received its inspiration, the result was unfortunate; for, instead of the general plan for all the Colonies which the convention had prayed for, as the alternative of being themselves allowed to form a constitution, Congress recommended to Massachusetts an awkward device, based upon a legal fiction, which found its sole precedent among the proceedings of the Long Parliament. This advice, which was frequently referred to by both parties in the troubles which ensued in Berkshire, was as follows: —

IN CONGRESS, Friday, June 9, 1775.

"*Resolved*, That no obedience being due to the act of parliament for altering the charter of the Colony of Massachusetts Bay, nor to a governor and lieutenant-governor who will not observe the directions of, but endeavor to subvert, the charter, the governor and lieutenant-governor are to be considered as absent, and their offices vacant.

"And as there is no Council there, and the inconveniences arising from the suspension of the powers of government are intolerable, especially at a time when Gen. Gage hath actually levied war, and is carrying on hostilities against his Majesty's peaceful and loyal subjects in that Colony; that in order to conform, as near as may be, to the spirit and substance of the charter, it is recommended to the Provincial Congress to write letters to the inhabitants of the several places which are entitled to representation in Assembly, requesting them to choose such representatives; and that the Assembly, when chosen, should elect councillors; which Assembly and Council should exercise the powers of government until a governor of his Majesty's appointment will consent to govern the Colony according to its charter."

It will be seen, that, so far from being explicit, this advice limited the duration of the temporary government to be set up under it by an event destined never to happen; and showed so little appreciation of the real condition of the country, that it did not contemplate the possibility of independence, which was declared within little more than a year.

Two days after the passage of this resolution, the Massachusetts Convention, not having yet received information of it, adopted a second address to Congress; meeting on Sunday for that purpose, and feeling the difficulties of their situation to be so grievous, that they sent a special messenger to Philadelphia, with an earnest entreaty that he should be despatched on his return as soon as possible with the advice which "the pressing nature of their distresses" rendered it necessary should be "immediate."

There is a marked difference between the tone of this address and that of its predecessor in May; the first being based upon the presence of a single great public danger, the second dwelling chiefly upon the insecurity of internal order, and the disturbance of business relations.

The Convention now forcibly represented, that, in many parts of the Province, alarming symptoms had appeared of a diminishing regard for the sacred rights of property; and that, although fewer enormities and breaches of the peace had occurred than it was natural to anticipate, yet there was extreme difficulty found in maintaining public order.

"The situation of no people or colony," it goes on to assert, "ever rendered it more necessary that the full powers of civil government should be exercised, than does the present state and situation of the Colony of Massachusetts Bay." Bitter complaint is made, that, "chiefly from the want of a settled civil polity, every undertaking necessary for the preservation of life, and still more of property, is subject to innumerable delays, embarrassments, disappointments, and obstructions; while whatever is accomplished in this direction is effected in the most expensive manner: so that, in times which require the most rigid economy, it is impossible to exercise it."

This piteous appeal was perhaps colored by the hypochondria with which Major Hawley, the chairman of the committee reporting it, was afflicted, and which soon after increased to such a degree as to compel the retirement of that ablest of the patriotic leaders from the public councils. The melancholy of so influential a member could hardly have failed to infect the whole convention. Nevertheless, something very like the condition of affairs depicted did exist.

Little, therefore, as the scheme of government proposed by Congress comported with the desire of Massachusetts as expressed in her first application, the temper of the Convention, when the response arrived, was in its favor.

Accordingly, on the 19th of June, circular letters were addressed to the several towns, requesting them to elect representatives to a Great and General Court, or assembly, to be held at Watertown on the 19th of July. With regard to the two measures, — the adoption of a new form of government, as proposed by the convention in May, and the travesty of the charter recommended by Congress in June, — the people of the eastern and western counties, says Sam Adams, who himself favored the charter, appeared to differ;[1]

[1] Frothingham's Warren, p. 377.

meaning, of course, that the predominant sentiment of those sections differed, for there was a considerable majority in each section which agreed upon this point with the minority in the other. There was much reluctance, almost everywhere, to accept the Congressional scheme; but the people of Berkshire and Hampshire had become reconciled in a far less degree than their eastern fellow-citizens to the losses which Massachusetts liberties sustained in the passage from a colonial to a provincial charter. That William of "glorious memory" had taken advantage of the wrong done by his predecessor of infamous story to rob the most devoted of Whig Colonies of her ancient privileges, was bitterly remembered and brooded over by men like the Rev. Mr. Allen, until it lacked little to render them eager to forswear all kings forever. They fretted under the evils which they justly ascribed to the innovations of the Provincial charter; hated cordially the aristocratic system which had sprung up under it; and, while they clung to what privileges it left them, they considered these always endangered until the choice of their own governor should be restored to the people, and a way thus prepared for further reforms. From the first uprising against the Regulating Acts, the most thoughtful of the Berkshire patriots looked to the restoration of the old and not of the new charter, as the ultimatum to be demanded of Great Britain; and that feeling strengthened and accommodated itself to the changing shapes of political affairs as the struggle went on, and day by day the deformities of King William's charter were demonstrated and denounced.

But, in June, Mr. Adams, writing from Philadelphia, represented to Dr. Warren that there was jealousy in the minds of some members of Congress, that Massachusetts aimed at total independency, not only of the mother country, but of the other Colonies also; and that, as her people were hardy and brave, they would in time overrun them all. These representatives privately assured Mr. Adams, that "their constituents would openly support Massachusetts, if her people were driven by necessity to defend their lives or liberties; but doubted whether they would ever be persuaded to think it necessary for them to set up another form of government." Mr. Adams, therefore, advised the adoption of the scheme devised in Congress, in order to avoid as much as possible the appearance of innovation, and thus preserve the unity among the Colonies which was so essential.[1]

[1] Frothingham's Warren, p. 378.

The people of Western Massachusetts were neither self-willed nor opinionated; and this reasoning, which commended itself to their good sense, prevailed while the condition of affairs which gave it cogency continued. If, as is probable, acceptance of the proposed plan was urged with the weight of Mr. Adams's personal influence, its effect was greatly increased; for, of all the Boston patriots, Sam Adams, in spite of differing opinions on the present point, was the leader most nearly after the heart of the mountain-men.

There was little, therefore, if any, opposition to the choice of representatives to the General Court, in response to the circular letter of June. Pittsfield elected two, — Capts. Charles Goodrich and Israel Dickinson, — one of whom only was to serve at a time.

The conditions which induced this submission were but of brief duration. During the summer of 1775, the minority, larger, — and growing with more rapidity than it dared believe, — longing for independence, advanced towards it by gradual and concealed approaches.

The theory of the day was, that an accommodation with Great Britain would be obtained at so early a date, that it was worth no man's while to concern himself greatly about the abstract principles of the government which should prevail in the interim. Even those who knew this theory false were often forced to accept it as the base from which, by the aid of favoring circumstances, to raise themselves to a higher plane.

But something very different from what appeared upon the surface was lurking beneath; and, as events crowded upon each other, opinions and sentiments engendered in the apt soil of New England ripened fast under the fervid sun of Revolution.

Their influence was not unfelt in Congress; so that when, early in November, advice was to be given to New Hampshire and South Carolina with regard to assuming the powers of civil government, it was couched in the following terms, — the language used to the two Colonies being of the same import: —

"*Resolved*, That it be recommended to the Provincial Congress of New Hampshire to call a full and free representation of the people, and that the representatives establish such a form of government as, in their judgment, will best produce the happiness of the people, and most effectually secure peace and good order in the Province during the continuance of the present dispute between Great Britain and the Colonies."

This was a great advance since June. John Adams, who looked upon it as the progress of the index upon the broad dial of national affairs, congratulated himself upon a triumph; although of the three phrases, "Colonies," "Province," and "Mother Country," which "by this time he had come mortally to hate," he had succeeded in eliminating only the last from the report.

In Massachusetts, the plan recommended to her sister Colonies, so nearly identical with that which she had asked for herself, but so widely variant from that which she had received, did not fail to conspire, with defects brought to light in the practical working of the government set up there, to provoke feeling against the new order of things; while, imbittering and giving direction to the opposition, memories of the old charter history, which the turmoil of recent events had obscured, were revived.

Among the reasons which suggested the peculiar Congressional device recommended to Massachusetts was the fact that she was one of the only three Colonies which possessed royal charters, conferring and limiting their powers of self-government, and prescribing the mode of their exercise; while the privileges of the other Provinces, obtained by prescription, or at best based upon what they claimed to be the indefeasible rights of Englishmen, were, in theory at least, more obscure and of less authority.

The constitutions of these latter had, however, taken form under successive legislatures, and been confirmed in the habits of thought of their peoples, until practically Massachusetts differed less from Virginia than she did from Connecticut.

The charters which Massachusetts, Connecticut, and Rhode Island received from Charles the First, under the broad seal of England, invested all alike, as to their internal affairs, with almost all the rights of independent States. These rights had been retained intact by Rhode Island and Connecticut; so that, when the Revolution came, it found their governments harmonious in all their departments, and prepared to throw off what little remained of foreign authority, without producing that confusion which ensued in Massachusetts.

The charter of the latter Colony, annulled in the reign of the second Charles by the decree of a servile tribunal, had, after an interval of seven years, been replaced in 1692 by a substitute obtained from William and Mary, not under the great but the privy seal. Earnest entreaty made to a Whig prince for the restitution of ancient privileges violently wrested from the Colony for her adherence to Whig principles availed little; and the new instrument fell so far short of the old, that the style of Massachusetts was, with just significance, changed from that of a colony to that of a province. Most essential of the losses sustained by the people in these transactions was the transfer from them to the king of the appointment of governor, lieutenant-governor, and secretary; of whom the first was invested with great powers, including the right to prorogue or dissolve the General Court, and to interpose a negative, not only to their ordinary legislative acts, but to the choice by the representatives of councillors, and even of their own speaker. All officers of the militia and the judiciary were also to be appointed by him with the advice and consent of the Council.

Thus the king, through his deputy, became the chief fountain of official honors and emoluments; and the places in his gift were sedulously used to attach the more substantial citizens to the party of the government.

When the decisive test came, the success of these seductive influences, although not inconsiderable, proved to be far short of what the royalist leaders had persuaded themselves to expect. An incidental result had, however, grown out of their system of politics which contributed largely to incite "the Berkshire troubles." In place of the old colonial "magistracy," the foundations had been very broadly laid for a new provincial aristocracy which was already burdensome to the people. Whether it was intrinsically more so than its Puritan predecessor, may be safely doubted; but, as a new evil, — and one incident to the subversion of their cherished charter, — it was hated as the grim old "magistracy" never had been. To most of the gentry of this class, from his honor the lieutenant-governor down to the village justice not of the quorum, the Revolutionary disturbances were extremely unwelcome and vexatious: the choice between king and country was hard to make, especially so long as the patriots professed to contend only for the preservation of the defective charter of William; a contest in which, however victory might nominally declare itself, the fruits of victory were sure to remain in the hands of the king's governor, and be the spoil of the king's supporters.

To ambitious country gentlemen of wealth and standing,

the dignities in the royal governor's keeping were tempting morsels in comparison with the poor seat in the trammelled legislature, or at the town council-board, which was the best the people had to offer.

Still, when the hour came in which all men were compelled to take sides, the greater portion of the tempted class, resisting the allurements which had been spread for them, adhered more or less promptly, and with differing degrees of zeal, to the cause of their country; and their familiarity with public business, as well as other reasons, led to the election of many of their number to the Provincial Congresses and to the General Court of 1775.

The selection of men of this class was undoubtedly wise: but it was not strange, that, upon the first occasion, suspicion should arise, among their less favored compatriots, of a design on their part to revive and perpetuate, under the new form of government, a system to which they owed so much under the old; nor was it unnatural, that whatever, short of popular election, was made the fountain of office should be the object of bitter jealousy.

The rule established under the advice of Congress owed its first opposition to the belief, that, in making selections for office, the General Court grossly favored its members and their friends, to the neglect of men at least equally meritorious. A Berkshire Convention, reciting the history of the county troubles, declared that it was the practice for the members to be called upon by counties "to make nominations in the civil and military line, who were then chosen by the House, and commissioned by the Council, in which effectual care was taken that those present should be in the nomination;" [1] "which procedure," continues the address, "roused our attention, that such persons should nominate and vote for themselves, or be elected in a form that the charter knew nothing of."

To the Berkshire fathers this greediness of office seemed the result of a deliberate design to foist one of the worst features of the old government upon the new; or, at the best, to be the inevitable fruit of a political system fatally defective, and which, it now began to be feared, there was no intention to limit in duration.

[1] Of the two representatives from Pittsfield, Capt. Goodrich secured the place of a justice of the sessions; Capt. Israel Dickinson was made high sheriff of the county. Every member of the House from Berkshire obtained civil office.

But, although opposition to the new rule was first aroused by a single grievance, it soon assumed a broader and more radical character; rising first to insist that a constitution and bill of rights were indispensable prerequisites to any government, and then to advise, as with authority, what principles should be incorporated in the fundamental law. As the anticipations of independence strengthened, what ideas should lie at the foundations of the new States — when the Colonies should assume that rank — became the subject of earnest and often of profound consideration, not only in legislative halls, but in country villages; and not less so were the constitutional provisions by which vitality could best be given to those ideas. We may be sure that rarely anywhere were these subjects earlier or more intelligently discussed than in the little meeting-house under the Pittsfield elm.

Certain great maxims, of undisputed authority, had been transmitted by the fathers of English freedom; a few safeguards of personal liberty had acquired traditional sanctity; the idea of a republic was dear to all hearts, even in colonies planted by cavaliers; but the statesmen of America could look nowhere for an example of republican government exactly adapted to their need.

Studies for the work before them were abundant: in the history of the ancient republics, and those of the middle ages; in the example of England under king and Commonwealth; and, best of all, in their own colonial experience. But model there was none. Years of experiment and devoted study, by the ablest and purest statesmen the world ever saw, elapsed before, from the lessons of history and the teachings of experience, an approach to perfection was obtained in the Federal Constitution, — years even before that scarcely less noble work, the Constitution of Massachusetts, was wrought out, chiefly from the broad learning of John Adams.

In the mean time, the country was flooded with tracts upon the structure of government.[1] The works of political essayists be-

[1] Of these the most popular was the essay of Thomas Paine, issued in 1775, in which that able although afterwards infamous author presented in a concise form, and clear, terse, and vigorous language, the arguments in favor of independence which had been used in the secret sessions of Congress and the private consultations of the Continental leaders. The work was admirably fitted to reach and influence the public mind, and its effect was widely felt. In the same tract had been included, with the advocacy of independence, certain loose but plausible theories of government, inculcated in the same winning style.

came popular reading; and some of them, — the disquisitions of James Burgh and Mrs. McCauley in particular, — of a higher tone than that of Paine, had many readers; while a host of native writers, sometimes of great ability, communicated their views through the periodical press.

Thus, while one class of minds was patiently and laboriously seeking material for the new structure in the treasured experience of the past, another was seizing eagerly upon whatever in the more recent and popular essayists seemed sustained by facts and adapted to the desired end. It was the age of free thinking in political creeds, and of a chaos out of which something very nearly perfect at last crystallized. The agitation and new thought developed by the writers of the day were not less indispensable to the grand result than were the researches of more scholarly statesmen. Between the two classes indicated, Rev. Mr. Allen occupied an intermediate position; although his natural impulsiveness, as well as other influences, led him generally to adopt the most advanced theory of human rights. A republican by birth and education, he was an ardent one by temperament. Inheriting a love for the political as well as the religious doctrines of the Puritans, he had been confirmed in them by the study of the best writers of that school, and, in the history of his theological denomination, had found the principles of his party so intimately interwoven with the articles of his creed, that they seemed almost equally a part of his religion. A disposition of mind naturally earnest had thus been trained in the direction of indignant protest against political wrong and oppression; and the desire for the purest possible form of government, which characterized the general mind of that era, became with him a passion.

The abrogation of the ancient charter by "that popish tyrant, Charles II.," had long been a subject of bitter and almost morbid contemplation with him; and while he admitted the instrument obtained from "King William of glorious memory" to be "of great value for the preservation of tolerable order," it was only "till we had grown to our present strength to seek that by force of arms which was then unjustly denied us."

When the few chartered privileges which the Colony retained were attacked by Parliament, we found him among the first to counsel resistance; and now, when it was proposed to restore the civil government — suspended in 1774 — upon the basis of "the defective and discordant charter" of King William, he became, to use the phrase employed both by himself and his enemies, "restless in his endeavors" to prevent it.

His mind thus busy with the political events of the day, Mr. Allen read diligently the current writers who treated upon them, and adopted the opinions of that school which enunciated the doctrines afterwards, in a more perfect form, championed by Thomas Jefferson. In these he conceived that he found the legitimate democratic development of republican principles.

Such were the characteristics and views which made the Pittsfield minister the founder and leader of that party in Berkshire which, to the end, successfully resisted the restoration in that county of civil government under the strange device which the Continental Congress had evolved from the Provincial charter.

The fundamental dogma of this party was, that political power can only rightfully be derived from the express consent of the people; that the charter government — itself but a mitigated usurpation — having been abrogated, the Province relapsed into a state of nature, from which it could rightly emerge only through the establishment of a constitution and bill of rights by the free vote of a majority of the people; that, antecedent to this, the only authority which ought to be submitted to should be, from its purely advisory character, incapable of making itself permanent.

Against those who favored the postponement of a new constitution until the return of peace, they urged that such a government as was proposed, *ad interim*, "if once allowed to take place, would be found very difficult to shake off ever after." Against the argument that the Continental Congress had proposed the obnoxious system, they maintained that Congress could not have intended to deprive Massachusetts of the right of framing a constitution for herself; and that, if it had such a design, it was entitled to no respect. Indeed, admitting that Congress in May intended to restrain the Colony from taking a step which too plainly betrayed the purpose of ultimate independence, that restraint was withdrawn in November; and the advice from which it was implied became every day more inapplicable to the altered circumstances of the Province.

In no view of the case could the Berkshire constitutionalists regard the new order of things as rightful. But a total renunciation of all connection with the powers instituted at Boston would have only been fraught with evil to both parties, and to the good cause which both had at heart. The device hit upon in this dilemma was to refuse obedience to a portion of the acts of the General Court, thus conceding to it only that advisory authority which had been accorded to the Provincial Congress.

It might reasonably have been argued, indeed, that neither the General nor Provincial Congress, having other than advisory authority, could invest another assembly with higher legislative powers than those with which they were themselves clothed; and that the people, in choosing representatives on their advice, did not *ipso facto* adopt that advice as the Constitution of the Province, much less as the fundamental law of the Commonwealth when it became an independent State. It was as competent, surely, for the Berkshire committees to assume that the Congresses could not have intended to exercise powers which had not been delegated to them, as for those assemblies to assume from the recusant position of Gage a vacancy in the gubernatorial office.

In selecting that department of government whose obstruction would sufficiently arrest attention at Boston, while it would least embarrass the State in its operations against the enemy, and the people in their efforts to obtain a constitution, the judiciary and civil magistracy suggested itself. Policy and feeling alike prompted a zealous response to every demand made by the Military Board; and the towns could not well refuse to send representatives to the General Court, which, however defective in its constitution, they were compelled to acknowledge as the only power which could carry on the war, or take the initiative in establishing government upon a rightful basis. The judiciary and the magistracy seemed thus the only department of the State which could at all be dispensed with; as it was also that whose place, for its most urgent purposes, could most readily be supplied by the municipal organizations. In fact, on the 26th of December, 1775, a Pittsfield town-meeting represented to the General Court, that, for the preceding eighteen months, — counting from the May term at Great Barrington in 1774, which was the last court actually held, — "The people of the county, under the lenient and efficient rule of their several committees, and in the most vigorous and unintermitted exertions in the country's cause, had lived together in the greatest love, peace, safety, liberty, happiness, and good order, except the disorders and dissensions occasioned by the Tories."

The suppression of the courts had thus attained its object in one instance, not only with no intolerable evils, but, as was claimed, with positive advantage to the happiness of the people. The town took care to disclaim any expectation that such a paradoxical paradise could long continue, and we may well question the perfect fairness of the picture; but there is no reason to doubt that a majority of the people felt themselves rather better off without such a judicial system as had existed under the Provincial rule than they would be with it.

Precedent sustained a resort to measures which had been so well tested and approved; and they were the more readily adopted as the chief grievance of which the people complained, under the old administration of the charter, had been the excessive cost of executing the laws; heavy fee-tables being established, as was alleged, in order to enrich swarms of magistrates and lawyers.

In truth, a more cumbrous judicial system could hardly have been devised than was inflicted upon this poor and scantily-peopled county, in common with the other shires of the Province; and resistance to its re-imposition, as a burden too grievous to be borne, had been resolved before the abstract principles which justified that resistance had been much considered by the masses.

There were held annually four terms each of the General Sessions of the Peace and of the Inferior Court of Common Pleas. The Sessions had jurisdiction in all matters pertaining to the conservation of the peace, and in all criminal cases where the punishment did not extend to deprivation of life or limb or to banishment; and also exercised the powers now held by the board of county commissioners.

The Court of Common Pleas had cognizance of all civil causes triable at the common law, when the matters in dispute exceeded the value of forty shillings.

From both the Common Pleas and the Sessions an appeal lay to the Superior Court of Judicature. This latter court had original jurisdiction in all cases which extended to deprivation of life or limb or to banishment; which removed from the county courts a large class of cases now tried by them. Each county had its own Common Pleas bench, which consisted in Berkshire of a chief Justice and three associates. And these, with the other justices of the peace in the county, numbering when the Revolution commenced about a dozen, formed the Court of General Sessions. Each court had its clerk and other officials. This clumsy organization performed the duties, which, in the present vastly more populous and wealthy county, devolve upon the commissioners and a single judge of the Superior Court.

Cases where a less sum than forty shillings was involved, and which did not affect the title of real estate, were cognizable by a single justice, as also were trivial misdemeanors. In civil cases, an appeal lay to the Common Pleas; in criminal, to the General Sessions: and the power of the magistrate in inflicting punishment was limited to confinement in the cage or the stocks for three hours, imprisonment for twenty-four, whipping not to exceed ten stripes, or a fine of twenty shillings, for which sum either of the other punishments might be commuted, at the option of the offender. The salaries of the judges individually were not large, but in the aggregate they were considerable; and the pay of the justices of the peace and of the Sessions, depending upon fees, was a more odious burden still. Another peculiarity, not impertinent to this discussion, may be enumerated: the judges were rarely men educated to the law. Before the Revolution, only four lawyers sat even upon the supreme bench of Massachusetts. The judgeships were held as rewards for political favorites in all walks of life.

A judicial system constituted like this was of necessity costly, and the fees proportionately large. It was believed to be intentionally thus framed, in order that as many as possible of the favored class might fatten upon the spoils of the poor and the unfortunate. The privilege of confessing judgment to avoid suit before a single magistrate, which had been earnestly sought, was thought to be denied for the same reason; and the presence of two magistrates and the clerk of a court of record was required for this very simple act. Whatever injustice there may have been in these jealousies, we may be sure that the judicial system of the Province was looked upon much more complacently by the lawyers and the mob of gentlemen who filled the bench than by the heavily-taxed parties to suits.

All this, together with the injudicious harshness almost universally exercised towards poor debtors, and in the punishment of the trivial misdemeanors of the lower classes, contributed to diminish, in no small degree, that filial reverence which should surround the tribunals of justice. It will serve also to explain what Mr. Allen meant in saying that "our fellow-citizens in this county have been ruled with a rod of iron."

Evils like these in a system of law could not fail to deprave even the vicious and impoverish the poor. To thoughtful observers, and especially to those ministers of the gospel who felt themselves commissioned to watch over the lowly and the miserable, these results were painfully apparent; and it was the hope of men with no desire, by shielding the wrong-doer, to impair the security of person or property, that the not intolerable consequences of a total suspension of the courts might be endured until, under a more equitable constitution, a system better adapted to attain the ends of justice should be organized.

But, while divers reasons thus directed the minds of the people of Berkshire to a single branch of government as that which ought to be suppressed, it must be remembered that the right to suppress any was based upon the absence of what was held essential to all legitimate rule, — establishment by an unmistakable expression of the popular consent. Nor must it be forgotten, that individual abuses were not attacked, primarily, to secure their own removal, but for the purpose of overthrowing a faulty whole, of which they were the most vulnerable parts. The town-meetings and county-conventions, while their action was at first directed to the redress of special grievances by specific means, at the very outset indicated the great principle from which their proceedings took rise, and continued to enunciate it with ever fuller emphasis and clearer utterance. In their minds, the ideas of national independence and of constitutional liberty advanced with equal step.

Among the Berkshire patriots, the belief became very early fixed that the British dominion over the Colony would never be restored; and it alarmed them that no disposition was shown by the General Court to ascertain the will of its constituents with regard to a new constitution. They deemed it evidence of a design to usurp power, that after the circumstances which might have been held by some to justify the advice given by Congress had ceased to exist, and even after that advice had been practically revoked, a determination was manifest at Boston to still build upon this undermined foundation, and with the most rotten material of the Provincial ruins.

Against this wrong, which appeared a very gross one from the Berkshire stand-point of 1775, Mr. Allen, in the fall of that year, took the field with even more than his accustomed ardor, resolved to agitate for a change until it should be effected; and, from that time forward, he was "restless in his endeavors" to that end, until, in 1780, Massachusetts obtained a Bill of Rights the most nearly perfect which had ever been constructed, and a Constitution which, although some of its provisions conflicted with his ultra-democratic notions, as a whole commanded his approbation, and which, having the sanction of that authority to which he always bowed, — the will of the people freely expressed, — he held to be entitled to the full allegiance of every good citizen.

During the four years of that contest, the Pittsfield minister was the apostle in Berkshire of constitutional government and democratic ideas; visiting every town, and urging his views everywhere by speeches, sermons, resolutions, conversations, and letters. His success was remarkable. A large majority of the people acceded to his doctrines. The towns and county conventions adopted resolutions, addresses, and memorials in accordance with them, and often drafted by him; while most of the committees of inspection were remodelled in order to secure vigor in prosecuting the measures adopted by his advice.

It is a conspicuous proof of the power of Mr. Allen's earnestness, eloquence, and personal consideration, that a single address by him was sometimes sufficient to revolutionize the entire sentiment of a town against the wishes of its own most prominent citizens, and that his teachings impressed upon the people of Berkshire political characteristics which remain strongly marked to this day; for it was in this fiery campaign, rather than in his subsequent political career, that he had the opportunity to inculcate those enduring principles whose deep root among these hills, and wide-spread influence wherever the sons of Berkshire have found a home, are ascribed to him by those most familiar with the intellectual history of the county. In argument, he was logical, and not unskilled in the subtler arts of oratory. In appeal, he was vehement and earnest; impassioned often to a degree that carried him to extremes in his expressions concerning opponents, and to something like exaggeration in his denunciation of measures. Righteous indignation was not greatly tempered by any thing in the composition of his mind. Exaggerated denunciation was, however, a fault of the day; and it is to Mr. Allen's credit, that in his papers we find none of that coarseness of epithet, or vulgarity of invective, which disgraced the pages of many of his contemporaries. His blade, if trenchant, was at least polished.

The first town action in the agitation for a constitution, of which we find a record, although some must have taken place earlier, was on the 26th of December, 1775, when the following memorial was adopted:[1] —

The Petition, Remonstrance, and Address of the Town of Pittsfield to the Honorable Board of Councillors and House of Representatives of the Province of Massachusetts Bay, in General Assembly, now sitting at Watertown.

MAY IT PLEASE YOUR HONORS, —

The inhabitants of the town of Pittsfield unalterably attached to the liberties of their country and in the fullest approbation of Congressional measures, with all humility, deference, and candor, beg leave to manifest the painful anxieties and distresses of our minds in this definitive crisis, not only in behalf of ourselves, but of this great and powerful Province, and declare our abhorrence of that constitution now adopting in this Province. Nothing but an invincible love of civil and religious liberty for ourselves and future posterity has induced us to add to your accumulated burdens at this great period.

Our forefathers left the delightful abodes of their native country, and passed a raging sea, that in these solitary climes they might enjoy civil and religious liberty, and never more feel the hand of tyranny and persecution; but that despotic, persecuting power which they fled reached them on these far-distant shores, the weight of which has been felt from their first emigration to the present day. After the loss of the charter of this Province in the reign of Charles the Second, a popish tyrant, a new one was obtained, after the Revolution, of King William of glorious memory, which was lame and essentially defective, and yet was of great value for the support of tolerable order till we had grown up to our present strength to seek that by force of arms which was then unjustly denied us.

The nomination and appointment of our governors by the king has been the source of all the evils and calamities that have befallen this Province and the united Colonies. By this means, a secret poison has been spread throughout all our towns, and great multitudes have been secured for the corrupt designs of an abandoned administration. Many of these men, who had drank of this baneful poison, could not be confided in to aid and assist their country in the present contest; which was one reason for the necessity of a suppression of government.

At this door all manner of disorders have been introduced into our constitution, till it has become an instrument of oppression and deep corruption, and would probably, had it been continued, have brought upon us an eternal destruction.

The want of that one privilege of confessing judgment in cases of debt

[1] This memorial, in the handwriting of Mr. Allen, is preserved in the State archives.

has overwhelmed great multitudes in destruction, and afforded encouragement to our mercenary lawyers to riot upon the spoils of the people.

We have been ruled in this county for many years past with a rod of iron.

The tyranny, despotism, and oppression of our fellow-subjects in this county have been beyond belief. Since the suppression of government, we have lived in peace, love, safety, liberty, and happiness, except the disorders and dissensions occasioned by the Tories. We find ourselves in danger of returning to our former state, and of undergoing a yoke of oppression which we are no longer able to bear.

We have calmly viewed the nature of our ancient mode of government, its various sluices of corruption, the danger and effects of nominating to office by those in power, and must pronounce it the most defective, discordant, and ruinous system of government of any that has come under our observation. We can discern no present necessity of adopting that mode of government so generally reprobated by the good people of this Province, or which will inevitably be so as soon as the great rational majority of the people have had time for proper reflection.

The adopting this mode of government to the length we have gone has, in our view, been hasty and precipitate. It was surprising to this town, and directly contrary to the instructions given to their representative. By this means, a considerable number of incurable enemies to a better constitution have been made; and, if ever adopted by the people, we shall never, perhaps, be able to rid ourselves of it again.

We have seen nothing done by the Continental Congress which leads us to conclude that they would limit us to this mode of government. We do not know of their having given us any advice that must necessarily be construed in opposition to what they gave the governments of New Hampshire and South Carolina, who, if they think it necessary, are to choose such a form of government as they in their judgment shall think will best promote the happiness of the people, and preserve peace and good order, during the present dispute with Great Britain.

Certainly the Continental Congress could have no intention of forcing upon us a constitution so detested by the people, and so abhorrent to common sense, and thus to reward us for our unparalleled sufferings. We have been led to hope for new privileges, which we still hope to obtain, or remain, so far as we have done for some time past, in a state of nature.

We have with decency and moderation attended to the various arguments of those gentlemen lately created our rulers; particularly we have heard it urged as the advice of the venerable Continental Congress. We have sufficiently attended to that and the various other arguments in favor of re-assuming our ancient constitution, and are of opinion there is no such advice, the qualifying expressions leaving ample room to new-model our constitution; but, if there is, we are of opinion that unlimited passive obedience and non-resistance to any human power whatever is what we are now contending with Great Britain, and to transfer that power to any other body of men is equally dangerous to our security and happiness.

We choose to be known to future posterity as being of the number of those who have timely protested against the re-assumption of this discordant constitution, and shall be restless in our endeavor that we may obtain the privilege of electing our civil and military officers. We assure your Honors that some of those who have been appointed to rule us are greatly obnoxious to people in general, especially those who have protested against the just proceedings of a Congress lately held in Stockbridge. We beg leave further to assure your Honors that a court has been held in this town in a clandestine manner, and great dishonor hereby done to the dignity of magistracy.

We therefore pray your Honors to issue out your orders to the good people of this Province, that their votes may be collected in the election of a governor and lieutenant-governor to act in concert with the Honorable Board and House of Representatives; after which we pray that every town may retain the privilege of electing their justices of the peace, and every county their judges, as well as the soldiers of every company of militia their officers. If the right of nominating to office is not vested in the people, we are indifferent who assumes it, — whether any particular persons on this or the other side of the water.

When such a constitution is formed, you'll find us the most meek and inoffensive subjects of any in this Province; although we would hope, in such a case, that the wisdom of our rulers would not admit of collecting private debts for the present, as we imagine that measure would be of great detriment to our common cause, as it would put much money into the hands of our enemies, and create divisions among ourselves.

But, if this just and reasonable request is denied us, we pray that, as we have lived in great love, peace, and good order in this county for more than sixteen months past, in the most vigorous unintermitted exertions in our country's cause, that you would dispense with a longer suspension of this ancient mode of government among us that we so much detest and abhor. The government of our respective committees is lenient and efficacious; but if it is necessary, for carrying into more effectual exertion the means of common safety, that some mode of government should be adopted, we pray that it may be *de novo*, agreeable to that fore-mentioned advice of the Continental Congress, and no more of our ancient form be retained than what is just and reasonable. We hope, in the establishment of such new constitution, that regard will be had for such a broad basis of civil and religious liberty, as no length of time will corrupt as long as the sun and moon shall endure.

And as in duty bound will we pray.

Per order of the town, ISRAEL DICKINSON, *Town Clerk.*

N. B. — Upon the foregoing premises, and on account of obnoxious persons being appointed to rule us, the court of this county of Quarter Sessions is ordered to desist from any future sessions.

Our resolves may be seen at Mr. Thomas's, which we entered into at the same time this petition was accepted by the town.

No record of the Congress at Stockbridge remains, and the Pittsfield resolutions are also lost: so that it is not known what measures they directed in order to exclude the new civil administration from the county; but their spirit may be inferred from the quaintly audacious postscript to the Pittsfield memorial, and from the subsequent action of the people. It was certainly recommended by one, and resolved by the other, effectually to resist the holding of the county courts, and the exercise of the magistracy by those who had lately received commissions signed by "a majority of the council," and running in the name of the king against whose authority their soldiers were fighting.

The justices of the Sessions, before the plans of the people were ripe, had made haste to hold a secret meeting, at which they had transacted business, so far at least as to license certain innholders, who paid six shillings each to the pockets of the justices for papers which proved worse than useless; for the towns, which had assumed the powers of this court, not only refused to recognize the validity of its licenses, but in many cases would not be persuaded to replace them with their own, — rigidly excluding from the honorable fraternity of Bonifaces the favorers of the new government as well as the friends of the king.

The next court appointed to be held was the term of the quarter sessions at Pittsfield on the last Tuesday of February, 1776; and, until the near approach of that day, it seems that public sentiment was not, in all the towns, ripe for obstructing the sitting; for Col. Ashley and others, in a petition to the next April session of the Legislature, asserted that the people of Richmond, having, only a short time previous, voted to sustain the government, Mr. Allen, on Sunday evening, Feb. 18, delivered them an address, "which, together with his private exhortations, had the desired effect, and the people were influenced to the degree the preacher designed."

It may perhaps be well to note, that, although an odor of sanctity, derived from its proximity to the "sabbath," pertained to Sunday evening with the New-England fathers, it was not "holy time" in the sense which the evening of Saturday was; but, if it had been otherwise, it is by no means certain that Mr. Allen would have considered it profanation to devote it to the defence of a cause which he held to be holy.

On the day previous to that fixed for the court, the several committees of inspection, &c., met at Pittsfield, summoned, as Col. Ashley charged, by Mr. Allen and his associates, to hinder the session from taking place. "Mr. Allen," continues Ashley, "although not a member of the convention, appeared as the chief agitator and spokesman, and, having read a pamphlet entitled 'Common Sense,' as his text, made great reflections upon the General Court as his doctrine and improvement, after which he produced a large number of resolves, by himself previously compiled, which were put and voted by a majority of those present."

Paine's "Common Sense" had been issued from the press in Philadelphia three months previous to this convention; and it had evidently powerfully impressed Mr. Allen, confirming and advancing his opinions of republican polity.

Adapted as it was, by the clearness and vigor of its style, to ready popular comprehension, it was a shrewd device in those days, when the circulation even of political tracts was limited, to read and enlarge upon it in an assembly of leading politicians from all parts of the county. The old meeting-house under the elm that day sent out one of those influences of which it was prolific, and which are felt to this day in every nook and corner of Berkshire. It is likely enough, too, that, in addition to laying down and applying general principles, Mr. Allen may have said severe things of the Great and General Court, being more than ever convinced, that, having assumed power without sufficient warrant, it intended to perpetuate it.

The influence of these harangues seems to have been as powerful with the people as with the convention; for Col. Ashley goes on to inform us that they "were so much influenced that no court was suffered to sit, and all commissions of civil officers upon which hands could be laid were taken away." The gentlemen of the Sessions went home unincumbered by the spoils of office, and holding that the county was reduced to a state of anarchy and confusion. The convention called it "a state of nature." It was, in fact, the somewhat arbitrary rule of town-meetings and revolutionary committees; something very different, to be sure, from the beneficent operation of established laws, but far removed also from anarchy, and that confusion which a relapse to unrestrained nature would entail.

The story of the Courts of Common Pleas throughout the Commonwealth does not show so much haste in re-establishing the tribunals specially designed for the protection of property as, according to the Provincial Congress, the direful circumstances of the Province demanded. In all the eleven counties of the State, except Worcester, impediments of one kind or another seem to have prevented the machinery of those courts from going into immediate operation; although in all, except Berkshire and Hampshire, commissions to the new judges were issued in October, 1775.

In Worcester, the court sat promptly on the 5th of the ensuing December; in Suffolk, in April; and in Middlesex, in May, 1776. In Plymouth, there is no record of any terms held by the judges first appointed; and those appointed April 10, 1777, did not take their seats until December of that year. Dukes was without a Court of Common Pleas until March, 1777; and Nantucket until 1783. The records of Essex, Barnstable, and Bristol are imperfect, but indicate more or less delay.

New judges for Hampshire were commissioned about the first of January, 1778, and probably took their seats in the course of the same year. No new commissions were issued for Berkshire until Feb. 26, 1779, when Col. John Ashley of Sheffield, John Bacon of Stockbridge, Col. William Whiting of Great Barrington, and Col. John Brown of Pittsfield, were appointed, but never attempted to hold courts.[1] The impediments to the courts in Hampshire were identical with those existing in Berkshire: although in the former county they yielded to the promise of a constitution; in the latter, only to its actual establishment. How far delay in the other counties, or in any of them, indicated a public sentiment similar to that which prevailed in Western Massachusetts, we have not at hand the means of ascertaining; but it would have been very strange if in no other part of the State the opponents of the Congressional scheme had been ready to adopt the measures of those in the west, with whom they sympathized in feeling.

In Berkshire, the ordinary channels of justice, obstructed, as we have seen, when the king's judges were crowded from their seats at Great Barrington in 1774, were not re-opened until the re-organization of the judiciary under the constitution of 1780; so that for six years no courts were held in the county. During the inter-

[1] Washburn's History of the Judiciary of Massachusetts.

regnum, the local authorities preserved public order, and restrained crimes against person and property, far from perfectly, it is true, but less imperfectly than was to have been expected; and the want of the civil courts was not so severely felt in business relations as it would have been in communities with larger and more complicated mercantile interests.

CHAPTER XIX.

THE BERKSHIRE CONSTITUTIONALISTS (CONTINUED).

[1775-1780.]

Pittsfield challenges legislative Attention to its Recusance. — Second Memorial. — Congress practically revokes its Advice. — Berkshire demands a Constitution, which the General Court neglects to provide. — Projected Constitution of 1777. — Pittsfield accepts it in Part, but the State rejects. — The Non-constitutionalists memorialize. — Their Statement. — The Legislature appeals to the People of Berkshire. — Consequent Action. — Vote of the Towns still excluding the Courts. — The County petitions for a Constitutional Convention. — Strong Language of the Petition. — The Legislature passes an act of Pardon and Oblivion. — Pittsfield denounces it as uncalled for and libellous. — The Legislature informs Berkshire of Measures towards complying with its Demands. — The County nevertheless excludes the Courts until the Constitution shall be actually adopted. — Final Memorial to the Legislature. — Instructions of Pittsfield to its Delegate in the Constitutional Convention. — Newspaper Libels. — Conclusion.

WHATEVER may have rendered tolerable the lack of civil government in Berkshire, the General Court could not have passed over in silence the flagrant rebellion existing there against its own authority, which had not only been brought formally to its notice by the memorial of Col. Ashley, and by the complaint of Justice Goodrich, who had been roughly handled by the Pittsfield committees for attempting to act under its commission, but had been boldly announced by the town for the very purpose of challenging the attention of the legislature.

A joint committee was therefore appointed to visit Pittsfield, and inquire into the causes of complaint, but did not do so; the desired information having come from other sources, among which the following paper from a Pittsfield town-meeting was prominent: —

TO THE HONORABLE COUNCIL AND THE HONORABLE HOUSE OF REPRESENTATIVES OF THE COLONY OF MASSACHUSETTS BAY IN GENERAL ASSEMBLY MET AT WATERTOWN, MAY 29, 1776.

The petition and memorial of the town of Pittsfield in said Colony humbly showeth, —

That they have the highest sense of the importance of civil and religious liberty, the destructive nature of tyranny and lawless power, and the absolute necessity of legal government to prevent anarchy and confusion.

That they, with their brethren in the other towns in this county, were early and vigorous in opposing the destructive measures of British administration against these Colonies; that they early signed the non-importation league and covenant, raised minute-men, agreed to pay them, ordered their public moneys to be paid to Henry Gardner, Esq., receiver-general, cast in their mite for the relief of Boston, and conformed in all things to the doings of the Honorable Continental and Provincial Congresses.

That they met with the utmost opposition from an unfriendly party in this town in every step, in every measure they pursued agreeable to the common councils of this Continent, which nothing but the most obstinate perseverance has enabled them to overcome and surmount, which, together with the inconveniences we have labored under, afford the true reason why we have been so behind in the payment of our public taxes.

That they, with the other towns in this county, have come behind none in their duty and attachment to their country's cause, and have exerted themselves much beyond their strength on all occasions.

A fresh instance of their zeal was conspicuous in our late defeat at Quebec, when a considerable number of men were raised and sent off in the dead of winter, and lay dying of sickness before the walls of Quebec, before any one man from this Colony had so much as left his own habitation for the relief of our distressed friends in Canada.

That from the purest and most disinterested principle and ardent love for their country, without selfish consideration, and in conformity with the advice of the wisest men in the Colony, they ordered and assisted in suspending the executive courts in this county in August, 1774.

That on no occasion have they spared either cost or trouble, without hope of pecuniary reward, vigorously and unweariedly exerting themselves for the support and defence of their country's cause, notwithstanding the most violent discouragements we have met with from open or secret enemies in this town and county, and in the neighboring Provinces.

That, till last fall, your memorialists had little or no expectation of obtaining any new privileges beyond what our defective charter secured to us.

That when they came more maturely to reflect on the nature of the present contest and the spirit and obstinacy of administration, — what an amazing expense the United Colonies had incurred, and how many of our towns had been burnt or otherwise damaged, what multitudes had been turned out to beg, and how many of our valiant heroes had been slain in the defence of their country, — and the impossibility of our being ever again dependent on Great Britain, or in any measure subject to her authority; when they further considered that the revolution in England afforded the nation but a very imperfect redress of grievances, — the nation, being transported with extravagant joy in getting rid of one tyrant, forgot to provide against another, — and how every man by nature has the seeds of tyranny deeply implanted within him, so that nothing short of Omnipotence can eradicate them; when they attended to the advice given this Colony by the Continental Congress respecting the assumption of our ancient Constitution, how early that advice was given, the reason of it, and the principles upon which it was given, which no longer exist; what a great change of circumstances there has been in the views and designs of this whole Continent since the giving said advice; that when they considered that now is the only time we have reason ever to expect for securing our liberties and the liberties of future posterity upon a permanent foundation that no length of time can undermine, — though they were filled with pain and anxiety at so much as seeming to oppose public councils, yet, with all these considerations in our view, love of virtue, freedom, and posterity prevailed upon us a second time to suspend the courts of justice in this county, after the judges of the Quarter Sessions had, in a precipitate and clandestine manner, held one court, and granted out a number of licenses to innholders at the rate of six shillings or more each, and divided the money amongst themselves with this boast, that "now it was going to be like former times," and had discovered a spirit of independence of the people, and a disposition triumphantly to ride over their heads, and worse than renew all our former oppressions.

We further beg leave to represent that we are deeply affected at the misrepresentations that have been made of us and the county in the General Court as men deeply in debt, dishonest, ungovernable, heady, intractable, without principle and good conduct, and ever ready to oppose lawful authority, as mobbers, disturbers of peace, order, and union, unwilling to submit to any government, or even to pay our debts; so that, we have been told, a former House of Representatives had it actually in contemplation to send an armed force, to effect that by violence which reason only ought to effect at the present day. We beg leave, therefore, to lay before your Honors our principles, real views, and designs in what we have hitherto done, and what object we are reaching after; with this assurance, that, if we have erred, it is through ignorance, and not bad intention.

We beg leave, therefore, to represent that we have always been persuaded that the people are the fountain of power; that, since the dissolution of the power of Great Britain over these Colonies, they have fallen into a state of nature.

That the first step to be taken by a people in such a state for the enjoyment or restoration of civil government among them is the formation of a fundamental constitution as the basis and ground-work of legislation;

that the approbation, by the majority of the people, of this fundamental constitution is absolutely necessary to give life and being to it; that then, and not till then, is the foundation laid for legislation.

We often hear of the fundamental constitution of Great Britain, which all political writers (except ministerial ones) set above the king, Lords, and Commons, which they cannot change; nothing short of the great rational majority of the people being sufficient for this.

A representative body may form, but cannot impose said fundamental constitution upon a people, as they, being but servants of the people, cannot be greater than their masters, and must be responsible to them; that, if this fundamental constitution is above the whole legislature, the legislature certainly cannot make it; it must be the approbation of the majority which gives life and being to it; that said fundamental constitution has not been formed for this Province; the corner-stone is not yet laid, and whatever building is reared without a foundation must fall to ruins;

That this can be instantly effected with the approbation of the Continental Congress; and law, subordination, and good government flow in better than their ancient channels in a few months' time; that, till this is done, we are but beating the air, and doing what will and must be undone afterwards, and all our labor is lost, and on divers reasons worse than lost;

That a doctrine newly broached in this county by several of the justices newly created without the voice of the people, that the representatives of the people may form just what fundamental constitution they please, and impose it upon the people, and, however obnoxious to them, they can obtain no relief from it but by a new election; and, if our representatives should never see fit to give the people one that pleases them, there is no help for it, — appears to us to be the rankest kind of Toryism, the self-same monster we are now fighting against.

These are some of the truths we firmly believe, and are countenanced in believing them by the most respectable political writers of the last and present century, especially by Mr. Burgh in his political disquisitions, for the publication of which one-half of the Continental Congress were subscribers.

We beg leave further to represent, that we by no means object to the most speedy institution of legal government through this Province, and that we are as earnestly desirous as any others of this great blessing.

That, knowing the strong bias of human nature to tyranny and despotism, we have nothing else in view but to provide for posterity against the wanton exercise of power, which cannot otherwise be done than by the formation of a fundamental constitution.

What is the fundamental constitution of this Province? What are the inalienable rights of the people? the power of the rulers? how often to be elected by the people, &c.? Have any of these things been as yet ascertained? Let it not be said by future posterity, that, in this great, this noble, this glorious contest, we made no provision against tyranny among ourselves.

We beg leave to assure your Honors, that the purest and most disinterested love of posterity, and the fervent desire of transmitting to them a fundamental constitution, securing to them social rights and immunities against all tyrants that may spring up after us, has moved us in what we have done. We have not been influenced by hope of gain, or expectation of preferment and honor; we are no discontented faction; we have no fellowship with Tories; we are the stanch friends of the union of these Colonies, and will support and maintain your Honors in opposing Great Britain with our lives and treasure. But even if commissions be recalled, and the king's name struck off them; if the fee-table be reduced never so low, and multitudes of other things be done to still the people, — *all is to us nothing* while the foundation is unfixed, the corner-stone of government unlaid. We have heard much of government being founded in compact: what compact has been formed as the foundation of government in this Province? We beg leave further to represent, that we have undergone many grievous oppressions in this county, and that now we wish a barrier might be set up against such oppressions, against which we can have no security long till the foundation of government be well established.

We beg leave further to represent these as the sentiments of by far the majority of the people of this county, as far as we can judge; and being so agreeable to reason, scripture, and common sense, as soon as the attention of the people of this Province is awakened we doubt not the majority will be with us.

We beg leave further to observe, that, if this honorable body shall find that we have embraced errors dangerous to the safety of these Colonies, it is our petition that our errors may be detected, and you shall be put to no further trouble from us; but, without an alteration in our judgment, the terrors of this world will not daunt us. We are determined to resist Great Britain to the last extremity, and all others who may claim a similar power over us. Yet we hold not to an *imperium imperio;* we will be determined by the majority.

Your petitioners, therefore, beg leave to request that this honorable body would form a fundamental constitution for this Province, after leave is asked and obtained from the Honorable Continental Congress, and that said constitution be sent abroad for the approbation of the majority of the people of this Colony; that, in this way, we may emerge from a state of nature, and enjoy again the blessings of civil government. In this way the rights and blessings of civil government will be secured, the glory of the present Revolution remain untarnished, and future posterity rise up and call the Honorable Council and House of Representatives blessed; and, as in duty bound, will ever pray.

Attest: ISRAEL DICKINSON, *Town Clerk.*

This paper, like the first memorial of the town, was from the pen of Mr. Allen; and the growth in his mind, and that of his fellow-citizens, of democratic ideas, and a desire for constitutional guaranties of free government, will be observed without a specific recapitulation of the points of the address. A nobler defence of the course pursued by the constitutionalists could hardly have been framed, or one based upon sounder political maxims.

It proved sufficiently explicit to forestall the proposed inquiry into the causes of complaint in Berkshire; and the General Court seems to have been so far satisfied, that no further action with regard to affairs in that county was had that year. The necessity of a more satisfactory basis of government, indeed, forced itself upon attention, and would not be put aside, even in that era of military disaster and extraordinary calls for exertion in the field; so that, for a time, the extreme measures adopting in the western counties attracted less notice.

Those who favored the retention of the baseless fabric of government, under which Massachusetts was neither Province, Colony, nor State, — maid, wife, nor widow, — were indeed puzzled to find a pretext for its longer continuance. The corner-stone of Congressional advice had, as we have seen, been sadly impaired by the adverse recommendations given to other Colonies; and the last fragment of support in that quarter had crumbled under the passage of the famous resolutions of May, 1776, declaring that "the exercise of every kind of authority under the king ought to be suppressed." At home, the legislature had previously entered upon measures to eradicate the king's name from all legal and official processes, and to replace all commissions under the regal authority with others under that of the Colony. But the use of the royal name and style, irritating to the masses, who had been taught by George III. heartily to detest them, was abhorrent to the constitutionalist thinkers chiefly as the symbol and the evidence of a determination by those in power at Boston to cling to a form of government which ought long before to have passed away. And, now that the symbol of royal authority would no longer be endured, the disposition to stop at mere superficial and palliatory reforms was so manifest as to excite the alarm of the advocates of a constitution, and to call for those paragraphs in the Pittsfield address which asserted the utter insufficiency of any thing short of a frame of government submitted to, and established by, a vote of the people. Statesmen of the highest ability and purest character, throughout the State, sympathized with the zeal of the men of Berkshire, although, perhaps, not generally with the measures by which they re-enforced their not excessively humble petitions.

Pretexts were, however, found to delay action until September, when the General Court appointed a committee "to prepare a new frame of government." But the body which had made no hesitation in taking up civil government upon the hint given by Congress was now struck with a sudden qualm, which forbade them to proceed further towards laying it down without the express consent of their constituents. Even the preparation of the groundwork of a constitution was therefore suspended; and a circular asking authority for that purpose was sent to the towns, who promptly returned a favorable response. Pittsfield voted, "That this town highly approves the handbill sent out on the 17th of September, relative to the present General Assembly forming a constitution, and to be sent to the several towns for their approbation."[1]

The decision of the people was ascertained at the May session of the legislature; and the ensuing summer and fall were spent in preparing a draft which was submitted to the people in March, 1778, with a proviso requiring the assent of two-thirds of the voters to give it validity. It is strange, that, upon a matter of such fundamental importance as this, only twelve thousand voters registered themselves, and one hundred and twenty towns made no return at all. Of those who took the trouble to vote, five-sixths, "under the lead of an almost unanimous public sentiment in Boston," declared against the instrument submitted to them.

What the special objections to it were is matter of conjecture. Hon. Charles Francis Adams, in a carefully-prepared sketch of the reconstruction of government in Massachusetts, speaks of it as "a very imperfect instrument, largely partaking of the haste and confusion of the time in which it was made, but yet very much better than none at all, or than the temporary system which necessity had created;" and expresses surprise that "interests had already grown up in the period of interregnum adverse to the establishment of any more permanent government."

[1] The town showed its deep interest in the task imposed upon the legislature of 1777, by sending to it an unprecedented number of representatives, choosing for that purpose three of its most trusted citizens, — Valentine Rathbun, Josiah Wright, and Eli Root. The committee of instruction was also of unusual ability, consisting of Cols. Williams and Easton, Capts. Isarel Dickinson, William Francis, and James Noble, Lieuts. William Barber and Amos Root.

The truth is, that those interests were as old as the Colonial magistracy; had sought shelter, in Province times, under the gubernatorial wing; had dictated the government of the interregnum, and now desired to retain it with only such modifications as should not make it less subservient to small ambitions. It may be shrewdly suspected that there were those engaged in framing the abortive ship of state who had no earnest desire that it should survive the launching. To frail construction, by ill-designing workmen, may be probably ascribed, in part at least, the ill-starred fate of the Constitution of 1778.

The people of Pittsfield, however, held the same opinion which Mr. Adams expresses of the proposed instrument; and although it denied their darling desire, — a bill of rights, — and in other respects fell far short of the standard which they had set up, their vote was unanimous for accepting it, save the 19th, 24th, and 26th articles.

The 19th article provided that all civil officers annually chosen, with salaries annually granted, should be elected by the General Court; all others appointed by the Governor and Senate. Articles 24th and 26th provided that the judges, justices of the peace, attorney-general, treasurer, &c., should hold office during good behavior.

The voters of Pittsfield were strenuous in their desire that all officers, civil, judicial, and military, should be elected by the people for a term of years.

By voting to accept a constitution which, in many respects, differed widely from its own notions, Pittsfield now gave evidence that it desired neither anarchy nor the rule of local committees; but only insisted upon a foundation of government created in such a way as to recognize the right of the people to model their own institutions, and remodel them whenever they should see cause.

A consistent earnestness in the same direction continued to be manifest in all the town action. It having been demonstrated that an ordinary legislative body was ill adapted to the work, Pittsfield united with the other towns in the county in a petition that a convention of delegates might be called, for the express purpose of framing a constitution and bill of rights; and, on the 17th of December, Col. John Brown, having in the previous May been chosen representative, was instructed to press it upon the House that the convention should be called as soon as possible.

In the mean time, the town, both by its separate action and by several votes in conjunction with the rest of the county, inflexibly maintained its determination "not to permit the holding of the Courts of Common Pleas or General Sessions."

On the 3d of June, 1776, shortly after the presentation of the second Pittsfield address, the House of Representatives received from Joseph Woodbridge of Stockbridge, Joseph Fairfield, Dan Cadwell, Jacob Ensign, Erastus Sackett, and Jacob Ward, of Pittsfield, and Ebenezer Doane, probably of Richmond, "a statement of the unhappy circumstances of this distracted county," in which they say,[1] —

"Numbers of these enthusiastic people[2] having got themselves into the office of committees of inspection and correspondence, inoculate the minds of their votaries, both by their example and doctrines, that they ought to pay no more obedience to the acts and doings of the General Court than they themselves think proper; and notwithstanding the General Court, by authority from the Grand American Congress, have adopted a free and salutary form of government, and have appointed suitable officers in this county to preserve peace and good order, by punishing the guilty and thereby protecting the innocent, yet the committees above mentioned, disregarding the authority of the whole continent, whilst they themselves are despising, defaming, assaulting, and abusing the civil officers your Honors have appointed in this county, they assume to themselves judicial authority, and in a most arbitrary manner execute the same, both in civil as well as criminal matters; and this presumption of the committees, your petitioners humbly conceive, will be attended with very pernicious consequences, if a very speedy stop should not be put to their illegal proceedings, as they will inevitably lay the foundation for a multiplicity of law-suits whenever order and legal government shall be restored in this county."

This statement affords a fair view of the aspect which affairs in the county bore in the eyes of the minority which advocated submission to the State government. The reader is already possessed of the different light in which it presented itself to those who regarded the necessity of a fundamental law as paramount to all considerations of immediate evils incident to a struggle for its attainment.

The legislature, whatever may have been its reasons, dismissed

[1] It is to be observed that Cadwell, Fairfield, and Sackett were afterwards prominent "Shay's rebels;" a fact which will be taken into consideration in estimating their present devotion to law and order.

[2] The constitutionalists.

the Woodbridge memorial, and, so far as appears from the record, paid no further attention to the Berkshire troubles until the 1st of February, 1777.

On that day, the question of a new constitution having in the previous September been referred to the people, the following preamble and order passed both houses: —

In the House of Representatives, Feb. 1, 1777.

Whereas our ancestors, the venerable and virtuous settlers of this country, who were no less remarkable for their attachments to the rights of mankind than their zeal for religion, did, in the early ages of this State, enact sundry laws for the encouragement of piety and virtue, and the preventing profane swearing, breaking of the sabbath, and other immoralities, for which the Supreme Being has usually punished a people;

And many laws having lately been passed by this and the last General Court to detect and punish those persons who are trying to subvert the liberty of these free States, which laws cannot be carried into execution without holding executive courts within the several counties of this State;

And whereas it is represented that the justices of the peace, in the counties of Berkshire and Hampshire, have neglected to hold courts of General Sessions of the Peace as the law directs; and grand jurors, who have always been deemed an order of men upon whom the well-being of society much depended, have not, in those counties, been chosen as usual, and the justices there have been prevented from punishing small offences within their cognizance, by reason of there being no Court of General Sessions of the Peace to appeal to, by which delay of distributive justice there is great danger of immoralities increasing; and as the power invested in civil magistrates is absolutely necessary to the preservation of the people, more especially while an army is on foot in the country:

It is therefore —

Ordered, That the justices of the said counties be, and they hereby are, directed to hold their courts of General Sessions of the Peace at the times and in the places by law prefixed therefor; and it is also recommended to the good people of these counties to consider how much the happiness and weal of society depends upon the orderly and regular execution of the laws, and to do all in their power to aid and support the civil magistrates in the execution of their office.

The General Court seems to have expected much from this paper; for in December, finding that it had not been properly distributed, it directed Daniel Hopkins, Esq., to send a copy to each town in Hampshire and Berkshire.

By this time, the Constitution, destined to be stillborn, had been framed; and, probably in anticipation of its early adoption rather than influenced by the document disseminated by Mr. Hopkins, the people of Hampshire permitted courts to be held at Springfield.

The Berkshire constitutionalists too shrewdly appreciated the tactics by which the proposed Constitution was manipulated, to trust to its establishment before it became an accomplished fact. A respectful consideration was, however, given to the appeal of the General Court; and a convention was held at Pittsfield on the 12th of August, — Col. William Williams presiding, William Walker of Lenox clerk, — to determine whether the county would admit the courts of law. The convention desired the several towns to take a vote, by yeas and nays, whether they wished the Court of Common Pleas and the Court of General Sessions, or either of them, to be holden in the county before a bill of rights and a constitution were framed and accepted by the people." The Pittsfield Committee of Correspondence was also requested to write to the committees of the different towns in Hampshire and Worcester for advice.

An adjournment was then had to the 26th of August, when the towns were expected to make their returns.[1]

At the adjourned meeting, the following result appeared; the yeas representing those who favored the opening of the courts: —

TOWNS.	Courts of Sessions.		Courts of Com. Pleas.	
	Yeas.	Nays.	Yeas.	Nays.
Richmond,	30	31	30	21
Alford,	18	0	0	18
Lenox,	1	69	0	63
Washington,	3	16	0	20
Hancock,	35	0	2	33
Lee,	9	12	9	12
Williamstown,	10	60	10	60
Carried forward,	106	188	51	227

[1] Only one response to the request for advice is preserved. It was from the town of Worcester; and was not written until December, — long after Berkshire had made its decision. It was a well-stated and temperately-worded argument against the position assumed in Berkshire, but was far from conclusive against the fixed idea of the western county, that government based on any thing but the express consent of the people was a dangerous usurpation. It was signed by Daniel Bigelow, Nathaniel Heywood, William Dana, Joseph Barbour, and Jonathan Price.

TOWNS.	Courts of Sessions.		Courts of Com. Pleas.	
	Yeas.	Nays.	Yeas.	Nays.
Brought forward,	106	188	51	227
Gageborough (now Windsor),	2	61	2	61
Partridgefield (now Peru and Hinsdale),	1	·61	1	61
Equivalent (now Dalton),	0	31	1	31
Sheffield,	41	0	0	41
Lanesborough,	3	60	3	60
New Ashford,	0	25	0	25
Great Barrington,	59	0	16	11
Stockbridge,	26	36	26	36
New Marlborough,	48	12	48	12
Sandisfield,	18	20	0	38
Loudon (Otis),	13	1	1	7
Pittsfield,	12	50	12	50
	329	545	161	660

The county having again, by this decisive majority, refused to admit the courts, the following gentlemen were appointed to draft still another petition for a constitutional convention: James Harris of Lanesborough, William Whiting of Great Barrington, William Williams of Pittsfield, Benjamin Pierson of Richmond, and William Walker of Lenox. The petition reported by them, like those which preceded it, recited the great military services of the county, its devoted faithfulness to the patriotic cause, the readiness of the people to fly to the assistance of their brethren on every alarm, and their abhorrence of Toryism. It then proceeds thus:—

"Nothwithstanding this our fidelity to the State and our exertions for the common cause, we have, by designing and disaffected men, been represented as a mobbish, ungovernable, refractory, licentious, and dissolute people; by means whereof we have been threatened with dismemberment, more especially, as we conceive, on account of our not admiting the course of common law.

"It is true we were the first county that put a stop to courts, and were soon followed by many others, — nay, in effect, by the whole State; and we are not certain but that it might have been as well, if not better, had they continued so, rather than to have law dealt out by piecemeal, as it is this day, without any foundation to support it; for we doubt not we should, before this time, have had a bill of rights and a constitution, which are the only things we at this time are empowered to pray for.

"And we do now, with the greatest deference, petition your Honors, that you would issue your precepts to all the towns and places within this State called upon to pay public taxes, requiring them to choose delegates, to sit as soon as may be in some suitable place, to form a bill of rights and a constitution for this State; without which we shall retain the aforesaid character, if grounded upon the non-admission of law, as abundantly appears to us this day by the yeas and nays from the respective towns we represent, taken in town-meeting officially called for that purpose, there being four-fifths of the inhabitants of said county against supporting the courts of law until a constitution be formed, and accepted by the people.

"If this our request is rejected, we shall endeavor, by addressing the first Committee of Safety, &c., in this State and others, that there be a State convention formed for the purpose aforesaid. And, if this Honorable Court are for dismemberment, there are other States, which have constitutions, who will, we doubt not, as bad as we are, gladly receive us; and we shall, to the utmost of our ability, support and defend authority and law, as we should, with greater cheerfulness, in the State to which we belong, were there any proper foundation for it.

"We are, with all submission, your Honors' youngest child, and are determined, to the utmost of our power, to protect and secure our just inheritance, and hope our parent will graciously concur and assist, by granting this our request.

"And, as in duty bound, will ever pray.

This appeal tells its own story, and shows a very serious complication of affairs between the State and the county. The General Court gave it earnest attention; in September, appointed a committee to consider "what was necessary to be done towards a new constitution," and immediately afterwards sent a deputation to meet the delegates of the Berkshire towns, at Pittsfield, "inquire into their grievances, and endeavor to remove them;" announcing to them, at the same time, the measures which had just been taken in regard to granting their demand for a constitution, and assuring them that the committee to whom that matter was referred would report upon it as soon as might be, and that it would be taken up at the next session.

The convocation was held Nov. 17; Valentine Rathbun, James Noble, and Josiah Wright representing Pittsfield. The result, in connection with a subsequent consultation with the Berkshire representatives in the legislature, was the passage of a very absolute act of pardon and oblivion, with the following provisions: —

"Whereas the situation of the county of Berkshire during the present troubles has been such as induced committees and other persons to do many acts which, in strict law, may be deemed criminal; therefore —

"*First.* All riots, unlawful assemblies, rescues, breaches of the peace, assaults, batteries, and imprisonments which had occurred in the county between the 10th of April, 1774, and the 1st of February, 1779, were pardoned, and put into utter oblivion.

"*Second.* It was enacted, that, without leave first had of the General Court, no action for damage should be brought against any person on account of any act done under the authority of any town, town-officer, or committee of correspondence and inspection, within the county.

"*Third.* It was ordered, that a term of the Superior Court of Judicature should be holden annually for the county of Berkshire, at Great Barrington, on the first Tuesday of May."

The act seems worded with a very tender consideration for the sensitiveness of those to whom it applied, and manifested genuine delicacy in classing among the acts which "*in strict law* MIGHT be deemed criminal," as well those done in suppressing the king's courts as those which obstructed the sessions of the State tribunals; for since all patriots acknowledged the first to have been praiseworthy in fact, whatever they might have been "deemed in strict law," no very severe condemnation could have been intended by the General Court of acts which it classed with them without discrimination.

It is not apparent how the legislature could have accomplished an object essential to the restoration of "the full course of law" in any other way, unless it had succumbed to the Berkshire theory, that its own authority was usurped, and thus thrown all the affairs of the State into confusion; a course which it could hardly have been expected to pursue, with whichever party the abstract right may have been.

But a clear comprehension of these considerations was not then to have been expected; and it is not strange, that, instead of giving satisfaction to those for whose benefit it was intended, the act excited their ire. Holding themselves to be the champions of legitimate government against the encroachments of its enemies, they claimed praise, and not pardon, as their due, and spurned indignantly the most remote intimation of the contrary.

The nature and strength of this feeling may be gathered from the instructions of Pittsfield to its representatives, Col. William Williams and Capt. James Noble, in which these paragraphs appear: —

"We give you the following instructions, viz.: —

"1st. That you do use your utmost endeavors that a constitution be formed at this time."

"3d. That a late act of the General Court, called and considered to be an act of oblivion respecting the county of Berkshire, be an object of your attention, and that your exert yourselves that the same may be repealed, as it was undesired by the county, and is fraught with reproach, discrimination, and such severe reflections upon the county as they utterly disdain, and are not chargeable with; not to mention the manifest injustice contained in it.

"4th. That the appointment of a Superior Court to be holden in this county on the first Tuesday of May current was unnecessary and premature, and that the gentlemen who proposed such a measure were not so instructed and directed."

"8th. And, as you are chosen to represent the town of Pittsfield, we expect that you will represent it as a town of a county which has acted as firmly and consistently as any county in this State; and, as you know the sentiments of the county, that you act conformably thereunto; and, if you are not treated with the same respect with representatives of other counties, that you return home, and give us the pleasure of your company."

These instructions are signed by Eli Root, John Strong, and James Easton; but the original draft is in the handwriting of Rev. Mr. Allen.[1]

The expectation announced to the people of Berkshire by the legislative committee was realized; and at its next session, — that to which Messrs. Williams and Noble were accredited, — the General Court submitted to the people of the State the question whether they desired to have a new constitution, and, if so, whether they would have it framed by a convention chosen expressly for that duty.

So sluggish was public sentiment outside of Berkshire and Hampshire on this great matter, that nearly one-third of the towns failed to make any return of their vote; and it was not until May that it was known that a majority had declared for a convention.

While uncertainty on this point continued to prevail, the day fixed for the new term of the Superior Court at Great Barrington approached; and a county convention met and adopted an address to the judges, written by Mr. Allen, and giving a brief *résumé* of the previous opposition to the courts, with the reasons which had induced it, showing that those reasons still existed, and closing as follows: —

"We are fearful of the consequences, should the operation of the law take place upon the present foundation, especially if it should be attempted

[1] The section of the act of oblivion which instituted the new term of the Superior Court was repealed. The rest continued in force.

to be enforced by violence, as some have insinuated; which insinuations we hope will appear to be groundless, as they have very much exasperated the people. We must, therefore, in duty to ourselves, our country, and our constituents, earnestly desire that your Honors would desist from attempting to sit in this county, until the explicit voice of the great majority of the freemen of this State may be taken, by yeas and nays, respecting the validity of the present form of government, by whose determination, when explicitly and regularly known, we are determined cheerfully and religiously to abide."

Thus, again and finally, did the men of Berkshire rest the defence of their course — where they had first placed, and ever consistently maintained it — upon the absolute invalidity of government based on no explicit consent of the governed; and thus did they reiterate their purpose to endure even the odious *débris* of the charter, if the majority should pronounce that to be their will.

Soon after these proceedings, it was ascertained that the voters of the State had decided for a convention; and it was called to meet on the 1st of the following September at Cambridge.

Pittsfield had voted unanimously that it wished, not only a constitution, but a bill of rights, "and that as soon as might be." It now chose Col. William Williams delegate to the convention, with the following committee of instruction: Valentine Rathbun, Thomas Allen, Eli Root, James Noble, and Lebbeus Backus.

Their report, prepared by Mr. Allen, was one of the most remarkable political papers which came from his pen, and offers a fitting culmination to the series whose introduction here has been deemed essential.

It must be remembered, in reading it, that the maxims laid down were not, in 1779, the accepted truths which most of them have become to later generations; for although some of them had already been incorporated into the new frames of government in Vermont, Virginia, and New York, and most of them had been more or less distinctly proclaimed by political writers, the sanctity which time has conferred upon them as well-defined propositions, integral parts of the Constitutions of Massachusetts and of the American Union, was yet to be attained. So that, while of course no claim to origination can be raised for this declaration of what Pittsfield desired to secure in the instrument which had so long been the star of her hope, no little political sagacity and right-mindedness must be inferred from the selection, out of the abounding dross, of so much which the test of experience has proved pure gold.

Report of the Committee appointed by the Town to draw up Instructions for their Representatives in State Convention is as follows: —

To Col. Williams.

Sir, — As you have been duly elected by the town of Pittsfield their representative to meet in a convention of this State at Cambridge, the 1st of September next, for the purpose of forming a new Constitution for the people of this State, which we view as a matter of the greatest consequence to the present and future generations, it will doubtless be agreeable to you to understand their sentiments for the government of your deportment. You are therefore hereby instructed to unite with said convention in drawing up a Bill of Rights and in forming a new Constitution for the people of this State. We wish you to oppose all unnecessary delay in this great work, and to proceed in it with the utmost wisdom and caution.

In the Bill of Rights, you will endeavor that all those unalienable and important rights which are essential to true liberty, and form the basis of government in a free State, shall be inserted: particularly, that this people have a right to adopt that form of government which appears to us most eligible, and best calculated to promote the happiness of ourselves and posterity; that as all men by nature are free, and have no dominion one over another, and all power originates in the people, so, in a state of civil society, all power is founded in compact; that every man has an unalienable right to enjoy his own opinion in matters of religion, and to worship God in that manner that is agreeable to his own sentiments without any control whatsoever, and that no particular mode or sect of religion ought to be established, but that every one be protected in the peaceable enjoyment of his religious persuasion and way of worship; that no man can be deprived of liberty, and subjected to perpetual bondage and servitude, unless he has forfeited his liberty as a malefactor; that the people have a right peaceably to assemble, consider of their grievances, and petition for redress; that, as civil rulers derive their authority from the people, so they are accountable to them for the use of it; that elections ought to be free, equal, and annual; that, as all men are equal by nature, so, when they enter into a state of civil government, they are entitled precisely to the same rights and privileges, or to an equal degree of political happiness; that the right of trial by jury ought to be perpetual; that no man's property of right can be taken from him without his consent, given either in person or by his representative; that no laws are obligatory on the people but those that have obtained a like consent, nor are such laws of any force, if, proceeding from a corrupt majority of the legislature, they are incompatible with the fundamental principles of government, and tend to subvert it; that the freedom of speech and debates and proceedings in the House of Representatives ought not to be questioned or impeached in any court, or place out of the General Court; that excessive bail shall not be required, nor excessive fines imposed, nor cruel and unjust punishments inflicted; that jurors ought to be duly impanelled and returned, and all jurors ought to be freeholders. These, and all other liberties which you find essential to true liberty, you will claim, demand, and insist upon, as the birthrights of this people.

In respect to the Constitution, you will use your best endeavors that the following things may be inserted in it amongst others: That the election of the representative body be annual; that no representative on any occasion shall absent himself from said House without leave first had from said body, but shall constantly attend on the business during the sessions. All taxes shall be levied with the utmost equality on polls, faculty, and property. You may consent to government by a Governor, Council, and House of Representatives. The Governor and Council shall have no negative voice upon the House of Representatives; but all disputed points shall be settled by the majority of the whole legislative body. The supreme judges of the executive courts shall be elected by the suffrages of the people at large, and be commissioned by the Governor. That all grants of money shall originate in the House of Representatives. The judges of the maritime courts, the attorney-general, and high sheriffs of each county, are to be appointed by the suffrages of people at large, and commissioned by the Governor. The justices of the Common Pleas and Quarter Sessions of the Peace in each county be elected by the suffrages of the people of said counties. That no person, unless of the Protestant religion, shall be Governor, Lieutenant-governor, or member of the Council or the House of Representatives.

The said Bill of Rights and Constitution you will move may be printed, and sent abroad for the approbation of the people of this State at large, and that each town be requested by said convention to show their approbation or disapprobation of every paragraph in said Bill of Rights and Constitution, and that it be not sent abroad for their approbation or disapprobation in the lump; and that the objectionable parts, if any such shall be, shall be pointed out by each town.

You are not to dissolve the convention, but to adjourn from time to time, as you shall find necessary, till said form of government is approved by the majority of the people.

On the whole, we empower you to act agreeable to the dictates of your own judgment after you have heard all the reasonings upon the various subjects of disquisition, having an invariable respect to the true liberty and real happiness of this State throughout all generations, any instructions herein contained to the contrary notwithstanding.

THOMAS ALLEN,
ELI ROOT,
JAMES NOBLE,
LEBBEUS BACKUS. } *Committee.*

Accepted. Attest:

ELI ROOT, *Moderator.*

In the instructions as originally drawn, the delegate was authorized to "consent that the supreme judges of the executive courts *should be nominated and chosen by the Governor, Council, and House of Representatives.*" In the copy attested by the moderator of the town-meeting, the italicized words are erased, and with a different ink, in a different handwriting, the following are substituted: "*Shall be elected by the suffrages of the people at large.*" A similar change occurs in the clause regarding the judges of the maritime courts, attorney-general, and the high sheriffs.

These alterations were evidently made as amendments in town-meeting, and indicate that even Mr. Allen was not so radical in his democracy as the dominant sentiment of the town. Mr. Rathbun, it will be observed, did not sign the report; and it may have been that the changes were made on his motion.[1]

It has been a mooted question whether slavery was abolished in Massachusetts by the deliberate intention of the people when voting for the Bill of Rights, or by a forced construction of that instrument in the courts. Those who have followed the record of Pittsfield will concede that one town at least meant the Bill of Rights to be no empty declaration of abstract principles, but a living law, requiring no legislative enactment to give it efficiency. Nor is it less apparent that the people of that town not only understood what they were doing when they cast their votes to ratify the Bill of Rights, but that they well knew, and clearly said what they intended to say, when they instructed their delegate to endeavor that it should be inserted among its prohibitions of wrong "that *no man can be deprived of liberty, and subjected to perpetual bondage and servitude, unless he has forfeited his liberty as a malefactor.*" Side by side with the God-given rights which they claimed for themselves, they placed their demand for universal freedom as equally the birthright of every human being.[2]

[1] A comparison of this paper with the Constitution of 1780, and the papers regarding it in the works of John Adams, will serve to give a correct idea of its character.

[2] The homogeneous sentiment, which the reader will have observed in the previous story as characterizing Berkshire, leaves no room to doubt, that, as regards the exclusion of slavery, the desire of all its towns was similar to that of Pittsfield. In the case of Stockbridge, we believe, there is direct evidence that it was so.

The clause in relation to religious liberty was far in advance of the article upon that subject which was actually inserted in the Bill of Rights, and of that proposed by Mr. Adams as well. It may reasonably be held to cover even that complete separation of church and state which was not attained until the abolition of taxation for the support of religious worship in 1834; for we may reasonably interpret the abstract declaration of 1779 in the light of the following extract from a letter which Mr. Allen wrote to the town in 1783, upon learning that a minority were dissatisfied with an increase, which, on account of the depreciation of the currency, had been voted to his salary: —

> "Having been made acquainted by several persons that the above-mentioned grant has occasioned uneasiness and dissatisfaction in the minds of some persons, I do hereby release the town from their vote; it never having been my intention to be supported in my office by compulsion. I wish for no other support than is freely granted, nor do I mean to continue any longer in office than I can obtain such support."

We have few means of ascertaining what influence the town, by its action, had in securing the provisions which it desired, and which were finally placed in the Constitution.

The convention met on the 1st of September; and, on the 6th, Col. Williams wrote to his wife that between two and three hundred delegates had arrived, "making a much more respectable body than he was apprehensive could be collected in the State." Before he closed his letter, the convention, "having chosen a grand committee to form a bill of rights and a constitution," adjourned to await their report. He was uncertain whether he should himself visit home in the interval, but directed his wife to inform Mr. Allen and Capt. Root of the contents of his letter, and request them to write him.

Mr. Allen was thus cognizant of the position of affairs in the convention as well as of the names of the committee, which Col. Williams had enclosed; and it is hardly conceivable that neither he nor Col. Williams, nervously anxious as both were upon the subject, placed at least the substance of the town's instructions in the hands of the committee, or of John Adams, who was commissioned by his associates to prepare the first draft of their work.

The Bill of Rights and Constitution prepared by the convention were established by the people in May, 1780.

The vote of Pittsfield in its favor was apparently unopposed and unanimous; although some of the provisions which it contained were at variance with the preconceived notions of its people.

The desire which they had expressed that the proposed form of government should be submitted to them "article by article, and not in the lump," was prompted by the fear of some such incongruous creation as that of 1777; and they must have seen, that, even if practicable, it would have been out of place to subject to such a process of revision as was requested the well-balanced production of 1780, which was prepared with all the skill of a profound and learned student of government, and from which one of the parts ignorantly torn away would have been very likely to impair the soundness of all.

This was so self-evident as not to be questioned; and, the State government being thus fixed upon the sure foundation which they had so assiduously sought, the majority of the citizens of Pittsfield, ever after — even when the Shays Rebellion agitated the western counties — were content to seek the reforms which remained to be effected in the laws through the channels provided by the Constitution.

In addition to the controversy which has been sketched between the General Court and the dominant party in Berkshire, regarding the measures which the latter adopted as a protest against the baseless government set up in the State, and as the means of securing a constituent law, a bitter and wordy dispute was carried on in the newspapers; poor Mr. Watson, of "The Hartford Courant," being specially afflicted with the communications on both sides. And, as usually happens in acrimonious political conflicts, each party grossly misrepresented and maligned the other. On the one hand, although among those who favored a recognition of the obnoxious government, and the admission of the courts, there were some of the truest patriots in Berkshire, on whom not the shadow of suspicion of treachery to the American cause could justly have rested, yet they were indiscriminately posted in the public prints, and charged by the public action of the towns, as "enemies of their country," in precisely the same phraseology that was used concerning the Tories. One not acquainted with the facts would infer from the record, that Capt. Charles Goodrich, for example, was, in the opinion of his townsmen, false to the Revolutionary cause; while, in fact, it had no more sincere supporter.

There was, however, something to give color of reason to this misconception, in the fact that the Tories of Pittsfield, almost without exception, favored the restoration of the courts under the old system, and the recognition of the State government as legitimate, — reserving the rights of the king. The polemical skill, the talent, and the style of Woodbridge Little are unmistakable in the ablest papers on the side of the non-constitutionalists. It was truly said, too, that Goodrich "consorted with the most ancient and implacable Tories of the town;" and, although it was only one of the strange combinations which are often effected in politics, its influence against him at the time was irresistible. And so, on the other hand, phases in the conduct and measures of the constitutionalists favored the assertion of their enemies, that they were a set of violent, turbulent, and dishonest fellows, who only desired to suppress the courts, lest they might be brought to account for their misdeeds, and be compelled to pay their honest debts.

So effectually, indeed, did the newspaper libellers affix this stigma to the rejection of civil administration in Berkshire, that it has not even yet been removed.

And yet, surely, love of license, and the hope of avoiding just responsibilities, never inspired such consistent devotion to constitutional law as the Berkshire fathers constantly manifested; never surely, before or since, were a people educated by the harangues of demagogues, and appeals to passion or selfish interests, up to the comprehension of, and desire for, the establishment of such principles of government as Pittsfield instructed Col. Williams to advocate in the convention of 1779. Tried by the decisive test of its effect upon the intellectual character of the people, the agitation of 1775–80 stands fully justified.

In argument and action, the Berkshire constitutionalists were better able to cope with their antagonists than in the arts of detraction. In the beginning, we saw them yielding to the apprehensions of their representatives in Congress their own convictions that a new form of government ought at once to be established; thus proving their subordination of local feeling to the general good. Roused by the selfish appropriation of official patronage in the General Court of 1775 to a new perception of the evils inseparable from unrestricted power, as well in the hands of elected representatives as of anointed kings, and the jealousy which forbade free action to Massachusetts being allayed, they renewed their demand for a fundamental law. To the suggestion that the opportunity annually to change their representatives ought to satisfy them, they replied, in substance, "What we crave is not the privilege of changing masters. Some of the powers inherent in the people we do not choose to delegate; some we would intrust, with carefully-guarded restrictions, to our representatives; all we would have exercised by ourselves as well as our deputies, in certain well-defined modes of operation, and in accordance with a fundamental law solemnly agreed upon. That is, we ask a constitution for the Commonwealth." Upon this simple demand they rang the changes through six years of angry political controversy.

Sorely pressed to forego this boon till a more convenient season, they at last pledged themselves to yield for the time even to the existing government, upon the single condition that it should first be submitted to a vote of the people, so that their will might thus be recognized as the proper source of all rightful authority. A Constitution once established, it received their fullest allegiance. From first to last there was nothing factious in their conduct.

For many things they expressed desire as component parts of the frame of government; but upon one only they insisted, and that was a distinct recognition of the people's right to model and remodel their institutions as they saw cause.

It was urged upon them, that their uncompromising demand for this disturbed the harmony which, while the war lasted, ought to be preserved in the patriotic ranks. Their reply was, that, if they were to be the subjects of arbitrary power, it mattered little whether its seat were in London or Boston, and that, if the government now set up were once quietly "permitted to take place," it would be very difficult ever after to shake it off. The example of Connecticut, and still more emphatically that of Rhode Island,— both which States retained charters far more liberal than that of Massachusetts as the bases of their independent governments,— show how just was that apprehension. Nor was there really much in the turmoil of the times to defer the task of framing and adopting a new form of government. The most perfect charters of freedom — so cunningly devised that tyranny cannot reach its victims without entirely setting them aside — were the work of disturbed eras. *Magna Charta* was not the child of

Peace, nor was the *Habeas Corpus* act. Trial by jury dates back to an age of perpetual war. The Declaration of American Independence was born of conflict; and the Constitution of Massachusetts, providing for the most complex relations of people and government, was none the less wisely constructed, that it was finally framed while war gave strength and tone to men's minds. Is it too much to claim that the Berkshire constitutionalists were wiser than their generation in their strenuous opposition to "the interests which had grown up in the State adverse to any more permanent form of government" than consorted with the small ambitions of the magisterial class?

CHAPTER XX.

THE BERKSHIRE CONSTITUTIONALISTS. — COMMITTEE GOVERNMENT OF THE INTERREGNUM.

[1774–1780.]

Committees of Correspondence, Inspection, and Safety. — Their Character and Origin. — Subordinated in 1776 to the Courts of Law. — The Berkshire Committees refuse Submission. — Their Administration of Justice. — Curious Surveillance of Morals and Manners. — Town Court established. — Its Rules of Practice and Fee-Table. — Discipline of Capt. Goodrich by the Committee. — He appeals to the Legislature. — Details of the Case.

ONLY brief allusion has been made in the foregoing chapters to the substitutes adopted in Pittsfield for the suppressed courts of law; but the reader will curiously inquire how, when the ordinary machinery of government was obstructed, "tolerable order was maintained."

It so happened that Massachusetts had retained, through all changes in her condition, what to her was of more worth than royal charters, — her system of town governments, each so complete within itself, that, in the lapse of exterior authority, it lacked little to become a perfect State; and each with citizens so accustomed to the conduct of public affairs, that they were capable of meeting whatever responsibilities were thrown upon them.

When, therefore, in 1774, the judicial system of the Province was broken up, the towns found little difficulty in assuming so much of its authority as the public necessity required should not utterly fail; resorting, in the absence of precedent, to divers plans for the proper execution of the duties newly devolved upon them. Occasionally the people, in town-meeting assembled, adjudicated directly upon matters brought before them. Sometimes they erected special tribunals; as in Attleborough, where the old Provincial fabric was imitated in miniature, with a superior court of four judges, and an inferior court of seven. But generally — and in Berkshire County universally — the improvised machinery of justice was much less complex; its entire powers being vested in the committees of inspection, with the occasional aid of a board of arbitrators, such as, immediately after the first suppression of the courts, was appointed in Pittsfield, and of which an account was given in the proper connection.

It must not, however, be supposed that the committee rule was formally devised, adopted, and organized as a substitute for the courts and magistracy. It was an outgrowth, developed little by little by the necessities of the times, from the New-England practice of placing every public business in the hands of a commission.

Under the different organizations known as committees of correspondence, inspection, and safety, it had played an important part in securing unity and vigor in the initiatory stages of the Revolution; and the powers recognized in those bodies by the State and Continental governments were formidable and extensive. Precisely what they were, we are informed by a report to the General Court in October, 1776. According to this paper,[1] the committees, originally existing by sufferance, acted upon their own discretion until the resolves of Congress, directed to them,[2] confirmed and in some measure defined their powers; but they continued to "act discretionally" when the resolves were not to be procured, or did not meet the case in hand. Originally the province of the committees of correspondence was, by the interchange of letters and the speedy communication of information, to apprise the community of dangers, and to concert measures for the public good, expose the designs of the enemies of liberty to public execration, and incite opposition to them. The committees of inspection took cognizance of unpatriotic importations of British goods, exerted themselves to suppress the sale of tea, and generally exposed and reprehended violations of the non-importation association, and denounced all acts detrimental to the common interests. The committees of safety were instituted to concert measures for the public safety of their respective towns, and the general safety of the community; "taking cognizance of measures afterwards taken up by Congress

[1] Mass. Ar., vol. cxxxvii. p. 118.

[2] The Resolves of Association, directed to the committees of inspection.

as well of lesser matters relative to internal police at a time when prostrate law gave no remedy against disorder and confusion."

"These," says the report, "were the powers these several committees had at their institution, although they afterwards received the sanction of the highest authority."

It will be perceived, that, in many particulars, the powers and duties of the three classes of committee were identical; and on the 13th of October, 1775, they were consolidated in one, by an act of the General Court, directing each town, at its annual election, to choose "a committee of correspondence, inspection, and safety for the especial purpose of attending to the general and political interests of the Colonies; to transmit intelligence to committees of the same denomination in other towns and counties, to the General Court and the Council, as they might deem expedient; to inspect the conduct of any inhabitants or residents in their respective towns or districts violating the Continental association, the resolves, directions, or recommendations of Congress, the acts or resolves of the General Court, or the proceedings of former Congresses of this Colony, respecting the struggle with Great Britain; to proceed according to the direction of Congress, and the laws and resolves of this Colony in such cases made and provided; to inform the General Court or the Council of all breaches of trust in the officers of state and other servants of the Colony; to use their influence in promoting peace and harmony; and, finally, to execute any order and resolves of this Court to them directed."

On the 6th of October, the Continental Congress, addressing the committees of inspection, empowered them to arrest and secure every person in their opinion endangering their Colony or the liberties of America.

On the 19th of August, 1776, the committees were directed by the General Court, —

> "To take possession of the personal and real estate of persons who had, in their opinion, fled to Boston — when in the possession of Gen. Gage — in the late times of trouble, to secure themselves, or have joined our enemies, or have withdrawn themselves out of the country with a view to aid their despotic measures; to take and let out such estates for one year, making an inventory of the personal property, and returning it with the rent of the real estate to the General Court; and to return a list of addressors, associates, and other unfriendly persons; and also the names and crimes of those who have fled to the British fleet or army, together with the evidence of facts against such persons, unless they have given proof of contrition, and made satisfaction to the public."

Afterwards, the Court empowered the committees to "send for, examine," and at their discretion cite, any person before a court of inquiry, and to prosecute their complaints to final judgment and execution.

By several resolves they were empowered "to call together regimental and alarm lists, and the train-bands of their respective towns, and, as some think, to execute law martial, while others think these resolves give no power to draft men, and refuse service under them."

The General Court also directed the committees to enforce the Test Act, the embargo on provisions, and similar laws; empowered them to remove stock, grain, and meal from exposed places, to return the names of persons skilled in making "flynts," and to regulate the price of salt.

In August, 1776, they were authorized by the Council to see that prisoners of war were kept within the limits assigned them, to supervise their conduct in general, and if they were found strolling, were refractory, or refused to work, to confine them in jail. In the same month, the Council exhorted them to exert themselves in executing the laws and orders concerning the Tories; and, about the same time, Congress enacted that none might discipline Tories or persons unfriendly to liberty, except by order of Congress, the General Assembly, Convention, Council of Safety of the Colony, or the committee of inspection of the district where they resided.

The authors of the report, apparently somewhat startled by the magnitude of the powers which had accumulated in the committees, — personal liberty, property, and perhaps even life itself, having been placed in their hands, — naturally urged that the most discreet prudent, and firm persons should be preferred to an office so liable to abuse, and of such vast importance if rightly administered. And as the General Court, being practically the only tribunal of appeal from the action of the committees,[1] was flooded with petitions for redress, an enactment was recommended, authorizing an appeal — with proper provisions for the immediate safety of public interests — to the Court of General Sessions, as well to relieve the General Court from business more properly belonging

[1] The action of the committees rarely differed from what the public sentiment of their respective towns approved; and an appeal from one to the other was not likely to secure any very valuable result to the appellant.

elsewhere as to provide a more easy and summary method of attaining the ends of justice.

In those counties where the authority of the General Court was fully admitted, the committees were thus brought into subordination to the ordinary courts of law, and, although an extraordinary, were not an inharmonious portion of the judicial system.

In Berkshire, also, the committees zealously executed the rules and orders which have been quoted, kept faithful watch and ward against both the internal and external enemies of their country, and rendered the best aid they could give in the collection of the taxes levied by the State. But, while they accepted and faithfully performed the duties assigned them by Congress and the General Court, they held that their powers were derived from a higher source, and exercised them as well in resisting the authority of the General Court when it conflicted with their paramount allegiance to the little town democracies, or to the county congresses when the towns consented to delegate their sovereignty to those assemblies. Under the commission of the town meetings, the committees continued until 1780 to exercise the jurisdiction which had been instituted to meet the necessities of 1774, in maintaining public order and restraining crimes and misdemeanors, as well as in guarding against and punishing the political offences of the partisans either of the king or of the non-constitutional civil administration of the State.

All the functions of the Court of General Sessions fell to the committees, except the control of such matters — the granting of licenses, laying-out of highways, and the like — as are now intrusted to the county commissioners; these latter the towns managed like ordinary municipal affairs.

It appears, also, that the committees "interfered" in civil cases which in ordinary times would have gone to the Common Pleas; for in 1776 the town, offended with Capt. Charles Goodrich for his adhesion to the obnoxious State government, instructed them not only not to take into consideration the action brought by him against certain young men for taking "watermillions" in 1774, but also "not to intermeddle in the affair between him and Ezra Strong relative to their water-mill."[1]

[1] The suit of Charles Goodrich against Ezra Strong, John Strong, and Warham Strong, in a plea wherein the said Goodrich demands one-quarter of a corn-mill standing on a stream of water which runs from the farm of said Ezra, was the

We have also the evidence, to the same effect, of Hon. Timothy Woodbridge, who, in his memorial of 1776, pointedly, and no doubt with truth, alleged that "the committees assumed to themselves jurisdiction in civil as well as criminal cases."

The committee alluded to in the Goodrich case was probably the board of arbitrators before mentioned. How long that board continued in existence we are not informed.

There is nothing, however, to show by what process civil cases were brought before the Pittsfield committees, nor by what rules of practice, or formalities of any kind, it guarded the exercise of its functions as a court of civil jurisdiction. And there is little to indicate of what classes of suits it consented to take cognizance, or whether it refused its intervention in any, save when the parties had outlawed themselves by adherence to the king, or by siding with the State against the committees. The Goodrich case, before cited, shows that refusal of protection in person or property was considered a legitimate mode of punishing political maleficence.[1] Protection to the rights of property, and the enforcement of the obligations of contracts, must have forced themselves upon the attention of the Revolutionary committees, as duties inevitably devolving upon those who seized the reins of government, and only to be postponed while the suspension of the courts was expected to be of brief duration. They did not, nevertheless, so far as we have information, take it upon themselves, like the Courts of Common Pleas, to compel the performance of obligations between man and man as such; but punished their violations as misdemeanors detrimental to the public interests, with whose care they were charged.

Obloquy would have surely fallen, both upon the obstruction of the courts and upon the party by which they were obstructed, if any had been permitted to pervert that measure to ends obviously selfish and unjust; and he who attempted to do so rendered himself amenable to the inspection of the committees.

With this view of their duties, these tribunals would aim at sub-

second on the docket at the re-opening of the Court of Common Pleas; the plaintiff being one of the judges, although, of course, not sitting when he was a party in the case. The jury found for Goodrich, and the Strongs appealed; but, apparently, the appeal was not sustained, as the case does not again appear on the Common Pleas docket.

[1] Outlawry, it must be remembered, was then, and is still, a part of the punishment of treason under British law.

stantial justice, or what would seem such to the popular judgment, rather than at a strict application of the law to the evidence. Thus they would aid in the collection of debts which they considered honestly due, when the debtor was able to make payment, and the creditor had not outlawed himself as a public enemy.

It is very easy to see that a substitute for courts of law so loose as this was, even in the hands of well-meaning men, liable to be made the instrument of gross injustice, and sure to create uncertainty and confusion in business relations. That it was so in Berkshire was confessed in the address to the superior judges, written by Mr. Allen, and adopted by the county convention of 1779, in which it is said, "We always had a sense of the necessity of law, especially in times of war: we feel the want of a due exercise of it, and in many instances the sad effects of not enjoying it." The fathers of Berkshire were by no means insensible to nor unregretful of the evils which they consented to endure rather than submit to the permanent establishment of a government without basis or limitation.

In its oversight of misdemeanors and minor morals, the Pittsfield Committee rule does not seem to have fallen at all short of the General Sessions and magistracy of earlier times. The town, indeed, through this and other agencies, kept rather a more stringent watch and ward than ever, both over its own citizens and the stranger that dwelt within its gates. In March, 1777, it ordered that "persons sixteen years old and over, who profaned the sabbath day by behaving indecently in the house of God in time of public worship, or otherwhere out of doors, should be by the tithing-man, or any other informing officer finding them so doing, *convented* before proper authority for trial, and punishment if found guilty." Children under sixteen, offending in the same way, were to be brought into the "broad alley," and there kept until the close of divine service. In addition to this, Rev. Mr. Allen was "desired by the town to speak aloud to such persons as should be found disorderly or *asleep* in the time of divine service on the sabbath day, and reprimand them for the same."

On the 12th of August, in the same year, it was voted, "that the practice of horse-racing is attended with many evil consequences, is productive of much mischief, and is totally contrary to the sense and approbation of this town; and that all persons who shall hereafter encourage, abet, or promote such evil practices shall not only be held in contempt in this town, but have their names published as persons counteracting and opposing the advice of the Honorable Continental Congress."[1]

The soldiers of Burgoyne's army, who, when taken prisoners, were hired as laborers by the citizens, were also objects of the town's solicitude; and, in August of 1778, it was "ordered, that if any of the foreign soldiers that are among us shall, after sunset, be seen sixty rods from the houses in which they respectively dwell, they shall be whipped at the discretion of the committee, and, upon a repetition of the offence, be committed to the common jail;" and "all innkeepers were forbidden to permit the said people to tipple in their houses, upon pain of the displeasure of the town." And the displeasure of the town, as then visited upon the offender, was not lightly to be challenged.

The judicial affairs of Pittsfield were thus administered until October, 1778, when the county having, with unusual deliberation and emphasis, again rejected the civil administration of the State, a more formal establishment for the administration of justice, with better-defined rules of practice, was deemed advisable; and a tribunal was established with all the powers of the old General Sessions, Chief-Justice Williams of the suspended Court of Common Pleas being placed at its head. The action of the town erecting the new tribunal was so characteristic, that it is well to here insert the record in full: —

MASSACHUSETTS BAY.

BERKSHIRE, SS.

Whereas the county of Berkshire, by a great majority of votes, have refused the admission of the course of law in its usual form; and whereas disorders of various kinds increase and abound amongst us, and there being no effectual way provided for the prevention thereof unless by the intervention and exertions of particular towns; and it being of the utmost importance that peace and good order be maintained and supported, — it is by this town resolved, —

1st. That the Selectmen and Constables, tithingmen, and all town-officers annually chosen by towns in the month of March, shall be upheld, supported, and protected by this town in the due execution of their respective trusts as by law prescribed and enjoined them.

[1] At the time of the Revolution, some of the people of Pittsfield were addicted to horse-racing, and had a course near the present Berkshire Pleasure Park. It was suppressed in accordance with the Continental Articles of Association, but was revived and flourished after peace was restored.

2d. That Col. William Williams, Dea. Josiah Wright, Capt. Eli Root, Capt. William Francis, and William Barber, be a committee, under oath to be administered by the town clerk, to hear and determine all breaches of peace and misdemeanors which, by the laws of this State now enacted and made cognizable by a justice of the peace or two justices (*quorum unus*), or by the the Court of General Sessions in all those cases where an appeal was by said laws the right of the defendant in the manner hereafter mentioned, to wit: in all cases where a justice of the peace by the law had the sole and final determination of the cause, the said committee to have the same power; and, in all cases where an appeal by law was grantable, the second and final trial to be by a jury of six men, if requested by the defendant. The determination of said jury shall be final and conclusive; which jury shall be formed and impanelled in this manner: —

The committee to nominate twelve men, being freeholders in this town, and the defendant twelve more; out of which number, six are to be drawn by the constable if present, or, in his absence, by such person as the committee shall appoint for the purpose. And, in case any person so nominated and drawn shall neglect or not be able to serve, the constable, or such person as shall be appointed by the committee, shall return a sufficient number of the bystanders to make up such deficiency.

3d. That any one of the committee be empowered to administer oaths to all witnesses who shall be called before them, in the usual form, and also to administer the following oath to the jurors who may attend upon any trial as afore mentioned, to wit: —

"You shall well and truly try, and true deliverance make between the people and prisoner now upon trial. So help you God."

4th. Whereas, the case of bastardy may be considered by the committee as cognizable by them by virtue of the second resolve, and as this case is exempt and distinct from all the cases which may come before them, it is voted, that the committee use their best discretion in all matters of this sort as the circumstances of the case may require.

5th. That, in all cases where by law fines and mulcts are to be inflicted for any offence, the said committee impose and order such fines to be paid, making the common and usual discount betwixt money as it now passes, and as it formerly passed, or as it may be at the time of trial; and that, in all cases where imprisonment is by law the punishment to be inflicted for any offence, the committee be empowered to inflict corporeal punishment according to the nature of the offence, not exceeding thirty-nine stripes for any offence.

6th. That the constable or constables for the time being shall serve and execute all warrants and processes of said committee or of either of them, and make due return thereof, and observe and obey all such orders as from time to time they shall receive from the said committee.

7th. That the said committee have power to appoint a clerk to attend them, and keep fair records of all their proceedings.

8th. That all retailers of spirituous liquors and all innholders be approbated by the selectmen of the town and licensed by the committee, and that no persons be authorized or qualified to be retailers or innholders unless so approbated and licensed.

9th. That all fines arising in consequence of the foregoing resolves shall be paid into the treasury of the town for the use of the town.

10th. That this town will support and uphold the committee above named in the due execution of the trust committed to them by the foregoing articles and resolves.

11th. That when any person shall be found guilty of any offence, and shall not forthwith, after the conviction and sentence, pay the charges and costs arising upon his trial such as shall be taxed by the committee agreeable to the rule hereafter given, the constable, by virtue of a warrant from the committee for that purpose, shall take and sell at a public vendue so much of his personal effects as shall be sufficient to defray said costs, and costs of sale, returning the overplus, if any there be, to the defendant; and, in case the defendant hath not estate wherewith to pay and defray such costs, he shall be disposed of in service for the payment of the same.

12th. That when it shall appear to the committee that any person commences a vexatious and malicious prosecution against another, and shall fail in supporting the same, he shall be liable to pay costs as aforesaid, and to be recovered in the manner above prescribed.

13th. That the committee above named exercise the power and authority wherewith they are hereby invested until the next March meeting, or until others shall be chosen in their room.

14th. That three of the foregoing committee shall be a quorum, and that no defendant shall in his bill of charge be feed for the attendance of any greater number.

A table of costs to be taxed by the committee in such cases as may come before them: —

The committee each per day	1*l.*	4*s.*	0*d.*
Warrant	0	6	0
Summons for witnesses	0	3	0
Summons for jurors	0	4	0
Clerk's attendance per day	0	4	0
Writ or warrant of execution	0	6	0
Constable fees, —			
Service of a warrant	0	3	0
Summons	0	2	0
Travel from defendant's place of abode to the place of trial, per mile	0	1	0
Attendance on a trial per day	0	18	0
Constable's necessary assistants per day	0	18	0

Jurors each per day	0*l.* 18*s.* 0*d.*
Witnesses' travel per mile	0 1 0
Attendance per day	0 18 0

Accepted,

WILLIAM WILLIAMS, *Per Order.*

At a legal adjourned meeting of the freeholders and other inhabitants of the town of Pittsfield, qualified to vote in town affairs, at the meeting-house in said town, on the nineteenth day of October, 1778, the foregoing resolves were read and accepted.

Attest: JOSIAH WRIGHT, *Moderator.*

CALEB STANLEY, *Town Clerk.*

We have no information of any cases tried in the town court established by the foregoing action; but of the previous doings of the committee several instances are more or less fully recorded, some of which, in regard to the Tories, are related in connection with their story.

But the most remarkable case was the attempt of the town to discipline Capt. Charles Goodrich for opposition to its policy in the matter of the State government. The election of this gentleman in 1775 to the General Court, where he was one of those careful to secure their own appointment to civil office, has already been mentioned. Capt. Israel Dickinson, elected high sheriff at the same time, declined to serve in opposition to the will of the people, and received their favor; but Goodrich, who was elevated to the populous bench of the General Sessions, clung to his commission, although the court was not permitted to sit. The consequence was, that in June, 1776, the town forbade him longer to represent them; to which he paid no attention. In February, they made against him the mild decree of outlawry, in connection with his lawsuits already alluded to; and, in May, they expressed by resolution their opposition to his "sustaining a civil commission," and instructed their committee to petition the General Court that the people might have the right of nomination, i.e., the right to choose their own magistrates.

Thus far the town record: but, at the September session of the Court, Capt. Goodrich presented a memorial, in which he related the story of his wrongs so piteously that they might have moved hearts less disposed to sympathy than those to which he appealed; declaring, that, on the 25th of March, the town committee assumed the power to hear, judge, and assess both private and public damages against him, for defending himself with blows when previously assaulted by one James Morey, who was probably engaged in executing some process of the committee, and that, in the course of the affair, he was forcibly dragged out of his house, and carried, late at night, before the committees, by a number of men claiming to act under their authority, and there detained until he gave a written agreement to pay the adjudged damages and costs; that, upon a late raising of every twenty-fifth man, he was informed, by report only, that he was ordered by the commissioned officers of Pittsfield either to serve as a drafted man or furnish a substitute; and that afterwards, being cited to appear before the committee to answer to a complaint not specified, he neglected to do so, supposing himself not bound thereto either in law, equity, or common prudence; whereupon he found his name included in a list given to John Graves, a notorious Tory, as one of those persons inimical to his country, with whom he was forbidden to hold intercourse; and also published, with a similar charge, in "The Hartford Courant" of Sept. 2, 1776.

Capt. Goodrich did not directly ask for redress in the matter of the costs and damages, but stated, that, in the publications named, his character had been "maliciously stabbed," and would suffer, until an impartial hearing could be had; and, the civil affairs of the county being so nearly in a state of nature that he could not then have such protection as society was instituted to give, he prayed the interposition of the legislature.

The committee having made answer to this complaint, the Council found that the principal reasons which they alleged for their proceedings against the memorialist were, that "he had procured himself a commission, in the king's name, to exercise authority over the people as a justice of the peace," which they seem to have considered as "submitting to the British authority;" his not paying proper attention when he was drafted in the alarm-list to serve in the expedition against Canada; and his having "joined himself with the most ancient Tories and implacable enemies among us."

This may have been a candid synopsis of the response from Pittsfield; but we cannot help regretting that the paper had not been preserved in full, so that we might have seen precisely how the committee put its defence, since it probably relied upon arguments which the Council were fain to consider foreign to the purpose. Their Honors, however, who may almost be regarded as judging their own case in that of their appointee, found that "Capt. Goodrich received his commission as justice from the major part of the Council, of such a tenor and form as they judged it proper to adopt, and such, as far as they could learn, as was agreeable to the practice of the other colonies, and agreeable to the sèntiments of Congress; and that the committee, therefore, in exhibiting this charge, discovered an entire ignorance of their line of duty, and great indecency towards the constituted authorities of the State."

With regard to the second charge, the Council excused Capt. Goodrich on the ground that he "did not consider himself liable to draft under the law;" and they declared the allegation that he consorted with Tories too general and unsupported by evidence to merit attention. And finally they resolved, with the concurrence of the House, "that Charles Goodrich, Esq., ought not to be stigmatized as an enemy to his country; but that, on the other hand, we consider him a friend to the rights of mankind, and the grand cause in which these United States are at present engaged."

This result was a natural one, as the judges were the very power for sustaining whose rightfulness Capt. Goodrich suffered; and the justice of their conclusion, regarded from their stand-point, was indisputable. Nor will any one at this day be inclined to doubt the sincere patriotism of the accused. We need not again recapitulate the reasons which inclined the Berkshire constitutionalists to place a different estimate upon his character. Political rancor, and perhaps personal dislike as well, gave them a weight which the calmness of after years denies.

If the action of the General Court had any effect in Pittsfield, it certainly was not in the direction of favor to their client: for on the 15th of October, in defiance of the legislative decision in the previous month, Capt. Goodrich was again summoned to attend the town meeting; and, not responding, six men were sent to "desire him to come, and, should he still refuse, to bring him forth." What the success of this expedition was, is not related. Very likely the stout-hearted old pioneer, who in the French war had transformed his house into a castle, now made his defence so formidable as to suggest delay in "bringing him forth." The meeting ordered a guard at his residence that night, and, after thanking the gentlemen from Lenox — the committee of that town — for their attendance, adjourned to the 19th. No mention is made of the presence of the defendant on that day; but the witnesses were examined, and it was resolved, "that it appeared from their evidence, that Capt. Goodrich, in his late conduct, had acted inimical to the cause of these States."

An "advertisement" was offered by the committee, and approved by the town. And thus the quarrel continued to be waged in "The Hartford Courant;" for the assailed was not one to suffer in silence what he considered a wrong.

But at Christmas, 1778, the lucky thought — inspired, perhaps, by the season consecrated to peace on earth and good will among men — occurred to some sensible fellow to get the controversy terminated by arbitration. On the 1st of January, 1779, the plan was adopted, and the following gentlemen, all eminent for integrity and good sense, were selected as referees: Col. Job Safford of Cheshire, Col. William Whiting of Great Barrington, and Gen. John Fellows of Sheffield; with James Harris, Esq., of Lanesborough, to fill the place of either of those first named who might fail to serve.

One of the conditions of the reference was, that the party which was found to have wronged the other should pay the costs of arbitration.

The arbitrators met at Col. Easton's tavern on the 8th of January; all the gentlemen named, including Mr. Harris, being present. Valentine Rathbun, Capt. James Noble, and Deacon Josiah Wright managed the case for the town. "After due investigation," says the award, it was decided that the parties had mutually wronged each other; but that as, on the whole, Capt. Goodrich had been the worst aggressor, he should be adjudged to pay the entire costs, which were taxed at £35. 9*s*. 6*d*." This decision practically recognized the rightfulness of the Berkshire opposition to the existing State government; for otherwise Capt. Goodrich would have been entirely justified, the town entirely in the wrong. While admitting the right of the county to oppose the non-constitutional civil administration, the coincident right to enforce that opposition followed of necessity; and the only ground of complaint which remained to Capt. Goodrich was the unjust imputation upon his character as a patriot. The publications on behalf of the town in "The Hartford Courant," so far as they related to his case, were not only unjust, but disingenuous, weak, and quibbling; placing the defence of the committee's action upon the lack of unessential formalities on the part of the legislature, and denying statements which the writers well knew to be substantially correct, because their allegations were made without technical precision. The style of composition, the logic, and the spirit of the committee's articles, all show that minds were engaged in the management of the case of a very different cast from those whose arguments, clearly stated, and founded upon great principles, have been quoted in our discussion of the Berkshire troubles.

The result of the arbitration was acquiesced in by both parties, apparently without objection; and the reconciliation which followed was cordial. Capt. Goodrich received honorable trusts from the next and following town meetings, and lived long, a respected citizen of the town. From 1781 to 1788, he was a judge of the county Court of Common Pleas. Thirty-three years after the termination, in 1778, of his political vexations, he held the plough at the first cattle-show of the Berkshire Agricultural Society. In 1815, he died at the age of ninety-six, and lies buried in the Pittsfield cemetery.

CHAPTER XXI.

THE SHAYS REBELLION.

1781–1786.

Its Causes. — Taxes. — Private Debts. — Harsh Laws and Customs. — County Conventions. — Popular Outbreaks. — Organized Rebellion. — The Peculiar Course of Berkshire County. — Convention at Lenox. — Courts obstructed at Great Barrington. — Gen. Lincoln establishes Headquarters at Pittsfield. — The Rebellion suppressed.

THE Constitution of 1780 was not permitted to have a fair trial before it was assailed by an opposition which, in 1786, culminated in the Shays Rebellion, — a popular convulsion which, although some of its features gave it a *vraisemblance* to the Berkshire troubles of 1775-80, essentially differed from them in principle and character; the earlier agitation having, in behalf of constitutional liberty, resisted the imposition of a government without basis or limitation, while the latter sought, by force of arms, to reform real or supposed grievances, for which the Constitution just established by the people provided a sufficient remedy through ordinary legislation.

The one movement was an attempted imitation of the other by men who entirely mistook its spirit and justification, or by demagogues who took advantage of the ignorance of others. But the resemblance of the two in some non-essentials, together with their proximity in time, will only serve to throw into stronger relief their intrinsic dissimilarity of character.

The popular ferment which prompted the Shays Rebellion had its origin chiefly in the circumstances of the Commonwealth at the close of the Revolution with regard to public and private indebtedness; aggravated by the harshness with which, by law and custom, debts and taxes were at that time collected. The acts in which that feeling manifested itself were the result of a false interpretation of precedent, and of the crude political knowledge of men who perceived clearly — what the experience of every day taught them — that they and their fellows were harshly dealt with, but who had not learned to trace effects to their causes with statesmanlike sagacity, and who did not comprehend that the same means which, in default of better, are legitimate for the overthrow of an oppressive government, become heinous offences when applied to the reform of even oppressive laws under the plastic institutions of a republic.

The financial situation of the Commonwealth was indeed most distressing, and such as, even in the most hopeful view, could find no perfect relief, except in long years of toil, endured by its people under the depressing influences of debt and enormous taxation. It seemed inevitable that the greater portion of the generation then living must go down to their graves in poverty, leaving the same bitter heritage to their children.

The debt of the State, contracted in its own name, was $4,333,000, exclusive of $833,000 due to the officers of the Massachusetts contingent in the army, which was as just a liability, to say the least, as any other. The Commonwealth's proportion of the national debt, for which, under the Confederation, it was specifically responsible, was not less than $5,000,000; making an aggregate of considerably over $10,000,000.

Besides this, every town was heavily indebted for money expended in local exigencies, such as filling quotas of men, demands for military supplies, &c. The payment of the interest alone upon this crushing accumulation of liabilities was an undertaking which might well have daunted the financiers of the impoverished State, even at a time of happier promise for the future; but the unwise impatience of the people, dissatisfied with paying interest, which was compared with a canker which consumed their substance without lessening their burdens, led to the imposition in 1784 of a tax of $466,000, and in 1786 of $333,000 additional, for the purpose of sinking that amount of the army debt.

As might have been expected, all the taxes were soon found to be largely and hopelessly in arrears, notwithstanding the depreciation of the certificates of indebtedness issued by the State treasury, which were made receivable for them.

But the tax-gatherer was not the only unwelcome visitor that was wont to haunt the doors of the citizens of Massachusetts in those unhappy days: the tap of the sheriff or the constable was no less familiar. Private debts which had, for various reasons, been postponed during the war, had accumulated fearfully, and a mania for bringing suits upon them seemed to possess creditors; so that the courts were fairly clogged with business.

No condition of things could have been imagined more unfavorable to the imposition of heavy taxes, and the collection of long-standing debts, than that which then existed in Massachusetts. A paralysis seemed to have struck the young vigor of the Commonwealth, for whose cure time, and a process quite other than depletion, were required. The febrile symptoms which manifested themselves everywhere were the pure results of exhaustion.

The sanctity of property and the obligations of contracts had become impaired, not from the license of the people, nor because courts were obstructed in Berkshire or elsewhere, but from the unsettling of values through the excessive, however unavoidable, emission of paper money, and from the legislation which vainly attempted to sustain its credit. Gold and silver had, long before the war closed, disappeared as a circulating medium; and the faith of the nation, which has since been found to furnish a not entirely inadequate substitute, was without the basis to do so then. The Continental currency, despite the exhausting efforts of Massachusetts to redeem her proportion of it, was fast sinking to an unappreciable value, and encumbered rather than facilitated the course of trade, until the only practicable relief was found in the formal recognition of its entire worthlessness.

Under circumstances of such overwhelming depression, manufactures, which, under the stimulus of the war, had attained a somewhat vigorous growth, now languished; the fisheries, fearfully narrowed in their markets, ceased to be that source of wealth which had enriched the Province; agriculture afforded but a scanty subsistence to farmers without the means of improving or stocking their lands, which were, indeed, in many cases, hopelessly mortgaged; while commerce had come to be little more than the means of draining what little of hoarded treasure yet remained in the State in payment for goods imported from markets which required few of the productions of Massachusetts in return.

We should fail to complete the picture of desolation without adding, that thriftless habits acquired in camp-life found little in the condition of things at home to stimulate or encourage reformation, and that intemperance prevailed to an extent which had never before been known, nor has been since.

Other results incident to a long and costly war conspired to inflame the discontent of the masses. Those who had served the great cause most faithfully had generally become impoverished, while men who deserved little had grown wealthy, and, for the most part, had invested what they had gained from the necessities of their country in something more substantial than the worthless paper which clogged the knapsack of the returning soldier and the hoard of the rural patriot.

In Boston, Salem, Newburyport, and other large towns, the ostentatious display of wealth and luxury by men of this class by successful naval adventures, and by others whom chance had favored in the general wreck, contrasted harshly with the struggling poverty of those whose long years of exposure and suffering had been cheered by the hope of a recompense very different from that which they received.

It may perhaps be pardoned to these latter, that some of them did not trace the causes of their disappointment with the nicety, or seek a remedy for it with the calm sagacity, of philosophers. They had left men at home charged with the care of these things; and their wisdom seemed almost as much confounded by the miserable entanglement of affairs as was their own; although it soon began to manifest itself in legislation which gradually brought, not only safety, but prosperity and harmony, to the Commonwealth.

Few are fully aware of the vast miseries which have been alleviated, and fewer still comprehend the measure of strength and stability which has been added to the State during the past seventy-five years, by the tender regard shown for the poor and unfortunate, even more in the amelioration of laws and customs than in the institutions provided for the direct relief of suffering.

When the Constitution of 1780 went into effect, the legal hardships of the poor were such as required years of liberal legislation for their relief; and how difficult it was to procure that legislation, the Pittsfield reader may learn by examination of the files of "The Sun," which for years was filled with pleadings for the abolition or mitigation of imprisonment for debt, by arguments which, although they seem simple enough now, were persistently resisted then.

The laws in force, and the customs universally in vogue, for the collection of debts and taxes, were cruel and irrational to a degree which almost passes belief; and they were carried out with less compunction than is now often wasted upon the fate of the most worthless criminal. Imprisonment for debt had no alleviation; and the sole remedy devised for inability to pay was enforced idleness. The prison-doors closed more remorselessly upon the poor debtor than upon the thief or the incendiary; for while bail or pardon might obtain the enlargement of the former, whose confinement at the worst had a fixed duration, no laws for his relief opened the prison-door of the latter, or fixed a period to his incarceration within walls where too little regard was had to health, comfort, or decency. His only hope — and a long-deferred one it often proved — was that his creditor might at last despair of extorting payment from the pity of his friends, or that his resentment might finally exhaust itself.

There are many yet living who remember how their young eyes were shocked by the gaunt forms, long, unkempt hair, grizzly beard, and claw-like hands, of men who, with sunken eyes, peered from behind grated windows, where they had lain for years, guilty of no worse crime than the incurring of a trifling debt, which, perhaps, some unforeseen political or commercial convulsion had rendered them unable to pay; and, in 1786, not a few of these poor creatures, blue with prison mould, were those who had fought long for freedom, and were still largely the creditors of the country whose laws made them the tenants of a debtor's jail.

But if, by chance, the poor man escaped a prison, and, despairing of a livelihood in his native place, sought it elsewhere, he was pretty sure to be met at the threshold of his land of promise by some such welcome as the following warrant, which we copy from the Pittsfield town-records, where the like are thickly scattered:—

BERKSHIRE, ss.

To the Constables of the Town of Pittsfield in the County of Berkshire, or either of them, greeting.

Whereas it has been represented to us that Elisha Eggleston, his wife and family; John French, his wife and family; Calvin Dunham, his wife and family, — are likely to become burdensome and chargeable to the town if they continue their residence in it, these are therefore to authorize and require you forthwith to warn and notify the above-named persons that they, with their families, immediately depart and remove out of the town, and not to return again, without giving security to the town.

Given under our hands this 22d day of May, Anno Domini 1782.

WOODBRIDGE LITTLE,
DAVID BUSH,
STEPHEN CROFOOT,
JAMES DN. COLT,
Selectmen of Pittsfield.

Constable Stephen Fowler returned service of this warning upon John and Calvin on the 7th of June; and doubtless they, their wives and little ones, thereupon resumed their weary pilgrimage; for, in default of obedience to the warning, the hard law required that the delinquents should be passed from constable to constable through the intervening towns, until they reached that of their proper settlement.

Eggleston appears to have obtained a respite: but in the more dreary month of February, 1784, he received a similar warning out, together with Isaac Churchill, his wife and nine children; Daniel Wheeler, his wife and seven children; Deborah Burrage, *alias* Deborah Lee, widow; Moses Lee, and several other unfortunates, who were suspected of circumstances which rendered them liable to become chargeable to the town. One can well comprehend that new-comers, with no other means of support than their daily labor, would be less welcome in those days of stagnant industries than they had been in the labor-dearth of war-times.

But while the poor were thus driven from pillar to post, and from post to pillar, in their struggles to better their condition, or at least "to keep the wolf from the door," taxation rested upon them with a weight which would now be considered grossly disproportionate; and the rates were exacted with a rigor which we should regard impolitic, as well as unmerciful.

Of all the taxes which the circumstances of the State demanded, as well as those large additions which were made without absolute necessity, one third part was assessed upon the ratable polls, which did not then number more than ninety thousand; and town charges were defrayed in a similar manner.

The severity with which these rates were collected, and the readiness of the courts to enforce the payment of debts due from towns, are illustrated in a case which, although it was in some respects extraordinary, was far from an extreme one.

Rev. Mr. Leavitt of Charlemont, a suspected Tory in politics and Arminian in religion, in 1777, on account of the depreciation of the currency, refused to receive his salary at the rate originally agreed upon; and, after various unsuccessful attempts at a compromise, the town voted to shut up the meeting-house, which was done, the constable guarding it. Upon this, Mr. Leavitt betook himself to a schoolhouse, where he preached to a few friendly families until more peaceful times, when he sued the town for his whole arrears of salary. He was nonsuited at the Common Pleas, but, on appeal to the Supreme Court, recovered £500; which sum was levied on the property of the inhabitants, from many of whom the last cow was taken to satisfy the claim of a minister whom they believed both a heretic and traitor, for preaching sermons of which they never heard a syllable.

Add to the picture we have attempted in the preceding pages, that which was given in a previous chapter of the onerous judicial system which the Commonwealth had inherited almost unchanged from the Province, and we shall be able to form some conception of the inflammatory condition of Massachusetts which developed itself in the Shays Rebellion.

The aspect of the general government offered still less of cheer. The shadowy powers of the Confederation had now reached that extreme of tenuity which compelled a resort to the forlorn hope — glorious as it proved — of the convention which framed the Federal Constitution. The confusion had grown to be utter. National credit, respect, power, and influence were rapidly approaching the vanishing point. Congress could do little to rescue either, and, with very inadequate powers to resist invasion, confessed itself destitute of any to suppress internal insurrection.

Imposts upon foreign trade, a prolific source of wealth to national treasuries, proved of little worth, when, the perquisites of rival seaport States, they were imposed by conflicting legislation, whose infinitely unwise attempts each to monopolize commerce and manufactures mutually ruined the interests it was their object to advance.

The citizen of Massachusetts who found gloom and confusion in the affairs of the Commonwealth, if he looked to the national government for relief was met by absolute darkness and chaos. The boundless hope which, in the Colony times, had been the dower of every American citizen, now awaited a more splendid resurrection under the Union, but no signs yet betokened the coming of the dawn.

Public affairs, which in their healthy condition exercise their benign powers imperceptibly, become, in their deranged state, even more apparently than really, the cause of individual misfortune; and governments are charged with malign influences for which they are not justly responsible. It so happened in Massachusetts at the epoch of which we write. There was lurking in the minds of the great mass of those who had returned poor from service in the Revolution, the not unnatural thought, "To what purpose have our blood and suffering secured the liberties of our country if our own are to be at the mercy of the tax-gatherer, the sheriff, and the jailer, or if, escaping from them, we are to be the serfs of toil which barely procures us a scanty subsistence, with a poorhouse for the hope of our age?"

In this prevailing discontent, there were not wanting men willing to make themselves leaders. Of these, the most prominent seem to have been sincerely convinced of the justice of their cause, but the victims of an overweening conceit of their ability to cope with the most knotty problems of state, or of that fanaticism which finds the root of every evil in the subject of its morbid contemplation. Grievances were abundant enough and real enough; but the peculiarity of the malecontent leaders was, that they rarely fastened odium upon any thing which deserved it, never traced an evil to its true source, and that, even before they resorted to arms, the remedies which they proposed for the undeniable sufferings of the people were the veriest nostrums of political quackery. Not one of those beneficent measures by which legislation, beginning soon after, has since removed all the hardships which we have enumerated, was so much as hinted at by the malecontent conventions; hardly one of these hardships was specified by them in their long list of "grievances." Their wrongs were as notional as their remedies were pernicious.

The leaders built their hopes upon a foundation which could sustain no such superstructure. They had seen the assumption of power by county conventions, supplemented by the obstruction of the courts, twice crowned with success; and, not comprehending the change which had been wrought by the adoption of the Constitution in the nature of the allegiance due from the citizen, they undertook to pursue the course which had in other cases led to the desired ends. The Constitution had, indeed, never been permitted to long have quiet sway. As early as 1781, it was represented to the General Court, "that sundry persons in the counties of Worcester, Hampshire, and Berkshire, enemies to their country, were endeavoring to subvert the Constitution of the Commonwealth, and poison the minds of the good people of the State." Commissioners were sent into the counties named to obtain evidence of the treasons concocting there.

Samuel Ely, the leader, was, in the spring of the next year, indicted for attempting, under the authority of a convention, to prevent the session of the Superior Court at Northampton, confessed, and was placed in jail at Springfield, from which he was released by a mob. The ringleaders in this affair were arrested; and, a mob collecting to rescue them, the militia were called out, and rallied with spirit to the number of twelve or fifteen hundred. The rioters were overawed when the parties met on the field, and the disturbance was quieted without bloodshed. But the Tender Act, under which judgment in private suits was satisfied by neat cattle or other specified articles at a fair valuation, followed so close upon the uprising, that, not without plausibility, it was claimed as its result; and the malecontents were encouraged to look upon insurrection as a legitimate as well as very effectual means of obtaining desired legislation. It was not, however, again resorted to for four years.

The conventions continued to be held, and, after 1784, with increasing frequency and violence of agitation. But, for the most part, they confined themselves to peaceable and lawful action; and, however unwise their utterances, they were, in manner and form, such as are now found to be perfectly consistent with the stability of government. We cannot participate at this day in the horror of the conservative historian of that, when he affirms that the conventions "undertook to censure and condemn the conduct of the public rulers; that they voted the Senate and judicial courts to be grievances, and called for a revision of the Constitution." The conservatives of Berkshire took a wiser view, met the malecontents on their own ground, outreasoned them, — a not very difficult feat, — and outvoted them.

A portion of the acts of the Hampshire and Worcester conventions was, according to Minot, of a less defensible character, in that they "attempted to collect a body of men as a general convention [for the revision of the Constitution] which might rival the legislature itself."

The Constitution of 1780, whether wisely or unwisely, made

no provision for its own amendment or revision previous to the year 1795, when the sense of the people was to be taken whether any were required. In the modern view, the absence of any express authority in that instrument would not be construed to impair the right of the legislature to submit the question of revision to the people at any time; but such was not the conservative opinion of 1784, while, as Minot alleges, the malecontent convention was called with the intention of subverting the existing Constitution, without awaiting legislative action. The Berkshire view, as in other cases, coincided with the modern.

Experience has shown, that, the difficulty inevitably arising from the distracted condition of national affairs being obviated by the Federal Union, the evils under which the people of Massachusetts were suffering were all removable through the medium of ordinary legislation, which would have been hindered rather than aided by any change in the fundamental law.

But, in 1786, a large portion of the people, groaning under burdens of which they imperfectly comprehended the nature, and still more imperfectly the remedy, impatient of the slow process and long results of legislative reforms, and suspecting the State government of indifference to their sufferings, were eager for a change in those provisions in the Constitution which, as they imagined, created an aristocratic element in the government, by removing its officers from the direct control of their constituents. Inspired by this idea, a clamor was raised for measures no less radical than the abolition of the Senate, a change in the basis of representation, and the dependence of all officers upon salaries annually granted.

Such were the amendments in the Constitution demanded by a convention in Hampshire County, Aug. 22, 1786; and the reforms upon which they insisted, as within the province of ordinary legislation, were no less radical, and most of them no less unwise, than those enumerated. It was asked that the courts of Common Pleas and General Sessions should be abolished; that the General Court should not sit at Boston; "to have a bank emitted of paper money subject to depreciation,"[1] making it a tender in all

[1] A more exact idea of this hopeful financial scheme will be found from the action of Conway, which, on the 24th of October, "instructed its representative in the General Court to use his influence to have a bank of paper currency emitted that should sink one penny a pound per month." —*Rev. C. B. Rice, in Conway Centennial Address.*

payments equal to gold and silver; that the system of imposing and collecting taxes should be remodelled, the fee-table reduced, and a general reform instituted in managing the finances of the Commonwealth.

They deprecated mob violence, and recommended a resort to only constitutional methods of redress, but denounced the government in terms, which, as their opponents alleged, led to the violent outbreaks which commenced on the last Tuesday of the same month, when nearly fifteen hundred men collected at Northampton, and prevented the session of the court at that place.

Be that as it may, the passions of a large part of the people were so much exasperated by real sufferings and supposed grievances, that the slightest spark was sufficient to set the interior counties aflame. The example of the Hampshire malecontents was followed, with similar success, by their brethren in Worcester and Middlesex; while in Bristol they made a formidable demonstration, which was only checked by the spirited course of the friends of order in the militia.

The course of the Berkshire people was peculiar. The insurgent leaders had evidently modelled their proceedings upon those of this county previous to the adoption of the Constitution, and from this circumstance, as well as from its defensible location, had counted upon this as their stronghold. But the six years' discussion of political and constitutional questions previous to 1780 had rendered the people here more familiar with the great principles of government, and less liable to be misled by false or ignorant teachers, than were those of most portions of the State. The inconsistency of seeking so soon to overthrow the edifice which they had erected at such infinite pains was instinctively felt by those who had been prominent in the struggles for a Constitution; and doubtless they were too familiar with the evils attendant upon an obstruction of the laws to favor a light resort to it. Few of them, therefore, were involved in the Shays insurrection. Rev. Mr. Allen, indeed, was so active in his opposition as to be the special mark of the rebel ire, and found it necessary to keep arms in his bedroom as a precaution when it was most rampart. His earnest preaching against the sin of rebellion at this time won him many bitter and lifelong enemies.

But the leading citizens of Berkshire had learned confidence in the people and in the flexibility of the laws, as well as respect for constitutional authority; and, instead of leaving the convention called in the county to be controlled by those who sought a violent remedy for sufferings perceptible alike to all, they tried their strength before the people, and elected a majority of moderate men. This was more important, as, in the imperfect organization of party politics which then existed, delegates were elected by the towns, and not, as now, by sections of the people, whose opinions alone they are entitled to represent. The County convention then carried with it something of the authority of the municipalities by which its members were chosen, and often instructed; and by many its authority, as being nearer the people, was held paramount to that of the legislature, — a heresy which, although it deserved no respect from the constitutionalists, was an element in the political situation which it was necessary for them to take into account.

The delegates elected from Pittsfield were Daniel Hubbard, Thomas Gold, and Major Oliver Root.

Gold was a demagogue, whose character afterwards came to be understood by the people. His present escapade is described in "The Berkshire Chronicle," printed in Pittsfield in 1789, as "an attempt to overthrow the present system of law and lawyers, and render the practitioners as bad as possible." The other delegates were old soldiers, and men of high character for probity and patriotism. They were themselves in good circumstances for those times, but were deeply imbued with the insurgent spirit through sympathy with the undeserved sufferings of less fortunate comrades.

The delegates were left uninstructed, and were also chosen a Committee of Correspondence for the town. The small number of citizens who at the close of the rebellion were found to have been implicated in it, and the known loyalty of most of the leading men of the town, indicate that the untoward result of this meeting was brought about by the activity of a minority, aided, no doubt, by the apathy or indecision of others.

The convention met at Lenox during the last week of August, while insurrection was raging in the lower counties, and pursued a course peculiar to itself, differing even from that of the people of Boston, who, although showing an admirable spirit and a charitable view of the errors of the insurgents, while entreating them to seek redress for grievances only in a constitutional method, could not truthfully express the same earnest desire for reform which was conspicuous in the Berkshire assembly.

The latter, says Minot, "explicitly approved the appropriation of the revenue arising from the impost and excise duties, and the grant of the supplementary funds to the United States; and they manifested a decent and respectful regard towards the administration of government in general. They disapproved of the plans for establishing paper money and of the Tender Act. They solemnly engaged to use their influence to support the courts of justice in the exercise of their legal powers, and to endeavor to quiet the agitated spirits of the people."

The wisdom of the Berkshire conservatives, in taking part in the county convention, was apparent in its effects; for, had that body given the warrant of its authority, even by implication, to the uprising, hundreds would have joined the ranks of the insurgents, who were now rendered the friends of law and order, or at least restrained from active participation in the disturbances of the day.

It does not appear, from the meagre report of its proceedings, whether the convention gave countenance to any of the preposterous political notions of the malecontents: but the contrary may well be inferred from their opposition to the Tender act; for this, of all the measures with which it was classed, was that least liable to modern censure, and most completely justified by the exigencies of the day. At a time when the circulating medium had been reduced to a point which rendered the possession of any considerable quantity of it impossible to men in ordinary circumstances, this much-maligned act simply provided that executions should be satisfied by property of a marketable kind, taken at a fair valuation, instead of being sacrificed under the hammer, with a moral certainty that it would be sold for a tithe of its value, perhaps being "bid in" by the creditor for a nominal sum, through the sheer inability of the impecunious neighborhood to compete with him. At the worst, a small harm was done to the creditor by the Tender Act in order to shield the debtor from a very grievous one; and it is difficult to see how bankrupt-laws can be justified by those who condemn this old measure of relief to those who would otherwise have suffered from the failure of the Commomwealth to provide a sufficient circulating medium. Its repudiation in the Berkshire convention affords a fair presumption that the follies which were enunciated by the similar assembly in Hampshire were not approved.

The influence of the convention did not, however, avail to save the county from participation in the insurrection; for it had hardly adjourned before a mob collected at Great Barrington, and not only prevented the session of the Court of Common Pleas, but broke open the jail, and released the prisoners. After which exploit they by threats induced three of the judges — among whom was our old friend, Capt. Charles Goodrich, who seems to have lost somewhat of his inflexibility — to sign an agreement that they would not act under their commissions until the grievances complained of had been redressed. To the credit of the fourth judge, Hon. Elijah Dwight of Great Barrington, as well as that of the rioters, it is related, that, upon his making a manful resistance, he was not compelled to sign the papers.

The mob was estimated at eight hundred men.

Traditions of incidents which occurred in Pittsfield and Lenox enable us to understand how the insurgent forces were recruited, and from what material. The village orators, previous to court day, gave out, either plainly or by innuendo, that the session must be prevented; and the word passed from mouth to mouth. On the evening preceding the appointed day, the disaffected farmers in the towns within a convenient distance, — or perhaps throughout the county, — as their men quitted work, said to them, "Well, boys, they say there's to be goings-on at Barrington to-morrow; and, if you like, you can have the day, and take the team and go down." One leader in Pittsfield sent his two sons in this way; and one in Lenox, his son and an apprentice. These were the better class of the insurgents; but in every town there were then an unusual number of unemployed men, ready for whatever excitement offered, and generally hostile to the government, which they regarded as the cause of their evil condition; so that, between those ready for any mischievous frolic and those earnestly hostile to the courts, a boisterous and excited crowd was easily collected, which soon received the additional inflammation of strong drink; and thus fitting instruments were ready to the hands of the designing leaders, who seized the opportunity to commit their followers so deeply to the rebellion that retreat was difficult.

Soon after the affair at Great Barrington, the insurgents, who had hitherto confined their opposition to the inferior courts, now dreading indictment by the Superior Court at Springfield, collected in such numbers at that place, that, although the court was protected by six hundred militia, the confusion was such that it was deemed advisable to adjourn without attempting to transact business, after passing resolutions that it was inexpedient to proceed to Berkshire.

When the day fixed by law for opening the court in this county came, the malecontents, nevertheless, assembled in considerable numbers at Great Barrington, believing, or pretending to believe, that the judges really intended to sit. Of course no court appeared: but the crowd became extremely riotous, and obliged several persons obnoxious to them to take flight; while armed men pursued one gentleman who held a very honorable office, searched private houses, and fired upon several of the inhabitants.[1]

About Christmas, 1786, the insurrectionary disturbances in the lower counties assumed the form of a pronounced rebellion. Daniel Shays, the renowned leader who clouded his fame as a faithful captain in the Revolution for the equivocal honor of giving his name to an unnecessary and unsuccessful rebellion, appeared first at Springfield, then at Worcester and elsewhere, with bands of armed men, of disorderly carriage and fluctuating material, but with some sort of a military organization.

Gov. Bowdoin intrusted the restoration of order to Major-Gen. Benjamin Lincoln, of Revolutionary fame, with a body of over four thousand militia.

Four hundred Berkshire men, under the leadership of Eli Parsons, were in Shays's army; but we know nothing of the recruits from Pittsfield who may have been among them, and we do not purpose to chronicle in detail the operations of the three months' campaign by which the insurrection was suppressed.

The spirit of the rebellion was broken on the 25th of January, when Shays, marching upon the post of Gen. Sheppard at the Springfield Arsenal, was met by a discharge of artillery, which sent his men flying in confusion, crying "Murder," and leaving three of their comrades dead upon the field.[2]

[1] History of Berkshire.

[2] An incident occurred in connection with this affair in which a boy, afterwards a prominent citizen of Pittsfield, was the hero.

Major Solomon Allen of Northampton, upon whom the command of the Hampshire militia, or a portion of it, devolved, dealt largely with Philadelphia drovers; and, when the outbreak occurred, he was in that city, having with him his little son of eight years, afterwards Hon. Phinehas Allen, the founder of "The

So weak at heart was this seemingly formidable uprising, that, upon a check so slight as this, the insurgents fell back from point to point, until they reached Petersham. Here Gen. Lincoln, by a forced march of thirty miles in the midst of a driving snow-storm, surprised them; and those who escaped capture were scattered.

Meanwhile small bodies of the disaffected appeared in Berkshire, with the intention of creating a diversion in favor of their brethren, and, as was feared, of forming a rendezvous upon the heights of the Hoosacs. As a countercheck to this movement, the friends of government formed a voluntary association, numbering perhaps five hundred men, and in slight encounters met with significant success. Still the malecontents, dispersed near Stockbridge, rallied again at South Adams, and, on the approach of the volunteers, scattered at that place to collect again, and again be dispersed, at Williamstown. However unfortunate in their essays, their disposition to embody was apparent; and it was understood that a considerable number were on their way to Washington to join the standard of one Major Wiley.

Gen. Patterson, commander of the Berkshire militia, apprehensive of the results of these movements, earnestly entreated assistance from Lincoln, who responded by promptly repairing to Pittsfield with two divisions of his army.

From this point he sent out parties in sleighs, — one, under the adjutant-general, to Dalton, where they captured Wiley's son and six others, Wiley having fled; one, under Capt. William Francis, to Williamstown, where, after a skirmish, they captured fourteen prisoners. The activity of the troops drove into banishment or concealment all those who had been in arms against the government in Northern Berkshire. But the truculent Eli Parsons, from his hiding-place, sent out an appeal to his "friends and fellow-sufferers" in the lower counties, — a paper of whose sanguinary vein the closing paragraph may convey an idea: —

"The first step I would recommend is to destroy Sheppard's army; then proceed to the county of Berkshire, as we are now collecting in New Leba-

Pittsfield Sun." Summoned home by his military duties, Major Allen reached Springfield in time to take part in the defence of the arsenal.

Here his little son, clad in red broadcloth, the gift of his father's customers, with whom he was a pet, was seated on horseback in the rear of the troops; and when, on the advance of the rebels, fire was opened, the little fellow, carried away with excitement, stretched himself up in the saddle, and gave a ringing huzza, to the great delight of the soldiers, who took up and prolonged the tiny cheer.

non in York State, and Pownal in Vermont State, with a determination to carry our point if fire, blood, and carnage will effect it: therefore we beg that every friend will immediately proceed to the county of Berkshire, and help us to Burgoyne Lincoln and his army."

There was more than mere bravado in this. Berkshire, with inaccessible hills on the east, and States north, south, and west upon whose soil the Massachusetts militia might not trespass, was surrounded by convenient lurking-places, of which the rebels did not neglect to avail themselves, to the great annoyance of the Commonwealth, until the friendly action of the sister States relieved her.

An occasion soon presented itself when an incursion might have been made with almost assured success by a small body of determined men; for the new contingent to supply the place of the militia, whose term of service expired on the 21st of February, not arriving promptly, Gen. Lincoln was left at Pittsfield with only thirty soldiers. The rebels were, happily, not informed correctly of the moment so opportune for them; and the danger passed. But, on the 27th, a body of between eighty and ninety men, under Capt. Perez Hamlin, entered the State from New York, pillaged Stockbridge, made prisoners of some of its most respectable citizens, and proceeded with their prisoners and booty to Great Barrington. Thence they went towards Sheffield in sleighs by a back road. In the mean time, Col. Ashley of Sheffield had collected the loyal militia of that town, and, uniting with a small body who had retreated from Great Barrington, had a force of eighty men.

With these he met the insurgents near the western boundary of Sheffield; and the most severe encounter of the rebellion ensued. The insurgents were defeated, with a loss of two killed and thirty wounded, one mortally; and Capt. William Walker of Lenox coming up opportunely with re-enforcements, one hundred and fifty prisoners were taken. Of the militia, two were killed and one wounded.

The borders of Berkshire, Hampshire, and Worcester remained in a disturbed condition for some months; but the energetic co-operation of the neighboring States, although that of Vermont was somewhat hesitating and tardy, finally removed all sources of apprehension from abroad. On the 13th of August, it was considered safe to reduce the number of troops to two hundred; and, on the 13th of September, the complete suppression of the rebellion was announced by the discharge of all the forces.

The wisdom, moderation, and firmness of Gov. Bowdoin and Gen. Lincoln, and the good conduct of the forces under their command, had saved, not only the Commonwealth, but the country, from dangers which threatened disastrous consequences whose extent it was impossible to foresee, and had relieved a widespread consternation of which it is difficult now to form an idea.

In the suppression of the rebellion, the legislature had co-operated with the executive, on the whole, with zeal and promptitude; although manifesting a natural repugnance to extreme measures against their misguided fellow-citizens. There now remained the more difficult task of re-establishing order, and composing the agitated minds of the people. Justice was to be tempered with mercy in such measure as would not give heart to new outbreaks. The majesty of the law was to be maintained, but in such manner that there should be not even the semblance of a vindictive spirit, either in the legislature or in the courts. Above all, the legislators of the Commonwealth were to enter earnestly upon the work of alleviating the burdens and sufferings which had maddened so many of its most patriotic and well-intentioned citizens. And, in all this, it was to be made apparent that nothing was conceded to intimidation, but that all was done through a sincere desire for the best interests of the people, and a pure regard for substantial justice. It is not our province to discuss in detail the measures by which these ends were sought; but the wisdom and moderation of Massachusetts legislation were never more conspicuous than in their adoption. Sufficient guaranties were exacted for future allegiance to law and order; but what was deemed the minimum of punishment was meted out for past offences. Six of the insurgent prisoners were condemned to death in Berkshire, six in Hampshire, and one each in Worcester and Middlesex; but none suffered that penalty. Of the Berkshire prisoners, three were pardoned, — one of them Samuel Rust, a Pittsfield veteran of the Continental Army, — two escaped, and the sentence of the sixth was commuted to imprisonment for seven years.

Large numbers were, however, convicted of seditious words and practices, many of them persons of consequence in their several localities. Among them was a member of the legislature, who was sentenced to pay a fine of fifty pounds, give security for five years' good behavior, and sit on a gallows with a rope around his neck; all of which sentence was carried out.[1]

Those who had participated in the insurrection were for a time disfranchised, and excluded from the jury-box; but these disabilities were soon removed, the offender being merely required to take the oath of allegiance. Measures of reform in the administration of the laws and of the finances were immediately entered upon, at first with somewhat of the crudity of thought which had prevailed before the insurrection. But the light soon began to break, and gleams of those beneficent reforms which have since prevailed began to streak the horizon. It is not the least among the compensations of the rebellion of 1786, that it directed the more earnest thought of cultivated statesmen to the imperfection of the laws, and to popular content as an element in the strength of government.

[1] The unfortunate legislator was Hon. Moses Harvey, senator from Hampshire County.

CHAPTER XXII.

PITTSFIELD IN THE SHAYS REBELLION.—PAROCHIAL DIFFICULTIES.

[1786–1789.]

Public Sentiment of the Town.—Its Comparative Prosperity.—Prominent Citizens labor for Law and Order.—Henry Van Schaack eulogizes the Town.—The Malecontent Movement modified in Pittsfield.—Instructions to Representative Childs.—A Stormy Town Meeting.—A Conservative Re-Action.—Military Occupation of the Town.—Anecdote.—Parochial Dissensions.—Reconciliation effected.—Joshua Danforth.—Henry Van Schaack.

IN considering the public sentiment which prevailed in Pittsfield during the memorable commotions just related, nice discrimination is required. Tradition affirms that the great majority of the inhabitants were averse to the insurrection; and, while it is certain that the malecontents more than once controlled the town meetings, it is equally clear that only a small fraction of the voters were, at the close of the rebellion, found to have been seriously implicated in it.

The population of the town was about eleven hundred, which would represent at least two hundred voters; but those who are recorded to have taken the oath of allegiance prescribed by the legislature as a condition of re-enfranchisement counted only thirty-one, of whom only eight are minuted as having "turned in their arms." Of these, some denied any guilty connection with the rebellion; and so slight was the evidence against them, that many were found to credit their plea. On the other hand, the names of Thomas Gold, and of two or three others known to have been active rebels, do not appear in the list. But the whole number of whom the oath could justly have been required could hardly have exceeded forty. It should be remarked, however, that some who had been led by a misinterpretation of precedents to consider the obstruction of courts as a very venial offence, if not an altogether justifiable mode of seeking reforms, shrank from the extreme measure of appearing in arms against the government, and especially after a "county congress" had expressly refused its sanction to any but constitutional measures of redress.

The list of thirty-one contains few names familiar to us, except those of the delegates to the county convention; and it is to be observed, that, with the exception of Col. Root and Deacon Hubbard, not one of the men who had been prominent as patriots in the Revolution, or who, as constitutionalists, had resisted the government of the interregnum, is known to have favored the insurrection of 1786; nor did any one of those implicated in the Rebellion ever afterwards rise to much political consequence in the town.

There were substantial reasons why this should be so. Pittsfield, although sharing in a degree in the general depression of affairs, was a thriving and prosperous village, with interests to be dangerously affected by popular tumults and indiscreet innovations. Manufactures were springing up; public improvements were anticipated; and possibly it may have been suggested that the course of the town in this emergency might influence the contest then pending with regard to new seats for the county courts. Col. Joshua Danforth, John Chandler Williams, Henry Van Schaack, and other gentlemen of influence, had recently removed to the town,[1] and with Rev. Mr. Allen, Oliver Wendell on his summer visits, Dr. Childs, and other eminent citizens of longer residence, united with Hon. Theodore Sedgwick and Judge Bacon of Stockbridge, Gen. Patterson of Lenox, and men of like stamp throughout the county, who at great sacrifice of personal comfort, and much exposure to personal danger and indignity, travelled from town to town, bringing their influence to bear in every possible way in favor of law and order.

Just before the outbreak, Major Van Schaack wrote a letter to his brother, from which we may be able to extract a fair idea of the double aspect of the times:[1] —

"Here I have made an advantageous purchase, and *live in the midst of those who owe*. I have made some other purchases about me, and I have a

[1] See note at end of this chapter.

[2] Life of Peter Van Schaack, LL.D., by his son Henry C. Van Schaack. New York: Appleton & Co.

number of mortgages in the neighborhood; so that I shall, in all probability, be a considerable landholder in a little time.

"The farm I live on I bought for four hundred and seventy-four pounds York money. It contains eighty-six acres good land, with a tolerably good house, barn, and a young orchard, and a pleasant lake[1] in sight of me. In my lifetime, I never lived among a more civil, obliging people. During my residence in Richmond,[2] I never was a witness to swearing, drunkenness, nor a breach of the sabbath, or, in short, any flagrant trespass upon morality. A purse of gold hung up in the public streets would be as safe from our inhabitants as it used to be in the great Alfred's time. Beggars and vagrants we are strangers to, as well as overbearing, purse-proud scoundrels. Provisions we abound in: beef, veal, mutton, and lamb, in the spring, summer, and fall, we buy at two pence lawful[3] per pound; in winter, beef and mutton at two and a half and three pence; every thing else in proportion, and very plenty. . . . I have just returned from Vermont. I took your son Harry and F. Silvester with me in the sleigh, who, as well as myself, were much pleased with the jaunt. . . . In travelling sixty-four miles and back again, four days out, lived extraordinary well all the time, and, among other things, dined upon boiled turkey and oyster-sauce at Manchester. The whole expense of our bill, while we were out, horse-keeping in the bargain, was twenty-six shillings eight pence York money apiece.[4] Add to the advantages of travelling, that your persons and property on the road and in the inns are perfectly safe. Murders, robberies, and burglaries, or petty larcenies, are scarce heard of in this country. So perfectly am I satisfied with the manners, customs, and laws of this Commonwealth, that I would not exchange them for any other I know of in the world.

"It will be difficult for you to believe, at so great a distance, that, immediately after the horrors of a civil war, the new government should have force and energy, the morals and religion of the inhabitants apparently as pure and uncorrupt as they were at the best a number of years before the late distractions. . . . It is true that the public calamities have brought heavy burthens; but these become lighter, and will be more and more so every year.

"The epitome of human misery — I mean the civil war — in this country has been accompanied by a failure of crops. . . If any of your friends wish to migrate, by way of encouragement you may assure them that lands are cheap and good in Berkshire. Building materials of every sort in great plenty. All that I want in my delightful retreat is a few people of your sort about me."

This picture is a good deal rose-tinted by Major Van Schaack, a prosperous gentleman of steady income, who had just saved from

[1] Melville.
[2] Where Major Van Schaack settled on his first removal to Berkshire.
[3] Lawful money.
[4] $3.25 Federal money.

the dangers of civil war more than he had expected of his own and his paternal fortune, who was likely to be enriched by the financial difficulties that impoverished his neighbors, who had secured a delightful estate, and was eulogizing the community where even his Whig opponents had received him with cordiality and confidence when he was exiled by those of his own section.

He had, however, but recently become a resident of the town, and there was much in it with which he had not yet come in contact. The Arcadian innocence which he paints so glowingly must be accepted, as a portrait, only with many grains of allowance. And the rich colors in which he depicts the physical comforts of his home were sadly obscured to those of his neighbors who "owed;" to the mortgagers, who saw little in the times to encourage the hope of *their* becoming or remaining "considerable landholders;" to the farmers, who found that it took a great deal of mutton at two pence a pound to pay such taxes as were levied upon them in order to "lighten the burthens" imposed by "the late public calamities." However it might be with some individuals, the masses of community could hardly felicitate themselves upon low prices, the result of insufficient markets and of a circulating medium utterly incapable of meeting the ordinary requirements of traffic.

Pittsfield, with a strong conservative element in its population, and with flourishing material interests which forbade it to favor rebellion, had thus also a large class, especially among its farmers, of men embarrassed, not only by the financial difficulties of the time, but by a succession of bad crops.

But there were also many, who, with no desire to overthrow the government, were painfully sensitive to the sufferings of the people, and sincerely believed that the legislature was criminally remiss in postponing the radical remedies which they deemed indispensable, who reiterated the complaints which had become chronic, if not morbid, in Berkshire, of the cumbrous and costly system of judiciary, and who perhaps joined in the charge that the counties of Hampshire and Berkshire had been unfairly assessed in the State valuation; and they were not unwilling that the apathy of the conservatives should be disturbed by popular tumults rising to the very verge of rebellion. It was a dangerous tampering with fearful elements; but if there were many among the influential classes, who, while rapt in admiration of the Commonwealth, thought it delightful "to live among those who owed," there was much to palliate their rashness.

It was by the votes, or the absence from town-meeting, of this class, which, although disaffected to the government, shrank from overt rebellion, that the open insurrectionists owed their triumphs. The malecontents, however, did not secure, and probably did not desire, town action in unison with that of their brethren in the lower counties. A fair indication of the extent to which the majority could be induced to yield its approval to measures for the reconstruction of government is found in the votes of September, 1785, concerning the instructions to be given Dr. Timothy Childs, who had some months before been chosen representative, and who was opposed to the insurrectionary movement, although doubtless, like most of the friends of law and order in Berkshire, earnestly desirous of thorough reforms by unintimidated legislation.

The committee to draft the instructions were Woodbridge Little, Joseph Fairfield, Daniel Hubbard, Major Simon Larned, and Eli Root, — two malecontents, and three who are supposed to have been of opposite views.

They reported seven paragraphs, of which four were adopted, expressing all to which a majority of the meeting would assent. The following is the report, as drafted, with the minutes of the town's action upon it: —

Sir, — In the present critical and disturbed situation of affairs in this Commonwealth, it is the wish of your constituents that you give the most early attendance possible at the General Court in their present session, and that you there use your influence that something may be done which may serve to quiet the minds, remove the uneasiness, and silence the complaints, of a great number of the good people of this State. And, for the purpose of effecting and obtaining this desirable object, your constituents recommend the following matters and articles to your consideration, which they imagine will be conducive to this end, and to which they expect you will give your particular attention in the General Court: —

1st, That you endeavor to obtain a suspension of the collecting of the last State tax, so far as it respects the redemption or payment of the public securities of every description or denomination, or the interest due on said securities, until some more easy and equal method of paying the same can be found and adopted. And it is the sense of your constituents, that some medium at which public securities of every kind have been sold and transferred from time to time shall be considered as the true value of the same, and that they be paid both principal and interest accordingly; and that the present appropriation of the impost and excise revenue be suspended in the mean time, if not forever. (Voted.)

2d, That the courts of Common Pleas and General Sessions of the Peace be abolished, and some other system instituted, calculated (if possible) to lessen the present expense of suits in law, and bring them to a more speedy decision. (Voted.)

3d. That particular attention be paid to the fee-table, and that the fees of justices of the peace, attorneys-at-law, sheriffs, and all other civil officers, be so far reduced as that they shall receive merely an honest and equitable recompense for their services, and not have it in their power to evade the true meaning and intention of the legislature in their establishment of fees; and that it be an object whether a reduction of salaries in many instances is not as proper as an augmentation in any. (Voted.)

4th, That you use your influence to obtain a law that no debt shall be collected by law which shall be contracted after a certain period to be fixed by the court, and that a tender act be made to ease all debtors as much as possible without doing manifest injustice to creditors. (Voted.)

5th, That a proper method be adopted to obtain the sentiments of the deople in this State respecting a present revision of our Contitution. (Voted.)

6th. [Your constituents being convinced that the town of Boston is an improper place for the General Assembly to hold their sessions in, they therefore request that you use your influence to have some other place fixed upon for that purpose.]

7th. [That the town clerk, or some other person, be appointed in each town to record the deeds of the town.]

Many other matters of importance will doubtless suggest themselves, or be brought into view in the course of the session, concerning which your constituents are not able at present to give you their opinion. Such matters they therefore cheerfully leave to your good sense and ability, to conduct therein according to your best skill and judgment; nothing doubting that you will use your utmost exertions to have such laws enacted, and such measures adopted, as will tend to the restoration and establishment of peace and good government through the Commonwealth.

A pleasant journey is wished you, and a safe return with happy tidings.

DR. TIMOTHY CHILDS.

The first paragraph was the fruit of the intolerable load of public indebtedness, from which had sprung, on the one hand, an unavailing attempt to reduce the principal by over-rapid instalments, and, on the other, projects derogatory to the faith of the Commonwealth; among which a favorite proposition was, that the public securities might justly be cancelled by paying the depreciated rates at which they had come into the hands of the last holders.

The legislature, struggling to maintain the public credit, had adopted an excise and impost tax for the purpose of paying the interest and reducing the principal of the State debt, and had, moreover, at the request of Congress, granted to the United States, in aid of paying the foreign debt, a further impost of five per cent. These acts the town instructed Representative Childs to oppose, as well as the collection of the State tax, in which it was alleged that the western counties were unfairly assessed.

The other paragraphs adopted merely favored the much-needed reform of the courts, and asked that the question of revising the Constitution should be submitted to the people. There was nothing, surely, very revolutionary in these votes. Nor would there have been even in the adoption of the others; which simply proposed to abolish the collection by law of debts incurred after a certain date, to substitute the registry of deeds by town instead of county officers, and favored that nine-lived folly, of which Gov. Hutchinson was the father,—a removal of the seat of government from Boston.

Another meeting was held Oct. 23, when the insurrection was approaching its armed outbreak; but, while again electing malecontent delegates[1] to the county convention to be held at Pittsfield, Nov. 5, it manifested the same repugnance to unnecessary innovation which its predecessor had exhibited. Its action was indeed even more conservative: for it declared emphatically against an emission of paper money; opposed a tender act; and, the former meeting having directed the collectors to retain the rate-bills in their hands, this promised the support of the town in their collection.

In the latter part of January, when the rebels at arms in the county were conducting with unbridled insolence, there was a stormy time at a town-meeting convened to consider the action of a recent county convention. Matters were carried with so high a hand by the insurrectionists, that the clerk, John Chandler Williams, withdrew; the moderator, Eli Root, refused to declare the votes; and Capt. John Strong, who was appointed clerk *pro tem.*, neglected to record the dissolution of the meeting.

The folly of tampering with the passions of the mob was now

[1] Joseph Fairfield, Daniel Hubbard, Samuel Rust, Dan Cadwell, and Capt. Daniel Sackett.

apparent; and the joy of the people was sincere, when, in the next month, the occupation of the town by Gen. Lincoln relieved them from the restraint which their indecision in the early part of the contest had invited.

Thenceforward the town meetings consistently favored, not only good order, but a sound policy. The best evidence of their real sentiment is found in their vote at the State election, April, 1787, when Gov. Bowdoin, whose energetic and fearless course had suppressed the rebellion, was a candidate for re-election, and opposed by John Hancock, who was supposed to be more favorably inclined to the insurgents. Such was the sympathy with the rebels in many parts of the Commonwealth, even among those who did not join in their extreme measures, that Hancock was elected mainly on that issue, with a legislature of the same complexion. But, in Pittsfield, the vote stood, — for Bowdoin, forty-seven; for Hancock, thirteen: while the popularity won by Lincoln in his local military administration was attested by a unanimous vote (eighty-two) for lieutenant-governor. A still more marked proof of the conservative re-action was the election of Henry Van Schaack as representative, in spite of the prejudice against him as a loyalist of the Revolution.[1]

During the military occupation of Pittsfield, the troops were quartered among the inhabitants in such manner as would cause the least inconvenience which the nature of the case admitted. The officers were assigned to the better class of houses, and were almost universally received with a cordial welcome, from which many enduring friendships arose; and doubtless, although unrecorded, the same was true of intimacies formed in humbler quarters.

Commendable discipline was maintained among the military; and the unavoidable wordy disputes between soldiers and citizens never resulted in serious disturbances.

With a large number of young men congregated in a place which afforded few legitimate channels for the relief of exuberant animal spirits, or means for dissipating the tedium of garrison life, the license of the camp sometimes assumed forms vexatious to the staid housekeeper. But the incidents related in illustration of these little annoyances betoken the roguish pranks of boyish men, and not the insolence of military hectoring. No doubt the pur-

[1] See note at end of this chapter.

suit of lurking rebels was varied by raids — such as college-boys make — upon orchards, cornfields, and poultry-yards; but, if the offenders were detected, punishment was sure and prompt.

Indeed, in the best-remembered instance, the injured party was prompt to right herself. It happened that a considerable squad was quartered in the tavern then kept by Capt. Jared Ingersoll, on the south corner of the present North and Depot Streets. Now, Capt. Ingersoll was a prisoner at Northampton, charged with participating in the rebellion, leaving his affairs in charge of his wife, the widow of Col. John Brown. The soldiers were perhaps encouraged by the unfortunate position of the landlord to make more free with the premises than they would otherwise have done; and a few of them, with a genuine Yankee appreciation of the fun of making money, placed in the bar-room a barrel of cider, from which they proceeded to retail by the glass. But the rogues had reckoned without their hostess; for the spirited and resolute landlady, appearing on the scene, unceremoniously pitched the intrusive commodity into the street, remarking, with quiet emphasis, that "*She* kept tavern *there*." It is safe to guess that order was preserved among the military guests of that household without reference to the provost-marshal.

But, well as the soldiery remembered that they were among the homes of their fellow-citizens, an extraordinary military bustle and disquiet pervaded the streets of Pittsfield during the spring and summer of 1787. The roll of the drum and the challenge of the sentinel were frequent; detachments were constantly marching and counter-marching, as alarms came from one quarter or another; and prisoners were continually brought in, to be sent forward to Great Barrington or Northampton jails: so that Pittsfield bore not a little of the sad aspect which always attaches to the head-quarters of the victors after a suppressed rebellion. For the clemency which afterwards marked the course of the government was not then assured or even probable; and the prisoners set out from Pittsfield with a well-grounded apprehension that the termination of their journey would be either a gallows or a felon's cell. Shadowy as the perils which the government and its opponents passed through in that day may now appear, we may be sure that they were realities fearfully vivid and palpable to those who were compelled to face them. And the consternation which the rebel, in his uprising, excited among the friends of the government, was fully brought home to his own breast, when, defeated, he found himself a prisoner in the hands of the law which he had undertaken to overthrow. Happily, the tremors of one party having been removed by the success of its arms, those of the other were quieted by the politic mercy of the victors. The general commanding the successful militia was earnest for the most liberal clemency, and the majority of the people shared his generous sentiments; while the most severe measures proposed by the minority were mild, as compared with the standard of that era in cases of treason.

But, long after the rebel spirit had been conciliated towards the government of the State, the effects of the divisions which it had created in counties, towns, and neighborhoods continued to manifest themselves in the relations of the people to each other. "Too much had been said and done," says Dr. Field, "to permit the people to become at once altogether friendly. Unhappy jealousies remained in neighborhoods and towns; the clergy who had favored the Revolutionary war opposed the rebellion, and thereby, in some instances, offended many of their parishioners; and this is understood to have caused the dismission of the ministers in Alford and Egremont, and created much disaffection in Sandisfield."

In Pittsfield, the dissensions were aggravated by other than political causes, and rose to such violence, that, in order to render life in the town at all tolerable, it became necessary to reconcile them. The mode in which this was attempted was so characteristic of the times and of the people that it merits a minute narration. The difficulties, although their exciting cause was chiefly political, developed themselves most conspicuously in connection with the affairs of the town as a religious parish, and were, in great part, the fruit of the unnatural connection between church and state.

In Pittsfield, the existence of other religious denominations than the Congregational was practically ignored. The town was simply a Congregational parish, which could not be divided, except by special act of the legislature. All its affairs were conducted in town-meeting, as of old; and the town retained all its rights and privileges as the secular organization which provided for religious worship. Cribbed so closely, the most pacific people would have fretted themselves into a passion in the most peaceful times. A great deal of good temper is preserved in our day by the large liberty we enjoy of dividing upon every difference. The good people of Pittsfield were more trammelled when, in 1788, they looked to peaceful separation as the alternative of the better if possible thing, unity, to remedy their troubles; and the warrant for the April meeting proposed to hear any suggestions which might be made "for uniting or dividing the town."

The meeting, it seems, did not despair of healing the existing dissensions, but appointed a committee "to attend to all matters which have been the cause or occasion of the late disunion in the town, and to such matters as may tend to a union and reconciliation, and make report as soon as may be of such measures as to them shall appear most likely to effect that desirable purpose."

The committee was made up with great care from men of influence and sound discretion in all parties, as well as some who had probably maintained a wise neutrality. Its members were Woodbridge Little, Deacon Daniel Hubbard, Joseph Farr, Capt. James Dn. Colt, Major Oliver Root, Deacon Joseph Clark, Capts. David Bush, Joel Stevens, and William Francis, Enoch Haskins and Stephen Fowler. A public hearing was given on the 3d of June to all interested; and "having fully considered all the matters of difficulty which were then or at any other time mentioned or suggested to them as causes of uneasiness," and after much consultation and investigation, the committee agreed upon a report, which was submitted to the town on the 26th.

They found that the causes of the dissensions were all reducible to the following heads: —

" *First.* The state of the pews in the meeting-house, including the manner in which they were obtained, and are now holden by their proprietors.

" *Second.* The Rev. Mr. Allen's having received an allowance from the town for the depreciation of money, notwithstanding the various public declarations which he has made.

Third. The Rev. Mr. Allen's having in times past, in his official character, repeatedly interested himself in the political affairs of the country, and publicly interposed therein in an undue and improper manner."

With regard to these allegations, the committee resolved, —

" *First.* That it should be recommended to proprietors of pews to relinquish their rights in them; and that the town take such measures to accommodate the inhabitants with seats as may be thought proper.

" *Second.* With respect to the second article, we do not find the Rev. Mr.

Allen to have been guilty of any immoral conduct therein; and we recommend it to every person who is aggrieved thereby to apply to Mr. Allen, who will doubtless give every reasonable satisfaction in his power; and, if any such person shall desire satisfaction of a pecuniary kind, we wish Mr. Allen, for the sake of peace, to grant it.

"*Third.* And, as to matters contained in the third article, we consider Mr. Allen to be liable to human frailties and error; and we are of opinion that much of the uneasiness and disunion subsisting in this town might have been prevented had he ever been silent with respect to political matters in his public performances; but we by no means charge him with any sinister or criminal intention therein.

"*Resolved, further,* That, whenever the town shall think proper to erect a meeting-house, the place for the standing of the same shall be submitted to the determination of three or more disinterested persons, not inhabitants of the town."

The reader will recall that proprietorship was originally acquired in the pews by some of the more wealthy early settlers, who were allowed to purchase for lack of funds otherwise to finish the house. The square pews were still held under these titles, and occupied an undue space in the little meeting-house. There arose a more serious difficulty, — that while the people were "sorted" by the committee, according to their notions of social position, upon the "long seats" and in the gallery, the pew-holders with their families, from year to year, marched to their prescriptive places with an odious dignity, free of official censorship.

Some further explanation than was at that time necessary is now requisite for a proper understanding of the pecuniary relations of Mr. Allen to the town.

His settlement in 1764, with an annual stipend of £80 and forty cords of wood, will be remembered. Twenty-four years had passed, and left him with a wife and eight surviving children, but no increase of salary, or, rather, with a fearful decrease by the depreciation of the currency. He had, however, during the war of the Revolution, been led by a noble zeal and faith in his country to "loan the Continent" the sum of $2,500, to obtain the means for which and for other local purposes of a similar character, as well as to support his family, he had alienated more than half of the valuable home-lot which had fallen to him as first minister of the town. At one time of his country's need, he had even sold his watch in order to turn the proceeds into a Continental "certificate of indebtedness." One can well pardon some untimely expression of a zeal which thus manifested itself. In 1788, these Continental certificates had depreciated in value to $606 Connecticut money; and the Confederation and the State then owed him, at these depreciated rates, $1,129, principal and interest.

It thus happened that in the year 1783, with his funds unavailable, he found himself considerably in debt, and, by the advice of friends, applied to his parish for relief. The request was promptly met by a grant of £300; but, learning that a few tax-payers felt aggrieved by this act of justice as well as generosity, he at once declined it.

He, however, accepted a loan of £200, for which he gave his bond, although he was led by the intimations of some of his parishioners to expect that repayment would never be required. We may anticipate our story by remarking that this not unnatural expectation was defeated by the contentions which continued to prevail. In 1792, Mr. Allen paid £150 of the principal; and, in 1809, he took up his note, devoting the whole of his salary for the preceding year to the payment of what remained due. He had paid more than £800, principal and interest, upon the loan of £200.

The report submitted on the 26th resulted in the following action. The owners of pews having released their rights "so that every person might have an equal right to seats therein until the town should be divided into two or more parishes," their action was voted perfectly satisfactory, although the idea of separation was still prominently held out.

With regard to the subjects of the second and third resolutions of the committee's report, it seems that Mr. Allen had made some personal communication to the meeting, — in part, probably, embodying some of the statements which we have given above. "These declarations," the town voted unanimously, "removed all uneasiness which had subsisted in the minds of the people now present, and they are determined to be satisfied therewith;" and they recommended "the inhabitants of the town not now present, who remain unsatisfied, to apply to the *town* for such pecuniary satisfaction as they may think they ought to receive for what they may have paid on the depreciation tax."

Notwithstanding this harmonious action of the meeting, "uneasiness continued to prevail to some extent among those who had absented themselves;" and a number of the discontented, the next year, applied for an abatement of their ministry tax, which was refused, except as regarded those legally exempt.

Mr. Allen's bond also continued to be the subject of discussion and negotiation until its final payment, as from time to time portions of it were discharged by "discounts on his salary," and by the release of his interest in the lots devoted to the support of the ministry. These transactions appear to have been conducted in good temper, and, at least during the closing years of that century, with due regard to the convenience of the debtor. Although some few were openly disaffected towards the minister, — and doubtless the sting of his plain preaching of political duty in time past secretly rankled in the bosoms of others, — still an era of comparative good feeling had been reached, as regarded the minister; and, for a few years, the contentious spirits of the town were engrossed by other matters.

NOTES.

JOSHUA DANFORTH was born at Weston in 1759; his father being Jonathan Danforth, who commanded a battalion with credit at the battle of Bennington. His preparation for college was interrupted by the Revolution, and he entered the army at the age of fifteen as clerk in his father's company. After serving for some months in this office, performing at the same time the duties of surgeon's mate, he was made ensign at sixteen, promoted first lieutenant in 1778, and paymaster, with the rank of captain, in 1781. He performed a gallant exploit in rescuing baggage from an exposed position at Roxbury in 1775, was present at the surrender of Burgoyne, and suffered with Washington's army the horrors of the following winter at Valley Forge, which he described as "incredible." In 1778, he took part in the battle of Monmouth Court-House, and, in 1781, was in command of a post on the Lower Hudson. From that year he served as paymaster until May, 1784, when he removed to Pittsfield, and engaged in mercantile business in company with Col. Simon Larned. Here he was postmaster and collector of internal revenue, and held other public offices, until his death in 1837. No citizen of the town was ever held in higher respect than Col. Danforth for sound sense, official ability and integrity, moral worth, and consistent piety.

HENRY VAN SCHAACK was born at Kinderhook in 1733. Having received the limited education which the common school of that town could give, he went to serve a mercantile apprenticeship with Peter Van Brugh Livingston of New York. At the age of twenty, he was lieutenant of the company commanded by Philip, afterwards Gen. Schuyler, in the expedition of 1755 against Crown Point; and, when Col. Ephraim Williams's regiment was cut up by the enemy, he was one of the party of two hundred and fifty who first went to their relief. He was afterwards paymaster and commissioner of musters, with the rank of major.

He carried on his mercantile business successfully; and, as early as 1757, he had an interest in trading stations at Oswego and Niagara. On the conquest of Canada, he extended his operations to Detroit and Mackinaw, then the *ultima thule* of British North America. He had by these means acquired, previous to the Revolution, an ample fortune.

When the Stamp Act passed, he was postmaster of the city of Albany, and a prominent business man. Falling under the suspicion of the "Sons of Liberty" that he intended to apply for the office of stamp-distributor also, the populace destroyed the balcony, windows, and furniture of his house, and compelled him to take an oath never to apply for the odious office, nor to accept it if offered him.

In 1769, he removed to his native town, Kinderhook, where he was immediately appointed justice of the peace, and elected supervisor, which offices he held until the Revolution.

Mr. Van Schaack was a member of the first Committee of Safety and Correspondence for the City and County of Albany, and a candidate for delegate to the Continental Congress. But, early in 1775, he withdrew from the committee, and declared himself a loyalist. He had reached the conclusion, that "the dispute with the mother country was carried on with too much acrimony;" that the Congress of 1774 "had left no back door open for reconciliation;" that there was "too much reason to believe that many citizens wished to shake off their dependence upon Great Britain;" and that "the people had got to that pass that they did not consider the qualifications of a king, for they would have no king." With regard to the two latter propositions, Mr. Van Shaack read the people better than they read themselves ; but he was less fortunate in predicting that "Great Britain will lower us, in spite of all we can do : the Fishing-bill will make us knuckle."

For all this, Mr. Van Schaack appears to have been a sincere lover of his country, and to have dreaded, not rejoiced in, the humiliation which he anticipated. But loyal by instinct as well as by principle, and reverencing the oath of allegiance which he had often taken, he craved the privilege of neutrality. This, however, could not reasonably be granted to a man of his prominence, while he remained at home ; and he was required by the Commissioners of Conspiracies to withdraw, while the contest lasted, into Connecticut or Massachusetts, and place himself under the supervision of their Committee of Inspection. He chose Berkshire County ; and, after trying Richmond and Stockbridge for a few months each, he purchased the beautiful estate which includes Melville Lake, and settled in Pittsfield. Here his desire to withdraw from political strife was gratified; and, although he watched the course of affairs with intense interest, he afforded no cause of complaint to the most jealous Whig. On the contrary, he won the confidence and friendship of many of the leading patriots to a degree which attests the worth of his character as a man and his pleasant qualities as a companion. The act of banishment against him was revoked, and Gen. Schuyler wrote inviting him to return. Mr. Van Shaack, however, was entirely satisfied with Massachusetts, as will appear from the letter already quoted, as well as from another to his brother Peter, in which he says, "So perfectly am I satisfied with the manners, customs, and laws of this Commonwealth, that I would not exchange them for any other I know of in the world."

At the close of the war, he became a citizen of the State ; and we shall continue to find him prominent in town affairs and in social life. But he finally returned to Kinderhook, where he died.

CHAPTER XXIII.

COUNTY COURTS IN PITTSFIELD.

[1761–1787.]

Courts on Unkamet Street. — Peculiarities of the Court of General Sessions. — Court-house Scenes. — Dissatisfaction with the Place of holding the Courts. — Contributions and Plans for a New Court-House. — Various Sites Advocated. — Change in the Shire-Towns proposed. — Popular and Legislative Action. — A County Convention decides for Lenox. — Opposition. — Delays. — The Legislature insists. — Court-House and Jail built.

LIEUT. GRAVES'S house, on Unkamet Street, was an important spot in the Pittsfield of old times, when the county courts held in its long room their quarterly terms; events of much greater public moment then than now, on account of the peculiar composition and functions of the General Sessions of the Peace.

This tribunal, in addition to its jurisdiction in criminal cases, was a sort of county parliament, in which not only were many important matters, now intrusted to the commissioners, officially decided by the justices; but the general affairs of the county were debated informally by all the gentlemen in attendance, and sometimes determinations reached to which the influence of those who participated in them gave almost the force of law. The personal influence of village magnates, powerful still, was then immeasurably more so; indeed, if united, irresistible: and, when matters of engrossing interest were agitated, a very large proportion of the men of wealth and standing were sure to congregate at "the Sessions."

Four justices composed this court in 1761, who, six years later, had increased to ten. Probably, when the Revolution broke out, the number of magistrates on its bench exceeded a dozen; but the records of the intervening period are missing, having, perhaps, been a part of those which, as traditions state, were destroyed with the house of Lieut. Graves when it was burned, just previous to the removal of the courts to Lenox.

After the Revolution, the number of justices was greatly augmented ; twenty-six being reported present at a session of 1800.

Besides the judges of the two courts, many of the principal gentlemen of the county were usually collected, as executive officers, lawyers, suitors, jurors, witnesses, or spectators interested in the civil matters before the Court of Sessions.

In Lieut. Graves's homestead, the most spacious room had been fitted up with the furniture necessary for the court; and, the winter terms being held at Pittsfield, a blazing fire roared up the huge old-fashioned chimney, and garrisoned the seat of justice against the besieging cold.

Among the groups gathered in the recesses of the courts around the cheery blaze, or those which no less ruddily illumined the windows of the neighboring taverns, might generally have been seen most of the men noted in the county annals of those times.

Some of these were in active correspondence with the leading spirits of the age at the centres of political influence ; all were readers of some of the few journals then published; and many were diligent students of State lore and of the polemical essays which flooded the country. Here they interchanged information and views, discussed the agitated course of events, and concerted measures in regard to them.

Nor has tradition forgotten the genial social intercourse of the gentlemen — many of them such in the best old use of that word — who were brought together in the long winter evenings of court-time. Many are the jokes, quips, quirks, and quiddits, the stories, anecdotes, and repartees, handed down of those whose sterling worth and brilliant talent are overshadowed to posterity by the quaintness with which their wit and humor, as well as their old-fashioned gentility, have invested their memory. They were good livers all, and, in the manner of its enjoyment, could impart an additional zest to either the haunch of venison, the gloriously-flavored wild turkey of the Berkshire woods, or the homely roast; to the fine old Madeira of Col. Williams, or the "bottled cider" of their own making, such as Major Van Schaack boasted "equal to the best champagne."

It must be confessed, that the social glass, unadulterated as it was, wrought its own work upon some of the noblest of the circle;

and it is true that the magnificence of spirit and nice code of honor which prevailed tolerated vices, especially the profanity and licentiousness peculiar to that age, which advancing civilization has since taught New England to ban, if not to banish.

Their vices, like their virtues, were those of the high-spirited gentlemen of the old school; and, if the groups gathered in that cosey and ruddy nook among the Winter-bergs is not a perfect model for the imitation of modern Berkshire, it is certainly a very picturesque one for the painter, whether he use pen or pencil. Nor is it for the present age, with its manifold creeping and crawling sins, to bestow its indignation in any Pharisaic spirit upon the more robust naughtiness of its predecessor.

In hours like those we have described, friendships grew up which endured for years, in which old men often manifested the most affecting tenderness for each other. Here, too, in the fierce conflicts of law and politics, were engendered feuds which sometimes became deadly and hereditary. But, upon the whole, the habitual attendants upon the courts acquired a friendly intimacy which rendered them almost a band of brothers.

Upon those pleasant days broke the distant rumblings which heralded the Revolution. In and around the little Pittsfield court-room at Unkamet's Crossing, as elsewhere, while the hour for resistance to tyranny was approaching, the encroachments of Great Britain were descanted upon; and, as one after another blow aimed at natural or chartered rights was announced, those who had clung to the hope of reconciliation one by one sorrowfully renounced it, until the few who adhered to the king stood miserably conspicuous, — aliens from the household in which some of them had lately been among the most honored members, excluded from social or commercial intercourse, and branded as "the enemies of American liberty."

But, before this division of those loyal to the king from those loyal to the country was complete, the courts of Berkshire had ceased forever to be held in the royal name; and the interregnum which ensued, until the new government was established in 1780, resulted incidentally in the removal of the courts from Great Barrington and Pittsfield, and their concentration at Lenox.

The insufficient accommodations for the courts at Pittsfield had, in 1774, long been a source of complaint; and, previous to that date, measures had been entered upon to provide better. The loss of the records, however, leaves us in the dark as to what those measures were, except as light is thrown upon them by the following unsigned draft of agreement, which was found among the papers of Col. Williams: —

BERKSHIRE, SS.

To the Honorable His Majesty's Justices of the General Sessions of the Peace and Inferior Court of Common Pleas, to be holden at Pittsfield, within and for the said County, on the fourth Tuesday of February next, being the twenty-second Day of said Month, A.D. 1774.

Whereas, for many years past, there has been great uneasiness in said county, that the courts appointed by law to be held at Pittsfield, within and for said county, should from time to time be holden at the house of Lieut. Graves, in said Pittsfield; and, from the extraordinary growth and increase of said county, said uneasiness has grown to a great degree of dissatisfaction, of which, if we are not mistaken, your Honors have heretofore been informed, and at a greater meeting than ever was known of his Majesty's justices of the General Sessions of the Peace for said county, whether it might be called a Court of the General Sessions of the Peace or not we are uncertain, they, the said justices, then and there did nominate and appoint a committee to repair to Pittsfield to view and determine the most suitable place for the erecting a court-house in said town, the major part of whom reported, as we are informed, that between the corners of Messrs. Jones, Fairfield, Goodrich, and Root was the most suitable place to accommodate the county and public: —

Wherefore we, the subscribers, for the sake of peace and unanimity, and for the accommodation of the public, do make over, dispose of, and assign to such person or persons as your Honors shall appoint, all and singular such lands, moneys, and articles as we have hereunto subscribed, for the ends and purposes following; viz., to erect a decent and commodious court-house for the use and benefit of said county, provided the house be erected at said place, and hereby bind and oblige ourselves, our heirs, &c., to the performance thereof, as fully and amply as we can or ought to be holden in any contract or bargain, however precisely and lawfully exemplified or expressed.

In witness whereof, we have hereunto affixed our names, and the articles which we promise for the purpose aforesaid.[1]

The location named is now Wendell Square, the ambitious early projects of whose abuttors, already narrated, were now revived, only to be again dashed almost in the moment of fruition. The interested parties tendered a gift of the land and building material; and tradition avers that the latter was actually collected, and long cumbered the ground. But the term of the court to which the tender was made, and by which it was undoubtedly accepted, was

[1] C. C. p. 237.

the last which Berkshire County saw for over six years. There were also efforts to secure the location of the court-house near The Elm and the meeting-house; but a more strenuous exertion was made by some proprietors of lands between Unkamet's Crossing and Silver Lake, who inherited Col. Stoddard's vision of a central village in that quarter, and wished the new building to be placed at the junction of Beaver and Dickinson Streets, on the lands now a part of the grounds of Hon. Messrs. Benjamin R. Curtis and Thomas Allen, and immediately in front of the house built, and in 1774 occupied, by Woodbridge Little. Here, as upon Wendell Square, land was tendered for the court-house, a public square was actually laid out, and materials for the building collected.

There was, of course, no occasion to discuss the location of court-houses while the courts were suspended, nor, in the absence of the General Sessions, was there any authority to build upon the spot already designated; and when, almost immediately after the re-establishment of civil government, the subject was again agitated, it was with a view to a change in the places of holding the courts.

Rev. Mr. Allen states positively [1] that the courts were removed for political reasons; and it is likely that the leading part which Pittsfield took in opposition to eastern sentiment regarding civil government during the Revolution may have been artfully used to influence the legislature in favor of the change. But it could hardly been the motive of the originators of the movement in the county.

What, if any thing other than local interests of the towns which wished to supplant the old county seats, really prompted this movement, it is difficult now to determine.

The population of the county, which in 1761 lay almost entirely south of the north line of Pittsfield, had now extended itself largely in the north, but not sufficiently to demand the transfer of the county seat in that direction. The preponderance of wealth and numbers was still with the lower towns.

Lanesborough was flourishing, and rivalling her next southern neighbor in business and population; but there were few spots among the sterile hills of the north to tempt the agriculturist from the broad and fertile meadows which extended along the Housa-

[1] Pamphlet of 1810.

tonic from Sheffield to Lanesborough, or from the superb uplands of Pittsfield and a few other towns in the south. Sheffield, Great Barrington, Stockbridge, and their neighbors, still retained the advantage in point of wealth which they had gained while Pittsfield, and all north of that point, was a wilderness, or was barely held by a military occupation against the savage. Those noble manufactures which have since brought such wealth and increase of people to Northern Berkshire were then but feebly dreamt of, if at all, by such enthusiasts as Parson Allen; and the railroads which now vein the county in all directions from Pittsfield were as yet not even prophesied by the poor foreshadowing of a single turnpike. There was nothing to indicate that the northern section of the county would ever equal — much less excel — its favored southern sister, either in wealth or people. Pittsfield was thus, in 1781, a more suitable place for holding the courts than when, almost upon the northern frontier of settlement, it was selected twenty years before; and there is no apparent reason other than the local ambition of rival towns why change should have been desired. The suggestion of the evils of a divided shire, so apparent as to show the necessity of concentration of all the courts at one place, evidently did not influence the *first* agitators of the subject.

The first recorded action in regard to a change was in November, 1782, when the legislature, upon the petition of Asa Barnes, a prominent citizen of Lanesborough, acting as agent for that and other towns, appointed a committee "to repair to the county of Berkshire, take a general view of it, and determine where the courts shall in future be held."

The committee — Charles Turner, Esq., Gen. Artemas Ward, and Hon. John Sprague — visited the county in June, met the delegates of twenty-two towns at Stockbridge, and made such an examination of the county as they thought necessary, or the delegates desired. The result was a recommendation, which the legislature adopted, that, after the 1st of January, 1784, the courts should be held at Lenox, in some convenient place between the meeting-house and the dwelling of Capt. Charles Dibble. This act passed in February, 1783; and, in the little parliament which assembled around the General Sessions at the Great Barrington term in May, a petition was set on, foot praying for an indefinite postponement of the proposed change, upon the ostensible ground that the county was too poor to erect the necessary buildings.

The legislature granted a delay of two years, until January, 1786; and the opponents of Lenox made a busy use of the respite. In the fall of 1784, a spirited movement was entered upon for what was doubtless the object of the Barnes petition, — alternate courts at Great Barrington and Lanesborough; but the project met little favor. The people, however, were so ill content, that the legislature submitted the matter again to a county convention, which assembled at Lenox, Sept. 28, sixteen towns being represented. This convention adjourned, after appointing Woodbridge Little of Pittsfield, Timothy Edwards of Stockbridge, and William Whiting of Great Barrington, a committee to receive the proposals of the several towns which desired to become the county seat.

On the 12th of October, this committee sent out circulars to all the towns in the county; of which the following paragraphs form the gist: —

" We, the subscribers, a committee of said convention, beg leave to inform you, that it is the wish and desire of said convention, that you, without fail, send one or more delegates to attend in a county convention to be holden by adjournment at Lenox, on the second Tuesday of November next, at the dwelling-house of Capt. Charles Dibble, at ten of the clock in the forenoon.

"The following proposals are submitted to your consideration; and it is desired, that, in your deliberations, you will attend to the same, and instruct and direct your delegate or delegates in what place or places it is the choice of your town that the courts in and for said county shall be holden.

" The proposals are as follows: —

" Great Barrington will repair the court-house in said town, and furnish and provide a sufficient jail in said town for the safe keeping of prisoners, and for this propose to give ample security, provided one-half of the courts be established in said town.

" Lanesborough will build and complete a good, sufficient, and elegant court-house in that town, and propose to give ample security therefor, provided one-half of the courts be established in that town.

" Pittsfield will be at the sole expense of erecting a court-house equal in value and elegance to the court-house in Northampton, and propose to give ample security therefor, provided one-half of the courts be established in said town, and the other half in Stockbridge.

" Stockbridge will give the sum of five hundred and seventy-eight pounds and ten shillings towards the public buildings for said county, provided one-half of the courts be established in said town, and the other half at Pittsfield; and further propose to give the sum of seven hundred and fifty pounds and ten shillings, if all the courts shall be established in Stockbridge; and propose to give ample security for the respective sums, as the case may require.

"Lenox will give the sum of eight hundred pounds towards the public buildings, and propose to give ample security therefor, provided all the courts are finally established in that town.

"And it is further proposed that the securities above mentioned be laid before said adjourned convention, that they may be able to determine upon them, as they shall judge proper.[1]

The convention met, according to adjournment, at the house of Capt. Charles Dibble, in Lenox, and chose Nathaniel Bishop scribe. Delegates were present from nineteen towns, viz.: —

From Sheffield, Col. Root, Mr. Raymond; Alford, Capt. Brunson; New Marlborough, Capt. Taylor; Sandisfield, Capt. Kellogg; Tyringham, Mr. Gaffield [Garfield], Mr. Jackson; Becket, Mr. Brown; Washington, Capt. Ashley; Lee, William Ingersoll, Esq., Capt. Bradley; Stockbridge, John Bacon, Esq., Jahleel Woodbridge, Esq., Timothy Edwards, Esq.; Richmont,[2] Gen. Rossiter, Nathaniel Bishop, Esq.; Lenox, Gen. Patterson, Col. Hyde, Israel Dewey, Esq., Capt. Gray, William Walker, Esq.; Pittsfield, Eli Root, Esq., Mr. [Dr.] Childs; Lanesborough, Gideon Wheeler, Esq.; Hancock, Samuel Hand, Esq.; Dalton, Capt. Cleveland; Partridgefield, Mr. Kenny; Great Barrington, William Whiting, Esq., Jonathan Nash, Esq., Mr. Elisha Lee, Major King, Mr. Younglove; West Stockbridge, Mr. Hooker.

The propositions from the several towns which had made offers in regard to the county seat were laid before the convention, and pronounced ample in each case.

The question was then put whether the courts "should in future be holden in two towns, or in one only;" and the vote stood as follows: —

For one town only, — Tyringham, Becket, Washington, Lee, Stockbridge, Richmont, Williamstown, Partridgefield, West Stockbridge, Lenox, — *ten.*

For two towns, — Sheffield, Alford, New Marlborough, Sandisfield, Pittsfield, Lanesborough, Hancock, Dalton, Great Barrington, — *nine.*

The convention then selected Lenox for the shire-town by the following vote: —

For Stockbridge, — Sheffield, Alford, New Marlborough, Sandisfield, Tyringham, Lee, Stockbridge, West Stockbridge, — *eight.*

For Lenox, — Becket, Washington, Richmont, Lenox, Lanesborough, Williamstown, Hancock, Dalton, Partridgefield, Great Barrington, — *ten.*[3]

[1] This circular, which is signed by Woodbridge Little in behalf and by order of the committee, is preserved in the archives of Pittsfield.

[2] The town of Richmond was originally incorporated, owing to a clerical error, as Richmont; and it was many years before the mistake was corrected by the legislature.

[3] The record of the November convention is in the collection of papers relating

Pittsfield did not vote; having probably determined to contest in the legislature the decision of the convention in favor of a single shire-town. There was, in fact, throughout the county, much dissatisfaction with the proceedings we have related; and, in 1785, so general and spirited was the opposition, that it appeared to the General Court that "the inhabitants of several towns in the county are dissatisfied that the courts should be held at Lenox, as by law established:" and, as it was "important that some place or places should be determined upon for that purpose as soon as might be," Hon. Caleb Strong, Warham Parks, and David Smead, Esqs., were commissioned to view the towns of Great Barrington, Stockbridge, Lenox, Pittsfield, and Lanesborough," — the prominent candidates for favor, — and such other places as might enable them to determine the object of their commission justly; to acquaint themselves with the roads passing through the county, and the communications between the interior and exterior towns; to pay due attention to situation, and the probability of future settlement; to hear such representations as might be made to them upon the subject; and then to fix upon some proper place or places, and, if they shall find more than one necessary, to determine what terms shall be held at each respectively, and which should be the shire-town."

The committee met the deputies of the towns at Pittsfield on the 11th of May, when all were represented except New Ashford, West Stockbridge, Becket, Sandisfield, and New Marlborough; "and it was agreed what the predilections of those towns severally were." A very thorough examination of the county, in accordance with the instructions of the legislature, was then made. The result was, that the committee "were clearly and unanimously of opinion that it would not be for the interest or peace of the county to have all the courts fixed at any one place; but that the inhabitants of the county would be best accommodated by having the courts held alternately at Stockbridge and Pittsfield, and that Stockbridge should be the shire-town," and that the terms of the Superior Court should be held at that place.

The legislature, governed by reasons of which we have no knowledge, adhered to its election of Lenox, notwithstanding the emphatically adverse report of its own able commission.

It would have been strange if the opposition of Pittsfield, dur-

to the history of Berkshire belonging to Charles J. Taylor, Esq., of Great Barrington.

ing the Revolution, to the courts set up by the legislature, and to the policy prevalent at the east, had not left a prejudice against her upon the minds of the public men of that section, of which it would have been easy for shrewd managers in the lobby or on the floor to have taken advantage; but the same could hardly be said of Great Barrington, which, in 1778, had been the only town in the county to vote, as it did almost unanimously, in favor of admitting the civil administration of the State. Lenox, although as perversely against the legislative policy as her neighbors, was less conspicuous. But Stockbridge was rather conservative in politics, was the residence of many eminent and influential men, and was already a lovely village, whose praise was in the mouths of people of culture and intelligence in the great centres of opinion.

It is observable, that when the movement for the change in the courts was begun, for the two years 1782 and 1783, Pittsfield was unrepresented in the General Court, and in the former year was fined £36. 6*s*. 3*d*. for neglecting to send a representative. In 1784 Dr. Timothy Childs, and in 1785 Capt. Charles Goodrich, were chosen, and probably commanded as much influence at Boston as any who could have been selected. In the same years, there were in the legislature, from Berkshire, such men as Theodore Sedgwick, Jahleel Woodbridge, and John Bacon, of Stockbridge; Elijah Dwight of Great Barrington; William Walker of Lenox; and Jonathan Smith of Lanesborough: and all doubtless exhibited the regard for their respective places of residence which is natural and creditable; and it would be pardonable if their judgments were warped by local predilections.

Geographically, as between the north and south, the centre of the county is nearly on the south line of Pittsfield, about equidistant from the Pittsfield Park and the Lenox Court-house; but, in 1785, the centre of wealth and population was considerably to the south of the latter point, probably in the neighborhood of "Old Stockbridge on the plain." If the courts were all to be held at one point, the selection of Lenox, therefore, favored the north rather than the south.

Even if the General Sessions manifested any great alacrity, which is not apparent, in complying with the act of the legislature in establishing the shire-town, the state of the county precluded an immediate provision to carry it out. The year 1786, it will be remembered, was that of the Shays Rebellion, and was certainly an unhappy one for raising taxes in Berkshire for any purpose, and most of all for the erection of court-houses and jails.

The court of General Sessions held at Pittsfield in May, 1786, nevertheless directed Eli Root, John C. Williams, and Simon Larned, all of that town, to prepare a plan for the public buildings to be built at Lenox, and report what materials would be required. Eli Root was also appointed to fill a vacancy caused by the resignation of Theodore Sedgwick on a commission previously named to select a proper site.

The succeeding terms of the court being obstructed by the Shays men, the committees had no opportunity to report until May, 1787, even if they desired to do so. But, early in that year, to have the Berkshire courts settled, the legislature, rendered impatient by the exciting events which had just transpired in the county, made a peremptory order that the Court of Common Pleas should be held at Lenox in the ensuing February, and the Supreme Court in May. The first term of the Common Pleas recorded to have been held there opened Sept. 11, 1787.

In the mean time, the Court of General Sessions, at the May term held at Great Barrington, selected Theodore Sedgwick and John Bacon of Stockbridge, and Major Azariah Eggleston of Lenox, to determine upon a site and contract for the erection of the buildings, which David Rossiter, Nathaniel Bishop of Richmond, and Benjamin Pierce were directed to superintend, and have finished as soon as possible. The county buildings were actually commenced in the spring of 1788. The jail was finished, and the prisoners were removed to it from Great Barrington, in the latter part of 1790; the court-house was completed in 1791 or 1792: the cost of the two buildings being £3,441. 5*s*., 3*d*., towards which, according to Dr. Field, "individuals in Lenox advanced, in building materials, £800." The court-house, a wooden building, now the Lenox town-hall, stood a few rods south of that now about to be abandoned by the courts, which was erected in 1815, and has been several times remodelled. The first jail was built upon a hill about half a mile south of the village, on the old Stockbridge Road.

CHAPTER XXIV.

THE MEETING-HOUSE OF 1790.

[1789–1793.]

Accommodations for Religious Worship in 1790. — Plans for a New Meeting-House. — Items from the Assessment of 1791. — Sale of Continental Money. — Materials for the New Meeting-House. — Location of the House. — Salvation of the Elm, and Creation of the Park. — Building of the House. — Disputes about Pews. — The First Bell. — Destruction of the Old Meeting-House. — Ball-Playing forbidden on the Common. — Town House and Academy erected. — Protection for the Burial-Ground. — John Chandler Williams. — Madam Williams.

MESSRS. Oliver Partridge and Moses Graves, in 1762, expressed to the General Court their opinion, that the little meeting-house then building, with perplexed and prolonged effort, by the poor proprietors of settling-lots at Poontoosuck, would be insufficient to contain the inhabitants when sixty families should be in town.

It was, however, made to answer, with no loud complaints of inconvenience, until, after thirty troubled years, Pittsfield, in 1790, had attained a population of two thousand, of which about two hundred were Baptists, Episcopalians, and Shakers.

The Baptists had a meeting-house, unfinished, in the West Part; the Shakers, another in the south-west; and the Episcopalians held divine service, with lay reading, oftenest in the spacious parlors of the Van Schaack mansion. But the attendance upon all these places of worship could not have sensibly diminished the congregation at the old meeting-house where Mr. Allen ministered to the "standing order."

Irreligious habits, contracted in years of war or popular tumult, contributed more sadly to lessen the number of constant worshippers; and the unattractive edifice drew within its narrow walls few whom the spirit of devotion, habit, or public opinion, did not compel thither.

But it appears from one of the resolutions quoted in the last chapter, that the growing necessity for a larger building was admitted, and that its location was one of the points in dispute among the people. Perhaps the existing dissensions had hindered the earlier undertaking of the work. Certainly the erection of a commodious and creditable house of worship was a task of no small magnitude as the town was then situated, and one for whose successful accomplishment united and amicable effort was so essential that it furnished a powerful inducement to that spirit of mutual forbearance which prevailed in the June meeting of 1788.

The first town action toward a new meeting-house was on the 13th of April, 1789, when the following committee was appointed to report a plan, with the estimated cost: Woodbridge Little, Daniel Hubbard, Timothy Childs, Joel Stevens, Simon Larned, Ebenezer White, Oswald Williams, David Bush,[1] and John Chandler Williams.

On the 23d of November, the committee reported, that, in their opinion, it was necessary to build a meeting-house seventy feet long, exclusive of porch and balcony, and fifty-one feet wide; that it was expedient to raise and cover the frame, paint, and glaze, in one year, of which the cost would be £701. 7*s.* 2*d.;* and that this would be about two-thirds of the entire expense. The question of finishing the interior they left to future consideration, with the design of postponing as long as possible the differences of opinion which were sure to arise regarding the mode of "seating the house."

The report was accepted, and the following committee was appointed to collect material: David Bush, Joel Stevens, John Chandler Williams, Simon Larned, John Partridge, Oliver Root, Josiah Moseley, Dan Cadwell, and Joel Dickinson.

This committee were instructed to give every person, as far as convenient, a chance to pay his proportion of the cost in material and labor, and to contract with the town debtors for payment in the same manner as far as they thought advantageous. The "Book of Credits" does not distinguish between the receipts on

1 There were at this time two citizens of the name of David Bush in active life, father and son; and the records rarely distinguish which is intended.

account of taxes and those in payment of debt; but otherwise they are very minute, and show from whose contribution almost every constituent of the building came, — from Dr. Timothy Child's eighty-feet stick of timber to the laborer's day's work or few bushels of lime. Thus, Stephen Fowler, who lies buried in the Pilgrim's Rest at the new cemetery, brought the ridgepole; Capt. Charles Goodrich, two sills; William Partridge, Josiah and Isaac Ward, a large stick; Col. Oliver Root, fifty feet of oak posts and forty-six feet of oak plates; Mrs. Stoddard and Mrs. Dickinson, widows of old friends, but leaders in opposing parties during the Revolution, united in contributing a pillar twenty feet long and a pine beam seventy feet; Zebulon Stiles, one of the earliest settlers, and now a slumberer in the Pilgrim's Rest, brought a sill fifty feet long; and Capt. Jared Ingersoll contributed, from his timber-land in Lenox, one of the pillars of the belfry: and thus through all the townsmen, or at least the Congregational portion of them.[1]

There is no intimation of any voluntary contributions, and there probably were none, as Joshua Danforth was in 1793 directed by a vote of the town to purchase a pulpit-cushion, — the article most likely to have been a gift. The only subscription-paper extant, connected with the building, is one to be paid in grain; and it expressly provides that the amounts contributed were to be deducted from the giver's next tax. A small portion of the taxes were paid in coin; and some who did not find it convenient to make payment either in this way or in the supply of material tendered neat cattle or grain, — a species of property which long afterwards continued, as it had been long before, the most convenient circulating medium within ordinary reach.

Some items of interest may be gathered from the assessor's books; and we take at random that of 1791, when £700 were assessed for "finishing the meeting-house."

The polls that year numbered 411; the real and personal estate and "faculty"[2] were valued at £3,626. 4*s*. 6*d*. The sum assessed for ordinary town charges was £297,— a little more than one-third of the expense of finishing the meeting-house. The poll-tax for town purposes was four shillings, two pence, the amount assessed

[1] It should be understood that the articles specified were only a portion of the contributions of most of the persons named.

[2] The faculty to obtain an income from skill in the learned professions, the arts, in mercantile business, or the like.

upon estates and faculty, one shilling, two pence, in the pound. The State tax of the town was £132; and that for the support of the minister, part of whose salary came from other sources, £58.

To raise the sum of £700 voted for finishing the meeting-house, a poll-tax of ten shillings, four pence, was assessed; which, if all had paid, — from Charles Goodrich down to Hazle-Blossom, negro, — would have produced £212. 7*s.* From estates and faculty, 2*s.* 9*d.* in the pound was levied; producing £496. 12*s.* 2*d.*

The heaviest real-estate tax-payers were as follows: Charles Goodrich, who owned more than a thousand acres in the east part, £10. 10*s.* 2*d.*; James D. Colt, who owned one thousand acres in the south-west, £9. 15*s.* 6*d.*; Henry Van Schaack, an Episcopalian, who was also assessed about £4. on personal property, £6. 15*s.* 6*d.*; Daniel Hubbard, £5. 7*s.* 11*d.*; Hannah, widow of Col. William Williams, £5. 6*s.* 10*d.*; Nathaniel Robbins, £5. 5*s.* 6*d.*

The well-to-do farmers paid from one pound to four; but by far the greater portion of the assessments were reckoned in shillings. Oliver Wendell, Margaret Phillips (grandmother of Mr. Wendell Phillips), Catharine Wendell, and other heirs of the first purchaser of the town, paid about £4 upon one thousand two hundred and sixty-eight acres still retained by them; and the non-resident heirs of Col. Stoddard paid a proportionate tax upon about eight hundred acres. John Chandler Williams was assessed £3. 17*s.* 8*d.* on real estate, 18*s.* personal, and £1. 4*s.* 9*d.* on faculty. This was the highest tax on faculty; the next being paid by Col. Danforth, who was postmaster, held other public offices, and was also in mercantile business. Col. Danforth also was honored with the largest assessment on personal property, — £7. On faculty, Daniel Weller, a tanner, paid £1. 2*s.*; Dr. Timothy Childs, 16*s.* 6*d.*; Thomas Gold, a lawyer, 13*s.* 6*d.*; Joel Dickinson, the master-builder of the meeting-house, 13*s.* 9*d.* Ministers of the gospel were exempt from taxation.

The sum of £600 thus assessed proved to be about one-third the whole cost of building; and as nearly one-third of that expense was defrayed by the application of the debts due the town, and from the sale of other property, a fair idea of the whole taxation for meeting-house purposes can be gained by doubling the items given.

The town in March, 1791, ordered the building committee to sell the "old Continental money and paper securities in the treasury for solid coin," and apply the proceeds to the purchase of lead for the meeting-house. The paper securities consisted of loan-office certificates, whose "specie value, by the scale," was $93.40, and "Hardy's indents" to the amount of $48. The Continental money amounted to £3,097; which had been handed down in sealed packages from treasurer to treasurer, awaiting the revival of the national credit. The whole was now sold for the pittance of £40. 10*s*., as appears from the record; although — owing to the use of that last resort of a lazy pen, an "et cetera" — the accounts do not show with absolute certainty whether the certificates were included in the sale.

The expenditure for lead was £39. 17*s*. 6*d*., and the freight upon it to Kinderhook was 12*d*.; so that this item seems to have been kept strictly within the appropriation.

From such various sources, means were obtained to meet the expenditures until they reached the sum of £2,188. 19*s*. 6*d*.; which proved to be the final cost of the structure.

This increase to double the original estimate was perhaps attributable in part to the natural proclivity of architects to under-estimates of cost, but was chiefly due to the increased size of the building over that of the plan accepted by the town, to the purchase of a bell, and probably to the addition, in the enthusiasm elicited by the progress of the work, of some luxuries which were not at first contemplated. The house, without any authority so far as appears from the record, was built ninety feet long, exclusive of the projecting porch, and fifty-five feet wide.

Although we find no intimation of any voluntary contributions, such as would now be made for a similar purpose, yet the whole assessment was only the equitable distribution of a burden which the community, with the eager consent of almost all its members, had imposed upon itself; and doubtless the great majority were more liberal in responding to the requisitions of the committee than they would have been in private bargaining. Tradition is, indeed, full of the zeal with which the fathers of the town sought out the choicest products of their forests, — for Berkshire woods were forests then, — and the glee with which they brought them to the appointed spot.

Certainly the material contributed for the new temple, which was to be the pride and the pet of the town, was not only abundant in quantity, but of the best quality which the rich forests of the neighborhood could afford. The spring of 1790 found the open space now occupied by the Park piled high with a still accumulating mass of stone, and such lumber as the valley has now not seen for many a long year.

But, before use could be made of it, a preliminary of no little difficulty remained to be settled. The vote, that the location of the new meeting-house should be determined by disinterested non-residents, seems to have been disregarded; for on the 5th of April, 1790, David Bush, jun., in behalf of a committee, reported that in their opinion "the meeting-house front door should face the south; that it should stand on the same ground that the old meeting-house covered; that the front sill should be on the north line of the highway; that the west side of the house should be about three feet west of the west side of the old meeting-house; and that the committee would have been willing to have carried it still farther west could it have been done without incommoding the monument of the late Col. William Williams."[1]

The meeting-house was located within a few feet of his monument, and, if it had not been in the way, would doubtless have been placed with only a small court-yard between it and North Street. The monument now stands south-west of St. John's Lake, in the new cemetery.

The report was adopted; but the location thus fixed was distasteful to a portion of the citizens, for a reason which curiously illustrates the delight which was anticipated in gazing upon the new building. Placed upon the proposed site, it would not be visible from the greater portion of West Street, while, if carried southward into the highway, the more ornamental portions would delight the eye of the traveller from the west on his way to church or to market; nay, some of the more favored denizens of that region could daily, in their homes, revel in the contemplation of its graces, perhaps—who could tell?—be made better Christians by this constant reminder of sacred things.

Twenty-three voters — principally those personally interested — accordingly requested a town-meeting, and were able to carry a vote to place the meeting-house seven feet further south than had been previously determined.

But for this it was necessary to fell the tall and graceful elm — fairer than any work of man's hand — which had been spared by the first settlers for its conspicuous beauty.

[1] Col. Williams died in 1785.

It must have even then entwined itself in the affections of many of the people; but its destruction seemed inevitable, and the first strokes of the axe had already wounded its devoted trunk, when it was saved by the spirited opposition of a noble woman.

It happened, by a fortunate chance, that, at the close of the Revolution, the handsome mansion on the site now between Park

JOHN CHANDLER WILLIAMS'S HOUSE.

Square and Williams Avenue had been purchased by John Chandler Williams, a gentleman of culture and refined tastes, who was also blest with an equally gifted wife.

It may well be imagined with what feelings they watched the impending destruction of the splendid old relic of the forest, which formed so unique an ornament of their neighborhood. So intense was the excitement of Mrs. Williams in view of the intended sacrilege, that she appeared upon the scene, and, finding the most passionate entreaties vain, threw herself between the tree and the axe, and at last procured a postponement of the work of destruction until the matter could again be considered by the town. The elm treasured the kindly act in its heart; and when it fell, full of years and honors, the tradition of its romantic salvation was found corroborated by the scars of three axe-strokes embedded in its annal of 1790.

The immediate danger past, Mr. Williams completed the good work which his wife had begun, by proposing to give to the town, for a common, so much of his land south of The Elm as they would leave of space between that point and the meeting-house. The generous offer was accepted; and thus Pittsfield acquired the ground for the beautiful little park now so attractive by its graceful circlet of elms and its sparkling fountain, and so hallowed by patriotic memories.

The first entry in the construction account for the meeting-house — it was a charge for the inevitable rum — was made on the same 10th of May, when the site was finally determined; and thenceforward the work went briskly on under the direction of Col. Joshua Danforth, John Chandler Williams,[1] and Daniel Weller, who in March had been elected a building-committee.

Col. Bulfinch of Boston, an architect of repute, furnished the designs, in accordance with which the new building became one of the finest specimens of those well-proportioned, cheery, wooden structures, with Grecian ornamentation, which, very similar in their general character, were about that time scattered through the more thrifty villages of New England; the contemporaries of those homes of stately comfort, the square, flat-roofed, and balustraded mansions, of broad halls and spacious parlors, like those erected in Pittsfield by Henry Van Schaack and Ashbell Strong.

Capt. Joel Dickinson, a skilful mechanic, was selected as master-builder, and took charge on the 18th of April.

The site selected was upon a ledge of hard, light-gray limestone, or marble, with a silicious intermixture ingrained; and the cellar, even under the costly edifice which now occupies the spot, is a very rude affair, excavated by enlarging the crevices of the rocks. So thin was the overlaying soil, that few graves had been made in it.

May was spent in preparing the foundation; the principal expenditures noted being for rum, powder, wedges, and fixing sheds. Rum, from the laying of the foundation to the dedication, was a large item in the construction accounts. One charge, a fair specimen of many, was "£4. 8*s*. for three hundred and fifty-two rations of rum in five weeks." The house was raised and covered, and probably painted and glazed, in 1790. Allusion is made to the raising in the record of a meeting in October in that year, which voted three shillings a day extra pay to David Ashley and Butler Goodrich for extraordinary services.

[1] See note at the end of this chapter.

The frame being extremely large and cumbrous, and the mechanical appliances for managing large timbers being very imperfect, it was necessary that workmen should go, at risk of life and limb, upon elevated or exposed portions of the unfixed roof and tower. This essential service was performed by Goodrich and Ashley, then young men of great activity, strength, and courage; and it was in this that they executed those feats which were rewarded by the town, and have been remembered by tradition. Ashley soon afterwards removed to the West; but his compeer lived to tell the story to his grandchildren, as the venerable "Deacon Goodrich."

The meeting of Oct. 4 also appointed a committee — John Chandler Williams, Daniel Hubbard, and Joshua Danforth — to provide material for finishing the house; and the following spring found the Common again cumbered with the contributions of tax-payers and town debtors.

But another of the local differences inevitable at every stage in the public works of the village arose; and a committee was appointed to consider in what form the pews should be made.

The committee was of the unusual number of eleven, attesting — as did also the character of the gentlemen composing it — the estimate which the town fixed upon the importance of its duties. It consisted of Daniel Hubbard, Oliver Root, David Bush, sen., Joseph Fairfield, Joshua Robbins, Eli Root, James D. Colt, J. C. Williams, Timothy Childs, and Daniel Sackett, — all men of weight in community, and most of them of advanced years.

This committee reported that it would be most convenient to finish the side-galleries with a set of pews on the sides, three feet and a half wide, and eleven feet and eight inches long; an alley of convenient width; and then two seats along the "breastworks," and two cross-alleys intersecting the whole at proper intervals.

Thus far the committee — eight being present — were unanimous. But, with regard to the arrangement of the lower part of the house, they divided; a majority recommending that the wall-pews should be made "of the length and width of a pattern which had been prepared," and that the body-pews should be seven and three inches long, five feet ten inches wide." This report was accepted by a small majority; but a petition was at once presented "to the gentlemen selectmen," for a new meeting, to see whether the town would reconsider its action, and adopt a more uniform plan for the lower part of the house; so that all the body-pews might be six feet three inches long, and five feet ten inches wide, and that the side wall-pews might be eleven feet eight inches long, and six feet wide, or that all the pews in the lower part of the meeting-house might be square, or as nearly so as the ground would admit."

In those days, habits of thought, social customs, and laws were slowly and reluctantly conforming themselves to the spirit of equality which the Revolution had infused into the Commonwealth; and there was often more in the apparently trivial village contentions than would appear from a casual inspection of the records. To use a Yankee illustration for a Yankee fact, the bird of freedom had burst its shell, but was still busily and sometimes testily engaged in pecking its young plumage to get rid of the adhering fragments. The present instance was a skirmish in the struggle to abolish that strange relic of the stiff old Puritan aristocracy,—the seating a congregation according to the estimate which a parish committee might happen to form of the relative "dignities" of the individuals composing it.

The signers of the petition for a more uniform style of pews, unlike the majority of the committee of eleven, although persons of respectable property and social position, were, with perhaps two exceptions, not those to whom the highest places in the synagogue would be likely to fall.

And as they could hardly hope to do away entirely with the unchristian distinctions which had crept into the temple of that worship whose Founder, when on earth, had not where to lay his head, they sought to render them less galling by making them less conspicuous. Although no record is found of the disposition which was made of the matter, it appears, from a plan of the house after its completion, that the first of the arrangements suggested by the petitioners was actually substituted for that recommended by the committee of eleven.

The meeting-house was completed in 1793, although some of the minor details of the work may have been left until the next spring.

The marble "step-stones"—the same which still serve in their old place before the new church—were drawn by a long string of oxen, and with jovial escort, from quarries in Richmond, about the 1st of February, 1793; and horse-blocks were brought about the same time to aid the fairer worshippers in dismounting from their pillions.

The first bell was a welcome new-comer in 1793. It was of the weight of seven hundred pounds only, but possessed a peculiarly silvery and musical tone, whose ringing echoes penetrated even to the summits of Washington Mountain in favorable conditions of the atmosphere. But the still-unsatisfied people must needs replace the tongue, which the maker had carefully adjusted to the strength of the sides, with one of heavier metal; and the experiment met the usual fate of overweening ambition.

The way being thus paved for a more ponderous successor, Col. Danforth — some extravagant propositions being set aside — was instructed to take the broken bell to some founder, and have

SECOND MEETING-HOUSE, AND FIRST TOWN-HALL.

it cast anew, adding *not more* than three hundred weight of metal; so that the second bell weighed about one thousand pounds.

It was further voted, "in order to secure the more speedy execution of the work," that "those gentlemen who may subscribe and pay any sum of money in advance shall have credit therefor on their next tax;" another of the frequent evidences of the scarcity of money in a community in which produce was, nevertheless, so abundant, that it was able, about the same time, to respond liberally to the application of the selectmen of Boston for aid to those left destitute by "the great fire" in that town.

The fate of the old meeting-house must not be omitted here. The intention of removing it to some convenient spot where it might continue to serve for a town-hall was abandoned; and a committee was appointed to sell it. But the sale was postponed so long that the old building became a source of danger to the new; for, the space between them being barely sufficient to admit the mortar-bed which was placed there, the lime caught fire, and it was with difficulty the flames were kept from spreading. The removal being doubtless hastened by the narrow escape, the old building was drawn a little way to the east, when its rotten timbers came crashing to the ground. One account says the destruction was intentional, and that a rope was attached to the top of the building at which the people pulled "with a will."

Whether the old men who had aided in its framing shed tears over the fallen hall of so many grave deliberations, and the walls which had echoed to so many pious exhortations, — as their descendants did over the fallen trunk of The Old Elm, — is not recorded; but the village urchins mounted the crushed roof in triumph, and held a gleeful jubilee over the deposed tyrant of their sabbath hours.[1]

In all the action of the town regarding the new meeting-house, it is noticeable that there is not a single allusion to the sacred purposes for which it was designed, in record, report, or petition; nor is there any indication that either the minister or the church was consulted in any matter connected with its construction. And it is still more remarkable, that there is no intimation, in the records of the church, of any knowledge on their part, that a work was in progress in which they naturally had so deep an interest, and for whose successful completion they doubtless often united in prayer. A similar statement is true with regard to the building of the first meeting-house; and, indeed, the records and papers of the town were always remarkably free from those pious phrases and professions with which public papers in Massachusetts were wont to be profusely interlarded.

Some minutes, however, might be looked for of provision for the dedication of the meeting-houses to divine service, either by the church or the town: but none has been found; and the only tradition of any, that is preserved, is of an account recently in existence which is said to have shown a generous consumption of the ingredients of punch.

[1] Among the urchin crowd was Jared Ingersoll, afterwards one of the most gallant captains in the war of 1812, and now a venerable citizen of eighty-two years, who distinctly remembers the scene.

There is abundant evidence, however, that their new house of worship was very precious in the eyes of the Pittsfield people of 1794, and that their hearts swelled with local pride as they introduced to its really beautiful interior the frequent strangers who were attracted to the town by the fame of its splendors.

Their regard for its neatness, if not for its sanctity, excluded town-meetings; and this resulted in the erection of a neat hall, as well as incidentally in a great improvement of the grammar-school.

After the destruction of their old haunt, the town-meetings were held in the "middle schoolhouse," which stood on the east of The Old Elm. This was exceedingly incommodious; and a meeting convened in it, and thus having a realizing sense of its utter unfitness for human occupation, appointed a committee to consider the most eligible mode of keeping a grammar-school, and to take into consideration the sale of the schoolhouse, and the erection of a new one, which might serve as a town-house.

The committee, consisting of J. C. Williams, Woodbridge Little, and Timothy Childs, reported that "a house ought to be built about forty-eight or fifty feet long by twenty-four or twenty-five wide, two stories high, with a flat square roof, a chimney at each end; that on the lower floor there should be two rooms, one for the grammar and one for the district school; that the chamber should be fixed with convenient seats, rising one above another in the form of a gallery, with a proper arrangement for the seats of the moderator, selectmen, and town-clerk, somewhat as in the chamber allotted to the use of the House of Representatives. This might also be convenient for learning to sing in, and for making exhibitions on quarter-day."

The committee thought the expense might be £200, or perhaps £250; and they submitted a plan by which it might be defrayed without any tax on the town.

In accordance with this report, a building for a town hall and academy was erected on the present site of St. Stephen's Church. The cost slightly exceeded the estimate; and the old schoolhouse, which probably was considered too luxurious for a hog-pen and not good enough for a barn, did not readily find a purchaser; but, by the aid of a tax of £75, the new town-house was completed and occupied by the March meeting of 1793.

The safety of the interior of the meeting-house being secured by the exclusion of the town-meetings, the exterior was protected by a by-law forbidding "any game of wicket, cricket, base-ball, bat-ball, foot-ball, cats, fives, or any other game played with ball," within eighty yards of the precious structure. As a matter of fact, however, the lovers of muscular sport were not absolutely excluded from the tempting lawn of the "Meeting-house Common," as the letter of the law would have excluded them.

It was, indeed, their favorite resort; but Chandler Williams was ever at hand, with his voice of courteous warning, to ward off the threatened bombardment, when the danger to the meeting-house windows became imminent.

Another incidental result which followed the building of the meeting-house was a more decent respect for the burial-ground; so that a vote was passed that it "shall no longer be improved for a pasture." A neat white fence was built along the Park-place front; and a curiously generous price was paid for a similar enclosure on North Street. In 1792, a committee appointed "to see if Dr. T. Childs might safely be permitted to build a medicine-store" on the west side of the meeting-house, reported that he might do so; and, upon their recommendation, the town granted to that gentleman, "a loan of the land" where P. Allen's bookstore now stands, to run as long as it should be used as a medicine-store, on condition that no family should ever live in it, and that the lessee should build, and keep in repair, a fence from the store to the corner of Park Place, similar to that with which it there connected.

It will thus be seen that the erection of the meeting-house, and the other buildings connected with it, in a few years created a marked alteration in the appearance of the centre of the village.

The meeting-house then built, having been injured by fire in 1855, was removed to the grounds of the Maplewood Young Ladies' Institute, and, having been slightly remodelled to adapt it to that purpose, is now the spacious and handsome gymnasium of that institution; the only material alteration in its exterior being the substitution of an observatory for the belfry.

The town-house long continued to serve for public meetings, and the multifarious purposes to which such a hall is put in New-England villages.

In the school-rooms on the lower floor, troops of Pittsfield children obtained the greater part of their education; and many now living in the town, with many more scattered far and wide, look back with pleasure to the days when their favorite sport of a summer evening was hurling pebbles at the swallows that swept and circled around the cupola and chimneys of the old academy.

In 1832, this building gave place to the Episcopal Church, and, having been entirely remodelled and renovated, is now a handsome residence on East Street.

NOTE.

John Chandler Williams was born at Roxbury in 1755. His father having been reduced in fortune, he repaired to Berkshire, then the land of promise for the ambitious poor, and, at the age of eighteen, held the office of deputy-sheriff, probably through the influence of his distant relative, the Chief Justice of the Common Pleas. When he first entered Pittsfield, a handkerchief held all his worldly possessions.[1] His term of office was brief; for, in 1774, he entered Harvard College, where he was supported by his own exertions, aided by his mother's family, the Chandlers of Worcester, and graduated in 1778. He, with many of his college-mates, was at the Battle of Lexington. On the 30th of April, the Provincial Committee of Safety summoned him to attend them, to be employed as an express. On the 23d of May, they furnished him with an order for horses and other necessaries " for his journey, he being in the country's service." On the 27th of June, his account of £4. 4*s.* 6*d.*, as " a rider in the service of the Colony," was allowed. The mission thus obscurely alluded to was, in part at least, the successful search for Gov. Hutchinson's letter-book, and other records of public moment, which were found in his country-seat at Milton Hills.[2]

It curiously happened that Chandler afterwards married the daughter of Col. Israel Williams, Hutchinson's Tory friend and correspondent, who was involved in serious trouble by the discoveries at Milton Hills.

Mr. Williams, after graduating at Harvard, studied law with Hon. John Worthington of Springfield, and commenced practice at Pittsfield in 1782. " As a lawyer," says Rev. Dr. George T. Chapman, "his standing was more than respectable. His mind was richly stored with legal knowledge; and of that knowledge he availed himself with the noble determination to be useful rather than splendid. . . . He acquired the esteem of the court, the bar, and the jury: he so ingratiated himself in the confidence of the community around him by the integrity of his conduct as to be proverbially eulogized as 'the honest lawyer.' "

He did not, however, confine himself to the practice of the law, but opened a store, which he conducted successfully, on the south side of the Park, where, soon after his removal to Pittsfield, he purchased the property which now lies on each side of Williams Avenue, and extends west to South Street, upon which the gambrel-roof mansion, now known as the Newton House, had then been just built.

His wife, Mrs. Lucretia, the preserver of the elm, was, as has been stated, the daughter of Col. Israel Williams, who commanded the Hampshire militia in the last French and Indian War, and was one of the most noted loyalists of the Revolution. Madam Lucretia inherited the Williams blood in all its pride and vigor. " She was," says the historian of the family, " a woman of uncommon spirit and *most* uncommon brilliancy of wit and intellect; always the centre of the circle in which she moved, and the point

[1] This is stated in the " History of the Williams Family " as being the case on his final settlement in Berkshire, which is clearly an error.

[2] Letter of Hon. E. A. Newton, in " History of Williams Family."

of attraction in all companies. She had a keen perception of the ridiculous; and the coxcomb, the frivolous, and the vicious received their due reward at her hands; but she was most kind and tender to the deserving." The most devoted of daughters, in the trouble which her father's political course brought upon him she was his chief solace and sustainer; and, when he was confined in Northampton jail as an enemy of his country, she, although but a girl of seventeen years, carried him his food daily from their home in Hatfield; submitting, for the sake of this sacred duty, to curb even her proud spirit under the annoyances and indignities inflicted by coarse and suspicious jailors. Naturally, her affections were not conciliated to the Whig party by this treatment; and, while she lived, she considered herself a subject of the English Crown, and invariably spoke of the war of the Revolution as "the Rebellion."

Some notable displays of the Williams spirit are related of her in Pittsfield. The house which Mr. Williams purchased on his removal to that town was originally surrounded by a fine growth of buttonwoods, then a favorite shade-tree. But the husband and wife agreed in preferring the more stately and graceful elm; and it was agreed, that, at some time, the buttonwoods must give place to their betters; but dread of the naked aspect which the place must for a while bear, postponed the change from year to year. But one spring, Mr. Williams set off for Boston to attend to his duties as a legislator; and, on his return, his wife triumphantly pointed him to a lawn as bare of forestry as his smoothest meadow. There was nothing to do but to introduce the long-desired elms. And to this incident, together with the skill used in selecting from the widely differing varieties of the elm, is due the noble colonnade of trees which now shade the new Court Square.

The other anecdote is no less characteristic of the times, and of the parties connected with it. It seems that a notorious demagogue had incurred the wrath of Thomas Allen, jun., by circulating some slander against his father; whereupon the younger Thomas, in accordance with a custom now passed away, lashed the offender across The Park and down East Street. Now, it happened that the houses of Chandler Williams and the Rev. Mr. Allen stood opposite each other at the head of that street; and, as the whipped and the whipper passed between, Madam Williams appeared at her gate, and, handing out a new whip, cheered on the excoriation with, "That's right, Tom! Give it to him well! Lay it on to the rascal!"

While, across the way, the venerable pastor stretched out his hands, crying, "Thomas, my son, forbear; forbear, Thomas, my son."

And Thomas, more gallant than dutiful, obeyed the lady.

Mr. and Mrs. Williams lie buried in the lot of their son-in-law, the late Hon. E. A. Newton, in the Pittsfield cemetery.

John C. Williams

CHAPTER XXV.

STRUGGLE FOR THE EQUALITY OF RELIGIOUS DENOMINATIONS.

[1772–1811.]

State of the Law. — Appropriations for the New Meeting-House resisted. — Baptists, Shakers, Episcopalians, and Methodists. — Protest of the Dissenters. — List of Dissenters in 1789. — Inquisition into Religious Faith. — Henry Van Schaack appeals to the Courts. — The Decision. — State Laws for the Support of Religious Worship remodelled. — Pittsfield Parishes.

THE means of defraying the cost of the new meeting-house were not raised without creating the usual village dissensions; and, as usual, these divisions formed a part of the struggle to make practical that equality before the law, which, although theoretically proclaimed by the Declaration of Rights, was still, in practice, denied, especially by the prevalent construction of the article in that instrument concerning the support of the institutions of religion.

In accordance with the new fundamental law, as well as with the ancient colonial statutes, towns in Massachusetts were constituted religious parishes, charged with the maintenance of public worship, and were required to compel the attendance upon it of such of their inhabitants as could conscientiously unite in the established exercises.

Against the incorporation of this portion of the colonial system into the institutions of the new Commonwealth, there had been an earnest but unavailing protest. Two classes of men had, in the Revolution, combined on the patriotic side, — those who would resist every encroachment, from whatever quarter, upon civil liberty or the natural rights of the individual, and those who simply desired to protect the ancient status of the Congregational and republican Colony against the attacks of Episcopal and imperial Britain. It was inevitable, therefore, that, the contest with the mother country being over, a new division of opinions should arise upon matters in which the spirit and practice inherited from colonial times seemed oppugnant to the liberty of the citizen. And thus a new struggle commenced, influenced more or less on both sides by selfish interests and personal prejudices, but nevertheless with a foundation of principle at bottom.

Two points of difference appeared, even before the colonists had any other assurance of success than the confidence which true men have in a just cause and in themselves, — protest being made against African slavery, and the compulsory support of public worship; the Baptists and Friends leading in the opposition to the latter.

The members of these denominations carried their efforts to effect a change into the constitutional convention of 1779, and there made a vigorous effort to do away with the whole system of State interference with religious matters, but in vain. Indeed, John Adams, as early as 1774, in an interview concerning this matter at Philadelphia with certain Pennsylvania Quakers, who wished to make it an element of national politics, had said somewhat petulantly, that he "knew they might as well turn the heavenly bodies out of their annual and diurnal course, as the people of Massachusetts from their meeting-house and Sunday laws."

The substance of the old statutes was therefore retained in the Declaration of Rights, which empowered the towns to tax polls and estates for the support of the public worship, which they were required to maintain, with the proviso that the tax-payers of a different religious denomination from that held by a majority of the town might require their assessments to be paid to teachers of their own faith, if there were any such, upon whose ministration they usually attended when in health; otherwise the payments to be made to the religious teacher or teachers of the parish in which they were levied.

The right of control, in religious as in other matters, pertained to the majority of voters, whatever their creed, provided it were Protestant and Christian. The Baptists, Friends, and Methodists were, however, opposed to the exercise of this right on principle, and the Episcopalians from policy; so that it was stated, with probable correctness, in the constitutional convention of 1820, that the Congregationalists alone had availed themselves of it, while by many even of that denomination it was looked upon with disfavor.[1]

Thus stood the law and public sentiment when the people of Pittsfield, in November, 1789, undertook to build the new meeting-house. But, in order to fully understand their bearing upon the subject of the new enterprise, some account is necessary of those in Pittsfield who dissented from "the standing order," as the dominant sect was called, and formed a considerable body of Baptists, Shakers, Episcopalians, and Methodists, perhaps numbering between two and three hundred souls in all, although represented by only thirty or forty tax-payers.

The Baptist faith was introduced into Pittsfield by Elder Valentine Rathbun. The reader is already familiar with the character of this gentleman as a political leader in Revolutionary times, when he was in excellent accord with Rev. Mr. Allen, except when his zeal incited him to even more radical measures than those which his Congregational brother favored.

His active and ardent temperament manifested itself in religion as in politics, rendering him restless and perhaps unquiet in pursuit of divine truth, and subject to quick sympathies, which sometimes led him astray, but of a sincere piety, which forbade him to persist in conscious error. He had received neither a classical nor theological education,— which might perhaps have preserved him from the delusion into which he fell for a time, — but has left evidence that he was not entirely unfitted for the office of a preacher, either in natural gifts, intellectual culture, or general information. Those who put faith in the indications of character afforded by chirography would attribute to him a nervous organization of extreme refinement and delicacy.

Shortly after his removal to Pittsfield, Mr. Rathbun began to hold meetings in his own house, and soon won to his faith several of his neighbors, who, in 1772, united themselves in a society of Baptists, or Anabaptists, — as they were more commonly called, from the prominence which their refusal of infant baptism held in the popular idea of their creed.

The new sect flourished for a while, but soon met with a sad in-

[1] The proposition to abolish it was introduced into the convention of 1820 by Dr. H. H. Childs, a Pittsfield Congregationalist, who championed it with ability and most persistent zeal, both in that body, and, when it was lost there, before the people, until it was finally carried in 1833.

terruption to its prosperity. In 1780, Mother Ann Lee, the Shaker prophetess, set out on her famous proselyting tour from Watervliet, N.Y., to Harvard, Mass. On their way, the apostolic party visited New Lebanon and Hancock, in which vicinity a most remarkable "revival of religion" had prevailed during the preceding year, having commenced in the fall of 1779 at New Lebanon, — then a part of the township of Canaan, — under the auspices of four women, exceedingly "gifted in prayer," who sent out their sweet influences from private houses, but most powerfully from "Darrow's barn," which stood where the Shaker Village at New Lebanon now does. These women, and other persons, chiefly Baptists, embraced the Shaker faith; so that when "Mother Ann, and the elders with her," in 1780, appeared upon the field so ripe for their reaping, the excitement was unbounded; and thousands flocked together from the neighboring towns in New York and Massachusetts to listen to her novel and marvellous doctrines.

It was not strange that a man like Mr. Rathbun should be carried away by the contagious enthusiasm of the hour, or that he should be fascinated by the new doctrines, among which the necessity of "personal purity" and "the mortification of the flesh" were prominently taught. It is not unlikely, also, that his sensitive and nervous mental system, which had been for years held at its extreme tension by his active duties in regard to the cruel contest with Great Britain, may have been ready to re-act to the other extreme of holding all war to be sinful. But, if the conversion of Mr. Rathbun to the Shaker faith is not unaccountable, it is still less strange that he soon found the practices of his new associates unsatisfactory, and hastened to renounce his connection with them, and publish a book opposing their creed, but more especially in denunciation of their practices.

Not content with this endeavor to repair the mischief in which he had been led to take part, Mr. Rathbun, in the March meeting of 1781, moved and carried a resolution appointing a committee to devise "some measures to take with those people known as Shakers," who, it seems, in his opinion, were exceeding the bounds of even Baptist toleration.

The committee consisted of Rev. Mr. Allen, Elder Rathbun, Elnathan Phelps, Eli Root, and Woodbridge Little; and, at the adjourned meeting in April, the following report, signed by Rev.

Mr. Allen "per order of the committee," was submitted and adopted: —

"The committee appointed on Mr. Rathbun's motion, respecting those people in town called and known by the name of Shakers, beg leave to report, —

"That they have attended to the object of their commission, so far as they imagined in duty and prudence they ought, and that they have reason to apprehend that those people called Shakers are, in many instances, irregular and disorderly in their conduct and conversation, if not guilty of some high crimes and misdemeanors. The committee therefore recommend it to the town to direct their selectmen to take such cognizance of all disorderly and idle persons in the town, and of their families, as in prudence and by law they may and ought; and, further, that the town give particular instructions to their respective grand jurors to be chosen for the next courts to inquire into all the conduct and practices of said people which are contrary to law, and make due presentment thereof, particularly all blasphemies, adulteries, fornications, breaches of sabbath, and all other breaches of law, which they may have been guilty of; and that all tithing-men and other persons use their best endeavors, according to law, to suppress all disorders and breaches of the peace of every kind; and also that the town direct their town-clerk to inform the commissioners, or other proper authority in the county of Albany, that great and manifest inconveniences and dangers arise from the correspondence and intercourse subsisting between the people of Niskeuna [Watervliet] called Shakers and some people of this town and county disposed to embrace their erroneous opinions, and that they be requested to co-operate with us in endeavoring to prevent such intercourse and correspondence by all possible ways and means.

"THOMAS ALLEN,
"*Per order of the Committee.*

"PITTSFIELD, April 2, 1781."

Mr. Rathbun did not succeed in leading back to the Baptist fold all who, with him, had wandered from it; some even of his own kinsmen adhering firmly to the Shaker faith: but he recovered, in a great degree, the confidence of community and of his co-religionists. He resumed his pastorate; and the church which, after his return to it, continued for seventeen years under the charge of its founder, was not unprosperous for the greater portion of that time, although doubtless weakened by the unfortunate lapse of 1780. In 1781, the Shaftsbury Association, comprising the Baptist churches within a wide circuit around that place, was formed; and in its ranks Mr. Rathbun's flock held at least a respectable position, reporting, in 1786, twenty-four members, of whom seven had been admitted during the year.

In 1790, as has been stated, the committee of the town, who manifestly were not inclined to enlarge the Baptist borders, reported twenty-one tax-payers indisputably connected with the society (besides Mr. Rathbun himself, who was exempted from taxation as a public teacher of religion), and several others whose claims to membership were disputed. This would indicate a still more numerous communion than in 1786; but in 1798, whether from the revival of old difficulties, or the engendering of new, the church had become so much reduced, that Elder Rathbun, with one of his deacons, appeared before the association, and requested that its name might be dropped from the rolls.

Mr. Rathbun immediately left Pittsfield, and settled at Scipio, N.Y. Whether his removal was the cause or effect of the decay of his church does not appear; but he maintained his reputation as a sincere Christian in his new home, and from him are descended some of the most respectable citizens of Western New-York, as well as of Pittsfield and the Valley of the Mississippi.

The church was re-organized in 1800, under the eldership of Rev. John Francis, who had been one of the early members of Mr. Rathbun's flock.

The manner in which Shakerism was introduced into this vicinity has been incidentally related above. The Pittsfield converts, or a portion of them, formed the nucleus of a family which established itself near the clothier-works of Mr. Rathbun, on the site still occupied by their successors. In their first days, they were charged with gross immoralities, or, as the more charitably inclined framed their indictment, indecencies. If there was any ground for these allegations in their conduct under the first excitement of an ill-regulated zeal, it was soon reformed; and, in 1790, the Shakers were recognized as upon an equal footing with other dissenting religious bodies, so far as regarded the payment of taxes for the support of public worship; and, by their industry and scrupulous morality, they have since won a high place in the esteem of their neighbors, although the Commonwealth has steadily refused to incorporate them.

The Methodist-Episcopal Church first obtained adherents in Pittsfield in 1788, through the preaching of Rev. Messrs. Lemuel Smith and Thomas Everett, who were then travelling the Stockbridge Circuit, and formed a class in the East Part.

Another was formed in the West Part by Mr. Smith, who preached his first sermon in 1791 at the house of Col. Oliver Root. With true Methodist zeal, these gentlemen held meetings in school-houses, private dwellings, barns, in the groves and the open fields, wherever two or three could be gathered to listen to their fervid words; and not without fruit.

Methodism was formally established in Pittsfield in 1792, by Rev. Robert Green, who, on his way to New Lebanon, was detained by a storm at the house of Capt. Joel Stevens, on the eastern base of the Taconic Mountains, and there made excellent use of his time in preaching, and organizing the Pittsfield Circuit.

The first local preacher was the eccentric and eloquent Lorenzo Dow; and, under a succession of faithful pastors, the denomination flourished throughout that century, as it has continued to do in this. In 1798, the Methodists built a meeting-house forty-two and a half feet long by thirty four and a half feet wide on the main street, west of Lake Onota, — the old black meeting-house of later years, dilapidated, but hallowed in many hearts by the memory of fervent prayer, and exhortation to repentance. Deacon Josiah Wright, one of the Revolutionary patriots most trusted for his hearty zeal tempered with sound discretion and practical judgment, was a leading member of the denomination; and his associates were distinguished for exemplary Christian deportment and warm devotion.

The Episcopalians were few in number, and had been loyalists of the Revolution; and perhaps sympathy with England insensibly inclined them to her church. But Mr. Van Schaack, educated in the Dutch Reformed creed, early became an Episcopalian, after much study and reflection. Four of the six tax-payers reported among them in 1790 were men of substance; while Henry Van Schaack, their chief, with the position and character ascribed to him in a former chapter, was well qualified to lead the dissenters of Pittsfield in their resistance to the assessment made upon them for the erection of the meeting-house of 1790. And upon him, indeed, fell the whole brunt of the battle, although he was supported, so far as their support was of avail, by all the Baptists and Episcopalians. The Methodists were not yet as sufficiently organized to take part in the legal contest; and the Shakers probably declined to appeal to the tribunals of the world's people.

The vote to build the meeting-house, the reader will remember, was passed in November, 1789; the first assessment of taxes to defray the expense (£500) was voted in March, 1790; and £250 additional followed in August of the same year.

The first recorded opposition by the dissenters was made at the last-named meeting, when the following spirited protest was entered, but secured no notice from the meeting, further than a vote that the taxes for the building of the meeting-house should be assessed separately from those for ordinary town-purposes: —

"We, the underwritten persons, beg leave to state to the town that the Presbyterians, being the most numerous sect of Christians in the town of Pittsfield, have of late obtained several votes in town-meetings for building a place of religious worship, and have, in some of those meetings, made various appropriations of town-property for erecting the same. And as the subscribers to this paper are freeholders and inhabitants of the town aforesaid, differing in religious sentiments with those for whose use the said place of worship is building, they do in this public manner disclaim any right or pretension to the same, under the idea that it cannot, in any construction, be considered as a town-building, but merely for accommodating a particular denomination of Christians; and that as we, in our several stations, contribute a share of our property voluntarily to the support of the gospel, according to our religious professions, we do claim it as our right to be exempted from any assessments, or other burthens, that have been, or which may be, imposed by any town vote, or otherwise, for building the place of worship aforesaid, or any other in the same predicament.

"Furthermore we do, in justice to ourselves and the Christian denominations we belong to, protest against any town-vote that now does, or which hereafter may, operate so as to assess or burthen one religious sect of Christians for building places of religious worship for another, or that any part of the town-property shall be applied for purposes but what are actually for town-uses. Contrary doctrines, it is conceived by the undersigned, tend to subordinate one sect or denomination of Christians to another, in direct violation of the Constitution of this Commonwealth, and contrary to the practice of Christians in general, in the United States of America.

"Dated and signed in Pittsfield, at a town-meeting held the —— of August, 1790.

John Branch.	Valentine Rathbun.
Andrew Langworthy.	John Baker.
John Jefferds.	Asa Branch.
Dyer Fitch.	Saxton Rathbun.
H. Van Schaack.	Stephen Jewett.

Protests and appeals having proved of no avail, occasion was found by the next town-meeting to promise indemnity to the assessors for the costs and damages which Henry Van Schaack might recover in the suit which he had commenced against them. John C. Williams and Dr. Timothy Childs were also appointed to aid the assessors with council and advice.

In December, 1791, and again in March, 1792, Mr. Van Schaack sent communications to the selectmen, stating, that, in the arrangements for "seating" the new meeting-house, a part of a pew had been assigned him, with the evident intention of giving countenance to the idea that he was to be considered as belonging to the "Congregational persuasion," and therefore liable to the collection of the oppressive taxes levied to build an expensive house of worship, beneficial only to the Congregational Society, and dedicated to God on principles of religion different from those which he professed. He therefore disclaimed in December all right and interest in the building, and reiterated his disclaimer in March, under seal and attested by witnesses. He states, in those papers, that he supports his own mode of worship in a neighboring town, Lenox,[1] and therefore considers that "to compel him to maintain that of another denomination bears an aspect too unfriendly to the sacred rights of conscience secured him by the Constitution, and therefore is an imposition not to be submitted to." He denies that the meeting-house was built in accordance with a town-vote, and asserts that the action regarding it was that of the Congregationlists alone.

In the December communication, Mr. Van Schaack demanded that it should be made part of the business of the next town-meeting, —

"*First*, That those who are not of the Congregational persuasion may have an opportunity publicly to give their reasons for disclaiming any right to seats in the new meeting-house; and that those objections might be lodged in the town-records.

"*Second*, That the town would call upon the committee appointed nearly two years ago to sell the school-lands, for a report of how this property has been disposed of, and how the avails have been appropriated."

[1] "The Episcopal Religious Society of Lenox, Pittsfield, Lee, and Stockbridge" was incorporated in 1805, Henry Van Schaack and Tertullas Hubby of Pittsfield being corporate members; but religious service in the Episcopal form had been previously held in Lenox.

The effect of Mr. Van Schaack's persistence, and of his appeal to the court, began now to manifest itself; and the town, March, 1792, appointed a committee to ascertain the names of those persons who had really been dissenters on the 1st of November, 1789, — when the building of the meeting-house was undertaken, — and still continued to be so.

The limitation as to time was due to the fact, that the religious opinions of some persons began to be seriously affected by the expectation that dissent from Congregationalism would exempt them from the meeting-house tax.

The committee selected for this delicate inquisition into the religious faith of the tax-paying community was John C. Williams, Woodbridge Little, Daniel Hubbard, Timothy Childs, Thomas Gold, John Baker. They reported in April the following list; which was accepted by the town, with the exception of the name of Stephen Jewett, who, in spite of his professed submission to Episcopal rule, was solemnly adjudged an Independent Congregationalist, — orthodox enough, at least, for taxation purposes.

DISSENTERS FROM CONGREGATIONALISM LIABLE TO TAXATION AS RESIDENTS IN PITTSFIELD, NOV. 1, 1789: —

Episcopalians. — Jonathan Hubby, James Heard, Henry Van Schaack, Esq., Eleazer Russell, Titus Grant, Stephen Jewett.

Shakers. — John Deming, Ephraim Welch, Josiah Talcott, Rufus Coggswell, Dr. Shadrach Hulbert, Joshua Birch, Daniel Goodrich, Hezekiah Osborn, Samuel Phelps.

Baptists. — John Baker, Solomon Deming, Saxton Rathbun, Benjamin Rathbun, Noadiah Deming, Ezekiel Crandall, John Francis, Josiah Francis, James Rathbun, Charles Lamb, John Branch, Asa Branch, David Ashley, John Jefferds, Andrew Langworthy, Williard Langworthy, Moses Merwin, Hubbard Goodrich, Jonathan Chadfield, John Remington, John Bryant.

Other tax-payers claiming that their dissent from Congregationalism had been unjustly disallowed, it was voted, at a subsequent meeting, to re-open the lists. What the result was is not recorded; but we may gather the character of the inquisition into the faith of individuals from the following paper filed in the town-archives, as —

Names of Persons who wish to be exempted from paying a Minister's Tax.

Robert Francis, — pleads conveniency.

John Francis, —

Charles Lamb, — a Churchman.

Dyer Fitch, — rather a Baptist in sentiment.

Uriah Betts, — a Baptist in sentiment, but can attend other meetings without injuring his conscience.

Walter Welch, — a Baptist by education, &c.

Augustus Crandall, — a Seventh-day Baptist, but now attends Mr. Rathbun's; never attended any other meeting.

Moses Wood, — a Baptist by profession.

Seth Janes, — a Baptist, as much as any thing, and now supports Mr. Rathbun on Sundays.

John Weed, — a Baptist in sentiment; ditto.

Daniel Rust, — profits most by hearing Mr. Rathbun; chooses to attend there from principle.

Abijah Wright, — a constant attendant on Mr. Rathbun.

Timothy Hurlbert, — an attendant on Mr. Rathbun.

David Ashley, — thinks it not right to support Mr. Allen by a tax.

David Ashley, jun., — an attendant on Mr. Rathbun's meeting from a child, and chooses to attend there still.

John Phelps, — thinks the Baptists to be most right.

Abiather Millard, — brought up a Baptist, and thinks it not right to support a minister by a tax.

Caleb Wadhams, — cannot attend on Mr. Allen, because he thinks it not right to support a minister by a tax.

Seth Dickinson, — can't pay his debts.

I do truly and absolutely believe in the Baptist persuasion. May this be recorded. — Seth Janes.

Nathan Davis, — a Baptist in principle.

Israel Miner, — never heard Mr. Allen, and can teach Mr. Allen, and thinks he ought not to pay his rates to him, and is a Shaker as much as any thing.

The March meeting, besides taking measures to ascertain the names of those "who were of a different denomination of Christians from that which is most prevalent in this town," had appointed a committee to consider whether the taxes of such persons should be abated in whole or in part.

The committee were Daniel Hubbard, Woodbridge Little, David Bush, John C. Williams, and Timothy Childs. Their report was in marked advance of previous action.

They acknowledged that it would be unreasonable and absurd for the town to dispute the equitable and constitutional rights and immunities of the dissenters; but that it ought, on the contrary, publicly to disclaim all wish or idea of compelling the payment of the tax assessed upon them towards building the meeting-house or the support of a public teacher in the town, to any use contrary to that which they had a right to request.

The committee, however, were quite as clearly of opinion, that it would be unsafe for the town, and repugnant to the undoubted intent of the Constitution, to abate the taxes of dissenters, and, indeed, that it had no right to do so; yet as, on account of some expectation of that kind, there had been delay in the collection of taxes, and as there "appeared to be a happy spirit of conciliation and a general disposition to peace, unity, and friendship prevailing," and a manifest unwillingness to take any undue advantage of the neglect or laches which had arisen, the committee advised "that the collection of taxes of dissenters should be suspended for three weeks, in order that they might have an opportunity to lodge with the treasurer a written request for the payment of the sums assessed upon them to the support of their respective teachers or elders; and if, previous to the collection of said taxes, any of the dissenters should produce to the treasurer an order, receipt, or discharge from such teachers, then the treasurer should give his orders to the collectors in accordance therewith; but, if no requisition for a different disposal of the taxes of any person should be filed within three months, they should be applied, in accordance with the requirements of the Constitution, to the support of the public worship of the standing order.

The committee did not touch upon the appropriation of the common property of the town, including that dedicated by law to the support of schools, for the benefit of a society composed of a portion of its citizens only. Its object seems to have been to lay the taxes for religious purposes equally upon all persons; but, while those of the Congregationalists were divided between the building of the meeting-house and the support of the minister, those of the other denominations were all to be paid to their respective ministers for their support: so that an inducement might not be held out to any to attach themselves to the denomination which supported its establishment in the cheapest manner; and, on the other hand, that religious societies might not be tempted, by the hope of securing this class of converts, to employ cheap and consequently ignorant preachers. It is probable that this was among the motives of the town from the first in its attempt to assess the meeting-house tax upon dissenters.

The difficulty was one inseparable from the interference of the State in religious matters, which in many respects operated to the injury of the apparently favored sect as well as of others.

The disposition of the matter recommended by the report to the April meeting was probably as fair as any thing which could have been devised, so far as taxation was concerned.[1] But the committee proposed no removal of one main cause of complaint; and for this, as well as perhaps for other reasons, it was unsatisfactory to the dissenters. Mr. Van Schaack therefore continued his legal proceedings, being encouraged to persist by letters from Bishop Seabury of Connecticut; Rev. Dr. Parker, afterwards Bishop of the New-England diocese; Rev. Dr. Stillman, an eminent Baptist divine of Boston, Gov. Eustis, and others.[2] He was non-suited in the Common Pleas, — "laughed out of Court;" but he at once carried the issue to the Supreme Bench, being sustained in his determination to do so by the opinion of Bishop Parker, that, "in spite of the horse-laugh of Judge Paine," the court of final resort was certain to pronounce in his favor. In the mean time, the town instructed the collectors not to "distress" any of the dissenters, recognized as such in the previous year, for their meeting-house tax; nor for the minister's previous to the second week in October, unless they were about to leave town.

In the first week of October, the case was decided by the Supreme Court in Mr. Van Schaack's favor.

In the warrant for the town-meeting of November, 1792, an article was inserted, probably at the instance of some dissenter, "to ascertain the sense of the town, whether, in case Mr. Van Schaack should recover damages and costs in his suit against the assessors, they were to be indemnified by a charge upon all ratable polls and estates, or only upon such as were of the Congregational persuasion."

No action is recorded upon this; but the meeting of November,

[1] The course recommended was that generally adopted at the east, in consequence of a decision of the Supreme Court in favor of the Baptists of Cambridge, in a suit against that town, which had also been sustained in other cases.

[2] Letters in the collection of Henry Van Schaack, Esq., of Manlius.

1794, directed the Committee on Accounts to ascertain the expense of the Van Schaack suit, and the amount paid by each dissenter towards it, and to give them credit for it in the next town-tax, which was correspondingly increased for the Congregationalists.

At the same meeting, it was voted to raise £125 for public worship; of which Mr. Allen was to receive £110, he furnishing his own wood: the remainder to go to the dissenters.

The system of accepting the certificates of their several pastors in discharge of the taxes assessed upon dissenters from Congregationalism for religious purposes continued until 1799, when the laws in regard to the support of public worship had, by a multitude of enactments and judicial decisions, became so vague and conflicting, that it was necessary to remodel them.

The new act required every town, precinct, or parish incorporated for religious purposes, to maintain a public teacher of morality, piety, and religion, — the designation then given to ministers of the gospel, — and conferred upon each of those corporations the power to tax its members for the support of a minister and the building of a suitable house of worship. By this law, every inhabitant in a town was presumed to belong to the original parish, unless he annually procured a certificate signed by the pastor of some other parish, and also by its committee specially elected for that purpose, that he commonly and usually, when in health, worshipped with them.

Under this system, the people of Pittsfield, in common with those of the rest of the State, lived until the amendment of the Constitution in 1834. Some amendments of the law were, however, made in 1811, which had a local as well as a general interest. Up to the year 1810, members of unincorporated religious societies were supposed to be entitled to the same privileges in the disposal of their taxes, and their pastors to the same exemption from assessment, with those of incorporated parishes. In that year, a judicial decision overthrew the commonly-received opinion, and an intense excitement was caused at the east, where scarce one dissenting society in ten was incorporated. The legislature of 1811, elected under the influence of this agitation, made the law to conform to the old practice, and further advanced one or two points in a liberal direction. Where two parishes of the same denomination existed in a town, members of one were permitted to transfer their connection to the other in the same manner as to one of a different creed; and non-resident tax-payers dissenting from the faith of the town-parish were granted the same right to direct the disposal of their taxes which residents possessed. The two latter clauses were of interest in Pittsfield, where a second Congregational parish, divided from the first upon political grounds, was springing up, and was favored by wealthy non-resident proprietors, including Oliver Wendell.

With regard to the rights of unincorporated societies, the interest was confined to the Shakers, whom the legislature have to this day steadily refused to incorporate, holding it inconsistent with sound policy to countenance a body hostile to the institution of marriage. All the other religious bodies in Pittsfield were specially incorporated, except the town (now the first Congregational) parish. With regard to this, a proposition was made, after the decision of the Van Schaack case in 1793, "to procure an act to incorporate the inhabitants of this town into a parish by the name of the Congregational Society in the Town of Pittsfield." Woodbridge Little, Timothy Childs, Simon Larned, Daniel Hubbard, and John Chandler Williams[1] were appointed to report upon the measure, and actually drafted a bill. The matter, however, was suffered to drop; and the First Congregational Parish of Pittsfield is such only by virtue of the general provisions in the old statutes, and in the constitutional amendment of 1834.[2]

The controversy in regard to the rights of dissenters, although sometimes giving occasion for unpleasant incidents, was, upon the whole, carried on with much less acrimony than usually attended the internal discords of the town. Public improvements were in the mean time made harmoniously; and Mr. Van Schaack was assigned prominent places upon the various committees, side by side with his leading opponents.

These who, upon principle, refused to pay their assessments for building the new meeting-house, were fain to confess the benefits which it conferred upon the whole town, and could not but show a local pride in its fame.

[1] Mr. Williams, who was so prominent in these affairs as a Congregationalist, became afterwards one of the most zealous Episcopalians.

[2] The First Congregational was a territorial parish, circumscribed by the town-boundaries. Those which were formed without regard to such limits, of such members as the corporation saw fit to admit, were known as *poll*-parishes, and often extended into several towns; as the Methodist Society of Pittsfield, Hancock, Dalton, and Washington, and the Episcopal parish before mentioned.

In the erection of the fine schoolhouse connected with the town-hall, and in the establishment of the excellent grammar-school which almost immediately ensued, the amount of money taken from the school-fund was more than restored; and, from 1793 to 1834, the different religious sects of Pittsfield lived together in as great harmony as the irritations which the law's interference with their mutual relations would admit.

APPENDIX.

A.

DEPRECIATION OF PROVINCIAL CURRENCY.

It would be impossible to obtain a correct idea of the prices paid in the purchase of lands, or in other pecuniary transactions mentioned in our story, previous to the year 1752, without taking into consideration the depreciation of the currency of the Province during that period.

When lawful money is specified in the account, silver is to be understood; gold not having been made a legal tender until 1761, when a law to that effect was obtained after a long and bitter struggle.

In 1690, in an emergency of the war then raging, the Province began the issue of treasury notes of the value of from five shillings to five pounds each; £40,000 in amount being emitted. Before the end of 1692, these bills depreciated at least one-third; but the General Court then made them a legal tender, and further enacted, that, in all public payments, they should be received at an advance of five per cent. By these means, the bills were restored to an equality with specie, and kept at par about twenty years.

But, in 1703, the government, yielding to a popular clamor for an expansion of the currency, began a financial system upon that principle. The effects of this inflation upon the paper currency were, however, not very apparent until about 1712, when the government, being compelled to extend the period for the redemption of its notes, the public confidence in them was shaken, and they began steadily to depreciate, and continued to do so year by year. Previous to 1712, the bills passed at the value of eight shillings for an ounce of silver. The depreciation from that time is represented in the following table:—

Years	Value
1710 1711	*8s.*
1712 1713	*8s. 6d.*

Year	Value
1714, 1715	9*s*.
1716, 1717	10*s*.
1718	11*s*.
1719, 1720	12*s*.
1721	13*s*.
1722	14*s*.
1723	15*s*.
1724, 1725, 1726, 1727	17*s*.
1728	16*s*. 6*d*. — 17*s*. — 18*s*.
1729	19*s*. — 19*s*. 6*d*. — 20*s*. — 21*s*. — 22*s*.
1730	21*s*. — 20*s*. — 19*s*.
1731	18*s*. 6*d*. — 19*s*.
1732	19*s*. 6*d*. — 20*s*. — 20*s*. 6*d*.
1733	21*s*. — 21*s*. 6*d*. — 22*s*. — 22*s*. 6*d*. — 23*s*.
1734	24*s*. — 25*s*. — 26*s*. — 26*s*. 6*d*. — 27*s*.
1735	27*s*. 6*d*.
1736	27*s*. — 26*s*. 6*d*.
1737	26*s*. 6*d*. — 27*s*.
1738, 1739, 1740	28*s*. — 29*s*.
1741, 1742, 1743, 1744	28*s*.
1745	35*s*. — 36*s*. — 37*s*.
1746, 1747, 1748	37*s*. — 38*s*. — 40*s*.
1749, 1750, 1751, 1752	60*s*.

In 1737, the General Court, perceiving the impossibility of restoring credit to the swollen mass of its notes, resolved to issue others of a new form, or tenor, although not discontinuing the use of the old; and thus came into use the terms *old* and *new tenor* in speaking of the bills of the Province. The different forms of the two bills are given below :—

OLD TENOR.

NO.—— 20*s.*

This Indented Bill of Twenty Shillings due from the Province of the Massachusetts Bay in New England to the Possessor thereof shall be in value equal to Money, and shall be accordingly. accepted by the Treasurer and Receivers subordinate to him in all publick payments and for any Stock at any time in the Treasury Boston November the Twenty-first Anno 1702 *By Order of the Great and General Court or Assembly*

NEW TENOR.

TWENTY SHILLINGS TWENTY SHILLINGS

This bill of Twenty Shillings due from the Province of the Massachusetts Bay in New England, to the possessor thereof, shall be in value equal to three ounces of coined silver, Troy weight, of sterling alloy, or gold coin at the rate of four pounds eighteen shillings per ounce; and shall be accordingly accepted by the Treasurer and receivers subordinate to him in all payments (the duties of Import and Tunnage of Shipping and incomes of the Light House only excepted,) and for any Stock at any time in the Treasury.

Boston,

By order of the Great and General Court or Assembly.

TWENTY SHILLINGS TWENTY SHILLINGS

....
.... } *Committee*
....

The law made one bill of the new tenor equal to three of the same denomination of the old; but the public passed them at the rate of one for four, and they depreciated together in that proportion. The old tenor continued the standard of value in ordinary usage.

The ruinous financial policy of the Province was not begun or continued without strenuous opposition at home and still stronger in England; and when, in 1748, the mother country agreed to pay an idemnity of £183,000 towards the expenses incurred by New England in the capture of Louisburg, nearly the whole of it coming to Massachusetts, it was resolved to appropriate her proportion to the redemption of the paper money of the Province, at depreciated rates. This now amounted to £2,200,000; but had depreciated, says Hildreth, since the issue, full one-half, the whole depreciation being at the rate of seven or eight for one.

In 1751, the specie for the Louisburg idemnity arrived, and the currency began to be redeemed at a rate about one-fifth less than its current value. It was enacted that future debts should be paid in silver, at the rate of 6*s*. 8*d*. the ounce. And treasury notes were not again issued by Massachusetts until the Revolution; although certificates of indebtedness were given by the treasury, and passed current, with more or less depreciation, among the people.

But, though the Province paper in 1752 ceased to be a legal tender, an account by an officer of the treasury, in 1753, showed that £131,996, equal in value to £17,599 lawful money, were still in the hands of the people.

The committee of the legislature had burnt bills, at the town-house in Boston, representing the amount of £1,792,236.

On the 29th of January, 1754, Harrison Gray, the Provincial Treasurer, issued a notice that all bills still out must be brought to him for exchange by the first day of the next June, or be forfeited; and that any person subsequently passing them would be subject to a fine of £10 for each offence. This appears to have effectually disposed of both the old and new tenor.

N. B. — For the facts above given, we are indebted generally to the "Historical Account of Massachusetts Currency," by Joseph B. Felt, published in 1839, — a valuable book, now out of print.

B.

REV. THOMAS ALLEN'S DIARY.

During some of the most interesting years of the Revolution, Rev. Mr. Allen kept a pocket diary; in which from time to time occur minutes and memoranda, sometimes of curious and often of instructive interest. Of the information contained in many of these, we have made use in the text of this volume: others find more appropriate places in the Appendix. The book in which the diary is kept is itself of interest; being "Aitken's General American Register, and the Gentleman's and Tradesman's Complete Annual Account Book, and Calendar, For the Pocket or Desk; For the Year of our Lord 1773. Published at Philadelphia; by Joseph Crukshank, for R. Aitken, Bookseller, opposite the London Coffee-House, Front Street." The Preface states that this was the first book ever published in America.

REVOLUTIONARY MARKET-PRICES.

January, 1779.

Wheat, twelve dollars per bushel.
Indian Corn, five dollars per bushel.
Tea (Bohea), sixteen dollars per pound.
Sugar (Maple), nine shillings per pound.
Sugar (Loaf), two shillings per pound.
Rum, twenty dollars per gallon.
Molasses, twenty dollars per gallon.

July, 1779.

New-England Rum, thirty dollars per gallon.
Bohea Tea, ten dollars per pound.
Brown Sugar, three dollars per pound.
Wheat, forty dollars per bushel.
Corn (Indian), twenty dollars per bushel.

1780.

Wheat, one hundred and ten dollars per bushel, or 9*s.* silver.
Bohea Tea, 12*s.* silver; 140 dollars Continental currency.

PRICES OF SOME OF THE ARTICLES AND NECESSARIES OF LIFE.

July, 1778.

Labor, four dollars per day.	Times as much as formerly....	8
Women's shoes, five dollars per pair.	" " "	5
Ploughing, eight dollars per day.	" " "	8
Rum, 17*s.* per quart.	" " "	11
Tea, twelve dollars per pound.	" " "	14
Clothing in general.	" " "	7
Salt.	" " "	30

MR. ALLEN'S LOANS TO THE CONTINENT.

Value of my Continental certificates as stated by Loan Office treasurer: —

11th June, 1777, of three hundred dollars, is..................	300
19th Jan., 1778, of two hundred dollars......................	200
17th March, 1778, of two hundred dollars, is..................	106.36.0
Connecticut..	606.36

2d June, 1778	$150\frac{45}{90}$
46th May, 1779	$045\frac{52}{90}$
Ditto	$045\frac{52}{90}$
	240
	606
	846
Interest of the end of 1785	277
	$1123

[Value of my Continental certificates: —

11th June, 1777, of 300 dollars, is	300
19th January, 1778, of 200 dollars, is	130
17th March, 1778, of 200 dollars, is	106
2d June, 1778, 400 dollars, is	150
26th May, 1779, 1200 dollars, is	89
5th October, 1779, 200 dollars, is	9
	784
May, 1785, interest supposed to be 260 dollars	260
	$1044]

The statement enclosed in brackets is crossed in the original by erasure lines.

Dec, 31. 1787. — What the Continent owes me at this time, reckoning interest from 1782, Dec. 31, to the above date: —

Connecticut certificates as on the opposite page, total	606 dol.
Massachusetts' total	150
	90
	846 dol.
Interest, five years	253
Dec. 31, 1787, this is	1099
I have by me a certificate for	30 dol.
	1129 dol.

RECEIPT TO MAKE INK.

Take of the bark of soft maple, of witch hazel, and alder, an equal quantity of the first with the two last, and boil them well in water, and add a small quantity of gum-arabic, and your ink will be good. Put some of the aforesaid gum into the ink when it is made of ink-powder.

DEPRECIATION OF CONTINENTAL CURRENCY.

In another memorandum book of Mr. Allen's, the following tables are found:—

State Scale, — 100 *Silver.*

1777.

January	105
February	107
March	109
April	102
May	115
June	120
July	125
August	150
September	175
October	275
November	300
December	310

1778.

January	325
February	350
March	375
April	400
May	400
June	400
July	425
August	450
September	475
October	500
November	545
December	634

1779.

January	742
February	868
March	1000
April	1104
May	1250
June	1342
July	1477
August	1630
September	1800
November	2300
December	2593

1780.

January	2934
February	3322
March	3736
April	4000

Date	Year		
March 1,	1778, D(ollar) Silver	=	$1\frac{3}{4}$
Sept. 1,	1778, 1	=	4
March 1,	1779, 1	=	10
Sept. 1,	1779, 1	=	18
Mar. 18,	1779, 1	=	40

Continental Scale.

1777.

September	1000
October	911
November	828
December	754

1778.

January	685
February	623
March	571
April	497
May	434
June	378
July	330
August	287
September	250
October	215
November	183
December	157

1779.

January	134
February	115
March	100
April	90
May	82
June	74
July	67

		1780.	
August	61	January	34
September	55	February	30
October	49	March	26
November	43	March	25
December	38		

1777.

February. — Died at Peekskill, Col. Seth Pomeroy; a good friend to his country. Pleurisy.

March 16. — Engaged in the Continental service.

March 20. — Was inoculated for the small-pox at Sheffield.

May 3. — Had twenty-seven old sheep, seventeen of which were ewes, and fourteen lambs; which is forty-one.

May 5. — Sowed flaxseed, and planted June potatoes.

May 29. — Finished planting.

May. — Tommy fell into a deep place in the river, and providentially escaped drowning by having timely assistance near. The Lord's name be praised!

May 28. — Brought a salmon from Northampton behind me without harm to it, though it was warm weather.

11th day of June. — Set out from home to join the army at Ticonderoga; returned home July 13.

18th July. — Green peas plenty, and, soon after, stringed beans.

1778.

March. — An uncommon season for a great depth of snow; drifts being over the fences in many places. It wasted fast March 12, 13, 14, 15.

March 23. — Began to make sugar, being too early.

May 16. — Load of shad from Kinderhook, or rather from Schodack.

July 9. — The first mess of green peas.

July 12. — Ended reading "The Family Expositor" for the first time in my family, and began to read it through again, July 19.

Oct. 30. —Finished getting in my sauce.

Aug. 2. — Lord's Day; cucumbers for the first time.

1779.

Little or no snow in February, and the most open winter I ever knew.

My sheep did not eat two hundred pounds of hay this winter, till March came in.

March 22, Monday. — Brunswicker came to live with me.

Sheared sheep April 30; too early.

Aug. 21. — This day received the melancholy tidings of brother Moses Allen's death, who was drowned in making his escape from a prison-ship near Savannah, beginning of January, 1779.

In September. — Sowed my wheat, being one week too late.

October, made a journey to Albany with my son. Returning, his horse fell and rolled quite over him, and yet he was preserved unhurt in any great degree, to my astonishment. How wonderful is the preservation of man! The Lord's name be praised!

1780.

As long and severe a winter as almost was ever known. Snow very much drifted and very deep.

Aug. 14. — Mowed my meadow, and finished mowing Tuesday, and got it all home Friday night. It is best to mow it all down the first day, if possible.

August 31. — Sowed my wheat, and finished dragging it the third day after.

Next year I am to sow some flax, peas, barley, and oats.

C.

NAMES OF EARLY SETTLERS.

Rev. Dr. Field, who made inquiries, when sources of information were more abundant than they now are, into the early settlement of the town, published the result in 1844. He appears to have relied chiefly upon traditions, and to have been entirely unacquainted with the measures for settlement before 1752, so that some errors naturally appear in his statement. We, however, here reproduce the essential portions, which may be compared with the text of the present work.

In 1752–3, Solomon Deming moved his family into the east part of the town. . . . . This year Charles Goodrich drove the first team and cart into the town, cutting his way for a number of miles through the woods. Nathaniel Fairfield also this year settled on the road running east from the house of the late Deacon Daniel Crofoot and Zebediah Stiles, on a rise of ground west of the dwelling of the late Dr. Childs.

It is understood that Abner and Isaac Dewey, Jacob Ensign, Hezekiah Jones, Samuel Taylor, Elias Willard, and Dea. Josiah Wright became settlers this year, and that Simeon and Stephen Crofoot, David Bush, and Col. William Williams became settlers the year following. . . .

In 1754, Eli Root, Esq., Ephraim Stiles, William Wright, and perhaps others, became inhabitants. . . .

On the road running west from the centre were Zebediah and Ephraim Stiles, Ezra Strong, Charles Miller, David Roberts, David Ashley, Amos and Oliver Root, and others by the name of Wright, Robbins, Belden, Hubbard, Francis and Wadhams; east were Rev. Mr. Allen, John Strong, Dr. Colton, the Crofoots. and Jacob Ensign; and further on to the north-east Josiah and Charles Goodrich, Israel Stoddard, Israel Dickinson, and Col. Wm. Williams; south were Col. Easton, Sylvanus Piercey, Ezekiel Root, Daniel Miller, James Lord, and Elisha Jones. Rufus Allen kept a public house on the corner now occupied by William B. Cooley [in 1868, by the Berkshire Life Insurance Company], and farther north, towards Lanesboro', were Joseph Allen, and the families by the name of Baker and Keeler. On the road eastward of Daniel Weller's, or near it, were the Fairfields, David Bush, Eli Root, Esq., Hezekiah Jones, Wm. Brattle, and Solomon Deming. Col. Williams early moved on to this road from the spot where Levi Goodrich now lives, and where Lieut. Graves settled after him. Charles Goodrich, Esq., left the farm on which he first lived, and settled near him.

A large portion of the early settlers were from Westfield, — all by the name of Ashley, Bagg, Bush, Cadwell, Dewey, Francis, Hubbard, Noble, Piercey, Sackett, Stiles, Taylor, and Weller. Hezekiah Jones was also from this town. Those of the name of Brattle, Deming, Goodrich, Gunn, Lord, Robbins, and Willard were from Wethersfield, Ct. The Allens, Bakers, Fairfields, Phelpses, Stoddards, Strongs, and Wrights were from Northampton; and the Crofoots from Belchertown.

1759. The following persons are understood from circumstances to have moved into the town this year; viz., Samuel Birchard, Daniel Hubbard, Daniel and Jesse Sackett, and Jonathan Taylor. I say are understood from circumstances to have moved in this year; for there is no inconsiderable difficulty in finding exactly, at this time, at what period the early settlers planted themselves here. . . . In 1760, David and Oliver Ashley, William Francis, and Gideon Gunn are understood to have become settlers. Joshua Robbins and Ezekiel Root became inhabitants before the incorporation of the town. . . . In 1761, Gideon Goodrich, James Lord, Charles Miller, Thomas Morgan, Daniel and David Noble, Wm. Phelps, and John Remington are understood to have become inhabitants.

In 1762–3–4, the following persons are understood to have settled here; namely, Phinehas Belden, Solomon Crosby, Israel Dickinson, Elisha Jones, John Morse, David Roberts, Aaron Stiles, Israel Stoddard, John and Caleb Wadhams, Aaron and Phinehas Baker, Wm. Brattle, Col. James Easton, Benjamin and Josiah Goodrich, Moses Miller, Joseph Phelps, Amos Root, John Williams, Rev. Thomas Allen, Jas. D. Colt, Ezra and King Strong, Dr. —— Colton, Rufus Allen, John Strong; and a number of others *probably* became inhabitants during these years. Not long after, Joseph Allen, David Bagg, Lieut. Moses Graves, Woodbridge Little, Esq., Col. Oliver Root, Ebenezer White, and many others, settled in town.

Most of the inhabitants who have been mentioned settled on the house-lots; some, on the squares.

Col. Williams and Elisha Jones were from Weston; Lieut. Graves and Israel Dickinson were from Hatfield; Thomas Morgan was from Springfield, and John Remington from West Springfield. Ebenezer White was from Hadley. David Roberts was from Hartford, and Jacob Ensign from West

Hartford, Ct. Col. Easton was immediately from Litchfield, previously from Hartford. Joseph Keeler was from Ridgefield, and Woodbridge Little, Esq., from Lebanon, and James D. Colt from Lyme, in the same State.

Valentine Rathbun, from Stonington, Ct., settled in this town about 1770; Dr. Timothy Childs, from Deerfield, in 1771; and Stephen Fowler and Josiah Moseley, from Westfield, about 1772. Col. John Brown, from Sandisfield, settled here in 1773. In 1775, Gad Merrill, from Hebron, Ct., settled to the north of the east branch of the Housatonic, near Dalton line; and, in the spring of 1780, William and John Partridge settled a little west of him.

D.

RECORDS OF THE REVOLUTIONARY SERVICE OF PITTSFIELD.

From the Military Rolls of the Commonwealth of Massachusetts.

In some cases, the companies whose rolls are here given were made up by levies from two or more towns; and, as it is impossible always to distinguish to which the soldiers should be credited, this list is printed without attempting to discriminate.

CAPT. NOBLE'S MINUTE MEN.

List of Capt. Noble's minute-men who marched to Cambridge on the Lexington alarm: —

Term of service, nine days; entered service April 22, 1775.

Captain, David Noble of Pittsfield. *First Lieut.*, Joseph Welch of Richmond. *Second Lieut.*, Josiah Wright of Pittsfield. *Sergeants*, Jeremiah Miller, Richmond; Joseph More, Pittsfield; Ambrose Hall, Richmond; Nathaniel Porter, Pittsfield. *Corporals*, Ebenezer Williams, Richmond; Solomon Martin, Pittsfield; Thomas Scott, Richmond; Jonathan Stoddard, Pittsfield. *Fifer*, George Leonard, Lenox. *Drummer*, Joshua Done, of Pittsfield.

Privates from Richmond.

—— Hill.
Benjamin Pynchon.
Paul Tupping [Tupper?]
Dan Tubs.
Amaziah Chapin.
A. Parmele.
Jonathan Hewley.
Isaiah ———.
B. Currier.
Joel Osborne.
Jose Hubbard.
Rufus Parmele.
William Lang.
Fred. Hill.
Wm. Raymont.
Reuben Coggwell.
David Gaston.

Privates from Pittsfield.

Phinehas Gilbert.
Hugh Mitchell.
Benjamin Deming.
Timothy Stearns.
Hugh Berry.
Wm. Cady.
Jonathan Blakesley.
Abraham Frost.
John Corbin.
Warham Strong.
Zebediah Stiles.
Joel Osborn.
Wm. Scott.
Joel Dickinson.
Nathaniel Dickinson.
Azariah Egleston.
Moses Goodrich.
Samuel Cross.
Aaron Miller.
Moses Noble.
Thomas Miller.
John King.
Jerry Butler.
Caleb Goodrich.
Ebenezer Wright.
Timothy Miller.
Joseph Elton.
Joseph Cotton.
Richard Rossiter.
Charles Belding.
John Gardner.
Jabez Chalmers.
Jonathan Bill.
Benjamin Austin.
David Beckwith.
Walter Welch.
James Elton.
Aaron Stiles.
Thomas Taylor.
Timothy Childs.

Jabez Chalmers, John Gardner, Jonathan Bill, volunteered in Arnold's expedition against Canada *via* the Kennebec.

Benjamin Austin and David Beckwith enlisted in "the train" early in July.

ROLL of Capt. David Noble's company of eight months' men in Col. Patterson's regiment at Cambridge, 1775: —

Officers.

Captain, David Noble, Pittsfield. *First Lieut.*, Joseph Welch, Richmond. *Second Lieut.*, Josiah Wright, Pittsfield. *Surgeon* [to the regiment], Timothy Childs, Pittsfield. *Surgeon's Mate*, Jonathan Lee, Pittsfield. *Sergeants*, Jeremiah Miller, Richmond; Joseph More, Pittsfield; Ambrose Hull [or Hall], Richmond; Nathaniel Porter, Pittsfield. *Corporals*, Ebenezer Williams, Richmond; Solomon Martin, Pittsfield; Thomas Scott, Richmond; Jonathan Stoddard, Pittsfield.

Privates.

Benjamin Austin.
George Butler.
Hugh Berry.
Jonathan Blakesley.
Jonathan Bill.
David Beckwith.
Samuel Cross.
John Cady.
Jabez Chalmers.
William Cady.
Benjamin Deming.
Azariah Eggleston.
Abraham Frost.
John Gardner.

Moses Goodrich.
Phinehas Gilbert.
John King.
Joshua Done (Doane), drummer.
Moses Noble.
Timothy Stearns.
Aaron Miller.
Thomas Miller.
Seth Macomber.

OTHER PITTSFIELD SOLDIERS in the eight months' service: —

Prince Hall, in Col. Wm. Prescott's regiment.

Thomas Parks, in Wm. Goodrich's company, Patterson's regiment.

Joseph Colson, drummer in Col. Jonathan Brewer's regiment.

Eleazer Keiler, sergeant in Capt. Asa Bower's company, Woodbridge's regiment.

John Lewis, surgeon's mate Eben Brewer's regiment.

PITTSFIELD MEN in Capt. Aaron Rowley's company, Col. Symond's regiment, called out by Gen. Gates, for Saratoga, from April 26 to May 19, 1777: —

Lieutenant, Wm. Ford. *Sergeant*, Joel Stevens. *Corporal*, Amos Delano, Samuel Coggswell, Isaac Coggswell, Ebenezer Phelps, Timothy Cadwell. Jehiel Wright, Jason Warren, Samuel Willard, Linus Parker [then of Lenox], Ozias Wright.

Gideon Gunn and Amos Root served in the same regiment.

BATTLE OF BENNINGTON.

PAY-ROLL of Lieut. Wm. Ford's Company in Col. David Rossiter's Detachment of Militia from the County of Berkshire for the Public Service at Bennington from Aug. 13, to Aug. 20, 1777 (Pittsfield): —

Lieutenants, Wm. Ford, Joseph Allen. *Sergeants*, James Easton, Charles Goodrich.

Privates.

James Noble.
Denam Tupper.
Rufus Allen.
James Brattle.
John Corbin.
Warham Strong.
Nathaniel Hale.
Francis Plumer.
Nathaniel Gorcester (?)
Rev. Thomas Allen.
Eleazer Goodrich
Timothy Cadwell.
Jehiel Wright.
Jaffry (negro).
Gideon Goodrich.

PAY-ROLL of Lieut. James Hubbard's Company in Lieut. Col. Rossiter's detachment of Militia from the State of Massachusetts Bay in the Service of U. S. A., commencing Aug. 17, 1777, and ending when they were discharged, Aug. 22: —

Lieutenant, James Hubbard. *Sergeants*, Aaron Noble, King Strong, Joel Stevens. *Corporals*, Joshua Narrimore, Amos Delano, Joseph Phelps.

Privates.

Oliver Root.
James Colt.
Paul Hutchinson.
Paul Hubbard.
Elnathan Phelps.
Zaccheus Hurlbert.
Oliver Burt.
Peter Wright.
Jacob Gleason.
Solomon Lothrop.
Jona'n Stoddard.
David Ashley.
Wm. Miller.
Nathaniel Davis.
Caleb Wadhams.
John Churchill.
Frederic Stanley.
Joseph Price.
Lemuel Phelps.
Calvin Cogswell.
Josiah Talcott.
Nehemiah Hopkins.
Aaron Drake.
John Deming.

AT STONE ARABIA.

A PAY-ROLL of the Field and Staff Officers of a Regiment of Levies commanded by Col. John Brown, late of Pittsfield, deceased, raised by the Commonwealth of Massachusetts for the term of three months:—

John Brown, Colonel, appointed July 14, 1780; served three months, three days; pay (per month), £22. 10s.

Oliver Root, Major, appointed July 8; served three months, twenty-four days; pay, £15.

James Easton, Adjutant, appointed July 17; served three months, fifteen days; pay, £12.

Elias Willard, Quartermaster, appointed July 17; served three months, fifteen days; pay, £85.

Oliver Brewster, Surgeon, appointed July 23; served two months, twenty-seven days; pay, £18.

A PAY-ROLL of Capt. Wm. Ford's Company in Col. John Brown's Regiment in the service of the U. S. A., commencing July 21, 1780, and ending Oct. 21, 1780:—

Captain, Wm. Ford. *Lieutenants*, Alpheus Spencer, Abel Pearson. *Sergeants*, Samuel Wheaton, Daniel Rathbone, Eleazur Slosson, Timothy Candee. *Corporals*, James Baker, Nath'l Tobie, Nathan Ingraham, Barth'w Bond. *Drummer*, Shubael Austin. *Fifer*, Thomas McKnight.

Privates.

Benoni Gleason.
John Cummington.
John Phelps.
Thos. Burt.
Jason Robbins.
David Taylor.
John More.
Nath'l Goodrich.
Levi Coggswell.
John North.
Ezekiel Smith.
Henry Bell.
Ezekiel Case.
Joel Ludd.

Wm. Milliken.
Wm. McKnight.
Jona'n Bateman.
Philon Stoddard.
Gilbert Goodrich.
David Clark.
Asahel Harrison.
Aaron Adams.
Zadoc Hewett.
Solomon Bliss.
John Lewis.
David Sears.
Oliver Belding.
Peleg Carlton.
Jehiel Stearns.
Wm. Baker.
Josiah Stiles.
Joseph Reed.
John Noble.
Calvin Easton.
Nathan Parks.
Wm. Hatch.
Reuben Carlton.
Calvin Dunham.
Warren Mace.
Elisha Carter.
Joseph Hardy.
Colman Andrews.
Moses Tomblin.
Joseph Porter.
Isaac Foot [or Israel].
Joseph Porter, jun.
Amos Woodruff.
Seth Newel.
Seth Bond.
Joel Dean.
Shubael Wollison.
James Ellison.
Warren Hall.
James Reed.
Charles Hyde.
Joseph Tuhel.

Thos. [Roll mutilated] R. M–rick, D. Sworn to before Justice Goodrich. Three names "forgotten," and reported in a supplementary roll, — John North, jun., Uriah Welch, John Slosson.

PAY-ROLL of Capt. Rufus Allen's Company of Militia of Matross in Col. Rossiter's Regiment in the Commonwealth of Massachusetts, Pittsfield, commencing Oct. 14, 1780, ending Oct. 17, 1780. Travel, 40 miles: —

Captain, Rufus Allen. *Lieutenants*, Oswald Williams and Joseph Allen. *Sergeants*, Elijah Crofoot, Thomas Taylor, Paul Hubbard. *Corporals*, James Brattle, Eli Root, Benjamin Judd.

Privates.

Thomas Miller.
Adoniram Hinman.
John Stearns.
Daniel Barber.
James Notting.
Hezekiah Wolcott.
Daniel Merrill.
Joseph Hall.
John King.
John Francis.
Thomas Keiler.
Wm. Miller.
Joel Walker.
Moses Bartlett.

PAY-ROLL of Detachment commanded by Lieut. Joel Stevens in Col. David Rossiter's Regiment, Pittsfield, Oct. 18, to Oct. 21, 1780. 40 miles travel allowed: —

Lieutenants, Joel Stevens, Aaron Noble. *Clerk*, Francis Plumer. *Sergeants*, Amos Delano, Martin Bagg. *Corporals*, Peter Sullard, Ebenezer Wright.

Soldiers.

Tim'y Cadwell.
Abel Branch.
Nathaniel Davis.
Enoch Baker.
Caleb Wadhams.
Edmund Wright.
John Deming.
Titus Wright.
Paul Guilford.
Daniel Burt.
Amos Root, Jr.
Timothy Cook.
Nathaniel Welch.

LIEUT. JOEL STEVENS'S DETACHMENT called out Oct. 15, 1780, to Oct. 18, 1780, in alarm at Fort Edward, allowed 40 miles travel: —

Lieutenants, Joel Stevens, Aaron Noble. *Clerk,* Francis Plumer. *Sergeants,* Amos Delano, Martin Bagg, Josh'a Narrimore. *Corporals,* Paul Sullard, Ebenezer Wright.

Privates.

Paul Guilford.
Elijah Ames.
Peter Wright.
Oliver Burt.
Nathaniel Davis.
John Jordon.
Daniel Brown.
Abel Branch.
George Butler.
Abiather Millard.
Benjamin Phelps.
Benjamin Coggswell.
Ambrose Booth.
Paul Hutchinson.
Caleb Wadhams.
Amos Root, jun.
Amos Welch.
William Cady.
Enoch Baker.
Matthew Wright.

PAY-ROLL of Capt. Joel Stevens's Company in Col. David Rossiter's Regiment, Pittsfield, Commonwealth of Massachusetts, on the alarm at Saratoga. Entered service Oct. 12, 1781. Discharged Oct. 25, 1781. Travel, 160 miles: —

Captain, Joel Stevens. *Lieutenant,* Lebbeus Backus. *Clerk,* Francis Plumer. *Sergeants,* James Brattle, Benja'n Chamberlain.

Privates.

Jonathan Lattimer.
Shubael Austin.
Martin Kingsbury.
Joshua Bigelow.
Wm. Bond.
Asa Silver.
Phinehas Cady.
Israel Phelps.
Phinehas Cole.
Wm. Williams.
Herman Jones.
Jonathan Loomis.
Simeon Babcock.
Levi Snow.
Josiah Goodrich.
Joshua Robbins.
Warren Cady.
Zenas Goodrich.

Calvin Sprague.
Henry Taylor.
Phillip Foot.
Amos Welch.
Abiather Millard.
Jonathan Noble.
Azariah Root.
Lyman Baker
Walter Walker.
Daniel Jones.
Caleb Wadhams.
David Ashley.
James DeWolf.
Thomas Davis.
Nath'l Davis.
George Concert.
Ezra Stearns.
John Wheelwright.
Calvin Chesman.
Benjamin Phelps.
Wm. Weller
Francis Belknap.
Jeremiah Blanchard.
Sol. Sackett.
Eben'r Wright.
Selah Lusk.
Stephen West.
Daniel Coggswell.
Benjamin Gallop.
Nicholas Cotterel.
Thomas Keiler.
Aaron Bigsby.
Palmer Sherman.
Ebenezer Williams.
Nathan Phillips.
Benjamin Judd.
Rufus Woodward.
Timothy Cook.
Thomas Lewis.
Nathan Taggard.

A Pay-roll of the six months' men raised by and for the Town of Pittsfield, and employed in the Continental service, in the year 1780. (*Continental pay.*)

Men's names.	Time marched.	Time discharged.	No. of miles.	Time in service. Weeks.	Days.	Wages due. £	s.	d.
Othniel Williamson	Aug. 2	Dec. 15	100	4	9	8	12	
Lieut. Williamson	" "	Feb. 12, 1781	110	6	5	12	6	8
John Ford	" 10	Dec. 21, 1780	110	4	16	9	1	4
Azariah Root	" 2	" 16, "	110	4	18	9	4	
Reuben Gunn	Sept. 3	March 3, 1781	110	6	5	12	6	8
Isaac Isaacs	Aug 28	Feb. 28	110	6	5	12	6	8
George Randow	" 3	March 3	110	7	5	14	6	8
Hosea Merrill	" 3	Dec. 19	110	4	21	9	8	
Abner Hathaway	" 23	Feb. 23	110	6	5	12	6	8
Jacob Wright	" "	Dec. 9	100	3	21	7	8	
Daniel Bad(b)cock	July 27	Jan. 21	110	6	5	12	6	8
Elijah Root	Aug. 3	" "	110	4	23	9	10	8
						£148	17	4

Moses Cook, supposed to have deserted.
Roger Welch, supposed to have deserted.
Samuel Spencer, supposed to have deserted.
Ebenezer Poppoonuck, died in the service.
Titus (Negro), died in the service.

A PAY-ROLL of the detachment of militia under the command of Capt. Wm. Wells, in the Third Regiment, in the County of Berkshire, on the alarm at Saratoga, Oct. 29, 1781: —

William Wells, *Capt.;* William Brattle, *Lieut.;* Caleb Culver, Zenas Root, Paul Hubbard, Jonathan Hewett, *Sergt.;* Phillip Lewis, Robert Francis, *Corporals;* Samuel Goodrich, *Drummer.*

Privates.

Cemyour Cutond [Seymour Cutting ?].
Amos Smith.
Bildad Clark.
John Root.
Isaac Isaacs.
Ebenezer Wheedon.
Joel Blinn.
John Treet.
Daniel Weller.
Peter Messenger.
Jason Warren.
Thomas Gates.
Ichabod Hamblin.
Abram Lambden.
Abram Northup.
Benjamin Stephens.
Elines [Linus] Parker.
Ashel [Asahel] Landers.
William Hostetter.
Daniel Keiler.
Daniel Osborn.
Truman Dibble.
Amos Root, jun.
Jehiel Wright.
Seth Jones [Janes].
Daniel Brown.
Josiah Ward.
Nathaniel Davis.
John Noble.
John Wright.
James Rathbun.
Ebenezer Austin.
Hoseah Merrells [Hosea Merrill].
Simeon Barber.
Jacob Barber.
Enos Henman.
John Fairfield.
David Martin.
Jonathan Fuller.
Joseph Chapin.
James Barber.

Time of service, eight days. Miles travelled, forty-five.

[This company appears to have been made up in Pittsfield and Lenox.]

STATEMENT OF MILITARY SERVICE.

1775 — Dec. 1779.

To the Hon'ble the Council and House of Representatives in General Court assembled.

The Petition of the Selectmen of the town of Pittsfield in the county of Berkshire Most Humbly showeth:

That the Town of Pittsfield have, ever since the commencement of the war, distinguished themselves in their readiness to assist in the common cause and, that they might come at some certainty of what proportion of service they have done the State and Continent, have overlooked their papers (which they are ready to produce), and find that their services are equal to one man

250 years, not to mention their situation, which has called them from home when their corn and grass were suffering, and deprived of opportunity of fixing their ground for seed; to which might be added the great supply of horses, teams, and carriages that we have been obliged to furnish, and the time expended by the Committees and Selectmen, that amount to hundreds, for which they have received no consideration.

The aforegoing, your petitioners humbly conceive are sufficient reasons for this Hon'ble Court to consider them in the present demand made for the supply of the Continental Army.

Which is humbly submitted to your Honors' wise, important, and just determination.

And as in duty bound shall ever pray,

WM. WILLIAMS.
ELI ROOT.
LEBBEUS BACKUS.

PITTSFIELD, Dec. 27, 1779.

The following is an account of the demands for men on the Town of Pittsfield since the commencement of the war with Great Britain: —

April 22, 1775, Capt. David Noble, Lieut. Tim'y Childs, Lieut. Josiah Wright, who marched to Cambridge, and served six months with the following men under their command, viz.: —

Thomas Miller.
Oswald Williams.
Aaron Stiles.
Ebenezer Wright.
David Noble, jun.
James Easton, jun.
Joel Dickinson.
Jabez Chaucer. [?]
Charles Belding.
Phinehas Gilbert.
John King.
Warham Strong.
Benjamin Deming.
Azariah Egleston.
Timothy Stearns.
Elijah Crane.
Jonathan Bill.
Hugh Berry.
Zebediah Stiles, jun.
Richard Osborn.
Moses Stiles.
Thomas Hudson.
Aaron Miller, jun.
George Butler.
Joseph Moore.
Samuel Straton.
Moses Noble.
Joseph Colton.
Solomon Lothrop.
Nathaniel Porter.
Hugh Mitchell.
John Gardner.
Jonathan Stoddard.
Solomon Martin.
Jonathan Blakely.
Joseph Easton.
Abraham Frost.
Benjamin Austin.
Caleb Goodrich.
John Corbin.
John Wait.
Joshua Done [Doane].

Richard Baxter.	David Beckwith.
William Cady.	John Tupper.
Moses Goodrich.	

Fifty-one men, twenty-six weeks; twenty-five and a half years of one man.

May 10, 1775, Capt. James Noble, Lieut. Joel Dickinson, Lieut. John Hitchcock, who engaged in Col. Easton's Regiment, and marched to Canada with the following men, and served until Dec. 30th 1775: —

William Killiard.	Daniel Oalds.
Timo'y Miller.	Timothy Baker.
Daniel Jones.	Daniel Burt.
John Noble.	Jacob Rathbun.
Mark Noble.	Moses Bartlett.
Ashbell Hale,	Wm. Little.
Eli Root, jun.	Shubael Dimock.
Nath'l Hale.	Sam'l Goodree.
Matthew Wright.	Elizur Goodrich.
John Brunt.	Col. James Easton.
James Brattle.	Maj. John Brown.
Josiah Moseley.	Q. M. Wm. C. Stanley.

Twenty-seven men, thirty-three weeks and four days; seventeen years of one man.

Aug. 4, 1775, Capt. Eli Root, Lieut. Stephen Crofoot, and Lieut. James Easton, who engaged in Col. Easton's Regiment, and marched to Canada, and were dismissed Dec. 30, 1775, with the following men under their command, viz.: —

Joseph Allen.	Gideon Goodrich, jun.
Oliver Miller.	Joseph Eldridge.
Aaron Stiles.	Simeon Tupper.
Stephen Phelps.	Joseph Easton.
Uriel Tupper.	Gideon Messenger.
Darius Tupper.	Aaron Foot.
Israel Phelps.	Richard Osbourn.
John Thorpe.	Enoch Dewey.
Wm. Jones.	Levi Miller.
David Wiley,	Asa Hill.
Adon'm Hinman.	

Twenty-four men, twenty-two weeks and two days; ten and a half years of one man.

Dec. 31, 1775, Capt. David Noble and Lieut. Solomon Martin, who marched to Boston, from thence to New York and to Canada, and were dismissed Dec. 31, 1776, with the following men, viz.: —

Jonathan Stoddard.	Joseph Colton.
John King.	Azariah ———
Moses Noble.	Timothy Stearns.

Warham Strong.
Thomas Miller.
John W. ———, jun.
Elisha ———
John Stearns.

[Some names partially and some wholly obliterated in filing. Margin indistinct.]

Jan. 1 1776, Capt. Eli Root, Lieut. Joel Dickinson, and Lieut. Joseph Allen, who engaged in Canada, and were dismissed May 2, 1776, with the following men: —

Moses Bartlett.
Ashbell Hale.
Joseph Eldridge.
James Brattle.
Gideon Goodrich, jun.
Levi Miller.

[Margin obscure.]

July 11, 1876, Capt. Oliver Root, who marched to New York, and was dismissed Dec. 5, 1776, with the following men: —

Caleb Stanley.
Robert Francis.
William Miller.
Peter Wright.
Valentine Rathbun.
Luther Coggswell.
Joseph Stoddard.
Oliver Miller.
Thomas Taylor.
Simeon Tupper.
John Thorpe.
John Cady.
Hugh Mitchell.
Jacob Ensign.
Jonah Jacobs.
Aaron Delano.

Seventeen men, twenty-one weeks; six years, forty weeks, of one man.

Jan. 23, 1776, men who marched to Quebec, and were dismissed Jan. 20, 1776: —

William Beard, Josiah Moseley, James Spear, Timothy Stearns.

[Margin obscured.]

Sept. 30, 1776, Lieut. William Barber, who marched to New York, and was dismissed Nov. 17, 1776, with the following men: —

Jacob Gleason.
Paul Hutchinson.
Aaron Noble.
Enoch Baker.
Elijah Janes.
Abel Branch.
Daniel Barber.
Benjamin Judd.
William Hinman.
Amos Root, jun.
Ezekiel Merrill.
David Warner.
Daniel Olds.
Phinehas Bagg.
Aaron ———

Rev. Thomas Allen, *Chaplain*, Col. Simonds's Regiment.

Seventeen men, seven weeks; one man, two years and fifteen weeks.

Oct. 17, 1776, Capt. William Francis, Lieut. Stephen Crofoot, who marched to Ticonderoga, and were dismissed Nov. 16, 1776, with the following men: —

Enoch Marvin.	Joseph Allen.
Timothy Parker.	Daniel Merrill.
Ebenezer Merry.	Gideon Goodrich.
Calvin Coggswell.	Joel Stevens.
William Wright.	Paul Hubbard.
Zebediah Stiles.	Francis Plummer.
Elijah Janes.	James Noble.
Joseph Phelps.	Andrew Spofford.
Josiah Talcott.	

Nineteen men, four weeks and two days; one year, twenty-nine weeks, of one man.

April 1, 1776, Col. John Brown, Capt. Joel Dickinson, and one more, who went to German Flats, and were dismissed May 16, 1777.

Three men, thirteen months, eighteen days; three years, twenty-one weeks, of one man.

Jan. 14, 1776, Capt. William Francis, who marched to Albany by order of Gen. Schuyler, and was dismissed Jan. 19, 1776: —

William Barber.	Gideon Goodrich.
William Ford.	Oswald Williams.
Caleb Goodrich.	John Thorpe.
Aaron Noble.	Hugh Berry.
Jedidiah Goodrich.	David Bagg.
Amos Delano.	Jacob Gleason.
Luke Noble.	Phinehas Bagg.
Ezra Stearns.	James Colt.
Timothy Miller.	Paul Hubbard.
Oliver Burt.	James Hubbard.
Zebediah Stiles.	Enoch Haskins.
Josiah Wright.	Aaron Miller.
Francis Plummer.	Thomas Taylor.
Benjamin Judd.	William Fenn.
Zuriel Tupper.	

Thirty men, five days; twenty-two weeks of one man.

Sept. 13, 1776, Capt. William Francis, and Lieut William Ford, who went to Williamstown by order of the general, and were dismissed Sept. 21, 1776, with the following men: —

Aaron Noble.	Martin Bagg.
Josiah Talcott.	James Taylor.

Timothy Cadwell.
Daniel Rathbun.
Enoch Baker.
Joel Stevens.
Nathaniel Davis.
Daniel Loomis.
Elijah Janes.
James Cahoon.
Enoch Marvin.
Calvin Coe.
Francis Plummer.
Paul Hutchinson.
Joshua Gates.
Jacob Gleason.

Twenty-one men, eight days; twenty-four weeks of one man.

Dec. 16, 1776, Lieut. James Hubbard, who marched to Ticonderoga, and was dismissed March 16, 1777, with the following men: —

Joseph Fairfield.
Jonathan Weston.
Levi Belding.
Daniel Weller.
Jonathan Hobby.
Gideon Gunn.
John Fairfield.
Wm. Little.
Israel Stoddard.
Ezekiel Root.
Dan Cadwell.
Charles Goodrich.
Elijah Ensign.
Benjamin Kieler.
John Horsford.
Ephraim Stiles.
Thomas Kellogg.
John Wait.

Nineteen men, thirteen weeks; one man, four years, three weeks.

April 25, 1777, Lieut. Stephen Crofoot, who marched to Ticonderoga, and was dismissed May 22, 1777, with the following men: —

William Brattle.
Uriah Judd.
Roswell Root.
Moses Yale.
Nehemiah Tracy.
Lebbeus Backus.
Timothy Miller.
Jacob Ward.
Ezra Kieler.
Luke Noble.
Daniel Jones.
Daniel Bagg.
Thomas Keiler.

Fourteen men, four weeks; one year and four weeks of one man.

May 4, 1777, Capt. John Strong and Lieut. James Hubbard, who went to Kinderhook after inimical persons, and were dismissed May 11, 1777, with the following men: —

Peter Sullard.
Reuben Rathbun.
Samuel Merry.
Aaron Stiles.
Asahel Stiles.
Benjamin Judd.
William Miller.
Caleb Goodrich.
Josiah Talcott.
James Noble.
Ezra Stearns.
Caleb Wadhams.
Eli Root.
Oliver Root.
Ezekiel Root.
Dan Cadwell.

Nathaniel Fairfield.
Titus Wright.
Abijah Hinman.
Enoch Haskins.
Timothy Miller.
Darius Tupper.
Calvin Coggswell.
Valentine Rathbun.
Paul Hubbard.
Ebenezer Chapman.
Joseph Easton.
Daniel Weller.
Daniel Hubbard.
Gideon Goodrich.

Thirty-two men, one week; thirty-two weeks of one man.

June 30, 1777, Capt. John Strong and Lieut. Caleb Goodrich, who marched to Fort Ann, and were dismissed July 26, 1777, with the following men, viz.: —

Aaron Noble.
Joseph Harrison.
Nathaniel Fairfield.
David Wells.
Lemuel Luddington.
Benjamin Austin.
Elijah Crofoot.
Daniel Bates.
Thomas Taylor.
John Remington.
Ezra Stearns
Ashbell Hale.
Benoni Gleason.
John Merry.
Peter Hubbard.
William Miller.
Daniel Merrill.
Oliver Miller.
Amos Root.
Adoniram Hinman.
Calvin Easton.
Paul Hutchinson.
Asahel Stiles.
William Cady.
Erastus Sackett.
Henry Tyler.
Willard Vernam.
Jonathan Taylor.
Nathaniel Davis,
William Lamson.
Elnathan Phelps.
William Beard.
Peter Wright.
Calvin Coggswell.
Lemuel Phelps.
Joseph Moore.
Reuben Rathbun.
Abijah Parks.
John Parks.
Elijah Lamphier.
Gideon Goodrich.
Nathaniel Welch.
Josiah Wright, jun.
John Branch.
Jacob Ensign.
Joseph Fairfield.
Asa Branch.
Prince (Negro).
Joshua Narramore.
Joshua Simonds.
Jacob Goff.
Joseph Chamberlain.

Fifty-four men, three weeks, ten days; one man, three years, ten months, forty-eight weeks.

July 8, 1777, Capt. William Francis and Lieut. Stephen Crofoot, who marched to Fort Edward, and were dismissed Aug. 26, 1777, with the following men, viz.: —

Lebbeus Backus.
Joshua Robbins.
King Strong.
Matthew Willard.
Ebenezer Wright.
Adoniram Waterman.
William Brattle.
Caleb Stanley.
John Stearns.
Uriah Judd.
John Babbitt.
Ethan Stone.
Joseph Phelps.
Jacob Gleason.
Phinehas Bagg.
Solomon Lothrop.
Oswald Williams.
Joel Dickinson.
Thomas Burt.
Enoch Baker.
Joseph Allen.
James Noble, jun.
Matthew Wright.
Daniel Hubbard.
Thomas Keiler.
Solomon Baker.
James Colt.
Roswell Root.
Oliver Root.
Stephen Fowler.
Richard Osbourn.
Nathaniel Hale.
Moses Bartlett.
Enoch Haskins.
Timothy Stearns.
Daniel Barber.
Jacob Ward.
Joshua Done [Doane].

Forty men, nine weeks; one man, five years, twenty weeks.

July 10, 1778, men who were drafted per order General Court, went to Albany and were dismissed Dec. 1, 1778: —

John Stearns.
Timothy Miller.
William Lamson.
Asa Narramore.
Joshua Simonds.
Solomon Baker.

Six men, twenty weeks; one man, two years, sixteen weeks.

July 18, 1777, Lieut. James Hubbard, who went to Manchester, and was dismissed July 28, 1777, with the following men: —

John Remington.
Matthew Barber.
John Deming.
William Barber.
Titus Wright.
David Bagg.
Martin Bagg.
Timothy Cadwell.
Jonathan Weston.

Ten men, one week, three days; one man, thirteen weeks.

Sept. 20, 1777, Capt. William Francis, who went to Stillwater, and was dismissed Oct. 10, 1777, with the following men, viz.: —

Martin Bagg.
Josiah Wright.
John Baker.
Caleb Stanley.
Solomon Lothrop.
Thomas Kellogg.
Stephen Crofoot.
Enoch Marvin.

Aaron Noble.	Aaron Baker.
Gideon Goodrich.	Nathaniel Robbins.
James Easton, jun.	Peter Wright.
John Stearns.	Josiah Wright, jun.
Joel Dickinson.	Paul Hubbard.
Timothy Childs.	Valentine Rathbun.
David Wells.	Ebenezer Keiler.
Eli Root, jun.	Oswald Williams.
Ezra Keiler.	Elijah Janes.
James Spears.	Samuel Bonney.

Thirty men, one week and four days; forty-seven weeks of one man.

April 25, 1777, Lieut. William Ford, who went to Ticonderoga, and was dismissed May 25, with the following men, viz.: —

Joel Stevens.	Timothy Cadwell.
Amos Delano.	Samuel Bonny.
Joshua Gates.	Jehiel Wright.

Seven men, four weeks, three days; thirty-one weeks of one man.

May 19, 1778, men who were raised to re-enforce the Continental army, and were dismissed Feb. 19, 1779: —

Ebenezer Hutchinson,	Jonathan Lee.
——— Davis.	Jonathan Stoddard.
James Lewis.	Samuel Bonney.
Patrick McGee.	

Seven men, nine months; one man, five years, three months.

June 1, 1778, men who marched to headquarters by order of General Court and were dismissed Feb. 1, 1779: —

Daniel Bates.	James Spears.
William Beard.	Ozias Wright.
Benoni Gleason.	Oliver Miller.

Six men, eight months; one man, four years.

Aug. 16, 1777, Lieut. William Ford, who marched to Bennington, and was dismissed Aug. 23, with the following men: —

James Easton.	Gideon Goodrich.
Rufus Allen.	Warham Strong.
James Brattle.	Nathaniel Hale.
Charles Goodrich.	Francis Plumer.
Joseph Allen.	Nathaniel Porter.
John Corbin.	Thomas Allen.
James Noble.	Elizur Goodrich.

Timothy Cadwell.
Jeffrey Hazard.
William Francis.
Jehiel Wright.
Abiather Willard.
Simeon Crofoot.
Josiah Wright.

Twenty-two men, one week; twenty-two weeks of one man.

Aug. 17, 1777, Lieut James Hubbard, who went to Bennington, and was dismissed Aug. 24, with the following men: —

Oliver Root.
Woodbridge Little.
Martin Bagg.
Joshua Narramore.
Jacob Gleason.
Aaron Noble.
Ezekiel Root.
Ephraim Stiles.
Israel Stoddard.
Aaron Hickocks.
Frederick Stanley.
Aaron Stiles.
Israel Dickinson.
James Taylor.
John Strong.
Abijah Hinman.

Seventeen men, five days; twelve weeks of one man.

July 8, 1778, men who went to Springfield, and were dismissed Jan. 8, 1779: —

Ebenezer Merry.
Noadiah Deming.
Amos Root, jun.
Asahel Stiles.

Four men, six months; two years of one man.

July 20, 1779, Lieut. Joel Stevens, who marched to New Haven, and was dismissed Aug. 25, 1779, with the following men: —

Azariah Root.
Ambrose Booth.
Thomas Keiler.
James Noble.
Solomon Baker.
Ashbel Hale.
Caleb Stanley.
John Ford.
William Drake.
Ozem Strong.
Silas Stiles.
William Phelps.
Calvin Easton.
Reuben Colton.

Fifteen men, five weeks, one day; one year, twenty-five weeks of one man.

July 16, 1779, men who were raised to re-enforce the Continental army for the term of nine months, viz.: —

Isaac Morse.
John Wright.
Daniel Bates.
Samuel Smith.
David Johnson.
Jonathan Morey.
Joshua Chapel.

Seven men, nine months, five years; three months of one man.

Oct. 26, 1779, men raised to re-enforce the Continental army, and were dismissed Nov. 30, 1779: —

Enoch Haskins.
Daniel Merrill.
John Noble.
Nathan Robinson.
Abner Hathway.
Phinehas Bagg.
Jonathan Graves.
Ezekiel Somers.
Joseph Hale.
Ambrose Booth.
Amos Root, jun.
Asa Woodward.
John Hosman.

Thirteen men, five weeks; one year, three months, of one man.

Sept. 6, 1777, Capt. John Strong, who went to Skenesborough, and was dismissed Oct. 1, 1777 (every man with a horse and meal-bag), with the following men: —

James Easton.
Benoni Gleason.
John Brown.
Ozem Strong.
Samuel Cross.
Jehiel Wright.
Joel Stevens.
William Lamson.
Francis Plumer.
William Hinman.
Thomas Taylor.
Samuel Davis.
Elijah Janes.
William Cook.
Ephraim Stiles.
Hezekiah Jones.
Lemuel Phelps.
John Hosford.
Timothy Cadwell.
Jonathan Hobby.
Nathaniel Fairfield.
David Bush.
Adoniram Waterman.
Aaron Drake,
John Wait.
Josiah Moseley.
John Thorpe.
Joseph Easton.
Caleb Waddams.
James Easton, jun.
Amos Root.

Three weeks, five days; two years, thirteen weeks, of one man.

A List of Continental Soldiers raised by the Town of Pittsfield during the War, or for Three Years.

NAME.	When Engaged.	Term of time eng'd for.	In whose company.	In whose regiment.
David Ingersoll	May, 1777	3 years	Capt. Watkins	Col. Brewer
Azariah Eggleston	May, 1777	D. W.	" Miller	" Vose
Hugh Berry	May, 1777	3 years	" Ashley	" Vose
William Cady	Dec. 7, 1776	3 years	Lient. Bailey	" Livingston
Ebenezer Stoddard	Dec. 7, 1776	D. W.	Capt. Burr.	" Bailey
Israel Peck	Dec. 7, 1776	3 years	" Ward	" Weston
James Peck	1776	D. W.	" Ward	" Weston
John Tupper	1776	D. W.	" Burr	" Bailey
Joseph Colton	April, 1777	D W.	" Belding	Sheldon's Lt. Dragoons
Mark Noble	Oct. 30, 1776	3 years	" Tucker	Col. Vose
Jeffrey Hazzard *	Nov. 4, 1779	D. W.	" Howard	" Bailey
Joshua Chappel *	July, 1779	D. W.		
Ebenezer Hutchinson *	Feb. 19, 1779	D. W.		" Bailey
Daniel Beckwith	April 9, 1777	3 years	" Miller	" Vose
Isaac Reed	April 4, 1777	3 years	" Stoddard	" Vose
Nathan Dart *	April 4, 1777	3 years	" Miller	" Vose
Josiah Jacobs	April 4, 1777	3 years	" Miller	" Vose
Solomon Lothrop	April 4, 1777	3 years	" Miller	" Vose
Joseph Handy	April 11, 1777	3 years	" Stoddard	" Vose
Hugh Mitchell	April 4, 1777	3 years	" Miller	" Vose
Samuel Goodree	April 9, 1777	3 years	" Ashley	" Vose
Jonathan Wright	April 11, 1777	3 years	" Stoddard	" Vose
David Goff (Luff)	April 4, 1777	3 years	" Miller	" Vose
John Cady	April 9, 1777	D. W.	" Miller	" Vose
James Spear *	April 9, 1777	3 years	" Burr	" Vose
John North	April 11, 1777	D. W.	" Ashley	" Vose
John Dennis	April 10, 1777	3 years	" Burr	" Vose
Daniel Rust *	April 4, 1777	D. W.	" Miller	" Vose
Lemuel Rowley	April 5, 1777	3 years	" Ashley	" Vose
Thomas Jenks	April 7, 1777	3 years	" Ashley	" Vose
Charles Stuart	April 7, 1777	3 years	" Ashley	" Vose
Ichabod Hiscock	May 5, 1777	3 years	" Warren	" Weston
Reuben Milbourn	April 9, 1777	D. W.	" Ashley	" Vose
Benjamin Dimock	May 15, 1777	3 years	" Miller	" Vose
Jonathan Briton	Jan. 10, 1778	D. W.	" Miller	" Vose
Moses Stiles		D. W.	" McKain	" Van Schaack
William Collins		3 years	" Stoddard	" Vose
Samuel Prindle *		3 years	" Stoddard	" Vose
Simeon Tupper *	April 4, 1777	D. W.	" Burr	" Bailey

Attest:

WM. WILLIAMS, ELI ROOT, STEPHEN CROFOOT,	*Selectmen.*	ELI ROOT, STEPHEN CROFOOT, WM. FRANCIS,	*Committee.*

JOHN STRONG, *Capt.*
STEPHEN CROFOOT, *Lieut.*
WM. FORD, *Capt.*
WM. FRANCIS, *Capt.*

N. B. — Nathan Dart was a Hancock man, enlisted for Pittsfield, and so certified. Jeffrey Hazzard, "mulatto fellow," enlisted out of Col. Chapin's regiment of levies; but he had fought in the Pittsfield company at Bennington.

Lemuel Halleck, chairman of the committee at Boston, certified to the enlistment of all the above list, except those whose names are starred, and to the following names not in the Selectmen's list: John Wood, Josiah Reed, Peter Dago, Aaron Hiscocks, George Atkins, Robert Milbourn.

The following additional names appear in the Continental rolls, in the State Archives, 1779: Isaac Moss (Morse?), John Wright, Jonathan Morey, Anthony Oliver, Thomas Tupper.

CLASSES AND BOUNTIES.

PITTSFIELD, April 20, 1781.

WE, the subscribers, selectmen of the town of Pittsfield, do hereby certify and inform all persons whom it may concern, That, in pursuance of a resolve of the General Court of the 2d of December last, the town of Pittsfield, by their committees appointed for that purpose, divided the ratable polls and estate of said town into as many classes as there were men required to be procured by said town; to wit, sixteen. And that fifteen of said classes did hire and procure the several men hereinafter named, and gave to them, as a bounty, the several sums annexed to their names, as appears by the receipts herewith trasmitted: —

John White,	£50	Simeon Tupper, jun.,	£60
Joseph Sharp,	50	Henry Smith,	55
Edward Davis,	50	Eliphalet Cobb,	60
Anoblos Moore,	50	Simeon Tupper,	60
Ambrose Booth,	50	David Taylor,	55
William Cady,	55	Allen Davis,	50
Jabez Albro,	50	Jehiel Stearns,	55
Nathan French,	55 7		

Amounting, in the whole, to the sum of £830. 7*s.*

And the said selectmen do further inform, that, although a number of receipts bear a later date, yet, to the best of their belief, the several persons above named (except one) were procured and mustered before the 20th day of January last, as will appear by the certificate of the muster-master; but some of the classes did not complete the payment and obtain receipts until afterwards.

And, as to one class in town, the subscribers would further inform, that the several members or individuals of said class did pay to the head of the class, to his full satisfaction, their respective sums and proportions sufficient to procure a man; and that, in consideration thereof, he did undertake to hire a man, and indemnify said class, but by some means hath neglected and failed to do so.

LEBBEUS BACKUS,
JOSHUA ROBBINS,
WM. BARBER,
JOHN STRONG,
OLIVER ROOT,
RUFUS ALLEN,
WOODBRIDGE LITTLE, } *Selectmen.*

Sworn to before Jonathan Lee, *Town Clerk.*

E.

CENSUS OF PITTSFIELD IN 1772.

[Number of families and persons in Pittsfield, Nov. 1, 1772.]

Name	Number
James Easton,	15
Thomas Allen,	8
John Strong,	7
Stephen Crowfoot,	9
Simeon Crowfoot,	8
Jacob Ensign,	8
Aaron Miller,	
Joseph Fairfield,	
Woodbridge Little,	4
Israel Dickinson,	8
Israel Stoddard,	8
Moses Graves,	
—— Birchard,	
—— Chamberlin,	
Charles Goodrich,	
William Williams,	12
Wm. Brattle,	9
Gideon Gunn,	7
Solomon Crosby,	9
Solomon Deming,	5
Josiah Moseley	3
Erastus Sackett,	8
William Barber,	3
Matthew Barber,	7
—— Keiler,	
Ezra Keiler,	3
Seth Keiler,	3
Benj. Keiler,	6
Phineas Belding,	9
Dan Cadwell,	9
Stephen Phelps,	2
—— Goodrich,	4
Jedidiah Goodrich,	2
David Bagg,	8
Thomas Morgan,	4
Timothy Cadwell,	7
Martin Bagg,	3
King Strong,	4
Aaron Noble,	5
—— Marvin,	4
Joseph Clark,	3
Aaron Baker,	15
Valentine Rathbun,	8
—— Branch,	9
—— Branch,	5
—— Branch,	6
Oliver Burt,	7
—— Morey,	7
Thomas North,	7
Zebediah Stiles,	11

Caleb Goodrich,	9
Ephraim Stiles,	5
Charles Miller,	9
Stephen Fowler,	3
John Corban,	5
Wm. Ford,	6
—— Gleason,	10
Amos Root,	8
Josiah Wright,	1
Joshua Robbins,	10
Daniel Hubbard, jun.,	8
Ebenezer Hutchinson,	3
Daniel Hubbard,	3
James Hubbard,	6
David Noble, }	
Widow Noble, }	20
—— Johnson, }	
William Francis,	9
—— Parker,	2
Ebenezer White,	6
Hezekiah Jones,	3
Hezekiah Jones, jun.,	6
—— Larribee,	8
Benjamin Kilbourn,	4
—— Hobby,	7
Lebbeus Backus,	6
Nathaniel Fairfield,	10
Eli Root,	7
Nathanael Phelps,	6
David Bush,	8
Ezekiel Root,	11
Daniel Weller,	9
Uriah Judd,	7
Elisha Jones,	
—— Hale,	4
Aaron Stiles,	7
Jonathan Blaxley,	4
—— Hopkins,	7
Joseph Allen,	7
Daniel Alexander,	3

—— Talcut,	
—— Talcut,	
Joseph Wright,	
Widow Wright,	

James Colt,	
Jonathan Kingsley,	5
Joshua Narramore,	6
John Narramore,	
Elnathan Phelps,	7
Wm. Phelps,	
Lemuel Phelps,	
—— Hopkins,	11
—— Hollister,	
Jos. More,	
Jacob Ellithorp,	5
Oswald Williams,	
James Noble,	
Gideon Goodrich,	
John Baker,	
John Remington,	2
John Remington, jun.,	
—— Hopkins,	
Ezra Strong,	8
Capt. North,	2

—— Loomis,	6
—— Turner,	
Oliver Root,	7
Amos Delano,	3
Wm. Wright,	7
Ebenezer Wright,	2
Solomon Lathrop,	3
David Ashley,	
John Clark,	
—— Grant,	4
—— Davis,	6
Zadock Hubbard,	2
John Demming,	
—— Cogswell,	
—— Janes.	
Paul Guilford,	7
—— Hicok,	
—— Plummer,	2
—— Squire,	2
Joseph Chamberlain,	
—— Doane,	2
Uriah Judd,	2
—— Austin,	3
Number of families,	138

N. B. — The census here given is a transcript from the records of the First Church. In some cases, blanks were left in the original, and in others the record is obliterated.

F.

ACCOUNT OF THE BATTLE OF BENNINGTON.

BY THE REV. THOMAS ALLEN.

[Mr. Allen, writing on the day of the battle, in the following account, gives the story of the Bennington fight according to his own observation, and the information which could be hastily collected at the time.]

From the Connecticut Courant, Aug. 25, 1777.

[The following particulars of the action between the militia, &c., and a part of the British army, on the 16th inst., near Bennington, have been transmitted to us by a letter of the 16th from the Rev. Mr. Allen of Pittsfield, who was present at the action.] — ED.

Saturday, Aug. 16, was a memorable day on account of a signal victory which the militia, under the command of Gen. Stark, obtained over a body of the king's troops commanded by Gov. Skeene, some account of which is here given by one who was himself in the action. It seems that Gen. Burgoyne had detached this corps, consisting of about fifteen hundred men, chiefly Waldeckers and Brunswickers, intermixed with some British troops and Tories, — a medly compound, — to penetrate as far as Bennington, and farther if it should be found practicable, with a view to increase the number of his friends, to disperse his "protections" in the country, to procure for his army provisions, and to wreak his wrath and vengeance on those who had disregarded his calls of mercy, and slighted with indignity his proffered protection. Gov. Skeene had advantageously posted this corps within about five miles of Bennington Meeting-house, where, in different places, they made breastworks for their own security. This digression was of such ill tendency, and savored so much of presumption, that Gen. Stark, who was at that time providentially at Bennington, with his brigade of militia from New-Hampshire State, determined to give him battle. Col. Simonds's regiment of militia in Berkshire County was invited to his assistance; and a part of Col. Brown's arrived seasonably to attend on the action; and some volunteers from different towns; and Col. Warner, with a part of his own regiment, joined him the same day. The general, it seems, wisely laid his plan of operation; and, Divine Providence blessing us with good weather, between three and four o'clock, P.M., he attacked them in front and flank, in three or four different places at the same instant, with irresistible impetuosity.

The action was extremely hot for between one and two hours. The flanking divisions had carried their points with great success, when the front pressed on to their breastworks with an ardor and patience beyond expectation. The blaze of the guns of the contending parties reached each other. The fire was so extremely hot, — and our men easily surmounting their breastworks, amid peals of thunder and flashes of lightning from their guns, without regarding the roar of their field-pieces, — that the enemy at once deserted their cover, and ran; and in about five minutes their whole camp was in the utmost confusion and disorder. All their battalions were broken in pieces, and fled most precipitately; at which instant our whole army pressed after with redoubled ardor, pursued them for a mile, made considerable slaughter among them, and made many prisoners. One field-piece had already fallen into our hands. At this point, our men stopped the pursuit to gain breath, when the enemy, being re-enforced, our front fell back a few rods for convenience of ground, and being directed and collected by Col. Rossiter, and re-enforced by Major Stratton, renewed the fight with redoubled ardor, and fell in upon them with great impetuosity, put them to confusion and flight, and pursued them about a mile, making many prisoners. Two or three more brass field-pieces fell into our hands, and are supposed to be the whole of what they brought with them. At this time, darkness came upon us, and prevented our swallowing up the whole of this body. The enemy fled precipitately the succeeding night towards the North River; and, unless they should be met with by a party of our army, may have reached there without further molestation. Gov. Skeene, in surprise and consternation, took horse and fled. This action, which redounds so much to the glory of the great Lord of the heavens and God of armies, affords the Americans a lasting monument of the divine power and goodness, and a most powerful argument of love to and trust in God.

Our loss is about forty or fifty killed, and more wounded. Their baggage fell into our hands. The number of prisoners taken is said to be about six hundred. Two of their colonels were among the prisoners, and mortally wounded. A number of their inferior officers have also fallen into our hands, and in particular the general's aide-de-camp. A good number deserted, and joined us. This victory is thought by some to equal any that has happened during the present controversy, and, as long as prudence, moderation, sobriety, and valor are of any estimation among these United States, will not fail to endear Gen. Stark to them. It is the opinion of some, that, if a large body of militia was now called to act in conjunction with our northern army, the enemy might be entirely overthrown. May all be concerned to give God the glory, whilst we commend the good conduct of the officers and soldiers in general on so important an occasion! The best account of the number of prisoners taken in the above action is as follows: —

2 Colonels,	1 Major,
1 Lieutenant-colonel,	5 Captains,
12 Lieutenants,	1 Judge advocate,
4 Ensigns,	1 Baron,
2 Canadian officers,	3 Surgeons,
37 British } privates,	2 Brass 4-pounders,
398 German } privates,	2 " 3-pounders,
175 Tories,	1 Medicine wagon, and a quantity of baggage.
680 besides, wounded,	

From Mr. Allen's Pocket Diary.

[The allusions to the Battle of Bennington in Rev. Mr. Allen's diary are brief, but suggestive, and read as follows]: —

"Aug. 16. — A memorable battle fought by the militia near Bennington. One thousand of the enemy killed, wounded, and taken prisoners.

"Expended on my tour to Bennington, seven shillings and sixpence.

"Expended for ammunition, nine shillings and sixpence.

"Aug. 21. — Received for horse-keeping and victualling [probably of soldiers and prisoners], two pounds, seventeen shillings, and sixpence.

"Received for use of my cart, and damage by prisoners, one pound, one shilling.

"Aug. 29. — Received for victuals for seventeen men, thirteen shillings and sixpence."

Rev. Dr. Field relates the following anecdote of Mr. Allen: —

"Once, when asked whether he actually killed any man at Bennington, he replied that he did not know; but that, observing a flash often repeated from a certain bush, and that it was generally followed by the fall of one of Stark's men, he fired that way, and put the flash out."

G.

PLAN OF PITTSFIELD IN 1794.

TRANSCRIBED FROM THE ORIGINAL IN THE MASS. STATE ARCHIVES.

A Plan of the Town of Pittsfield, in the County of Berkshire, taken in Obedience to a Resolve of the General Court, passed June 26, *A.D.* 1794.

The south line of this town is 2,111 rods in length; the east line is 1,897 rods long; the north line in the whole is 2,048 rods; and the whole of the west line 1,892 rods in length. This town was intended to be, and perhaps is, in a square form. The very steep mountain [Honwee], near the north-west corner, may make a difference in measuring the lines. The original plans of the town, one of which we had, taken thirty-four years ago, set forth the town as square, and the points from the south-west corner, as running east 19 degrees south; but in running the same line at this period, and setting the compass so as to strike the north-west corner of the town of Lenox, which is in the south-west line of Pittsfield, and 684 rods from our south-

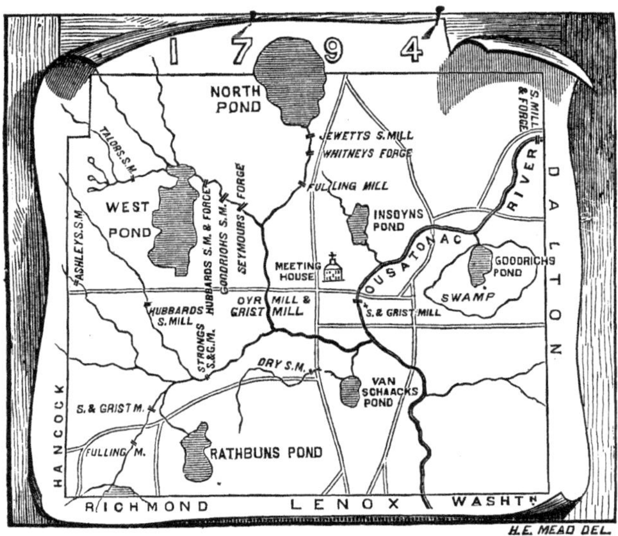

west corner, the line was found to run east sixteen degrees and fifteen minutes south. The lines at each corner are at right angles, and the ancient boundaries and marked trees are yet remaining.

Pittsfield by estimation, on the route through Northampton, is 140 miles from Boston. Its meeting-house is six miles and a half from Lenox Court House. The Ousatonac River, at its entrance on the east side of said town, is six rods wide; and on the south side of the town, where it crosses the line, it is eight rods wide.

There are five ponds which lie wholly in Pittsfield, and two others, part of one of which is in Lanesborough, and the other in Richmond, which we estimate as follows, to wit: —

Goodrich Pond, 50 acres; Ensign's Pond, 40 acres; Van Schaack's Pond, 40 acres; Rathbun's Pond, 45 acres; West Pond, 520 acres; North Pond, 300 acres; South Pond, 80 acres.

We know of no mines, or minerals, in this town. The ore used here is brought from Richmond, &c. This survey was taken in the months of November and December, A.D. 1794. The dotted lines represent the county roads; the green lines, the streams and rivers, over which are bridges, where roads cross them. The bridges over the Ousatonac River are five in number. Dalton, S. W. corner. Washington, N. W. corner.

JOHN C. WILLIAMS,
OLIVER ROOT,
SIMON LARNED,
NATHANIEL ROBBINS,
ELI ROOT,
} *Committee.*

DEC. 8, 1794.

N. B. — The committee do not seem to have been aware of the sixty-eight rods allowed in addition to the original town boundaries.

H.

WHILE this work has been passing through the press, a few facts have come to our knowledge, which are worthy of record.

Dr. Charles S. Goodrich of New York furnishes us with the following traditions regarding his grandfather, Capt. Charles Goodrich.

East Street was opened under his direction; and four or five fine elm-trees were left standing where Park Square now is, among them The Great Elm. Dr. Goodrich often heard his grandfather say that one of his axe-men struck two blows into the tree, with the intention of felling it; but Capt. Goodrich, admiring its beauty, — it was then tall, straight, and limbless, to the height of some fifty feet,— ordered his axe-men to "spare that tree," which they did, with three or four others near it. The Elm was then about a foot in diameter.

Dr. Goodrich states that his grandfather owned six thousand acres of land in Pittsfield and the neighboring towns; among which was the farm upon which the popular mineral springs of New Lebanon, N.Y., were afterwards found.

Once, when eighty years old, Capt. Goodrich rode a Narragansett pony from Pittsfield, Vermont — which was named by him, and where his son lived,— to Pittsfield, Massachusetts, a distance of a hundred and four miles; starting after sunrise, and sleeping at home the same night.

Capt. Goodrich died at the age of ninety-six, leaving two sons, — Rev. Charles Goodrich, who is now living, at the age of ninety; and James G., who is now eighty-nine years old, — and one daughter, Mrs. Lucy G. Pratt, who died three years since, at the age of ninety.

The last deer known in Pittsfield were slaughtered in the winter of 1780, when the snow was so deep that it was possible for the hunters to kill them, without the possibility of their escape, in the yards which they had beaten out for themselves among the snow-drifts. The demand for buckskins for the manufacture of breeches for the military was then urgent, and the hunters were diligent to supply it.

The initials I. M. W., on the Plan of Pittsfield in 1759, refer to John Mico Wendell, son of Col. Jacob, who married Catherine Brattle, a descendant of Thomas Brattle, the founder of the Brattle family of Massachusetts, a branch of which was thus introduced into Pittsfield, where some of its members still reside. John Mico Wendell and his wife were both descendants of Governors Bradstreet and Dudley.

Of Col. Israel Williams's nine children, four settled in Pittsfield and vicinity: Deacon William Williams, who was one of the first trustees of Williams College, and who should be distinguished from Col. William Williams of Pittsfield; Sarah, who married Dr. Marsh of Dalton; Eunice, who married Major Israel Stoddard of Pittsfield; and Lucretia, who married John Chandler Williams. Of Dr. Marsh's daughters, Sarah married Israel Peck; Martha married Thomas Gold; Eunice, Darius Larned; Lucretia, William Millen; Elizabeth, Jonathan Allen; and Sophia, Fordyce Merrick, — all of Pittsfield.

INDEX.

A.

B.

C.

D.

E.

F.

G.

H.

I.

J.

K.

L.

M.

N.

O.

P.

Q.

R.

S.

T.

U.

ALPHABETICAL LIST

OF

SOLDIERS NAMED IN THE RECORD OF PITTSFIELD REVOLUTIONARY SERVICE (APPENDIX D).

A.

Austin, Benjamin
Allen, Rufus
Ames, Elijah
Ashley, David
Austin, Ebenezer
Adams, Aaron
Andrews, Colman
Austin, Shubael
Allen, Joseph
Allen, Rev. Thomas
Albro, Jabez

B.

Berry, Hugh
Butler, Jerry
Bill, Jonathan
Beckwith, David
Belding, Charles
Butler, George
Blakesley, Jonathan
Brattle, James
Burt, Oliver
Bateman, Jonathan
Bliss, Solomon
Barber, William
Barber, Daniel
Bagg, Martin
Branch, Abel
Baker, Enoch
Burt, Daniel
Brown, Daniel
Booth, Ambrose
Backus, Lebbeus
Bigelow, Joshua
Branch, Asa
Bond, William
Babcock, Simeon
Belknap, Francis
Blanchard, Jeremiah
Bigsbee, Aaron
Barber, Simeon
Barber, Jacob
Burt, Thomas
Brown, John
Brewster, Oliver
Bell, Henry
Bond, Seth
Bartlett, Moses
Baxter, Richard
Baker, Timothy
Beard, William
Barber, Phinehas
Bagg, Phinehas
Bagg, David
Belding, Levi
Bagg, Daniel
Brattle, William
Bates, Daniel
Barber, James
Babbit, John
Burt, Thomas
Baker, Solomon
Barber, Matthew
Bonney, Samuel
Bush, David
Briton, Jonathan
Baker, James
Bond, Bartholomew
Belding, Oliver
Baker, William
Bond, William
Badcock, Daniel
Baker, Lyman
Blinn, Joel
Brunt [Burt ?], John
Branch, John

C.

Collins, William
Chapin, Amaziah
Coggswell, Reuben
Currier, B.
Cady, William
Corbin, John
Cross, Samuel
Cotton, Joseph
Chalmers, Jabez
Childs, Timothy
Cady, John
Colson, Joseph [Colton ?]
Coggswell, Samuel
Coggswell, Isaac
Cadwell, Timothy
Colt, James D.
Coggswell, Calvin
Churchill, John
Coggswell, Levi
Cummington, John
Case, Ezekiel
Clark, David
Carlton, Peleg
Carlton, Reuben
Cady, John
Cahoon, James
Coe, Calvin
Cadwell, Dan
Chamberlain, Joseph
Coggswell, Benjamin
Chesman, Calvin
Cady, Warren
Cady, Phinehas
Cole, Phinehas
Coggswell, Daniel
Cotterel, Nicholas
Cook, Timothy
Concert, George
Clark, Bildad
Chapin, Joseph
Crofoot, Stephen
Colton, Reuben
Chapel, Joshua
Cotterel, Nicholas
Colton, Joseph
Coggswell, Luther
Candee, Timothy
Collins, William
Chappel, Joshua
Carter, Elisha
Crofoot, Elijah
Cadwell, Timothy
Chamberlain, Benjamin
Cutond, Cemyour [Seymour Cutting or Cotton ?]
Chaucer, Jabez ?
Crane, Elijah
Chapman, Ebenezer
Cook, William
Cobb, Eliphalet

D.

Dago, Peter
Dickinson, Nathaniel
Deming, Benjamin
Dickinson, Joel
Davis, Nathaniel
Drake, Aaron
Deming, John
DeWolf, James
Davis, Thomas
Dibble, Truman
Dunham, Calvin
Delano, Aaron
Delano, Amos
Dickinson, Israel
Deming, Noadiah
Drake, William
Davis, Samuel
Dimock, Shubael
Done, Joshua [Doane]
Dart, Nathan
Dennis, John
Dimock, Benjamin
Dean, Joel

E.

F.

G.

H.

I.

J.

K.

L.

M.

N.

O.

P.

www.ingramcontent.com/pod-product-compliance
Lightning Source LLC
LaVergne TN
LVHW021259110826
845150LV00003B/430